CONFUCIAN SPIRITUALITY
Volume Two

World Spirituality
An Encyclopedic History of the Religious Quest

Volume 11B of
World Spirituality:
An Encyclopedic History
of the Religious Quest

CONFUCIAN SPIRITUALITY

VOLUME TWO

Edited by
Tu Weiming
and
Mary Evelyn Tucker

A Herder and Herder Book
The Crossroad Publishing Company
New York

The Crossroad Publishing Company
481 Eighth Avenue, Suite 1550, New York, NY 10001

Printed in the United States of America

Library of Congress Cataloging-in-Publication Data

Confucian spirituality / Edited by Tu Weiming and Mary Evelyn Tucker.
    p. cm.
   "A Herder and Herder Book."
   Includes bibliographical references and index.
   ISBN 0-8245-2254-0 (v. 2) (alk. paper)
   1. Confucianism. 2. Confucian ethics. 3. Philosophy, Confucian.
I. Tu, Wei-ming. II. Tucker, Mary Evelyn. III. Title.
BL1855.C66 2003
299'.512—dc21
                                    2003005752

1   2   3   4   5   6   7   8   9   10   07   06   05   04

Contents

**Part Three
Confucian Humanism as a Manifestation
of East Asian Spirituality: Self-Cultivation
as Spiritual Praxis**

vii

Part Five:
The Third Epoch of Confucian Humanism in the Global Community

Preface to the Series

THE PRESENT VOLUME is part of a series entitled World Spirituality: An Encyclopedic History of the Religious Quest, which seeks to present the spiritual wisdom of the human race in its historical unfolding. Although each of the volumes can be read on its own terms, taken together they provide a comprehensive picture of the spiritual strivings of the human community as a whole—from prehistoric times, through the great religions, to the meeting of traditions at the present.

Drawing upon the highest level of scholarship around the world, the series gathers together and presents in a single collection the richness of the spiritual heritage of the human race. It is designed to reflect the autonomy of each tradition in its historical development, but at the same time to present the entire story of the human spiritual quest. The first five volumes deal with the spiritualities of archaic peoples in Asia, Europe, Africa, Oceania, and North and South America. Most of these have ceased to exist as living traditions, although some perdure among tribal peoples throughout the world. However, the archaic level of spirituality survives within the later traditions as a foundational stratum, preserved in ritual and myth. Individual volumes or combinations of volumes are devoted to the major traditions: Hindu, Buddhist, Taoist, Confucian, Jewish, Christian, and Islamic. Included within the series are the Jain, Sikh, and Zoroastrian traditions in order to complete the story, the series includes traditions that have not survived but have exercised important influence on living traditions—such as Egyptian, Sumerian, classical Greek and Roman. A volume is devoted to modern esoteric movements and another to modern secular movements.

Having presented the history of the various traditions, the series devotes two volumes to the meeting of spiritualities. The first surveys the meeting of spiritualities from the past to the present, exploring common themes

A longer version of this preface may be found in Christian Spirituality: Origins to the Twelfth Century, *the first published volume in the series.*

that can provide the basis for a positive encounter, for example, symbols, rituals, techniques. The second deals with the meeting of spiritualities in the present and future. Finally, the series closes with a dictionary of world spirituality.

Each volume is edited by a specialist or a team of specialists who have gathered a number of contributors to write articles in their fields of specialization. As in this volume, the articles are not brief entries but substantial studies of an area of spirituality within a given tradition. An effort has been made to choose editors and contributors who have a cultural and religious grounding within the tradition studied and at the same time possess the scholarly objectivity to present the material to a larger forum of readers. For several years some five hundred scholars around the world have been working on the project.

In the planning of the project, no attempt was made to arrive at a common definition of spirituality that would be accepted by all in precisely the same way. The term "spirituality," or an equivalent, is not found in a number of the traditions. Yet from the outset, there was a consensus among the editors about what was in general intended by the term. It was left to each tradition to clarify its own understanding of this meaning and to the editors to express this in the introduction to their volumes. As a working hypothesis, the following description was used to launch the project:

> The series focuses on that inner dimension of the person called by certain traditions "the spirit." This spiritual core is the deepest center of the person. It is here that the person is open to the transcendent dimension; it is here that the person experiences ultimate reality. The series explores the discovery of this core, the dynamics of its development, and its journey to the ultimate goal. It deals with prayer, spiritual direction, the various maps of the spiritual journey, and the methods of advancement in the spiritual ascent.

By presenting the ancient spiritual wisdom in an academic perspective, the series can fulfill a number of needs. It can provide readers with a spiritual inventory of the richness of their own traditions, informing them at the same time of the richness of other traditions. It can give structure and order, meaning and direction to the vast amount of information with which we are often overwhelmed in the computer age. By drawing the material into the focus of world spirituality, it can provide a perspective for understanding one's place in the larger process. For it may well be that the meeting of spiritual paths—the assimilation not only of one's own spiritual heritage but of that of the human community as a whole—is the distinctive spiritual journey of our time.

EWERT COUSINS

Acknowledgments

T HE EDITORS would like to thank the East-West Cultural Centre in Singapore for making possible the initial Harvard conference in August 1997 from which these volumes on Confucian Spirituality arose. Laura Epperson of the Harvard-Yenching Institute was most gracious in helping to organize the conference at the Harvard Center for the Study of World Religions.

Gratitude is also due to Deborah Sommer for providing the pictures for these volumes, to John Berthrong for the glossary and general bibliography, to Man Lung Cheng and Li Ruohong for assistance with the photos, and to Ronald Suleski for myriad contributions.

Special thanks is extended to Ewert Cousins for his tireless efforts on behalf of the World Spirituality series.

This book is dedicated to our teachers, Wing-tsit Chan, Wm. Theodore de Bary, and Thomas Berry.

Introduction

MARY EVELYN TUCKER

T
HE ART OF CONFUCIAN SPIRITUALITY might be described as
discovering one's cosmological being amidst daily affairs. For the
Confucian the ordinary is the locus of the extraordinary; the secular is the sacred; the transcendent is in the immanent. What distinguishes Confucian spirituality among the world's religious traditions is
an all-encompassing cosmological context that grounds its world-affirming
orientation for humanity. This is not a tradition that seeks liberation outside the world, but rather one that affirms the spirituality of becoming
more fully human within the world. The way of immanence is the Confucian way.[1]

The means of self-transformation is through cultivation of oneself in
relation to others and to the natural world. This cultivation is seen in connection with a tradition of scholarly reflection embedded in a commitment
to the value of culture and its myriad expressions. It aims to promote flourishing social relations, effective educational systems, sustainable agricultural patterns, and humane political governance within the context of the
dynamic, life-giving processes of the universe.

One may hasten to add that, while subject to debate, aspects of transcendence are not entirely absent from this tradition, for example, in the idea of
Heaven in classical Confucianism or the Supreme Ultimate in later Neo-
Confucianism.[2] However, the emphasis of Confucian spirituality is on cultivating one's Heavenly-endowed nature in relation to other humans and
to the universe itself. There is no impulse to escape the cycles of samsaric
suffering as in Hinduism or Buddhism or to seek otherworldly salvation as
in Judaism, Christianity, or Islam. Rather, the microcosm of the self and

the macrocosm of the universe are implicitly and explicitly seen as aspects of a unified but ever-changing reality.

The seamless web of immanence and transcendence in this tradition thus creates a unique form of spiritual praxis among the world's religions. There is no ontological split between the supernatural and the natural orders. Indeed, this may be identified as one of the distinctive contributions of Confucian spirituality, both historically and in its modern revived forms.

How to describe this form of spirituality is part of the challenge of these two volumes, which are intended to give the reader an overview of the remarkable array of Confucian spirituality from the classical period to the contemporary period. This is the first time such a comprehensive collective perspective has been offered to Western readers interested in exploring the varied dimensions of Confucian spirituality. We hope that by examining these distinctive forms of Confucian spirituality the very notion of spirituality in the larger human community will be broadened and enriched.

These essays are intended as an invitation for further research into the religious and spiritual dimensions of Confucianism. We trust that future research on East Asia, in both its premodern and modern phases, will include more extensive interdisciplinary collaborative reflection on the significant topic of the multiform spiritual dimensions of Confucianism.

What Is Confucian Spirituality?

Among the world's religious traditions Confucianism has the distinction of being the tradition that is least understood as having religious or spiritual aspects. Part of the complexity of the problem regarding the religious nature of Confucianism lies in sorting out a series of interlocking questions. Foremost among them is how one defines Confucianism—as a political system, as ethical teachings, as social norms, as a humanistic philosophy, or as a religious worldview.[3] We acknowledge all of these features as being part of Confucianism. However, we aim here to explore Confucianism not necessarily as a "religion" per se, but as a religious worldview with distinctive spiritual dimensions.

We are refraining from using the term "religion" to describe Confucianism, as "religion" tends to be associated with formal institutional structures and most often with characteristics of Western religions such as theism, personal salvation, and natural/supernatural dichotomies.[4] The term "religion" may thus obscure rather than clarify the distinctive religious and spiritual dimensions of Confucianism.[5] Therefore, instead of claiming Confucianism as a religion (which is problematic in itself for many people), we are suggesting that Confucianism manifests a religious worldview in its cosmological orientation.[6] This cosmological orientation is realized in the connection of the microcosm of the self to the macrocosm of the universe through spiritual practices of communitarian ethics, self-transformation, and ritual relatedness.

A religious worldview is that which gives humans a comprehensive and defining orientation to ultimate concerns.[7] Spirituality is that which provides expression for the deep yearnings of the human for relatedness to these ultimate concerns. While a religious worldview may be assumed as part of a given set of cultural ideals and practices into which one is born, spirituality is the vehicle of attainment of these ideals. The Confucian religious worldview is distinguished by its cosmological context, in which humans complete the triad of Heaven and Earth. Confucian spirituality requires discipline and practice along with spontaneity and creativity. Confucian spirituality establishes different ethical responsibilities for specific human relations, deepens subjectivity in its methods of self-cultivation, and celebrates communion of cosmic and human forces in its ritual connections. It aims to situate human creativity amidst concentric circles of interdependent creativity from the person to the larger universe.

One way to appreciate the distinctiveness of the Confucian religious worldview and its spiritual expressions is to observe broad characteristics of religions with a common geographical place of origin. In this spirit it is significant to note that the flowering of the world's religions that took place in the sixth century B.C.E. was labeled by Karl Jaspers as the Axial Age.[8] This period of flowering can be characterized as having three major centers of origin: those in West Asia—Judaism, Christianity, Islam; those in South Asia—Hinduism, Jainism, Buddhism; and those in East Asia—Confucianism and Daoism. The first can be described as prophetic and historically based religions; the second can be seen as mystical religions and religions of liberation; the third can be understood as religious worldviews of cosmic and social harmony.[9] It is precisely the interaction of the cosmic and social that underlies the spiritual dynamics of Confucianism.

The Dimensions of Confucian Spirituality

The cosmological orientation of Confucianism provides a holistic context for its spiritual dimensions, namely, communitarian ethics, modes of self-transformation, and ritual practices. The integrating impetus of these spiritual practices can be described as celebrating the generativity and creativity of the cosmos in the midst of changing daily affairs. These three forms of spirituality are interrelated, and they set in motion patterns of relational resonance between humans and the ever-expanding, interconnected circles of life.

The *cosmological orientation* of the Confucian religious worldview has been described as encompassing a continuity of being between all life forms without a radical break between the divine and human worlds.[10] Heaven, Earth, and humans are part of a continuous worldview that is organic, holistic, and dynamic. Tu Weiming has used the term "anthropocosmic" to describe this integral relatedness of humans to the cosmos.[11] The flow of life and energy is seen in *qi* (material force or vital energy), which unifies the plant, animal, and human worlds and pervades all the elements of reality. The identification of the microcosm and the macrocosm in Confucian thought is a distinguishing feature of its cosmological orientation.[12]

Humans are connected to one another and to the larger cosmological order through an elaborate system of *communitarian ethics*. The five relations of society are marked, for example, by virtues of mutual exchange along with differentiated respect.[13] Reciprocity is a key to Confucian ethics and the means by which Confucian societies develop a communitarian basis so that they can become a bonded "fiduciary community."[14] Moreover, the cultivation of virtue in individuals is the basis for the interconnection of self, society, and the cosmos. As P. J. Ivanhoe observes, the activation of virtue evokes response: "This mutual dynamic of *de* 'virtue' or 'kindness' and *bao* 'response' was thought to be in the very nature of things; some early thinkers seemed to believe it operated with the regularity and force of gravity."[15]

In all of this, Confucian spirituality aims at moral *transformation* of the human so that individuals can realize their full personhood. Each person receives a Heavenly-endowed nature, and thus the potential for full authenticity or even sagehood is ever present. Nonetheless, to become a noble person (*junzi*) is an achievement of continual self-examination, rigorous discipline, and the cultivation of virtue. This process of spiritual self-transformation is a communal act.[16] It is not an individual spiritual path aimed at personal salvation. It is, rather, an ongoing process of rectification so as to cultivate one's "luminous virtue."[17] The act of inner cultivation implies reflecting on the constituents of daily experience and bringing that experience into accord with the insights of the sages. The ultimate goal of such self-cultivation is the realization of sagehood, namely, the attainment of one's cosmological being.[18]

Attainment of one's cosmological being means that humans must be attentive to one another, responsive to the needs of society, and attuned to the natural world through *rituals* that establish patterns of relatedness. In the Confucian context there were rituals performed at official state ceremonials as well as rituals at Confucian temples. However, the primary emphasis of ritual in the Confucian tradition was not liturgical ceremonies connected with places of worship (as in Western religions), but rituals involved in daily interchanges and rites of passage intended to smooth and elevate human relations. For the early Confucian thinker Xunzi, rituals are seen as vehicles for expressing the range and depth of human emotion in appropriate contexts and in an adequate manner.[19] Rituals thus become a means of affirming the emotional dimensions of human life. Moreover, they link humans to one another and to the other key dimensions of reality—the political order, nature's seasonal cycles, and the cosmos itself. Thus Confucian rituals are seen to be in consonance with the creativity of the cosmic order.

Confucian spirituality, then, might be seen as a means of integrating oneself into the larger patterns of life embedded in society and nature. P. J. Ivanhoe describes this effort succinctly when he observes that the Confucians believed "that a transformation of the self fulfilled a larger design, inherent in the universe itself, which the cultivated person could come to discern, and that a peaceful and flourishing society could only arise and be sustained by realizing this grand design. Cultivating the self in order to take one's place in this universal scheme describes the central task of life."[20]

The Appeal of Confucian Spirituality

Scholars in the field of religious studies may be able to make certain helpful clarifications toward elucidating the rich and varied nature of Confucian spirituality. While historians in the last fifty years have analyzed the development of Confucian texts, lineages, and institutions, and while social scientists have examined individual, family, and political patterns of Confucian-influenced behavior, only a few scholars have as yet explored the religious and philosophical dimensions of the Confucian tradition.[21] Further interpretations of the religious and philosophical nature of Confucianism may be important for understanding the endurance and appeal of Confucianism across East Asia, both traditionally and in the modern period.[22]

As David Keightley observes: "The strength and endurance of the Confucian tradition, ostensibly secular though its manifestations frequently were, cannot be fully explained, or its true nature understood, unless we take into account the religious commitment which assisted at that tradition's birth and which continued to sustain it."[23] Clearly, Confucian thought had an appeal to individuals and groups in East Asia for centuries beyond its political or ideological uses. Individual scholars and teachers engaged in the study and practice of Confucianism for intellectual inspiration, personal edification, spiritual growth, and ritual expression. We can see this in the spread of Confucianism to Korea, Japan, and Vietnam. This was especially evident in Japan, where there was no civil service examination system to advance personal careers. In the Tokugawa period (1603–1868), for example, many Japanese scholars and teachers studied Confucianism for its inherent value and assisted its spread in the society by establishing schools.[24]

Confucianism is more than the conventional stereotype of a model for creating social order and political stability sometimes used for oppressive or autocratic ends. While Confucianism aimed to establish stable and harmonious societies, it also encouraged personal and public reform, along with the reexamination of moral principles and spiritual practices appropriate to different contexts.[25] This is evident in Confucian moral and political theory, from the early classical concept of the rectification of names in the *Analects* to Mencius's qualified notion of the right to revolution. It is likewise seen in the later Neo-Confucian practice of delivering remonstrating lectures to the emperor and, when necessary, withdrawing one's services from an unresponsive or corrupt government.

On a personal level, the whole process of self-cultivation in Confucian spiritual practice was aimed at achieving authenticity and sincerity through conscientious study, critical self-examination, continual effort, and a willingness to change oneself.[26] "Learning for oneself," not simply absorbing ideas uncritically or trying to impress others, was considered essential to this process.[27] Thus, authenticity could only be realized by constant transformation so as to bring oneself into consonance with the creative and generative powers of Heaven and Earth.[28] These teachings sought to inculcate a process in tune with the dynamic, cosmological workings of nature. It thus affirmed change as a positive force in the natural order and in human affairs. This process of harmonizing with changes in the universe can be identified as a major wellspring of Confucian spirituality expressed in various forms of self-cultivation.

This focus on the positive aspects of change can be seen in each period of Confucianism as well as in its spread to other geographical contexts. Change in self, society, and cosmos was affirmed and celebrated from the early formative period, which produced the *Classic of Changes* (*Yijing*). Later Han Confucianism emphasized the vitality of correspondences between the human and the various elements in nature.[29] Eleventh- and twelfth-century Song Neo-Confucianism stressed the creativity of Heaven and Earth. Confucian spirituality in all its diverse expressions was seen in

East Asia as a powerful means of personal transformation. Furthermore, it was a potential instrument of establishing social harmony and political order through communitarian ethics and ritual practices. It emphasized moral transformation that rippled outward across concentric circles rather than the external imposition of legalistic and bureaucratic restraints. It was precisely this point that differentiated the Confucian aspirations and ideals from those of the Legalists, such as Han Fei Tzu, who felt humans could be restrained by law and changed by punishment.[30] It is a tradition that has endured for more than two and a half millennia in varied historical, geographical, and cultural contexts and is still undergoing transformation and revitalization in its contemporary forms.[31]

Overview of the Historical Development of the Confucian Tradition

The Confucian tradition has assumed distinctive expressions in China, Korea, Japan, Vietnam, Hong Kong, Taiwan, and Singapore. Viewing Confucianism as a singular tradition is problematic because of its geographic spread, its historical development, and its varied forms, ranging from Imperial State Confucianism to local and familial Confucianism. Nonetheless, this overview will try to make some distinctions in the various kinds of Confucianism in order to highlight its religious dimensions.[32]

While originating in the first millennium B.C.E. in China, the tradition includes the transmission and transformation of Confucianism that took place in different East Asian cultural and geographical contexts. In examining the reasons for its spread and its appeal, it is important to highlight the spiritual dynamics of the tradition and the ways in which it interacted with native traditions in China and across East Asia. Confucianism, for example, responded to and mingled with Daoism and Buddhism in China, with shamanism in Korea, and with Shinto in Japan.[33] Thus, although these two volumes explore the nature of Confucian spirituality, the borrowing and creative interaction among the various religious traditions in East Asia need to be underscored. Indeed, the so-called unity and syncretism of the three traditions of Confucianism, Daoism, and Buddhism in China should be noted. This was especially pronounced in the Ming (1368–1644) and Qing (1644–1911) periods.[34]

While recognizing this dynamic cross-fertilization of religious traditions in East Asia, we can also identify historically four major periods of Confucian thought and practice. The first stage in China is that of classical Confucianism, which ranges from approximately the sixth century B.C.E. to the second century before the common era. This is the period of the flourishing of the early Confucian thinkers, namely, Confucius and Mencius. The second period is that of Han Confucianism, when the classical tradition was shaped into a political orthodoxy under the Han empire (202 B.C.E.– 220 C.E.) and began to spread to other parts of East Asia. This period saw the development of the theory of correspondences of the microcosm of the human world with the macrocosm of the natural world. The third major period is the Neo-Confucian era from the eleventh to the early twentieth century. This includes the comprehensive synthesis of Zhu Xi in the eleventh century and the distinctive contributions of Wang Yangming in the fifteenth and sixteenth centuries. The influence of Confucianism as an educational and philosophical system was felt throughout many parts of East Asia during this period. The last phase is that of New Confucianism in the twentieth century, which represents a revival of the tradition under the influence of scholars who came to Taiwan and Hong Kong after Mao's ascendancy in 1949.[35] Four decades later, in October 1989, the International Confucian Society held two major conferences in Beijing and in Confucius's birthplace, Qufu, to explore the future of the Confucian Way. These conferences were intended to mark the 2540th anniversary of Confucius's birth and they both signified the interest of Confucian practitioners in looking toward the future.

The acknowledged founder of the Confucian tradition was known as the sage-teacher Kongzi (551–479 B.C.E.).[36] His name was Latinized by the Jesuit missionaries as Confucius. Born into a time of rapid social change, Confucius was concerned with the goal of reestablishing political and social order. He taught that this could be done through rectification of the individual and the state. This involved a program embracing both political and religious components. As a creative transmitter of earlier Chinese traditions, Confucius, according to legend, compiled the Appendices to the *Classic of Changes* and compiled the other classics, namely, the *Classic of Documents, Poetry, Rites,* and the *Spring and Autumn Annals.*[37]

The principal sayings and teachings of Confucius are contained in his conversations recorded in the *Analects.* Here he emphasized the cultivation of moral virtues, especially humaneness (*ren*) and the practice of civility or ritual decorum (*li*), which entails the practice of filiality (*xiao*).[38] Virtue and civility were exemplified by the noble person (*junzi*) particularly within the five relations, namely, between ruler and minister, parent and child, husband and wife, older and younger siblings, and friend and friend. The essence of Confucian thinking was that to establish order in society one had to begin with individual cultivation and then create harmony, filiality, and decorum in the family. Like concentric circles, the effect of virtue would thus reach outward from the individual and family to society. Likewise, if the ruler was moral, it would have a "rippling out" effect to the whole country.

At the heart of this classical Confucian worldview was a profound commitment to humaneness and civility. These two virtues defined the means of human relatedness as a spiritual path. Through civility, beginning with filiality, one could repay the gifts of life to one's parents, to one's ancestors, and to the whole natural world. Through humaneness one could extend this sensibility to other humans and to all living things. In doing so one became more fully human. The root of practicing humaneness was considered to be filial relations. The extension of these relations from one's family and ancestors to the human family and to the cosmic family was the means whereby these primary biological ties provided a person with the roots, trunks, and branches of an interconnected spiritual path.

The personal and the cosmic were joined in the stream of filiality. From the lineages of ancestors to future progeny, intergenerational connections and ethical bonding arose. Through one's parents and ancestors one became part of human life. Reverence and reciprocity were considered a natural response to this gift of life and a means of participating in its creativity. Great sacrifices were made for the family, and utmost loyalties were required in this spiritual path.[39] Analogously, through developing reverence for Heaven and Earth as the great parents of all life, one came to realize one's full cosmological being.

Confucian thought was further developed in the writings of Mencius (385?–312? B.C.E.) and Xunzi (310?–219? B.C.E.), who debated whether human nature was intrinsically good or evil and what were the consequences for the development of the human. Mencius's argument for the inherent goodness of human nature gained dominance among Confucian thinkers and gave an optimistic flavor to Confucian educational philosophy and political theory. This perspective influenced the spiritual aspects of the tradition as well because self-cultivation was seen as a natural means of uncovering this innate good nature. Mencius contributed an understanding of the process required for self-cultivation. He did this by identifying the four seeds of virtues he believed are innate in every human. He then suggested ways in which these seeds could be cultivated toward their full flowering as virtues. Analogies taken from the natural world (like the seeds and the stories of the man from Song and Ox mountain[40]) extended the idea of self-cultivation of the individual for the sake of family and society to a wider frame of reference that also encompassed the natural environment. This can be described as a path of botanical cultivation, where images of nurturing, tending, weeding, gathering, and harvesting are used to illustrate how spiritual practices of self-cultivation are analogous to agricultural rhythms.[41]

Xunzi, on the other hand, contributed a strong sense of the importance of ritual practice as a means of self-cultivation. He noted that human desires need to be satisfied and emotions such as joy and sorrow need to be expressed in the appropriate degree. Rituals provide the form for such expression in daily human exchange as well as in rites of passage such as marriage and death. Moreover, because Xunzi saw human nature as innately flawed, he emphasized the need for education to shape human nature toward the good. Finally, he had a highly developed sense of the interdependent triad of Heaven, Earth, and humanity, which was emphasized also by many later Confucian thinkers. He writes: "Heaven has its seasons; Earth has its riches; humans have their government."[42]

Confucianism blossomed in a Neo-Confucian revival in the eleventh and twelfth centuries, which resulted in a new synthesis of the earlier teachings. The major Neo-Confucian thinker, Zhu Xi (1130–1200), designated four texts from the canon of historical writings as containing the central ideas of Confucian thought. These were two chapters from the *Classic of Rites*, namely, the *Great Learning* and the *Mean*, as well as the *Analects* and the *Mencius*. He elevated these Four Books to a position of prime importance over the Five Classics mentioned earlier. These texts and Zhu Xi's commentaries on them became, in 1315, the basis of the Chinese civil service examination system, which endured for nearly six hundred years until 1905. Every prospective government official had to take the civil service exams based on Zhu Xi's commentaries on the Four Books. The idea was to provide educated, moral officials for the large government bureaucracy which ruled China. The influence, then, of Neo-Confucian thought on government, education, and social values was extensive.

Zhu Xi's synthesis of Neo-Confucianism was recorded in his classic anthology, *Reflections on Things at Hand (Jinsilu)*, which he co-edited with Lu Zuxian (1137–1181).[43] In this work he provided, for the first time, a comprehensive metaphysical basis for Confucian thought and practice. In response to the Buddhists' metaphysics of emptiness and their perceived tendency toward withdrawal from the world in meditative practices, Zhu formulated a this-worldly spirituality based on a balance of cosmological orientation, ethical and ritual practices, scholarly reflection, and political participation. The aim was to balance inner cultivation with outward investigation of things. Zhu used the *Explanation of the Diagram of the Supreme Polarity (Taijitu shuo)* as a cosmological framework to orient spiritual practice and self-cultivation.[44]

Unlike the Buddhists, who saw the world of change as the source of suffering, Zhu Xi, and the Neo-Confucians after him, affirmed change as the source of transformation in both the cosmos and the person. Thus Neo-Confucian spiritual discipline involved cultivating one's moral nature so as to bring it into harmony with the larger pattern of change in the cosmos. Each moral virtue had its cosmological component.[45] For example, the central virtue of humaneness was seen as the source of fecundity and growth in both the individual and the cosmos. By practicing humaneness, one could effect the transformation of things in oneself, in society, and in the cosmos. In so doing, one's deeper identity with reality was recognized as forming one body with all things, thus actualizing one's cosmological being. As the *Mean* stated it: "being able to assist in the transforming and nourishing powers of Heaven and Earth, one can form a triad with Heaven and Earth."[46] All of this for Zhu was part of a dynamic process of the mutual interaction of the *qi* of the person interacting with the *qi* of the cosmos. As Zhu put it: "Once a person's mind has moved, it must reach the *qi* [of Heaven and Earth] and mutually stimulate and interact with this [*qi*] that contracts and expands, goes and comes."[47]

To realize one's cosmological being, a rigorous spiritual practice was needed. This involved a development of poles present in earlier Confucian thought, namely, a balancing of religious reverence within and ritual propriety manifested in daily life. For Zhu Xi and later Neo-Confucians, such spiritual practices were a central concern. Interior meditation became known as "quiet-sitting," "abiding in reverence," or "rectifying the mind." Moral self-discipline was known as "making the will sincere," "controlling the desires," and "investigating principle."[48] All of this was expressed in a broad understanding of spiritual cultivation known as the "learning of the mind-and-heart" which became a primary instrument of the transmission of Confucianism throughout East Asia.[49]

Through conscientious spiritual effort and study one could become a noble person (*junzi*) or even a sage (*sheng*) who was able to participate in society and politics most effectively. While in the earlier Confucian view the emphasis was on the ruler as the prime moral leader of society, in Neo-Confucian thought this duty was extended to all people, with a particular responsibility placed on teachers and government officials. While ritual was primary in earlier Confucianism, spiritual discipline became even more significant in Neo-Confucian practice. In both the early and later tradition, major emphasis was placed on mutual respect and reciprocity in basic human relations. Zhu Xi helped to identify the dimensions of family rituals that were essential for the flourishing of the Confucian family.[50]

Confucian thought and practice spread to Vietnam, Korea, and Japan, where it had a profound effect on their respective cultures. Confucianism was transmitted to Korea as early as the Three Kingdoms period (57 B.C.E.–935 C.E.) where its political and educational ideas were utilized, especially as a philosophy to encourage unification of the disparate political groups on the peninsula. A Royal Academy based on Confucian texts was established in 651, and government civil service examinations were instituted in 788. While Buddhism was a major influence during the Koryo dynasty (918–1392), at the same time a strong central government with a civil bureaucracy emerged based on Confucian principles. With the founding of the Yi dynasty (1392–1910), Neo-Confucian ideas reached a new peak of influence in politics, society, and education.[51] A nationwide system of public schools was established, and local associations were set up to propagate Confucian ethics. Moreover, there were widespread intellectual debates on Neo-Confucian philosophy, especially regarding the nature of principle (*li*) and material force (*qi*). This debate was the focus of the two leading Neo-Confucian thinkers, Yi T'oegye (1501–1570) and Yi Yulgok (1536–1584).[52]

Confucianism gained official recognition in Japan at the end of the third century, when a Korean official brought the *Analects* to the emperor Oji. With the adoption of Prince Shotoku's constitution in 604 and with the Taika Reforms of 645 and 646, Confucianism became a useful political philosophy to overcome the clan-based politics of the earlier period. During the Kamakura (1185–1336) and Muromachi (1336–1598) periods, Confucianism was closely tied to the Zen monasteries, where it was carefully studied by the Zen monks, who were attracted by its sophisticated forms of Chinese learning. During the Tokugawa era (1603–1868) Confucianism flourished primarily in the world of scholarship and education, in addition to its political uses.[53] One of the leading thinkers of this period was Kaibara Ekken (1630–1714), who passed on the learning of the mind-and-heart through texts written for wide distribution.[54] Ekken also continued the debate regarding the nature of the relationship of *li* and *qi* as a means of both grounding spiritual self-cultivation and investigating the natural world.

In the modern period, Confucianism continues to have a major influence in many aspects of East Asian society, including the importance given to education and to social mores. Despite the effects of modernization on traditional ways, Confucianism persists as a cultural DNA passed on in the family. Its influence extends to political attitudes, to how businesses operate, and even to broad-based economic policies. Indeed, earlier studies have suggested that the success of the Japanese in modernizing after the Meiji Restoration of 1868 and in achieving rapid economic development after

World War II, may have been due in part to the Confucian values, which emphasized particular social obligations and duties and helped shape the educational system. Similar arguments have been made for the economic achievements of the other "four mini dragons," which have also been influenced by Confucianism, namely, South Korea, Taiwan, Hong Kong, and Singapore. Some of this thinking is being revised in light of the economic crises in the region in the 1990s.

After 1949 the government of the People's Republic of China repudiated Confucianism, especially during the Cultural Revolution of the 1960s and 1970s. However, the Confucian tradition is currently being reexamined in China, often relying on publications of European and American scholars. Several conferences have been held in recent years in China on the thought of Confucius, Zhu Xi, and Wang Yangming and an official Confucian association has been formed. The direction and outcome of this revival of interest in Confucianism remain to be seen. This is in large part because of the contested nature of the tradition in China and because of the disruptive impact of westernization and modernization in the region over the last century.

Reinterpreting Confucianism: From Repudiation to Reevaluation

Even before the Maoist era, the nature and uses of Confucianism were subject to significant debate, especially in the nineteenth and twentieth centuries in both East Asia and the West. For Chinese intellectuals struggling with the burden of tradition in relation to Western imperialism in the nineteenth century and modernization in the twentieth century, the legacy of Confucianism has been seriously reevaluated. From the late-nineteenth-century reforms to the May Fourth movement of 1919, from the New Culture movement of the 1920s to the New Confucianism of the post-Mao era, the reinterpretation of the Confucian legacy has been a paramount concern for Chinese intellectuals as well as for Western scholars of China.[55]

In this struggle between traditional and modern values in East Asia, the question arises as to whether Confucianism should be regarded as simply a hierarchical, "feudal" system to be set aside in favor of Western individualistic values, scientific methods, democratic principles, and free market capitalism. Many feel that the two approaches to social organization and economic exchange are mutually incompatible. Some of the leading lines of argument are whether Confucianism should be seen primarily as a political ideology often fostering authoritarianism or whether it can accurately be viewed as a humanistic ethical system capable of supporting individual autonomy and democratic processes.[56] This is often linked to the debate as to whether Confucianism has, in fact, contributed positively or negatively to economic growth and modernization in East Asia.[57] Furthermore, there has been reflection on whether a distinctive form of modern Confucianism may still be emerging in East Asia.[58] Of particular interest for these two volumes is the fact that the religious and spiritual dimensions of Confucianism are being rediscovered in East Asia and in the west at the same time as contemporary scholars are reexamining the varied political, economic, and social roles of Confucianism.[59]

There are many related questions regarding Confucianism that have been raised by these scholars and deserve further examination. These include: What are the problematic aspects of Confucianism which may have hindered individualism or dissent from authoritarian structures? What can be learned from the failures of Confucianism, especially in the challenges to building infrastructures to support civil society?[60] How can we evaluate the human cost of modernization for many individuals and groups in East Asia? What can be said about the clash of traditional and modern values in East Asia in the face of growing environmental degradation that industrial processes have helped to create? What accounts for the different rates of economic development in East Asian countries? Has Confucianism helped or hindered this process, or both assisted and obstructed this process? Are there positive features of Confucianism that have encouraged education and the development of human resources in contemporary East Asia? Are human rights recognized within Confucian cultures?[61] What role has Confucianism played in fostering "Asian values"? Can Confucianism contribute to a broader understanding of environmental ethics?[62]

These topics are clearly vast, singularly important, and frequently interlocked. In acknowledging the complexity of the arguments involved and the growing literature on these subjects, it would appear that various multidisciplinary efforts will be required to sift through the data, the texts, and the historical record before any satisfactory solutions to some of these questions might emerge. In addition, a more complex understanding of the production and uses of ideology will be needed, as well as greater attention to texts, contexts, and intertextuality.[63] Both in China and in the West, twentieth-century intellectuals have been preoccupied with understanding the nature of ideology as an oppressive force as a result of the rise of totalitarianism and fascism that led to the world wars and imperialist conquest. In this reading, religion has often been relegated to the category of ideology, and thus the appreciation for religion and for spirituality as potentially liberating forces has been eclipsed.[64]

Furthermore, an understanding of the religious dimensions of Confucianism has been obscured by the absence of or ambivalence regarding the term "religion" in East Asia and by a circumscribed view in the West of the nature and function of religion in other cultures. It is important to note that there was no term for "religion" in the Chinese language before it was introduced by the Japanese in the late nineteenth century through translations of European works. This was picked up by one of the leading reformers of late-nineteenth-century China, Kang Youwei (1858–1927). Kang used the term *kong jiao/k'ung chiao* (meaning the teaching or lineage of Confucius) to indicate Confucianism as a religion.[65] The term that came to be used for religion in general was *zong jiao/tsung chiao*. Similarly, there was no term for philosophy until *zhexue/che hsueh* was adopted under Western influence in the late nineteenth century. Instead, it was customary simply to use *jiao/chiao* (meaning teaching or philosophical school) to represent broad philosophical or religious lineages such as Confucianism, Daoism, and Buddhism. Moreover, there was no fundamental distinction in Chinese thought between religion and philosophy. In addition, the three dominant traditions in China interacted in complex ways, often resulting in creative syncretism or in claims that the three traditions were one. The exclusive separation of religious traditions, such as we see in the West, was not operative in the same way in East Asia. Within the Neo-Confucian tradition, particular lineages or schools of thought become distinguished, such as the School of Principle (*lixue*), associated with Zhu Xi, and the School of Mind (*xinxue*), associated with Wang Yangming.[66]

Confucianism in this context has thus been viewed by Westerners as either simply a humanistic ethical system or as a religious cult connected to state rituals. For widely divergent reasons, seventeenth-century European Christian missionaries, eighteenth-century French *philosophes,* and nineteenth-century translators such as James Legge[67] interpreted Confucianism as a rationalistic and ethical system without an idea of a personal God and without institutional structures such as were evident in Christianity.[68] Confucius was seen as agnostic, and Confucianism was not viewed as particularly religious. Herrlee Creel noted, however, that the view of Confucius as agnostic was most likely a result of the influence of post-Enlightenment valuing of rationalism by Western scholars which was also appropriated by Chinese intellectuals.[69] Consequently, Confucianism was understood to be a humanistic, rational, bureaucratic, political system, perpetuated by civil service examinations[70] and linked to a state cult. Elements of the tradition that might be viewed as spiritually enriching and personally transformative were overlooked or ignored.

In the twentieth century, Chinese intellectuals such as Hu Shi (1891–1962) tried to distinguish nonreligious from religious Confucianism so as to identify the dimensions of Confucianism that might be capable of contributing to the modernization of China. Hu saw the religious aspects of Confucianism, which he associated with the state cult, as being backward and feudalistic. He especially condemned the attempted revival of religious Confucianism by President Yuan Shikai after the reestablishment of the Republic in 1912. On the other hand, the sociologist of religion C. K. Yang accepted the dichotomy of two distinct systems of belief and practice and described the coexistence of Confucian thought with Chinese religion. He categorized the former as rational and ethical and the latter as supernaturally oriented and popularly based. He suggested that a dominant–subordinate working relationship existed between these two areas.[71] For twentieth-century Chinese, the legacy of Confucianism was clearly mixed, and its role as a religious tradition was far from clear in its function or efficacy.

This is especially true because of the destructive impact of Western imperialism in nineteenth-century China and the seductive power of modernization and westernization in twentieth-century China. The preoccupation of many nineteenth-century reformers throughout East Asia was whether one could effectively combine "Eastern morality," especially Confucian thought, as substance (*ti*) with Western technology as function (*yong*). The elaborate and at times anguished debates on this subject reflect an important new stage of the Confucian legacy in China, Korea, and Japan. Over the last one hundred years Confucianism has been seen by some interpreters, both in East Asia and in the West, as an ideology used to enforce class hierarchy, subservience, and conformity. Indeed, Confucianism has sometimes been identified with an *ancien régime* style of political order or solely with conservative modes of thinking. As a support for a repressive feudal past, it has been regarded by some as unenlightened at best and autocratic at worst. In short, for many individuals in East Asia and in the West, it appeared that modernity would proceed most effectively after the abandonment of Confucian-dominated thinking and the adaptation of Western scientific, political, and social values.[72]

This was particularly true of the New Culture movement leaders in the early part of the twentieth century. The movement was inspired by the writings of Chen Duxiu (1879–1942) and Hu Shi (1891–1962) and was joined by those embracing the slogan "Destroy the old curiosity shop of Confucianism." Its adherents championed science and democracy along with pragmatism and individualism. Yet this was also mingled with a swing toward disillusionment with the West, especially after World War I. This was especially true with the materialism and decadence of European society in evidence. Skepticism toward aspects of both Western and Confucian thought has been part of the complex legacy of Chinese intellectuals.

In the second half of the twentieth century a reevaluation of the role and relevance of Confucianism has been a major preoccupation of several philosophers in China as well as among the New Confucians in Hong Kong and Taiwan and the West.[73] Xiong Shili (1895–1968) is considered to be a primary inspiration of the New Confucian movement. Drawing on the *Classic of Changes* and the notion of the continuing creativity of the universe, he emphasized the virtue of humaneness, which forms one body with all things. Another important philosopher who remained in China during the Maoist regime was Liang Shuming (1893–1988). He published a comparative study of Chinese and Western civilization that celebrated Confucian moral values rather than the indiscriminate adoption of Western values and institutions. Both Xiong and Liang survived the attacks on Confucianism under Mao and persisted in writing on the philosophical and religious dimensions of Neo-Confucian thought.[74]

They were joined in this effort by the New Confucian philosophers who had escaped to Hong Kong and Taiwan after Mao's ascendancy. These included Zhang Junmai, Tang Junyi, Xu Fuguan, and Mou Zongsan. The publication of their "Manifesto for a Reappraisal of Sinology and the Reconstruction of Chinese Culture" in 1958 was a watershed moment for the revival of Confucianism in the modern period.[75] Some New Confucians also called for a more comprehensive understanding of the religious dimensions of Confucianism. This is true, for example, of Mou Zongsan, who affirmed Confucianism as one of the world's great religions. [76]

Categories for the Study of Confucianism

It may be helpful to distinguish various kinds of Confucianism so as to reframe the questions surrounding the emergence and manipulation of political ideologies and separate them from the spiritual dimensions of Confucianism. At the same time, we can acknowledge the ambiguous nature of many religions or philosophies in their frequent appropriation for manipulative or distorted ends.

Gilbert Rozman has proposed several types of Confucianism in his analysis of the "Confucian heritage and its modern adaptation" in East Asia.[77] He suggests a hierarchical categorization following the stratification of East Asian societies, which may include some overlap. At the top is *imperial Confucianism*, involving ideology and ritual surrounding the emperor. While this has often been seen as authoritarian, *reform Confucian-*

ism has been regarded as invoking principles of renewal or dissent to benefit society. This may intersect at times with *elite Confucianism,* which
reflects the interests and concerns of the educated scholar-official class.
Next is *merchant-house Confucianism,* which includes business groups in
both the premodern and modern periods. Finally, there is *mass Confucianism* which embraces the vast numbers of peasants and ordinary citizens in
East Asian societies.

Another classification of types of Confucianism has been made by Kim
Kyong-Dong.[78] He speaks of the *religious aspects* in reference to ideas of
Heaven and rituals of ancestor worship or veneration of the sages. Next he
cites Confucianism as a *philosophical system* that includes cosmology and
metaphysics, theories of human nature, ways of knowing, and ethics. Confucianism, he notes, also embraces *visions of governance* based on political
theories and *social norms* guiding human relations. Finally, Confucianism
can be seen as a system of *personal cultivation* aimed at achieving inner
equanimity and thus extending harmony to the world.

While Rozman's categories are quite apposite, they are limited by the
perspective of social classification and may be appropriated by those who
see Confucianism only as a political ideology. Similarly, Kim's categories
are fitting but curiously separate the religious and philosophical aspects
from social norms and personal cultivation. In evaluating the complex role
of Confucianism as a religious worldview from a more comprehensive perspective than social classifications or ideology, we will first identify four
broad categories of Confucianism as having had a significant impact on
East Asian history and society. Then we will discuss the religious worldview of Confucian cosmology and its expression in three distinctive forms
of spirituality previously described, namely, *communitarian ethics, modes of
self-transformation,* and *ritual practices.*

It should be clear that these broad categories of Confucian spirituality
are intended to be suggestive and illustrative, not exhaustive or rigid classifications. Other dimensions may be identified in the future as more scholars become engaged in the study of Confucian spirituality. One should
thus allow for the inevitable and often fruitful overlapping in the categories
that are proposed here. Despite their limitations, the usefulness of these
categories is in describing distinctive strands of Confucian spirituality
which coexist and are used in different periods for distinctive ends.

Let us turn first to identify some broad descriptive categories of Confucian spirituality that are distinct from, yet overlap with, religious Confucianism:

1. *Political Confucianism* refers to state or imperial Confucianism, especially in its Chinese form, and involves such institutions as the civil service

examination system and the larger government bureaucracy from the local level to the various ranks of court ministers. In Korea, Confucian bureaucratic government was adapted in the Koryo dynasty, and in 958 the civil service examination system was adopted as a means of selecting officials. Confucianism was further established as official orthodoxy under the Yi dynasty in 1392, and civil service examinations were inaugurated. In Japan there were no civil service examinations, but Confucian ideas were used in the Nara government and in Prince Shotoku's "constitution" of 719, as well as in legitimizing the Tokugawa Shogunate and later in the Meiji government's "Imperial Rescript on Education."

2. *Social Confucianism* alludes to what one might call family-based or human relations–oriented Confucianism. This involves the complex interactions of individuals with others both within and outside of the family. It has been described by Thomas Berry as a cultural coding and by Tu Weiming as a cultural DNA, or "habits of the heart" passed on from one generation to the next through the family. These interactions both reflect and create the intricate patterns of obligations and responsibilities that permeate East Asian society. In Japan, for example, these patterns are expressed in concepts such as *on* and *giri* (mutual obligations and debts requiring repayment).

3. *Educational Confucianism* encompasses public and private learning in schools, in families, and by individual scholars and teachers. It refers, although not exclusively, to the curriculum of study of the Four Books— the *Great Learning,* the *Mean,* the *Analects,* and the *Mencius*—selected as the canon by Zhu Xi. This was used as the basis of the civil service examination system in China and Korea. Educational Confucianism incorporates the adaptation of that curriculum to other educational institutions and venues in East Asia. In Japan and Korea, for example, it includes the various schools set up both privately and by national and provincial governments, especially in Yi-dynasty Korea and Tokugawa Japan. In addition, it refers to some of the moral training that continued to be part of the educational system in Korea and Japan in the twentieth century.[79] Educational Confucianism can be said to go beyond schools, institutions, and curriculum to include at its heart the notion of learning as a means of self-cultivation, an approach that is emphasized in the *Analects* and *Mencius.*[80]

4. *Economic Confucianism* describes business company forms of Confucianism in the modern period and merchant-related Confucianism in the premodern period, especially in Qing China, Yi Korea, and Tokugawa Japan.[81] It includes the idea of familialism and loyalty as critical principles for the transmission of family-based Confucian values into organizational

structures within the business community. This seems to be particularly widespread in East Asia, especially in the last fifty years.[82] It also includes the transmission across society of values often associated with Confucianism such as frugality, loyalty, and industriousness.

Religious Confucianism and Its Forms of Spirituality

As described earlier, a Confucian religious worldview is distinguished by its cosmological orientation. This is realized through the three dimensions of Confucian spirituality, namely, communitarian ethics, modes of self-transformation, and ritual practices.[83] The essays in these volumes represent a rich cross-section of discussion concerning these interrelated topics.

The *cosmological orientation* of the Confucian religious worldview involves the recognition that humans are embedded in and dependent on the larger dynamics of nature. The fecundity of cosmic processes is not simply a static background but a fundamental context in which human life flourishes and finds its richest expression. To harmonize with the creativity and changes in the universe is the task of the human in forming one body with all things. This is the anthropocosmic vision that Tu Weiming has articulated:

> Human beings are . . . an integral part of the "chain of being," encompassing Heaven, Earth, and the myriad things. However, the uniqueness of being human is the intrinsic capacity of the mind to "embody" (*ti*) the cosmos in its conscience and consciousness. Through this embodying, the mind realizes its own sensitivity, manifests true humanity and assists in the cosmic transformation of Heaven and Earth.[84]

To activate these dimensions of one's cosmological being spiritual practice is necessary through ethics, cultivation, and ritual.

The *ethical dimensions* emphasize the communitarian nature of Confucian moral philosophy. The individual is always seen in relation to others, not as an isolated, atomistic individual. The embeddedness of a person in a web of relationships involves mutual obligations and responsibilities rather than individual rights. A series of relationships expressed as correspondences is thus established between the person, the family, the larger society, and the cosmos itself. Humans are considered to be in relational resonance with other humans as well as with animals and plants, the elements and the seasons, colors and directions. Communitarian ethics thus involves an elaborate patterning that binds together the society and the cosmos. There is a rich moral continuity between persons and the universe at large.

The *self-transformational dimensions* of Confucian spirituality entail various modes of personal cultivation. These include a variety of practices ranging from the aesthetic arts of music, poetry, painting, and calligraphy to spiritual disciplines such as quiet-sitting, abiding in reverence, and being mindful when alone. One is encouraged to observe one's inner state of tranquillity before the emotions arise (centrality) and to achieve the appropriate balance in expressing emotions (harmony).[85] One cultivates the inner life so as to return to the original mind-and-heart of a child, thus expressing the deepest spontaneities and clearest responses of the human to others and to the larger cosmos. Tu Weiming has described such cultivation as "self-transformation as a communal act."[86] One of the main concerns of religious Confucianism is with moral and spiritual cultivation for the benefit of self, society, and the cosmos. This process of learning, reflection, and spiritual discipline is based on the understanding that to be fully human one aims to be a noble person (*junzi*) who is in harmony with the creative powers of Heaven and Earth and in accord with the larger human community. The goal of becoming a sage is an overarching goal of Confucian self-cultivation,[87] but always with the larger purpose of being of service to society and participating in the cosmological processes of the universe. Thus Confucian spirituality encompasses forms of practice that are attentive to the intersection of nature, of community, and of the self.

The *ritual dimensions* of Confucian spirituality involve the ties that link these intersections. Thus individuals and groups are joined together for a larger sense of social harmony, political coherence, and cosmological relationship. In China, state rituals at the altars of Heaven and Earth were a central component of this category, as were rituals at Confucian temples and in educational institutions. In addition to these forms of public display, private rituals were carried out at ancestral altars as well as within families and even between individuals. These included rituals for rites of passage such as birth, marriage, death, and mourning. From the more public state ceremonies to the more private family interactions, these ritual structures became a means of reflecting the patterns of the cosmos, linking to the world of the ancestors and binding individuals to one another.[88]

Spiritual Dimensions of Confucianism

It is appropriate to turn now to a fuller discussion of the religious worldview of Confucian cosmology as a way of appreciating its distinctive spiritual dynamics. This discussion is important for three reasons. First, it may help to shed some light on the varied roles and appeal of Confucianism in East Asia. Second, it is a valuable area of research because Confucianism is so little studied or understood within the discipline of the history of religions or comparative religions. Third, by elucidating the spiritual dimensions of Confucianism we may be able to broaden our understanding of the nature of spirituality in the human community at large.

Confucianism does not fit into the conventional definitions of religion, which have arisen from within the framework of the Western theistic traditions. As has been noted by various scholars, the absence of a personal Creator God in Confucianism and the lack of a strong distinction between the transcendent and immanent realms are just two examples of how Confucianism differs from western religions. Consequently, for many people Confucianism would not be characterized as a religion. [89] However, if we broaden our understanding of religion and place Confucianism in a comparative context, we will see more clearly the interaction of the Confucian religious worldview as a comprehensive cosmological orientation with particular dimensions of spiritual practice.

A fruitful way to illustrate this understanding of Confucianism is through Clifford Geertz's concept of "Religion as a Cultural System."[90] Geertz speaks of religion as consisting of a people's worldview and ethos, which become mutually reinforcing entities. The mediating relationship between cosmology and ethics is seen as crucial to an understanding of religion in different cultural contexts. As a cultural anthropologist, Geertz straddles the views of those concerned with analyzing religious experience (e.g., Rudolf Otto) and those more focused on a sociological analysis (e.g., Emile Durkheim). He acknowledges his debt to Max Weber, who was interested in studying not just social interactions but their underlying significance and cultural import as well. Likewise, he cites Wilfred Cantwell Smith as an influence in his formulation of religion as both faith and cumulative tradition, thus linking it to persons and culture.[91] These three areas of concern, namely, meaning, persons, and culture, are keys to Geertz's view of the role of religion.

Geertz observes that religion as a symbolic system cannot exist apart from a cultural context. Symbols, he suggests, mutually shape and are shaped by worldviews and ethos. When these two dimensions reinforce each other, there is a sense of coherence and order in a society. When they no longer function as patterns of meaning, a crisis of belief and practice occurs. Geertz points out that this is one way in which modern societies are in conflict with traditional beliefs and practices. In such circumstances, long-standing religious symbols appear to be unable to validate human action or substantiate a cosmology.

Geertz summarizes his concept of people's worldview and ethos, their cosmology and their spiritual practices, as mutually confirming entities expressed in symbols and ritual, in the following statement:

> As we are to deal with meaning, let us begin with a paradigm: viz., that sacred symbols function to synthesize a people's ethos—the tone, character and quality of their life, its moral and aesthetic style and mood—and their world-view—the picture they have of the way things in sheer actuality are, their most comprehensive ideas of order. In religious belief and practice a group's ethos is rendered intellectually reasonable by being shown to represent a way of life ideally adapted to the actual state of affairs the world-view describes, while the world-view is rendered emotionally convincing by being presented as an image of an actual state of affairs peculiarly well arranged to accommodate such a way of life.[92]

The religious worldview of Confucianism is evident in its dynamic cosmology interwoven with dimensions of spirituality, namely, communitarian harmony of society, moral cultivation of the individual, and public and private ritual expressions. This linking of self, society, and cosmos was effected through elaborate theories of correspondences.[93] Geertz's conceptual framework of worldview and ethos helps to elucidate further the interaction of Confucian cosmology and Confucian spirituality.

Worldview and Ethos: Organic Cosmology and Communitarian Ethics

The Confucian religious worldview, while by no means singular or uniform, is one that can be described as having an organismic cosmology[94] characterized as a "continuity of being"[95] within an "immanental cosmos."[96] There is no clear separation, as in the Western religions, between a transcendent, otherworldly order and an immanent, this-worldly orientation. As the *Mean* (*Zhongyong*) states: "The Way of Heaven and Earth can be described in one sentence: They are without any doubleness and so they produce things in an unfathomable way. The Way of Heaven and Earth is extensive, deep, high, brilliant, infinite, and lasting."[97]

Without an ontological gap between this world and an other world there emerges an appreciation for the seamless interaction of humans with the universe. The Confucian cosmological worldview is one that embraces a fluid and dynamic continuity of being. In terms of ethos or ethics this involves working out the deep interconnections of Heaven, Earth, and humans. This profound symbolic expression of the triadic intercommunion of an immanental cosmos is invoked repeatedly in both the Confucian and Neo-Confucian texts cited across East Asia.[98] As Tu Weiming notes, this cosmology is neither theocentric nor anthropocentric, but rather anthropocosmic.[99] In this sense the emphasis is not exclusively on the divine or on humans, as is the prevailing model in the west. Rather, the comprehensive interaction of Heaven, Earth, and humans is what is underscored by the term anthropocosmic. Thus the worldview of an organic cosmology creates a context for the intricate communitarian model of social ethics that distinguishes East Asian societies.

The mutual attraction of things for one another in both the human and natural worlds gives rise to an embedded ethical system of reciprocal relationships. The instinctive qualities of the human heart toward commiseration and empathy is what is nurtured and expressed in human relations and ritual practices (*Mencius* 2A:6). The human is not an isolated individual in need of redemption by a personal God, but is deeply embedded in a network of life-giving and life-sustaining relationships and rituals. Within this organic universe the human is viewed as a microcosm of the macrocosm where one's actions affect the larger whole, like ripples in a pond, as expressed in the *Great Learning*. Thus, there is a relational resonance of personal and cosmic communion animated by authenticity (*cheng*), as illustrated in the *Mean*.[100] The individual is intrinsically linked via rituals to various communities, beginning with the natural bonding of the family and stretching out to include the social-political order and to embrace the symbolic community of Heaven and Earth.[101] Humans achieve their fullest identity as members of the great triad with Heaven and Earth. Within this triad Heaven is a guiding moral presence, Earth is a vital moral force, and humans are co-creators of a humane and moral social-political order.

Cosmology and Cultivation:
Creativity of Heaven and Transformation of Humans

The Confucian organic cosmological order is distinguished by the creativity of Heaven as a life-giving force that is ceaselessly self-generating.[102] Similar to Whiteheadian process thought, the Confucian universe is seen as an unfolding, creative process, not as a static, inert mechanistic system controlled by an absent or remote deity.[103] As a protecting, sustaining, and transforming force, Heaven helps to bring all to their natural fulfillment as cosmological. This is because humans are imprinted with a Heavenly-endowed nature that enables them to transform themselves through self-cultivation.[104]

The ethos, then, of this creative cosmology is one that encourages education, learning, and self-transformation. The optimistic view of humans as receiving a Heavenly nature results in a Confucian educational and family

ethos that ideally create a value system for nurturing innate human goodness and the creative transformation of individual potential. This ethos is
one that encourages a filial sense of repayment to Heaven for the gift of life
and for a Heavenly-bestowed nature. The way to repay these gifts is
through ongoing moral cultivation for the betterment of self and society.
The symbol or model that joins this aspect of the worldview and ethos
together is the noble person (*junzi*), or the sage (*sheng*), who "hears" the
will of Heaven and is able to embody it naturally in the ongoing process of
learning and self-cultivation. The sage is thus the highest embodiment of
the spiritual aspirations of the Confucian tradition.[105]

Vitalism of the Earth and Co-creativity of Humans: Cosmological Correspondences and Human Ritual

The creativity of Heaven in the Confucian cosmological worldview is paralleled by the vitalism of the natural world. From the early text of the *Classic of Changes* (*Yijing*), through the Neo Confucian reappropriation of this
classic, the sense of the vitality of the natural world infuses many of the
Confucian writings.[106] This vitality is understood as part of the seasonal
cycles of nature, rather than as the developmental, evolving universe discussed by contemporary process philosophers and theologians. It is
expressed in an elaborate series of correspondences (seasonal, directional,
elemental) and rituals that in Han Confucianism were seen as patterns suggestive of the careful regulation needed in the social and political realms.[107]
This cosmological view of the integral cycles of nature reinforces an ethos
of cooperating with those processes through establishing a harmonious
society and government with appropriate ritual structures. The rituals
reflect the patterned structures of the natural world and bind humans to
one another, to the ancestral world, and to the cosmos at large.

The vital material force (*qi*) of the universe is that which joins humans
and nature, unifying their worldview and ethos and giving humans the
potential to become co-creators with the universe.[108] As Mencius notes, it
is *qi* that unites rightness (ethos) and the Way (worldview), filling the
whole space between Heaven and Earth.[109] The moral imperative of Confucianism, then, is to make appropriate ethical and ritual choices linked to
the creative powers of the Way and thus contribute to the betterment of
social and political order.

The Confucian worldview, then, affirms change, as is manifest in the creativity of Heaven and in the vitality of Earth. In particular, the varied and
dynamic patterns of cosmological change are celebrated as part of a life-
giving universe. Rituals and music are designed to harmonize with these

cosmic changes and to assist the process of personal transformation. Rituals help to join the worldview of cosmic change with the ethos of human changes in society, thus harmonizing the natural and human orders. Rituals and music are a means of creating grace, beauty, and accord. Thus, the natural cosmological structures of the Earth provide a counterpoint for an ethos of social patterns expressed in ritual behavior and music. Harmonizing with the universe in a cosmological sense is balanced by an ethos of reciprocal resonance in human relations and is expressed in the patterned behavior of rituals.

Conclusion

The religious worldview of Confucianism encompasses a dynamic cosmological orientation that is interwoven with spiritual expressions in the form of communitarian ethics of society, self-cultivation of the person, and ritual expressions integrating self, society, and cosmos. This tapestry of spiritual integration, which has had a long and rich history in China and in other countries of East Asia, deserves further study. These volumes are a contribution to such investigations. We trust they will also point the way toward future forms of Confucian spirituality in new and creative expressions.

Notes

1. In this introduction, except where noted, we are using the terms "Confucian" and "Confucianism" to refer to the tradition in a broad sense without necessarily distinguishing between the early classical Confucian expressions and the later Neo-Confucian forms in China, Korea, and Japan.

2. As Tu Weiming puts it, "Despite the difficulty of conceptualizing transcendence as radical otherness, the Confucian commitment to ultimate self-transformation necessarily involves a transcendent dimension" (*Confucian Thought: Self-hood as Creative Transformation* [Albany: State University of New York Press, 1985] 137). This is not "radical transcendence but immanence with a transcendent dimension" (*Centrality and Commonality: An Essay on Confucian Religiousness* [Albany: State University of New York Press, 1989], 121). See similar arguments made earlier by Liu Shu-hsien, "The Confucian Approach to the Problem of Transcendence and Immanence," *Philosophy East and West* 22, no. 1 (1972): 45–52. Roger Ames and David Hall have argued that the Confucian tradition, especially in its classical forms does not focus on transcendence. See their books *Thinking Through Confucius* (Albany: State University of New York Press, 1987) and *Thinking from the Han: Self, Truth and Transcendence in Chinese and Western Culture* (Albany: State University of New York Press, 1998). See also Roger Ames, "Reli-

giousness in Classical Confucianism: A Comparative Analysis," in *Asian Culture Quarterly* 12, no. 2 (1984): 7–23.

3. Liu Shu-shien and others have observed that Confucianism as a cultural ideal embodying certain spiritual values and aspirations should be differentiated from Confucianism as embedded in social and political ideologies and institutions. See his chapter in Tu Weiming, *Confucian Traditions in East Asian Modernity: Moral Education and Economic Culture in Japan and the Four Mini Dragons* (Cambridge, Mass.: Harvard University Press, 1996). See also Liu Shu-sien, *Understanding Confucian Philosophy: Classical and Sung-Ming* (Westport, Conn.: Praeger, 1998).

4. While one could utilize certain Western definitions of religion to illustrate that Confucianism is a religion, these definitions may limit the understanding of the nature of Confucian spirituality. For example, we can draw on both Paul Tillich's and Frederick Streng's definitions of religion. For Tillich, religion focuses on ultimate concern, while Streng suggests that religion is a means of ultimate transformation. See Paul Tillich, *The Dynamics of Faith* (New York: Harper & Row, 1957); idem, *The Courage to Be* (New York: Harper & Row, 1952); and Frederick Streng, *Understanding Religious Life* (Belmont, Calif.: Wadsworth Publishing Co., 1985).

Both of these broad definitions are applicable to Confucianism. Ultimate concern in Confucianism is evident when a person is responding to the will of Heaven that is discovered in one's Heavenly-endowed nature and manifest in temporal affairs. Ultimate transformation in Confucianism involves modes of self-cultivation that are intellectual, spiritual, and moral. The goal here is to become more fully human, namely, more deeply empathetic and more comprehensively compassionate. Ultimate transformation leads one toward sagehood. Still, this attainment is within the phenomenal world, not apart from it, and for the benefit of the larger society, not for one's salvation alone. This distinguishes Confucian religiosity from Western forms of religion. See also Wilfred Cantwell Smith, *The Meaning and End of Religion* (New York: Macmillan, 1963) for a discussion of the nature of religion.

Articulating the Confucian worldview (both philosophically and religiously) apart from Western categories has been the concern of Roger Ames and David Hall, who suggest that Confucianism is at once nontheistic and profoundly religious. See their commentary on the *Mean* in *Focusing the Familiar: A Translation and Philosophical Interpretation of the Zhongyong* (Albany: State University of New York, 2001).

5. Tu Weiming has observed: "The problem of whether Neo-Confucianism is a religion should not be confused with the more significant question: what does it mean to be religious in the Neo-Confucian community? The solution to the former often depends on the particular interpretive position we choose to take on what constitutes the paradigmatic example of a religion, which may have little to do with our knowledge about Neo-Confucianism as a spiritual tradition" ("Neo-Confucian Religiosity and Human-Relatedness," in *Confucian Thought*, 132).

6. I am indebted to the work of Wm. Theodore de Bary and Tu Weiming in

ﯾﮟ

this area. For one of the first comprehensive discussions of the religious dimensions of Confucianism, see de Bary's introduction to *The Unfolding of Neo-Confucianism* (New York: Columbia University Press, 1975). Similarly see Tu Weiming, *Centrality and Commonality.* In addition, the work of P. J. Ivanhoe and Roger Ames and David Hall has been significant. See P. J. Ivanhoe, *Confucian Moral Self Cultivation* (Indianapolis: Hackett, 2000); and Roger Ames and David Hall's numerous books including their most recent, *Focusing the Familiar.*

7. We are using worldview here in its singular form, yet we recognize worldviews as having various formative components.

8. Karl Jaspers, *Origin and Goal of History* (London: Routledge & Kegan Paul, 1953).

9. John Berthrong, *All Under Heaven: Transforming Paradigms in Confucian-Christian Dialogue* (Albany: State University of New York Press, 1994), 216.

10. See Tu Weiming, "The Continuity of Being: Chinese Visions of Nature" in *Confucian Thought.*

11. Ibid., 137–38.

12. See, e.g., John Henderson, *The Development and Decline of Chinese Cosmology* (New York: Columbia University Press, 1984); *Explorations of Early Chinese Cosmology,* ed. Henry Rosemont (Missoula, Mont.: Scholars Press, 1984); Charles LeBlanc, *Huai-nan tzu: Philosophical Synthesis in Early Han Thought* (Hong Kong: Hong Kong University Press 1985).

13. The five relations are between ruler and minister, parent and child, husband and wife, older and younger siblings, and friend and friend.

14. Tu Weiming, *Centrality and Commonality.*

15. Ivanhoe, *Confucian Moral Self Cultivation,* xii.

16. Tu Weiming, *Centrality and Commonality,* 94–96.

17. This is from the *Great Learning (Daxue).* See *Sources of Chinese Tradition,* ed. Wm. Theodore de Bary and Irene Bloom (New York: Columbia University Press, 1999), 330.

18. For discussion of sagehood as the goal of Confucian spiritual practice, see Rodney Taylor, *The Religious Dimensions of Confucianism* (Albany: State University of New York Press, 1989); and idem, *The Cultivation of Sagehood as a Religious Goal in Neo-Confucianism: A Study of Selected Writings of Kao P'an-lung (1562–1626)* (Missoula, Mont.: Scholars Press, 1978). For an insightful discussion of the various models of self-cultivation in the Confucian and Neo-Confucian tradition, see Ivanhoe, *Confucian Moral Self Cultivation.*

19. *Hsun Tzu, Basic Writings,* trans. Burton Watson (New York: Columbia University Press, 1963). The importance of ritual practice for the Confucian spiritual path has been emphasized by Robert Neville; see especially his *Boston Confucianism: Portable Tradition in the Late-Modern World* (Albany: State University of New York Press, 2000). Edward Machle sees Xunxi's sense of ritual as reflecting a kind of cosmic dance; see his *Nature and Heaven in the Xunzi: A Study of the Tien Lun* (Albany: State University of New York Press, 1993).

20. Ivanhoe, *Confucian Moral Self Cultivation,* xiv.

21. Some of this work has been led by the New Confucians in Hong Kong and Taiwan such as Tang Junyi and Mou Zongsan and their students, such as Tu Weiming and Liu Shu-shien. Scholars who have especially focused on the religious and philosophical dimensions of Confucianism include Roger Ames, John Berthrong, Julia Ching, Cheng Chung-ying, Antonio Cua, Wm. Theodore de Bary, David Hall, P. J. Ivanhoe, Young Chan Ro, Rodney Taylor, Mary Evelyn Tucker, and Lee Yearley. See especially the multiple volumes of David Hall and Roger Ames as well as John Berthrong, "Trends in the Interpretation of Confucian Religiosity, in *All Under Heaven;* Julia Ching, *Chinese Religions* (Maryknoll, N.Y.: Orbis Books, 1993); Liu Shu-hsien, "The Religious Import of Confucian Philosophy: Its Traditional Outlook and Contemporary Significance," in *Philosophy East and West* 21, no. 2 (1971): 157–75; Tang Chun-I, "The Development of Ideas of Spiritual Value in Chinese Philosophy," in *The Chinese Mind,* ed. Charles Moore (Honolulu: University Press of Hawaii, 1967); Taylor, *Religious Dimensions of Confucianism;* Tu Weiming, *Confucian Thought;* idem, *Centrality and Commonality.*

22. See Wm. Theodore de Bary, *The Trouble with Confucianism* (Cambridge, Mass.: Harvard University Press, 1991). The work of philosophers and Sinologists such as Roger Ames and P. J. Ivanhoe is especially important in this regard.

23. David Keightley, "The Religious Commitment: Shang Theology and the Genesis of Chinese Political Culture," *History of Religions* 117 (1978): 224.

24. See Richard Rubinger, *Private Academies of Tokugawa Japan* (Princeton, N.J.: Princeton University Press, 1982).

25. Wm. Theodore de Bary, "A Reappraisal of Neo-Confucianism," in *Studies in Chinese Thought,* ed. Arthur Wright, *The American Anthropological Association* 55, no. 5, part 2, memoir no. 75 (December 1953).

26. See Wm. Theodore de Bary, *Learning for One's Self: Essays on the Individual in Neo-Confucian Thought* (New York: Columbia University Press, 1991).

27. See ibid.

28. See Tu Weiming's discussion of this in *Centrality and Commonality.*

29. It is important to note that this ordering of cosmos and society can have both life-enhancing and life-constraining dimensions. When used as political ideology in the Han period the record becomes more mixed.

30. The Confucians were, however, caught in matters of pragmatic politics of governance that often required not only an appeal to personal moral transformation and ritual practice as a means of restraint, but also recognized that law and punishment had their function, although as a secondary measure.

31. Many of the writings of Western Confucian scholars are being translated into Chinese as part of the renewed interest in Confucianism in China. These include works by Wm. Theodore de Bary, Tu Weiming, Roger Ames and David Hall, Robert Neville, John Berthrong, and these two volumes on Confucian spirituality.

32. Clearly, the tension of acknowledging the historical particularity of Confucianism along with identifying certain overarching religious elements in the tradition is present here.

33. For example, in Japan Confucianism linked itself to Shinto during the seventeenth century, was separated from it by the nativists of the eighteenth century, and was rejoined to Shinto again in the late nineteenth century. Japanese Confucianism as a worldview and as a form of spiritual cultivation is still part of many of the new religions in Japan and deserves further study. See Helen Hardacre's discussion of "The World View of the New Religions," in *Kurozumikyo and the New Religions of Japan* (Princeton, N.J.: Princeton University Press, 1986), ch. 1.

34. See Judith Berling, *The Syncretic Religion of Lin Chao-en* (New York: Columbia University Press, 1980).

35. Tu Weiming speaks of the New Confucians as the "Third Epoch of Confucian Humanism" after the classical and Neo-Confucian periods; see *Confucianism: The Dynamics of Tradition,* ed. Irene Eber (New York: Macmillan, 1986), 3–21. John Berthrong has outlined six periods of Confucianism which separate out the Han, Tang, and later Qing Evidential Learning; see *All Under Heaven,* 77–83, 191–92.

36. The following nine paragraphs have appeared in slightly different form in "An Ecological Cosmology: The Confucian Philosophy of Material Force," in *Ecological Prospects: Scientific, Religious and Aesthetic Perspectives,* ed. Christopher Chapple (Albany: State University of New York Press, 1994).

37. The actual compilation and editing of these texts are the subject of numerous scholarly debates.

38. John Berthrong has translated *li* not only as "ritual" but as "civility," so as to encompass the area of politics and human rights (*All Under Heaven*).

39. Likewise, often great distortions were demanded by parents or in-laws and, this dark side of Confucianism was highlighted in the New Culture movement of the twentieth century. See, e.g., the novel *Family,* by Ba Jin.

40. The fours seeds or four beginnings (pity and compassion, shame and aversion, modesty and compliance, sense of right and wrong) in *Mencius* 2A:6 contain incipient tendencies toward the four virtues in all humans (humaneness, rightness, propriety, wisdom). The man of Song in *Mencius* 2A:2 describes a man who tried to help his seedlings to grow by pulling them up. Ox Mountain in *Mencius* 6A:8 describes a mountain that has been deforested as comparable to one's innate good nature that languishes because it is not cultivated.

41. See a discussion of this in Julia Ching, *The Religious Thought of Chu Hsi* (New York: Oxford University Press, 2000), 124–25. See also Sarah Allan, *The Way of Water and the Sprouts of Virtue* (Albany: State University of New York Press, 1997).

42. *Hsun Tzu, Basic Writings,* trans. Watson, 80. Publications on Hsun Tzu (Xunzi) have grown in recent years. See Machle, *Nature and Heaven in the Xunzi;* Paul Ratika Goldin, *Rituals of the Way: The Philosophy of Xunzi* (LaSalle, Ill.: Open

Court, 1995); T. C. Kline and P. J. Ivanhoe, *Virtue, Nature and Moral Agency in the Xunzi* (Indianapolis: Hackett, 2000). See also Eric Hutton, "Virtue and Reason in Xunxi" (Ph.D. diss., Stanford University, 2001).

43. Wing-tsit Chan, trans. *Reflections on Things at Hand: The Neo-Confucian Anthology* (New York: Columbia University Press, 1967).

44. For a comprehensive discussion see Ching, *Religious Thought of Chu Hsi.* See also Wing-tsit Chan, *Chu Hsi: Life and Thought* (New York: St. Martin's Press, 1987), especially 139–61 ("Chu Hsi's Religious Life").

45. This appears in the *Classified Conversations of Chu Hsi* (*Chu-tzu yu-lei* 94:12a); see Ching, *Religious Thought of Chu Hsi,* 95.

46. The *Mean* (*Zhongyong*) ch. 22 in *Sources of Chinese Tradition,* ed. de Bary and Bloom, 338.

47. Yung Sik Kim, *The Natural Philosophy of Chu Hsi 1130–1200* (Philadelphia: American Philosophical Association, 2000), 219.

48. For a discussion of Neo-Confucian spiritual practice, see Wm. Theodore de Bary, "Neo-Confucian Cultivation and Enlightenment," in *Unfolding of Neo-Confucianism,* ed. de Bary. See also Ivanhoe, *Confucian Moral Self Cultivation.*

49. This is the important thesis of Wm. Theodore de Bary in *Neo-Confucian Orthodoxy and the Learning of the Mind-and-Heart* (New York: Columbia University Press, 1981).

50. Patricia Ebrey, trans., *Chu Hsi's Family Rituals: A Twelfth-Century Manual for the Performance of Cappings. Weddings, Funerals, and Ancestral Rites* (Princeton, N.J.: Princeton University Press, 1991).

51. On Korean Neo-Confucianism, see *The Rise of Neo-Confucianism in Korea,* ed. Wm. Theodore de Bary and JaHyun Kim Haboush (New York: Columbia University Press, 1985).

52. See Michael Kalton, trans. and ed., *To Become a Sage: The Ten Diagrams on Sage Learning by Yi T'oegye* (New York: Columbia University Press, 1988); and Young-Chan Ro, *The Korean Neo-Confucianism of Yi Yulgok* (Albany: State University of New York Press, 1989).

53. For an excellent survey of the history of Japanese Confucianism, see Martin Collcutt, "The Legacy of Confucianism in Japan," in *The East Asian Region,* ed. Gilbert Rozman (Princeton, N.J.: Princeton University Press, 1991), 111–54. See also Wm. Theodore de Bary and Irene Bloom, *Principle and Practicality: Essays in Neo-Confucianism and Practical Learning* (New York: Columbia University Press, 1979); *Confucianism and Tokugawa Culture,* ed. Peter Nosco (Princeton, N.J.: Princeton University Press, 1984); and Mary Evelyn Tucker, "Confucianism in Japan," in *Encyclopedia of Chinese Philosophy, ed.* Antonio Cua (Westport, Conn.: Garland Publications, 2002).

54. See Mary Evelyn Tucker, *Moral and Spiritual Cultivation in Japanese Neo-Confucianism: The Life and Thought of Kaibara Ekken (1630-1714)* (Albany: State University of New York Press, 1989).

55. One of the richest discussions of this reinterpretation of the Confucian legacy in light of Social Darwinism occurs in James Pusey's book *China and*

Charles Darwin (Cambridge, Mass.: Council for East Asia Studies and Harvard University Press, 1983).

56. This debate has been explored by Wm. Theodore de Bary in *Trouble with Confucianism;* and in his book *The Liberal Tradition in China* (New York: Columbia Press, 1983).

57. This discussion was in part initiated by Max Weber's critique of Confucianism as an inhibiting force in the modernization process. See *The Religion of China: Confucianism and Daoism,* trans. Hans H. Gerth (Glencoe, Ill: Free Press, 1951). The view of Confucianism as a static tradition has been challenged by Wm. Theodore de Bary and others. See, e.g., de Bary's introduction to *Unfolding of Neo-Confucianism;* and Thomas Metzger, *Escape from Predicament: Neo-Confucianism and China's Evolving Political Culture* (New York: Columbia University Press, 1977).

58. This is especially the concern of Tu Weiming; see his *Confucian Traditions in East Asian Modernity.*

59. See, e.g., Neville, *Boston Confucianism.*

60. See Wm. Theodore de Bary, "Introduction," in *Confucianism and Human Rights* (New York: Columbia University Press, 1998), 25, and his book *Trouble with Confucianism.*

61. The debate regarding human rights in China and the role of Confucianism has been vigorously discussed in the last decade. See especially *Confucianism and Human Rights,* ed. Wm. Theodore de Bary and Tu Weiming (New York: Columbia University Press, 1998); *The East Asian Challenge for Human Rights,* ed. Joanne Bauer and Daniel Bell (New York: Cambridge University Press, 1999); and Daniel Bell, *East Meets West: Human Rights and Democracy in East Asia* (Princeton, N.J.: Princeton University Press, 2000).

62. See *Confucianism and Ecology: The Interrelation of Heaven, Earth and Humans,* ed. Mary Evelyn Tucker and John Berthrong (Cambridge, Mass.: Harvard Center for the Study of World Religions and Harvard University Press, 1998).

63. See, e.g., the work of Peter Bol, Benjamin Elman, Lionel Jensen, and Hoyt Tillman noted in the bibliography.

64. This preoccupation with ideology has been especially strong in the field of postmodern deconstruction.

65. Kang advocated the preservation of Confucianism and even its reestablishment as an institutional religion. He was particularly adamant that Confucius was a reformer and that therefore his ideas could be used to back the reforms being recommended by the Self Strengthening movement in the late nineteenth century. This in turn would help to preserve China from Western exploitation. See James Pusey, "K'ang Yu-Wei and *Pao Chiao:* Confucian Reform and Reformation," *Papers on China* 20 (December 1966). Published by East Asian Research Center, Harvard University. See also Chen Hsi-yuan, "Confucianism Encounters Religion: The Formation of Religious Discourse and the Confucian Movement in Modern China" (Ph.D diss., Harvard University, 1999).

66. Wm. Theodore de Bary claims, however, that these schools were not as rigidly distinguished as later historians have delineated (*Neo-Confucian Orthodoxy*).

67. See Norman J. Girardot, *The Victorian Translation of China: James Legge's Oriental and Oxonian Pilgrimage* (Berkeley: University of California Press, 2001), 35.

68. For further studies on this, see *Discovering China: European Interpretations in the Enlightenment*, ed. Julia Ching and Willard Oxtoby (Rochester: University of Rochester Press, 1992); Julia Ching and Willard Oxtoby, *Moral Enlightenment: Leibniz and Wolff on China*, Monumenta serica monograph series 26 (Nettetal: Steyler Verlag, 1992); J. J. Clarke, *Oriental Enlightenment: The Encounter Between Asian and Western Thought* (London/New York: Routledge, 1997).

69. Herrlee Creel, "Was Confucius Agnostic?" *T'oung Pao* 39 (1932): 55–99.

70. John Chaffee, *The Thorny Gates of Learning in Sung China: A Social History of Examinations* (New York: Cambridge University Press, 1985).

71. C. K. Yang, "The Functional Relationship Between Confucian Thought and Chinese Religion" in *Chinese Thought and Institutions*, ed. John Fairbank (Chicago: University of Chicago Press, 1957). Thomas Wilson, on the other hand, raises the question of how the separation arose in China between religion and rational philosophy: "Yet it is not clear whether this 'transition' occurred in Confucius' day or whether it is the effect of a much later modernist separation between ritual, religion, activities of the body on the one hand, and ethics, rational philosophy and thoughts of the mind on the other" (*Geneology of the Way: The Construction and Uses of the Confucian Tradition in Late Imperial China*, ed. Thomas Wilson [Stanford: Stanford University Press, 1995], 10).

72. This was, in part, the assumption of the May Fourth movement of 1919 in China, which had such strong anti-Confucian tones. This critical tone continued with such writers as Lu Xun and others who wished to "Destroy the old curiosity shop of Confucianism." See James Pusey, *Lu Xun and Evolution* (Albany: State University of New York Press, 1998); and Lin Yu-sheng, *The Crisis of Chinese Consciousness: Radical Antitraditionalism in the May Fourth Era* (Madison: University of Wisconsin Press, 1979). The Maoists also wished to overthrow Confucianism as "feudalistic," especially during the Cultural Revolution in the 1970s. This was also part of the appeal of John Dewey's ideas during his two-year stay in China (1919–1921) and even down to the present. See David Hall and Roger Ames, *Democracy of the Dead: Dewey, Confucius and the Hope for Democracy in China* (LaSalle, Ill.: Open Court, 1999).

73. See de Bary, *Sources of Chinese Tradition*, 546–50.

74. See *The Limits to Change: Essays on Conservative Alternatives in Republican China*, ed. Charlotte Furth (Cambridge, Mass.: Harvard University Press, 1976).

75. For an abbreviated version of the Manifesto, see Wm. Theodore de Bary and Richard Lufrano, *Sources of Chinese Tradition* (New York: Columbia University Press, 2000), 2:550–58. For the full version, see Carsun Chang, *The Development of Neo-Confucian Thought* (New York: Bookman Associates, 1962), 2:455–83.

76. See Berthrong, *All Under Heaven*, 191.

77. Gilbert Rozman, ed., *The East Asian Region: Confucian Heritage and Its Modern Adaptation* (Princeton, N.J.: Princeton University Press, 1991). These various categories are described on p. 161.

78. Kim Kyong-Dong, "Confucianism and Modernization in East Asia," in *The Impact of Traditional Thought on Present-Day Japan,* ed. Josef Kreiner (Munich: Iudicium-Verlag, 1996), 51–53.

79. Wm. Theodore de Bary and John Chaffee, *Neo-Confucian Education: The Formative Stage* (Berkeley: University of California Press, 1989).

80. See de Bary, *Learning for One's Self.*

81. See, e.g., the study by Tetsuo Najita, *Visions of Virtue in Tokugawa Japan: The Kaitokudo Merchant Academy of Osaka* (Chicago: University of Chicago Press, 1987).

82. See Tu Weiming, *Confucian Traditions in East Asian Modernity.* See also the articles on modernization and development by Ronald Dore, Tu Weiming, and Kim Kyong-Dong in *Impact of Traditional Thought on Present Day Japan,* ed. Kreiner.

83. Robert Neville, "Introduction," in Rodney Taylor, *Religious Dimensions of Confucianism,* ix, x.

84. Tu Weiming, *Confucian Thought,* 132.

85. See the *Mean* in *Sources of Chinese Tradition,* ed. de Bary and Bloom, 333–39.

86. Tu Weiming, "Neo-Confucian Religiosity and Human Relatedness," in *Confucian Thought,* 133.

87. Taylor, *Religious Dimensions of Confucianism;* idem, *The Cultivation of Sagehood as a Religious Goal in Neo-Confucianism: A Study of Selected Writings of Kao P'an-lung (1562-1626)* (Missoula, Mont.: Scholars Press, 1978).

88. *The Ways of Heaven,* ed. Rodney Taylor (Leiden: Brill, 1986); *Genealogy of the Way: The Construction and Uses of the Confucian Tradition in Late Imperial China,* ed. Thomas Wilson (Stanford: Stanford University Press, 1995); Patricia Ebrey, *Confucianism and Family Rituals in Imperial China: A Social History of Writing about Rites* (Princeton, N.J.: Princeton University Press, 1991); and eadem, *Chu Hsi's Family Rituals* (Princeton. N.J.: Princeton University Press, 1991).

89. As we noted earlier, part of the difficulty in describing Confucianism as a religion or as religious are the assumptions and agenda one brings to the topic. For many people the term "religion" has negative associations with antiquated ways of thinking that need to be superseded by more rational, humanist, and modern modes of thought. This was true for Westerners such as the Enlightenment *philosophes* of the eighteenth century and for Chinese reformers such as Hu Shi in the twentieth century. These thinkers applauded the move from so-called superstition and ritual to rationalism and ethics as being a mark of the progress or development of a culture. For others, religion has positive associations of bringing a culture into dialogue with other cultures or worldviews where religion is valued. Some examples of this are the attempts of the Jesuits in seventeenth-century China and the Christian missionaries in the nineteenth century to identify monotheism in the Confucian tradition as present in the early cult of the Lord on High (*Shangdi*) and in the concept of Heaven (*tian*).

90. See his article with this title in *Reader in Comparative Religion: An Anthropological Approach,* ed. William A. Lessa and Evon Z. Vogt (New York: Harper & Row, 1972), 167–78.

91. Smith, *Meaning and End of Religion.*

92. Clifford Geertz, "Religion as a Cultural System," in *Reader in Comparative Religion: An Anthropological Approach,* ed. William Lessa and Evon Vogt (New York: Harper & Row, 1972), 167.

93. This is especially evident in Han Confucian thought, but it continued to influence the later Neo-Confucian tradition as well.

94. Joseph Needham, *Science and Civilisation in China* (Cambridge: Cambridge University Press, 1956), 2:291–93.

95. See Tu Weiming, *Confucian Thought.*

96. This is a term used by Roger Ames and David Hall in *Thinking Through Confucius,* 12–17.

97. Translated by Wing-tsit Chan, *A Source Book in Chinese Philosophy* (Princeton, N.J.: Princeton University Press, 1963), 109.

98. These include, among others, the *Book of Changes* (Third Appendix); the *Book of Ritual* (ch. 7); the *Mean* (ch. 22); Dong Zhongshu, *Luxuriant Gems of the Spring and Autumn Annals* (ch. 44); the *Diagram of the Great Ultimate* of Zhou Dunyi; the *Western Inscription* of Zhang Zai; the *Commentary on the Great Learning* by Wang Yangming. See these texts in *Sources of Chinese Tradition,* ed. de Bary and Bloom.

99. Tu Weiming, *Centrality and Commonality,* 102–7.

100. See chs. 22, 25, 26 of the *Mean* in *Sources of Chinese Tradition,* ed. de Bary and Bloom.

101. See Thomas Berry's article "Affectivity in Classical Confucian Tradition," ch. 5 in this volume.

102. *Book of Changes* Appendix HI 2:1/8. See also the chapter on "Creative Principle" in Hellmut Wilhelm, *Heaven, Earth and Man in the Book of Changes* (Seattle: University of Washington Press, 1977). The Neo-Confucians frequently refer to the productive and reproductive forces of the universe (ch. *sheng sheng,* Jp. *sei sei*).

103. See Berthrong, *All Under Heaven.*

104. See the *Mean,* ch. 1 in *Sources of Chinese Tradition,* ed. de Bary and Bloom.

105. Taylor, *Religious Dimensions of Confucianism.*

106. See Kidder Smith, Peter Bol, Joseph Adler, and Don Wyatt, *Sung Dynasty Uses of the I Ching* (Princeton, N.J.: Princeton University Press, 1990).

107. See *Explorations in Early Chinese Cosmology,* ed. Henry Rosemont (Chico, Calif.: Scholars Press, 1984); Sarah Queen, *From Chronicle to Canon: The Hermeneutics of the Spring and Autumn According to Tung Chung-shu* (New York: Cambridge University Press, 1996); Robert Eno, *The Confucian Creation of Heaven: Philosophy and the Defense of Ritual Mastery* (Albany: State University of New York Press, 1990); Henderson, *Development and Decline of Chinese Cosmology.*

108. See Tu Weiming's use of the term co-creator in *Centrality and Commonality,* 70, 78, 98, 102, 106.

109. *Mencius* 2A:2.

Part Three

CONFUCIAN HUMANISM
AS A MANIFESTATION
OF EAST ASIAN SPIRITUALITY:
SELF-CULTIVATION
AS SPIRITUAL PRAXIS

17

From Cosmic to Personal: Shao Yong's Narratives on the Creative Source

JOANNE D. BIRDWHISTELL

Theoretical Considerations

COMPARATIVE STUDIES SUGGEST that there are many ways to be religious, for diverse phenomena fall within the scope of what is, and has been, considered religion. Although religious systems differ widely in their particular characteristics and in the approaches that they emphasize, a common tie, according to scholars, is their concern with "ultimate reality," however that is conceived. Employing a variety of practices and beliefs, religious participants attempt to bring themselves near to, and establish an appropriate relationship with, ultimate reality. While religious phenomena may be studied from different perspectives, one helpful framework for investigating and comparing the diverse phenomena proposes six fundamental ways of being religious. These consist of the ways of right action, sacred rite, reasoned inquiry, mystical quest, shamanic mediation, and devotion.[1]

Whether seen in terms of these six ways or from some other perspective, religion may further be understood as involving a system of symbols and symbolic actions that help the participants fulfill their aims relating to ultimate reality. Symbols are diverse and include such things as narratives, scriptures, words, gestures, objects, places, and moral codes. Not only do religions vary in the symbols they emphasize, but the symbols within a religion may also be interpreted in different ways, both over time and by different people at the same time. Symbols are dynamic entities, constantly changing and continually open to new uses. They are an important key to understanding the dynamics of a religion.

Shao Yong represents both his own creativity and his historical-cultural context, and his spiritual position will be discussed here in light of these six ways of being religious along with the symbols important in his thought. First, a look at a few characteristics of Shao himself may help us appreciate Shao's views.[2] Shao Yong (1012–1077 C.E.) was a thinker, charismatic teacher, writer, and poet who lived during a prosperous and relatively peaceful period of the Northern Song dynasty (960–1125 C.E.). His writings and those of others indicate that he was familiar with all kinds of texts, including those associated with the religious traditions of Daoism, Buddhism, and Confucianism. He studied the Confucian classics but never took the official examinations, and he traveled extensively, in part at least to further his education. He maintained friendships with contemporary political and intellectual leaders who identified with Confucianism, and he participated in discussion groups that advocated Confucian ideas and practices. He also engaged in various Daoist practices.

His teachers included his father, who is thought to have specialized in learning based on the *Book of Changes* (*Yijing*), and the government official Li Zhicai, who taught him the *Yijing*-based learning called the "learning of the images and numbers" (*xiangshu xue*). Li's version of this form of *Yijing* learning is generally traced to the esoteric Daoist learning of Chen Tuan (tenth century C.E.) of the Tang dynasty, while its roots go back at least to the Han dynasty, if not earlier. Shao's importance in the Neo-Confucian tradition was due, in part, to the widely accepted view that he was the first thinker to reveal to a broader audience this hitherto secret system of knowledge. He was regarded as one of the five founders of the "learning of Dao" (*Daoxue*), often called Neo-Confucianism in English, and his thought influenced many later thinkers. From hindsight, we can also say that Shao truly was a transitional type of thinker, who incorporated Confucian, Daoist, and Buddhist elements in his thought. His major writings consist of the *August Ultimate Traversing the Ages* (*Huangji jingshi*, hereafter cited as HJJS, and also translated as the *Supreme Principles Ordering the World*), a philosophical-religious-historical work, and a compilation of poetry, *Collection of the Yi River Teacher's Beating the Rang* (*Yichuan jirangji*, hereafter cited as JRJ).

The Primary Symbol in Shao Yong's Thought

The symbol or symbolic form at the center of Shao's thought was a story or narrative that Shao told in various ways in both prose and verse. His narrative was a sacred narrative, for it was concerned with ultimate questions about human existence and with "ultimate reality," conceived by him as being the creative source of the cosmos and all things. Shao's story consisted of an account of the emergence and theoretical structure of three inter-related entities: the cosmos itself, civilization as a moral-social-political-cultural realm, and human beings in society. In other words, he told the story about how the cosmos, civilization (that is, Chinese civilization), and human beings each emerged from Dao (Way), the creative source. In addition, he related how each of these three entities could symbolically be rein-tegrated into the precosmic whole.[3] For the individual person, this meant achieving a unity or harmony with the creative source, while for the cos-mos and civilization, this meant attaining a harmony that was symbolic of the precosmic condition. Although Shao often used the term Dao (Way) to refer to this ultimate reality, he employed other terms too, such as Heaven (*tian*).

Shao's "master narrative" focused both on the particular entities that appeared at each stage of development and on the underlying patterns that ordered each stage. For instance, particular entities included Heaven and earth in cosmic development, the ancient sage Fuxi, King Wen, and the Han dynasty in the development of civilization, and human nature (*xing*) and the heart-mind (*xin*) in the formation of human beings. Underlying patterns included bipolar pairing and alternation, as well as quaternary grouping and correlations, and they were represented by the symbols of *Yijing* learning. These symbols were called "images" and "numbers."

Since the motifs and elements comprising both perspectives had exten-sive symbolic importance, Shao's accounts made a variety of interpreta-tions possible. Consequently, the sacred narrative recounted so effectively by Shao, but told by others too, gained usefulness as a religious symbol in at least four of the six ways mentioned above. These four were the ways of right action, reasoned inquiry, mystical quest, and devotion.

Shao's narrative supported the way of right action by using historical precedents to illustrate the importance of moral action and to serve as mod-els for behavior. In the Chinese context, moral action was understood both as proper behavior in the family and society and as positive political action that contributed to the welfare of the people and the state. Moral behavior led to harmony in the cosmos, state, and individual.

His narrative supported the way of reasoned inquiry by making public and explaining the esoteric *Yijing*-learning that was believed to offer an understanding of the patterns of nature, or the cosmos, society, and all things. This understanding would enable a sagely ruler to respond effec-tively in the human world to the many changes of nature (or Heaven). Whether in a personal or political context, reasoned inquiry could aid one in making appropriate, moral responses, an act known as adaptive behavior or situational weighing (*quan*), an important concept in Shao's thought and in Confucianism.

Along with right action, the way of mystical quest was the ultimate goal for the individual person. The quest was to realize a complete unity with the ultimate, that is, Heaven or Dao, and this unity was to be achieved by a method of reflective contemplation or visualization (*fanguan*), which enabled one to dissolve the subject–object distinction. This method seems to have been influenced by both Buddhist and Daoist views.[4]

The fourth way supported by Shao's narrative was the way of devotion. It involved a conception of Heaven as a personification of the ultimate, as well as High Heaven and the Sage (Confucius) as divine, creative powers. Devotion to Heaven and to High Heaven and the Sage led to a commitment to Chinese culture, which was understood as embodying the moral way of Heaven. Devotion to Heaven also aided in personal mystical quests.

Shao's commitment to Dao was passionate and total. Closeness to Dao represented a personal life of moral fulfillment, peace, and joy, as well as a harmonious and well-ordered society and world, for which he and his elite class felt responsible. Shao was especially concerned about telling the story, for he claimed that people would not be committed to Dao and the values of civilization unless they had knowledge of it. Although he presented his accounts in both of his major works, he held that poetry was especially good for presenting the narrative of Dao, for poetry was concerned with people's feelings and commitments (for instance, "Song about poetry and painting" [JRJ 18.111b–112b], "Song about rejoicing in things" [JRJ 10.144b–145a], and selected stanzas from "Song about heads and tails" [JRJ 20.137a, 142b, 149b, 150a, 156b]).

The Narrative of Cosmic Development

As indicated above, Shao's accounts of cosmic development or cosmogony combined two kinds of interest. One was concerned with the emergence of the particular things (*wu*) that made up the world, and the other focused on the abstract patterns according to which things developed and were related to each other. The broad outline of the sacred story as told by Shao related how Dao, as the ultimate source or root, produced Heaven and earth, the two largest things of the cosmos, and how Heaven and earth in turn produced the myriad things (HJJS 5.1a–6.27b, *Sibu Beiyao* ed.). Shao said that there were no larger things (*wu*) than Heaven and earth, but since even they were things, they depended on something else for their existence. It was the interaction of *yin* and *yang qi*, the dark and light energy configurations, that completed Heaven, and the interaction of *gang* and *rou qi*, the hard and soft (or firm and yielding) energy configurations that completed earth.

The completion of Heaven next entailed the completion of the four seasons, and, in a comparable fashion, the completion of earth entailed the completion of the four directions. Shao called the four seasons and the four directions the "four treasuries" (sifu) of Heaven and of earth. Heaven and earth formed a bipolar pair, and their respective entities were correlated with each other in groups of four, based on the four treasuries. Together there were thus eight fundamental entities that in turn served as symbols of an extensive system of correlations and associations. (Also translated as orbs, the fu or zangfu were a central concept in Chinese medical thinking and were important in religious Daoism.[5])

Shifting to a more theoretical or metaphysical version and using Yijing-related concepts, Shao elaborated on these cosmic developments in the following way. Heaven emerged from movement (dong) and earth from stillness (jing), and the interaction of movement and stillness led to the completion of the ways (dao) of Heaven and earth. That is, movement gave rise first to yang, then yin, and stillness gave rise first to softness (rou), then hardness (gang). The interaction of these four types of qi led respectively to the "functions" (yong) of Heaven and earth. The four types of qi (yang, yin, rou, gang) each divided into a greater and lesser, so that eight functions (yong), also called "images" (xiang), were the result, namely, greater yang, lesser yang, greater yin, lesser yin, greater rou, lesser rou, greater gang, lesser gang. Correlated with the eight trigrams and the numbers (one through eight), these eight images interacted and produced all the things of the world.

From this theoretical and metaphysical perspective using the images and numbers, Shao continued his narrative by focusing on the processes that produced the numerous things of the world. Shao correlated the eight images (that is, the functions) of Heaven and earth with the eight interacting "substances" (ti) of Heaven and earth. The substances of Heaven and earth, which were also images, consisted of the sun, moon, stars, and asterisms (or planets or constellations) for Heaven, and water, fire, earth, and stone for earth.

Based largely on bipolar and quaternary (four-part) divisions and correlations, the creative process continued, as the "changes" (bian) and "transformations" (hua) of the eight substances (the images of sun, moon, stars, and asterisms of Heaven and water, fire, earth, and stone of earth) led to the emergence of the myriad things (and the categories that they symbolized) in the world. While Heaven and earth formed a bipolar pair, quaternary groupings dominated in their respective realms. In the realm of Heaven, for instance, sun changed to heat and moon to cold, while in the realm of earth, water transformed into rain and fire into wind. In this way, such things as heat, cold, rain, and wind emerged. Further cosmic interactions, referred to as the movements (*gan*) and responses (*ying*) of the myriad things, ensued and resulted in further phenomena of the cosmos. For instance, some things appeared that were classified as walkers and flyers, while other things appeared that were aspects of things, such as feelings and forms, eyes and ears. Shao also wrote about great cosmic cycles of Heaven and earth, based on the numbers of ten, twelve, and thirty.

Coming to the pinnacle of cosmic development, Shao narrated how the ways of human beings and things were completed as a result of the interactions between humans and things. The interaction was possible because of the marvelous human characteristic called *ling* (numinous, spiritual, creative, efficacious). For example, the eyes and ears of humans received the appearances and sounds of things, and thus humans experienced seeing and hearing. The substances (*ti*) of the myriad things, that is, their sounds, appearances, odors, and tastes, interacted with the functions (*yong*) of humans, that is, the functioning of the ears, eyes, nose, and mouth, to complete the ways of humans and things. Shao claimed that humans were more *ling* than other living things and so were able to participate in the development of this further dimension of the cosmos, namely, such subjective human experiences as seeing and hearing, which relied on the "outer" existence of visual forms and sounds.

Shao offered simplified versions of this complex account. He wrote, for instance, that Heaven emerged (*sheng*) from Dao, and earth was completed (*cheng*) from Dao (HJJS 6.8b). Things received their forms (*xing*) from Dao, and humans received their behavior (*xing*) from Dao. While the category of the myriad things included all things, even humans, human beings constituted the highest category of things, and so Shao gave them special consideration. Dao thus produced the four major types of things—Heaven, earth, the myriad things, and human beings. These entities were correlated according to bipolar and quaternary patterns. Heaven and earth, humans and things (broadly conceived), and High Heaven and the Sage (Confucius) constituted three important bipolar pairs. The four treasuries of Heaven and of earth and the images correlated with them formed the quaternary pattern.

Shao made a strong distinction between Dao as the ultimate creative source of all things and the phenomenal things (*wu*) of the world. Dao had no boundaries. It had no shape or form and could only be seen in actual affairs (HJJS 6.8b). In contrast, all things, no matter how large, even Heaven and earth, did have limits. Although each type of thing had its own respective way (*dao*), that is, its patterns and modes of being and behaving, the particular ways all emerged from the one ultimate Dao. Shao emphasized that all things depended on other things for their existence, that no thing was eternal or self-created, and that no thing stood alone. In other words, to become a thing, it must form a pair with something else.

A major issue in the narrative for Shao was how the cosmos developed, from the perspective of systematic patterns of order—that is, what kinds of regularities or patterns worked together to produce the cosmos, to the point that eventually the four major realms (or things) emerged—Heaven, earth, things, and humans. For Shao, the notion of development or emergence was inseparable from ideas of orderly behavior and activity. The emergence of any thing depended on its particular patterns of activity of *qi*, and these patterns became symbols, variously called images (*xiang*), functions (*yong*), or substances (*ti*). The regularity of these patterns allowed the trigrams and numbers, both symbols as well, to be used as substitutes.

In this kind of thinking, and in contrast to some Greek and European thought, the "stuff" out of which things were made was not the issue, since everything consisted of *qi*. Rather, *how* things behaved, or *how qi* acted, was the concern. The notion of Dao in this cosmic narrative emphasized that Dao was the source of cosmic patterns of activity and of *qi* too. Moreover, since *qi* was constantly active, there were no absolute distinctions between "active" manifestations of *qi*, such as the alternation of day and night, and "thinglike" or "still" manifestations of *qi*, such as the two great things called Heaven and earth. Dao itself was beyond ordinary human sensory-based knowledge but could be known through the functions and substances of the world.

This account by Shao, which was based on an esoteric tradition of cosmic development, drew primarily on ideas found in classical Daoism, religious and liturgical Daoism, and Han Confucianism. Although his master narrative had many similarities to that of Daoism, unlike the Daoists he did not elaborate on stages or conditions of cosmic development before Dao. In addition, unlike the early Daoists, he approved of the emergence of civilization and Confucian morality. Earlier texts that contributed ideas to his narrative included the *Classic of Changes,* the *Classic of Documents,* the *Classic of Odes,* the *Huainanzi,* the *Laozi,* and a few later Daoist scriptures, although he generally did not give credit to the Daoist works.

The Narrative of the Development of Civilization

Shao's narrative proceeded without interruption from his account of cosmic development to that of civilization. Continuity prevailed both in terms of specific things that emerged and in terms of the underlying patterns of activity, especially the patterns of bipolar pairing and quaternary grouping. The notion of development or emergence did not imply an inevitable or unchanging linear progression toward a better or worse state of affairs. While Confucian thinking held that ancient civilization marked a high point in moral attainment with the ancient sages, the goal was always to achieve again a condition of moral harmony and order. Shao's view of the emergence of civilization did not address the question of whether there was a necessary moral direction existing by itself, separate from specific historical contexts. Rather, he was concerned with the issue of moral behavior in context. His was a moral narrative, the main point of which was not to show inevitable "decline" or "progress" but to show the workings of morality, which occurred in particular contexts usually according to a bipolar pattern.

Following the emergence of the four primary "things," that is, Heaven, earth, things, and humans, and their specific ways, Shao continued his narrative with High Heaven (*haotian*) and the Sage (Confucius). High Heaven and the Sage formed a correlated, bipolar pair, with High Heaven responsible for completing (*jin*) the way of things and the Sage responsible for completing the way of humans. High Heaven was an anthropomorphic type of diety, personifying the functioning of Heaven and earth, while the Sage was a deified Confucius, seen as responsible for the emergence of certain aspects of civilization.

Shao said that High Heaven in completing things and the Sage in completing the people (*min*) each had four treasuries (*sifu*), a concept encountered above in relation to the completion of Heaven and earth. The four treasuries of High Heaven were the seasons: spring, summer, autumn, and winter, and those of the Sage were the classics: the *Changes, Documents, Odes,* and *Spring and Autumn.* Shao observed that *yin* and *yang* rose and fell in the midst of the seasons, while the rites and music flourished and declined in the midst of the classics. In other words, the changing of the seasons was due to the interaction of *yin* and *yang qi,* and the contents of the classics were related to the changing political and moral relations of ancient society. Continuing his account, Shao then correlated the seasons and the classics with each other and with the four-part cycle of birth, growth, harvest, and death. Thus, for example, the season of spring, the *Classic of Changes,* and the stage of birth were correlated with one another.

Demonstrating how civilization emerged in an orderly and patterned way and how everything in the world was interrelated, Shao proceeded with numerous further correlations that involved things, concepts, and historical figures, all of which had symbolic importance. The sets of correlations included, among others, (1) thoughts, words, images, numbers; (2) benevolence, ritual, duty, wisdom; (3) human nature, feelings, form, body; (4) sages, worthies, talents, adepts; (5) the three sovereigns, five emperors, three kings, five hegemons; (6) Shun, Yu, Tang, the Zhou ancestor; (7) King Wen, King Wu, Duke of Zhou, Duke of Shao; (8) Mu of Qin, Wen of Jin, Huan of Qi, Zhuang of Chu; (9) transforming, teaching, exhorting, leading; (10) the Way, virtue, accomplishments, force; (11) naturalness, yielding, correctness, struggle; and (12) non-action, kindness and good faith, impartiality and correctness, cunning and strength. As part of the development of civilization, there was also the emergence of the people (*min*), who were characterized by their division into the four classes of scholar-officials, farmers, artisans, and merchants.

These quaternary sets of correlations were a way of organizing historical particulars by demonstrating their interdependent relationships. The correlations established a type of narrative that did not take chronological sequence as its most important organizing principle, although changes over time were certainly recognized. Rather, the correlations brought attention to the theoretical pattern of how the moral-political way of ancient civilization functioned. In particular, the rulers chose methods of rule that involved appropriate responses (*ying*) to the movements of Heaven and the conditions of society. Shao referred to this phenomenon as adaptive behavior (*quan*) by the rulers.

In presenting this sacred narrative, Shao did not isolate ancient historical figures and events from their broader contexts, for the basis of their very selection, or what made them significant, was the cosmic and cultural contexts, which involved the movements of Heaven and human responses. Shao pointed out that his mention of a historical figure—for example, King Wen—not only referred to that specific person but also symbolized anyone who behaved in a morally similar way. Thus, the classics gave accounts of specific historical affairs and people that in turn became symbols of moral contexts, concepts, and ideal behavior.

In his account of civilization, Shao addressed certain perennial moral questions, one of which was the question of why strive to be morally good, if one's destiny was perhaps fated anyway. Shao maintained that Heaven had certain powers and humans had others. For instance, a person's achievement of wealth and high rank was a matter of Heaven, not humans, but good works and virtue were a matter of human effort, not Heaven. Even though there was no necessary correlation between the morality of one's acts and one's destiny, or "Heavenly fate," and even though Heaven could (and did) send down calamities to both good and evil people, the morally good person attempted to achieve as much good as possible.

Shao illustrated these beliefs with historical figures and incidents, noting, for example, that Yu of the Xia dynasty and Tang of the Yin dynasty both gained the empire because of their achievements, while Jie of the Xia and Zhou of the Yin both lost the empire because of their cruelty (HJJS 5.19b). On the other hand, he noted that King Ping was given credit for restoring the royal house and preventing the fall of the Zhou dynasty simply because he moved the capital east and not because he performed any meritorious actions. In addition, King Nan moved the capital west and even without having committed any cruel deeds, he lost the royal house, for he surrendered to the state of Qin and thereby ended the Zhou dynasty.

Shao claimed that those rulers who were benevolent to the people supported life and were loved by the people, whereas those who were cruel to the people supported death and were hated by the people. The Zhou and Han states fit into the former category, while the Qin and the Chu fit into the latter. Thus, Shao held that the moral actions of rulers were strongly connected to the conditions of life and the feelings of the people. Just as the alternation of *yin* and *yang* characterized the way of Heaven (or nature), so goodness and depravity characterized the way of humans. A good ruler would be able to encourage many, but not all, of the people to behave morally, and a tyrannical ruler would cause many, but not all, of the people to behave immorally. Shao thus saw such moral contrasts as the superior man and the petty man, rightness and private benefit, and goodness and depravity as human counterparts to the bipolar pattern of the way of Heaven and earth. Shao did not suggest, however, that specific actions of humans were predestined, for one could choose one's actions and what one chose to do in part involved one's *qing* (feelings, desires, commitments).

Shao's account of civilization presented the entire course of Chinese political history, from the mythological beginnings to his own times. He wrote that the human way (*rendao*) began with the shattering of primal simplicity (*pu*) and that regulations first appeared with Fuxi, the Yellow Emperor, and the ancient sages (for instance, "Song about contemplating the greatness of the foundations" [JRJ 1:4a–9a]; "After writing the *August Ultimate Traversing the Ages*" [JRJ 8.103b–104a]; "The book from Peace and Happiness Nest" [JRJ 9.128a]). Periods of order and disorder then followed, alternating with each other. Shao described the span of history as four thousand years of flourishing and decline, a time when the numerous states had many varied characteristics.

The first four ancient periods differed somewhat from later periods in that they established the basis of the quaternary pattern. Shao usually described these early periods as the times of the three sovereigns, the two (or sometimes, five) emperors, the three kings, and the five hegemons. He used a slightly different political framework in other versions, for instance, the Xia, Shang, Zhou, and Qin dynasties. Shao then told about the seven states (of the Warring States period), the Qin, the two Han, the Three Kingdoms, the Western Jin, the Xiongnu hordes, the Eastern Jin, the Song, the Qi, the Liang, the Chen, the Later (Northern) Wei, the Eastern and Western Wei, the Northern Qi, the Later (Northern) Zhou, the Sui, the Tang, the Five Dynasties, and the Song, his own dynastic period. Some accounts were in abbreviated form, for example, referring simply to the sixteen states and the northern and southern dynasties, while others gave details of the particular states and dynasties. Important in all his accounts, however, was the theme of order and disorder, the human counterpart of the cosmic alternation of *yin* and *yang*.

Holding onto the Central Plain was a critical theme and symbol. The Central Plain was regarded as the geographical site of the foundation of the Chinese state and civilization, and thus it was a symbol of the state and civilization, by definition both moral entities. When the Central Plain was lost to the barbarians, so were political and moral order. Political order came from the center, the ruler, and it came from the Chinese, not from the barbarians. Moral order also came from the cosmic center, in that it came from Dao. The Way of Heaven (or Dao) was conferred on humans by Heaven and was "located" in the human heart (heart-mind). The moral heart of humans was thus derived from the "heart" of Heaven. From different perspectives, then, the center (the source of morality) was Heaven itself, the Chinese state and civilization, and the heart of human beings—all three. In other words, the Way of Heaven not only was the natural order of *yin* and *yang*; it also was the moral and political order of the human world, which was ultimately based in the heart of all human beings. The sacred story of civilization thus emphasized that the human world, as well as the natural world, was a manifestation of Dao and that the particular patterns that characterized Dao led to the kind of order that provided the necessary conditions of life. Order, life, and morality were inseparable.

The Narrative of the Development of Human Beings

Shao's accounts of human beings followed his narratives of civilization and cosmic development without interruption. Here he was interested in humans, as opposed to other kinds of things in the world, and especially their unique capabilities. The prior narratives of the cosmos and civilization were important, for the cosmic context was relevant in looking at humans from a metaphysical viewpoint, and the cultural context was relevant from a social-political-moral viewpoint. A human being was never a "self-contained" entity. Shao's story, in effect, was one of how human beings developed from the creative source and how they were able to use their special abilities to return to the creative source.

Shao favored the terms Dao and *xin* (heart, heart-mind) to refer to the creative source when speaking about humans, but he used other terms too, just as he did in the cosmic and cultural contexts. Some of these were *xiantian* ("before Heaven," a stage or condition of precosmic development that was before Heaven and earth and perhaps before Dao), *taiji* (Supreme Ultimate), *yi* (the One), *shen* (spirit), and *zhong* (the center). These and other related terms had rich histories and various meanings in Daoist and Confucian thought, but Shao seldom attempted to define these terms in any extensive way. His learning was widely known, however, as "the learning of *xiantian*" (*xiantian xue*).

From a metaphysical viewpoint, or according to his *xiantian* learning, humans (and all things) followed the same sequence of development as the cosmos. That is, there was a progression from *taiji* to the two forces, the four images, the eight trigrams, and so forth (HJJS 8xia.9b). Shao also conceived of humans from the perspective of the psychological and sensory realms of human experience and so developed what may be considered a "psychosomatic" view of humans. Here he drew on many ideas from his cultural tradition, ideas that had originally derived separately from Daoist, Confucian, and Buddhist sources. We see, for instance, an interesting adaptation of the Buddhist view of humans as composed of interrelated layers of components (the five skandhas) and a certain similarity to Xunzi's view regarding the emotions as a motivating source of human actions.

Shao viewed the formation of human beings, in a psychosomatic sense, somewhat like a set of concentric circles. His narrative employed a spacial image to represent activity from center to periphery, and his ideas were presented in verbal form and in diagrams. This view was in part based on a biological model, emphasizing growth from a root and cycles of life and death, waxing and waning, which were correlated with the *yin* and *yang* pattern of alternation. The bipolar pairs formed, in Manfred Porkert's terms, a "functional yoke." Also relevant was a military type of model, with outer defenses protecting the center.

Shao presented his narrative in outline form in his preface to his collection of poetry and expanded on it in numerous passages elsewhere. Employing territorial and defense terminology, he envisioned the human being as a set of interrelated layers with Dao at the center surrounded by a number of "arenas" or "fields." The ineffable source from which everything emerged, Dao was also the innermost core of a human being, the basis of life and its patterns of order.

The first field outward from Dao was a human being's nature (*xing*). Although the term *xing* is usually translated as "human nature," this translation does not truly convey Shao's emphasis on behavior or activity. For Shao, *xing* referred to the actions and natural patterns of behavior that made a human being distinct from other kinds of things. Viewing it as the first stage in the manifestation of Dao, Shao said that "*xing* is the embodiment (*xingti*) of Dao." Next outward was the heart-mind (*xin*), which Shao said formed "the city walls (*fuguo*) of one's human nature." Next outward was the self (*shen*), "the empire or territory (*quyu*) of the heart-mind." And lastly, there were things (*wu*), "the vehicle (*zhouche*) of the self." In appreciating some of the implications of this view, it is helpful to realize that these references to the aspects of a person were references to functional systems of activity (like the orbs in medicine), not to static things; that comparing the body to the state was common in Chinese thought, especially since the Han; and that the metaphor of the vehicle and the idea of sheaths were central to Buddhism.

Comments scattered throughout Shao's works enable us to construct the significance of these sheathlike layers. A fundamental difference between Dao and the outer aspects was that there was no truly appropriate description or name that could be applied to Dao. Entities in the phenomenal world, however, had various characteristics, including a spacial aspect. That is, things were somewhere in relation to other things. Using spirit (*shen*) as an alternate term for Dao, Shao referred to this spacial perspective, for instance, by asserting that there is no place where spirit is and no place where spirit is not (HJJS 8xia.16b–17a).

Human nature (*xing*) differed from Dao in that it appeared in this world of distinctions and so was part of a *yin* and *yang* type of functional yoke or bipolar pair. Human nature was the beginning aspect of a thing and was distinguished from the completing, "structive," or "substantive" aspect of a thing, which Shao referred to as *qi* (matter-energy, energetic configurations) or, alternately, as *ti* (body, substance). No oppositions could be made, however, with Dao. Although distinguishable for analytic purposes, Shao held that *xing* and *qi* were inseparable and did not (and could not) exist apart from each other. He said, for instance, that *qi* nourishes *xing* and *xing* rides on *qi*, and that the existence of *qi* entails the existence of *xing*, while the movement of *xing* entails the movement of *qi* (HJJS 8xia.27b). Alternately employing the concept of *ti* (body, substance) in place of *qi*, Shao said that "human nature (*xing*) does not exist ("is not completed") without substance (*ti*) and substance does not exist ("does not emerge") without human nature. *Yang* takes *yin* as its substance (*ti*) and *yin* takes *yang* as its nature (*xing*). Moving is [human] nature and being still is substance. In Heaven, *yang* moves and *yin* is still. On earth *yang* is still and *yin* moves . . ." (HJJS 8xia.22a). Human nature, the layer next to Dao, thus was correlated with *yang* and with the beginning of both things and movement, while *qi* (energetic configurations) or *ti* (substance) was correlated with *yin* and the completion of things and movement.

Continuing with Shao's view, one's human nature was "surrounded" by the heart-mind (*xin*). Whereas human nature and *qi* (or, alternately, *ti*) were opposed to each other, the heart-mind functioned in a different field of reference with different possible oppositions. It was paired with the self (*shen*) and was seen as its ruler or director. The heart-mind involved such activities as thinking, feeling, and making commitments. Distinguishing between the self and the person (*ren*), a difference somewhat similar to a psychological and social distinction, Shao said, for instance, that the heart-mind brought order to the self and the self brought order to the person ("Song about ordering the heart-mind," JRJ 18.114a-b). The heart-mind was not only the "site" from which one's aims, desires, intentions, feelings, and thoughts, arose; it was those activities. Just as the root is responsible for the plant's development, the heart-mind was the root of the self, the self the root of the family, the family the root of the state, the state the root of the empire. If one's heart-mind could manage well or order one's self, then one's family, the state, and the empire could be similarly well ordered (HJJS 8xia.34a).

Next outward from the heart-mind was the self (*shen*), a field consisting of intellectual, physiological, psychological, and emotional dimensions. The distinction between the heart-mind and the self may be compared to one that Xunzi made and one also found in Western thought between the "I," which cannot be described except to say that it is that which thinks, desires, aims, feels, and directs action, and the social-psychological "me," the condition of which can be observed and described. The "me" was the self that could, for instance, be at peace or be agitated.

The outermost field consisted of things (*wu*), conceived as the vehicle carrying the self. This field tied human beings in with all other things. Although Shao did not explain what he meant by "things," his comments suggest that things could refer to the physical kinds of things in one's environment, one's physical body, or one's family, the state, and the empire. If, or when, "things" were understood in the sense of one's bodily aspects, then "things" were possibly an alternate concept for one's visible form (*xing*), discussed below.

From Shao's perspective, which was similar to the view expressed in the *Great Learning*, each field was intimately related to the ones next to it, and the state of health or well-being of each field had a primary influence on that of the next outer or next inner one. Shao stressed that harm or disease spread from the outer to the inner fields, while good order or health proceeded from the inner to the outer fields. Thus, harming one's nature also harmed Dao; harming one's heart-mind also harmed one's nature; harming one's self also harmed one's heart-mind; and harming one's things also harmed one's self. As a remedy, Shao advised that one should contemplate or visualize (*guan*) one's nature from the viewpoint of Dao, one's heart-mind from the viewpoint of one's nature, one's self from the viewpoint of one's heart-mind, and one's things from the viewpoint of one's self. If the latter (inner aspect) were well ordered, so would the former (outer aspect) be. And the implication was that the outer could not be well ordered unless the inner was first.

Shao did not stop here, but proceeded with his narrative to a next stage. If one contemplated or visualized any of these fields from the viewpoint of another field, one was still caught in the mundane issues of harm versus well-being. Shao wished to go beyond these distinctions to a personal state of joy, an ultimate, religious state in which the separateness of these fields was no longer a concern and one's own entanglements were forgotten. To do this, one had to contemplate or visualize each from the viewpoint of itself—Dao from the viewpoint of Dao, nature from the viewpoint of nature, the heart-mind from the viewpoint of the heart-mind, the self from the viewpoint of the self, and things from the viewpoint of things. If one could do this, one could also visualize the family from the viewpoint of the family, the state from the viewpoint of the state, and the empire from the viewpoint of the empire.

If successful, one then achieved a unity (*yi*) with all things. Shao said that if one's heart-mind were unified and not divided, one could respond to the myriad things, and this was how the superior man had an empty, still heart-mind (HJJS 8xia.29a). That is, one no longer made a distinction between the perceiving subject and the perceived object. There was no "I" or "ego" (*wu wo*) (HJJS 8xia27b). It was not just a matter of unifying or merging with the visible, outer forms (*xing*) of the myriad things, but of merging with the inner feelings (*qing*) of the myriad things (HJJS 6:26b). One achieved this ultimate state by a method that Shao called reflective contemplation or visualization (*fanguan*). Shao thus contrasted the visible forms of human beings with their feelings (*qing*), which were the basis of human action and vitality. Human beings possessed feelings, moreover, as long as they had *ling*, their marvelous spiritual and creative power ("Song about human spirituality," JRJ 18.114b).

The feelings and forms of humans thus formed a bipolar pair that paralleled their nature and *qi* or their nature and substance (*ti*). For Shao, both feelings and human nature referred to the *yang* aspect that initiated activity, while the visible form and *qi* or substance (*ti*) referred to the *yin* aspect, the completing or structive aspect. A distinction between one's nature and feelings was that the latter was applied to behavior occurring in response to things outside of oneself (JRJ preface 1a), whereas the former was applied to behavior seen as arising from one's natural endowment received from Heaven (HJJS 8xia.9b). This view implied that human behavior resulted both from "inner stimuli" and from "outer responses." Thus it was important to have knowledge and commitments.

One further idea important in Shao's account of human beings was his view that Heaven and humans shared the same heart (heart-mind). Here, using an anthropomorphic conception of Heaven, he held that both Heaven and humans had the same kind of feelings, desires, aims, and guiding norms. The heart was thus an alternate term for Dao. Shao said, for instance, that human feelings (*renqing*) and Heaven's intentions (*tianyi*) were not two different things ("Song about Heaven and humans," JRJ 15.65b). Feelings were the human counterpart of Heaven's intentions. Shao also wrote that it was Heaven that began things by dividing the "one center" and that the Way was embodied in human actions ("Song about contemplating the *Yijing*," JRJ 15.60a). As a manifestation of Heaven or Dao, the heart of human beings was the source of both the constant norms and the feelings, and these two were not seen to be in conflict.

Summary

To summarize this discussion of Shao's Yong's religious position, the most prominent among his ways of being religious were the ways of right action, reasoned inquiry, mystical quest, and devotion, while the symbolic form central to his thinking was the sacred story. His narrative recounted the emergence of the cosmos, civilization, and human beings from Dao, the creative source, and provided ways symbolically to return to, or merge with, that source. In narrating the sacred story, Shao emphasized both particular entities and abstract patterns. His narrative illustrated moral norms of Chinese civilization and models for personal behavior; it entailed an analytic type of understanding of the nature of the world; it encouraged personal mystical quests through various meditative and ritual practices; and it manifested a sense of devotion to High Heaven and the Sage, and also to Heaven as the source of the cosmos, as the ruler and regulator of the world, and as the "power" that endowed human beings with their abilities and characteristics. Use of the sacred story, in any of these ways, helped a person to strive to attain unity with Dao, to achieve that ultimate state of wholeness or genuineness (*cheng*), and to return to the undifferentiated creative center from the multiplicity of worldly things.

Notes

1. Dale Cannon, *Six Ways of Being Religious: A Framework for Comparative Studies of Religion* (Belmont, Calif.: Wadsworth Publishing, 1996). This work presents a theoretical framework for investigating and understanding diverse religious phenomena, along with helpful case studies and bibliographies.

2. See Anne D. Birdwhistell, *Transition to Neo-Confucianism: Shao Yong on Knowledge and Symbols of Reality;* and Alain Arrault, *Shao Yong (1012–1077): Poète et Cosmologue.*

3. For discussion of the precosmic as opposed to cosmic stage and for related ideas that were part of the Daoist background of Shao's thought, see N. J. Girardot, *Myth and Meaning in Early Taoism: The Theme of Chaos (hun-tun).*

4. See *The Taoist Experience: An Anthology,* ed. Livia Kohn, 221–47, concerning visualization as part of Daoist meditational techniques; and *Traditions of Meditation in Chinese Buddhism,* ed. Peter N. Gregory.

5. See Manfred Porkert, *The Theoretical Foundations of Chinese Medicine: Systems of Correspondence* (Cambridge, Mass.: MIT Press, 1974), and *Taoist Experience,* ed. Kohn, 161–88.

Suggested Reading

Arrault, Alain. *Shao Yong (1012–1077): Poète et Cosmologue.* Paris: Collège de France, Institut des Hautes Études Chinoises, 2002.

Birdwhistell, Anne D. *Transition to Neo-Confucianism: Shao Yung on Knowledge and Symbols of Reality.* Stanford: Stanford University Press, 1989.

Chan, Wing-tsit. *A Source Book in Chinese Philosophy.* Princeton, N.J.: Princeton University Press, 1963.

Fung Yu-lan. *A History of Chinese Philosophy.* 2 vols. Translated by Derk Bodde. Princeton, N.J.: Princeton University Press, 1952, 1953.

Girardot, N. J. *Myth and Meaning in Early Taoism: The Theme of Chao (hun-tun).* Berkeley: University of California Press, 1983.

The Taoist Experience: An Anthology. Edited by Livia Kohn. Albany: State University of New York Press, 1993.

Traditions of Meditation in Chinese Buddhism. Edited by Peter N. Gregory. Honolulu: University of Hawaii Press, 1986.

Smith, Kidder, Jr., Peter K. Bol, Joseph A. Adler, and Don J. Wyatt. *Sung Dynasty Uses of the I Ching.* Princeton, N.J.: Princeton University Press, 1990.

18

Forming One Body:
The Cheng Brothers and Their Circle

THOMAS W. SELOVER

Your servant humbly states that the Dao of Confucius was transmitted to Zeng Zi, Zeng Zi transmitted to Zi Si, and Zi Si transmitted to Mencius. After Mencius there was no transmission. Coming to our dynasty, Cheng Hao and Cheng Yi of Loyang transmitted his Dao more than a thousand years afterwards. Those engaged in learning shouldered satchels and hiked up their garments [in hurrying] to personally receive their instruction, spreading it to the four directions. Some in secret and some openly—none can exhaust the record![1]

Every religious and spiritual tradition lives and develops in history through a continuous interaction between the resources of the tradition and the hearts-and-minds of each new generation of participants. There are also special moments when a spiritual tradition is renewed and revivified through a powerful combination of circumstances and remarkable human beings. For the Confucian tradition, the late eleventh century in China produced such a moment. The memorial quoted above is the earliest official statement of the pedigree of the Confucian revival movement known as *Daoxue* (Dao learning). In it, Cheng Hao (1032–1085) and his younger brother Cheng Yi (1033–1107) are identified as the preeminent teachers of the *Daoxue* revival. Primarily through direct interaction, the Cheng brothers inspired a circle of disciples that continued to widen in future generations, becoming a major stream of Chinese thought.[2]

The Cheng circle described their new encounter with the truth of the classics in terms of the "discovery" of the "untransmitted learning" of the sages. The emerging "Dao learning" was characterized by an acute sense that although the *Analects* and other records of Confucius's teaching had been transmitted over many centuries, the authentic meaning and import of the texts had been lost. In 1085, Cheng Yi eulogized his brother Cheng

Hao as having discovered this "untransmitted learning," which had been obscured for fourteen hundred years, and as having been intent on "using this Dao to awaken this people."[3] The *Daoxue* Neo-Confucians felt themselves to have both the opportunity and the responsibility to recover and realize this Dao. Alternatively, one could say that their sense of the loss of transmission was retrospective, after they had "rediscovered" the authentic meaning. Their sense of discovery led to an optimistic, almost "perfectionist" zeal; those who constituted the *Daoxue* fellowship shared an exuberant sense of being newly able to emulate the Sage himself through their study and practice.[4]

No doubt, the transmitted image of such exemplary teachers is fundamentally cast by their direct disciples and successors. These immediate students were the questioners and recorders of the "sayings" by which the Chengs' teachings are primarily known.[5] As an event, therefore, the Song dynasty *Daoxue* movement, with its perception of a renewed authentic transmission from the ancient sages and wise teachers, cannot be fully understood by focusing on the Cheng brothers alone. Those who received teaching from the Chengs, their disciples and friends, were an integral part of the matrix of the *Daoxue* revival, in the reciprocity of teaching and learning.

As the memorial above describes, students traveled considerable distances to study with the Chengs, to learn directly from their example. Like Confucius's original disciples, they engaged in question-and-answer learning encounters with their exemplary teachers. The main threads of these teaching encounters were drawn from the repertoire of Confucian scriptural classics. The Cheng brothers and their circle practiced a reflective discipline known as "savoring the text" (*wanwei*) in the study of the scriptural classics. Prominent among these classics was the *Analects* (*Lunyu*), itself a "sayings" collection of brief teaching encounters between Confucius and his disciples. The touchstone of the *Analects*, and also of the Chengs' teaching, is the venerable Confucian theme of *ren* (human kindness, humanity), expressing the ideal quality of human relatedness. Cheng Hao and his followers spoke of realizing *ren* as sensitivity and awareness that "forms one body" with others. These three aspects of the Cheng circle—exemplary teaching, savoring the text, and realizing *ren* as forming one body—were thoroughly interwoven.

Exemplary Teaching

In their words and practice, the Cheng brothers articulated anew the spiritual resources of the Confucian tradition, bringing them powerfully to bear upon their contemporary generation. As exemplary teachers, they were able to mobilize the cultural resources of the common tradition in a way that drew their disciples (as listeners or as readers) into a deeper personal encounter and identification with the tradition and its ideals.

In an anecdote of encounter between Cheng Hao and Xie Liangzuo, one of the Chengs' prominent disciples, Cheng Hao caught Xie's attention at a time when Xie was showing off his knowledge and redirected his sense of vocation in an opportune moment of teaching:

> At first, Master Xie took rote memorization to be learning and had a high opinion of himself as erudite. In front of Master Mingdao [i.e., Cheng Hao], he recited a book of history without leaving out a single character. Mingdao said, "My worthy friend, you have indeed memorized a great deal. This could be called 'trifling with things and losing purpose.'" When Xie heard these words, he perspired all over and became red in the face. Mingdao then remarked, "That is precisely 'the heart-and-mind of natural compassion.'"
>
> When it later came to seeing Mingdao himself reading histories, determining the lines and reading through without mistaking a single character, Xie felt very resentful. Afterwards, he reflected and came to a realization.[6]

At its most incisive, the dialogical encounter of exemplary teaching impacts the personal consciousness and conscience, such that even the disciple's "blood and breath" are affected. Cheng Hao induced an intense reaction in Xie through adroit use of the common scriptural heritage and then pointed to Xie's visceral response as a manifestation of "natural compassion," the "beginning" of *ren*.

The Cheng's exemplary teaching included a meditative or reflective discipline known as "quiet-sitting" (*jingzuo*). In contrast to lengthy discourses on meditation in the Buddhist tradition, Confucian guides to "quiet-sitting" are sparse indeed. It seems that the Chengs modeled the practice of quiet-sitting and let their followers work out the details for themselves. Cheng Hao once criticized his students for only studying his words, urging them to devote themselves to practice. When they indicated that they were not sure what to practice, Cheng Hao said, "Then do quiet-sitting" (*Jinsilu* 4/63; *Reflections on Things at Hand*, 151). In an account that likely describes Cheng Hao's own practice of quiet-sitting, Xie remarked, "When Mingdao sat down, he was like an earthen figure, but when he associated with people, he was completely a sphere of peaceful disposition" (*Jinsilu* 14/21; *Reflections*, 304). The description of Cheng Hao as an "earthen figure" is reminiscent of passages describing meditation or trance in the Daoist classic *Chuang-tzu*. It was one of the *Daoxue* discoveries that this kind of meditative spirituality, shared by Buddhist and Daoist practitioners, could also take place within the resources and resonances of the Confucian tradition. For the Cheng circle, quiet-sitting and thoughtful study both came under the rubric of *jing* (reverence, seriousness, composure).[7] The discipline of quiet-sitting, as an aspect of ritual cultivation of the body, is at once the training of the heart-and-mind, as the two are synergistically one.

These disciples found in the Cheng brothers exemplary teachers that taught them to believe in the possibility of re-creating the transformative power of the classic sages. As Xie Liangzuo remarked of Cheng Hao, "I've been in the school of [Cheng] Mingdao from early on and am able to free myself, for 'he transforms all whom he passes by'" (*Shangcai yulu* 1/9b, alluding to *Mencius* 7A:13). Yang Shi described Cheng Yi as "greatly understanding" and able to open doors for others when he lectured on the classics (*Yang Guishanji* 13:17b). The Chengs provided an exemplary pattern of encounter with the scriptural classics, encouraging their followers and students to savor the texts for themselves.

Savoring the Text and the Pattern

In praising Cheng Hao's methods of teaching the *Odes*, Xie Liangzuo commented that instead of getting bogged down in analyzing phrases Cheng Hao just "savors them in a carefree way, intoning them high and low, and thus brings it about that people get something from it."[8] The Chengs' hermeneutic practice of "savoring the text" coincided with their easy and close relationship with their followers; after describing Cheng Hao's teaching the *Odes*, Xie mused, "This is why the ancients highly valued being intimate with and influenced [by sage teachers]" (*Jinsilu* 3/44, with an allusion to *Mencius* 7B:15; see *Reflections*, 106). Encounter with the text in the community of teacher and disciples, thus returning the "living voice," re-created the sagely community in which the meanings of those texts were originally shared. This re-creation was especially vivid when the text at hand was the *Analects*. Cheng Yi recommended:

> Just take the Sage's words and savor them for a while, then naturally there will be something gained. You ought to seek deeply in the *Analects*, taking the disciples' questions as your own questions and the Sage's answers as what your ears have heard today, then naturally you will get something out of it. If Confucius and Mencius were to live again, they would not go beyond this in teaching people.[9]

For these Neo-Confucians, "reading" in the context of oral teaching restored the orality of the *Analects;* that is, it restored the dialogical encounter recorded in the text. In this sense, the *Analects* was treated as the original *yulu* (record of conversations), a record of the Sage's teaching that preserved the impact of direct encounter. Thus, proper study of the *Analects* should be a transformative process; as Cheng Yi put it, "if after having studied the *Analects*, one is still just the same old person as before, that's to have never studied it" (*Jinsilu* 3/30; see *Reflections*, 100).

It was central to the process of "savoring the text" that it be done in a hermeneutic circle of like-minded fellow students. In such a circle, one can grapple with the text's difficulties on several levels. Indeed, the text thematizes the give-and-take in the hermeneutic circle of learning. In the collected conversations of the Cheng circle, their constant use of scriptural citations and allusions evinces what could be called a "scriptural voice," an authentic "ring" of scriptural and classical phrases resounding in their discourse.

The newly important term *li* (principle, pattern, coherence) can also be understood in terms of "savoring the text." As Peter Bol has pointed out, the Neo-Confucian understanding of *li* as the inherent pattern of things draws on, among other sources, earlier uses of *li* to refer to the constant, normative pattern present in literary elaborations (*wenzhang*).[10] The discernment of *li* takes place in the words and phrases, in the pattern of thought, and also in the way the pattern of thought sheds light on the pattern of things.

The oral teachings and scriptural commentaries of the Cheng brothers and their disciples show examples of how to savor the text, so that its meaning can be personally experienced by the reader. "Knowing the flavor" of the text is thus a form of skill-knowing based on practice. In turn, the learning to which such reading of the text leads is also in a sense a skill, of knowing how to be a cultivated humane human being, a person of *ren*. *Ren* in its various dimensions informs the "savoring" process in Confucian humane learning. In the Cheng circle, *ren* was understood and sought as the awareness of forming one body with others and all things.

Forming One Body: The Learning of *Ren*

The core of Confucian spirituality, in the Song dynasty as before and since, is to be sought through *ren* (human kindness). In many ways, the Cheng brothers' teaching on *ren* was their most essential teaching, the one that most inspired their followers. The opening line of Cheng Hao's celebrated *Shi ren pian* (On Understanding/recognizing *ren*) is key: "A person of *ren* is undifferentiatedly the same body (*tongti*) together with things."[11] It was Cheng Hao who first articulated this theme of "forming one body" as central to Confucian spirituality, and later developments of it by Wang Yang-ming and others can be traced back to him.

Ren as embodied sensitivity extends through three interwoven arenas. The first is the experience of vital interconnection within one's own psychophysical body. This bodily experience is further extended in two other arenas: between fellow human beings in community, and in unity with the cosmos of all things. Though these three levels can be articulated separately, in practice there is mutual ramification. Moreover, each of these three dimensions of *ren* as "sensitive awareness forming one body" is intimately related to "exemplary teaching" and "savoring the text."

One Body and Sensitivity: Pain and Itch

The first of the three interwoven arenas of somatic unity or embodied sensitivity is the root experience of vital interconnectedness within one's own immediate body itself, the "lived body" made whole through the sensitivity of "pain and itch." In another well-known passage from his collected conversations, Cheng Hao says:

> Medical books describe numbness of the hands and feet as "*bu-ren.*" This is an excellent description. For the person of *ren*, Heaven-and-earth and the myriad things are one body; none is not myself. (*Jinsilu* 1/20)[12]

Here Cheng lauds a medical usage of the term *buren* (literally, "not-*ren*") as suggesting a key characterization of *ren* in its wider meanings. This medical definition is also drawn upon by Xie Liangzuo: "And what is *ren*? What is living is *ren*, what is dead is not-*ren*. These days when someone's body is numb and does not feel pain and itch, it is called not-*ren*" (*Shangcai yulu* 1/2b). The medical terminology is found in *Basic Questions on the Internal Classic of the Yellow Emperor* (*Huangdi neijing suwen*).[13] In the *Internal Classic*, *buren* is a common designation for numbness and lack of sensitivity of the four limbs (not feeling pain and itch, hot and cold).

In this medical theory, the bodily situation is *buren* when the flow of *qi* (psychophysical energy) is somehow blocked or unbalanced. Just as a medical model of the body developed on the basis of the anatomy of cadavers stands behind the modern Western understanding of the body as a machine, so Confucian thought draws upon an Eastern medical model based on the synergy of "vital energy," or *qi*, in the living body. This medical model supports many forms of East Asian thinking about the cultivation of personal well-being. The particularly Confucian emphasis is on the extension of this Chinese medical model to apply also to the wider social and cosmic body, through "forming one body with all things" (*yi wanwu wei yiti*).

Bodily awareness of pain and itch as opposed to numbness and paralysis is Cheng Hao's characteristic metaphor for the quality of *ren*.[14] Bodily awareness would include not only the acute awareness of actual pain and itch but also the latent potential to feel pain and itch at any moment.[15] There is no separation posited here between bodily awareness and the heart-and-mind's awareness, for a psychophysical unity is assumed. In contrast to Western models, the posited dichotomy is not between mind and body but rather between being-alive and being-dead, sensitivity and insensitivity. Moreover, the Neo-Confucians are saying something different than simply employing the medical usage as a metaphor for the extended implications of *ren*; rather, the same underlying principle is operative throughout.[16] The experiential dimensions of "forming one body" were expressed by Xie in terms of understanding *ren* as sensitivity and awareness (*jue*). For Yang Shi, the connection is thematized in terms of *cheng* (integrity, sincerity), another key term in Confucian reflection, especially developed in the *Zhongyong* (*Doctrine of the Mean*).[17]

Further evidence of this psychophysical dimension of "forming one body" is the effect that savoring the Confucian classics is affirmed to have on one's very mental and physical composition. Cheng Yi promises that when the study of the *Analects* and the *Mencius* is properly carried out, the beneficial effects will transform the whole psychophysical person: "If you can search deeply in the *Analects* and *Mencius* and savor them, then your cultivation will become complete to the point of extraordinary endowment of *qi!*" (*Jinsilu* 3/36; see *Reflections*, 103). The benefits of this practice were expected to reach all the way to transforming one's *qi*-endowment, the basic "stuff" of one's personality; surely this would be a great impetus for the study of classical texts! The expectation of a physical and psychic improvement as a result of cultivated study serves as a reminder that the basic Chinese conception of the body and heart-and-mind differs substantially from modern Western models. Again quoting Cheng Yi, one's sensitivity and perceptivity can become such that while reading the text, one joyfully responds with the whole body:

> There are people who have read the *Analects* without having anything happen to them. There are others who are happy after having understood a sentence or two. There are still others who, having read the book, love it. And there are those who, having read it, "unconsciously dance with their hands and feet." (*Jinsilu* 3/38; see *Reflections*, 103)

The phrase about "unconsciously dancing with hands and feet" is cited from the "Great Preface" to the *Odes*, showing again the connection with that poetic tradition of reading. These sayings of the Chengs indicate that "savoring the text" is a process of nurturing a joyful unity of heart-and-mind and body, centered on reading the text.

Ren is a matter of both sensitivity and activity (*ren* as forming one body is both sensory and motor). When asked how to make effort in seeking *ren*, Xie replied, again referring to the *Analects*, that one could either emulate Yan Hui and work on seeing, hearing, speech, and conduct (*Analects* 12:1) or emulate Zeng Zi and work on expressions, gestures, words, and tones (*Analects* 8:4). Certain ritualized bodily actions, such as "producing words and tones" (*chu ci qi*) became paradigmatic for the development of *ren*. The bodily actions of exemplary teachers, including the ancient disciples of Confucius, served as present models for the personal embodiment of *ren*. Naturally, "ritualization of the body" takes place within the social matrix that is also key to the practice of manifesting *ren*.

Animating the Social Body

Confucian spirituality is fundamentally relational; the "five relations" form the nexus of personal cultivation and human flourishing.[18] The traditional Confucian understanding of *ren* in human relations is both broadened and made more intimate when interpreted as forming "one body," with the connection of sensitivity and awareness as mode and meaning. Just as the Confucian perspective does not assume a mind/body dualism, so also there is no presumption of an individual/society dichotomy. The social "body" and the individual "body" are understood on a continuum, and regulating social relations is a natural extension of personal cultivation.

The Cheng circle developed their thought and practice in social relations in two main arenas, the family and the "body politic." The family is the natural arena for cultivating human relatedness; three of the five relations are family ties. In particular, filiality and serving one's parents are keynotes of Confucian cultivation practice. The examples given by the Chengs evince a bodily sense of connection with one's parents' well-being:

> When one gets some food, one must first feed one's parents. Why is this? It's because father's and mother's mouths are more important than one's own mouth. When one gets some clothing, one must first clothe one's parents. Why is this? Because father's and mother's bodies are more important than one's own body. (*Jinsilu* 6/13 in Zhang Boxing's *Jinsilujijie*)

> When one's parents are sick in bed, to leave them to an incompetent doctor is tantamount to being unkind and unfilial. In serving parents, one should know something about medicine. (*Jinsilu* 6/14; see *Reflections*, 177-78)

In describing how to "know *ren*," or recognize the "savor" of *ren*, Xie Liangzuo recommended reflection on such actual occasions of serving one's parents.

With reference to realizing *ren* in the family, it would seem natural to consider one's relations not only to both parents but also to sisters and brothers, and above all to one's spouse. This is surely the most glaring deficiency in the records of the Cheng circle. They had very little to say about the women in their families, let alone women's practices of cultivating *ren*. Cheng Yi's account of their mother provides a glimpse of what is missing:

> She was humane (*ren*), altruistic, liberal, and earnest. She cared for and loved the children of my father's concubines just as she did her own. . . . She was skillful in ruling the family. She was not stern, but correct. She did not like to beat servants but, instead, looked upon little servants as her own children. . . . Mother had six sons. Only two are still living. Her love and affection for us were of the highest degree. But in teaching us she would not give in a bit. (*Jinsilu* 6/17; *Reflections*, 179-80)

Cheng Yi's reference to the concubines and servants shows in a flash some of the social conditions under which these texts were generated, and which they assumed. The terms of appreciation and praise for a mother's role in education are common in (male) Confucian writings, going back at least to Mencius, but little mention is made of women's own course of cultivation and achievement. Nor was it considered proper or decent to discuss male–female relations openly; the theme of "forming one body" in marriage is significantly absent. As a result, vast areas integral to human cultivation and flourishing have passed without comment.[19]

The body politic is a natural extension and application of the image of "forming one body" in human society and would come readily to mind for Confucian scholar-officials. These Confucian teachers were typically also civil officials with governing responsibilities. For them, the public sphere was a realm for personal cultivation, and exhortations to practice were often kept at hand. The local gazeteer of a prefecture where Cheng Hao once governed records that he kept on the right side of his official desk the saying, "Regard the people as if [treating] the wounded." Drawing the connection between this saying and *ren*, Yang Shi remarked:

> A ruler who does not have a *ren* heart-and-mind will not be adequate to win the people. Therefore [only if] ministers can induce the ruler to "Regard the people as if [treating] the wounded" will the royal way proceed.[20]

This visceral image of "the wounded" evokes the tender compassion of benevolent rule while at the same time suggesting that the people are parts of the body of state.

The Cheng circle itself provided another social arena for the manifestation of *ren*. There was a comraderie of spirit among them that was particularly important during the later years of political disfavor.[21] As the example of Cheng Hao's admonishing Xie Liangzuo shows, the quality of the teacher–disciple relationship in the Cheng circle was such that there was an intimate, almost visceral connection between them. In seeking to realize *ren*, the Cheng circle exhorted each other not to have a "selfish" opposition between oneself and others; this humane quality of give-and-take would then open out to the wider cosmos of all things.

Forming One Body with All Things

In the distinctive spirituality of the Cheng circle, *ren* was understood as extending beyond interhuman relations to include the cosmos of all things (*wanwu*). In this third arena, the language of the sensitivity that forms one body is applied in relation to the realm of "all things." Returning to Cheng Hao's teaching that *ren* forms one body with Heaven, earth, and the myriad things, he emphasized that this somatic unity (*tongti*) extends to everything and not only to other human beings or human phenomena. It is only humans, however, who consciously respond to this unity.

Humane awareness, as receptivity and true resonance, is the way of experientially "forming one body with all things." The implication is that rather than an egoistic expanding of some kind of "self" to include things, the desire to realize *ren* (*qiuren*) already assumes that one is an integral part of the cosmos of myriad things (*wanwu*), both responsive and responsible to the cosmos. Because of the inherent model of what Tu Weiming has called "the continuity of being," "forming one body" is not the imposition of an alien unity upon disparate elements, but rather there is in *qi* the ontological underpinnings for realized awareness. But the metaphysics of *qi*, or the continuity of being, differs from a concept of material continuity in an important way, in that it is fundamentally constituted by sensitivity and responsiveness.[22] Because *qi* is more than matter, something different than a materialistic common stuff is implied. The human heart-and-mind as the organ of sensitivity is also *qi*; therefore sensitive responsiveness is the characteristic activity of the most refined *qi*.[23] "Forming" one body is not simply the formal recognition of a kind of consubstantiality with things but the lived experience of vital connection with others and with "all things" in one's affective life.

"Savoring" is extended to the patterns in things; as Cheng Yi said, "Things are especially good for savoring." Discovering the pattern of things is both a matter of "investigation" (as in the common translation of "*gewu*") and a process of receptivity. The Chengs taught that the pattern is actually present in the cosmos and in the text, and also latent in the understanding heart-and-mind. In human beings, the *li* is present as our "nature" (*xing*). To know *li*, therefore, is to know one's own nature, and the pattern and standard by which to live. Though the Cheng brothers differed in their approach to *li*, with Cheng Hao placing more emphasis on internal awareness and Cheng Yi on encountering *li* in things and affairs (*gewu*), they nonetheless agreed on the vital connection between the two. Really "knowing" the *li* is not just a matter of being able or inclined to give a certain discursive account. The organ of knowing is the whole body, including the heart-and-mind; genuine knowing is referred to as *ti ren* or *ti hui*—embodied knowing, or whole-body knowing. Pattern discovery is a hermeneutic act, both of meaning formation and of being (in)formed by the meaning. Thus, each person is both the subject and the object of the hermeneutic act of savoring that forms one body.

The discovery of *li* as the meaningful pattern of things was verified both by a communal process in which insights were confirmed in the teacher–disciple interaction and by a reflective personal savoring of those patterns in life experience. The discovery of pattern through the text also assists in finding one's right relationship to the cosmos. In turn, a deep appreciation of the scriptural classics depends on clearing away habitually selfish patterns of give-and-take through study and practice. As Xie commented,

> When one's discrimination between things and self is too profound, and in one's breast there is a lance and sharp spear (a deep sense of alienation and defensiveness), then in reading of "reciprocity (*shu*) which can be practiced for one's whole life" (*Analects* 15:24), can one really know the taste of it?[24]

The converse also holds true: by taking the words of the Sage and early disciples seriously, personally, there is leverage for grappling with those habitual patterns. "Forming one body" with all things is a matter of overcoming the false separation between oneself and things, connecting to the cosmos in dialogical encounter.

There is a basis in this notion of one-bodiness or somatic unity based on sensitivity for the development of a Confucian ecological vision.[25] Although past Confucians did not "flesh" out the implications, the notion of "forming one body"—both as being the center of the wider affective body and as a "part" of the cosmos—does lay out a direction for increased sensitivity to the state of the earth. Here the Cheng brothers' uncle Zhang Zai's famous *Western Inscription* is exemplary:

> *Qian* (cosmic masculine) is (my) father, *Kun* (cosmic feminine) is (my) mother. . . . Therefore, that which fills the universe I regard as my body and

all that which directs this universe I consider as my nature. (*Jinsilu* 2/32; see *Reflections*, 76)

The *Daoxue* teachers were not only exemplary in their personal conduct and in their educative relationships with others; they were also teaching and practicing a principle that unites human beings and the cosmos through paths of sensitive understanding. Thus, Zhang Zai's *Western Inscription* is both a "savoring" of the classical patterns in the *Yijing* (*Qian* and *Kun*) and an evocative instance of exemplary teaching.

The Confucian ideal of "forming one body" through humane sensitivity is a cultural construction of embodiment that leads directly to expanding circles of relatedness. Indeed, the lived body is embedded in all three realms of embodiment simultaneously, and becoming increasingly aware on all three levels is a continuous process of cultivation. The Cheng circle's concern with the apprehension of *li* and their excitement over the discovery of *li* are directly related to the tasks of personal cultivation. To "know the *li*" of something or, generically, to "know Dao" is a matter of experiential learning, knowing with one's whole body and mind, heart and limbs. According to this understanding, that unity is precisely the realization of *ren* as the active sensitivity and sensitive activity that forms one body with Heaven-and-earth and the myriad things.

Conclusion

The Cheng brothers and their circle shared several common understandings that shaped the dynamics of their fellowship. First among these was that the ancient Confucian texts are profoundly meaningful and provide an authoritative guide for living. A corollary to this is that inherited understandings and uses of these classic texts had placed undue limitations on the ways those meanings might be apprehended in the present. Nevertheless, the overall lineaments of the tradition were sound—what the ancients thought of as important, the Cheng brothers and their circle also recognized as important, central in human life. In other words, there was a traditional continuity of ideals and also of special texts. The key to coming to a direct apprehension of the "original meaning" of the texts, they felt, was to savor them in reflective practice, perceiving that those meanings and guides are directly applicable to one's own spiritual practice in learning to be fully human.

Three aspects of Confucian spirituality have been considered here: exemplary teaching, savoring of texts and principles, and *ren* as sensitivity that forms one body. The phenomenon of the Cheng circle brought these three aspects together in an inspirational and coherent way. The long-lasting sense of a revived authentic transmission of Confucian learning in the circle of the Cheng brothers and their disciples is illustrative of another dimension of sensitivity "forming one body." By striving to re-create the interpretive circle of Confucius's original disciples, through collectively "savoring" the text of the *Analects* and other Confucian scriptural classics, the Cheng circle was "forming one body" with their forebears and ancestors on the path of Confucian cultivation.

Further, a common understanding of the Cheng circle was that the significant methods and meanings embodied in these texts are both discoverable and shareable, and that group study with an accomplished teacher was the most direct way to unfold these meanings. The meanings in the classic encounters between Confucius or Mencius and their disciples reverberated in their present lived reality, including the developing qualities of their own characters, the like-minded community engaged in learning, and the whole order of the cosmos. Their sense of being able to feel, know, and live the real "pattern of things"—and therefore to realize fundamental "one-body unity" with all things and with that pattern—was indeed cause for excitement. Likewise, the fact that Confucian humane learning is one of the pathways of spiritual practice still available today is in part an inheritance from the Cheng brothers and their circle.

Notes

1. This memorial was submitted by Zhu Zhen to the Song emperor Gaozong (r. 1127–1162) in 1136 C.E. and may be found in *Dao-ming lu* [Record of the Destiny of the Dao] compiled by Li Xinchuan, Ming Hongzhi edition 3/2a–b. See Hoyt Tillman, *Confucian Discourse and Chu Hsi's Ascendancy*, 20–21; and Wing-tsit Chan, *Chu Hsi: New Studies* (Honolulu: University of Hawaii Press, 1989), 321.

2. For an overview of the Cheng brothers' lives and thought, see A. C. Graham, *Two Chinese Philosophers*, and their biographies by Wing-tsit Chan in *Sung Biographies*, ed. Herbert Franke (Wiesbaden: Franz Steiner, 1976). For more on the *Daoxue* movement, see the chapters by A. Birdwhistell, D. Gardner, J. Adler, and Wm. T. de Bary in this volume.

3. Cheng Yi, "Mingdao xiansheng mubiao" [Epitaph for master [Cheng] Mingdao] in *Henan Chengshi wenji* 11, *Er-Cheng ji*, 640. The citation is from *Mencius* 5A:7.

4. The felicitous characterization of *Daoxue* as a "fellowship" was suggested by Hoyt Tillman in *Confucian Discourse*, 2–9.

5. The Cheng brothers had many direct disciples; the core group included Xie Liangzuo (ca. 1050–ca. 1120), Yang Shi (1053–1135), You Zuo (1053–1123), Yin Tun (1071–1142), and Lü Dalin (1046–1092). Many of the Chengs' sayings

recorded by these disciples were included by Zhu Xi (1130–1200) and Lü Zuqian (1137–1181) in their very influential collection entitled *Jinsilu*, translated by Wing-tsit Chan as *Reflections on Things at Hand*.

6. The incident is described in the *Yi-Lo yuanyuan lu* 9/4a, and also in *Shangcai yulu* #102. This interaction shows the way that scriptural phrases were embedded in the discourse; "trifling with things and losing purpose" (*wanwu sang-zhi*) is from *Shujing* 25 and "the heart-and-mind of natural compassion" (*ceyin zhi xin*) is from *Mencius* 2A:6.

7. Julia Ching has drawn a helpful connection between the Confucian practice of "reverence" and the Christian contemplative practice of "recollection"; see "Chu Hsi on Personal Cultivation," in *Chu Hsi and Neo-Confucianism*, ed. Wing-tsit Chan (Honolulu: University of Hawaii Press, 1995), 281. Both Christian reflection and Confucian quiet-sitting may be described as disciplined spiritual reflection on the "experiential landscape."

8. *Jinsilu* 3/44; see *Reflections*, 105, and also Steven Van Zoeren, *Poetry and Personality*, 214. Van Zoeren has well expressed the communal dimension of this "savoring" practice: "It seems that exploring the savor of a passage was not necessarily an "internal," private activity, but something that could be done out loud, for other people. . . . [Cheng Hao] thus restored to the text the animating and defining presence of the living voice, removing ambiguities and opening the way to understanding" (p. 214). The *Odes*, one of the Confucian *Five Classics*, is an ancient anthology of court poetry and popular verse, traditionally thought to have been edited by Confucius.

9. *Er-Cheng Yishu* 22A, *Er-Cheng ji*, 279. This passage is partially included at *Jinsilu* 3/36; see translations in *Reflections*, 103, and Van Zoeren, *Poetry and Personality*, 215.

10. See Peter K. Bol in *"This Culture of Ours": Intellectual Transitions in T'ang and Sung China*, especially his chapter on Cheng Yi.

11. The *Shi ren pian* is a passage from the records of Cheng Hao's oral teaching, found in *Er-Cheng Yishu* 2A, *Er-Cheng ji*, 16. For a full translation and discussion of this passage, see Wing-tsit Chan, *Source Book in Chinese Philosophy*, 523-24.

12. See *Reflections*, 19; and *Source Book*, 530. The last line can be interpreted as, "nothing is alien to me."

13. This foundational work in Chinese medical philosophy was recently edited and reissued under imperial auspices when the Cheng brothers were teaching. It was presented during the reign of Shenzong, in the decade 1068–1078. See Ilza Veith, *Huang Ti Nei Ching Su Wen: The Yellow Emperor's Classic of Internal Medicine* (Berkeley: University of California Press, 1966), 8–9, 87–90.

14. A. C. Graham explains, "Not to feel a disinterested sympathy with others is to lose the consciousness that they are one substance with oneself. It is like numbness in a limb—a simile which recurs frequently in Ming-tao's sayings and which in unattributed sayings can be taken as almost certain evidence that he is the speaker" (*Two Chinese Philosophers*, 98).

15. This latent potential is connected in Chinese medical theory with the free

flowing of *qi* along specific pathways known as meridians. The meridians do not correspond exactly to any Western anatomical feature such as neural links or blood channels; rather, they are known and plotted by connecting acupuncture points. On the discovery that some hypersensitive patients can internally "feel" the location of acupuncture points, see Yuasa Yasuo, *The Body: Toward an Eastern Mind-Body Theory* (Albany: State University of New York Press, 1987), 220.

16. The modern Chinese expression for apathy and insensitivity, *mamu buren*, maintains this correlation between sensory and affective numbness.

17. Alison Jameson has nicely expressed the similarity between Xie's identification of *ren* as *jue* (sensitivity) and Yang's use of *cheng* as both describing "awareness of the links between oneself, the myriad phenomena and the Dao itself, of which the product is necessarily a feeling of tenderness and empathy toward all" (see M. A. Jameson, "South-Returning Wings: Yang Shih and the New Sung Metaphysics" [Ph.D. diss., University of Arizona, 1990], 91).

18. As given in *Mencius* 3A:4, the five relations are: father/son, ruler/minister, husband/wife, elder/younger siblings, friends. See also *Zhongyong* 20.

19. For more on the "treacherous terrain" of mapping women's spirituality in the Confucian tradition, see V. Nyitray's article in this volume.

20. The saying "Regard the people as if [treating] the wounded (*shi min ru shang*)" is found in the *Zuozhuan*, fourth month of the first year of Duke Ai (494 B.C.E.) and also in *Mencius* 4B:20. The local gazeteer referred to is [*Guangxu*] *Fugou xianzhi*, 5/32a. Yang Shi's comment is from *Guishan yulu*, 1/23b.

21. For an account of the political disfavor into which *Daoxue* fell, and also its later rise to prominence, see James T. C. Liu, *China Turning Inward: Intellectual-Political Changes in the Early Twelfth Century* (Cambridge, Mass.: Harvard University Press, 1988).

22. As Tu Weiming expresses it: "Our nature, that particular way in which vital energy [*qi*] crystallizes, endows us with the ability to feel the presence of an ever-expanding network of relationships. Since there is no limit to our sensitivity, the network is always an open system" ("A Confucian Perspective on Embodiment," 93). See also Tu's "Continuity of Being," in *Nature in Asian Traditions of Thought: Essays in Environmental Philosophy*, ed. J. Baird Callicott and Rogert T. Ames (Albany: State University of New York Press, 1989).

23. For a helpful discussion of *qi* in Zhu Xi's thought in relation to the heart-and-mind and also to spiritual beings (*guishen*), see Daniel Gardner, "Ghosts and Spirits in the Sung Neo-Confucian World: Chu Hsi on *kuei-shen*," *Journal of the American Oriental Society* 115, no. 4 (October–December 1995): 598–611.

24. This passage is from Xie's "Preface" to his commentary on the *Analects*, found in *Song Wenjian* 92. For further discussion of Xie's *Analects* commentary and its significance, see Selover, *Kernel of Humanity*.

25. See the essays in *Confucianism and Ecology*, ed. Mary Evelyn Tucker and John Berthrong (Cambridge, Mass.: Center for the Study of World Religions, Harvard University, 1998).

Suggested Reading

Bol, Peter K. 'This Culture of Ours': Intellectual Transitions in T'ang and Sung China. Stanford: Stanford University Press, 1992.

Chan, Wing-tsit, trans. Reflections on Things at Hand: The Neo-Confucian Anthology. New York: Columbia University Press, 1967.

Chan, Wing-tsit, ed. and trans. A Source Book in Chinese Philosophy. Princeton, N.J.: Princeton University Press, 1963.

Fung Yu-lan. A History of Chinese Philosophy, volume 2. Translated by Derk Bodde. Princeton, N.J.: Princeton University Press, 1953.

Graham, A. C. Two Chinese Philosophers: The Metaphysics of the Brothers Ch'eng. Foreword by Irene Bloom. La Salle, Ill.: Open Court, 1992.

Selover, Thomas W. The Kernel of Humanity: A Neo-Confucian Exploration of Humane Learning and Scriptural Exegesis. Atlanta: Scholars Press, 1998.

———. Hsieh Liang-tso and the Analects of Confucius: Humane Learning as a Religious Quest. New York: Oxford University Press, 2004.

Tillman, Hoyt. Confucian Discourse and Chu Hsi's Ascendancy. Honolulu: University of Hawaii Press, 1992.

Tu Weiming. "A Confucian Perspective on Embodiment." In The Body in Medical Thought and Practice, ed. Drew Leder, 87–100. Dordrecht: Kluwer Academic Publishers, 1992.

———. Confucian Thought: Selfhood as Creative Transformation. Albany: State University of New York Press, 1985.

Van Zoeren, Steven. Poetry and Personality: Reading, Exegesis, and Hermeneutics in Traditional China. Stanford: Stanford University Press, 1991.

19

Zhu Xi's Neo-Confucian Spirituality

WM. THEODORE DE BARY

W HEN IN 1958 Tang Junyi, Carsun Chang, Mou Zongsan, and others of the so-called New Confucians issued their Manifesto for a Reappraisal of Sinology and Reconstruction of Chinese Culture,"[1] among those Confucian values they most pointedly reaffirmed were the religious and spiritual values. This was not the way most people thought of Confucianism at that time, and there was indeed an injured, almost petulant tone to these scholars' defense of Confucian spirituality, as if it were provoked by the prevalent misrepresentation of Confucianism on this score. Nor is it difficult to imagine the possible grounds of such a perception on their part. Much of the twentieth-century critique of Confucianism in revolutionary times had seen it as primarily a political doctrine identified with a discredited imperial regime. This perception was powerfully reinforced by the easy acceptance in both the West and East Asia of a marxist view—reflecting the influence on Marx of Hegel and early-nineteenth century British thinkers—that India and China had been stagnant societies and, in the Chinese case, that a socially and politically repressive Confucianism was much to blame for this retarded condition.

Contributing to this view of Confucianism as essentially a social and political system was its awkward fit into the usual categories of intellectual and especially academic discourse. Confucianism, judged by Western standards, was not a real philosophy; much less was it a religion, since it failed, despite its heavy emphasis on ritual, to conform to the familiar pattern of Indo-European or Semitic religions. Indeed, the seeming secularization of Confucian ritual only confirmed this judgment.

Nevertheless, one cannot dismiss the question as simply one of Western misperceptions. If Confucianism were perceived as essentially a form of humanism, and the latter was already counterposed in many modern Western minds to theism or religion, the needed corrective to this inadequate taxonomy was certainly not to deny the centrality of the "human" to the essential Confucian vision. Rather, it is better to think of Confucianism as a form of humanism with a strong religious dimension (among other humanistic traditions that have their own religious or spiritual dimensions).

In the Confucian case, what warrants the special claim that it has been centered on the "human" is that it takes human life as the starting point of its reflections on the divine, celestial, and cosmic orders—in other words, that it takes human life itself as revelatory of the divine, rather than "divine revelation" as the primary reference point for defining the human.

As for the perception of Confucianism as primarily political in character, this too has some basis in fact and cannot easily be dismissed as just another Western invention or oversimplification. Long before the West entered on the scene, syncretic representations of the three major traditions (the "Three Teachings" as they were called) typically assigned each a special sphere of competence, identifying Daoism with the cultivation of the body (*shen*) (i.e., physical regimens, longevity cults, alchemical techniques, etc.); Buddhism with the "mind" (*xin*) (meditation); and Confucianism with social and political order (*zhi*).

Facile though these stereotypes were, they accorded with a Chinese sense of letting everyone have his own place while at the same time sharing somehow in the total vision of things. Just how they could be seen as one ("The Three Teachings are One" *Sanjiao heyi*), remained a mystery, necessarily indefinable but somehow traceable back to an ineluctable source. Nevertheless, to say that Confucianism's center of gravity was to be found in governance and social order had strong scriptural and historical support. Confucianism had more than one home; it subsisted and persisted in the family, the school, and the state; but lodged in government it had no serious rivals. Buddhism and Daoism might have their own "families" and "schools" but, for all the personal patronage they at times enjoyed from condescending Chinese rulers, neither religion succeeded in developing a public philosophy or political ethos that could guide and give definite shape to the conduct of government.

Religiously speaking, Confucian success in the political department came at some cost. Over the long course of history its schools served the ruling elite better than the general populace, and its rationalism served scholarship better than popular religion, which Confucianism dealt with at arm's length with great skepticism and notable diffidence. Hence, for all the efforts of Confucians historically, and especially the Neo-Confucians, to revive the old-time religion of the Zhou aristocracy and resurrect the classic rituals, they had little success in winning over the general populace and experienced almost constant frustration, if not despair, over their failure to wean the masses from their seeming bewitchment by the magic of Buddhist and Daoist liturgies and religious spectacles.

A further implication of this estrangement is that, by thus distancing itself from popular religion, Confucianism not only delimited its religious role but also, in the process, defined its own cultural level. It has long been recognized how Confucianism tended to become identified with custody of the classical language and literature, wherefore, contrary to the Confucians' own egalitarian professions, their very fidelity to tradition—if not often their belletristic preciosity—cut them off from much that was vital in the vulgate and popular culture. Still more pertinent to the present discussion, this distinctive course of cultural evolution had its effect on the subsequent development of Confucian spirituality, which emerged not as an incremental refinement to popular religiosity but as a further, higher dimension of the Confucian noble man's vocation to public service, that is, *noblesse oblige* as the highest ideal of elite culture. The elaboration of this ideal came with the rise of Neo-Confucianism in the Song, Yuan, and Ming, and later in Korea and Japan as well.

The Heroic Ideal in Secular Society

After Buddhism's long dominance of the religious and philosophical scene in Tang China, a new concern for the secular order for civil society and the public welfare arose with the Song's reunification of China and its revitalization of the civil bureaucracy. Intellectually this had been preceded by Han Yu's bold challenge in the ninth century to the idea that Buddhism and Confucianism were compatible manifestations of essentially one Way. For him the Confucian Way was bound up with human culture and the arts of civilization, whereas Buddhism undercut civilizational values by its insistence that self-awakening and self-deliverance—the search for spiritual emancipation and freedom from illusion and suffering—must come first. In Han Yu's view this brought a disjunction between personal religiosity and public philosophy, whereas Confucian intellectual and moral self-cultivation, as outlined in the *Great Learning*, prepared one, step by step, for increasing social involvement and the assumption of successively greater social and political responsibilities.

The epitomization of this Confucian conception in memorable utterance guarded by generation after generation as expressing most succinctly the Confucian ideal of public service came with Fan Zhongyan's characterization of the noble person (*junzi*) as one who is "first in worrying about the world's worries and last in enjoying its pleasures." What is translated here as "the world" is more literally "All-under-Heaven" and carries the implication that all creation, but especially humankind, exists under the moral aegis of Heaven as the creative, providential power that fosters and protects all life. It is for the noble person who, as Mencius said, "awakens" first to the true needs of humankind and feels the obligation to "awaken those who come after"—it is for such as these, awakened to the concern they share with Heaven for the fostering of all life, to dedicate themselves to this cause of arousing others to it and to find self-fulfillment in the midst of acting out day by day this Heavenly humane concern. Being "first in worrying" means not putting one's own peace of mind first by striving for Enlightenment and only after that returning to "save the world," but rather from the outset seeing worry and hard struggle as the means of one's own self-fulfillment.

Some time ago a leading sinologue of the mid-twentieth century saw this heroic ideal as Confucianism's appropriation of the bodhisattva ideal to its own secular mission. The comparison is apt insofar as it acknowledges the parallelism of the two ideals, which should each be recognized as embodying its own distinctive form of spirituality, rather than the one being labeled "religious" and the other "secular." But in fact Fan Zhongyan's language is the language of Mencius, not that of the Buddhist Santideva (to whom it had been mistakenly attributed), and Fan's whole conception, though it may well have been evoked by the contemporary challenge of the bodhisattva ideal, was thoroughly grounded in Mencius. Hence, too, Fan's motto proved apposite as an expression of the Neo-Confucian life ideal in the Song and after, which went back to the Mencian view of the mind-and-heart as the basis for its reintegration of the religious and secular, the Heavenly and the human.

Another major thrust of this movement was focused on the practice of sagehood. In its earlier phase, so much devoted to political and social activism, Neo-Confucian reformism had held up the sage-king as the embodiment of the social ideal. Here the model of the sage-king was advanced by Confucians to provide critical moral leverage on the ruler, hoping thereby to convert him to the need for radical reform and claiming authoritative precedents for this in the ideal institutions of the ancient sage-kings. When, however, major reform efforts in the eleventh century failed to achieve the millennium, attention was redirected to the sage as a personal ideal, embodying certain constant moral and spiritual values transcending (or underlying and persisting through) ephemeral, secular change.

Exemplary of this redirected effort were the Cheng brothers, who had participated in the earlier reform movement, believing that "a great reform could produce great government" (*dagai ze dazhi*), but who at the same time were deeply concerned with sagehood as a spiritual ideal accompanying politics. In fact, as a young man Cheng Yi had written a memorable essay entitled "What Master Yan Loved to Learn." Master Yan referred to Yan Hui, a favorite disciple of Confucius described in both the *Analects* and *Mencius* as one living in humble circumstances, so devoted to learning that he cared nothing for worldly position or personal comfort so long as he could dedicate himself to the pursuit of a goal referred to by Cheng Yi as "learning to be a sage" (*shengxue*).

The brief description of Yan Hui in the classic texts lends itself to only modest elucidation of what this spiritual ideal consisted in. Nevertheless, it is fair to say that, while clearly represented as an ascetic lifestyle, it was understood to be neither self-denying nor self-sacrificing but rather self-confirming and self-fulfilling.

This conception of sagehood, thought of as achievable in the humblest of conditions, became the keynote of Neo-Confucian spirituality. Although it overlaps to some extent the conception of the noble person (*junzi*), insofar as both would be devoted to learning, the ideal of sagehood is free of any consideration of social status and does not necessarily call for the assumption of leadership responsibilities such as those that attach to the Neo-Confucian scholar-official, whose self-conception as a "noble person" or "superior man" could sometimes appear "elitist." The prominence of Yan Hui in later Neo-Confucian literature and the frequency with which he was enshrined in Confucian temples, including many temples dedicated specifically to him in the Song, Yuan, and Ming, testify to the importance of this religiosity and spirituality to the developing Neo-Confucian movement. Further, this egalitarian aspect of Neo-Confucian sagehood as accessible to all, might serve as one respect in which Neo-Confucianism moved in a distinctly religious direction, since most major religions including Mahayana Buddhism itself exhibit this leveling tendency on the spiritual plane.

Contributing to this development were the speculations of other Song thinkers whose ideas became incorporated into the great synthesis of Zhu Xi. Here I shall mention only a few whose contributions are most directly pertinent to Neo-Confucian spirituality. Zhu's own paternal and scholastic filiations are with the Cheng brothers, and much of his philosophy derives from them, but he also thought of himself as heir to a wider range of Song thought and scholarship, and believed it important to include these more recent contributions in his attempted reconstitution of the Confucian tradition in a form suitable for his own time.

Zhu did this against the background of a contemporary culture pervasively influenced by Chan Buddhism, with its concept of spiritual authority expressed as a direct "transmission from mind-to-mind." This, Chan claimed in the Song, had been passed on by different lineages of Chan masters "outside the scriptures." Zhu, by contrast, attached importance to literate discourse as the basis of a public philosophy, and even though he had his own doubts about the authenticity of many received texts in the Confucian tradition, he thought it imperative that this textual tradition be both critically and sympathetically rehabilitated, as the discursive ground on which to base a consensus on moral values and public policy. Hence, Confucian Learning, as Zhu defined it in contradistinction to the Chan line of mind-to-mind, extratextual transmission, exhibited a spirituality based on actual texts, subject to critical scholarly examination but creatively reinterpreted by large-minded men with a broad vision. Hence, it was not just mind alone, or private communication, but insight and inspiration working out in the open, on some record or artifact of human experience, that grounded Zhu's spirituality in the practical order; and it was his inclusion of recent thinkers in his reformulation of the Way that rendered it timely—and thus again, practical.

The implications of this idea that the Way was propagated through creative interplay between mind and text were not limited to the sages and worthies who figured prominently in the *Daotong* as the Succession to the Way. The same interplay between mind and text took place in the ordinary process of education. Anyone's study of the classics should, ideally and most effectively, involve one's own personal reflection on the texts, drawing something out of oneself in the process of engaging the text and making sense of it for oneself. Unless the reading were to be simply mindless and mechanical, one had to address the text seriously and mindfully which is as much as to say, in the language of the Confucian tradition, "reverently" (*jing*), showing due respect for the text as a hallowed product of one's honored spiritual forebears. It was not something to be treated frivolously, "used," or exploited simply for one's own benefit, but rather to be handled with care and passed on as a legacy, perhaps with some interest (in both senses of the term) to one's successors. Showing respect for the text meant showing respect for oneself and reverence for the Way.

To do this one had to bring to it the best of oneself. One could not find the Way in the text without at the same time finding the Way in oneself, that is, as Mencius put it, one could not really "get it" without getting it by and in oneself (*zide zhi*). Then, having done this at least to some degree, one had to try one's own understanding of the original classic text out on one's fellow students and teachers, before going on to consult past commentaries for their understanding of it. Thus Zhu's reading and study method corresponded closely with the traditional Western sense of "education," from the Latin *e-duco*, as a "leading or drawing out" of one's own inner potential.

Zhu's own pursuit of sagehood emerged from his earlier pursuit of "Learning for One's Self" (*weiji zhi xue*), an aim that his father had put before him at a young age. Here "for One's Self" meant learning for one's own self-development and self-realization, a precondition to and priority over any learning that was merely success-oriented (understood in China primarily in the form of success in the civil service examinations). Since Yan Hui too was identified with this kind of nonmaterial, nonworldly ideal, it is understandable how Learning for One's Self could lead Zhu to Cheng Yi's "Learning to be a Sage." Both constitute a form of personal spirituality.

It was natural for Zhu, in explaining his reconstitution of the Succession to the Way (*Daotong*), to credit the Cheng brothers, as his own spiritual forebears, with having recovered the Way after a long lapse in its proper exposition since the time of Mencius. But in his pursuit of learning to be a sage, Zhu was led to a slightly senior contemporary of the Chengs, Zhou Dunyi (1017–1073), whom he then installed as the first of the Song masters to carry out the rearticulation of the Way in their own time.

One can say, therefore, that there are two reasons for Zhu's exhumation of Zhou Dunyi and posthumous elevation of him into the Neo-Confucian hall of fame, by editing and publishing Zhou's writings and by quoting him first among the Song masters in his anthology of the Learning of the Way (known in English as "Reflections on Things at Hand" [*Jinsilu*, which could also be translated as "Record of Recent Thought"]). Both reasons are contained in the selections Zhu made for this anthology, but the second in order of presentation is the first for us to consider in the present context. It is from the early chapter on Essentials of Learning:

> Master Lienxi [Zhou Dunyi] said: The sage aspires to become Heaven, the worthy aspires to become a sage and the gentleman aspires to become a worthy. . . . Yan Yuan "did not transfer his anger; he did not repeat a mistake" [*Analects* 6:2], and "for three months there would be nothing in his mind contrary to humanity (*ren*)." If one desires what Yiyin desired and learns what Yen Tzu learned, he will become a sage if he reaches the highest degree and a worthy if he reaches the proper degree. Even if he does not, he will not miss a good reputation.
>
> The Way of the Sage is to be heard through the ear, to be preserved in the heart, to be deeply embraced there to become one's moral character, and to become one's activities and undertakings when it is put into practice. . . .

Master Yichuan [Chengyi] said: "It was to learn the way of becoming a sage."

"Can one become a sage through learning?"

"Yes." . . .

This established "Learning to be a Sage" as something anyone could aspire to, even if everyone might not achieve the same success. Thus, Zhou and Zhu affirmed it as a spiritual ideal accessible to all as something that could be "learned" and was not just an innate gift of the specially endowed. This is as much as to say, the potentiality for sagehood in every human being, rooted in one's nature, represented a kind of lowest common human denominator, a spiritual capability shared by all and a Confucian equivalent of the universality of Buddhahood proclaimed in the Lotus Sutra. Since in the *Analects* of Confucius sagehood had stood as a remote ideal, here Zhou and Zhu were expanding on Mencius's assertion that all men had the potentiality for sagehood—and doing so now on a philosophical level and in terms such as were needed to meet the challenge of Buddhism.

The second reason appears in the very first quotation cited in this anthology, from Zhou's "Explanation of the Diagram of the Supreme Ultimate." It involved a subtle metaphysical formulation: "Non-finite and yet the Supreme Ultimate (Pole or Norm)," a characterization of the ultimate reality principle. The importance of this for our purposes is that, again, it provided the cosmological basis for Zhu's concepts of human nature and sagehood. Here the directive principle of the Supreme Ultimate is seen as guiding the process of change, understood as a growth process, rather than as one destructive of any enduring or substantial self-nature (as in Buddhism). This explanation of change as ordered and yet open-ended (not fixed), served to ground Zhu's philosophy of human nature in an organic process and to establish his concept of the moral nature (the potential for sagehood) in the world of emerging physical reality.

To expand further on this concept of the natural world as a process of psychophysical evolution, manifesting both a moral and rational order, was the contribution Zhu found in the work of Zhang Zai (1020-1077), also prominently featured in Zhu's *Reflections on Things at Hand.* Therein Zhu included Zhang's *Western Inscription,* which linked the human moral relations to a larger cosmic order in a manner illustrative of the Cheng brothers' doctrine concerning "the humaneness which forms one body with Heaven-and-earth and all things." "Forming one body" meant that the natural moral sentiments (natural bodily affections), properly cultivated, could unite one to the creative process and thus to all of creation.

Here again Zhang and Zhu were expanding Mencius's earlier concept of moral cultivation as also a process of psychophysical expansiveness (the expanding spirit of *qi*) that could unite one to all of Heaven-and-earth. As a form of ethical mysticism, further elaborated upon by Zhu Xi, this became the basis for the mystical experience of many later Neo-Confucians.

Corollary to this holism, as conceived by the Cheng brothers and Zhu Xi, was the doctrine of "the unity of Principle and its diverse particularizations" (*liyi fenshu*). As an example, one could cite Zhu Xi's comment on a passage in the *Analects* wherein Confucius discusses the particular quality of each of the so-called Three Ages—the Xia, the Shang, and the Zhou. Each had its own characteristics in the process of historical and civilizational development, but in each the Five Constants of humaneness, rightness, ritual decorum, wisdom, and trustworthiness endured from age to age.[2] In each age, then, these human constants were expressed in a manner reflecting the particular conditions, spirit, or quality of the age.

Here principle was identified, in the human order, with humaneness, but humaneness itself, as a genetic principle, manifested an expansive power conjoined to the cosmic energy of the universe, as if all existence were linked together by a mutual attraction, and this universal magnetic attraction constituted the unity of all creation ("Heaven and earth and the myriad things"). Another way of expressing this "unity of principle" in the Cheng-Zhu formula above is as a universal genetic coding, a growth principle (*sheng-sheng*) and directive principle (*ji*) inherent in all things which gives them a fundamental affinity.

According to this view, each of the myriad things manifests its own particular growth principle and distinctive function in the emerging universe of psychophysical existence (*qi*), just as each seed of grain has its own inner structure (perceivable as its "grain"), which is not just a static configuration but an organic, genetic principle that guides its functioning and development.

In this conception, the unity and diversity of principle are equally real and irreducible. In the human order one cannot realize this unity without attending at the same time to one's proper function. Merely to intuit or grasp the "unity" of all things in some "transcendent" experience of enlightenment would not do; such unity could be genuine only if "realized" through the practical fulfillment of one's own particular functions. For human beings, this meant fulfilling one's moral nature in action, that is, fulfilling moral constants (principle) in relation to one's given condition and situation in life, with one's corresponding personal obligations seen as the differentiated duties ("diverse particularizations") of the underlying principle of human nature: one's humaneness.

Zhu Xi strongly insisted on this point in his interpretation of Zhang Zai's *Western Inscription*. He was concerned lest it be misunderstood either as a vague mystical holism, an intuitive enlightenment that transcended the moral and rational order, or as a diffuse humanitarian sentiment unguided by moral norms and practical reason. Either fallacy could lead to a facile syncretism that equated Confucian humaneness with an undifferentiated, undefined Buddhist compassion. Thus, Zhu pointed out how Zhang Zai "specified the particular" ways in which one was to perform one's personal obligations in achieving the "oneness with Heaven-and-earth" he elegized in the *Western Inscription*.

Zhu Xi also took special pains to explain the exact procedures by which one could accomplish this result: that is, as Zhou Dunyi had affirmed it, how one could learn to be a sage or, at the least, if one fell short of perfection, how one could achieve personal fulfillment. This Zhu did in more than one way, but two of the most fundamental methods are found in his choice of the *Great Learning* (*Daxue*) and the *The Mean* (Zhongyong) for inclusion along with the *Analects* and *Mencius,* in the basic, elementary texts of his learning method.

The first of these that bears on Zhu's method, and one quite recognizable as a method of spiritual praxis, is the sixteen-word formula that became known as the "Method of the Mind" (*xinfa*) and also as the key to Zhu Xi's Learning of the mind-and-heart (*xinxue*). The sixteen words come from an apocryphal text in the *Classic of Historical Documents* (*Shujing*), and Zhu's overriding of his own doubts about the authenticity of the text is a measure of the prime value he attached to it as an illustration of his method; in other words, its provenance was a less vital concern for Zhu than its rhetorical or symbolic value.

The sixteen words (characters) may be translated as "The human mind-and-heart is precarious; the mind-and-heart of the Way is subtle. Be discriminating and unified. Hold to the Mean!" This laconic utterance, attributed to the sage-kings Yao and Shun, is cryptic enough to call for some interpretation and allows for more than one rendering.

First, "the human mind-and-heart is precarious" refers to the instability of the human psyche, precariously poised between selfish and unselfish desires. Here "selfish desires" are literally "human desires," an expression found in the *Book of Rituals* (*Liji*), where it stands in contrast to the "mind of Heaven," with the latter understood to represent Heaven as a beneficent moral power impartially concerned with the welfare of "all-under-Heaven." In the original context of the *Liji*, the reference to the human mind is to that of the ruler, who should, like Heaven, rule impartially out of a concern for benefiting all his subjects, yet who all too often proves concerned only with his own position of power and his own selfish enjoyment ("human desire"). In this political context, the "mind of Heaven" stood for all that was fair, just, and open and in the shared interest of all, presiding as Heaven (the moral order) did over the common or public interest (kung), for which the ruler, as Heaven's surrogate, also bore the responsibility.

Furthermore Heaven's concern, expressed as the "mind-and-heart of Heaven," was implicit in the so-called Mandate of Heaven (*tianming*) conveying Heaven's moral and political charge to the ruler. Yet, as the opening lines of the *The Mean* (*Zhongyong*) put it, this moral charge was also the basis of the human's Heavenly-endowed moral nature. Thus, every human being (not just the ruler) had implanted within him this innate moral conscience, expressive of Heaven's mind, and equated in the sixteen-word formula with "the mind of the Way."

For Zhu Xi's audience of would-be scholar-officials (*shidafu*), this language addressed to members of the ruling aristocracy in ancient China still had relevance; they understood that the education available to anyone who enjoyed the leisure and freedom from manual toil necessary for the pursuit of learning thereby incurred a special moral burden: the expectation of one's meeting higher social responsibilities. This called for conscientious self-scrutiny of one's motivations in the exercise of one's power over others. But further, once this "mind of the Way" became recognized as inherent in human nature generally, all human beings shared to some degree that "charge," that moral imperative known as the "mind of the Way," and with it the obligation to curb the potentially selfish desires that naturally arose in the human mind-and-heart.

According to Zhu Xi's view of human nature, desires need not necessarily be a source of craving or delusion; they could be entirely legitimate if not inordinate or satisfied at the expense of others. Desires arose naturally as functions of the bodily self; indeed, human life itself was energized and sustained by such appetites. Good and necessary in themselves, they became harmful only when overindulged or misdirected. Consequently there was a need for the Mind of the Way, acting on behalf of what was fair and just (*gong*), to direct the desires and control them within reasonable limits or, in the terms of the sixteen-word formula, to hold to the Mean.

To guide the desires properly, however, was not easy. Indeed to judge fairness (*gong*)—that is, what was fair to oneself or to one's own, as well as fair to others; to control the appetites and be firm of will; to refrain from self-deception by indulging self-serving rationalizations—sometimes required fine moral judgment, what in the West might be called delicacy of conscience. Hence the dual emphasis on the difficulty of perceiving the "mind of the Way" (what was right and fair) and the precariousness of the human mind in dealing with powerful passions and conflicting desires.

Those who followed Mencius's doctrines of the goodness of human nature, as the Neo-Confucians did, have sometimes been thought over-optimistic and insufficiently aware of the weaker, even evil, side of human nature. Zhu Xi, it would seem, is not liable to this charge. Indeed, some critics have accused him of the opposite tendency—leaning too far in the direction of Xunzi's and the Legalists' darker view of human nature, and thus of being too strict and repressive of human desires.

For a reasonable judgment of this issue, one must further consider what was meant by "being discriminating and unified." Discriminating (*jing*) could be understood as being careful and precise in making reasonable judgments concerning the "unity of principle" (general or constant values) and the "diversity of its particularizations." Since all human affairs were compounded of universal human values and their particularization in given situations, to follow the Mind of the Way through the sixteen-word "method of the mind" consisted in a balanced attention to this irreducible combination of "the unity of principle" (being at one) and its diverse particularizations (exercising refined discrimination). In other words, it meant "holding to the Mean" that recognized the unity of principle in the midst of its diverse particularizations (for instance, what was fair [*gong*] both to oneself and to others, or how humaneness might be expressed in different applications, functions, or duties).

Since the sixteen-character formula does not appear in the text of the *Mean* (*Zhongyong*), for Zhu Xi so pointedly to introduce it in his preface suggests that he meant it to explain and reinforce an injunction that does appear prominently in both the *Mean* and the *Great Learning:* "to be watchful over oneself when alone." "Being self-watchful" meant to be attentive to and on guard concerning "what was unseen and unheard," that is, the fine prompting of the moral mind (Mind of the Way) and invidious "human desires" (*renyu*) that could lead one astray. "When alone" meant when no one else was watching. It stood for interiority of conscience; for "finding the Way in one's self," as Mencius had put it; for achieving that integrity of the mind-and-heart that should ensure a proper response to others or resistance to external pressures.

Because the Confucian sense of mutuality, reciprocity, and responsiveness to others was seen as fundamental to the virtue of humaneness, with its empathetic feeling for the interrelatedness of all being, an undue sensitivity to others' approval has sometimes been adduced as the basis for calling Confucianism "other-directed" (in contrast to "inner-directed") or for referring to it as a "shame ethic," guided less by interior conscience than by social pressures. Closer to the truth would be to say that the Confucian, while exhibiting particular social sensitivities, also was attentive, at his best, to this cultivation of the inner conscience, out of a special responsiveness and fidelity to the Mind of the Way).

As this sensitivity in matters of conscience spread with Zhu Xi's "method of the mind and heart" to later generations of Neo-Confucians, it gave rise to many issues concerning integrity of personal character versus hypocrisy, pretentiousness, and self-serving rationalization. It could easily be overdone or underdone, resulting in either an excessive rigidity, rigorism, or even puritanism, or else in a lax and permissive attitude as the extreme to which one might carry spontaneity or naturalness in the expression of one's unfeigned sincerity or inner integrity.

The values and functions involved here cover a wide range of human activities, and the "method" or "formula" of the mind-and-heart could be applied to almost any matter or affair, since the unity of principle and diversity of its particularizations applied to all human experience. This being the case, it is difficult to draw a clear line between what might be called intellectual, moral, and spiritual functions. Zhu Xi's spirituality is not dissociated from learning including book-learning as we have seen in his view of the Succession to the Way (*Daotong*) as a process of interaction between classic texts and a sensitive or inspired mind-and-heart. It is important to remember too that principle in human nature is rooted in the human affections, particularly common moral sentiments. Thus, knowing and learning are directly connected, in the eight items of the *Great Learning*'s process of self-cultivation, to "rectifying the mind-and-heart" and "making one's intentions sincere." Learning cannot be genuine or real unless it is grounded in a clarification of one's moral stance and is accompanied by an empathetic effort to enter into whatever is being studied or dealt with.

Perhaps the best statement of this view is found in the special note Zhu Xi added to the *Great Learning*'s "Investigation of Things" and extending of knowledge. Here "knowledge" must be understood not primarily as something known objectively or quantitatively but as something qualitatively appreciated by the knowing mind. Hence the need sometimes to translate *zhi* as "knowing" in order to convey the idea that one's knowing or learning capacity is even more involved than the object apprehended. (In English, the word "cognize" may express the notion that there is something originally and basically cognate between the knower and the known, brought together in the recognition of principle in the mind-and-heart and things.)

In traditional Neo-Confucian discourse Zhu Xi's special note is one of the most pivotal formulations of this idea, and we also have the benefit of his clarification of it in *Questions on the Great Learning*. The special note reads:

> The foregoing fifth chapter of the commentary explained the meaning of "investigation of things and the extension of knowledge," but it is now lost. I have ventured to draw upon the ideas of Master Cheng [Yi] to supply it. That the "extension of knowledge consists in the investigation of things" means that, wishing to extend one's knowledge, one must fathom the principles in each thing or affair as it presents itself to us. The spiritual intelligence of man always seeks to know, and the things and affairs of this world all have their principles. But if there are principles yet unfathomed, man's knowledge is incomplete. Therefore the *Great Learning*, at the outset of its instruction, insists that the student, in regard to the things and affairs of the world, proceed from what he already knows of their principles and fathom them to their utmost limit. After exerting himself for a long time, one day he will experience a breakthrough to integral comprehension. Then there will be nothing in the multiplicity of things external or internal, fine or coarse, that is beyond one's reach, and nothing in the whole substance and great functioning of the mind that will not be fully clarified. This is what is meant by the investigation of things, the extension of knowledge.[3]

Now for Zhu's further explanation in the *Questions and Answers on the Great Learning:*

> In the pursuit of learning what one studies is nothing but the mind and principles. Though the mind is the master of this one person, its empty, spiritual substance can command all the principles under Heaven, and though the principles are dispersed in things, their operation [or function], in all its subtlety and refinement, does not lie beyond this one man's mind. Initially there is no distinction to be made between the internal or external, fine or coarse, but if one is unaware of the spirituality of the mind-and-heart and thus unable to preserve it, obscurations and vexations will prevent one from fathoming the fine subtlety of the principles. Unable to understand their fine subtlety and having no way to fathom them, one would be prevented by partiality, narrow-mindedness, and obstinacy from exhaustively exercising the whole substance of the mind-and-heart.
>
> Thus the sage provided instruction so that man would become aware of this spiritual intelligence in the silence of his own mind and preserve it in dignity [of demeanor] and single-minded composure [quiescent unity] as the basis of his fathoming of principle; and [it was also] so that man would understand the subtlety of principles, fathom them through scholarly study and discussion, and accomplish the work of exhaustively exercising the mind, so that the broad and narrow interpenetrate one another and action and quiescence sustain one another. From the start there is no distinction to be made

between what is internal or external, fine or coarse, but with the persistent and genuine accumulation of effort, there will be a breakthrough to integral comprehension, and having come to understand all things in their undifferentiated unity, in the end there will be no distinctions of internal or external, fine or coarse to speak of.

Nowadays people want to oversimplify the matter and wrap it up in mystery so as to make it seem like a profound and impenetrable doctrine of some very special sort. They would have scholars misdirect their minds to something outside words and letters, saying that only in this manner can the Way be apprehended. This is all attributable to the seductive and misleading doctrines of Buddhism in recent times, and it would be a great error to let this be put forward to the detriment of the ancients' real learning of "clarifying virtue" (i.e., manifesting the moral nature) and "renewing the people."[4]

The direct meaning and significance of these passages may be summed up as: (1) the need to study things and affairs in order to understand their principles; (2) a belief in the intelligibility of principle; (3) the characterization of the mind as "empty and spiritual" (in the sense of unlimited receptivity and permeability) while at the same time replete with principle (in the sense of the mind and things being similarly structured so that there is a natural affinity between them); (4) the view of the cumulative nature of learning and the increasing coherence of principles as pursued both extensively in things and intensively within the self; (5) the culmination of this learning in a comprehensive understanding of things in their undifferentiated unity or wholeness (guantong), which eventually dawns on one (i.e., an understanding that is not necessarily an exhaustive knowledge of things in their particularity but which brings a fusion of cognitive awareness and affective response, overcoming the dichotomy of self and other, inner and outer, etc.); (6) the view that this holistic understanding, though it goes beyond words, is not to be confused with a Buddhist enlightenment which transcends morality and reason; and (7) the conviction that growth in learning leads to the fullest possible manifestation of the "whole substance and great functioning" of man's nature and of individual selfhood or personhood.

Admittedly, the text is not without its ambiguities, and these led to controversy among later Neo-Confucians. How extensive did the search for an exhaustive knowledge of the principles in things need to be? For some later critics, this seemed to require a lifetime of prolonged study, as if scholarly achievement had become a prerequisite to achieving sagehood. Zhu undoubtedly believed that study and investigation were lifelong pursuits, yet here he is talking about a certain stage in the pursuit of learning when one's understanding finally brings a sense of being at home with oneself and the world. Zhu does not actually stipulate that this sense of wholeness and fulfillment requires a mastery of all the principles in things; it is more likely that what he has in mind is a process of learning, both cognitive and affective, which brings one's capacity for empathetic understanding to the point where nothing in the world seemed alien to one.

Presumably, this deep sense of being at home with oneself and things, of overcoming the dichotomy between self and other, inner and outer, also meant understanding one's own role and destiny in a manner similar to Confucius's "learning the imperative of Heaven" (*tianming*) at the age of fifty. This is now seen in Zhu Xi's terms under the two basic aspects of knowing the principle or the ground of one's being (*soiran zhi gu*) and the principle of what a thing should be (*sodangran zhi ze*). Since each individual has his own principle and Supreme Ultimate, his integrated comprehension of the wholeness of things would include an insight into Heaven's imperative under both of these aspects as the basis of his individuality in relation to the Way as a whole.[5] Moreover, being established through the conjunction of humanity's Heavenly nature (principle) with its physical nature, like the principle inherent in each seed of grain, this particularity of the individual would be recognized as a compound of the physical and emotional nature with the moral and rational. It was not just an abstract norm.[6]

As a succinct statement of Zhu Xi's mature views on the method and goal of self-cultivation, and one that appeared prominently in a basic text of the Neo-Confucian school—the first among the Four Books in the new curriculum the special note in Zhu's commentary on the *Great Learning* had extraordinary importance and influence. The further attention that Zhu gave to it in *Questions and Answers on the Great Learning* not only amplified the rather terse language of the *Sentences and Phrases* and expanded its significance but also demonstrated that this idea was no mere afterthought or casual comment of Zhu's. Rather it came as the culmination of a long development in his thinking about the central concepts in Song philosophy.

This philosophical dialogue goes back almost to the start of his intellectual and spiritual quest in colloquy with his teacher Li Tong (1092–1162). It transpired in fulfillment of his father's injunction to Zhu that he should pursue "learning for one's self," something that Zhu said he only seriously began under the tutelage of Li Tong.[7] Zhu Xi's *Responses of Yen-p'ing* (*Yen-ping dawen*) records his conversations and correspondence with Li in the years from 1157 to 1162. In the immediate background of this exchange is Zhu's youthful fascination with Chan Buddhism, and in the direct foreground of the discussions are issues arising from the Buddhist–Confucian encounter. They are issues that significantly affect our understanding of Zhu Xi's holism as well as the alternatives he considered before arriving at his final position. Though we cannot review here the whole sorting-out process he went through, neither can we bypass it completely if we are to grasp the significance of Zhu's holistic conception of self-fulfillment as compared to others proposed at that time.

The key terms in which this holism is discussed came down to Li Tong and Zhu Xi from the Cheng brothers (Cheng Yi taught the teacher of the teacher of Li Tong) and their uncle Zhang Zai (1020–1077). One of these expressions was the aforementioned "unity of principle and diversity of its particularizations" (*liyi fenshu*). Another was Cheng Hao's doctrine of the "humaneness which forms one body with Heaven-and-earth and all things" (*tiandi wanwu yiti zhi ren*),[8] also spoken of by him holistically as "totally forming the same body [substance] with things" (*hunran yuwu tongti*).[9] Zhu drew on these conceptions while also qualifying them in important respects. Together they provide the context for Zhu's enigmatic expression, "a breakthrough to integral comprehension" (*huoran guantong*), which is the culmination of the learning process and the fulfillment of self-cultivation as described in Zhu's commentaries above.

As Li Tong explained to Zhu the significance of the "unity of principle and diversity of its particularizations," he took issue with the idea of principle or substance as separable from practice or function, as well as with those who held that there was no essential difference in principle between Confucianism and Buddhism, since Confucian "humaneness" (*ren*) could be equated with Buddhist "compassion" (*ci*). According to this latter view, the only significant difference between the two teachings lay in the functional aspect—that is, Buddhism's lack of a practical program such as Confucianism offered for dealing with the needs of human society. Li, however, and Zhu following him, contended that the difference in practice also pointed to a difference in principle. One could not expect Confucian practice to follow from Buddhist principle, nor could one accept as true principle what did not lead to Confucian ethical practice. Hence, there could be no dichotomizing, as in Buddhism, of principle and practice to represent two different orders of reality: principle real and undifferentiated, practice less real because it pertained to the world of differentiation and discrimination.[10] To substantiate principle, one must realize one's humanity in the midst of practice, that is, by coming to terms with one's individual lot (*fen*) or station in life and its differentiated duties, thus fulfilling one's own particular nature as well as joining oneself to the creative principle underlying all things. This is what was meant by realizing the unity of principle and the diversity of its particularizations.[11] It was also what distinguished Confucianism as "real or practical learning" from the "empty learning" of Buddhism, which viewed the world of action as a secondary or qualified order of reality in comparison to the essential truth of Buddhist emptiness.[12] In this way the reality of the individual was affirmed along with the unity of principle, so that self-realization involved no loss of individuality through absorption into the whole. In the end, true individuality merged with, rather than being submerged in, holistic unity.

Li Tong was willing to concede neither the Buddhist bifurcation of reality on two levels of truth nor the need for transcendental enlightenment as the precondition for coping with the world. For him, on the contrary, true self-realization and spiritual freedom were to be attained in the performance of the moral task.[13] To describe the characteristic spirit of the sage, Li borrowed an expression from Huang Tingjian's (1045–1105)[14] portrayal of Zhou Dunyi as having achieved a state of mind that was "free, pure, and unobstructed [saluo] like a breeze on a sunny day or the clear moon."[15] This characterization later was included by Zhu Xi in his presentation of the "Dispositions [or Characteristics] of the Sages and Worthies" in Reflections on Things at Hand.[16] Zhu also expressed his admiration for like qualities in Li Tong, who had overcome his own wayward disposition to achieve a lofty state of mind, serenity of soul, and unfathomable profundity. It was a freedom of spirit attained by liberating oneself from all selfishness, obstinacy, and rigidity. In this state one's mind was completely impartial and open to reality. Principle inherent in one's nature could then express itself freely and clearly, with no selfish obstructions.[17]

As Li is quoted in the Responses of Yanping:

> If in encountering things and affairs one can have not one iota of selfish obstinacy or rigidity, then that is to be "free, pure and unobstructed." In other words, this is to be large-minded, open and fair. It is to be completely one with principle and the Way. If in encountering things one is not able to enter into them completely [it means that] in one's mind-and-heart, one has not freed oneself from all trace of partiality, or in other words that one is still obstinate and rigid. None of this will do.[18]

Elsewhere Li likened this state of mind to the "evening spirit" spoken of by Mencius, a spirit nourished by the restorative influence of the night (Mencius 6A:8).[19] He also explained that it was a state of mind in which one naturally followed principle and the latter imposed no restraint. Indeed, if one felt any constraint, said Li, he would know he was not proceeding on the right course.[20]

Achieving this state, in which the mind and principle had become one, was not something to be accomplished in one stroke or by a headlong effort. It required constant attentiveness to one matter or affair after another, in the manner of Cheng Yi's "holding to reverence" (zhijing) or "abiding in reverence" (jujing). The mind should be allowed to dwell on each matter until principle in the mind and principle in things became completely fused.[21] "If you go from one thing to another without really comprehending each in turn, it is of no use."[22] After a long while this cumulative exercise would produce a natural sense of ease and freedom in the mind-and-heart.[23]

Zhu Xi saw this method of Li in the light of the practice of the investigation of things and the fathoming of principle (kewu qiongli). In the Reflections on Things at Hand, he quoted Cheng Yi as saying "When the mind is at ease, it naturally perceives principle."[24] And again, "One must investigate one item today and another tomorrow. When one has accumulated much knowledge, he will naturally achieve a thorough understanding like a sudden release."[25] This is similar to Zhu Xi's own account of the investigation of things culminating in a breakthrough to integral comprehension and a sense of total clarity, as set forth in his commentary on the Great Learning and elaborated in the Questions and Answers on the Great Learning. His final view, as expressed in the latter text, summed up a lifetime of study and reflection on the Neo-Confucian kōan Li Tong had passed on to him and Cheng Yi's teachings had helped him solve.[26]

As a form of praxis in self-cultivation Li Tong strongly recommended quiet-sitting (jingzuo), which he also described as "sitting in silence and clearing the mind" (mozuo chengxin).[27] Influenced though it was by Chan Buddhism's "sitting in meditation" (zuochan), this practice had been adapted to Neo-Confucian purposes and conformed to its own lifestyle.[28] Li believed that quiet-sitting would settle the mind and leave it with the transparency of still water, in which Heaven's principle and one's own moral stance in relation to a given matter would emerge clearly.[29]

> The way of learning does not lie in too many words. It is just sitting silently, clearing the mind, and experiencing Heavenly principle. Then even the slightest sign of selfish desire will not go undetected or unchecked. . . .
> Generally speaking, if one has doubts as to how to proceed, one should sit silently and look within oneself. Then one's moral obligations are sure to be revealed clearly, Heavenly principle is sure to be observed and one can detect the point at which one's effort should be applied in daily affairs.[30]

For Li Tong, this introspective practice was intended as a spiritual discipline to nourish the mind and keep it in a constant state of attentiveness, mindfulness, or readiness for action in daily life. While it focused on the unmanifest state of the mind-and-heart, before the activation and articulation of the feelings, it was not understood as opposed to rational discourse or scholarly learning. Li Tong rejected the notion of "sudden enlightenment" in Chan Buddhism, with its transcendence of discursive knowledge. When Zhu came to Li after his experiments with Chan, Li directed him to study the Confucian classics, which would engage him in rational discourse concerning the moral life. The kind of insight or enlightenment sought by Confucius should not be limited to words, but neither could it dispense with them. "Holding to reverence" through quiet-sitting went hand in hand with book learning, that is, study of the classics.[31] Thus, the deep personal experience of truth, as taught by Li, should be of the wondrousness or mystery that is at the very heart of discursive knowledge itself. In other words, it should help one to understand the wonder of creation in the most ordinary things and to recognize in the numinous aspect of things something of enduring value, rather than the momentary reflection of an emptiness about which nothing can finally be predicated. Here the magic of the word expresses the wondrous functioning (*miaoyong*) of substantial Confucian principle, as contrasted to the "mysterious being" (*miaoyou*), which arises from Emptiness but which, in Chan Buddhism, one should not try to capture in words (*buli wenzi*).

Combining as it did objective observation and personal intuition, this method could produce a kind of enlightenment (*juewu*), but Li Tong preferred to express it as "finding the Way in oneself through personal experience" (*tiren zide*).[32] Though Zhu Xi also spoke of "finding the Way in oneself" and of "personal realization," in the passages cited above from his commentaries, he preferred to express it in terms of achieving the "whole substance and great functioning" of the mind. The reasons for this are better understood if we look at the alternative formulations which Zhu considered before arriving at his final position.

Zhu had some reservations about the method of quiet-sitting precisely because it smacked too much of quietism and because, as a means of "nourishing principle in the mind," it seemed to concentrate on substance (i.e., the mind in its quiescent state) at the possible expense of function a concern he felt even over Cheng's emphasis on the unity of principle.[33] Zhu sought a formulation that would better express Li's own insistence on the need to combine the "unity of principle" with the "diversity of its [functional] particularizations."

Among the theories that Zhu evaluated in this connection was Cheng Hao's "humaneness which forms one body with Heaven-and-earth and all things."[34] Properly understood, this was a doctrine to which Zhu could give his blessing, and with that it remained one of the most influential Neo-Confucian concepts down into modern times.[35] But without some qualification, it could easily be misinterpreted as putting primary stress on the sense of man's unity with the universe at the expense of the differentiated functions through which man's humaneness must in fact be realized. That is, a subjective experience or mystical feeling of oneness with the universe could become the counterfeit of a true holistic self-realization through moral effort and practical action. For Zhu Xi, a genuine holism could only mean the simultaneous realization of the "whole substance and great functioning" (*quanti dayong*) of human nature because the humaneness which forms "one body with Heaven, earth and all things" cannot be simply a subjective experience of undifferentiated unity—it must also express itself in loving actions of a particular sort.

Cheng Yi had also raised this issue in his discussions of humanity with his students, and Zhu quoted him in *Reflections on Things at Hand* in a way that expressed the irreducibly individual, and at the same time holistic, character of its realization:

> It is up to you gentlemen to think for yourselves and personally realize what humanity is. Because Mencius said: "The feeling of commiseration is what we call humanity" [6A:6] later scholars have therefore considered love to be humanity. But love is feeling, whereas humanity is the nature. How can love be taken exclusively as humanity? Mencius said that the feeling of commiseration is the beginning of humanity. Since it is called the beginning of humanity, it should not be called humanity itself.[36]

In his "Treatise on Humanity" (*Ren shuo*) and his "Lecture at the Jade Mountain" (*Yushan jiangyi*), Zhu developed the distinction between humanity as the principle (substance) of love and love as the functioning of humanity. Confusion of the two led, at one extreme, to the identification of human nature or humanity with raw emotion or a diffuse humanitarian sentimentality, and, at the other, to a kind of undifferentiated consciousness that denied the value distinctions so vital to the practice of genuine humaneness. To avoid these pitfalls, Zhu would ground human love in a larger cosmic principle, the life-giving energy and creature-loving mind-and-heart of Heaven-and-earth, while also subordinating it to the higher end of perfecting human nature to attain the Supreme Ultimate. At the same time he would confirm as function the concrete reality of the love expressed in the mind-and-heart of man and given specific, practical application in human society.

In Zhu Xi's words:

> In the teachings [of Confucius], it is said, "conquer self and restore ritual decorum." This means that if we can overcome and eliminate selfishness and return to the Principle of Nature [*tianli*, Principle of Heaven], then the sub-

stance of this mind [that is, *ren*], will be present everywhere and its function will always be operative. It is also said, "Be respectful in private life, be serious in handling affairs, and be loyal in dealing with others." These are also ways to preserve this mind. Again, it is said, "Be filial in serving parents," "Be respectful in serving elder brothers," and "Be loving in dealing with all things." These are ways to put this mind into practice.

Furthermore, to talk about ren in general terms of the self and things as "one body" may lead one to be vague, confused, neglectful, and make no effort to be vigilant. The bad effect—and there has been such—may be to consider other things as oneself. [On the other hand] to talk about love exclusively in terms of consciousness [function] will lead people to be nervous, impatient, and devoid of any quality of depth. The bad effect—and there has been such—may be to take desire in itself as principle. In one case, the mind is forgetful [and careless]. In the other case there is an artificial effort to get results. Both are wrong.[37]

Here Zhu argues against a concept of the self and things as forming one body if it means an identification so vague and a compassion so diffuse that one fails realistically to meet the concrete needs of the self and things in their own particularity, as in the case of the bodhisattva's sacrificing himself to feed the starving tiger, a gesture so extravagant and unrealistic as to be meaningless.[38] This is to put undue emphasis on substance to the neglect of function. On the other hand, if one pursues consciousness—"using the mind to pursue the mind"—without regard to the larger vision that should guide the emotion of love, it can lead to an impatience for getting immediate results that is detrimental to one's true emotional and moral development. This is to put undue emphasis on function (immediate utility) at the expense of the "whole substance" (the perfecting of one's humaneness).

In his commentary on the "extension of knowledge" in the *Great Learning*, Zhu had described cognitive learning as the initial stage in a process of self-cultivation that should lead to the realization of the "whole substance and great functioning" of man's nature. By "whole substance" he meant "humanity," seen in the larger dimensions of man's oneness with Heaven, earth, and all things and also as the directive principle which gave ultimate meaning and significance to human life. By "great functioning" he meant the exercise of the full range of human faculties intellectual, moral, emotional and spiritual which could participate in the creative work of Heaven-and-earth, especially in meeting the needs of human society.

When in the *Questions and Answers on the Great Learning* Zhu speaks of the mind as "empty and spiritual yet replete with principle," he alludes to the nonfinite and limitless (*wuji*) aspect of the unity of the Supreme Ultimate, which is also the "utmost good" to be realized in man on the basis of the "unity of principle and diversity of its particularizations." "The utmost good," in the language of the *Great Learning*, represents the Supreme Ultimate in each individual as defined by his own share in Heaven's endowment, his station and duties in life, and the circumstances which condition his actions. It is what is most appropriate for him in the context of these givens.[39] As for the "Supreme Ultimate," which in the language of the *Changes* and Zhou Dunyi, is the rough equivalent of the "utmost good," Professor Wing-tsit Chan has summed up Zhu Xi's view as follows:

> According to him, the Supreme Ultimate is at once the one principle and the sum total of all principles. At the same time, since everything has principle, everything has the Supreme Ultimate in it. Consequently, the Supreme Ultimate involves all things as a whole and at the same time every individual thing involves the Supreme Ultimate. In other words, the universe is a macrocosm while everything is a microcosm. In a sense the pattern was hinted [at] by Zhou Dunyi in his *Tongshu* [*Comprehending the Changes*] where he said, "The many are [ultimately] one and the one is actually differentiated in the many. The one and the many each has its own correct state of being. The great and the small each has its definite function."[40]

When Zhu describes the culmination of the learning process as a "breakthrough to integral understanding," he expresses the idea of an enlightenment that comprehends both the unity and diversity, the infinity and ultimacy, of principle in the mind and things. This implies an understanding of the total functioning of the substance of the mind in all its dimensions and faculties—an "enlightenment" that includes the cognitive and affective aspects of the mind-and-heart, yet goes beyond them in the same sense that Zhu intended when he spoke of humanity as the guiding principle of love.

This, then, was the ideal of spiritual and moral self-cultivation for Zhu Xi, which would define the kind of individual fulfillment he envisaged for humankind. It is also "finding the Way in oneself" in the deeper sense of *zide* spoken of in Zhu's summing up of the significance of the *Doctrine of the Mean*, which, he says, "speaks of the meritorious achievements and transforming influence of the sages and spiritual men in the highest degree. It was Zisi's desire that the learner should search within himself and find it [the Way] within himself."[41] For Zhu, too, it represented the final fruit, even if it could not be a "definitive" result, of his lifelong search to achieve "learning for one's self."

The doctrine of the "whole substance and great functioning" of human nature, in the terms it is expressed here, remains true to Zhu's conception of the Supreme Ultimate as a nature that is both formed and yet-to-be

formed, possessing in humanity an essential goodness that is still to be perfected. Among the various tendencies in Song Neo-Confucian thought, it
was the Cheng-Zhu school that particularly insisted on the goodness of
human nature. This was a goodness that implied human freedom to choose
the path of self-improvement and self-perfection, to transform one's actual
nature so as to achieve, or as least approximate, sagehood. Understood as
yet-unformed and, indeed, limitless (*wuji*), that nature contained within it
the possibility of achieving self-transcendence as well as self-fulfillment.
Accepting the limits imposed by what was given (one's lot, station, condition, and disposition as "decreed" by Heaven), and while still living within
the form of things, one could by the exercise of that freedom pass beyond
the limits of the given. In this sense Zhu was affirming both the inherent
dignity of the person and his inalienable freedom to opt for a self-fulfillment yet to be discovered within himself.

If this sounds rather too free-wheeling for "orthodoxy," it must immediately be said that Zhu tried to hedge it around with safeguards, conscious of the dangers that attended such a sense of freedom—the danger of
self-delusion, which may arise from failure fully to exercise one's cognitive
faculties in relation to knowable facts and principles; the danger of being
carried away by vague mystical feelings not substantiated in actual conduct
or experience; and the danger, on the other hand, of pursuing immediate
utility without due regard for the nature of oneself and things, and so on.
The balance Zhu sought to achieve through self-cultivation was a precarious one, as he himself implied in his discussion of the mind of man as
unstable and the mind of the Way as barely perceptible. Holism could easily become its own worst enemy if its component parts were not kept in
line with the Way. So embracing was Zhu's synthesis that later scholars—
including Wang Yangming himself—could find some warrant there for
views much in contrast to other emphases in Zhu's thought.

Zhu Xi's system has long been recognized as the great synthesis of the
philosophical speculation and dialogue carried on in the Song. Here we can
see that it also serves as the practical synthesis of the methods for attaining
sagehood or enlightenment discussed in that time. In the words "integral
comprehension" (*guantong*), Zhu Xi's description of individual fufillment
expresses one of the highest ideals of Song thought and scholarship.

Whether succeeding ages could sustain this magisterial synthesis of learning and spirituality would be a real question, but that it challenged them to
achieve such an ideal of individual fulfillment was attested to by the successive generations of scholars and thinkers who set themselves to this task in
Yuan, Ming, and Qing China, Yi-dynasty Korea, and Tokugawa Japan.

Notes

1. Reprinted in Carsun Chang, *The Development of Neo-Confucian Thought*, 2 vols. (New York: Bookman Associates, 1957, 1962), 2:455–83.

2. *Lun-yü jizhu* I, Zizhang wen shi shi.

3. *Daxue zhangju*, 6a–b (17–18).

4. *Daxue huowen*, 20b–21a (39–41).

5. Zhu Xi, "Weizheng" [Governing], in *Lunyu jizhu* [Collected Commentaries on the *Analects*], in *Sishu jizhu* 2.9a; *Daxue huowen*, 4b–7a (8–13); *Zhuzi yulei* 1.1a–b, 23.16b, 117.9a (1, 892, 4491).

6. *Zhu Zi yulei* 94.8a–b (3769–70).

7. *Zhu Zi wenji* 38.34a–b (first letter in response to Jiang Yuanshi). For the sequence of Zhu's learning experiences, see Wing-tsit Chan, "Patterns for Neo-Confucianism: Why Chu Hsi Differed from Ch'eng I," *Journal of Chinese Philosophy* 5, no. 2 (June 1978): 101–26; and Tomoeda Ryūtarō, *Shushi no shisō keisei* (Tokyo: Shunjusha, 1979).

8. Cheng Yi, *Yishu* 2A.2a.

9. Ibid., 2A.3a; Tomoeda Ryūtarō, *Shushi no shisō keisei*, 110.

10. Okada Takehiko, "Shushi no chichi to shi," *Seinan gakuin daigaku bunri ronshū* (March 1974): 14, pt. 2, 70.

11. Zhu Xi, *Yenping dawen* (Kinsei kanseki sōkan, shisōhen ed.), 70, 89–92, 99–103. Iki Hiroyuki, *"Empei tomon wo yomu"* [On Reading *Responses of Yen-p'ing*], in *Tōyōno risō to eichi* [The Ideals and Wisdom of the East], ed. Okada Takehiko (Fukuoka: Tōyō Shisō Kenkyūkai, 1963), 51–64.

12. Although Buddhist enlightenment transcended this dichotomy, it also subsumed it, and to the extent that it accepted the mysterious view, yielded no determinate principle on which to ground the moral and social order.

13. Zhu Xi, *Yenping dawen*, 111.

14. Huang Tingjian, *Songshi* [Song History], 444.1; *Song-Yuan xue-an* 19.28.

15. Zhu Xi, *Yenping dawen*, 65, quoting Huang Tingjian's preface to the poetry (*shi*) of Chou Tunyi found in *Yuzhang Huang xiansheng senji* [Collected Writings of Mr. Huang of Yü-zhang] (SPTK ed.), 1.14b.

16. Mao Xinglai, *Jinsilu jizhu* 14.6a; Chan, *Things at Hand*, 298.

17. *Yenping dawen*, 83–84.

18. Ibid., 67–68.

19. Ibid., 60, 63–64.

20. Ibid., 62.

21. Ibid., 61–62.

22. *Yenping dawen fulu* [Supplement to the *Responses of Yen-ping*] (Kinsei kanseki sōkan, shisōhen ed.), 135.

23. Ibid.

24. Mao Xinglai, *Jinsilu jizhu* 3.11a, no. 25; Chan, *Things at Hand*, 7.

25. Cheng Yi, *Yishu* 18.5b; Mao Xinglai, *Jinsilu jizhu* 3.5b, no. 9; Chan, *Things at Hand*, 92.

26. *Yenping dawen*, 72, 109; Mou Zongsan, *Xinti yu xingti* [Substance of Mind

and Substance of Its Nature], 3 vols. (Taipei: Cheng-chung Book Company, 1969), vol. 3, chs. 2–4; Tomoeda Ryūtarō, Introduction to *Yenping dawen* (Kinsei kanseki sōkan, shisōhen ed.), 1–11; Okada Takehiko, "Shushi no chichi to shi," 85, 93.

27. Zhu Xi, *Yenping dawen*, 93, 111, 114; Okada Takehiko, "Shushi no chichi to shi," 86.

28. Cf. my "Neo-Confucian Cultivation and Enlightenment," in *The Unfolding of Neo-Confucianism*, ed. Wm. Theodore de Bary (New York: Columbia University Press, 1975), 170–72.

29. Zhu Xi, *Yenping dawen*, 42, 63, 114; Okada Takehiko, "Shushi no chichi to shi," 86.

30. Zhu Xi, *Yenping dawen*, 114.

31. Tomoeda Ryūtarō, Introduction to *Yenping dawen*, 9–10.

32. Zhu Xi, *Yenping dawen*, 92, 102, 107, 109; Tomoeda Ryūtarō, *Shushi no shisō keisei*, 248; Okada Takehiko, "Shushi no chichi to shi," 81–82.

33. Tomoeda, *Shushi no shisō keisei*, 60; Chan, "Patterns for Neo-Confucianism," 112–13.

34. Cheng Yi, *Yishu*, 24.2a.

35. The classic study of the evolution of this doctrine and its relation to modern reformism and radicalism is Shimada Kenji, "Subjective Idealism in Sung and Post-Sung China: The All Things Are One Theory of *Jen*," Tōhōgaku-hō 28 (March 1958): 1–80.

36. Cheng Yi, *Yishu* 18.1a; Mao Xinglai, *Jinsilu jizhu* 1.31b–32a (translated in Chan, *Things at Hand*, 27).

37. "Ren shuo," in *Zhu Zi wenji* 67.21b; translation adapted from Chan, *Source Book*, 596.

38. *Zhu Zi yulei* 126.20b (4858).

39. *Daxue zhangzhu*, 4a–5a (13–15); *Daxue huowen*, 4a, 5b, 7b, 8b, 11a, 13a–14a, 18b, 31b (7, 10, 14, 16, 21, 25–27, 36, 62).

40. Chan, "Patterns for Neo-Confucianism," 110.

41. Zhu Xi, *Zhongyong zhangzhu* [Commentary on the *Mean*], in *Sishu jizhu*, 49.

Bibliography

Chan, Wing-tsit. *Neo-Confucian Terms Explained: The Bei-xi Ziyi by Chen Chun, 1159–1223*. New York: Columbia University Press, 1986.

———. *A Source Book in Chinese Philosophy*. Princeton, N.J.: Princeton University Press, 1969.

de Bary, William Theodore. *Learning for One's Self: Essays on the Individual in Neo-Confucian Thought*. New York: Columbia University Press, 1991.

———. *The Message of the Mind in Neo-Confucianism*. New York: Columbia University Press, 1989.

———. *Sources of Chinese Tradition*. Revised edition, chapters 19–24. New York: Columbia University Press, 1998.

de Bary, William Theodore, ed. *Self and Society in Ming Thought*. New York: Columbia University Press, 1970.

———. *The Unfolding of Neo-Confucianism*. New York: Columbia University Press, 1975.

Wang Yangming. *Instructions for Practical Living and Other Neo-Confucian Writings*. Translated by Wing-tsit Chan. New York: Columbia University Press, 1963.

Zhu Xi. *Reflections on Things at Hand*. Translated by Wing-tsit Chan. New York: Columbia University Press, 1967.

20

Attentiveness and Meditative Reading in Cheng-Zhu Neo-Confucianism

Daniel K. Gardner

One day a man of the people said to Zen Master Ikkyu: "Master, will you please write for me some maxims of the highest wisdom?"

Ikkyu immediately took his brush and wrote the word "Attention."

"Is that all?" asked the man. "Will you not add something more?"

Ikkyu then wrote twice running: "Attention. Attention."

"Well," remarked the man rather irritably, "I really don't see much depth or subtlety in what you have just written."

Then Ikkyu wrote the same word three times running: "Attention. Attention. Attention."

Half-angered the man demanded: "What does that word 'Attention' mean anyway?"

And Ikkyu answered gently: "Attention means attention."[1]

"ATTENTION" AS A RELIGIOUS PHENOMENON has attracted considerable scholarly interest in recent years, especially in the Hindu and Buddhist traditions of the East, and increasingly in the Judaic, Christian, and Islamic traditions of the West.[2] But very little has been written on its role in China's Neo-Confucian tradition, despite its central importance there. Indeed, neither Cheng Yi (1033–1107) nor Zhu Xi (1130–1200), leading architects of the Neo-Confucian school, would feel especially uncomfortable or out of place standing in for Master Ikkyu (1394–1481) in the above story. Their writings reveal a profound concern with the concept of *jing*, "inner mental attentiveness," and a deep conviction that by means of such attentiveness followers of the Neo-Confucian school could hope to achieve illumination of their true selves and the world as it is.

Inner Mental Attentiveness

For entering into the Way nothing is better than inner mental attentiveness. (Cheng Yi, *Yishu* 71:7)[3]

Practicing inner mental attentiveness is of the greatest importance to the Confucian school. From beginning to end there mustn't be even a moment's interruption. (Zhu Xi, *YL* 210:6)[4]

Religious traditions that call for the training or retraining of attentiveness, no matter how different their attentional techniques, share one fundamental assumption: the human mind, in its normal condition, is *not* attentive. Be it Zen, Hinduism, Sufism, Hasidism, or Neo-Confucianism, the mind in its ordinary state is thought to be distracted and fragmented; divided within itself and from the phenomenal world; unfree, enslaved by habitual modes of perception; ruled by false opinions; and unconscious of the true nature of things. The various attentional techniques—*zazen* meditational practices, the concentrative prayer of the Hasids (*kavvanah*) and of the Sufis (*dhikr*), and one-pointed attention or concentration (*citta-ekâgratâ*) of the Hindus, all aim to give the mind freedom from the distractions and the "noise" of daily life; taking leave of its normal state, the mind can shed itself of its routine modes of perception and see the world in a new and clearer way.

Very early on, in the first millennium B.C.E., the Confucian tradition expressed, in somewhat cryptic terms to be sure, anxiety over the mind and its ability to remain undispersed and concentrated. The *Book of History* says: "The human mind is precarious, the Dao mind is subtle. Be discriminating, be undivided, that you may sincerely hold fast the mean."[5] Whatever the precise meaning intended here in the *Book of History,* the passage comes to serve as a constant source of philosophic inspiration and reflection for Cheng Yi and, even more so, Zhu Xi. The distinction between the human mind (*renxin*) and the Dao mind (*daoxin*) is one they return to over and over again in their writings and conversations. Indeed, for them, the entire Neo-Confucian program of self-cultivation centers on the struggle between these two minds. It is, I think, worth citing a portion of Zhu Xi's explication of the brief passage from the *Book of History,* not only because his view of the mind represented there warrants our attention, but because the reader will also get from it a good sense of the Neo-Confucian mode of reflection on the canonical tradition:

The mind—unprejudiced, spiritual, and conscious—is one. But that there is a distinction between the "human mind" and the "Dao mind" is due to this: the mind at times arises in the self-centeredness of the psychophysical being (*xingqi*) and at times originates in the perfect impartiality of the moral nature decreed by heaven, so the resulting consciousnesses are different. Hence the mind can be precarious and unsettled, or abstruse and almost imperceptible. Yet all men have a psychophysical being, so even the very wisest will always have a human mind; and all men have a moral nature, so even the very stupidest will always have a Dao mind. If the human mind and the Dao mind become mixed in the heart and one does not know how to control them, the precarious will become even more precarious, the imperceptible will become even more imperceptible, and the impartiality of the heavenly principle in the end will be unable to overcome the selfishness of human desires.

A few brief remarks are in order here. First, and most generally, Zhu's reading of this passage on the mind found in the venerated *Book of History* is fully understandable in terms of his Song metaphysics of *qi* ("psychophysical stuff"), *li* ("principle") and *xing* ("human nature"). By this I mean that the metaphysical outlook Zhu brings to the canonical text informs his reading of the passage, even as the metaphysical outlook itself is informed and shaped by such serious reflection on the canonical sources. Second, in Zhu's reading of the passage, the human mind and the Dao mind are not two separate entities but rather two aspects of the one mind. Third, the so-called human mind is the aspect of mind associated with our psychophysical (*qi*) being and thus is precarious, that is, susceptible to selfish desire, prejudice, and imbalance; this is the mind we must carefully control and restrain, lest such selfish desire, prejudice, and imbalance arise there and lead us away from the Dao mind (which is what makes it "precarious"). Fourth, the so-called Dao mind is the aspect of mind associated with the moral nature (*xing*) endowed by heaven in each and every one of us at birth; this mind embodies moral principle (*li*) in all its manifestations and so is always in accord with what should be. Fifth, as all human beings, according to Zhu's Neo-Confucian vision, have both a psychophysical being and a moral nature, all human beings naturally are possessed of both a human mind and a Dao mind. The challenge for each of us, as Zhu remarks further on in his explication of the passage, is "to make certain that the Dao mind always acts as master of the body and the human mind always obeys its orders," in which case, "the precarious will become settled and the almost imperceptible manifest."[6] Thus, commenting on this early passage in the Confucian tradition, Zhu places an enormous burden on the mind. For each and every individual, the mind is *the* locus of the human battle to conform to heavenly principle: "As for the mind of man, if heavenly principle is preserved, human desire will disappear. But should human desire prevail, heavenly principle will be blotted out" (*YL* 224:4). The mind must not waver, be distracted, nor be overcome by selfish desire or prejudice.

Since antiquity, sages and worthies have all considered the mind to be the root. (Zhu Xi, *YL* 199:4)

The mind then matters dearly to Cheng Yi and Zhu Xi, for it is the mind that enables one to actualize heavenly principle and thereby achieve a clear and comprehensive understanding of the world; but it is the same mind that can become burdened by excessive desire and prejudice and thereby lose its original equilibrium and balance, the consequence of which is that principle becomes obscured and remains unrealized. The mind thus must be cultivated, to protect it against falling prey to selfish desire and prejudice or to rescue it in cases where it has already succumbed. Zhu Xi, and Cheng Yi earlier, speaks frequently of "preserving the mind" and "seeking the lost mind." As Zhu puts it: "It's simply because man has let go of his mind that he falls into evil" (*YL* 203:2); or elsewhere, "If a person is able to preserve his mind so that it is exceptionally clear, he'll naturally be capable of merging with the Way" (*YL* 205:8). Thus, the mind is "the root," just as the sages and worthies of antiquity had asserted. It is, in Zhu's words, the "master" of the person. If the mind be not preserved, "your entire person will be without a master," he informs his disciples (*YL* 199:7).[7] This mind therefore has to be tended to, has to be kept refined. As Zhu opines, "Man simply has a mind. But if he doesn't control it, what sort of man will he be?" (*YL* 199:10).

The will, *zhi*—which Zhu describes as the intention or inclination of the mind or, literally, "where the mind is headed" (see passages in *YL* 96)—can help guide the mind in the right direction. One thus has to strive to keep one's will firmly fixed; for if it is strong and determined, it will lead the mind along the right path toward the good nature and away from insidious human desires.[8] That is, intemperate desires and emotions will not have the opportunity to develop, if man so wills. *Lizhi*, "to establish or fix the will," is one of Zhu's most common refrains in discussions with disciples (e.g., comments in *YL* 133–34). The mind thus functions as the indeterminate element in Zhu Xi's Neo-Confucian program of self-cultivation, the element that makes realization of heavenly principle a possibility, but not by any means an inevitability.[9]

In consequence of its indeterminacy, we find Zhu, throughout his conversations with disciples, urging them variously to "control" the mind, "hold on to it," "gather it in," "possess it," "keep it constantly alert," and so forth (especially ch. 12 of *YL*, pp. 199–221). In different ways he is telling them the same thing: prepare the mind for its confrontation with things and affairs in the world.[10]

Someone asked, "What effort is required in inner mental attentiveness?"

Cheng Yi responded, "Nothing is better than making unity the ruler."

Su Jiming said, "I've been troubled by unsettled thoughts. At times, before I think through one matter, other matters occur to me, entangled like hemp fibers. What's to be done?"

Cheng said, "This must be avoided; it is the source of disintegration. You must practice. When by practicing you become capable of concentrating, things will be all right. Whether in thought or in action you must always seek unity." (Cheng Yi, *Yishu* 223:9)[11]

Inner mental attentiveness is simply the mind being its own master. (Zhu Xi, *YL* 210:13)

Inner mental attentiveness is the mind in a fully concentrated state. It is the mind without any distractions whatsoever. It is the mind unified, preserved in its whole. To be *jing*, to be mentally attentive, is to be fully present, fully in the moment, fully responsive to the matter before one. For Cheng Yi and Zhu Xi, one is to be mentally attentive at all times; it is not an exercise reserved for a special time or special place. In greeting a parent one is to be attentive; so too in reading a book, in entering a temple, in practicing quiet-sitting, in doing calligraphy, in enjoying the scenery, even in doing one's toilet. As Zhu says, "there mustn't be even a moment's interruption." In this respect, *jing* may be likened somewhat to mobile *zazen* in which one "enters fully into every action with total attention and clear awareness."[12]

To practice inner mental attentiveness is to sharpen the mind's alertness, to awaken it totally to the matter at hand, so that one better sees that matter as it really is (and, of course, responds to it entirely as one should). The mind ordinarily is bombarded by multiple stimuli that leave the individual confused and incapable of seeing any one thing or matter for what it is. Inner mental attentiveness is meant to banish such stimuli—both internal and external—by focusing the mind's energy entirely on the one matter, object, or affair. As Zhu casually says to a student, "It's simply to collect your own mental energy and concentrate it on a certain spot" (*YL* 215:16). The chances of the mind becoming fragmented and divided are thereby considerably lessened.

In the view of Cheng Yi and Zhu Xi, most of us simply do not see things as they are. Bringing to our perception of the world a mind distracted by numerous stimuli, cluttered with selfish desire and prejudice, we stand little chance of apprehending the true nature (*li* or principle) of the things we come into contact with, or even our own true nature. In Zhu's words, "Man's mind is originally bright. It's just that it gets covered over by things

and can't get out from under them; hence, illuminating principle is difficult. Let's strip away the things covering over the mind and wait for it to
come out and be itself" (*YL* 205:9). *Jing*, inner mental attentiveness, is the
stripping away;[13] it is the emptying of the mind (*xuxin*)—to use a phrase
Zhu Xi himself uses frequently—of the distractions and habituated thought
that obscure true understanding.

Emptying the mind, then, is to put the noise and distractions of the
world aside, leaving the mind "open" (*xu*) to experience things and affairs
directly without prejudice or preconceptions.[14] It is to encounter the phenomenal world with a mind different from the one we normally bring to
it.[15] To practice *jing* or inner mental attentiveness is thus, in a sense, to
dehabituate, to clear the mind of its ordinary state of consciousness, its
ordinary contents—"the attempt to quiet the automized activities of the
mind through concentrated attention"[16]—so that we may see reality anew,
with a mind now fully concentrated and "one" (*YL* 210:12).

No longer subject to mental turbulence, the mind, in the state of attentiveness, achieves a calm and tranquility.[17] Tranquil, it recovers its original
balance, and thus again is in full possession of itself, its own "master." This
is the mind that readily keeps evil at bay;[18] this is the mind that apprehends
heavenly principle and its myriad manifestations in the world;[19] this is the
mind that appreciates one's own true self.[20] In short, it is the mind, the
fully attentive, concentrative mind, that by transcending our normal condition, allows the self-manifesting quality of truth, residing in ourselves
and in the world out there, to disclose itself.[21]

Although inner mental attentiveness refers to a state or quality of mind,
Cheng and Zhu both believe that certain physical attitudes help to promote its practice. Cheng Yi on different occasions advises disciples to "be
orderly and solemn," "control your countenance," and "regulate your dress
and dignify your gaze" (*Yishu* 165:4, 165:8, 205:14). As he says, "to be digni-
fied and grave is not the way of inner mental attentiveness; but to practice
inner mental attentiveness you must begin here" (*Yishu* 188:3). Zhu, echo-
ing Cheng Yi as well as the canonical *Book of Ritual*, offers a physical pre-
scription for synchronizing the mind and body in attentiveness:

> "Sit as though you were impersonating an ancestor, stand as though you were
> performing a sacrifice."[22] The head should be upright, the eyes looking
> straight ahead, the feet steady, the hands respectful, the mouth quiet and
> composed, the bearing solemn[23]—these are all aspects of inner mental atten-
> tiveness. (*YL* 212:4)

For the Cheng-Zhu school, then, such external demeanor does not merely
reflect one's internal state of mind, but does much to assist the mind in

more fully developing its concentrative powers and thus seeing the world as it is.

This concern here with physical demeanor speaks, even if only indirectly, to a number of interesting and related points. First is the general cultural assumption that mind and body cannot be separated; the attentive mind naturally yields an attentive body, and the attentive body naturally yields an attentive mind. The mind and body function organismically. Second, and related to the first, is the belief, explicitly held at least since the time of Confucius, in the power of ritualized behavior on the part of the body to effect fundamental transformations in one's mind-and-heart (*xin*). Perform the *li*, or rituals, of a gentleman and with time one indeed becomes in mind-and-heart a gentleman. In the same manner, if the physical body can be trained or habituated, through the sort of ritualized regimen outlined by Cheng and Zhu, to be fully attentive, one's mind too—organismically—becomes fully attentive. In fact, the central role that *li* and ritualized behavior play generally in the Chinese philosophical tradition can be related, in large part, to the assumption that body and mind are inseparable. Third, and again related to the first and second, is the respect for the physical body in the Chinese tradition. There is no clear spirit/matter dichotomy in which the physical is denigrated. The body as flesh is not evil, something to be overcome. Rather, Cheng and Zhu here urge their followers to entrust themselves to their physical bodies. They suggest that by taking the proper posture a person may achieve bodily stability (much as the lotus position is thought to do for the practitioner of Zen), and that the body, when stable and unwavering, can sense the distractions and stimuli that threaten the mind and, through an attentive demeanor, help keep them at bay. The body, from this perspective then, is capable of sustaining the mind and giving it guidance.[24]

What is meant by "the extension of knowledge lies in fully apprehending the principle in things" is, that if we wish to extend our knowledge to the utmost we must probe thoroughly the principle in those things we encounter. It would seem that every man's intellect is possessed of the capacity for knowing and that everything in the world is possessed of principle. But, to the extent that principle is not yet thoroughly probed, man's knowledge is not yet fully realized. Hence, the first step of the instruction in greater learning is to teach the student, whenever he encounters anything at all in the world, to build upon what is already known to him of principle and to probe still further, so that he seeks to reach the limit. After exerting himself in this way for a long time, he will one day become enlightened and thoroughly understand [principle]; then, the manifest and the hidden, and the mind, in its whole substance and vast operations, will be completely illuminated. This is called "fully apprehending the principle in things." This is called "the completion of knowledge." (Zhu Xi)[25]

An illuminated understanding of the world is theoretically open to all, in the Cheng-Zhu school. Any person might choose to engage in *gewu*, the process of apprehending the principle in things. This is a process that charges the individual with seeing beyond the superficial or material nature of the things he encounters, with uncovering the abiding nature of those things. There is, for Cheng Yi and Zhu Xi, an underlying reality to things and affairs, but most of us simply do not make the effort to apprehend it. Rather we perceive things in their psychophysical (*qi*) form, rarely probing into their inner nature, their inner being. By probing beyond the "appearance" of things, we can hope to understand things as they truly are. And over time, as one thing after another becomes clear, reality in its whole becomes accessible—and our minds become totally illuminated.

This program of self-cultivation, which assumes a privileged position in the Neo-Confucian tradition until the early years of the twentieth century, places a heavy responsibility on the mind. But there is a fundamental, ontological premise that makes successful apprehension of the truth by the mind possible, in the view of Cheng Yi and Zhu Xi: the underlying principle in all things, all affairs, all matters in the world out there, resides in human beings as well, in their minds. Zhu remarks, "Principle in things and in our mind are essentially one. Neither is deficient in the slightest. What's necessary is that we respond to things, that's all. Things and mind share the same principle" (*YL* 220:4). Thus, in probing beyond the superficial nature of the thing or affair that it encounters, the mind, through a sort of resonance, is able to sense its principle, its underlying truth or reality. That is, a natural response occurs between principle in one's mind and in the things before the mind. With effort and over time this process cannot but lead to a clearer and clearer understanding of principle.

Quite obviously, the uncluttered, attentive mind, the mind that is concentrated entirely on uncovering the true nature of what is before it, is more likely to see beyond superficial or material appearances. *Gewu* is the process by which one may become illuminated and the world clear; *jing* or inner mental attentiveness is the mental attitude, the state or quality of mind that one ideally is to bring to the process. For Zhu Xi, the relationship between *gewu* and *jing* is a rather complex one, dialectical in nature. He comments: "Adhering to inner mental attentiveness is the basis of probing principle. Probing principle until it is clear is an aid to nurturing the mind" (*YL* 150:16). It is thus not simply that the practicing of attentiveness makes probing principle more efficacious, which of course it does; for as Zhu Xi tells his students, "If one is able to probe principle, one's efforts at practicing inner mental attentiveness will improve daily" (*YL* 150:9). In short, the *gewu* program of self-cultivation is enhanced considerably by an attentive mind; but this mind, being further refined and cultivated by the *gewu* process, is capable, in turn, of practicing inner mental attentiveness with even greater efficacy—thereby enhancing the process of *gewu* still further. (Or, to put it another way, once principle in the mind is made less distracted, less obscured, its resonance with principle out there is sure to be stronger; strong resonance of principle brings with it greater clarity of mind, thus strengthening the resonance further and making the "apprehension of the principle in things" even more successful.) Indeed, Zhu on occasion concludes that practicing inner mental attentiveness and probing principle are "in actual fact simply one matter" (*YL* 150:9).

Meditative Reading

In each thing there is a manifestation of principle; it is necessary to probe principle to the utmost. There are many ways of probing principle—the study of books, and the explanation of the moral principles in them; the discussion of prominent figures, past and present, and distinguishing what is right and wrong in their actions; handling practical affairs and managing them appropriately. All are ways of probing principle. (Cheng Yi, *Yishu* 209:7)[26]

Cheng Yi is confident that *li*, principle or truth, inheres in all things, including the human mind; that, with effort, principle or truth is totally knowable; and that by appreciating fully the principle or truth of things, a person at the same time becomes true to his own inherently good, moral nature. It is for this reason that he urges students to look to heaven and earth, to seek principle in the myriad things and affairs out there as a way of fulfilling themselves.[27] For Cheng Yi and his followers, the field of study, the subject matter of their investigation, is the entire universe and all things in it.

As a self-proclaimed "disciple" of Cheng Yi, Zhu Xi enthusiastically embraces the proposal to investigate principle in the universe. Indeed, throughout his life he works hard to fashion *gewu* into as systematic and coherent a process as possible, making it the very foundation of his philosophical program. But where I think Zhu Xi differs from Cheng Yi, and where I think one of his great original contributions to the Neo-Confucian tradition lies, is in narrowing the field of the study of principle. For Zhu, as for Cheng, principle is to be found everywhere and thus is to be pursued everywhere. But Zhu wants to give more guidance to the inquiry, wishing to make principle as readily accessible to students as possible. Thus, he roots the study of principle firmly in the study of books, and in particular, the Confucian classics. In short, what he does is to take Cheng Yi's more abstract, discursive discussion of principle and nature and ground it thoroughly in the canonical tradition. I naturally do not wish to suggest here that Cheng Yi is not interested in the classics—he is, and he urges his students to turn to them in the study of principle.[28] But, in the end, Cheng Yi views the canon as just a small part of the students' wider field of investigation. Zhu, by contrast, makes the canon *the* field of study, *the* place to turn to apprehend principle;[29] and, in turn, for him the meaning of practicing inner mental attentiveness is more pointed than for Cheng Yi, as its practical field of application is circumscribed quite considerably. He is completely confident that, even though principle inheres in all things, it is most readily revealed in the works of the sages, men who themselves had fully realized principle in their daily lives. This, of course, helps to explain why Zhu Xi—and not Cheng Yi—gives so much consideration to the development of a special Neo-Confucian curriculum and hermeneutics.[30] It also helps to explain why, for Zhu, reading becomes a deeply affective, spiritual exercise, similar in many respects to the roughly contemporaneous *lectio divina*, divine or sacred reading, of the Latin West.[31] Reading in Zhu Xi's program of learning can be characterized as spiritual for three principal reasons: by virtue of what is to be read; by virtue of the way it is to be read, the attitude and quality of mind that are to be brought to the act of reading; and by virtue of the purpose and goal of reading.[32]

> If people today simply did ten days of reading, lowering their heads and ignoring all unrelated matters, I guarantee that they'd become transformed people. Even if they were to read for only a day—no need to speak of ten— they'd see results. (Zhu Xi, *YL* 197:10)

Zhu Xi has a profound faith in the transformative power of reading, in the ability of the text to enable the individual to strip away distractions, desires, and biases and to awaken to the true self. But, in his view, his contemporaries do not appreciate the affective influence reading can have, concerned more, as they are, with the worldly success—in the civil service examinations and in office—knowledge of texts can provide. People of the time read with quantity as their goal, not quality of understanding; they race through texts, eager to turn to the next one; they read their own ideas into the texts, rather than letting the texts speak for themselves; and, in general, the powers of concentration they expend on the texts are severely deficient. Zhu is deeply dismayed by and highly critical of the current practices and asks his followers to engage in an entirely different sort of reading.[33] True reading, he argues throughout his writings and conversations with disciples, is to be a disciplined and reverential encounter with the words of the great sages and worthies of the past.

For Zhu, the texts in the Confucian canon have a special efficacy: "All things in the world have principle, but its essence is embodied in the work of the sages and worthies. Hence, in seeking principle we must turn to these works" (*Wenji* 59.5a).[34] It is not, of course, that other works in the Chinese tradition do not embody principle as well, for, after all, principle inheres in all things. But the sages and worthies, men who themselves had been awakened to their true natures, manifesting principle fully in their daily lives, transmitted this principle in their writings extraordinarily clearly, without obscuration.[35] It is here, in the canonical tradition, then, that principle is most accessible, that one can hope to arrive at a penetrating understanding of the true nature of things. Read the Four Books first—the *Greater Learning*, the *Doctrine of the Mean* (both chapters from the *Book of Ritual*), the *Analects*, and the *Mencius*—then the so-called Five Classics—the *Book of Changes*, the *Book of Poetry*, the *Book of History*, the *Book of Ritual*, and the *Spring and Autumn Annals*—Zhu repeatedly exhorts his followers. For Zhu Xi the texts in the canon are sacred and deserving of the deepest commitment:

> The sages wrote the Classics to teach later generations. These texts enable the reader to reflect on the ideas of the sages while reciting their words and hence to understand what is in accordance with the principle of things. Understanding the whole substance of the proper Way, he will practice the Way with all his strength, and so enter the realm of the sages and worthies. Although the texts are concise, they treat all matters under heaven, the hidden and the manifest, the great and the small. If he who wishes to seek the Way and thereby enter into virtue abandons the Classics, he will have nothing to which to apply himself. (*Wenji* 83.26a)

The student of Zhu's Neo-Confucianism is to devote his life to the canonical works—the words of the tradition's most revered sages; only after apprehending them fully may he fruitfully proceed to other valued texts in the cultural tradition, such as *Records of the Grand Historian* and the *Zuo Commentary* (*YL* ch. 11, *passim*):

When students today read a text, it's just as if they had never read it. When they haven't read it, it's just as if they had. (Zhu Xi, *YL* 171:14)

If these sacred texts, the Four Books and Five Classics, are to have meaning, if they are to reveal truth to the reader, the reader must approach them with the proper mental disposition. In reading, Zhu asserts, students nowadays let their minds wander, as they are preoccupied with making their way through the texts as quickly as possible, or with the gain they might realize in mastering the texts for the examinations. A wandering mind, however, does not produce genuine understanding. The mind must give itself entirely to the text in front of it, concentrating on its every word, its every sentence, its every paragraph: "In reading, you want both body and mind to enter into the passage. Don't concern yourself with what's going on elsewhere and you'll see the principle in the passage" (*YL* 177:15). The mind that is deeply attentive, freed of all other concerns and distractions, is more likely to apprehend the message of the sages, a message, by Zhu's own admission, made extremely difficult by the great expanse of time separating the sages from the present (*Wenji* 82.26a). He advises, "Keep your mind glued to the text. Only when every sentence and every character falls into place have you done a good job of thinking through the work" (*YL* 177:3).

A mind "glued to the text" is one whose concentration is totally devoted to the text. Again, the relationship here between reading and practicing inner mental attentiveness is not a simple one. For the fully attentive mind—so uncharacteristic of contemporary readers, in Zhu's view—is essential to grasping the profound truth of the sages' writings. It is what makes the reading efficacious: "In reading . . . you should put aside unimportant matters, stop engaging in idle thought, and concentrate the mind in order to get a real sense of moral principle. In this way the mind will become sharp, and once the mind's sharp, it'll become intimately familiar with moral principle" (*YL* 164:9; cf. *YL* 177:9).

Reading is thus made open to the truth transmitted in the text by a mind free of the distractions and clutter that normally plague it. But, at the same time, reading is an exercise that assists in concentrating the mind, that focuses it on the "thing"—the text—at hand, pushing out all other thoughts, distractions, and desires. Thus, reading sharpens the mind, as Zhu says above. In this sense, reading is itself the practice of inner mental attentiveness; fully absorbed in the text, the mind becomes collected, undivided, detached from worldly concerns, and, consequently, fully sensitive to things as they really are. The text, in short, becomes a vehicle by which inner mental attentiveness may be achieved. As Zhu tells students, "If a person reads constantly, he can pretty much control his mind and thereby keep it constantly preserved. Hengqu [i.e., Zhang Zai] said: 'Books are the way to maintain the mind. The moment you put them down is the moment your virtuous nature grows lax.' How then can one neglect reading?" (*YL* 176:7).[36]

> If you just hold a piece of fruit in your hand, you don't know if its inside is acidic or salty, bitter or harsh. You must chew it, then you'll appreciate its flavor. (Zhu Xi, *YL* 145:5)

Genuine reading is more than merely passing the eyes over the text. As Zhu is fond of saying, the reader has to "experience" the text personally, he has to make the text his own. Experiencing the text requires that the reader "read and reread it, appreciating each and every paragraph, each and every sentence, each and every word" (*YL* 162:1). To this end, he urges disciples to recite a text over and over, even fifty to a hundred times or more, until they no longer see it as "other" (see comments in *YL* 168–69). Indeed, Zhu tells them that when he himself was seventeen or eighteen he would recite both the *Greater Learning* and the *Doctrine of the Mean* ten times every morning (*YL* 319:2). In his view, there is no prescribed number of times a text is to be read; he simply advises that "when the number's sufficient, stop" (*YL* 169:3).

Repeated recitation of the classics allows the reader to internalize or embody the words of the sages. But for those words to have true meaning, the reader must take them in slowly and deliberately, becoming "intimately familiar" with each and every one of them. Zhu advises:

> In reading, keep the curriculum small but the effort you make on it large. If you are able to read two hundred characters, read only one hundred, but on those one hundred make a truly fierce effort. Understand them in every detail, recite them until you are intimately familiar with them. . . . If you read a great deal, but race through what you read, it will be of no benefit at all. (*YL* 165:14)[37]

The Neo-Confucian reader, according to Zhu, is to practice a slow, meditative reading, in which he takes the writings of the revered sages and reflects deeply and patiently on them, going beyond the superficial meaning of words to their deeper layers of significance (e.g., *YL* 162:12 and 162:13).[38]

To describe this reflective, meditative reading, Zhu Xi frequently resorts to the imagery of rumination. The reader is to "chew" the words of the text over and over, savoring their flavor. The slower he chews the longer the flavor lasts. As Zhu remarks, "If we take big bites and big gulps, in the end we don't know the flavor" (*YL* 169:14; cf. *YL* 167:14 and 145:5). Savoring the flavor fully, the reader will come to appreciate the true taste.[39] Such imagery is especially apt in a culture of reading where the text normally is recited aloud, by the lips and the mouth.[40] It is also apt here because the words of the sages are thought by Zhu Xi to provide nourishment and spiritual sustenance. Indeed, just as "we are what we eat," so Zhu hopes that, by his process of reading, the words of the sages will become our own words and transform us thereby into our true selves: "Generally speaking, in reading, we must first become intimately familiar with the text so that its words seem to come from our own mouths. We should then continue to reflect on it so that its ideas seem to come from our own minds. Only then can there be real understanding" (*YL* 168:11). It is at this point that the reader has truly embodied or experienced the text, that he has truly made its words his own; he now has become one with it—and with the mind of the sage whose words it is. In other words, his human mind now is in total conformity with his Dao mind.

Students mustn't compromise the words of the sages with their own ideas. (Zhu Xi, *YL* 185:7)

Meditative reading is thus capable of drawing the reader into a communion with the sages and worthies of antiquity. In fact, Zhu Xi likens the reading of the sages' texts to "speaking with them face to face" (*YL* 162:9). The reader, accordingly, is to approach the canon with a certain awe and reverence, and indeed a faith, if you will, that the truth is fully manifest there, and accessible to one ready to receive it. Opening the mind (*xuxin*) is an essential part of this meditative reading; for only the mind that is empty of all distractions, preconceived ideas, subjective opinions, and the like, is capable of apprehending the truth directly from the sages without any impediment.[41] Only this open mind can experience a clear, sharp resonance with the principle embodied in the words of the sacred texts.

Of course, "opening" the mind, making it fully attentive to the profound message of the sages, requires deliberate effort. Zhu remarks: "There is a method to book learning. Simply scrub clean the mind, then read. If you don't understand the text, put it down for the moment, wait until your thoughts have cleared, then pick it up and read it again. Now we speak about the need to open up our minds. The mind, how can we open it? We just have to take it and keep it focused on the text" (*YL* 177:13). All opinions, prejudices, and selfish desires that over time have come to collect in the mind are thus to be "cleansed" or "washed away" (e.g., *YL* 185:16 and 186:6), which can be accomplished by practicing *jing*, or inner mental attentiveness, in approaching the canonical text.

Scrubbing it clean is but one of Zhu's metaphors for opening the mind. Another is "settling" the mind: "Presently, should you want to engage in book learning, you must first settle the mind so that it becomes like still water or a clear mirror. How can a cloudy mirror reflect anything?" (*YL* 177:11). To reflect accurately the words of the sages, the reader's mind has to have achieved a clear, settled state, free from unchecked emotions and desires. Undistracted and fully focused on the words of the sages, the reader is thus prepared to hear the truth in the text. To help his students attain this state of mind Zhu urges them to practice *jingzuo*, or quiet-sitting,[42] once even suggesting that it would be best to give half a day to quiet-sitting and the other half to reading (*YL* 2806:4). Zhu's hope is that in their time off from reading, students will sit quietly in meditation, ridding the mind of any personal thoughts or desires that might interfere with a fair and faithful reading of the text. For only if the mind is made completely unobstructed and calm will the principle in the reader, which resides in the mind, be unimpeded. Unimpeded, it will resonate clearly with the principle—and the mind—of the sages.[43] In this way, communion with the revered sages of antiquity will be truly meaningful.

Conclusion

For Zhu Xi, then, the Confucian canon, approached properly, is a mirror in which one could recognize oneself.[44] In his words:

> In reading, we cannot seek moral principle solely from the text. We must turn the process around and look for it in ourselves. Since the Qin-Han period, no one has spoken about this; people simply have sought it in the text, not in themselves. We have yet to discover for ourselves what the sages previously explained in their texts—only through their words will we find it in ourselves. (*YL* 181:8; cf. *YL* 188:3)

Hence, while Zhu's program of meditative reading calls for a deeply reverential and attentive attitude toward the classical texts, and for probing "rumination" over their every word, the aim clearly is not acquisition of knowledge per se or scholastic advancement. This, of course, is why for all of his emphasis on reading, he could tell students, "Book learning is of secondary importance" (*YL* 161:5; cf. *YL* 161:4). Meditative reading for Zhu Xi, and in the later Cheng-Zhu tradition, is primarily a spiritual practice, bringing the reader ever closer to a union with the paragons of the Confucian tradition; in this encounter with the sages, the reader, through a resonance made possible by principle, could hope to awaken fully to his true self, as well as to the true nature of all things and affairs of the world. With this, his spiritual transformation will be complete and his understanding of the world all-penetrating.

It would be appropriate, given the subject of this volume, to be more explicit about what I mean here by spiritual transformation. For the very word spiritual can be a problematic and confusing one when applied to a tradition in which there is no clear boundary between matter/spirit or body/soul, as there has been in the West. Through attentiveness and meditative reading, the Cheng-Zhu school of Neo-Confucianism is advocating the cultivation of one's *qi*, one's psychophysical endowment. Body and mind together are to be refined and transformed. The aim of such transformation is a transcendence, but not to an "other" realm; rather it is a transcendence of our normal, chronic condition, to realization of our authentic self. Meditative reading for Zhu Xi then is a quest of inner discovery, a quest to awaken the sage within us. The recovery of our ontological self through communion with the sages of the past is to become one in mind and humanity with those sages. At the same time, it is to become acutely aware that our humanity—our principle fully manifest—binds us inextricably to all other beings and creatures in the universe.

A brief comparison of the meditative reading of the Cheng-Zhu school of Neo-Confucianism and the divine, meditative reading—*lectio divina*—of the western monastic tradition can, I think, be instructive here. The structural similarity between the two is striking. Each prescribes for its followers a core curriculum: the one based on the Confucian classics, the words of the sages, and the other based on scripture, the Word of God. Each develops an elaborate religious hermeneutics, urging readers to approach the texts in an attentive, "prayerful" manner, memorizing their every word, savoring fully their flavor, and thereby making the texts and the truths in them one's own. Finally, each takes as its ultimate end more than mere comprehension of the texts, seeking instead the union of reader and "author."[45]

But for all the structural similarity, there is a wide cosmological schism separating Cheng-Zhu meditative reading from *lectio divina*. Union with the sages of the past and union with God are, presumably, not the same experience. The sages are fully human. They are ontologically one with the reader, making "resonance" with them possible. With a resolute will and determined effort, the reader can hope to traverse the centuries and millennia to apprehend their words and, indeed, the mind that gives these words expression. Union of this sort with the sages—these fully perfected men of antiquity—brings to perfection the humanity, the truth, and the understanding ontologically endowed in the reader. God is other and, so, not ontologically conterminus with the reader. *Lectio divina* provides the opportunity to commune with God, to come to know God fully, but the reader's will alone cannot be sufficient; approaching scripture with the proper attitude, the reader, steeped in original sin, can only hope to be offered insight into the divine and "other" by the grace of God. Union with God here, as with the sages, to be sure, results in the perfection of the reader's humanity, but a perfection that is a transcendence of his endowed capabilities, one that is a gift from without. *Lectio divina* thus, in part, is a quest to know and participate in the divine, in the "otherly."

The point here, in conclusion, is that there is nothing divine or "otherly" in the meditative reading of the Cheng-Zhu school. Union with the sages is but union with one's true self, and apprehension of their mind through the recitation of the classics is apprehension of a mind that "is no different from your own mind today," as Zhu puts it (*YL* 225:3). Nonetheless, through meditative reading devout Neo-Confucians could hope to achieve a transformation of body and mind, which would, in turn, profoundly transform the way they experience themselves and the world around them.

Notes

I am grateful to Cynthia J. Brokaw for her thoughtful reading of earlier drafts of this essay.

1. Philip Kapleau, *The Three Pillars of Zen: Teaching, Practice, and Enlightenment* (Boston: Beacon Press, 1965), 10–11. This translation from Kapleau is based on that found in E. Steinilber-Oberlin and Matsuo Kuni, *The Buddhist Sects of Japan: Their History, Philosophical Doctrines and Sanctuaries* (London: George Allen & Unwin, 1938), 167–68. The translation, according to Steinilber-Oberlin and Kuni, is of a passage found in a collection of dialogues of Zen masters, *Zensô mondô* (unavailable to me).

2. For example, see the fine overviews of "attention" as a category of religious practice and experience by Philip Novak, "Attention," in *The Encyclopedia of Religion*, ed. Mircea Eliade (New York: Macmillan, 1985), 1:501–9; and Carol Zaleski, "Attending to Attention," in *Faithful Imagining: Essays in Honor of Richard R. Niebuhr*, ed. Sang Hyun Lee, Wayne Proudfoot, and Albert Blackwell (Atlanta: Scholars Press, 1995), 127–49. For a more popular and sometimes problematic overview, see Daniel Goleman, *The Meditative Mind: The Varieties of Meditative Experience* (New York: Putnam, 1988).

3. *Yishu* is an abbreviation for Cheng Hao and Cheng Yi, *Henan Chengshi yishu*

(*Guoxue jiben congshu* ed.). The passage cited here is from the comment that begins on line 7 of p. 71.

4. *YL* is an abbreviation for *Zhuzi yulei*, ed. Li Jingde (Beijing: Zhonghua shuju, 1986). The passage cited is from the comment that begins on line 6 of p. 210.

5. *Shangshu* (*Shisan jing zhu shu*, 1815 ed.), 4.8b; the second sentence of this translation is from *The Chinese Classics*, trans. James Legge, 5 vols. (1871; repr., Hong Kong: Hong Kong University Press, 1960), 3:61–62.

6. This explication of the passage from the *Book of History* is found in Zhu Xi's "Preface" to his commentary on the *Doctrine of the Mean*, "Zhongyong zhangju xu (in *Sishu jizhu* [*Sibu beiyao* ed.]) 1a–b. For less detailed explanation by Cheng Yi, see, e.g., *Yishu* 280:14 and 302:2. For a summary of Zhu's views of the human mind and the Dao mind, see W. T. de Bary, *The Message of the Mind in Neo-Confucianism* (New York: Columbia University Press, 1989), 9–12.

7. See many similar comments in *YL* 199–201.

8. Pertinent questions here that Zhu Xi never addresses entirely satisfactorily include: How does the individual whose will is not inclined in the right direction in the first place determine to fix the will? What is it that incites this individual to change the direction in which the mind is headed? What motivates him, in the absence of a properly disposed will, to engage in a program of study and self-cultivation that leads to the necessary reinclination of the will, redirection of the mind, and thus realization of his good nature?

9. See ch. 5 of *YL*, pp. 82–98, for Zhu Xi's remarks on the mind and the will.

10. The summary of the mind and the will presented in the last few paragraphs is from Daniel K. Gardner, *Learning to Be a Sage: Selections from the Conversations of Master Chu, Arranged Topically*, 51–52.

11. Translation based on A. C. Graham, *Two Chinese Philosophers: Ch'eng Ming-tao and Ch'eng Yi-ch'uan*, 70.

12. Goleman, *Meditative Mind*, 89. The term *jing* has also been variously translated as "reverence," "seriousness," and "composure." Attentiveness would seem to capture the flavor better, for as Cheng Yi and Zhu Xi describe it, it is the mind in a concentrated, focused state. Indeed, the term *attentiveness* subsumes the meanings of reverence, seriousness, and composure; for the attitudes or feelings of reverence, seriousness, and composure can only be produced by a mind in its fully attentive state.

13. Elsewhere, in *YL* 206:1, Zhu says: "The effort required of students entails pruning away superficial and extraneous ideas."

14. Zhu comments (*YL* 155:3): "Open the mind to observe principle."

15. This is one of the defining features of sagehood for Zhu (*YL* 219:9): "The sage, in activity, is quiescent. By contrast, the multitude, in activity, is confused and disturbed. When people today want to do something, they're never capable of concentrating on it or dealing with it efficiently and without confusion. For as they deliberate on it, they want to do this and at the same time want to do that. This is why in times of activity there isn't that quiescence."

16. Novak, "Attention," 502. On this process of dehabituation or "de-automization," see Arthur Deikman, "Deautomization and the Mystic Experience," *Psychiatry* 29 (1966): 324–38.

17. Both Cheng Yi and Zhu Xi describe the attentive mind as one that is tranquil. See, e.g., *Yishu* 174:5 and *YL* 204.10.

18. Both Cheng Yi and Zhu Xi remark that "inner mental attentiveness will overcome the hundred moral depravities." See *Yishu* 132:3 and *YL* 210:11.

19. Cheng Yi remarks (*Yishu* 165:8): "Inner mental attentiveness is simply making unity the ruler. If unity is made the ruling consideration, the mind goes neither East nor West and thus remains in equilibrium; it goes neither this way nor that way and thus remains within. If you preserve this, heavenly principle will spontaneously become plain" (translation based on Graham, *Two Chinese Philosophers*, 71–72).

20. Zhu Xi comments (*YL* 205:15): "Only when the mind attains its proper balance is it capable of appreciating the goodness of human nature."

21. See Novak, "Attention," 505–8.

22. From *Liji* (*Shisan jing zhu shu*, 1815 ed.), 1.8a.

23. From *Liji* 30.23a–b.

24. For these reasons, it can be argued that the term *jing* might be better translated simply as "attentiveness." "Inner mental attentiveness" implicitly draws a distinction that neither Cheng nor Zhu would have made. Still, in the writings and conversations of Cheng Yi and Zhu Xi, it is clear that when they speak of *jing*, their main concern is with concentrating the mind and keeping it attentive. Thus, while *jing* governs the physical as well, it is the relationship of *jing* to the mind that really matters to them.

For recent work that treats the relationship between body and mind in Asian thought, see, e.g., Yasuo Yuasa, *The Body: Toward an Eastern Mind-Body Theory* (Albany: State University of New York Press, 1987); Thomas P. Kasulis with Roger T. Ames and Wimal Dissanayake, eds., *Self as Body in Asian Theory and Practice* (Albany: State University of New York Press, 1993); and Tu Weiming, "The Continuity of Being: Chinese Visions of Nature," in *Confucian Thought: Selfhood as Creative Transformation* (Albany: State University of New York Press, 1985), 35–50.

25. Zhu Xi's so-called "supplementary chapter" to the *Greater Learning*; *Daxue* (in *Sishu jizhu*) 5a. Translation from Daniel K. Gardner, *Chu Hsi and the Ta-hsueh*, 104–5. By Zhu Xi's own admission, the statement here is fashioned out of various remarks made earlier by Cheng Yi; see *Daxue huowen* (in *Sishu daquan* [Japanese edition of 1626 based on *Yongle* edition of 1415]), 33a–51a. Wing-tsit Chan lists the passages in the *Yishu* that Zhu draws upon in writing the supplementary chapter ("Chu Hsi's Completion of Neo-Confucianism," in *Etudes Song: In Memoriam Etienne Balazs*, ed. Françoise Aubin, ser. 2, no. 1 [Paris: Mouton, 1973], 50).

26. Translation based on Graham, *Two Chinese Philosophers*, 76.

27. See Peter Bol, *"This Culture of Ours": Intellectual Transitions in T'ang and Sung China*, 300–342.

28. See, e.g., his remark in Wing-tsit Chan, *Reflections on Things at Hand* (New York: Columbia University Press, 1967), 47–48.

29. Not surprisingly, Cheng Yi spends little time annotating and commenting on the classical texts, with the notable exception of the *Book of Changes*; Zhu, on the other hand, as is well known, consumes much of his adult life writing and refining commentaries on the classical canon.

30. Gardner, *Learning to Be a Sage*, 73–74. On Zhu's program of learning and hermeneutics in general, see the "Introduction" to *Learning to Be a Sage;* and Gardner, "Principle and Pedagogy: Chu Hsi and the Four Books," *Harvard Journal of Asiatic Studies* 44, no. 1 (1984): 57–81.

31. On *lectio divina*, see Monica Sandor, "Lectio Divina and the Monastic Spirituality of Reading," *American Benedictine Review* 40, no. 1 (March 1989): 82–114; and Jean Leclercq, *The Love of Learning and the Desire for God: A Study of Monastic Culture* (New York: Fordham University Press, 1982), esp. 15–17 and 71–86.

32. Sandor argues that it is these three reasons that make the *lectio*, the reading, of the medieval monastic tradition *divina* ("Lectio Divina").

33. For criticism of contemporary reading, see especially chs. 10 and 11 of *YL*; for the pernicious influence of the examination system on reading, see ch. 13.

34. *Wenji* is an abbreviation for *Hui'an xiansheng Zhu Wengong wenji* (*Sibu congkan* edition).

35. Ichikawa Yasuji, *Tei I-sen tetsugaku no kenkyû* (Tokyo: Tokyo University Press, 1964), 131–37.

36. On one occasion Zhu succinctly remarks to students (*YL* 177:1): "It's essential that preserving the mind and reading books constitute one matter; only then will you succeed." Cf. *YL* 176:9.

37. Chapter 10 in *YL* is filled with such advice.

38. On one occasion he provides a rather graphic account of what is involved (*YL* 162:10): "You must frequently take the words of the sages and worthies and pass them before your eyes, roll them around and around in your mouth, and turn them over and over in your mind."

39. In *YL* 191:5, Zhu remarks, "You must take the classical text and read it until you've become intimately familiar with it. Savor each and every word until you know its taste." Earlier Cheng Yi and Cheng Hao had called for students to "get the real taste" of what they read; see Chan, *Reflections*, 101–5, passim.

40. Zhu remarks often that recitation is the proper way to read a text; see, e.g., *YL* 170:3, 170:13, 179:1.

41. On *xuxin*, see comments throughout ch. 11 of *YL*.

42. E.g., *YL* 177:7 and 216:14 and numerous comments in *YL* 216ff.

43. Daniel K. Gardner, "Transmitting the Way: Chu Hsi and His Program of Learning," *Harvard Journal of Asiatic Studies* 49, no. 2 (1989): 160–61.

44. To paraphrase Sandor, "Lectio Divina," 99.

45. See Sandor, "Lectio Divina"; and Jean Leclercq, "Lectio Divina," *Worship* 58, no. 3 (May 1984): 239–48.

Recommended Reading

Bol, Peter K. *"This Culture of Ours": Intellectual Transitions in T'ang and Sung China.* Stanford: Stanford University Press, 1992.

Chan, Wing-tsit, ed. *Chu Hsi and Neo-Confucianism.* Honolulu: University of Hawaii Press, 1986.

de Bary, Wm. Theodore. *Neo-Confucian Orthodoxy and the Learning of the Mind-and-Heart.* New York: Columbia University Press, 1981.

de Bary, Wm. Theodore, and John W. Chaffee, eds. *Neo-Confucian Education: The Formative Stage.* Berkeley: University of California Press, 1989.

Gardner, Daniel K. *Chu Hsi and the Ta-hsuih: Neo-Confucian Reflection on the Confucian Canon.* Cambridge, Mass.: Harvard University Press, 1986.

———. *Learning to Be a Sage: Selections from the Conversations of Master Chu, Arranged Topically.* Berkeley: University of California Press, 1990.

Graham, A. C. *Two Chinese Philosophers: Ch'eng Ming-tao and Ch'eng Yi-ch'uan.* London: Lung Humphries, 1958.

Henderson, John B. *Scripture, Canon, and Commentary: A Comparison of Confucian and Western Exegesis.* Princeton, N.J.: Princeton University Press, 1991.

Tillman, Hoyt. *Confucian Discourse and Chu Hsi's Ascendancy.* Honolulu: University of Hawaii Press, 1992.

Zhu Xi and Lü Zuqian. *Reflections on Things at Hand.* Translated by Wing-tsit Chan. New York: Columbia University Press, 1967.

21

Varieties of Spiritual Experience: *Shen* in Neo-Confucian Discourse

JOSEPH A. ADLER

> Gongsun Chou asked, . . . "May I ask you,
> Master, in what do you excel?"
> "I understand words, and I am good
> at nourishing my flowing *qi*."
>
> *Mencius* 2A:2

Preliminaries: Understanding Words

BOTH OF MENCIUS'S STRONG POINTS are highly relevant to our inquiry into Neo-Confucian spirituality. We need to be very self-conscious about the words we bring to the Confucian texts (such as "spirituality") and the words we take from them in translation. Comparative studies always involve the potential risk of built-in biases caused by projecting foreign concepts onto the subject matter. In the present case, the entire project embodied in this volume is open to the criticism that the very concept of "spirituality" is problematic in the Chinese context. Basic dictionary definitions as well as common usage of the word "spirit" and its derivatives carry the clear implication of contradistinction from "matter" and "body," and this is simply and emphatically not true of the concepts we will be examining. The various Chinese terms sometimes translated as "spirit" or "spiritual"—of these, *shen* is the most common—are explicitly understood as being forms or modes of the *qi* that Mencius was skilled at nourishing. And *qi*, as many of its translations imply (psychophysical stuff, material force, vital energy), clearly bridges the conceptual gap described (or constructed) by the terms "spirit" (or energy) and "body" (or matter). Thus, we need at the outset to establish good grounds for retaining or rejecting such words as "spirituality," and for choosing which Chinese words they will translate.

In terms of etymology, it is probably *qi* that bears the closest resemblance to "spirit." The original meaning of *qi* was "mist," or the vapor rising from a sacrificial offering;[1] "spirit" comes from the Latin *spiritus*, meaning "breath." Note also the various English words with the same root (respiration, inspiration) that still refer explicitly to breath, and the analogous words in Hebrew, classical Greek, and Sanskrit (*rûaḥ*, *pneuma*, and *prana*), which similarly cover the range of meanings from wind and breath to spirit. Some modern colloquial usages of *qi* are similar to such terms as "high spirits" and *esprit de corps*.[2]

Most uses of *qi* in Neo-Confucian discourse, however, do not carry the religious implications that "spirit" in English would convey. In fact they tend to emphasize more the physical end of the psychophysical spectrum, as in the key term *qizhi zhi xing*, or physical nature (as opposed to the moral nature). In addition, *qi* is not commonly used as an adjective; thus if we translated *qi* as "spirit," we would have few, if any, occasions to use the adjective "spiritual." *Shen*, on the other hand, is used in ways that suggest all the variations: "spirit," "spirits," "spiritual," and "spirituality."[3] And since *shen* is understood to be the finest form of *qi*, it is implicitly related to breath or vapor.

Therefore, with the proviso that we think of "spirit" in a sense closer to its Latin roots than to its Cartesian dualistic usage as a completely nonphysical entity or quality, I will use "spirit" in its various forms to translate *shen*. I will use "psychophysical stuff" for *qi* when necessary, but in general I will leave *qi* untranslated, as it is becoming common enough in English to stand on its own. Finally, another word sometimes translated as "spiritual," *ling*, will be translated here as "numinous." *Ling* is used in compounds that suggest the spiritual *efficacy* of gods, ancestral spirits, and ghosts—for example, their power to effect the seemingly miraculous, to arouse awe, dread, and fascination.[4] Since this is precisely how Rudolf Otto defines "numinous" (a word he coined in his book *Das Heilige* [The Holy] in 1923), "numinous" serves as an apt translation of *ling*.[5]

In this chapter I will use the concept of *shen*, in its various forms, as a thread to link together four levels of Neo-Confucian discourse: cosmology, physiology, epistemology, and sagehood. The boundaries between these categories, especially in the Chinese intellectual context, are admittedly fluid and somewhat arbitrary; in any case, the focus of the discussion will be on their holistic interrelationships in terms of *shen* and its related terms. I will argue that this religio-philosophical system is an elaboration of the fundamental Confucian belief that human values are rooted in the natural world, and that it describes a form of religious life best characterized as a system of ultimate transformation and ultimate orientation.[6] We will see that Confucian spirituality is not limited to the "interiority" of moral reflection and mental (or spiritual) cultivation—although it is highly developed in those respects—and that in no way does it exclude or even de-emphasize the body and the physical world. Indeed, the ontological *continuity* of body, mind, and spirit is the key to understanding Neo-Confucian spirituality.

Since we are interested here only in a general depiction of Neo-Confucian discourse, I will focus on the Cheng-Zhu school, which after the twelfth century dominated the Confucian intellectual scene in China. I will use as one of my chief source texts the *Xingli daquan shu* (Great Compendium on Human Nature and Principle), compiled by Hu Kuang in 1415, a seventy-chapter classified collection of writings and conversations of the Cheng-Zhu school, covering the Song and Yuan dynasties (960–1368).[7] It was these thinkers, dominated by Zhu Xi (1130–1200), whose ideas were the basis of the civil service examinations from the fourteenth century to the early twentieth, and who therefore exerted tremendous influence over intellectual life in China (including those who rejected their ideas) for roughly seven hundred years.

Spirit and Cosmology (*qi, yin-yang, gui-shen*)

The concepts of *qi* and *yin-yang* are well known enough not to require much explanation here. Suffice it to say that *qi*, or psychophysical stuff, is the substance of which all existing phenomena are constituted, including all the phases of matter, energy, mind (*xin*), and even the various forms of spirit (*shen*). The term is used in both a general sense, referring to the primordial stuff of which all things are composed, and more specific senses. For example, Zhu Xi uses both general and specific senses in one sentence, in reference to the human body: "The pure *qi* is *qi* [here meaning something like "breath"]; the turbid *qi* is matter (*zhi*)."[8] It is convenient, although oversimplified, to think of *qi* as a fundamental vapor that can condense into solid matter and disperse into finer and finer forms. It is much like the *aer* of the pre-Socratic Greek philosopher Anaximenes, who claimed that it (like *qi*) was the fundamental substance or nature (*physis*) of all things.[9]

Yin and *yang*, whose root meanings are "shady" and "sunny" (or dark and light), are not substances or things but rather functional *modes* of *qi*. *Yin* is *qi* in its dense, dark, sinking, wet, condensing mode; and *yang* denotes the light, bright, rising, dry, expanding mode. Together *yin* and *yang* represent the principle of bipolarity or complementarity, which was almost universally considered in China since the Han dynasty to be the most fundamental ordering principle of the cosmos—in Neo-Confucian terms, the most fundamental, universal *li* (principle, pattern, or order). Zhu Xi called this most fundamental, universal ordering principle *Taiji*, a term with largely Daoist roots that had been used by the Northern Song Confucian Zhou Dunyi (1017–1073). Thus *Taiji*, as understood by Zhu Xi, is best translated as "Supreme Polarity" (although it is usually translated "Supreme Ultimate").[10]

Guishen, as a paired term going back at least to Zhou times (eleventh to third centuries B.C.E.) refers to ghosts and spirits. Ghosts (*gui*) are unfriendly, dangerous spirits of the dead, especially those who died in unnatural or otherwise extraordinary ways, those for whom the proper burial rites were not performed, and those whose descendants have neglected them, leaving them with no proper place in the social order (which includes both the living and the dead). Spirits (*shen*) are those whose deaths were natural and properly observed, and whose descendants honor them properly with sacrificial offerings. In other words, these spirits are ancestors (*zu*, or *zuxian*).

But the word *shen*—in the Song dynasty as well as the present day—also refers to gods, of which there are several varieties. There are gods of nature (mountains, rivers, etc.); there are gods who were once powerful people—and therefore also ancestors (e.g., Guan Yu, the famous warrior of the post-Han period);[11] there are household gods (e.g., Caojun, the stove god); there are bureaucratic gods (e.g., Chenghuang, the city god); and there is the master of them all, the Jade Emperor (Yuhuang dadi, or Yuhuang shangdi). All of these are *shen*, who were and are clearly and unambiguously worshiped as gods.

Then there are the spirits of the Confucian Sages (*sheng*) and Worthies (*xian*), such as Confucius and his chief disciples and Mencius, who were installed in government-established temples and accorded special rites. (Later, the very Neo-Confucians we will be examining here would join them.) Whether these are to be considered gods, heroes, or ancestral spirits—in this case not of families but of the class of scholar-officials—is open to question. Functionally they seem to be parallel to the patron gods of various occupations (e.g., shoemakers, printers, dyers), who were also once historical individuals. But since the word *shen* covers them all, this is not a problem we really need to solve. In any case, there will be no definitive answer, as different worshipers have different conceptions of them.

Confucius was famously reticent concerning ghosts and spirits, and the Neo-Confucians were very much aware of this. Confucius had said, for example, "Respect ghosts and spirits, but keep them at a distance" (*Analects* 6:20). And when a disciple asked about "serving ghosts and spirits," he replied, "When one is not yet able to serve other people, how can one serve ghosts?" When the disciple asked about death, Confucius said, "When one does not yet understand life, how can one understand death?" (*Analects* 11:11).

Statements like these do not mean that Confucius did not believe in ghosts and spirits; they reflect, rather, his attempts to redirect the attention of the literati of his day to the urgent social, ethical, and political tasks of restoring harmony to a society wracked by war and political strife. He felt that what was most urgent was the moral revitalization of the ruling class, and that the way to achieve this was not to court the favor of gods and ancestors but to revive the idealized Way or ways of the benevolent sage-kings who had founded the Zhou dynasty some five hundred years earlier. While this Way included worship of ancestors and various gods, such worship without proper understanding and reverence was meaningless and ineffective and, even with understanding and reverence, was no substitute for good government. So Confucius stressed learning, thinking, and moral self-cultivation as the key to good government and meaningful ritual. "If one is not humane (*ren*), what can he have to do with ritual? If one is not humane, what can he have to do with music [part of court ritual]?" (*Analects* 3:3).

But the Neo-Confucians went considerably further than Confucius in distancing themselves from popular worship of ghosts and spirits—except for ancestral spirits, which will be discussed below. While not denying the existence of apparitions and ghosts, Cheng Yi, Zhu Xi, and their followers "rationalized" or "naturalized" them to a considerable degree. That is, they interpreted them as functions of the natural processes of *qi*, implying that at least some forms of ghosts and spirits lacked conscious, personal wills. In this respect they were in line with the rationalistic and skeptical traditions of Xunzi (third century B.C.E.) and Wang Chong (first century C.E.). Zhang Zai, for example, said, "Ghosts and spirits are the inherent potential (*liangneng*) of the two [modes of] *qi*."[12] Cheng Yi said, in a similar vein, "Ghosts and spirits are traces of the creative process."[13] Zhu Xi said, "The same principles (*li*) apply to human beings, heaven and earth, ghosts and spirits."[14] Chen Chun, Zhu Xi's pupil, said, "Ghosts and spirits are nothing more than the contraction and expansion, coming and going, of *yin* and *yang qi*."[15]

As these statements suggest, the terms *gui* and *shen* were thoroughly integrated into Neo-Confucian "natural philosophy." They were even used in reference to such phenomena as phases of the weather, in which case they definitely lacked consciousness. Zhu Xi's explanation of the terms relied in part on the traditional etymologies of *gui* and *shen*, relating them to the homophones "returning" (*gui*) and "extending/expanding" (*shen*).[16] But he was primarily interested in correlating the terms with the most fundamental polarity, *yin* and *yang*, thereby making it possible to incorporate all aspects of spirit and spirituality into his comprehensive religio-philosophical system. For this he relied primarily on his Northern Song predecessors, Zhang Zai and Cheng Yi, arguing that the terms *gui* and *shen* could be used to describe impersonal, empirically observable manifestations of *qi*: According to Zhu:

> *Gui* and *shen* are nothing more than the growth and dispersion of *yin* and *yang*.[17]

> That which contracts and expands, back and forth, is *qi*. Within Heaven-and-earth there is nothing that is not *qi*. Human *qi* and the *qi* of Heaven-and-earth are constantly interacting, with no interruption. (*Xingli daquan shu*, 28:2b, p. 609)

> *Shen* is expanding (*shen*); *gui* is contracting (*qu*). For example, the moment when wind and rain, thunder and lightning, first appear is *shen*. And when wind stops and rain passes, thunder stops and lightning ceases, this is *gui*. (*Xingli daquan shu*, 28:2a, p. 609)

Moreover, since—contrary to popular belief—*gui* and *shen* operated according to the natural principle of *yin* and *yang*, they were capable (at least theoretically) of being rationally understood:

> By the time we have attended thoroughly to ordinary daily matters, the principles governing *gui* and *shen* will naturally be understood. (*Zhuzi quanshu*, 51:2a)[18]

> [Most] explanations of *gui-shen* take them to be uncanny. But the world itself has a moral principle (*daoli*). We cannot say that these [phenomena] are not unusual, [but neither can we say] that they are not regular aspects of the creative process. (*Zhuzi quanshu*, 51:5a)

In *Analects* 7:20, it is said that Confucius "did not discuss the uncanny (*kuai*), force (*li*), disorders (*luan*), or spirits (*shen*)," with no distinctions noted among the four items. But Zhu Xi introduced a qualification. He said that the first three items

> are not regular aspects of principle (*fei li zhi zheng*), and are definitely what the Sage did not discuss. [But] "ghosts and spirits are traces of the creative process" [quoting Cheng Yi]. Although they are not irregular (*fei bu zheng*)

[i.e. they are "principled" or ordered], nevertheless they are not the goal of fathoming principle. There are things which are not easily understood; therefore one does not lightly discuss them with others. (*Sishu jizhu*, 4:5a)[19]

Zhu was willing to acknowledge the possible existence of bogeys, monsters, or uncanny apparitions (*kuai*), but he insisted that they are not outside the natural order (*tianli*):

For example, the *Jiayu* (Sayings of the Confucian School) says, "The monsters of the mountains are called *gui* and *wangliang*; the monsters of the water are called *long* (dragons) and *wangxiang*; and the monsters of the earth are called *fenyang*." All these are produced by confused and perverse *qi* and are surely not without *li*—you mustn't stubbornly think they are without *li*. It's like the winter's being cold and the summer's being warm; this is the regular (*zheng*) *li*. But there are times when suddenly in the summer it turns cold and in the winter it turns warm—how can we say there isn't a *li* for this! Still, because it isn't the ordinary (*chang*) *li* we consider it uncanny. (*Zhuzi yulei*, 3:37)[20]

It is clear that Zhu Xi was determined to show that everything that actually existed in the world—or had at least been attested in books that he accepted as canonical or trustworthy—was part of the natural/moral order (*tianli/daoli*). Some of the strange or uncanny phenomena that filled the Chinese popular imagination, such as ghosts and hauntings of various sorts, fell into this category for him. When it came to ancestral spirits, of course, it was not a matter of accepting or rejecting popular beliefs. Since ancestor worship had been incorporated into Confucian thought and practice from the very beginning, and had been philosophically elaborated in the doctrines of filial piety (*xiao*) and ritual propriety (*li*, originally referring primarily to ancestral sacrifice), the Neo-Confucians never questioned the real existence of ancestral spirits. But here too these spirits (*shen*) or ancestors (*zu*) were very nearly stripped of their personal identities. They were simply "traces of the creative process" or "the expansion and contraction" of *qi*.

Zhu Xi's explanation of death is a straightforward application of his basic theory of *qi* in terms of the *yin*-soul, or *po*, and the *yang*-soul, or *hun*, which are the *yin* and *yang* portions of *qi* in the body and mind. These were and are widely used concepts in popular Chinese religion, although there are numerous variations of belief concerning their number and their natures.[21] Zhu's theory represents the simplest, most systematic version. He said, for example:

While humans have much *qi*, there must come a time when it is exhausted. When it is exhausted, then the *hun qi* returns to Heaven and the physical *po* returns to earth, and they die. When humans are about to die, the warm *qi* rises upward, which is called the *hun* ascending; the body down below gradually cools, which is called the *po* descending. This is why when there is life there must be death; when there is a beginning there must be an end. What gathers and disperses is *qi*. (*Xingli daquan shu*, 28:13a, p. 614; also *Zhuzi yulei*, 3:37)

This might appear at first to be a rather mechanistic account that would preclude the ancestral spirits' having consciousness. Were this the case, then the efficacy of ancestral sacrifice would be called into question. But a naturalistic explanation based on *qi* did *not* preclude consciousness on the part of the ancestral spirits, because the prevailing view among the Neo-Confucians was that conscious awareness is in fact an attribute of the purest, finest grades of *qi*, which is what constitutes spirits. For example, as Zhu Xi's student (and son-in-law), Huang Gan, explained:

Human biology [lit., human life] is simply *jing* (vital essence) and *qi*. What constitutes hair, bones, flesh and blood is *jing*. What constitutes breath, cold, and warmth is *qi*. But humans are the most numinous (*ling*) of the myriad things;[22] they are not trees and rocks. Therefore their *jing* and their *qi* are full of spirit (*shen*). The spirit of *jing* is called *po*; the spirit of *qi* is called *hun*. What enables the eyes and ears to see and hear is the *po*; what enables this mind to think is the *hun*. Together, the *po* and *hun* are the spirit of *yin* and *yang*, and yet they are full of *li*. Only in the *hun* and *po* is there the fullness of *li* (moral order/principle). (*Xingli daquan shu*, 28:24a, p. 620)

The *Yijing* says, "*Jing* and *qi* constitute things." (*Xici* A.4.2; *Zhouyi benyi*, 3:4b).[23] "*Jing*" means vital essence and blood; "*qi*" means warmth and vapor. . . . Vital essence and blood, warmth and vapor each have pure, numinous awareness (*xuling zhijue*) within them. The pure, numinous awareness of vital essence and blood is the *po*. The pure, numinous awareness of warmth and vapor is the *hun*. This pure, numinous awareness is not a pure, floating object. It is composed simply of abundant [or many] moral principle(s). (*Xingli daquan shu*, 28:25a, p. 620)[24]

"Pure, numinous awareness" (*xuling zhijue*) is thus characteristic of *qi* itself, at least in its finer phases, and is inherently moral. We shall return to this topic later. Suffice it now to suggest that it is the inherent capacity of consciousness in the finer forms of *qi* that make ancestral sacrifice efficacious. While a more naturalistic or mechanistic notion of affinity or resonance might account for the impersonal connection itself between the *qi* of the ancestor and that of the descendant during the rituals of ancestor worship, it is difficult to see how it would explain their *efficacy* (i.e., the ancestor's presumed awareness of and meaningful response to the petition, for example).

Thus, while in certain respects Neo-Confucian theories about *gui* and *shen* were reminiscent of the rationalistic and naturalistic theories of Xunzi and Wang Chong, most Neo-Confucians differed radically and fundamentally from these forebears in insisting on the linkage between the natural world and the human world—in particular, the immanence and naturalness of human values (implied by "the fullness of *li*") and the potential for consciousness in the fundamental substrate that constitutes all things in the natural world.

Spirit and Physiology (*jing-qi*, *hun-po*)

Analysis of the constituents of the human body had already had a long history by the time of the Song revival of Confucianism. *Yin-yang* and *wuxing* (Five Phases) theory had been applied to medicine as early as the *Yellow Emperor's Internal Classic* (*Huangdi neijing* [sixth century B.C.E.]), considered to be the foundation of Chinese medical theory. In terms of tangible substances, the fundamental concept was of course *qi*. But this term was also used in such dyadic terms as *xie-qi* and *jing-qi*. *Xie* is blood; *jing*, or "vital essence," is epitomized by sexual fluid (male or female). Both blood and vital essence represent the liquid, life-giving phase of psychophysical stuff; *qi* in these pairs stands for the gaseous or energetic phase.

In various forms of Daoist meditation that had developed from pre-Qin times (in Huang-Lao Daoism) up into the Song, *jing*, *qi*, and *shen* (spirit) were the three primal substances of the body that were manipulated through visualization techniques to synthesize an immortal "Perfected Person" (*zhenren*).[25] While most of the Song Neo-Confucians disapproved of such practices, they were well aware of them and did not reject them entirely. Even such a partisan as Zhu Xi gave credence to the ability of some Daoist adepts to prevent the decomposition of their bodies after death by "nourishing their vital essence and spirit" (e.g., *Xingli daquan shu*, 28:15b, p. 615). There were also scattered references to these terms in the appendices of the *Yijing* (*Book of Changes*), which were attributed to Confucius and were important textual sources for the Neo-Confucian movement. One of these passages (*Xici* A.4.2) discusses how the first primordial sage, Fuxi, created the hexagrams of the *Yi*:

> Gazing up he observed the heavenly patterns [the movements of the heavenly bodies]; looking down he examined the earthly order [geography]; thus he understood the characteristics of the dark and light. He traced things to their beginnings and anticipated their ends; thus he understood the meaning of life and death [as follows]: *Jing* and *qi* constitute things; the *hun* floating

away constitutes their change [death]. In this way he understood the characteristics of ghosts and spirits.

Zhu Xi's comment on this passage gives us a summary statement of the relationships among the key terms:

> Change (*yi*) is nothing other than *yin* and *yang*. Dark and light, life and death, ghosts and spirits, are all the alternation (*bian*) of *yin* and *yang*. This is the Way of Heaven-and-earth. . . . *Yin* is vital essence (*jing*), *yang* is *qi*; these collect to become things. Spirits (*shen*) are expansion (*shen*). The *hun* floats away and the *po* descends. This dissipation constitutes the change [of death]. Ghosts (*gui*) are returning (*gui*). (*Zhouyi benyi*, 3:4a–4b).[26]

In a conversation with his students, Zhu elaborates on the relationship of these terms:

> The differentiation of the two *qi* [i.e. *yin* and *yang*, or dark and light] is equivalent to the circulation of the one *qi*. It is what is meant by [Zhou Dunyi's statement in the *Taijitu shuo*] "Activity and stillness alternate; each is the basis of the other. In distinguishing *yin* and *yang*, the Two Modes are thereby established."
>
> In humans, in terms of the [aforementioned] differentiation, the vital essence (*jing*) is *yin* and *qi* is *yang*; thus the *po* becomes the ghost and *hun* becomes the spirit. In terms of the circulation, dispersion is *yin* and growth is *yang*; thus expansion is the spirit and returning is the ghost.

Up to this point Zhu's explanation is little more than an array and clarification of the terms under the *yin-yang* principle of bipolarity. But his reference to Zhou Dunyi's "Explanation of the Supreme Polarity Diagram" in the first paragraph is the critical link to Zhu's more significant concerns. As he continues:

> But the nature of the *hun* is activity (*dong*); thus just when it is expanding it is not without *po*, and yet it must have *hun* as its ruling [principle]. The nature of *po* is stillness (*jing*); thus when it is on the point of returning, it is not without *hun*, yet it must have *po* as it ruling [principle]. So, from the first there are not two principles (*wu er li*). (*Xingli daquan shu*, 28:12b, p. 614)

What Zhu Xi does with these terms, in his published commentaries and in his discussions with students, is to integrate the bipolar terminology of *jing* and *qi*, *hun* and *po*, into his theory of *li* (order, principle) and *taiji* (Supreme Polarity). The Supreme Polarity—that is, the principle of *yin/yang* or the principle of polarity—is a single, "non-dualistic" (*wu er*) principle of coherence, and, as the most fundamental ordering principle, it is fully inherent in all things, including the human mind. More specifically, based on the writings of his eleventh-century predecessor Zhou Dunyi,

Zhu stresses that the most basic, natural form of this principle—the most basic form of polarity—is *activity and stillness* (*dong-jing*). And according to Zhou Dunyi, the relationship of activity and stillness is not merely temporal alternation but metaphysical *interpenetration*.[27]

By relating all these spiritual-physiological terms, despite their various provenances, to this central conception and interpretation of *li*, Zhu is doing two things. First, he is synthesizing an intellectual system that incorporates (and perhaps co-opts) elements from Daoism and popular religion, thereby constructing a "respectable" Confucian alternative to these "heterodox" or "vulgar" (*su*) Ways. Second, in terms of the specific agenda of "learning to be a sage" (*shengxue*) in his system, he is emphasizing here the crucial linkage between the metaphysical principle of *li*—the single order that incorporates both the natural order (*tianli*) and the moral order (*daoli*) —and the phenomenal world constituted by *qi* in all its forms. The significance of this linkage within the framework of this system is that it provides access by the functioning human mind (*xin*), which is also a form of *qi*, to the inherent goodness of human nature (*xing*), which is the principle (*li*) of being human. This is what is necessary in order to transform oneself into a sage, and "spirit" (*shen*) plays a significant role in this process. Thus we shift to the possibly more familiar level of "spirituality" as the interior life of moral reflection and cultivation.

Spirit and Epistemology (*xin, zhi, shenming*)

As mentioned earlier, Daoist theories that were well established long before the Song posited three primal "fluids" or substances of the human body: *qi, jing* (vital essence), and *shen* (spirit), which corresponded to deities known as the "Three Pure Ones" (San Qing). These substances could be manipulated and synthesized into guardian spirits and deities by means of various kinds of meditation, visualization, breath control, diet, and sexual practices. Thus, by the time of the Song Confucian revival there was a considerable history of discussion of "spirit" (*shen*) itself as a psychophysical component of human life, apart from the more personalistic notion of "ghosts and spirits" (*gui-shen*). But of course, in the eyes of most of the Neo-Confucians (at least after some early but serious dalliances with Daoism and/or Buddhism by many of them), the texts containing these discussions and the practices associated with them were highly suspect.

One text that was solidly canonical, though, was the *Scripture of Changes* (*Yijing*), which, in its Appendices attributed to Confucius, dealt with *shen* as a general quality of human *qi*. As mentioned above, these texts—especially the *Xici*, or "Appended Remarks" (also called the *Dazhuan*, or "Great

Treatise")—were important textual sources for Song Neo-Confucianism.[28] Zhou Dunyi, in particular, based much of his work on the *Yijing*, and Zhou was later declared by Zhu Xi to have been the first true Confucian sage since Mencius.[29] Moreover, Zhou's discussions of *shen* are in the context of a theory of mind and the practice of moral self-cultivation as a means of transforming oneself into a sage. It is not surprising, then, that much of the Neo-Confucian discussion of *shen* revolves around Zhou Dunyi and passages from the *Yijing*. But to understand these discussions we need first to look briefly at Neo-Confucian ideas about mind and sagehood.

The self-realization, or self-transformation, that was known as "learning to be a sage" in the dominant Cheng-Zhu school of Neo-Confucianism was a process of realizing or actualizing the inherent goodness that constitutes human nature (*xing*), or the principle (*li*) of being human. This premise is based on Mencius, who had said:

> He who fully develops his mind knows his nature; knowing his nature he knows Heaven. To preserve the mind and nourish the nature is the way to serve Heaven. (7A:1)

What this involves is coming to realize—that is, to know (*zhi*) and to actualize in practice (*xing*)—the Heaven-endowed (i.e., natural) moral *potential* that is inherent in all human minds in the form of feelings or dispositions (*qing*), such as commiseration with the suffering of others, shame at one's own faults, deference to superiors, and approval/disapproval of the actions of others (*Mencius* 2A:2). Because these feelings and the principles they embody appear spontaneously in the human mind, they were considered to be objective features of the natural world, which is to say, they were "given" or "decreed" (*ming*) by Heaven (*Zhongyong* 1). To know and to actualize them in practice—that is, to realize one's own nature—is therefore to know Heaven (*tian*), which is unconditioned and absolute, and to actualize the Way of Heaven (*tiandao*).[30]

Zhu Xi argued that it was very difficult to achieve self-knowlege directly. Since the mind is composed of *qi*—albeit the most refined and pure *qi*—this physical nature of the mind obscures or clouds one's self-awareness of the principle of the mind, giving rise to selfishness (*si*) and partiality or one-sidedness (*pian*). These are the basic Neo-Confucian "evils." It is because of the difficulty of overcoming the cloudiness of one's *qi* and achieving self-knowledge directly that Zhu, drawing directly on Cheng Yi, stressed "the investigation of things" (*gewu*), including the need to rely on the wisdom of sages recorded in the classics, in his program for becoming a sage. Thus, Cheng and Zhu said that it is usually easier to perceive the underlying order or principles of things outside oneself, in nature, human affairs, and books. Then, in combination with self-reflection, one can extend these principles (*tui li*) to higher levels of generalization that comprehend the outer and inner realms, natural and human, fact and value.

The difficulty in achieving this integrated understanding of self and world was caused by the clouding or blockage of the fundamental nature (*benxing*) and the "moral mind" (*daoxin*) by the physical nature (*qizhi zhi xing*) and the "human mind" (*renxin*). Only in the mind of the sage is the human mind congruent with the moral mind, the feelings and dispositions (*qing*) in line with the moral nature (*xing*).

As a solution to this problem, Zhu Xi adopted the doctrine of "transforming the physical endowment" (*bianhua qizhi*) from Zhang Zai and his nephews, the Cheng brothers. Zhang had distinguished the physical nature (*qizhi zhi xing*) from the nature of Heaven and Earth (*tiandi zhi xing*), saying that when the former was reformed the latter would be preserved.[31] The physical nature, according to this theory, is not in itself evil. But when the originally formless *qi* condenses, it gives rise to differentiation, opposition, and conflict, which in turn result in feelings, desires, and behavior that are selfish—that is, directed at private (*si*) instead of public (*gong*) ends—and partial or one-sided instead of harmoniously in accord with the "mean" or the "centrality" (*zhong*) of human nature.[32] These tendencies result in part from the mere fact of the physical nature, since physical individuality itself—the fact that we each have a body distinct from others—naturally gives rise to egoistic or selfish desires. Thus there is an element of intractability to the problem of evil. But there is also an aspect of the physical nature that can be changed, namely, the clouding or blockage of the mind by its own endowment of *qi*. This blockage can be corrected by learning: "The great benefit of learning is to enable one to transform the physical nature by oneself."[33] Hence in Neo-Confucianism there is a moral imperative for learning, and the process of learning is a psychospiritual transformation that refines and clarifies one's *qi*.

But what is the connection between learning and *qi*? This question addresses the crux of Neo-Confucian spirituality. The answer is based on the often acknowledged but insufficiently appreciated fact that the concept of *qi* covers the entire spectrum of body, mind, and spirit. As Benjamin Schwartz has put it, "*qi* comes to embrace properties which we would call psychic, emotional, spiritual, numinous, and even 'mystical.'"[34] The *qi* that constitutes the mind is pure and invisible and circulates throughout the body, residing primarily in the heart.[35] This *qi* (like all *qi*) is inherently dynamic and is informed by *li*, or principle, which is to say that it is *ordered*. Thinking is the "movement of the mind" (*Zhuzi quanshu*, 15:6b); knowledge of external things involves the outflowing of mind-*qi* from the body to the thing, where it penetrates (*tong*) the thing and conforms itself to its principle or inherent order. This is the aspect of the cognitive process by which the mind is said to "respond to things" (*ying wu*) after being "stimulated" (*gan*) by them, and to "fully realize the principles of things" (*qiong li*).[36] According to Zhu Xi, "The learning of the Sages is to base one's mind on fully investigating principle, and to accord or conform with principle by responding to things."[37]

The distinctive feature of mind-*qi* is that, because of its exceptional purity and refinement, it is capable of conforming itself or "responding" to any *li*, thus becoming further ordered, or ordered in greater detail, or on a higher level of complexity. Knowledge of a particular principle, then, is the ordering or conforming of mind-*qi* to that principle, so that when a principle is known it is concretely embodied by the mind. That is, when mind penetrates and responds (or conforms) to the order or principle of a thing, the mind itself is transformed in the process. This is how mind-*qi*, or the physical nature, is transformed by learning. The extent of this capability in a particular person depends on the degree of purity or clarity of his or her mind-*qi*. Thus, while every person is theoretically capable of achieving the spiritual clarity (*shenming*) of mind that characterizes a sage (and a very few are even born with it[38]), differences in endowments of *qi* result in differences in the likelihood of achieving it.

Zhang Zai, the source of much of this theory, said:

> By enlarging one's mind one can enter into all things in the world. As long as anything is not yet entered into, there is still something outside the mind. . . . The mind that leaves something outside is not capable of uniting itself with the mind of Heaven. Knowledge coming from seeing and hearing is knowledge obtained through interaction with things. . . .[39]

Zhu Xi, commenting on this passage, interpreted *ti wu* (enter into things) as the mind flowing out of the body to penetrate external things:

> "Enter into" (*ti*) is like humanity (*ren*) entering into all things with nothing left out. It refers to the principle of the mind circulating [as if] through the interpenetrating [network of] arteries and veins so that nothing is not reached. If one thing is not yet entered into, then there is a place not reached and the inclusion is incomplete. This means that there is something outside the mind. If there are selfish wishes separating the self and things into opposing positions, then even the utmost intimacy will not necessarily be capable of including everything.
>
> *Question* on the meaning of *ti* (enter into). *Reply:* This is to place the mind within a thing, to dig into and perceive its principle. Its meaning in the case of "investigating things and extending knowledge" is not the same as the *ti* of *ti-yong* (substance and function).[40]

When the mind's capacity for psychophysical intercourse with things—its ability to penetrate, enter into, or pervade things, even in some cases the minds of others[41]—is developed to the highest degree, it is called "spiritual" (*shen*), or "spiritual clarity" (*shenming*). Thus Zhu Xi said:

> Mind is human spiritual clarity (*shenming*). It is that by which one embodies the multitudinous principle and responds (*ying*) to the myriad phenomena. (*Sishu jizhu* 7:1a)[42]

Mind endows a person with "spiritual clarity" when its *qi* is purified enough to be able to penetrate all things and to conform, respond, or resonate with their principles. *Shen* in this sense is the finest, most free-flowing *qi*, with the capacity for unlimited responsiveness and penetration. The potential to be *shen* is inherent in all *qi*, but in humans it functions most clearly in the mind of the sage.

Returning now to the mind of the ordinary person, let us see how our formulation of mental activity applies to Zhu Xi's well-known "supplement" to the *Great Learning*'s section on "investigating things and extending knowledge," in which he describes what is often called the Neo-Confucian experience of enlightenment:

> "The extension of knowledge consists in the investigation of things" means: If we wish to extend our personal knowledge, it consists in contacting things and fully investigating their principle. No human consciousness is without knowledge, and nothing in the world is without principle. It is only because there are principles not yet investigated that a person's knowledge is incomplete. For this reason the *Great Learning*'s first instruction is that it is necessary to have the student contact all things in the world. By basing [this contact] on the principles already known, none will fail to increase and complete [his knowledge], and so to seek to reach its ultimate limit. When he reaches the point where he has exerted effort for a long time, one day [everything] will suddenly interpenetrate (*guantong*). Then the external and internal, subtle and gross [qualities] of all things will be apprehended, and there will be no unclarity in the total substance and great functioning of our mind.[43] This is called the investigation of things. This is called the perfection of knowledge. (*Daxue zhangju* [in *Sishu jizhu*] 5a)[44]

Elsewhere Zhu Xi describes the sudden "interpenetration" or "thorough comprehension" of all the aspects of principle one has gradually and laboriously come to know as a "liberating" event (*Zhu wengong wenji*, 15:14b), a "spontaneous awakening" requiring no effort (*Jinsi lu jizhu*, 3:13a),[45] a "broad interpenetration" by which one "increases to the limit" the principle contained in the mind (*Zhu wengong wenji*, 67:19a),[46] and a "sudden bursting open into a spontaneous penetration" (*Zhuzi quanshu*, 6:17a).

In terms of the model described above, this can be understood as the progressive conforming of mind-*qi* to the order or principles embodied in the things contacted by the mind. When the final connection or inference is made, a unified order instantaneously emerges, like a single piece of a jigsaw puzzle falling into place and transforming what was a chaotic jumble of forms into a coherent image.

This final step is more than a quantitative accretion of knowledge; it is a qualitative transformation of consciousness—an enlightenment experience —in two ways. First, whenever a new cognition results in the apprehension of a principle of a higher order of generality or abstraction, we can say that on that higher level there has been a transformation of disorder (or chaos) into order (as suggested by the jigsaw puzzle analogy above). This would apply to intermediate levels of awareness as well as to the final state described by Zhu Xi.

Second, the experience is, as Zhu Xi describes it, a "liberating" event in which the final obstruction to one's psychophysical interpenetration with all things falls away. This freedom implies a moral transformation, for the absence of blockage in one's physical nature, with the moral nature no longer obscured, means that one is free of partiality and selfishness. This is not a freedom *from* worldly cares, but a freedom *to* participate in the cosmos—"to assist in the transforming and nourishing processes of Heaven and earth" (*Zhongyong* 22)—without sacrificing (in fact, to the contrary, fulfilling) one's essential humanity. It is an existential freedom that fulfills, rather than transcends, morality; the freedom described by Confucius when he said, "At seventy, I could follow what my heart desired without overstepping the rules" (*Analects* 2:4).

What Zhu Xi has described is an enlightenment experience and a soteriological act brought about by mental effort[47]—although the final step occurs effortlessly and cannot be willfully attained ("if you try to rush it, you will not achieve it" [*Jinsi lu jizhu*, 3:3a]). The result is a kind of spiritual unification of the fundamental polarities that constitute (in Zhu Xi's thought) the human being: nature and feelings (*xing/qing*), moral mind and human mind (*daoxin/renxin*).[48] One of the symbols of that unification is the sage.

Spirit and Sagehood (*sheng*)

On this fourth level of discourse, the *Yijing* and Zhou Dunyi again provide the source texts on which Zhu Xi constructs his synthesis. The *Xici* appendix to the *Yijing*, in a passage explaining the oracular function of the text, says:

The *Yi* does not think and does not [deliberately] act (*wusi wuwei*). Silent and inactive, when stimulated it then penetrates all situations under Heaven. If it were not the most spiritual (*shen*) thing under Heaven, how would it be capable of doing this? (*Xici* A.10.4; *Zhouyi benyi* 3:12b)

The *Yi* as an oracle is "spiritual" in part because of its transcendence of the ordinary conditions of temporality and causality. But this mysterious oracular ability is a form of *knowing*, and in that sense the *Yi* can be compared to the human mind. Thus Zhu Xi, commenting on the passage, says, "The mystery of the human mind, in its activity and stillness, is also like this" (*Zhouyi benyi* 3:13a). And the same passage is the basis for section 4 of Zhou Dunyi's *Tongshu*, which discusses Sagehood. Here is that section, with some of Zhu Xi's comments:[49]

4.a. That which is "silent and inactive" is authenticity (*cheng*). That which "penetrates when stimulated" is spirit (*shen*). That which is active but not yet formed, between existence and nonexistence, is incipient (*ji*).[50]

   [Zhu's comment on the second sentence:] That which is aptly responsive yet unfathomable is the functioning of the actualized order (*shili*).

  b. Authenticity is essential (*jing*) and therefore clear (*ming*). Spirit is responsive, and therefore mysterious. Incipience is subtle, and therefore obscure.

   [Zhu's comment:] To be clear and bright in body, with a will like that of a spirit, is to be "essential" and "clear." "To hurry without haste, to arrive without going" (*Xici* A.10.6; *Zhouyi benyi* 3:13a) is to be "responsive" and "mysterious." Although [in incipience] the order (*li*) has already developed, events are not yet apparent; they are "subtle" and "obscure."

  c. One who is authentic, spiritual, and incipient is called a sage.

   [Zhu comments:] If one is "by nature like this, at ease like this,"[51] then one is essential and clear, responsive and mysterious, and has the means to see into the obscure and subtle.

Spirit is associated here with the penetrating and responsive qualities of mind and *qi* that, when developed in a human being to the highest degree, produce the seemingly miraculous or numinous phenomena that are commonly associated with gods and spirits. In a conversation between Zhu and his students about Zhou's use of the term *shen* there is the following exchange:

Question: Does "spirit" refer to the mysterious? *Reply:* Yes. There is also the line, "That which 'penetrates when stimulated' is spirit." Hengqu [Zhang Zai] explained spirit in another way, referring to that which is in two places [at once] and therefore cannot be fathomed, indicating [the processes of] creative transformation. He said, "Suddenly here, suddenly there: it is spirit." *Question:* How do you speak of it within human beings? *Reply:* Consciousness (*zhijue*) is certainly spirit. If you cut your hand then your hand perceives pain. If you cut your foot then your foot perceives pain. This is certainly spirit. "Spirit is responsive, and therefore mysterious."

And in reference to his own written commentary on the middle paragraph of *Tongshu* 4 (above), Zhu says:

"A will like that of a spirit" is precisely the Way of perfect authenticity (*cheng*), the idea that one can have foreknowledge (*qianzhi*). (*Zhou Lianxi ji*, 5:19a)

This is an allusion to *Zhongyong* 24, which says:

It is characteristic of absolute authenticity to be able to foreknow.... Therefore one who has absolute authenticity is like a spirit. (*Zhongyong zhangju* [in *Sishu jizhu*] 17a–b)

Shen is thus a cosmological-psychological category that describes the infinite mutability, sensitivity, and responsiveness of *qi* in general, especially in processes that seem to defy the laws of cause and effect. *Shen* also applies to such mysterious epistemological phenomena as divination and precognition. Again, the *Xici* says:

The virtue of the milfoil [stalks used in *Yijing* divination] is round and spiritual; the virtue of the hexagrams is square and wise; the meanings of the six lines change in order to inform. With these the Sage purifies his mind and retires into secrecy. He suffers good fortune and misfortune in common with the people. Being spiritual, he knows the future. Being wise, he stores up the past. Who is comparable to this? [It was] the ancients, with broad intelligence and astute wisdom; those who were spiritually martial and yet non-violent.

Zhu Xi comments:

"Round and spiritual" means the unboundedness of transformation. "Square and wise" means that things have definite principles. ... The Sage concretely embodies the virtues of the three [milfoil, hexagrams, and lines], without the slightest worldly tie. When there is nothing happening, then his mind is silent, and no one can see it. When there is something happening, then the operation of his spiritual understanding responds when stimulated. This means he knows good fortune and misfortune without divination. "Spiritually martial and yet non-violent" means he apprehends principle without recourse to things. (*Xici* A.11.2; *Zhouyi beny*, 3:13b)

The sage, by virtue of his spirituality, can spontaneously respond to the incipient signs of good fortune and misfortune or the subtle tendencies of events and can thus know their direction of change without using divination. This understanding is nonempirical in that it does not depend on prior exposure to things. He has the ability to transcend the usual limitations of cause and effect, for example: "To hurry without haste, to arrive without going" (A.10.6), and to know the future. In this way he is "like a spirit"—or a god (both *shen*).

The belief that any person is at least theoretically capable of becoming a sage dates to Mencius (2A:2; 6A:7). How to become a sage is the basic problematic of Neo-Confucianism. In the Cheng-Zhu school it was often stated in terms of the relationship of the "moral mind" (*daoxin*)—the clear understanding of the natural/moral order that is inherent in every person—and the "human mind" (*renxin*)—the actual functioning of the embodied mind, normally clouded by human desires. Let us look more closely now at that relationship, as Zhu Xi discussed it in the preface to his commentary on the *Zhongyong* ("Centrality and Commonality"):

> Why was the *Zhongyong* written? It was written because of Master Zisi's concern that the propagation of the learning of the Way might be lost. The propagation of the succession of the Way (*daotong*) began with the Sage-spirits of high antiquity, who "succeeded Heaven" and established the Ultimate. . . . "The human mind is precarious; the moral mind is subtle. Be refined, be singleminded, and sincerely hold fast to the Mean" is how Shun passed it [the Way] on to Yu. . . .[52]
>
> The mind's pure consciousness (*xuling zhijue*) is simply one. Yet there is a difference between the human mind and the moral mind: the one arises from the selfishness of tangible *qi*, and the other originates in the correctness of human nature's endowment. . . .[53] No person lacks this tangible form, so no matter how wise they are, no one can be without the human mind. And no person lacks this human nature, so no matter how dull they are, no one can be without the moral mind. As the two are mixed in the square inch [of the heart], if we do not know how to govern them, then . . . the impartiality of the natural order [or Heavenly principle] will have no way of overcoming the selfishness of human desire.
>
> "Refinement" means to reflect on the difference between the two and not to confuse them. "Singlemindedness" means to protect the correctness of the original mind and not to depart from it. If one manages one's affairs like this, without the briefest interruption, this will certainly cause the moral mind always to be the master of the self, and the human mind always to hear the decree from it [i.e. to do what is right]. (*Zhongyong zhangju xu* [in *Sishu jizhu*] 1a–b)

Careful distinction must first be made between the two aspects of the mind, but eventually the distinction is transcended. No fundamental dualism is implied by the "mastery" exerted by the moral mind over the human mind, for it is "an all-pervading control and command existing in the mind itself" (*Zhuzi quanshu*, 45:4b);[54] that is, it is an inherent quality or capacity of the mind. Furthermore:

> When one takes the moral mind as master, then the human mind will be transformed into the moral mind. (*Zhu wengong wenji*, 51)[55]

> When the individual mind is rectified, it will be none other than the mind of the Sage and Heaven-and-earth. (*Zhu wengong wenji*, 42)[56]

By first distinguishing the moral mind from the human mind one learns to recognize in oneself that which is identical with the ultimate reality, and one finds that it is nothing other than the principle of the mind, or human nature. Fundamentally there is only one mind-stuff, which can manifest its principle in varying degrees:

> Mind is unitary. When it is held and preserved, then moral principle is illuminated and we call it the moral mind. When it is let go and lost, then material desires are indulged and we call it the human mind. To be "lost" is not to be non-existent; it is just to go out [uncontrollably] after external things. When the human mind is recovered it is the moral mind. When the moral mind is abandoned it is the human mind. (*Zhu wengong wenji*, 40)[57]

Thus, a characteristic of the mind of the sage is its ability not to allow external stimuli to deflect it from its inherent nature. Its responses to stimuli are always perfectly appropriate to the situation and morally correct. For example, emotions such as anger or joy are not to be avoided, rather:

> When one becomes angry at the right time, he will be acting in the proper degree. When the matter is over, anger disappears, and none of it will be retained. (*Zhuzi quanshu*, 45:15a)[58]

The sage neither injects private dispositions into a situation, nor retains any residue of the situation in his mind once it is past; thus things are perceived as they are, without prejudice. In this respect the mind of the sage, being a fully realized expression of the moral principle of human nature, is equivalent to the "mind of Heaven-and-earth," that is, the same moral order inherent in the natural world. As Cheng Hao said in his well-known "Letter on Stabilizing Human Nature" to his uncle, Zhang Zai:

> The constant principle of Heaven-and-earth is that its mind pervades innumerable things, and yet it has no mind of its own. The constant principle of the Sage is that his dispositions (*qing*) follow the innumerable phenomena, and yet he has no dispositions of his own. Therefore, in the education of the superior person (*junzi*) there is nothing like being completely broad and

impartial, and responding in accordance with things as they come. (*Mingdao wenji* 3:1a–b)[59]

Zhu Xi comments on this:

> "Pervading innumerable things" and "following innumerable phenomena" mean that the Sage is "completely impartial" toward things. "Having no mind and no dispositions" means that the Sage is able "to respond in accordance with things as they come." (*Zhuzi quanshu* 45:13b)[60]

Correlating Cheng Hao's terminology with that of the *Yijing* (*Xici* A.10.4), Zhu says:

> "Extremely broad and impartial" means "completely silent and inactive." "Responding in accordance with things as they come" means "stimulated and then penetrating." (*Zhuzi quanshu* 45:13a)[61]

By using the terminology of the *Yijing* and Zhou Dunyi's *Tongshu* to explain Cheng Hao's description of the sage, Zhu Xi is drawing attention to the notion that the characteristics of the human mind are also characteristics of the spiritual aspects of *qi* itself. This is, of course, a way of legitimizing the Confucian understanding of human values. But it also provides a philosophical basis for the Confucian belief that the human mind, simply by perfecting its natural, ordinary mode of functioning, can achieve a spiritual interpenetration with all-under-Heaven.

Spirit or spirituality, then, is the quality that enables the mind of the sage to penetrate even the most mysterious things, to detect even the most subtle principles and incipient changes, and to comprehend the totality of the natural/moral order (*tianli/daoli*). While most people will never actually become sages, they can, by cultivating the "spiritual clarity" (*shenming*) of their minds, transform themselves and those around them, thereby manifesting the creative principle of the cosmos and helping to actualize its moral potential.

Conclusions

We have located Neo-Confucian spirituality on a number of levels. First, there are certain continuities between Neo-Confucian thought and popular ideas of ghosts and spirits and practices related to them. The most significant of these from the perspective of the basic Neo-Confucian project is ancestor worship. But underlying both ancestor worship and the acceptance by Neo-Confucians of the existence of ghosts, demons, and other occult (*yin*) phenomena is a systematic theory of mind and *qi* that provides for what we might call "emergent spirituality." By this I mean

that "spirit" is an inherent characteristic of *qi* that is expressed or manifested only at the highest level of purity. It is found both in nature and in
human beings. In nature it is observable only in the most subtle processes,
where it accounts for continuity and responsiveness where no empirical
mechanism is observable:

> The unfathomability of *yin* and *yang* is called spirit. (*Xici* A.5.9; *Zhouyi benyi*
> 3:6a)

> *Qi* has [the two modes] *yin* and *yang*. When it proceeds slowly, it is transfor-
> mation (*hua*). When it is unified and unfathomable, it is spirit.[62]

> Spirit is responsive, and therefore mysterious.[63]

In human beings, spirit is a quality of mind—specifically mind-*qi* in its
finest, most free-flowing state—which accounts for the capacity of the
human mind to penetrate, respond to, and conform itself to the most subtle aspects of the natural/moral order. To embody this epistemological
potential—so that the "human mind" embodies the "moral mind"—is to
actualize the principle (*shi li*) of being human, which is to be a fully authentic (*cheng*) human being, a sage.[64] Although all people have the moral mind
inherent in them, and therefore have the potential to become sages, very
few actually do. Only sages have minds that can penetrate and comprehend
the totality of the natural/moral order. This ability also gives them "talents," such as precognition, that make them appear "like spirits" to ordinary people.

Nevertheless, the chief significance of spirit and spirituality in Neo-
Confucianism is not a transcendence of the natural order but a continuity
with it. The epistemological function of spirit is what gives it its "soteriological" function.[65] Spirit, or spirituality, is the perfection of human understanding—*ordinary* human understanding. That is, the natural capacities of
the human mind, when perfected, give one the spiritual characteristics of a
sage. Thus, every person is a potential sage; self-transformation is self-
realization; the capacity to *transcend* one's given condition or endowment
is *immanent*. By "knowing one's mind" and "knowing one's nature," any
human being can come to "serve Heaven" (*Mencius* 7A:1). By actualizing
the principle of being human—that is, being "authentic" (*cheng*) and "real"
(*shi*)—one can "assist in the transforming and nourishing process of Heaven
and Earth" and "form a trinity with Heaven and earth" (*Zhongyong* 22).

Frederick Streng's definition of religion as "a means to ultimate transformation" has been used by many scholars of East Asian religions, as it
focuses on an aspect of religion that is particularly prominent there. "Ulti-

mate transformation" implies (1) a given human condition that is in some way flawed, unsatisfactory, or caught in a dilemma; (2) a goal that posits a resolution of that problem or dilemma; and (3) a process leading toward the achievement of the goal. The qualifier "ultimate" means that the starting point, process, and goal are defined in relation to whatever the tradition in question believes to be absolute or unconditioned.

Confucianism clearly fits this definition of religion. The unsatisfactory human condition is that the Way "does not prevail" (*Analects* 18:6): individuals fail to realize their true natures, leaders fail to set moral examples, and societies fail to provide nourishing environments in which people can cultivate their moral potentials. The goal is sagehood for the individual, humane government, and peace throughout the world. The process is self-cultivation, education, public work, and responsibility for the larger social and natural environment.[66]

Every religious tradition, it would seem, has a central problem or dilemma analogous to this. The ultimate referents differ, the formulations of the initial problem differ, and so on. But ultimate transformation of some sort seems to be universal.

Still, not all religious behavior fits clearly into this model. Ordinary popular worship at a local shrine or temple, for example, may only indirectly be understood—by the worshiper or by an observer—as involving an ultimate transformation. What it does clearly involve, however, is *orientation* to the ultimate. Devotional religion—which is often expressed in petitions for rather mundane goods—is a way of locating oneself in a meaningful cosmos, orienting oneself to an absolute frame of reference, and *participating* in a life that is felt to be real.[67] These are all ways in which human beings define themselves and construct their worlds.

The Confucian worldview, despite its intellectual and social distance from Chinese popular religion, concerns ultimate orientation just as much as ultimate transformation. Its *axis mundi*, the central connection between the human realm and the absolute realm that provides a point of orientation and an anchorage to something deemed to be ultimately real, is the relationship between Heaven and human beings, expressed in many different ways: "Heaven and humanity are one,"[68] "Heaven produced the virtue in me" (*Analects* 7:22), "What is given by Heaven is human nature" (*Zhongyong* 1), and so on.

By focusing on the various levels of "spirit" in Neo-Confucian discourse, particularly its epistemological function and its role in self-cultivation, we have drawn attention to some of the ways in which the human realm (mind, moral values, etc.) and the Heavenly realm (in this context both the natural world and the metaphysical principle by which it is ordered) are intimately connected in this tradition. Indeed, the function of spirituality as a human faculty here is precisely to illuminate and to facilitate those connections. By illuminating the immanent order of Heaven, earth, and humanity, the "spiritual clarity" of the human mind *orients* humanity in relation to the unconditioned reality of Heaven. And the very process of illuminating, responding to, and nourishing the linkages among the natural world, the human world, and their metaphysical basis is what constitutes ultimate transformation in the Neo-Confucian tradition.

Notes

1. See Benjamin I. Schwartz, *The World of Thought in Ancient China*, 179–84.
2. Ibid., 181–82.
3. See Stephen Teiser's brief discussion in his "Introduction" to *Religions of China in Practice*, ed. Donald S. Lopez, Jr. (Princeton, N.J.: Princeton University Press, 1996), 32–36.
4. See Valerie Hansen, *Changing Gods in Medieval China, 1127–1276*, chs. 1–2.
5. See Rudolf Otto, *The Idea of the Holy*, trans. John W. Harvey, 2nd ed. (New York: Oxford University Press, 1950). Some have used "numen" (the root of "numinous") to translate *shen*, since the numen in ancient Rome was a local spirit very much like a local god in China or a *kami* in Japan, both of which are denoted by the word *shen*. See, e.g., Harold D. Roth, "The Early Taoist Concept of *Shen*: A Ghost in the Machine?" in *Sagehood and Systematizing Thought in Warring States and Han China*, ed. Kidder Smith, Jr. (Brunswick, Me.: Asian Studies Program, Bowdoin College, 1990), 11–32; and idem, "The Inner Cultivation Tradition of Early Daoism," in *Religions of China in Practice*, ed. Lopez, 123–48. I find that using "the Numen" in reference to a general quality of *qi* in the human body and mind—as *shen* is used in Neo-Confucian discourse—does not convey enough meaning in English to be worthwhile. It also misleadingly suggests an elemental substance instead of a mode or quality of *qi*.
6. "Means to ultimate transformation" is Frederick J. Streng's definition of religion, in *Understanding Religious Life*, 3rd ed. (Belmont: Wadsworth, 1985), 2. I believe that this definition becomes more inclusive and in the present case illuminates another significant feature of Neo-Confucian spirituality if we add to it "ultimate orientation," a point that will be developed in the concluding section of this essay. Nevertheless, I do not believe that we must have a single, all-inclusive "definition" of such a complex set of phenomena as that which we associate with the concept of religion. "Open," rather than exclusive, definitions are appropriate to the subject. See W. Richard Comstock, "Toward Open Definitions of Religion," *Journal of the American Academy of Religion* 52, no. 3 (1984): 499–517. Note also that Ninian Smart would eschew definitions of religion altogether because of the danger of essentialism (*Dimensions of the Sacred: An Anatomy of the World's Beliefs* [Berkeley: University of California Press, 1996]).

7. Citations will be to the Taiwan reprint of the Siku quanshu edition (Taibei: Commercial Press, 1986), volume 710.

8. *Xingli daquan shu*, 28:13a, p. 614; also *Zhuzi yulei* [Master Zhu's Classified Conversations], comp. Li Jingde (1270; repr., Beijing: Zhonghua shuju, 1986), 3:37.

9. G. S. Kirk and J. E. Raven, *The Pre-Socratic Philosophers* (Cambridge: Cambridge University Press, 1971), 143–62.

10. See Joseph A. Adler, "Zhou Dunyi: The Metaphysics and Practice of Sagehood," in *Sources of Chinese Tradition*, 2nd ed., ed. Wm. Theodore de Bary and Irene Bloom (New York: Columbia University Press, 1998), ch. 20.

11. He is one of the heroes of the much-loved historical novel *Sanguo yanyi* [Tale of the Three Kingdoms] and is worshiped as Guangong or Guandi.

12. *Zheng-meng* [Correcting Youthful Ignorance], in *Zhangzi quanshu* [Zhang Zai's Complete Writings] (Sibu beiyao ed.), section 10; cf. Wing-tsit Chan, trans. and comp., *A Source Book in Chinese Philosophy* (Princeton, N.J.: Princeton University Press, 1963), 505; quoted frequently, e.g., by Chen Chun in *Xingli daquan shu*, 28:6a, p. 611. Chen explains *liang-neng* as "the spontaneous ability of the two [modes of] *qi* to expand and contract, or go and come" (ibid.)—that is, the inherent dynamism of *qi*. See also Ch'en Ch'un, *Neo-Confucian Terms Explained: The Pei-hsi tzu-i*, trans. Wing-tsit Chan (New York: Columbia University Press, 1986), 143.

13. *Yichuan Yizhuan* [Cheng Yi's Commentary on the *Yijing*] (Congshu jicheng ed.), 2, p. 82; and *Er Cheng quanshu* (Sibu beiyao ed.), 1:7b. Cheng had also referred to *gui* and *shen* as "functions of Heaven and earth" (quoted by Zhu Xi, *Zhongyong zhangju* in *Sishu jizhu* [Sibu beiyao ed.], p.8b), and "products of the creative process" (*Xingli daquan shu*, 28:1a, p. 608).

14. Zhu Xi, *Zhouyi benyi* [The Original Meaning of the *Yijing*] (1177; repr., Taibei: Hualian, 1978), 1:9a, comment on *Wenyan*, hexagram 1.

15. *Xingli daquan shu*, 28:6a, p. 611; cf. *Neo-Confucian Terms Explained*, p. 143. Daniel K. Gardner has thoroughly documented Zhu Xi's beliefs on *gui-shen* in "Ghosts and Spirits in the Sung Neo-Confucian World: Chu Hsi on *Kuei-shen*," *Journal of the American Oriental Society* 115, no. 4 (1995): 598–611, where he places them under three categories: (1) contractive and expansive forces, (2) ghosts, monsters, and spirits, and (3) ancestral spirits. See also Gardner's "Zhu Xi on Spirit Beings," in *Religions of China in Practice*, ed. Lopez, 106–19.

16. See, e.g., Wang Chong, *Lun Heng* [Balanced Essays] (Sibu beiyao ed.), 20:9b, and Zhu Xi, *Zhouyi benyi*, 3:4b.

17. *Xingli daquan shu*, 28:2a, p. 609, and *Zhuzi quanshu* [Zhu Xi's 'Complete Writings'], comp. Li Guangdi (1713; rpt. Taibei: Guangxue, 1977), 51.2b.

18. Trans. Chan, *Source Book*, 644.

19. Zhu's comment on *Analects* 7:20.

20. Trans. Gardner, "Ghosts and Spirits in the Sung Neo-Confucian World," 605–6 (slightly modified).

21. See, e.g., David K. Jordan, *Gods, Ghosts, and Ancestors: Folk Religion in a Taiwanese Village* (Berkeley: University of California Press, 1972), 31–33.

22. Paraphrasing Zhou Dunyi's *Taijitu shuo*.

23. See next section for the passage in which this line occurs and Zhu Xi's commentary on it.

24. Although *xu* is more literally translated as "empty," I use "pure" here, in the sense of "pure consciousness" (i.e., consciousness without an object), which conveys a clearer and more appropriate meaning in this context.

25. See Kristofer Schipper, *The Taoist Body* (Berkeley: University of California Press, 1993); *Taoist Meditation and Longevity Techniques*, ed. Livia Kohn (Ann Arbor: University of Michigan Center for Chinese Studies 1989); Harold D. Roth, "Psychology and Self-Cultivation in Early Taoistic Thought," in *Harvard Journal of Asiatic Studies* 51, no. 2 (1991): 599–650.

26. Although these are simply folk etymologies based on homonyms for *gui* and *shen*, note the similarity to the French word for ghost, *revenant* ("returner").

27. See Zhou's *Taijitu shuo* and *Tongshu*, ch. 16.

28. See Kidder Smith, Jr., Peter K. Bol, Joseph A. Adler, and Don J. Wyatt, *Sung Dynasty Uses of the I Ching* (Princeton, N.J.: Princeton University Press, 1990), chs. 6-7. The *Xici* was originally a separate text dating probably to the early Han, with close affinities to the last few chapters of the *Zhuangzi*. See Gerald Swanson, "The Concept of Change in the *Great Treatise*," in Henry Rosemont, Jr., ed., *Explorations in Early Chinese Cosmology* (Chico, Calif.: Scholars Press, 1984); and Willard Peterson, "Making Connections: 'Commentary on the Attached Verbalizations' of the *Book of Change*," *Harvard Journal of Asiatic Studies* 42 (1982): 67–116.

29. Joseph A. Adler, "Zhou Dunyi: The Metaphysics and Practice of Sagehood," in *Sources of Chinese Tradition*, 2nd ed., ed. de Bary and Bloom, ch. 20.

30. Cf. *Analects* 15:28: "Humans can broaden the Way; it is not the Way that broadens humans."

31. Zhang Zai, *Zhengmeng*, ch.6, in *Zhangzi quanshu* (Sibu beiyao ed.), 2:18b-19a. Cf. Chan, *Source Book*, 511.

32. See Wing-tsit Chan, "The Neo-Confucian Solution to the Problem of Evil," in *Studies Presented to Hu Shih on his Sixty-fifth Birthday* (Bulletin of the Institute of History and Philology, Academia Sinica, 28 (1957), 773–91. Reprinted in *Neo-Confucianism, Etc.: Essays by Wing-tsit Chan*, comp. Charles K. H. Chen (Hanover, N.H.: Oriental Society, 1969), 88–116; and Tang Junyi, "Chang Tsai's Theory of Mind and Its Metaphysical Basis," *Philosophy East & West* 6 (1956): 113–36.

33. Zhang Zai, *Yulu*, in *Zhangzi quanshu* (Sibu beiyao ed.), 12:3a. Trans. Chan, *Source Book*, 516.

34. Schwartz, *World of Thought in Ancient China*, 181.

35. See *Zhuzi quanshu*, 44:4a; Kim Yung Sik, "The World-View of Chu Hsi (1130–1200): Knowledge About Natural World in Chu Tzu Ch'üan-shu" (Ph.D. diss., Princeton University, 1980); and Hidemi Ishida, "Body and Mind: The Chinese Perspective," in *Taoist Meditation and Longevity Techniques*, ed. Livia Kohn, 41–72.

36. This is the meaning of "investigating things" (*gewu*), according to Zhu Xi (*Daxue zhangju* [in *Sishu jizhu*], 2a).

37. *Zhu Wengong wenji* (Sibu beiyao edition, entitled *Zhuzi daquan*), 67:19b ("Treatise on the Examination of the Mind"). Cf. Chan, *Source Book*, 604.

38. See Zhu Xi, "Notes on the rebuilding of Master [Zhou] Lianxi's library in Jiangzhou," *Zhu Wengong wenji* (Sibu beiyao ed.), 78:12a–13a, where he makes this claim in regard to Zhou Dunyi (p. 12b).

39. Zhang Zai, *Zhengmeng* [Correcting Youthful Ignorance], ch. 7, loc. cit., 2:21a. Trans. Chan, *Source Book*, 515, substituting "interaction" for "contact" in the last sentence.

40. Ibid., 2:21b. Cf. Chan, *Source Book*, 629; *Zhuzi quanshu*, 28:13a–b (Zhu Xi's comments on *Yijing, Wenyan, Qian*/1: "The superior person embodies humanity"); and ibid., 44:11b–12b. See also Tu Weiming, "'Inner Experience': The Basis of Creativity in Neo-Confucian Thinking," in *Humanity and Self-Cultivation: Essays in Confucian Thought* (Berkeley: Asian Humanities Press, 1979), 103–4, for a discussion of various uses of the word *ti* in the sense "to embody."

41. Kim Yung Sik, "World-View of Chu Hsi," 318–19.

42. Comment on *Mencius* 7A:1.

43. For a discussion of "total substance and great functioning," see Okada Takehiko, "Practical Learning in the Zhu Xi School: Yamazaki Ansai and Kaibara Ekken," in *Principle and Practicality*, ed. Wm. Theodore de Bary and Irene Bloom (New York: Columbia University Press, 1979), 281.

44. For a full discussion of Zhu Xi's use of the *Great Learning*, see Daniel K. Gardner, *Chu Hsi and the Ta-hsueh: Neo-Confucian Reflection on the Confucian Canon* (Cambridge, Mass.: Harvard University Council on East Asian Studies, 1986).

45. Collected Comments on *Reflections on Things at Hand* (Sibu beiyao ed.).

46. Chan, *Source Book*, 604.

47. In this respect it differs from Chan/Zen Buddhist enlightenment (*wu*, or *satori*).

48. The possibility of such unification is based on the premise that *li* and *qi*, although ontologically distinct, are never separate in their actual existence; there has never existed *li* without *qi*, and vice versa; *li* is the order of *qi*, and *qi* is the "container" or substrate in which *li* becomes manifest. See *Xingli daquan shu*, ch. 26 , and *Zhuzi yulei*, ch. 1.

49. *Zhou Lianxi xiansheng quanji* [Zhou Dunyi's Collected Works], comp. Zhang Boxing (1708; reprinted in *Zhengyi tang quanshu* [Baibu congshu jicheng ed.]), 5:17b–18a. Hereafter cited as *Zhou Lianxi ji*. For further discussion of this section, see Joseph A. Adler, "Response and Responsibility: Chou Tun-i and Confucian Resources for Environmental Ethics," in *Confucianism and Ecology: The Interrelation of Heaven, Earth, and Humans*, ed. Mary Evelyn Tucker and John Berthrong (Cambridge, Mass.: Harvard University Center for the Study of World Religions, 1998).

50. For a discussion of "incipience" in Zhu Xi's thought, see Smith et al., *Sung Dynasty Uses of the I Ching*, 190–99.

51. Quoting the previous section of the *Tongshu*.

52. See *Shujing*, trans. Legge, *The Chinese Classics*, 3:61–62. Shun and Yu are two of the sage-kings who, in Confucian myth, established the tradition of benevolent rulership.

53. Alluding to the first line of the *Zhongyong*, "What is endowed [or 'given'] (*ming*) by Heaven is human nature."

54. Trans. Chan, *Source Book*, 631.

55. Quoted by Qian Mu, *Zhuzi xin xue'an* [A New Scholarly Record of Zhu Xi] (Taibei: San Min Book Co., 1971), 2:114.

56. Quoted in ibid., 2:104.

57. Quoted in ibid., 2:115. The idea of "recovering" and "abandoning" the mind comes from Mencius 6A:11: "The Way of learning is none other that seeking for the abandoned mind."

58. Trans. Chan, *Source Book*, 632. See also Fung Yu-lan, *A History of Chinese Philosophy* (Princeton, N.J.: Princeton University Press, 1953), 2:525–26.

59. In *Er Cheng quanshu* (Sibu beiyao ed.); cf. Chan, *Source Book*, 525–26.

60. Trans. David C. Yü, "Chu Hsi's Approach to Knowledge," *Chinese Culture* 10, no.4 (1969): 11–12 (slightly modified).

61. See above, where the same terms from *Xici* A.10.4 are used by Zhou Dunyi.

62. Zhu Xi, quoting Zhang Zai, commenting on *Xici* B.5.4 (*Zhouyi benyi*, 3:21a). See also *Zhu wengong wenji*, 67:2a, "Discussion of [the terms] Essence, Fluctuation, and Spirit in the *Yi*."

63. Zhou Dunyi, *Tongshu*, sec. 4 (quoted above).

64. *Cheng*, or authenticity, is the defining characteristic of the sage, according to Zhou Dunyi (*Tongshu* 1-2). Zhu Xi defines *cheng* as "actualized principle" (*shi li*), that is, the condition in which the original human nature (*benxing*), or the principle of being human, is fully actualized or put into effect in practice. One is *cheng* when one is truly being or actively manifesting what one truly is by nature, when one is a morally actualized agent. For Zhu's definition, see *Zhou Lianxi ji*, 5:2b, 9a, 10b. For further discussion of *cheng*, see Joseph A. Adler, "Response and Responsibility: Chou Tun-i and Confucian Resources for Environmental Ethics."

65. "Soteriology" in this context is not intended literally to mean "salvation," because the religious goal in Confucianism is more a *fulfillment* of the given conditions of human life than a release from them.

66. On this last point, see Joseph A. Adler, "Response and Responsibility: Chou Tun-i and Confucian Resources for Environmental Ethics."

67. Mircea Eliade's theories of sacred space and sacred time are relevant in this respect. See, e.g., *The Sacred and the Profane* (New York: Harcourt, Brace, 1959).

68. See Julia Ching, *Mysticism and Kingship in China* (Cambridge: Cambridge University Press, 1997).

Suggested Readings

Ching, Julia. *Mysticism and Kingship in China: The Heart of Chinese Description.* Cambridge: Cambridge University Press, 1997.

Ebrey, Patricia Buckley. *Chu Hsi's Family Rituals.* Princeton, N.J.: Princeton University Press, 1991.

———. *Confucianism and Family Rituals in Imperial China: A Social History of Writing about Rites.* Princeton, N.J.: Princeton University Press, 1991.

Fingarette, Herbert. *Confucius—The Secular as Sacred.* San Francisco: Harper & Row, 1972.

Gardner, Daniel K. *Learning to Be a Sage: Selections from the Conversations of Master Chu, Arranged Topically.* Berkeley: University of California Press, 1990.

Hansen, Valerie. *Changing Gods in Medieval China, 1127–1276.* Princeton, N.J.: Princeton University Press, 1990.

Kalton, Michael C. *To Become a Sage.: The Ten Diagrams on Sage Learning by Yi T'oegye.* New York: Columbia University Press, 1988.

Schwartz, Benjamin I. *The World of Thought in Ancient China.* Cambridge, Mass.: Harvard University Press, 1985.

Smith, Kidder, Jr., Peter K. Bol, Joseph A. Adler, and Don J. Wyatt. *Sung Dynasty Uses of the I Ching.* Princeton, N.J.: Princeton University Press, 1990.

Smith, Richard J. *Fortune-Tellers and Philosophers: Divination in Traditional Chinese Society.* Boulder, Colo.: Westview Press, 1991.

Taylor, Rodney L. *The Religious Dimensions of Confucianism.* Albany: State University of New York Press, 1990.

———. *The Way of Heaven: An Introduction to the Confucian Religious Life.* Leiden: E. J. Brill, 1986.

Tucker, Mary Evelyn, and John Berthrong, eds. *Confucianism and Ecology: The Interrelation of Heaven, Earth, and Human.* Cambridge, Mass.: Harvard University Center for the Study of World Religions, 1998.

Tu Weiming. *Centrality and Commonality: An Essay on Confucian Religiousness.* Albany: State University of New York Press, 1989.

———. *Confucian Thought: Selfhood as Creative Transformation.* Albany: State University of New York Press, 1985.

———. *Humanity and Self-Cultivation: Essays in Confucian Thought.* Berkeley: Asian Humanities Press, 1979.

22

Learning to Be Human: Spiritual Exercises from Zhu Xi and Wang Yangming to Liu Zongzhou

TU WEIMING

CONFUCIUS INSISTED THAT AUTHENTIC LEARNING is for the sake of the self rather than for the sake of others; unless we take self-cultivation as the root of moral education, we cannot really help others (*Analects* 14:24). The common impression that Confucian humanism, as a form of social ethics, advocates that society (often symbolized by the family) takes precedence over the individual is clearly a misreading of the Master's message. The message of self-learning features prominently in the writings of all major Confucian thinkers; and, indeed, self-cultivation is a defining characteristic of the Confucian Way. As the *Great Learning* specifies, self-cultivation is the root of regulating the family, governing the state, and establishing world peace, and thus should be the core concern of all human beings, from the Son of Heaven to ordinary people (*Great Learning*, ch. 1). Yet this common misreading of Confucian humanism is understandable, because Confucians do view the self as a center of relationships rather than as the independent and somewhat isolated individual so frequently encountered in Western thought. The idea that Confucian self-cultivation does not lead to social service is mistaken, as is the idea that self-cultivation is a purely spiritual exercise solely aimed at one's own salvation.

Nature, Heart, and Feeling

The newly discovered bamboo strips from the tombs excavated in Hubei at Guodian, the so-called Guodian texts, clearly indicate that heart, nature, and feeling are three fundamental categories of thought in the Confucian philosophical universe.[1] Strictly speaking, not only are these categories psychological, but they also have social and religious significance.

The heart is the domain in which the conscious activity of self-cultivation takes place. The seemingly paradoxical notion that learning is the quest for the "lost heart" is tantamount to stating the obvious: self-cultivation consists of spiritual exercises of the heart.[2] In English, the classical Chinese word *xin* is often rendered as "heart-mind," since this definition highlights the importance of both its cognitive and affective dimensions. The purpose of the spiritual exercises of the heart is not only for the formation of a mental discipline. Actually, the focus is on better managing one's emotional life, such as how to deal properly with the volatile passions of anger and joy. Since this spiritual exercise of the heart necessarily involves the physical body, it may be more appropriate to conceive of it as an exercise of the "body and mind."[3] Indeed, the Confucian idea of the heart as embracing a complex notion of self-cultivation, is fruitfully ambiguous. If we probe its nuances, however, we can acquire a taste of its subtlety and its profound implications for understanding the Confucian way of learning to be human.

The question of human nature is equally complex. Mencius's assertion that human nature is good has led to the accusation that the epistemological optimism in the Confucian view of the human condition is incompatible with the post-Marxist and post-Freudian notion of the modern man. Following this line of reasoning, the Confucian belief in human perfection, in light of class analysis and psychoanalytical insight, is elitist and naïve. Yet the idea of nature, including human nature, is predicated on a sophisticated metaphysical vision that points to the uniqueness of being human. According to Confucianism, while Heaven bestows the same nature on all beings, the Mandate of Heaven obligates humans alone to realize themselves through self-effort. The ancient Chinese saying that "Heaven engenders and the human completes"[4] inspired the Confucians to envision a "covenant" between Heaven and the human. Since both are involved in a joint venture, human beings are not merely creatures, but should rather be seen as co-creators.

However, as co-creators obligated to bring to fruition what the cosmic process has initiated, human beings must of necessity form a relationship of consanguinity with other animals, birds, plants, and even rocks. This experienced sense of continuity with all other modalities of being in the universe is so widespread among humans and so much an integral part of human uniqueness that we can affirm human nature, as nature, is shared by

Heaven, Earth, and the myriad things. We may want to qualify the statement that human beings alone can realize themselves through self-effort. Animals and birds can, in principle, also learn to realize themselves. Without stretching our imagination, we can also envision plants and all other growing things as learning to become themselves. Even a piece of rock, as a particular configuration of vital energy, is constantly changing and transforming. It may not be farfetched to suggest that jade or turquoise is continuously evolving and thus developing itself. If this is true, someday science will let us see these changes. Yet, while the uniqueness of humanity lies not in its separation from but in its connectedness with all other beings in the universe, it is the human potential for full self-actualization that defines who we are. According to the strong claim of the *qi* philosophy, everything is alive and consciousness is omnipresent, but the intensity and refinement of human reflexivity for complete self-realization, either as an evolving property or as a created quality, is still unique.

Taken against the background of heart and nature, the categories of feeling and emotion are also complex. From the outset, it is important to differentiate moral sentiments such as sympathy and compassion from emotive states such as joy and anger. In simplified terms, we can define the Confucian project of self-cultivation as a dual approach to feeling: to enhance the supply of moral sentiments and to harmonize emotive states. Moral sentiments, such as commiseration, rightness, propriety, and wisdom (the famous "four seeds" in Mencius), are derived from the innate capacities such as feeling, willing, sensing, and knowing (*Mencius* 2A:6). As long as we can feel the suffering of others, are willing to improve ourselves, can sense what is appropriate and know what is right, we can fulfill the minimum requirements of being human. The quest for the lost heart is none other than the recovery of the innate capacities for human sensitivity. The harmonization of emotive states, such as joy, anger, sorrow, pleasure, love, hatred and desire (the so-called seven emotions), refers to a learned ability to transform potentially harmful energy into creative self-expression.

Self-cultivation, in sum, involves the conscientious activity of the heart; the proper mediation of feeling discloses the inner disposition of human nature. This line of thinking, often designated by Mencius as the "learning of the heart-mind" is noted for two salient features: (1) humanity and rightness (by implication, all the moral sentiments) are intrinsic qualities of human beings, and (2) the inner dispositions of human nature are manifested through the concrete activities of the heart, or, more appropriately, the heart-mind.

Zhu Xi's Meditation on Centrality and Harmony

In struggling to apply Mencius's teaching to his life and times, Zhu Xi (1130–1200) meditated on the precise relationships among heart, nature, and feeling. His famous reflection on "centrality and harmony" (zhonghe) began with the question of core identity. If, as Mencius taught, all human beings possess a core identity (centrality) that remains intact despite the "fleeting experiences" of daily existence, what kind of spiritual practice will allow us constant access to it? In Mencius's early letters to the Hunan scholars, he wrote that the enlightening ability of the heart itself guarantees that our inner core (the centrality inherent in our nature) is always accessible to us. Later he modified his view and accepted Master Cheng Yi's (1033–1107) assertion that access to our core self is not automatic; it requires self-cultivation. He also accepted Cheng Yi's admonition that we should not seek our "centrality" until we can address our feelings as they arise. The proper method of self-cultivation is not to suppress our emotions but to harmonize them as they arise. This requires constant alertness and daily practice.

Scholars in Zhu Xi's time, in their desire for ready access to the centrality that they saw as the core identity inherent in our nature, hoped to find a "simple and easy" solution to the complex issue of human existence.[5] Zhu Xi decided that this attempt to find a shortcut was incompatible with the spirit of Confucian teaching, because of the Confucian insistence that human beings engage in relationships with others and experience all aspects of daily living, a process that requires prolonged and multilayered interactions. Eventually, Zhu decided to endorse a "hard and bitter"[6] method as the most authentic Confucian approach to human existence. He made it clear that the Confucian "cultivated person" sees himself as a human being among other human beings. We can add that, unlike the Greek philosopher, the Hebrew prophet, the Christian priest, the Buddhist monk, the Hindu guru, or the Daoist master, the Confucian "cultivated person" focuses on the concerns of this world and serves primarily as teacher, bureaucrat, scholar, writer, official, clerk, or scribe as well as farmer, merchant, or soldier.

By the "hard and bitter" method, Zhu Xi meant that we must deal actively with the complexities of managing our daily life; we must reflect on the things at hand and order our conduct by establishing a systematic and programmatic routine. The challenge for full self-realization for Confucians lies in the details of our daily existence. We should learn the art of "investigating things" in order to search for each thing's inherent pattern (the principle). By encountering a variety of things through such experiences as reading a text, discussing a historical event, taking care of the elderly, instructing a student, deciding a court case, taking an examination, sending a memorial to the court, settling a dispute at home, having an intimate talk with one's spouse, or visiting a friend, our understanding of the multidimensional principle underlying each thing (affair, event, or occurrence) evolves. This empiricist approach enabled Zhu Xi to take Cheng Yi's dictum as the most balanced instruction for our conduct: "Reverence is the most efficacious way for cultivating and nurturing (our virtue); the extension of knowledge is essential for advancing learning."[7]

As a result, Zhu Xi became critical of two definitions of humanity advocated by Cheng Hao (1032–1085): sensitivity and forming one body with Heaven, Earth, and the myriad things. Zhu believed that it is not the sensitivity of the heart itself but the disciplined cultivation and appreciation of the principle inherent in the heart that really matters; it is not the grandiose vision of the unity of all things but rather the analytical understanding of the subtle differences among human beings in concrete situations that sustains human flourishing.

Zhu Xi's view of the necessity of self-cultivation for reaching one's inner core prompted a well-formed counterresponse from his contemporary, Lu Xiangshan (1139–1193). Lu insisted that by a close reading of the original text he obtained on his own what the Mencian teaching truly is.

Lu Xiangshan propounded a strong thesis that "establishing the will" (*lizhi*) is the precondition of moral self-cultivation. Underscoring Mencius's distinction between the "great body" (*dati*) and the "small body" (*xiaoti*), Lu proposed that the first task in learning to be authentically human is to establish that which is potentially "great" in us. Since the "great body" refers to the heart and the moral sentiments inherent in nature and the "small body" refers to the instinctual demands (such as desires for food and sex) that are an integral part of our emotive states, Lu insisted that, according to Mencius, the critical exercise in self-cultivation is to recognize the subtle differences between human beings and other animals.[8]

Lu's analysis was straightforward: All animals, including humans, share instincts for survival and perpetuation. Human beings alone, however, can embrace moral sentiments to give meaning to their survival and to perpetuate themselves as co-creators of the cosmic order. The uniqueness of being human lies in the seemingly "small" difference between humans and other animals. Once this "small" difference is fully recognized and vigorously cultivated, its potential can be infinitely expanded. This can help us to regulate the family, govern the state, and bring peace throughout the world.

Indeed, if we recognize the subtle difference (that makes us uniquely human) and continue to develop and extend it through constant effort, we can ultimately form one body with Heaven, Earth, and the myriad things.

Accordingly, Lu Xiangshan had serious problems with Zhu Xi's systematic and programmatic approach to learning. Lu asserted that human beings must have a sense of priority which means, specifically, first establishing the will to develop that which is great in us. If we lack this sense of priority, no matter how hard we try to investigate things and probe the principle underlying them, we will fail to embark on the right path of self-cultivation. He continued by saying that although it is important to recognize that the process of learning to be human is "hard and bitter," we must also be able to mobilize our inner resources for spiritual self-transformation. To avoid the danger of fragmentation and incoherence in our ordinary daily conduct, we should be acutely aware that we do not automatically have intimate and direct access to our inner identity. Thus, to establish the will or to identify our "great body" as the starting point on our journey of self-realization is not "hard and bitter" but "simple and easy." Indeed, the "simple and easy" way, in the long run, will endure.

Wang Yangming's Learning of the Heart

Wang Yangming (1472–1529), inspired by Lu Xiangshan's critique, insightfully elaborated on the Learning of the Heart. He first formulated the idea of the "unity of knowledge and action" as a result of his abortive attempt to acquire an experiential understanding of Zhu Xi's instruction on the investigation of things. If the investigation of things as a method of apprehending the underlying principle is simply to obtain external knowledge for its own sake, Wang queried, how is this knowledge relevant to our self-cultivation? To make learning (such as investigating the bamboo grove in front of his house) significant for self-knowledge, should there not be a prior consideration framing the intellectual enterprise in a proper context? What is knowledge for? Surely its purpose is not simply to be informed by the vicissitude of the external principles? What kind of knowledge can transform as well as inform us?

According to Wang, knowledge is not merely the consequence of knowing the results of the investigation of things, no matter how valuable and significant such information is. Surely a great deal of knowledge is essential to conduct our lives reasonably and intelligently, but the kind of knowledge that we possess as our own must be embodied in our very existence. It is not merely an internalized skill but a learned competence, indeed a cultivated quality, that defines who we are. Wang noted that we cannot have true knowledge of filial love unless we put it into practice. It is inconceivable that a filial son would not actually perform filial acts for his parents. Accomplished lute players, calligraphers, archers, or charioteers must have internalized the necessary skills to perform their art well. Furthermore, they must have mastered the skills of the art to the extent that they are enabled to become thoroughly competent in their work. Actually, their internalized skills and learned competencies fully qualify them to perform the arts in a manner fundamentally different from those who only dabble in them. Indeed, they are musicians, calligraphers, archers, or charioteers to themselves as well as to their admirers. This awareness encouraged Wang Yangming to generalize his vision of knowledge in terms of experiential understanding.

Genuine knowledge, he held, as contrasted with information (from "hearing and seeing"), is not merely to "know that" (to know about something) but also to "know how" (understanding how to learn and what has been learned). As internalized skill, learned competence, and embodied quality, genuine knowledge is not simply a form of knowing but also a transformative act. In Wang Yangming's words, in terms of sequence, "knowledge is the beginning of action, and action is the completion of knowledge"; in terms of connection, "the real intimacy and solid groundedness of knowledge is action and the brilliant awareness and refined discernment of action is knowledge."[9] In practice, Wang Yangming proposed that through embodied knowing, we persistently transform our heart-mind and our body by allowing each act of self-cultivation to endure and continue to be part of our nature. As the moral sentiments (such as the feeling of commiseration) permeate our hearts, we no longer merely act in accordance with humanity and rightness. Rather, we live a life flowing out of humanity and rightness. What was once the beginning of the action (conscious self-cultivation to achieve a moral good), became a naturally occurring expression of the goal of the action (acting morally).

Having firmly established the thesis of the unity of knowledge and action, Wang Yangming began to advocate Cheng Hao's earlier teaching: "preserve the Heavenly Principle and eliminate human desires."[10] On the surface, this spiritual exercise may imply that the purpose is to deny the legitimacy of basic human instincts such as the desires for food and sex. In fact, contemporary critics of Neo-Confucianism often cite this dictum as the functional equivalent of puritanical asceticism. What Wang Yangming had in mind, however, was rather a logical question of priority reminiscent of Lu Xiangshan's clear-headed process of "establishing the will," "honoring our moral nature," or "first firming up that which is great in us." The "Heavenly Principle" as Cheng Hao understood it is our true nature. It is what we are ontologically and what we should learn to become existentially. In undertaking spiritual exercise, we should constantly remind ourselves that our true nature is not merely the instincts that we share with other animals, but, more importantly, it encompass the moral sentiments that make us uniquely human.

The idea of the "Heavenly Principle" is predicated on the classical Confucian assertion that "nature is that which is conferred by Heaven."[11] The faith in the mutual responsiveness between Heaven and human beings underlies the thesis that there is a transcendent referent in human nature because our natural gifts are not only biologically determined but are also cosmologically circumscribed. To preserve the Heavenly Principle inherent in our human nature is tantamount to the Mencian teaching that self-cultivation entails the quest for the lost heart. While we fully recognize the need to satisfy our basic needs for survival and perpetuation, we should never allow the *higher* meaning of life to be totally subsumed by the biological and physiological demands for food and sex. We need to care for our "great body" as the highest priority, so that it will naturally find a proper niche for our "small body." By contrast, if we are obsessed with the "small body," our life of the mind will be impoverished to the extent that even our basic instincts cannot be properly satisfied. "Human desires" should be eradicated precisely because, in the long run, they will overwhelm and obscure what is best for our self-realization. However, it must be understood that a pragmatic calculation based solely on instrumental rationality cannot help us figure out the most efficacious course of action. "To preserve the Heavenly Principle and eradicate human desires" is not about self-interest, but is instead about self-knowledge.

When Wang Yangming turned fifty, having endured what he poignantly depicted as "a hundred deaths and a thousand hardships,"[12] he encapsulated the message of what he had learned in an incisive three-character phrase "*zhi liangzhi*" (expanding primordial awareness). The term *liangzhi*, originally from Mencius, has been variously translated as "innate goodness," "good knowledge," "conscience," or "conscientious consciousness." It refers to an innate capacity of the heart to be awakened by encountering a thing, affair, event, or situation. This awakening is a form of knowing, and it is necessarily a transformative act; it is, without fail, enlightening. Wang Yangming, then, adopted Lu Xiangshan's "simple and easy" method of reaching one's inner core (attaining one's centrality) by recommending a direct appeal to the sensitivity of the heart. He believed that our "primordial awareness" has its own dynamism and direction. If we learn to "expand" our awareness by extending its orbit of concern to an ever-enlarging circle of relationships (family, clan, village, nation, world, and beyond), we can experientially form one body with Heaven, Earth, and the myriad things. This view, Wang Yangming made clear, is not an overly romantic view of the unity of all things without differentiation. Rather, it is a properly measured and finely tuned idea of how our "primordial awareness" can sympathetically resonate with all modalities of being in the universe without losing its own sense of order and coherence.

To Wang Yangming, the spiritual exercises that enable us to develop fully our capacity to realize the ultimate meaning of life in ordinary daily existence are neither contemplation nor meditation. Instead, they are "embodied knowing" (*tizhi*), an interplay between disinterested engagement and concerned impartiality. Through rigorous mental discipline in the midst of daily routine, or, in Wang Yangming's own words, "tempering oneself through handling concrete affairs (*shishang molian*)," we attain a state of equilibrium. The challenge is twofold: First, to engage ourselves actively and responsibly in the world without, even for a moment, severing the intimate relationship with our "centrality" (the inner identity) and thus losing the ability to wrestle with complex details of life in a spirit of tranquility. Second, to remain impartial yet deeply concerned about the relationships that socially define who we are.

Wang Yangming's learning of the body and mind, involving such seminal theses as "the unity of knowledge and action," "the preservation of the Heavenly Principle and the eradication of human desires," and "the expansion of our primordial awareness," offers a holistic vision of learning to be human through spiritual exercises that integrate the heart, nature, and feeling. According to this vision, a salient feature of human nature as a manifestation of the Heavenly Principle is the continuous realization of its inner dispositions through self-reflection. The principle, the innate pattern that defines who we are, is not an abstract ontological idea. Our inner pattern is dynamic and ever renewing as well as a "ground of being" with transformative power. Feelings, like ocean waves, are both natural expressions of the heart and concrete manifestations of our nature. Human desires are inevitable; they must be transformed and harmonized through self-cultivation so that their pernicious egoistic tendencies will be reversed and instead, enrich our moral sentiments. For example, anger becomes moral indignation, aggressiveness becomes courage, and resentment becomes a wholesome critical attitude.

Wang Yangming's faith in self-realization through personal effort, his hope for transforming politics through moral education, the promise of attaining the good life by way of self-cultivation as a communal act, and his conviction that it is not only humanly possible but an unavoidable human responsibility to bring peace throughout the world were succinctly presented in his celebrated essay "Inquiry on the Great Learning." He declared that the capacity to form one body with Heaven, Earth, and the myriad things is and always has been intrinsic to human nature. Ordinary people as well as worthies and sages are endowed with this capacity. The human heart is, in principle, receptive to all modalities of being in the universe (it can embrace and respond to a stranger, an alley cat, a blade of grass, a distant star) and, therefore, in practice, is sympathetically connected to all human beings, animals, trees, and rocks. The primary task of learning to be human is to expand this sensitivity (primordial awareness) of the heart so that it will not be restricted to only the immediate family environment. While it is essential that we ground our emotional life in the warmth of the hearth, we must transcend all structural impediments in our psychic universe (negative qualities such as egoism, nepotism, parochialism, ethnocentrism, and anthropocentrism) in order to fully realize our inherent humanity.

Wang Yangming's positive assessment of the human potential for self-transcendence has been characterized as an epistemological optimism or the belief in a moral perfectionism. However, in a deeper sense, his vision is grounded in an anthropocosmic vision that intimately connects personal spiritual exercises with the cosmic order. The implication is that what we do in the privacy of our homes is not only socially and politically significant, but is also "ecologically" meaningful. Surely people possessing different amounts of material and symbolic resources may affect the outside world differently, but, in a qualitative way, each of us is a co-creator of the cosmic process. We can all, to varying degrees but in the fullest sense, "take part in the transforming and nourishing processes of Heaven and Earth." The path to human flourishing is never closed. Even the most materially or physically underprivileged are empowered, by their humanity and moral self-awareness, to be an integral part of this joint venture.

However, underlying Wang Yangming's optimism and perfectionism, is a critical awareness that, far from being "simple and easy," the concrete steps to harmonize our basic human relationships and to proficiently handle the daily ritual of living are "hard and bitter." In the *Doctrine of the Mean*, Confucius confessed that he failed at the seemingly simple and easy tasks of a cultivated person: to treat his father as he expects his own son to treat him; to treat his lord as he expects his minister to treat him; to treat his older brother as he expects his younger brother to treat him; and to treat his friends as he expects them to treat him. While Confucius may have criticized himself out of humility and modesty, it seems that the Master also wanted to make it clear that the gap between actuality and expectation is often unbridgeable. Realistically, living up to the expectations we often demand of others is painfully difficult. As a scholar-official, immersed in bureaucratic routine and repeatedly confronted with crucial decisions, Wang Yangming knew well the "hard and bitter" taste of human existence.

Liu Zhongzhou's Philosophy of the Will

Nevertheless, in presenting the human condition, Wang Yangming's faith, hope, and promise significantly outweighed his concern about skepticism, deprivation, wickedness, or the human propensity for evil. Yet the issue of the precariousness of the human heart (including the classical Greek conundrum of "the weakness of the will"), which loomed large in Zhu Xi's teaching on self-cultivation, must be addressed. Liu Zongzhou's (1578–1645) philosophy of life was a creative response to this *Problematik*. While Liu acknowledged Wang Yangming's "expansion of primordial awareness" as a seminal idea, he criticized its efficacy in dealing with human frailties. He argued that when we become aware of our mistakes, even though the realization itself is a transformative act, it is inevitably a postmortem reflection on what has already happened. Consequently, he recommended a more proactive approach: to anticipate the subtle activation of the heart in order to predispose it to right action.

As Tang Junyi notes, Liu was not satisfied with initiating the spiritual exercise at the level of "primordial awareness." Instead, he suggested an even more basic domain: the "root of the will" (*yigan*). According to Tang's interpretation, Liu Zhongzhou felt that the light emitted from "primordial awareness" must be augmented by the heat generated by the "root of the will" to make self-cultivation a completely integrated project.[13] In concrete terms, we must learn to nip the negative consequences of our emotive states in the bud. Even before emotions are aroused, the corrective measure prompted by willpower is already present and ready to transform and harmonize them. Indeed, "primordial awareness" as a form of knowing must wait for the thing to occur before it can exercise its function of reflection, whereas "the root of the will" as a deliberate act conscientiously and decidedly orients the incipient manifestation of a feeling toward an appropriate expression.

Liu took a radically different approach to learning to be human. He insisted that, despite the great human potential for self-transcendence, we must truthfully acknowledge that, in any existential situation in our daily living, we are, in various degrees of seriousness, flawed. The point of departure of self-cultivation is not the abstract idealistic aspiration of what we may become but the concrete realistic assessment of what we are. No matter how we have conducted our lives, there is always room for improvement. We must be continuously mindful of our shortcomings and constantly alert that our behavior, attitudes, convictions, and quality of the heart all require vigilant attentiveness for further refinement. In the lived concreteness of our daily existence, there is always a deficiency that needs to be corrected and a deviation that demands to be adjusted. In short, learning to be human, in practical terms, is to learn to correct mistakes.

Understandably, Liu Zhongzhou's *Human Account* (*Renpu*), contains a comprehensive phenomenological narration of human frailties. Faults ranging from obvious behavioral blunders to subtle (hidden) traces of improper ideas are all accounted for. The six categories of human frailties (subtle, hidden, obvious, great, miscellaneous, and habitual), covering a whole range of behavioral, attitudinal, mental, and unconscious faults, offer a detailed analysis of the physical and psychic energy required for human flourishing. Liu's strategy is paradoxical: our nature is endowed with the Heavenly Principle, which holds the full potential for realizing our stature as a co-creator of the cosmic process and is intrinsic to our heart-mind. However, the concrete step we must take is to correct the errors we have committed, so that we can return to the right path. To put it succinctly, in an ontological sense, every human being is a sage, and yet existentially no one can ever fully embody sagehood. Learning to be human through a ceaseless process of spiritual exercises is, therefore, open to and significant for all human beings.

By introducing the idea and practice of the "root of the will," Liu presented a new constellation of heart, nature, and feeling. Surely the ability of the heart to experience the world through embodied knowing is a defining characteristic of human nature, but the depth of our feeling which truly connects us to Heaven does not spontaneously reveal itself to us if we are conditioned by habitual negative thoughts and constrained by selfish desires. Only in "vigilant solitariness," when we are totally unencumbered by inauthentic attachments, will we connect to the sympathetic resonance that empowers us to take part in what Mencius depicted as "immersing in the flow of Heaven above and Earth below." To Liu, "vigilant solitariness" is both an inner tranquility and a center of creativity, accessible to us only through rigorous discipline of the body and mind.[14]

Among Mencius's "four seeds" (feeling, willing, sensing, and knowing), Liu singled out the ability to will for focused investigation. He believed that the unending task of self-cultivation involves the deconstruction of habitual thoughts and the transformation of selfish desires. Unless habitual thoughts are totally deconstructed and selfish desires thoroughly transformed into moral sentiments, the true feelings of the heart will not reveal themselves and the original nature will not be disclosed. It is in the "vigilant solitariness" that we experience firsthand the subtle inactivation of the "root of the will." Therefore, to make the will sincere, true, authentic, and real is the vitally important spiritual exercise that none of us can afford to ignore.

All of the Confucian philosophers discussed here were, we must acknowledge, dealing with capricious human nature. They were searching for ways to cultivate and to refine what were natural human urges and responses. They all recognized that human beings are something greater than merely living organisms. They felt that heaven gives to humans the potential to be in complete harmony with all of nature. To achieve this complete harmony, the natural and strong human emotions that exist in all of us must be channeled. They suggested that this channeling can take place through self-discipline and constant striving.

Notes

1. Although no scholarly articles in English are available, several collections of essays in Chinese have been published. See *Guo Yi, Guodian Chujian yu xianQin xueshu sixiang* [The Bamboo Strips of Guodian and pre-Qin Thought] (forthcoming), ch. 3, pp. 265–97.

2. The idea of the "lost heart" came from *Mencius* 6A:7.

3. For a discussion of the learning of the body and mind, see Tu Weiming, "The Confucian Perception of Adulthood," in Tu Weiming, *Humanity and Self-Cultivation: Essays in Confucian Thought* (repr., Boston: Cheng & Tsui Company, 1998), 44.

4. Although I cannot identify the locus classicus for this expression, I am quite sure that this was a pre-Confucian idea.

5. This idea has often been attributed to Zhu Xi's rival, Lu Xiangshan (1139–1191).

6. This is the expression Zhu Xi used to describe his life experience as a Confucian.

7. See Wing-tsit Chan, *A Source Book in Chinese Philosophy* (Princeton, N.J.: Princeton University Press, 1963), 562, for a different translation.

8. For a brief discussion of this issue, see Tu Weiming, "Mencian Perception of Moral Development, " in Tu Weiming, *Humanity and Self-Cultivation*, 66–68.

9. Wing-tsit Chan, trans., *Instructions for Practical Living and Other Neo-Confucian Writings by Wang Yang-ming* (New York: Columbia University Press, 1963), 11. My translation is significantly different.

10. Wing-tsit Chan, *Source Book*, 523.

11. This is the opening statement of the *Doctrine of the Mean*. See Tu Weiming, *Centrality and Commonality: An Essay on Confucian Religiousness* (Albany: State University of New York Press, 1989), ch. 1.

12. *Nianpu* (chronological biography), under 50 sui, in *Wang Yangming quanshu* [The Complete Works of Wang Yangming] (Taibei: Zhengzhong Book Co., 1955), 14:125.

13. Tang Chun-I [Tang Junyi], "Liu Tsung-chou's Doctrine of Moral Mind and Practice and His Critique of Wang Yang-ming," in *The Unfolding of Neo-Confucianism*, ed. Wm. Theodore de Bary (New York: Columbia University Press, 1975), 305–31.

14. For a general discussion of this issue, see Tu Weiming, "Subjectivity in Liu Tsung-chou's Philosophical Anthropology," in *Unfolding of Neo-Confucianism*, ed. de Bary, 215–38.

23

Confucian Spirituality
and Qing Thought

RODNEY L. TAYLOR

FOR AS LONG AS SCHOLARS HAVE STUDIED the Confucian tradition, there has been a question about its religious nature. Historically the tradition has more often been seen as a form of humanism or ethics rather than as a religious tradition.[1] The cumulative effect of this issue over the years has been largely to discount the question of the religious nature of Confucianism and to perpetrate much of the stereotype of the tradition as an ethical-humanistic teaching in which religious motivation plays a small role, if any at all.

By contrast to this representation of the tradition, in more recent years a small number of scholars have focused specifically on the capacity of the tradition to reflect religious meaning.[2] I have argued for the religious integrity of the Confucian tradition based largely on a definition of religion grounded in the work of Frederick Streng, who said that religion was a "means of ultimate transformation."[3] On the basis of this definition, several major characteristics of religious phenomena can be identified, including (1) a belief in life as meaningful and the universe as purposeful, (2) a belief that meaning is associated with the identification of an absolute, (3) a process of transformation, leading the individual from the present condition to that which is identified with the absolute, and (4) the identification of religion as a total life orientation for the individual in which all activities potentially take on religious meaning.[4]

The definition utilized both speaks to the capacity for the identification of what is considered ultimate or absolute and, in addition, suggests the relationship between the individual and the absolute in terms of a process of transformation. Religion, therefore, is not only the identification of an absolute but, most importantly, the process whereby the individual is transformed from the present condition toward that which is regarded as absolute in nature. When these characteristics are applied to the Confucian tradition, we find (1) the search for ultimate meaning and (2) the identification of an absolute with *tian* (Heaven), in the classical tradition and *tianli* (Principle of Heaven), in the Neo-Confucian tradition. In turn, (3) the process of transformation and (4) the primacy of religion can both be identified with the cultivation of sagehood, *shengxue,* the learning of the sage or learning to be a sage.[5]

The identification of the absolute with *tian* and *tianli* represents the most frequently found categories that might match the way in which the absolute is identified. Their use does not, however, exclude the possibility of other terms also being identified as possible absolutes in combination with or separate from those identified. Other possible candidates for an absolute might include *taiji,* Great Ultimate; *qi,* Material Force or Vitality; or *Dao,* Way. Particularly relevant for our discussion of Qing thought is the use of Dao as a potential absolute.

While it is true that the sages and the records of their thoughts and actions play a central role in the Confucian tradition, the cultivation of sagehood described by the models of learning found in *lixue,* School of Principle, and *xinxue,* School of Heart and Mind, do not necessarily apply to *all* forms of Confucianism. Not unlike the concept of the *daotong* (orthodox tradition), the model of sagehood is not inclusive of all materials or individuals who could be described as part of the Confucian tradition.[6] It was during the Qing period that the *daotong* model became less significant, as scholars sought to return to the very periods that had been ignored and excluded by the *daotong,* that is, Han and Tang Confucian learning. The Qing period became the champion of these studies and through these efforts appeared to change the agenda of Confucian learning. Any attempt to understand the larger question of the religious nature of the Confucian tradition must be able to account for the relation between Qing thought and Confucian spirituality.

It is *Hanxue,* Han learning, and *kaozhengxue,* evidential research learning, that often are used to characterize Qing thought,[7] in part because they appear to represent the unique contribution of the period and in turn the most radical break with the traditions of Confucianism associated with classical Confucianism and Neo-Confucianism.[8] While that radical break may be more apparent than real, there is still the strong emphasis of those within the Han learning and evidential research movements that they were rejecting much of what they themselves saw as the errors of the past in Song and Ming learning.

The critical question is whether, in this rejection of the Song and Ming models of learning and self-cultivation, which had been advanced by the School of Principle and the School of Heart-and-Mind, there was also a rejection of much of what could make the case for the religious understanding of the Confucian tradition. In other words, most arguments for the religious nature of the Confucian tradition, or even a religious dimension to the tradition, have been based on the salient role played by the Song and Ming models of interpretation of the intent and purpose of the tradition as a whole. This argument applies equally to both Neo-Confucian and classical Confucian materials because of the dominance of Neo-Confucian hermeneutics in the interpretation of the classical heritage until the advent of the Qing period Han learning. Though Han and Tang commentary traditions presented a challenge to the later Neo-Confucian hermenutical tradition, the issue was largely ignored by their exclusion from the *daotong* lineage, a lineage that persisted as the dominant model of interpretation of Confucian thought until the Qing challenge. As a result, the classical Confucian heritage has been interpreted largely through a Neo-Confucian process of textual exegesis. When that entire process is challenged, as it was in the Qing period, religious meanings of the tradition as a whole are subject to question.

This line of reasoning leads to several questions. Do we see in Qing thought a rejection of the religious heritage of Confucianism and a substitution of it for a form of scholarly pursuit whose endpoint is measured in terms of a classical heritage of only ethical and humanistic teachings, not religiously infused ethical teachings or ethically infused religious teachings? That is, is the Qing quest for scholarship secular rather than sacred? Or, on the other hand, is the Qing experience, even in Han learning and evidential research, still potentially a deeply and profoundly moving religious orientation and outlook in and of itself, and is this a form of religious meaning that needs to become part of the total understanding of Confucianism as a religious tradition?

Han Learning and Evidential Research

There has been much debate around the question of the origins of the *Hanxue,* or Han learning movement, and the *kaozhengxue,* or evidential learning movement. In spite of their seemingly radical departure from Song and Ming thought, many scholars have sought to see a connection between the movements and the periods of thought they appeared to reject or radically reform. In this respect, the movement of thought known as practical learning (*shixue*), with its newfound emphasis on *qi* (material or vital force), is potentially highly relevant to the understanding of the emergence of these dominant strains of Qing thought. Figures such as Luo Qinshun, Wang Fuzhi, Huang Zongxi, Gu Yanwu, and Yan Yuan all potentially play an important role in terms of turning their attention to a more practical and applied form of learning that focused on the real and concrete nature of things and their relevance for the understanding of self and other. Wm. Theodore de Bary has referred to this trend as a form of "vitalism" that gave rise to the "realism" of Qing empiricism.[9]

Han learning and evidential research are both characterized by rigorous methods of scholarship and learning as well as a rejection of so-called abstract thought. Such learning and scholarship were chiefly defined in terms of philology, etymology, phonology, paleography, and, in general, close textual studies. The part of the movement referred to as Han learning reflects the newfound admiration for the Han-period commentaries on the classics and the belief that such commentaries represented a closer understanding of the meaning of the classics than the distance represented both historically and philosophically by the Song and Ming interpretations of the classics. The reference to Han learning as *puxue* (unadorned learning), is a reflection of the belief that the movement represented a return to a simpler and more direct access to the understanding of the classics. It is also referred to as *Zhengxue*, that is, the learning of Zheng Xuan (127–200 C.E.), the Han Confucian chiefly responsible for the high standards of Han scholarship.

Kaozhengxue, evidential research—also called inductive research, textual criticism, or even empiricism—is a more broadly based movement than the Han learning movement. Han learning, as the title implies, focused its attention on the Han-period commentaries; evidential research became a method that was applied across a range of fields and without particular attention to the Han period as the final arbiter for correct meanings. In this sense the application of "empiricism" as one translation of *kaozheng* is suggestive of the degree to which the movement represents a broad-based method for conducting learning and scholarship.

The question that arises with both Han learning and evidential research is whether these movements are simply methods for learning and research, highly critical of the speculative and abstract nature of Confucian thought before them, but generally free of a philosophical point of view themselves, or whether they are creating and/or maintaining a philosophical discourse with the tools and methods advocated through their focus on close textual scholarship. If the latter is the case—that is, that they are creating and/or maintaining a philosophical agenda—then their goals raise the question of continuity and discontinuity with past models of learning and self-cultivation, and the pursuit of a common or different agenda as the intent of Confucian teaching and practice.

Qing Thought: Philosophy or Philology?

De Bary has characterized the roots of Qing thought in the development of a broad appreciation for and development of a philosophy of "vitalism" arising in the Song and Ming and seen in terms of a particular focus on a philosophy of *qi* (material force or vital force).[10] On-cho Ng, emphasizing de Bary's sense of vitalism, has suggested that while Qing thought represented a "dismantling" of the *Daoxue* tradition of Confucianism, in its place was substituted a "vitalist ontology,"[11] that is, a newfound interest in practical, naturalistic, and materialistic teachings, which were seen in and of themselves as a new and fresh point of view, a point of view with philosophical significance. Thomas Metzger has phrased the problem in terms of an ontology of "concrete fact" in which the focus became the recovery of "exact meanings" from the classics,[12] equally a philosophical agenda. Kai-wing Chow has suggested that the central role played by the classics for the evidential scholars only reinforces the degree to which the classics stood as a respository of truth, that is, knowledge of Dao, and their agenda was measured in terms of the philosophical pursuit of this truth, what he calls the commitment to "purist hermeneutics."[13]

While attention shifted to "concreteness" of things and the role of *qi* for the evidential scholars, they also saw the paradigmatic and root-metaphor definitions of truth as the object of their pursuit. Such a pursuit suggested a continuity of ontology, not the radical rejection of philosophical concern seen as a consequence of their criticism of Song and Ming learning. The possibility of a continuity of thought giving rise to Han learning and evidential research suggests that the Qing preoccupation with text and analysis is not necessarily at odds with a philosophical agenda, but simply represents a different approach to a common problem of meaning and truth.

Benjamin Elman, in what is the classic study of the evidential research movement of the Qing period, suggests a changing agenda "from philosophy to philology," but at the same time does not minimize the capacity of philology to provide a continuing philosophical agenda.[14] Elman suggests that the goal of sagehood was no longer the central aim of the Qing Confucian, at least understood in terms of a process leading toward the internalization and/or realization of a rationalistic or intuitive understanding of the teachings of the sages, that is, the Song and Ming models of learning and self-cultivation as represented by both the School of Principle and the School of Heart-and-Mind. Rather, the agenda had become a return to what the classics could tell us about the sages of antiquity.

In this quest for philological accuracy and terminological analysis, focusing only on questions of textual analysis, it is possible that questions of textual meaning supplemented questions about or even interest in the teachings of the sages contained in the classics. Such a move would justify the full sense of moving from philosophy to philology. On the other hand, it may be the case that a philological agenda could lead to or even be in itself a philosophical project. The clarification of this question potentially distinguishes evidential research as a method of study from a form of philosophical discourse.

The towering figure of Qing thought, Dai Zhen (1723–1777), was himself a master of evidential research and representative of the potential for evidential research to advance learning and research. To what end did Dai Zhen see the evidential research movement? Tu Weiming suggests that Dai Zhen was engaged in "a systematic inquiry into the underlying structure of classical Confucian thought."[15] His focus is evidential scholarship, but his larger vision is the understanding of the Confucian tradition itself. The following words of Dai Zhen are illustrative of the intent with which Dai pursued his evidential research and scholarship:

> The Classics provide the route to the Tao. What illuminates the Tao is their words. How words are formed can be grasped only through (a knowledge of) philology and paleography. From (the study of) primary and derived characters we can master the language. Through the language we can penetrate the mind and will of the ancient sages and worthies.[16]

The goal of sagehood may have been less of a central concern for the Qing evidential scholars, at least as it had been understood by the dominant forms of Song and Ming learning, but the intent to attend to the Dao (Tao) remained a salient concern, at least for Dai Zhen. Dai Zhen shows a very different agenda from the Song and Ming models of Neo-Confucian learning. Instead of an attempt to intellectualize upon or "abstract" the meanings of the teachings of the sages and realize them within oneself, Dai Zhen suggests that close textual analysis is the path toward an understanding of the Dao. To reinforce the importance of the philological method of seeking philosophical truth, he suggests that knowledge of the absolute is entirely dependent on philological method. "If there is one character that is not precisely understood, then understanding the meaning of what is said necessarily falls short and the way is lost thereby."[17] For Dai Zhen, the classics contain the essence of truth of the sages, but it is not accessible through philosophical discourse and abstraction. It is available through the most exacting of textual analysis and only such analysis. For Cynthia Brokaw, Dai Zhen did not see philology as a way to approach philosophy, but as philosophy itself.[18] Through his learning and scholarship, philology becomes philosophy in the pursuit of the truth believed to reside in the sayings of the sages of the past and recorded in the classics.

The commitment to the pursuit of a philosophical agenda was also expressed by Dai Zhen in very personal terms. He considered the pursuit of the Way to be the goal of his life, a pursuit that was to be carried out through the most exacting of scholarly methods.

> Since the age of 17 sui, I set my mind on hearing the Way, and I believed that if I didn't seek the Way in the Six Classics, Confucius and Mencius, I would not find it; if I did not set myself to the task of learning the meaning of the characters, institutions, and terms in the Classics, then I would have no basis from which to understand their language. I have worked at this goal for over thirty years and thus know the source of order and disorder throughout all time.[19]

The Qing evidential scholar Wang Mingsheng (1722–1798) illustrates a similar point of view to Dai Zhen's.

> The Classics are employed to understand the Tao. But those who seek the Tao should not cling vacuously to "meanings and principles" (*i-li*, that is, moral principles) in order to find it. If only they will correct primary and derived characters, discern their pronunciation, read the explanations and glosses, and master the commentaries and notes, the "meanings and principles" will appear on their own, and the Tao within them.[20]

Wang's statement represents a strong endorsement of the primacy of the philological method in deriving meaning. In this case Wang directly contrasts his own method with the attempt to derive meaning by way of understanding an abstract level of meanings and principles, *yili* (*i-li*). Interestingly, he does not criticize the end point of "meanings and principles," but suggests that any such understanding must simply be based on the method of evidential research. And the end point of such research? The end point is nothing short of knowledge of the Dao itself as contained in the sayings of the sages of the past and recorded in the classics.

There is no doubt that for these individuals at least, the classics contained the Dao, and the chief motivation in pursuing the forms of scholarship developed under the rubric of these movements was to approach and attain an understanding of the Dao. The term *yili* (meanings and principles), is key both in terms of what it was that the evidential scholars were rejecting from the Song-Ming model of Neo-Confucian learning and in terms of what it was that they sought through their own method of evidential research. Quoting Dai Zhen,

> Thus, if ancient glosses are clear, the ancient Classics will be clear. If the ancient Classics are clear, the meanings and principle (*i-li*) of the sages and worthies will be clear. Moreover, what unites my mind (with these meanings and principles) will accordingly also be clear.[21]

Yili were not to be the product of a process of an abstract intellectual process, the "rationalism" of the School of Principle, let alone a form of "intuitive" knowing, the innate knowing, *liangzhi*, of the School of Heart-and-Mind. Meanings and principles were to be derived by evidential means. As these meanings and principles emerged in the context of evidential research they represented the teachings of the sages and worthies.[22] Philology in this context is clearly philosophical method whose aim is the discovery of truth.

When Philology Is Not Philosophy

If the purpose of scholarship is not set upon *yili*, then there is a question of what end is served by such research and learning. Does philology become an end in itself? And does it then compromise its potential as a method for attaining knowledge of Dao by no longer seeing the end point of Dao? Elman's study of the evidential research movement demonstrates that a figure such as Dai Zhen was very concerned about those for whom the value of evidential research was *without* philosophical focus. Brokaw's study demonstrates that the evidential research movement, on the other hand, was also largely dissatisfied with Dai Zhen and his agenda. For many other evidential scholars, research was aimed at the construction of meaning free of a philosophical agenda, and Dai Zhen was seen as yet another example of someone trying to do philosophy—and in this case, in the guise of philology.[23] His agenda is the reason that Dai Zhen in his own day and particularly from those with whom he interacted could get so little hearing for his philosophical works and was in general repudiated for engaging in philosophical issues.

Dai Zhen's own goal was philosophical, and anything less than this was seen as a failure to attend properly to the real and pressing questions. Philology without philosophy for Dai Zhen appears to have no direction or goal and can result only in the accumulation of what he saw as scattered and disjointed knowledge. Such knowledge was not in itself a path to an understanding of the Dao. Dai Zhen was in the minority of the evidential movement in this view, and the concluding phase of the evidential movement, according to Elman, was eventually brought about by the frustration experienced by those who felt the need for attention to philosophical issues.[24] Dai Zhen himself had anticipated the problem that would bring about the greatest challenge to the very movements that played such a dominant role in Qing thought. Against the backdrop of Qing thought as a whole, evidential research and Han learning were seen as appropriate methods of research when they were set in the context of a broader philosophical agenda, but they fell short when they lacked that philosophical agenda.

Evidential Pursuit of Dao: Material or Spiritual?

Establishing that at least some of the members of the evidential research movement saw their goal as the pursuit of Dao suggests that the pursuit was more then merely method or an empty critique of the philosophy of their predecessors. There was a philosophical agenda in their pursuit. It was a pursuit of Dao and, as such, raised questions of truth, its transmission and inculcation, and the meaning of Dao in the lives of these individuals. While sagehood is not normally associated with the ideals of the evidential research scholars and in fact has been suggested as no longer relevant by Elman,[25] there is a question of whether the only sagehood models rejected were those associated with Song and Ming thought and whether there still existed an ideal of the sage representing a different agenda. Sagehood itself possesses a rich spectrum of meanings,[26] and a continuing evidential ideal of sagehood was not only possible, but far closer to the Ming ideals of a practical learning with a sage representing *shixue* (practical learning), than the often stereotyped rejection of sagely goals.

It is possible, of course, that the movement, which has at times been seen in its capacity to represent a form of empiricism, may simply be a form of materialism.[27] If that is the case, there is little to draw our attention further on the question of the potential for finding religiosity within the pursuit of knowledge of Dao. Thomas Metzger has addressed the issue of materialism. Suggesting that Western materialism took God out of the formula—that is, it is simply the world as raw data with no organizing principle within which questions of purpose or meaning can be raised—Metzger sought to differentiate the Chinese experience and expression of the philosophy of *qi*. For Metzger what we find in Qing thought and its predecessors of the philosophy of *qi* is not a materialism but what he calls a "concrete reality teleologically infused with divine meaning."[28] Metzger is explicit in his remarks

that Qing thought was never meant as a rejection of Neo-Confucian ontology, that is, a movement toward materialism; but rather it was meant as a
redefining of the terms or "ground," if you will, of that ontology.

De Bary has suggested a similar point in seeing Qing thought developing
around a form of "vitalism" that emphasizes the productivity of the cosmos, *sheng sheng* (constant production and creativity),[29] a principle intended
to convey not a sense of random or capricious outpouring but ordered
development. Such a view of the cosmic unfolding speaks not to a philosophy of materialism but to the capacity of things and principle to be indivis-
ible within the context of "concreteness"—what Metzger captures by the
phrase "equilibrium of imminent issuance."[30] The world represents or,
more accurately, *is* a balanced, purposeful, and meaningful process of production and creativity, and it is this very reality that constitutes Dao
defined as the *yili* of things in themselves. The focus is on the concrete
nature of the process of production, but it is a view that the physical universe itself is the very nature of this ultimate ground of existence, a ground
fully meaningful for what it reveals of the absolute nature of things. Ng has
referred to *qi* as the ultimate principle of reality in Qing thought precisely
because *qi* is seen as at the center of this ordering and productive nature of
the cosmos.[31] The concept of materialism is inadequate to capture the full
meaning of the Qing movement in evidential research, a movement capable of articulating its own ontological, if not teleological, agenda—at least
for Dai Zhen and like-minded scholars. But if it is not materialism, then in
what way might the tradition be thought of as "spiritual"? That is, it can be
seen as a philosophically meaningful tradition, but how does its meaning
move from philosophy to religion? In this light Metzger's phrase "teleologically infused with divine meaning" suggests the possibility that Qing
thought represents not only a philosophically meaningful tradition, but
one that can be discussed for its potential of religiosity as well.

An Evidential Model of Sagehood

For Qing thought, the world of concrete things is, at least for some, teleologically meaningful. There is a Dao, and its meaning and understanding
are to be pursued. Its understanding is not the product of the models of
learning suggested by the traditional schools of Neo-Confucianism, the
School of Principle and the School of Heart-and-Mind. Rather, Dao is associated with concrete things, the actual nature of things in the world, *qi*.
What the Qing scholars saw as the ruinous dichotomy of *li* and *qi*, principle and material or vital force, has been brought together by giving priority
to *qi*. The pursuit of understanding, *yili*, is to be found in the pursuit of

knowledge of things, not the abstraction of meanings and principles apart from things or prior to things. The degree to which *yili* is an a priori understanding of things is the degree to which it represents only the old models of learning and is therefore mistaken from the perspective of the evidential scholars. The degree to which *yili* emerges within the context of the study of things is the degree to which it provides a method for the understanding of Dao itself.

The role of the absolute for the evidential scholar, or some evidential scholars, is a matter of philosophy, but is it a matter of religion? Our initial definition of religion requires both the identification of an absolute and, in addition, the movement of the individual toward that absolute, that is, the transformation of the individual. Is there the retention of an absolute within this point of view? One can speak only for those who chose to see evidential research within the context of the pursuit of Dao. For those focused on Dao, it should be said that Dao was absolute. Is there any evidence of a conscious process of transformation, what we have described in earlier models of Confucian learning and self-cultivation as the ideal of sagehood? There is much less direct attention given to discussions of the cultivation of sagehood in Qing thought, and this in part because of the rejection of the Song and Ming models of learning. But the pursuit of evidential research, when it is defined in terms of a philosophical quest for understanding of Dao, becomes a pursuit of the ideal of the sage.[32]

Whether it is called sagehood or the pursuit of Dao, there was a process of attempting to pursue the understanding of what was regarded as the absolute. The process was not, however, defined in terms of the traditional models of learning and self-cultivation defined through the schools of Neo-Confucianism except in the broadest terms of learning and scholarship. At the center of the evidential movement was a series of strategies for conducting research and scholarship by exacting and demanding methods and techniques. It is this quest of scholarship itself that lies at the heart of the quest for understanding of the Dao, the quest for sagehood. Brokaw has described the process of learning in Dai Zhen as a quest for sagehood, describing the focus of Dai Zhen's thought as a "faith in the possibility of sagehood."[33] Dai Zhen says in this respect, "The purpose of studying is to nourish a man's innate goodness (*liang*), to make him develop into a worthy or a sage."[34]

Metzger has enticingly explicated the capacity for movement or transformation in pursuit of an understanding of the Dao or the quest for sagehood by suggesting that evidential scholars were involved in a process of "reifying the experience of academic study as the *kung-fu* which themselves constituted the Tao."[35] In other words, the act of study is itself the effort toward understanding Dao and thus a process of action. To suggest that study became the *gongfu* (*kung-fu*) (moral effort or action) is to suggest that there was the perception of the need for action or effort to occur to move the individual from where he/she is to the position of understanding Dao, that is, a movement from what "is" to what "ought to be." The condition of the "ought" is sagehood, the realization of the Dao. Such movement is a process of transformation and as such may bear the capacity for religiosity. In this interpretation, the sage in his/her very scholarship may be exercising greater religious potential than has normally been associated with the interpretation of Qing thought.

Conclusion

The capacity for transformation toward sagehood and thus the possibility of an evidential model of religiosity is a very different interpretation of the evidential movement from that normally encountered. The degree to which the movement represents continuity with what preceded it, even though it sought to redefine much of what it saw as the Confucian agenda, makes it somewhat easier to understand a potential continuity of belief around a teleologically meaningful world. The capacity of the tradition to *continue* to hold to belief in an absolute and thus provide a means whereby the individual can transform himself/herself toward that absolute is suggestive of the continuation of a fundamental Confucian agenda even if defined in terms of concrete goals. The particularity of the object of focus, that is, the nature of the absolute, does not in itself define religion from nonreligion. Having established an absolute,[36] it is the manner in which the object of focus is held and the resulting orientation toward self and cosmos that become meaningful for the question of religiosity.

We have, it is true, only isolated the thought of Dai Zhen for interpretation as a form of spirituality. The degree to which much of the evidential movement opposed Dai Zhen does not make it a simple task to discuss the broad capacity of the evidential movement to demonstrate religious motivation. However, the establishment of Dai Zhen as a religious person is significant for its capacity to demonstrate that the evidential movement could provide an avenue toward religious meaning, even if not all its adherents followed its potential. Certainly Dai Zhen saw evidential research as a way not only of doing philosophy, but of being religious as well. Dai Zhen's religiosity has been described by Tu Weiming as a project to "reorient the spiritual direction of his age from metaphysical speculations on the ultimate reality to lived experience of ordinary people."[37] The depth of spirituality is identified within the very attentiveness to concrete things that was the subject of his study of Dao. To interpret this agenda as anything other than religiosity is to diminish the capacity of Dai Zhen's thought to manifest the spiritual depth offered by the Confucian tradition.

In turn, on the basis of Dai Zhen even as a single example, one cannot simply dismiss Qing thought as failing to address issues of religious meaning in its own past, nor deny it the possibility of positing its own religious response to questions of its own time. Qing thought, contrary to most interpretation, suggests that the Confucian tradition can still be thought of as a religious tradition, even with the inclusion of the Han learning and evidential research movements. There are admittedly individuals for whom religion plays little or no role, but this observation in turn may be no different from any other religious tradition. Participation in a tradition exists for some without faith or belief, and there will probably always be nonreligious people even within the context of a religious tradition. On the other hand, for those who are religious and committed to the pursuit of a religious goal, there is little that cannot serve to facilitate that goal. The traditions of Han learning and evidential research offered to some a path to pursue the Dao and transform their lives in terms of the understanding of the Dao. To see the capacity of the Confucian tradition to include religious meaning even in these activities only serves to demonstrate more fully the religious intent with which the Confucian agenda was pursued and the seriousness with which we must entertain the possibility of a profound and deep Confucian spirituality stretching across the expanse of the tradition.

Notes

1. See, e.g., standard studies such as Fung Yu-lan [Feng Youlan], *A History of Chinese Philosophy,* volume 1, *The Period of the Philosophers,* trans. Derk Bodde (Princeton, N.J.: Princeton University Press, 1952); and Wing-tsit chan, *A Source Book in Chinese Philosophy* (Princeton, N.J.: Princeton University Press, 1963).

2. See, e.g., Tu Weiming, *Humanity and Self-Cultivation;* idem, *Confucian Thought: Self-hood as Creative Transformation;* idem, *Centrality and Commonality;* Julia Ching, *Confucianism and Christianity;* Mary Evelyn Tucker, *Moral and Spiritual Cultivation in Japanese Neo-Confucianism;* Michael Kalton, *To Become a Sage;* and Rodney L. Taylor, *The Religious Dimensions of Confucianism.* For summaries and evaluations of the current study of Confucianism as a religious tradition, see Rodney L. Taylor, "The Study of Confucianism as a Religious Tradition," *Journal of Chinese Religions* 18 (1990): 143–59; Rodney L. Taylor and Gary Arbuckle, "Confucianism" in "Chinese Religions: The State of the Field," ed. D. Overmyer, *Journal of Asian Studies* 54, no. 2 (May 1995): 347–54. See also John Berthrong, *All Under Heaven,* 189–207.

3. Frederick J. Streng, *Undertstanding Religious Life,* 1–8.

4. See Taylor, *Religious Dimensions;* see also the introduction to Rodney L. Taylor, *The Illustrated Encyclopedia of Confucianism* (New York: Rosen Publishing Group, 2004), and a more technical form of the piece, "The Religious Character of the Confucian Tradition," *Philosophy East and West* 48, no. 1 (January 1998): 80–107.

5. Taylor, *Religious Dimensions;* "Introduction," and "Religious Character."

6. On *Daotong,* see Wm. Theodore de Bary, *Neo-Confucian Orthodoxy and the Learning of the Mind-and-Heart* (New York: Columbia University Press, 1981).

7. Tu Weiming has discussed the intellectual agenda involved in characterizing Qing thought by way of Han learning and evidential research. See Tu Weiming, "Perceptions of Learning (Hsüeh) in Early Ch'ing Thought," in Tu Weiming, *Way, Learning, and Politics,* 117–23.

8. For a general discussion of the *kao-zheng* movement and the milieu within which it arose, see R. Kent Guy, *The Emperor's Four Treasures: Scholars and the State in the Late Ch'ien-lung Era* (Cambridge, Mass.: Council on East Asian Studies, Harvard University, 1987). For the most complete study of this movement, see Benjamin A. Elman, *From Philosophy to Philology.* I am particularly indebted to Elman's analysis of the evidential research movement for my present understanding of Qing thought.

9. Wm. Theodore de Bary, "Neo-Confucian Cultivation and the Seventeenth Century 'Enlightenment,'" in *The Unfolding of Neo-Confucianism,* ed. de Bary, 194–95.

10. Ibid.

11. On-cho Ng, "Toward an Interpretation of Ch'ing Ontology," in *Cosmology, Ontology, and Human Efficacy: Essays in Chinese Thought,* ed. Richard J. Smith and D. W. Y. Kwok (Honolulu: University of Hawaii Press, 1993), 36.

12. Thomas A. Metzger, *Escape from Predicament,* 161.

13. Kaiwing Chow, "Purist Hermeneutics and Ritualist Ethics in Mid-Ch'ing Thought," in *Cosmology, Ontology, and Human Efficacy,* ed. Smith et al., 186.

14. Elman, *From Philosophy to Philology,* 28.

15. Tu, "Perceptions of Learning in Early Ch'ing Thought," 119.

16. This passage is a key to understanding Dai's thought and thus is quoted in most studies. See Elman, *From Philosophy to Philology,* 29. Also quoted in Benjamin Elman, "The Revaluation of Benevolence (*Jen*) in Ch'ing Dynasty Evidential Research," in *Cosmology, Ontology, and Human Efficacy,* ed. Smith et al., 69; Chung-ying Cheng, *Tai Chen's Inquiry into Goodness* (Honolulu: University of Hawaii Press, 1971), 52; Cynthia J. Brokaw, "Tai Chen and Learning in the Confucian Tradition," in *Education and Society in Late Imperial China, 1600–1900,* ed. Benjamin A. Elman and Alexander Woodside (Berkeley: University of California Press, 1994), 270.

17. Quoted in Brokaw, "Tai Chen and Learning," 270.

18. Ibid., 259.

19. Quoted in ibid., 271.

20. Quoted in Elman, *From Philosophy to Philology,* 28.

21. Quoted in Elman, "Revaluation of Benevolence," 65.

22. For evidential research that was centered on investigation of works other than the classics, meanings and principles emerged from the concreteness of things. This will be covered later in the essay.

23. Brokaw, "Tai Chen and Learning," 259, 279.

24. The Chang-Zhou School of New Text Confucianism or the Gong-yong School arose in many respects as an attempt to reintroduce issues of "abstraction" into Confucian discourse, that is, a committed philosophical orientation. See Elman, *From Philosophy to Philology,* 234–37, for a study of the role of the New Text School. For more detail, see his separate study of the New Text School: Benjamin A. Elman, *Classicism, Politics, and Kinship: The Ch'ang-Chou School of New Text Confucianism in Late Imperial China* (Berkeley: University of California Press, 1990).

25. Elman, *From Philosophy to Philology,* 6.

26. See Wm. Theodore de Bary, "Sagehood as Secular and Spiritual Ideal in Tokugawa Neo-Confucianism," in *Principle and Practicality,* ed. de Bary and Bloom, 127–88; idem, "Neo-Confucian Cultivation and the Seventeenth-Century 'Enlightenment,'" in *The Unfolding of Neo-Confucianism,* ed. de Bary, 141–216.

27. This is the position taken by Hou Wai-lu. See Tu Weiming's discussion of this interpretation ("Learning in Early Ch'ing Thought," 120).

28. Metzger, *Escape from Predicament,* 163.

29. De Bary, "Neo-Confucian Cultivation," 194–95.

30. Ibid.

31. Ng, "Toward an Interpretation of Ch'ing Ontology," 54.

32. It is also significant that evidential scholars represented a major shift of attention away from the Four Books and back to the classics. On the issue of sagehood, this shift is significant in that it was the Four Books that had in many respects represented the *locus classicus* for the relevance of the ideal of sagehood. The classics in turn tend to see sagehood as at a distance, restricted to figures of high antiquity, not an ideal brought from the past for the cultivation of those of the present. Sagehood as an ideal was not an articulated goal, but it is still implicit in the quest for the understanding of Dao. See Taylor, *Religious Dimensions,* 32–36.

33. Brokaw, "Tai Chen and Learning," 279.

34. Quoted in ibid., 280.

35. Metzger, *Escape from Predicament,* 163.

36. In the case of Dai Zhen, this absolute is Dao, which might best be spoken of in terms of its concreteness and materiality, rather than the earlier focus on *tianli,* Principle of Heaven.

37. Tu, "Learning in Early Ch'ing Thought," 120.

Suggested Readings

Berthrong, John. *All Under Heaven: Transforming Paradigms in Confucian-Christian Dialogue.* Albany: State University of New York Press, 1994.

Brokaw, Cynthia J. "Tai Chen and Learning in the Confucian Tradition," in *Education and Society in Late Imperial China, 1600–1900,* edited by Benjamin A. Elman, Alexander Woodside, 257–91. Berkeley: University of California Press, 1994.

Cheng Chung-ying. *Tai Chen's Inquiry into Goodness: A Translation of the Yüan Shan, With an Introductory Essay.* Honolulu: East-West Center Press, 1971.

Ching, Julia. *Confucianism and Christianity: A Comparative Study.* Tokyo: Kodansha International, 1977.

De Bary, Wm. Theodore. "Individualism and Humanitarianism in Late Ming Thought." In *Self and Society in Ming Thought,* ed. Wm. Theodore de Bary, 145–247. New York: Columbia University Press, 1970.

————. "Neo-Confucian Cultivation and the Seventeenth-Century 'Enlightenment.'" In *The Unfolding of Neo-Confucianism,* edited by Wm. Theodore de Bary, 141–216. New York: Columbia University Press, 1981.

————. *Neo-Confucian Orthodoxy and the Learning of the Mind-and-Heart.* New York: Columbia University Press, 1981.

————. "Sagehood as Secular and Spiritual Ideal in Tokugawa Neo-Confucianism." In *Principle and Practicality: Essays in Neo-Confucianism and Practical Learning,* edited by Wm. Theodore de Bary and Irene Bloom, 127–88. New York: Columbia University Press, 1979.

————. *The Trouble with Confucianism.* Cambridge, Mass.: Harvard University Press, 1991.

De Bary, Wm. Theodore, ed. *Self and Society in Ming Thought.* New York: Columbia University Press, 1970.

————. *The Unfolding of Neo-Confucianism.* New York: Columbia University Press, 1975.

————, and Irene Bloom, eds. *Principle and Practicality: Essays in Neo-Confucianism and Practical Learning.* New York: Columbia University Press, 1979.

Elman, Benjamin A. *From Philosophy to Philology: Intellectual and Social Aspects of Change in Late Imperial China.* Cambridge, Mass.: Council on East Asian Studies, Harvard University, 1984.

Kalton, Michael. *To Become a Sage: The Ten Diagrams on Sage Learning by Yi T'oegye.* New York: Columbia University Press, 1988.

Metzger, Thomas A. *Escape from Predicament: Neo-Confucianism and China's Evolving Political Culture.* New York: Columbia University Press, 1977.

Streng, Frederick J. *Understanding Religious Life.* 3rd ed. Belmont, Calif.: Wadsworth, 1985.

Taylor, Rodney L. *The Confucian Way of Contemplation: Okada Takehiko and the Tradition of Quiet-Sitting.* Columbia: University of South Carolina Press, 1988.

————. *The Cultivation of Sagehood as a Religious Goal in Neo-Confucianism: A Study of Selected Writings of Kao P'an-lung (1562–1626).* Missoula, Mont.: Scholars Press/American Academy of Religion, 1978.

————. *An Illustrated Encyclopedia of Confucianism.* New York: Rosen Publishing Group, 2004.

————. "The Religious Character of the Confucian Tradition." *Philosophy East and West* 48 no. 1 (January 1998): 80–107.

————. *The Religious Dimensions of Confucianism.* Albany: State University of New York Press, 1990.

————. *The Way of Heaven: An Introduction to the Confucian Religious Life.* Leiden: E. J. Brill, 1986.

Tucker, Mary Evelyn. *Moral and Spiritual Cultivation in Japanese Neo-Confucianism: The Life and Thought of Kaibara Ekken (1630–1714).* Albany: State University of New York Press, 1990.

Tu Weiming. *Centrality and Commonality: An Essay on Confucian Religiousness.* Albany: State University of New York Press, 1989.

————. *Confucian Thought: Self-hood as Creative Transformation.* Albany: State University of New York Press, 1985.

————. *Humanity and Self-Cultivation: Essays in Confucian Thought.* Berkeley: Asian Humanities Press, 1979.

————. *Way, Learning, and Politics: Essays on the Confucian Intellectual.* Albany: State University of New York Press, 1993.

Part Four

THE TRANSMISSION
OF THE CONFUCIAN WAY

Korea   Japan   Vietnam

24

Sage Learning

MICHAEL C. KALTON

T HE TITLE OF THIS CHAPTER, "Sage Learning," is deliberately ambiguous. Does it mean the learning taught and transmitted by the sages, or does it mean learning to become a sage? By and large, Confucians down to about 1000 C.E. would have had little trouble in answering this question, taking the first alternative and negating the second. The ancient affirmation that every man could become a sage was safely enshrined in the tradition, but sagehood was not really taken as the practical goal of spiritual cultivation.

All this changed with the advent of the great Confucian movement that revitalized and reshaped the tradition in the first two centuries of the second millennium. One of the founding fathers of this Neo-Confucian movement, Zhou Dunyi (1017–1073), wrote a chapter entitled "Sage Learning." In it he boldly asked, "Can sagehood be learned?" He answered with a resounding, "Yes!" and set about describing how. In this enterprise he had many cohorts; the time was ripe for Confucians to discover an analogue to the sophisticated techniques for cultivating the inner life of the mind that led the Buddhists toward the perfection of enlightenment. For too many centuries it had been easy to dismiss the Confucian tradition as rather simple and mundane, a worldly code for dealing with society that usefully complemented the more transcendent dimensions elucidated by Buddhists and Daoists.

These early Neo-Confucians created a new core within the ancient classics as they centered their attention on texts that seemed to speak to questions of inner cultivation or to offer the basis for a metaphysical description of existence. Metaphysics was a necessary prelude; the Buddhist and Daoist examples clearly illustrated that a spiritual path leading to an ultimate perfection could be worked out only on the basis of a clear vision of the nature of reality. Knowing reality, one could comprehend the ultimate potential open to humans and see how it might be realized.

The result of these efforts was a new Confucian synthesis; the traditional Confucian social and moral concerns were now metaphysically grounded and incorporated into a path of spiritual cultivation that might make one a sage. The contributors to this synthesis were many, but the final architect of the integrated system was Zhu Xi (1130–1200). His school of thought became the predominant or "orthodox" line in both China and Korea. In China the fifteenth century saw the rise of a rival Neo-Confucian school, that of Wang Yangming (1472–1529). Wang's school for a time overshadowed that of Zhu Xi in China, but it had little impact on the more tightly organized society of Korea, which prided itself on preserving the "true Dao," that is, the vision of Zhu Xi.

Korean Neo-Confucian spirituality, then, is essentially the spirituality of Zhu Xi's school; and of the interpreters of Zhu Xi none has been held in higher esteem than Yi Hwang (1501–1570), better known by his honorific name, T'oegye. T'oegye's superlative mastery of Zhu Xi's thought made his work a constant reference point for later generations of Korean scholars. Although he made major contributions to the more technical or theoretical aspects of Neo-Confucian thought, his overriding interest was practical self-cultivation or spiritual formation. In particular he poured over Zhu Xi's voluminous correspondence with his students, seeking the spirit and attitudes that were the constant underpinnings of the varied instructions addressed to men of different temperaments, accomplishments, and circumstances. Of T'oegye's many writings, one in particular is suited to form the basis of our inquiry into Neo-Confucian spirituality as practiced in Korea: the *Ten Diagrams on Sage Learning*. In ten brief chapters, each introduced by a diagram, T'oegye leads one step by step from the great metaphysical vision of the universe to a discussion of an appropriate daily routine from rising to bedtime. The *Ten Diagrams* was composed for the young King Sônjo by T'oegye when he was sixty-eight years old and too sick to continue his personal instructions. As the distillation of the wisdom of his long lifetime, it became the best known and most popular of all his works, going through some twenty-nine printings during the next four centuries.

The *Ten Diagrams* excels in completeness: unlike the many spiritual guides that are little but a collection of pithy maxims inculcating correct discipline and values, it integrates spiritual practice with the full metaphysical framework and mediates the transition between them with a description of the metaphysically based psychological theory that informed

Neo-Confucian ascetical theory and practice. The *Ten Diagrams* also is exceedingly compressed, a crystallization of the Neo-Confucian vision rather than an elaboration of it. Fortunately, T'oegye's lengthy correspondence with his students offers us a wealth of material to fill out the fundamental structure given us in the text.

The topics we have mentioned—metaphysics, psychology, ascetical theory and practice—are vast; what we can do within the allotted scope of this chapter can only be an overview that introduces the major lineaments of these closely interrelated areas. To do this, we will follow the essential structure of the *Ten Diagrams*, beginning with the theoretical foundations and working toward a presentation of the actual spiritual discipline or practice elaborated on those foundations.

Metaphysics: The Vision of the Universe

The first of the ten chapters of the *Ten Diagrams* is devoted to Zhou Dunyi's *Diagram of the Supreme Ultimate*, the work that was the cornerstone of Neo-Confucian metaphysics. Neo-Confucian metaphysics is much like other eastern metaphysical systems in that the controlling interest goes beyond the speculative: it describes the nature of existence in order to clarify how we should live if we are to reach our fullest potential. T'oegye comments: "This diagram has been placed at the very beginning of this work for the same reason that its explanation was placed at the beginning of [Zhu Xi's] Reflections on Things at Hand. That is, one who would learn to be a sage should seek the beginning here" (*Ten Diagrams*, ch. 1; *TC*, A, 7.12a).[1]

Zhou's *Diagram* presents the origin and the ultimate dimensions of all existence. The first thing that would strike a Western reader would probably be the absence of some familiar features: no God or Creator, no afterlife or heaven or hell. We know already that the goals of this spirituality will be something quite different from an intense personal relationship with a personal God or the assurance of eternal life. What one finds instead is a philosophical elaboration of a worldview that had long been common in East Asia. This worldview is often described as "organicism," for it assumes a single organic unity running through everything, making the universe something like a single great living body or organism. No creator is required, for it is assumed that the stuff of existence was always there, evolving and transforming in accord with its own inner law or pattern. The same inner law or pattern furnishes direction, meaning, and purpose, being a transcendent ground of existence that is immanent within the universe itself.

Neo-Confucian philosophy gives conceptual precision to this traditional vision in terms of two essential concepts, material force (Korean *ki*, Chinese *qi*), the stuff of existence, and principle (*li*), the term for the inner law or pattern of all things ("the Dao" in traditional parlance; *dao* is often used almost interchangeably with *li* in Neo-Confucian writings). Material force is subtle, formless, and invisible in its pure condition, but it also condenses to more coarse, concrete, differentiated shapes. In persons, pure material force is the stuff and vital energy of the psyche, while coarser material force accounts for physicality; thus the single concept covers much of the terrain the West treats as the dichotomy of spirit and matter. In this view, then, humans are entirely of the same stuff as the rest of the universe.

Principle (*li*) is the guiding, shaping, normative element within material force. There is nothing abstract about this kind of principle: it is the actual structuring pattern that makes everything be what it is and act as it does. Thus, principle is identified as the inner nature of all things. But although there are many things and many kinds of things, principle is ultimately one, or as a much-favored dictum puts it, "principle is one but manifest in distinct ways." The physicality of material force makes multiplicity possible, and its degrees of coarseness are a limiting factor that accounts for the diverse manifestations of the one inner principle. One might think here of a human body, which is one (it's all me and all human) but many (toes are not ears). As one, principle is the Supreme Ultimate, the single pattern or Dao running throughout the universe; as many, it constitutes the natures of the many diverse creatures.

As we shall see, material force and principle serve as central concepts in Neo-Confucian psychological theory and so have great importance for the approach to spiritual self-cultivation. But on a more general level, the type of worldview explicated by these concepts sets the broadest parameters for Neo-Confucian spirituality. First, unlike typical Indian forms of monism that emphasize unity to such an extent that multiplicity is reduced to some sort of illusory or unreal status, there is nothing unreal about multiplicity in this view. Material force really can condense into separate beings. But this multiplicity is unlike the pluralism typical of Western traditions, for underlying the multiplicity there is a unity running throughout all being: in spite of its diverse manifestation in the many beings, principle or the Dao is ultimately one. Although we often experience division and conflict, integration and harmony are the final reality, and a personal realization of that condition is a fundamental element of the spiritual quest. But true to long Confucian tradition, this realization is more a matter of moral perfection than mystical insight. As we shall see, the new metaphysics does ground a meditative practice and even a kind of enlightenment experience, but its final importance is the new grounding it provides for traditional Confucian social morality.

This is made clear by the second chapter of the *Ten Diagrams,* which is devoted to Zhang Zai's *Western Inscription,* a famous essay that explicates the social and ethical consequences of the new metaphysics. Its tenor may be readily seen in the following passage:

> All people are from the same womb as I, all creatures are my companions. The Great Ruler is the eldest son of my parents, and his great ministers are the household retainers of the eldest son. By honoring those who are advanced in years, I carry out the respect for age which is due my aged, and by kindness to the solitary and weak, I carry out the tender care for the young which should be paid to my young. The Sage is at one with the character [of Heaven and Earth], and the wise man is of their finest [stuff]. All persons in the world who are exhausted, decrepit, worn out, or ill, or who are brotherless, childless, widowers, or widowed, are my own brothers who have become helpless and have none to whom they can appeal. (*Ten Diagrams,* ch. 2; *TC,* A, 7.13b)

Confucians had long pondered the implications of physical and psychic continuity in a family line, and this understanding of the family provided the most basic norm for proper self-understanding. Thus filial piety, behaving as befits one who exists as an extention of the existence of parents and ancestors and is entrusted with transmitting the life of the family forward to another generation, constitutes the fundament of human existence. But the virtue of virtues in the Confucian tradition is humanity (Korean *in;* Chinese *ren*), the virtue of relating in the proper way with other people. Zhang Zai's brilliant essay used the familiar language of family continuity and filial piety to discuss relationships within a sweeping cosmic framework in which Heaven and Earth are parents in a more than metaphorical sense. The well-worn path of grounding family conduct on a single shared wellspring of vital force in effect becomes the paradigm to provide the whole of Confucian social ethics with a new kind of cosmic or metaphysical grounding. T'oegye comments:

> For Heng-ch'ü [Zhang Zai] in this inscription repeatedly reasons out and clarifies how the principle shared by oneself, Heaven and Earth, and all creatures is fundamentally one. He formulates the substance of humanity in order to break down the selfishness of the self, expand on the impartiality of selflessness, and make the stonelike obstinate mind-and-heart dissolve and fuse with no separation between the self and others, allowing no place for the least bit of self-centered intentions between them. One can thus see that

Heaven and Earth are as a single family, the whole nation as a single person, and that the suffering and distress [of others] is truly that of one's own person; [understanding this] one attains the tao of humanity. (*TC*, A, 7.49b)

One can see here the spiritual vision this metaphysics serves. But as T'oegye constantly emphasizes, this is not just some vast, abstract ideal. It must become a matter of personal experience and personal conduct, and that requires a very serious application to the task of self-cultivation. Although the nature of the universe and our own innermost nature would have us be like this, there are obstructions that call for a demanding process of self-cultivation before the ordinary person can become what he most truly is. A consideration of the Neo-Confucian description of the human person and his or her psyche will help us better understand this situation.

Psychological Theory: The Human Person and the Person's Psyche

We have seen that *li*, or principle, constitutes the inner nature of the various creatures, while the concrete stuff of their existence is *ki*, or material force. But how does the one principle account for many different kinds of beings? The Neo-Confucian answer is that material force, with its many gradations of purity and coarseness or turbidity, is a limiting factor that differentiates principle into the many kinds of beings. Strictly speaking, the difference between humans and other creatures is a difference not so much of kind as of degree: human beings are constituted of material force of such purity that they possess principle in its integrity. Thus, while other creatures are limited to various degrees in their capacity to respond and deal with situations, humans are essentially unlimited: possessing all principle, there is nothing with which they are not involved, nothing that is not included in their response structure. Humanity thus joins Heaven and Earth to form the ultimate triad responsible for the nurture and well-being of all things. They share, as it were, a single mind:

But what is this mind [of which we speak]? In Heaven and Earth it is the inexhaustible disposition to produce and give life to creatures; in men it is the warm love for others and the disposition to benefit all creatures.[2]

Just as differences in material force on the macro level limit principle and constitute different species, so within the species variances in turbidity or purity also function to explain the relative adequacy or inadequacy with which the perfection of nature is realized. The crucial application, of course, is the human one, where the turbidity of the psychophysical stuff of our being accounts for our lack of moral perfection. Neo-Confucians sometimes used the vivid image of the paralysis of a limb in discussing this: we become insensitive to our vital unity with other beings and are incapable of acting responsively to them. We share a single body, but act as if we did not belong to it; the perfect responsiveness inherent in our nature is obscured and blocked up by the turbidity of material force.

These fundamental ideas already contain the seeds of an approach to the problem of spiritual self-cultivation. Notice the way the problem is posed: it does not start with free will and the human person poised between alternative choices of good and evil. Rather, it assumes that the person is a responder within a situation; humans are constituted to respond properly, and the question is what causes them to deviate from a proper response. The ideal person, the sage, responds to any situation with spontaneous perfection; the ordinary person must deliberate carefully, a witness to the fact that something renders us less than perfectly in touch with the situation or with our own deepest responses. Spiritual cultivation, then, must begin by identifying the factors that hinder and distort our inherently proper responsiveness and follow this up with appropriate remedies. In view of the ideal of spontaneity, we might look for a methodology with elements of "saturation," which can somehow overcome the ordinary dividedness and perplexity that beset the inner life of uncertain human beings.

Before we can get to a specific methodology, however, we must first identify more exactly the nature of the human spiritual problem. This means that we will have to take up some of the complexities of Neo-Confucian psychological theory. T'oegye devotes chapter 6 of his *Ten Diagrams* to this matter; it provides the essential framework for the practical ascetical teaching of the final four chapters.

Chapter 6 has as its title and topic a famous saying of Zhang Zai: "The mind combines and governs the nature and the feelings" (*Zhang Zi quan shu*, 14.2a). Nature and feelings are intimately related: nature (principle) is a person's inner structuring, and feelings are the active manifestation of that structuring. The mind, when it is still and quiescent, may be thought of as simply possessing its nature or structure; when it becomes active in response to something, feelings move in accord with its inner structure. For Confucians, "feelings" include matters such as approving of right and disapproving of wrong and a sense of modesty and deference as well as the more familiar items such as joy, anger, sorrow, and so on. Since there is no basic differentiation made between feeling and intellect as separate faculties, there is no tendency to glorify the one and suppress the other.

In fact, the feeling response of the mind would be perfect if it were not for the disruptive turbidity of material force. As the concretizing and energizing component of human being, material force constitutes the psychic being of our mind-and-heart as well as the physical being of our bodies. Thus, the influence of material force is present in all mental activity, its imperfection being manifest as the distorting thrust of self-centeredness that can disrupt the spontaneous appropriateness of the feelings. The turbidity of material force and the isolated insensitivity of self-centeredness, then, express on the metaphysical and moral levels respectively the essential spiritual problem. Human nature is perfect, but our physical separateness and psychic opacity may disrupt our natural responsiveness and leave us literally blocked up inside ourselves.

These observations bring us to what has historically been the great divide between the major schools of Neo-Confucian thought and spirituality, those of Zhu Xi and of Wang Yangming. Unlike Zhu Xi's emphasis on the role of material force in the functioning of the mind, Wang and his followers tended to identify the mind with principle. Thus, we have only to recover our true mind and we will respond to all situations with the spontaneous perfection of a sage. This form of Neo-Confucianism, as followers of Zhu Xi often observed, comes very close to Chan (Zen) Buddhism.

In Korea, however, Wang had little influence. In part this was because T'oegye made subtle and controversial distinctions regarding the way material force functions in relation to principle as the various kinds of feelings originate. The debate that ensued became central to the Korean intellectual agenda for centuries. Its details need not concern us here, but we should be aware that since all involved assumed, like Zhu Xi, that the mind included the functioning of material force as an essential and problematic element, the prevalent spirituality paid close attention to techniques that might prevent distorting forces in the wellspring of our psychic activity. T'oegye specifies the critical point as follows:

> The essence of the matter is this: that which includes both principle and material force and combines and governs the nature and the feelings is the mind; and the moment of the nature's issuance as feelings is the subtle wellspring of the whole mind, the pivot of ten thousand transformations, the separation point of good and evil. (*Ten Diagrams*, ch. 6; *TC*, A, 7.24b)

The distortion that may be introduced by the material force component (selfish desire) makes the transition from quiet to activity, from nature to feelings, a critical moment, for the role of material force begins with activity. But the mind is not only the passive locus of this transition ("combines the nature and the feelings"); it also has the distinctive function of presiding over it ("governs the nature and the feelings"). Thus, the alert governance of the mind emerges as the central feature of the spirituality premised on this psychology. The remarks with which T'oegye concludes the sixth chapter clearly reflect the dominant tone of this type of spirituality:

> If one who pursues learning is truly able to recollect himself through maintaining mindfulness, and not confusing principle with human desires brings the greatest caution to bear on this matter, if his application to the composure [of his mind] and the nurturing [of his nature] before the mind is aroused is profound, and he is well-versed in the exercise of reflection and discernment after it is aroused, and if he accumulates truth and is constant in his effort for a long time and does not stop, then the learning of sagehood . . . and the method of cultivating the mind wherein it is composed in substance and [accurately] responsive in function, need not be sought elsewhere, but will all be attained in this. (*Ten Diagrams*, ch. 6; *TC*, A, 7.24b–25a)

This single sentence is a summary of his spiritual theory. It alludes to topics and contains terminology that will require the remainder of this chapter to explicate fully, but the emphasis on constant watchfulness and unremitting hard work over an extended period of time are marks of the Zhu Xi school that are not easily missed.

The Essential Method: The Investigation of Principle

We have seen that the proper responsiveness of the mind-and-heart is a central concern in this spirituality. It would be wrong to conclude from this, however, that such spiritual cultivation is mainly inward-looking. The same *li* structures both the external world and the internal life of our psyches, so our internal responsive structures equip us to respond appropriately to every situation. But ordinary people do not enjoy such a perfect and unhindered integration of their interior with the world they encounter. The imperfection of our psychophysical constitution introduces a twofold problem: externally we may imperfectly apprehend the world, and internally our selfish proclivities may distort our responsive impulses. Of course these are intimately related facets of a holistic spiritual situation, for looking at the world through self-centered eyes is a systemic distortion encompassing at once misapprehension and impaired responsiveness. Cultivation must address both facets of this situation.

Our proclivity to misapprehend must be remedied by study or "the investigation of principle," as it was often called. The investigation of principle had as its aim the attainment of objective truth, but it was far different from the kind of detached, "objective" method that typifies modern science. Misapprehension of the kind addressed by "the investigation of principle" certainly included the dimension of needing accurate information, so ordinary study and learning could not be neglected. But beyond that, this quest for objectivity attended with particular care to the many games we play with ourselves. Thus, the emphasis was on the subject rather than the object as detached from the subject; one sought self-transformation through a personal grasp and appropriation of the moral truth as the truth of one's own being. As T'oegye instructed in a typical case:

> As for the interpretation of humanity, righteousness, propriety, and wisdom, if one only looks at their terminological meaning, though in the recitation or interpretation [of texts] one does not make the slightest error, in the end what profit is there in it? It is necessary to make the meaning of these four words one's [personal] subject matter; entering into thought on their meaning sit quietly, immerse your mind in them, and investigate them deeply, mulling them over and getting their real flavor with a personal understanding and personal examination. (Letter to Yi P'yŏngsuk; TC, A, 37.25b)

Virtually anything, from current events and the affairs of daily life to the sayings and writings of the ancient sages could be matter for the investigation of principle. Books, of course, were an important source, but this kind of investigation required a reading method quite different from the extensive reading and memorization of texts pursued by those studying for the civil service examinations:

> [Kim Sŏngil] asked about the method of reading books. Master T'oegye said: It is only a matter of ripening. In all reading of books, although one may clearly understand the meaning of the text, if it is not ripened, as soon as it is read it is forgotten, and it is certain that one cannot preserve it in his mind-and-heart. After study one must further apply oneself to becoming thoroughly versed and ripened in it; only then will he be able to preserve it in his mind-and-heart and be thoroughly steeped in its taste. (Ŏnhaengnok [Record of T'oegye's Sayings and Deeds], 1.7a; TC, B, p. 792)

This idea of "ripening" occurs frequently in texts dealing with the pursuit of learning. It indicates the gradual absorption and personal assimilation and complete mastery of principle until it becomes second nature—or in Confucian terms, a recovery of our "original nature." In this kind of learning, of course, study and practice are complementary aspects of a single process, for there can be no such ripening without long practice.

T'oegye composed his *Ten Diagrams* in a format that is premised on this methodology. I have mentioned the extremely compressed nature of this work. This was deliberate: T'oegye's idea was that it should be not only a book but also a work that could be made into a ten-panel screen that might be set in the king's personal quarters. For it is not so much a text to be read, as it is a crystallized vision to be lived with and absorbed over the years as ordinary activity alternates with quiet contemplation in the routine of daily life:

> If one takes up one diagram for consideration, he should entirely focus his attention on that diagram, as if he did not know there were any others; if one takes up one matter for practice, he should entirely focus his attention on that one matter as if ignorant that any other existed. Whether morning or night, there should be constancy; from one day to the next there should be a single continuity. At times one should go over [what one has learned] and become steeped in its savor in the restorative atmosphere of the early predawn hours when the mind is clear; at others he should deepen his personal experience of it, nurturing and cultivating it in his interaction with others in his daily life. (*Chin sônghak sipdo* [Address Presenting the *Ten Diagrams* to King Sônjo]; *TC,* A, 7.8a–8b)

This describes the life of earnest and continual self-cultivation that is the context within which a work such as the *Ten Diagrams* can find a place and a use. There is a single technical term in Neo-Confucian discourse that encompasses this entire lifestyle: the practice of mindfulness (Korean *kyông;* Chinese *jing*). "Mindfulness" is the absolute core of what T'oegye understands as the spiritual teaching transmitted by Zhu Xi and the focal point of T'oegye's own spiritual methodology. But in order to understand its role in synthesizing every aspect of spiritual self-cultivation, we must first consider two fundamental modes of cultivation and their attendant practice.

Cultivation in Quiet and in Activity

The classical foundation for the Neo-Confucian analysis of the basic states of the mind comes from the famous first chapter of the *Doctrine of the Mean:*

> Before the feelings of pleasure, anger, sorrow, and joy are aroused, it is called equilibrium. When these feelings are aroused and each and all attain due measure and degree, it is called harmony. Equilibrium is the great foundation of the world, and harmony its universal path. When equilibrium and harmony are realized to the highest degree, heaven and earth will attain their proper order and all things will flourish.[3]

What this meant to Neo-Confucians is summed up in the sentences that express the structure of the mind in the diagram attached to chapter 6:

> The mind as perfectly still and not active is the nature; as stirred and going forth penetratingly it is the feelings. The not-yet-aroused state, the nature, is

the substance of the mind; the aroused state, the feelings, is the function of the mind.

Here we have the nature (principle) as the inner structure or substance of the mind; that is all that is there in the absence of activity. Correlated with this are the feelings, the activity issuing from and manifesting the substantial structure as the mind responds to various situations. With the *Doctrine of the Mean*'s description of equilibrium and harmony in mind, one can readily see that the entire order and well-being of the universe are contingent on cultivating the perfection of these two states or aspects of the mind.

Based on this framework, Neo-Confucian spirituality is thus structured on an alternation of quiet and activity. To a certain extent this reflects the background of traditional *yin-yang* thought, for quiet and activity were two of the primary qualities associated with these primordial cosmological symbols. It is noteworthy, however, that the interpretation given these states in the Neo-Confucian reading of the *Doctrine of the Mean* is not simply the alternation of relative quiet and activity, but absolute quiet (quiescence) and activity. Centuries of familiarity with Buddhist meditation practices had made it natural to posit objectless consciousness as a fundamental mental condition, and the analytical distinction of the mind in terms of substance and function, nature and feelings, likewise invited such an interpretation. In any case, here we find a systematic basis for meditative practice to enter the Confucian tradition.

All that we have discussed regarding the investigation of principle belongs to the cultivation of the mind in activity: study, practice, reflection, and understanding belong on this active side—any conceivable activity. What then is left for the cultivation of the other side? What content and what significance could a Confucian find in absolute quiescence? The answer is, very much. So much, in fact, that for a time this side of cultivation threatened to overshadow the attention paid to cultivating the mind in its active state. Early masters developed a practice called "quiet-sitting," which was the practice of sitting in a condition of objectless consciousness. At times this practice was attacked as dangerously close to Zen, but Neo-Confucian suppositions about the mind almost necessarily demanded something of the kind. T'oegye cautioned his students against one-sided quietism, but he also felt that this practice was fundamental:

> Only after [practicing] quiet-sitting can one's mind and body become recollected and moral principles finally all come together and be anchored. If one's form and bones are heedlessly relaxed and without restraint, then the body and mind are darkened and disordered and moral principle no longer has a place to which to gather and be anchored. Therefore Kao-t'ing [Zhu Xi]

quiet-sat facing Master Yen-p'ing for an entire day, and after he had parted from him likewise did so on his own. (*Ŏnhaengnok*, 1.16b, *TC*, B, p. 796)

Similar meditation practices may take on a quite different significance in the context of different religious traditions. In T'oegye's words we begin to see what this profound quiescence meant in a Neo-Confucian context. Recalling that all principle, that is, the undifferentiated Supreme Ultimate, is wholly present as the substance of the mind, we may understand how a profound quiet with no discernible object or activity may be understood as simply putting the mind in union with the pure and perfect Source; as T'oegye puts it, "all moral principle has a place to which it can gather and be anchored." An unrestrained and distracted mind is certainly out of touch with principle, hence calm and control become in themselves positive values, and this is the perfection of calm and control.

If one goes only this far, however, we are still in the context of a kind of transcendentally oriented mysticism—the slippery Zen side of this practice that masters continually warned against. Its fully Neo-Confucian significance demands a relation to activity and morality. This emerges if we return to the fundamental Neo-Confucian approach to good and evil as a matter of proper response to a situation. From quiet union with its substance, the mind can move to an undistorted active response:

> [Yi] Tôkhong asked: As for not a single thing being permitted [to have a hold] within the mind-and-heart, does this mean that even such a thing as a norm of what is appropriate likewise should not be permitted? [T'oegye] said: No, that's not it. The integral substance of the mind is perfectly empty and perfectly still, like a clear mirror that reflects things. When something presents itself one responds to it but it does not clog up [the mind]; when it goes, one is as previously, empty and clear. If [the mind] becomes fixated with something it is like a mirror soiled with mud; it is entirely unable to attain its empty, clear, quiet, undivided condition. (*Ŏnhaengnok*, 1.14a; *TC*, B, p. 795)

In its precise sense, Tôkhong's question addresses the issue of mindfulness, a practice that includes cultivation of both quiet and active states. T'oegye's answer, however, clearly reflects the value of the empty, clear, still state of quiet. For a Confucian, the characteristics of this state are valued not as ends in themselves but because such mental qualities obviate distortion and make one more perfectly responsive to the ever-changing situations encountered in dealing with the affairs of the world.

This having been said, however, these developments still could undermine the effort devoted to the active side of cultivation. We have seen that the nature is the substance of the mind; if one just cultivated quiet integration with that fundamental inner structure, would not activity evidence the spontaneous perfection of sagehood? Such an inference might easily be made, but in the view of Zhu Xi's school it is only partially true: in practice it would lead to quietism, and it is one-sided in neglecting the need for the external investigation of principle. Having natural feelings of hunger and an instinct to eat is not yet, after all, an adequate grasp of proper nutrition. As T'oegye explains, the need to find a more appropriate balance called forth a further conceptualization of the cultivation process:

> The purport of making quiet the primary thing has been spoken of by Confucius, Mencius, Zhou [Zhou Dunyi], and the Chengs; in the school of Kuei-shan [Yang Shi] what was passed on as the essential key until it reached Hui-am [Zhu Xi] likewise consisted in this. How much more is it so since it is the medicine which fits your particular problem! But if one makes a single slip in this matter he will fall into Zen. Therefore Master Cheng [Cheng Yi] and Master Zhu also have a thesis about employing mindfulness rather than quietness. This was because they feared people would mistakenly slip into [Zen] and so they put forth this explanation to save them; it was not that they regarded making quiet the primary thing as impermissible. Nevertheless one likewise should not get fed up with the complexity of broad study and restraining oneself with propriety, and exclusively devote oneself to concentrating on quietness. (Letter to Kim Ijông; *TC*, A, 28.29b–30a)

This brings us to mindfulness, the central theme of the self-cultivation taught in the *Ten Diagrams*.

Mindfulness

Historically the balance between the external and internal, the active and the quiet sides of self-cultivation in the Zhu Xi school proved difficult to maintain. The doctrine of mindfulness was explicitly developed to include both sides and to embrace every aspect of self-cultivation. With this doctrine the substance-function differentiation of quiet and activity recedes into the background and is replaced by the notion of a simple yin-yang like alternation between quiet and activity; this alternation is just the ordinary rhythm of life, and mindfulness applied appropriately to each is the essence of self-cultivation.

In the *Ten Diagrams* the last two chapters are devoted entirely to mindfulness. In chapter 8 T'oegye quotes a text that may serve as a useful introduction:

> In sum, the essence of applying one's efforts is nothing other than a matter of not departing from constant mindfulness, for the mind is the master of the

entire person and mindfulness is the master of the mind. If one who pursues learning will but thoroughly master what is meant by "focusing on one thing without departing from it," "being properly ordered and controlled, grave and quiet," and "recollecting the mind and making it always awake and alert," his practice will be utterly perfect and complete, and entering the condition of sagehood likewise will not be difficult. (*Ten Diagrams*, ch. 8; *TC*, A, 7.29b)

Early Chinese masters each developed slightly different approaches or descriptions of mindfulness; the phrases that crystallize three of them are used above. To them we might add another that was highly regarded by T'oegye: "not allowing a single thing [to have hold on one's mind]."

One can see running throughout these expressions the influence of a psychology that identified mastery as the distinctive function of the mind and viewed such mastery as the key to the mind's proper responsiveness. "Focusing on the matter at hand" is necessary for an appropriate reading of the situation; "being always awake and alert" has a similar rationale and recognizes the problem of dullness as well as wandering; "not allowing a single thing to have hold on the mind" maintains the mind's own mastery and signifies the absence of the kind of selfish desires that give things the power to control us.

But T'oegye commonly advised his students to approach the practice of mindfulness through the "properly ordered and controlled, grave and quiet" description. Utilizing the terminology of traditional Confucian propriety and decorum, this is the most externalistic and nonmental of the four approaches, but it also attains the calm focused condition aimed at more directly by the others:

> Now, in seeking where to begin applying your effort, you should take Master Cheng [Cheng Yi]'s "properly ordered and controlled, grave and quiet," saying as the first matter. If you practice it for a long time and are not neglectful, you will personally experience that you have not been deceived by his saying that, "then the mind will become single and will not offend by wrong or depraved thoughts." If your exterior is grave and quiet and your mind within is single, then what is referred to as, "Focus on one thing; do not depart," what is described as, "The mind is recollected and does not allow a single thing [to have hold on it]," and what is called "always being bright and alert," will all be included in it without having to depend on a separate particular form of practice for each item. (Letter to Kim Ijông; *TC*, A, 29.13a–13b)

T'oegye's preference is based on the reliability of this sort of approach: "In this there is no place for searching after [a particular mental condition] or trying to manage [the mind] in a particular way" (*Ŏnhaengnok*, 1.15a; *TC*, B, p. 796). The control and self-discipline inculcated by strict propriety would of itself involve the kind of recollected and focused condition of mind signified by mindfulness. Especially for beginners it is more suitable than attempting the direct control of mental states.

As a technique of self-cultivation, mindfulness is a matter of maintaining continual presence of mind. Initially it was addressed to the active, engaged state of mind as a balance to an early emphasis on quiet-sitting, but eventually it came to be regarded as including the quiet state as well. Thus, as in the case of T'oegye, it could be emphasized as the single methodology that encompassed everything: it entailed a presence of mind that simply assumed different forms, ranging from a meditative objectless consciousness to alert reflective awareness of the matter at hand, depending on one's situation.

This much, however, describes the technique without adequately accounting for the values or attitude that motivated it and gave such practice its particular Confucian significance. We may begin by noting that the description of mindfulness in terms of propriety was not only for beginners. It was valued not only as less open to mistaken understanding and practice, but also because it includes an element that might be missed in the more mentalistic descriptions that only emphasize some sort of recollection, focus, or presence of mind. Confucians had long emphasized that propriety that does not flow from reverence is empty show, and it is this same sense of reverence that is the inner wellspring of mindfulness.

In fact, the classical meaning of the term we have been translating as "mindfulness" is "reverence." The traditional meaning still pertains even when the term takes on a special technical sense in the context of Neo-Confucian discourse; an alternative translation is called for only because on the surface "reverence" does not suggest the concern for a recollected and focused consciousness that became a critical factor in the framework of Neo-Confucian ascetical theory. Reverence is manifested outwardly in propriety, but within it involves a condition of self-possession and attentiveness and in this respect the term was well suited for the technical meaning given it by Neo-Confucians.

Reverence for what, and why? For outsiders, who must assimilate the complex Neo-Confucian discourse on principle and material force as a system of philosophy, the question is perplexing, for here we are dealing with the religious character of the tradition. It is important to be aware that theistic language is still fraught with meaning for Neo-Confucians. One of T'oegye's favorite passages in his own beloved guide to self-cultivation, the *Classic of the Mind-and-Heart,* quotes from the *Book of Odes:* "The *Book of Odes* says: 'The Lord on High watches over you; do not be of two minds.' And again it says: "Do not be of two minds, do not be negligent; the Lord on High watches over you."[4] These passages, written before the time of Confucius, reflect a sense of religious awe and reverence that was not lost as the worldview subsequently took a less theistic form. Rather the nonpersonal and immanent pattern or structure that largely supplanted the figure of a personal divine being as the governing or directive agency of the universe became the object of the same sort of religious feeling. That is why Neo-Confucians are perfectly at home using the imagery of a personal God to express their own religious sense. T'oegye exhorted young King Sônjo:

> Thus the *Book of Odes* speaks of reverence for the Tao of Heaven, saying: "Reverence it, reverence it! Heaven is lustrous, its Mandate is not easy! Do not say it is lofty and high above; ascending and descending, it watches daily over your affairs." For with regard to the issuing forth of the principle of Heaven, there is nothing in which it is not present and no time that it is not so. If in one's daily conduct there is a slight deviance from the principle of Heaven and one slips into following [selfish] human desire, this is not how one reverences Heaven. . . . The oversight of Heaven is bright and perceptive; how can it but be feared! Therefore the *Odes* again says: "Fear the majesty of Heaven; at all times maintain [your awe]." (*Ŏnhaengnok*, 3.23a–23b; *TC*, B, p. 830)

Such passages make it clear that the fact that the Dao or principle is an immanent and constituent element of the world does not thereby render them mundane; rather they point to an ever-present transcendent or absolute element within the mundane that demands our ultimate seriousness and reverence in everything we do. This is the religious spirit of reverence that animates the practice of mindfulness.

Lifestyle

Up to this point we have seen major features of the broad framework and spiritual cultivation practice typical of the form of Neo-Confucianism prevalent in Chosôn dynasty Korea (1392–1910). But within the various elements we have discussed, there is an implicit lifestyle, a mode of living that might be regarded as maximally beneficial for someone who is serious about such cultivation. T'oegye concludes his *Ten Diagrams* with a chapter that depicts this lifestyle in the form of an ideal day. The material he used was a Song dynasty Chinese text, the *Admonition on "Rising Early and Retiring Late,"*[5] but it very much reflects his own ideal: "The *Admonition on Rising Early and Retiring Late* fully expresses the way of pursuing learning. Although I have not been able personally to carry it out [fully], it is what I wish to practice" (Letter to No Susin; *TC*, A, 10.14a).

The text of the *Admonition* presents an ideal day in seven divisions. I have added numbers to the text for ease of reference:

1. When the cock crows and you awake, thoughts gradually increase their pace; at this time how can one but compose himself and bring order to them. Sometimes reflect on your past faults; at others follow out what has been newly apprehended. With proper order and sequence, lucidly ponder this matter in silence.

2. The foundation being thus established, as day breaks, rise, brush your teeth, comb your hair, and don your robes and cap. Then, sitting erect, compose your body and recollect your mind, making it as luminous as the rising sun; become solemn and silent, ordered and even, empty and lucid, still and undivided.

3. Then open your books and enter the presence of the sages and wise men; Confucius is seated, Yan Hui and Zeng Zi attend before and behind. Personally and reverently attend to the words of the Sage Master; carefully going over and reconsidering the questions and discussions of the disciples, settle them [in your own mind].

4. When some matter arises, respond to it; then you may experience [what you have been learning] in actual practice. The clear Mandate will shine forth; keep your attention constantly upon it. When the matter has been responded to and is finished, be as you were before, with your mind clear and calm. Recollect your spirit and dispel distracting thoughts.

5. Over the cyclic alternation of activity and quiet, the mind alone presides; it should be possessed in quiet and discerning in activity. Do not allow it to become divided into two or three. In the time left over from reading, from time to time take a swim to relax your mind and refresh and nourish your feelings and nature.

6. As the sun sets one tends to slacken and a dull spirit easily comes upon one; purify, refresh, order and settle yourself, reinvigorating your mind. When the night is far gone, go to bed, lying with your hands at your sides and your feet together; do not let your mind wander in thought, but make it return to abide [in repose]. Nurture it in the restorative atmosphere of the night; after Steadfastness there is a return to Origination.

7. Be mindful of the matter at hand, industrious day and night. (*Ten Diagrams*, ch. 10; *TC*, A, 7.34a–34b)

Mencius had said that the night tends to restore things to their original and proper condition after the stress and distortion of the day, and that in the early predawn hours a man's nature would thus be nearest its originally good condition. Thus no. 6 speaks of nurturing the mind "in the restorative atmosphere of the night," and in no. 1 we see how the day begins before dawn when one can utilize the restored mind to think things over before any distorting influences can take effect. The rest of this day is well summarized in no. 5: "Over the cyclic alternation of activity and quiet, the mind alone presides; it should be possessed in quiet and discerning in activity." Continual mental self-possession is the theme throughout, as we move from quiet-sitting (no. 2), to the investigation of principle by reading (no. 3), to various sorts of more active tasks and then back again to quiet (no. 4). If one can maintain this mental condition, then in every situation "the clear Mandate will shine forth," that is, principle, the proper way of acting and responding, will be evident. In sum, the vision and practice of self-cultivation we have discussed are fully embodied in this kind of daily routine.

It is noteworthy that the whole flavor of the day presented here as ideal is that of the quiet life of a scholar living in retirement, far from the distracting cares of the world. It is certainly quite different from the busy life of a government official that was the traditional Confucian ideal. Where in earlier Confucianism there was one clear ideal type of life, that of a government official, now there seem to be two.

It is not difficult to see how this happened in the context of the sophisticated mind-and-heart–centered spirituality developed by the Neo-Confucians. There was no deliberate intent to displace the traditional Confucian orientation toward active participation in society and government. Quite the contrary: this spirituality was carefully framed so as to provide for a serious pursuit of spiritual cultivation that would not detract from the active life. T'oegye writes:

> In general, the way one should pursue learning does not take into account the presence or absence of affairs [to be dealt with] or the presence or absence of intention; one should only regard mindfulness as the primary thing and then neither activity nor quiescence will miss the norm. Before thoughts have arisen the substance of the mind will be empty and clear and its fundament deep and pure; after thoughts have arisen moral principle will be clearly manifest and [selfish] desire will recede and be cut off. The problem of a confused and disordered [state of mind] will gradually diminish in proportion as one accumulates [practice] and approaches becoming fully accomplished. This is the essential method. (Letter to Kim Tonso; *TC*, A, 28.17a)

Recalling that this mental recollection is sought as a means of ensuring proper responsiveness to every situation, one can even say that an active life is presupposed in this spirituality. It is a working out of the classic Confucian injunction to cultivate oneself in order to perfect one's family, one's state, and finally the whole world.

But while such values remain intact, the very nature of this spirituality invites an alternative lifestyle. The investigation of principle and the cultivation of continual mental calm and self-possession are demanding and engrossing tasks. They have a direct relevance for the perfection of one's activities, but certainly one must already have a solid spiritual foundation in order to continue with such cultivation in a busy round of daily activities. The milieu described in the *Admonition* is the kind in which one could develop such a foundation as an ideal preparation for an active life in government and society. But if for any reason one did not choose such a career, such pursuits could easily be taken as the main task of one's life. Neo-Confucians as a matter of fact emphasized that this kind of self-cultivation required years of continual serious application. If one was serious about spiritual cultivation and perhaps even sagehood, then clearly the quiet life depicted here would be more suitable than the busy turmoil of public life.

It is only a short step from this to a negative evaluation of "the world" and a "worldly" career. As T'oegye wrote to a young friend about to begin a promising career in government:

> If you allow a slight gap you will not be able to avoid your mind becoming lazy, your intention becoming lax, and your thoughts being turned about. The worldly notion of what constitutes profit and loss, disaster or blessing, consequently acts as a pressure and threat that gradually dissolves and melts [one's original resolve]; thus there are few who do not change from the ends they initially served and come to regard accommodation with the world as acceptable and turning their backs on the Tao for the pursuit of gain as the most profitable course. This is the most fearful thing of all. (Letter to Ki Myôngôn; *TC*, A, 16.6a–6b)

On the one hand, the world may be regarded as the stage upon which one acts to bring about the perfection of one's society; but, on the other, it can also be regarded as typifying the wrong kind of mentality or motivation. When the "nonworldly" mentality is also crystallized into an alternative lifestyle, one begins to hear even in the deliberately worldly Confucian tradition echoes of the pejorative note common to monastic discourse in all traditions. For years T'oegye himself sought to escape from an official career of the sort ordinary persons longed to attain. His eyes were on values invisible to those who live for profit and aggrandizement:

> Worldlings all alike race along the path of honor and profit. If they succeed, they regard it as happiness; if they fail, they feel it a matter for anxiety and lamenting. The multitude are all like this. They do not understand what the wise find in the mountains and forests that they can plant themselves there and are able to forget about such values. But there is certainly something there! There is certainly something they attain! There is certainly something which they preserve and find peace in! There is certainly something which

brings happiness to their hearts, but which others cannot understand as they do. (Letter to Cho Konjung, *TC*, A, 10.3a–3b)

As this passage reflects, those who seriously devoted themselves to the kind of self-cultivation we have described were a self-conscious minority: rigorous self-cultivation is not a mass phenomenon.

These men were a strong social and political influence, however. The monastic tone of such passages does not signify a real break with the world. Even those who retired to the mountains and forests were closely connected with active life insofar as they attracted young students eager to learn and to try to carry out their ideals in active careers. The spirituality practiced by Korean Neo-Confucians was strongly centered on Zhu Xi's investigation of principle and on continual mental self-possession or mindfulness, but these practices served the final goal of becoming the kind of person described in Mencius's classic description of a fully-realized human being:

> He dwells in the wide house of the world; he stands in the correct seat of the world; he walks in the great path of the world. When he attains his desire [for office], he shares the pursuit [of his principles] with the people; when he does not attain it, he practices them alone. Wealth and high position cannot corrupt him; poverty and low estate cannot move him; majesty and might cannot bend him. Such is what is meant by the Great Man. (*Mencius* 3B:2)

Notes

1. All references to *T'oegye chônso* (The Complete Works of T'oegye) (hereafter *TC*) are to the two-volume edition, Seoul: Sônggyun'gwan Taehakkyo Taedong Munhwa Yôn'guwôn, 1958, photo reprint.

2. From Zhu Xi's *Treatise on Humanity*, quoted in *Ten Diagrams*, ch. 7, *TC*, A, 7.27a.

3. As translated by Wing-tsit Chan, *A Source Book in Chinese Philosophy* (Princeton, N.J.: Princeton University Press, 1963), 98.

4. *Hsin-ching fu-chu* [The Classic of the Mind and Heart, Amplified and Annotated], 1.4b. The passage quotes *Odes* #236 and #300 respectively.

5. The author was a Song dynasty scholar named Chen Bo. The title is a reference to a passage in *Book of Odes* #256.

25

A Confucian Spirituality in Yi T'oegye: A Korean Neo-Confucian Interpretation and Its Implications for Comparative Religion

E D W A R D   Y.   J.   C H U N G

YI T'OEGYE (1501–1570), a leading figure of Korean Neo-Confucianism in the Chosôn dynasty (1393–1910), has been known in Western scholarship.[1] In short, he was a great scholar-teacher respected as the "Zhu Xi of Korea" or the Korean Neo-Confucian synthesizer.[2] As a creative thinker and spiritual practitioner, he not only exerted a profound influence on the philosophical and scholarly development of Neo-Confucianism in Korea but also left behind a lasting legacy of original moral ideas and spiritual insights. Current scholarship on T'oegye's thought makes a significant contribution to our growing understanding of Korean Neo-Confucianism, although most works are primarily concerned with its philosophical, historical, and related patterns. Accordingly, we need to know more about the spiritual-religious significance of T'oegye's thought.

This essay discusses T'oegye's understanding and practice of Confucian spirituality with a textual and hermeneutical approach. Its first section discusses his interpretation of Confucian sagehood and self-cultivation according to his major works. Our related concern in the second section is to examine the way in which T'oegye intensifies this key element of Confucian spirituality in relation to certain Neo-Confucian ideas and practices.

The final section of the essay presents relevant questions and reflections in a contemporary and comparative context of religion and spirituality. For example, What is significant about T'oegye's Neo-Confucian spirituality? How does it differ from, and relate to, the major types of Western spirituality? What about in terms of "faith," "transcendence," and "immanence"? What can we say about the T'oegye paradigm in connection to the general patterns of Confucian "humanism" and Confucian "religiosity"? Why is this relevant to the academic discipline of comparative religion/theology and its growing field of interreligious (or interspiritual) dialogue? I conclude by pointing out that T'oegye's spiritual practices and insights are paramount not only to a deeper comprehension of Confucian scholarship but also to our global appreciation of religion and human spirituality.

Sagehood and Self-Cultivation

At the core of the Confucian and Neo-Confucian tradition lies the fundamental project of self-cultivation and its ultimate quest for sagehood.[3] In their reformulation of the Confucian Way, Song and Ming Chinese Neo-Confucians, including Zhu Xi (1130–1200) and Wang Yangming (1472–1529), generally agreed that sagehood is an attainable goal that could in principle be personally cultivated and experienced by every individual. Fundamental Confucian teachings were reinterpreted and revitalized in this light.

In Korea, T'oegye frequently discussed the same topic in terms of the central Confucian project of "learning to be a sage" (shengxue). His major works such as the monumental Sŏnghak sipto (Ten Diagrams on Learning to Be a Sage) and Four-Seven letters[4] emphasize the dedicated practice of self-cultivation as the true way of Confucian spirituality, presenting his own experiences and hermeneutical elements. He did so without ignoring the Zhu Xi school's textual and theoretical traditions. For T'oegye, however, orthodoxy never meant one's blind lip service to the texts and words of the Confucian sages and worthies, but rather involves a penetrating understanding of their meanings and implications as well as a proper practice of moral-spiritual cultivation. In other words, the Confucian way of sagehood is a continuous and gradual spiritual process, one that ought to integrate one's intellectual insights and moral effort as well.

In a well-known lecture to the king, T'oegye emphasized that "for the true (Confucian) learning it is never enough just to read the teachings of the sages and worthies." More specifically, "When the mind-heart (xin) is tranquil at night, one must experience Heaven's Principle (tianli) in oneself.

One should examine what one has done and work at self-reflection and self-rectification every day. Once you get used to this practice, you will realize the truth of learning to become a sage (*shengxue*)" (*TC*, vol. 4, p. 209).[5] T'oegye emphasized Heaven's Principle as the transcendent/ultimate reality of human nature (to use the contemporary terminology of comparative religion), or the absolutely "good" and "pure" mind-heart (*xin*), from which moral principles and virtues are manifest. Because it represents the sagely *xin* embodied in human nature, the practice self-cultivation means "to preserve Heaven's Principle" (*TC* 37.28b), involving a personal realization of it in the moral-spiritual mind. This path to sagehood is "to get rid of evil and follow good" (*TC* 29.15a). In the *Ch'ŏnmyŏng tosŏl* (Diagrammatic Treatise on Heaven's Mandate), one of his major essays, T'oegye also identified Heaven's Principle as the classical notion of Heaven's Mandate. Accordingly, Confucian spirituality necessarily requires one's moral and spiritual self-cultivation. For this reason, T'oegye consistently engaged himself in the interiorized way of contemplation and spiritual cultivation, without doing away with the classical and Cheng-Zhu tradition of intellectual learning and moral action. This represents, as I pointed out elsewhere, a major Korean revitalization of Zhu Xi's Neo-Confucianism, one that enhanced the inner Confucian enterprise of sagehood and spirituality.[6]

The idea of Heaven's Principle was previously mentioned by the Chinese Neo-Confucians such as the Cheng brothers, Zhu Xi, and their leading followers like Chen Duxiu (1178–1235).[7] In his preface to the *Doctrine of the Mean* (which was cited by Chen and others, including T'oegye), Zhu Xi stated, for example, that all human beings have the moral mind-heart inherent in human nature. But he contrasted the "precariousness" and "instability" of the ordinary mind (*renxin*) with the inherent impartiality and goodness of the moral-spiritual mind (*daoxin*; literally, the mind of Dao).[8] On the whole, Confucian self-cultivation requires one to overcome selfish material, physical, and psychological desires and to exercise a sincere and serious effort at preserving and nourishing the moral-spiritual *xin*.

T'oegye incorporated the classical and Cheng-Zhu teachings into his understanding of Heaven's Principle. In the *Sŏnghak sipto* and Four-Seven letters, he emphasized the key Confucian teachings on the "original goodness of human nature" (Mencius), "Heaven-endowed human nature" (*Doctrine of the Mean*), "original human nature" (taught by Zhang Zai and Zhu Xi), "human nature is principle (*li*)" (Cheng Yi and Zhu Xi), and "the nature of Heaven and Earth" (Zhang Zai and Zhu Xi).[9] Heaven's Principle is identified with these key phrases, representing the ultimate source of self-cultivation, and its authentic manifestation is said to be sagehood. For T'oegye, then, Confucian spirituality ought to be based on a penetrating and committed understanding of the ontological and conceptual distinction between the moral-spiritual qualities aroused by Heaven's Principle, on the one hand, and the ordinary physical and psychological desires and external stimuli, on the other. Otherwise, there will be an "unfortunate consequence" of misidentifying the latter with the former (*TC* 16.12a). The existential reality of human nature is subject to physical-mental dispositions and external factors, which can lead to good or evil; for this reason, one must hold to the truth and goodness of Heaven's Principle embodied in the moral-spiritual *daoxin*.

In the context of Zhu Xi's line of reasoning as well, the heart-mind, or *xin*, is viewed as the "master of the self," which should apprehend and control the physical, intellectual, and psychological phenomena of human existence. In other words, it is the dynamic and creative director of all ideas, values, emotions, desires, and so on. T'oegye's major works frequently mention the *xin* as a vital moral-spiritual being embodying its transcendent ground of being, that is, Heaven's Principle. In addressing Confucian learning to become a sage, he therefore emphasized a sincere and serious effort at "transcending [selfish] cravings and preserving Heaven's Principle" (*TC* 37.28b). T'oegye's understanding of sagehood and Heaven's Principle is not merely a philosophical matter, but rather reveals its ontological and spiritual significance.

For T'oegye, this spiritual practice must be grounded in the cultivation of reverence (*jing*). The question is, Why did he emphasize reverence as the most important virtue for Confucian spirituality of sagehood (*shengxue*)? In the *Sônghak sipto*, he declared personal cultivation of *jing* as "the beginning and end of learning to become a sage" (*TC* 7.33a). This commitment resulted from his creative synthesis of Zhu Xi's thought.[10] In the Chinese Neo-Confucian tradition, *jing* has several meanings for the practice of self-cultivation.[11] Zhu Xi, for example, taught that one should apply reverence to one's moral cultivation. In general, he and his followers saw *jing* as an attitude of reverence toward Heaven and Earth, as well as an intellectual seriousness and moral uprightness in handling things and human relationships.

In Korea, T'oegye, an engaged spiritual master, went further in seeing *jing* as a religious reverence for Heaven's Principle. According to his *Ch'ônmyông tosôl* (Diagrammatic Treatise on Heaven's Mandate), one should take reverence as "the first principle of Confucian learning" (*TC*, vol. 3, p. 144). Otherwise, it is not possible to realize and extend what T'oegye (and other Neo-Confucians) called the fundamental mind-heart (*ben-xin*). In the *Sônghak sipto* as well, he asserted that one's practice of holding fast to *jing* and preserving Heaven's Principle makes "the effort of self-examination and self-rectification" sincere and deep, leading to "the refined state of single-mindedness (*TC* 7.24b). "One should personally experience an insight into the meaning of reverence. Be cautious and discerning by incorporating it into self-reflection in the course of daily life and whatever comes to the *xin*" (*TC* 7.33a). T'oegye's biographical accounts also state: "When I am inactive, I am watchful of myself and cultivate reverence" and "Remain at the center of the myriad phenomena and make sure that reverence and the myriad phenomena do not deviate from one another" (*TC*, vol. 4, pp. 175–76).[12] Self-cultivation should therefore be maintained "with solemnity as [one's self is] controlled and united" (*TC*, vol. 4, p. 238).

These statements seem to emphasize a contemplative, religious approach to one's inner search for Heaven's Principle, which is identified with human nature in itself (*xing zhi benti*) (*TC*, vol. 4, p. 176). This Confucian activity of attentive self-reflection certainly indicates a spiritual path to solitude and self-awakening. The *benti* of our nature is full of truth and goodness, representing what T'oegye meant by "the center of the myriad phenomena." To use a religious-theological langauge here, it is begotten of Heaven's Principle (Dao), the ultimate reality of self-transcendence. As Rodney Taylor pointed out, "the soteriological relationship between Heaven and the sage becomes a religious model for the tradition as a whole."[13] The religious significance of T'oegye's interpretation seems to be grounded in a reverential piety for Heaven's Principle and a spiritual practice of self-transformation.

True understanding, in T'oegye's view, requires careful contemplation and spiritual cultivation. For this reason, he practiced quiet-sitting contemplation as a regular spiritual routine in his self-cultivation; this Neo-Confucian form of meditation helps to grasp what he calls true knowledge. T'oegye's biography (e.g., *TC*, vol. 4, pp. 176 and 246) indicates that it was a relevant and inspiring topic in his instructions to his disciples, even though he knew that it was not the sole choice of the Zhu Xi tradition of Neo-Confucianism.[14] T'oegye used quiet-sitting to control and overcome selfish/distracting feelings, desires, and thoughts. Equally important, it is a way of experiencing the mind-in-itself (referred as *benxin* or *xin zhi ti*), or the *xin* in its unmanifest state of tranquility and solitude, before feelings and desires are aroused (*TC*, vol. 4, p. 176). However, as T'oegye said, this experience should maintain a continuous relation with the conscious and active mind in the manifest state. According to his "Diagrammatic Treatise on Heaven's Mandate" (*Chônmyông tosôl*), self-cultivation means "to preserve and nourish the substance of the *xin* when it is tranquil," and "to examine and rectify the function of the *xin* after feelings and desires are aroused" (*TC*, vol. 3, p. 144). T'oegye also instructed his disciples by emphasizing that "Only after the practice of quiet-sitting, can one collect the body and the mind so that moral principles (*daoli*) can be united together. If the self is dispersed and not collected, one's body and mind will be in darkness and disorder" (*TC*, vol. 4, p. 176).[15]

Heaven's Principle is identified with one's search for human nature in itself (*xing zhi benti*), which is understood interchangeably as the fundamental *xin* (*benxin*), moral-spiritual *xin* (*daoxin*), Heaven-endowed human nature, and so on. Although some attention is given to the preservation of the "unmanifest *xin*" (substance) in the practice of meditation, the role of the "manifest *xin*" (function) is essential in the whole process of learning to become a sage. For T'oegye, Confucian spiritual practice demands a return to intellectual learning and moral effort. Its contemplative art is to recollect his spiritual interiority and peace and to purify the "dispersed self" of physical and psychological dispositions. This Neo-Confucian paradigm is a religious path that engages a realization of the illuminated, sagely self in the world. It relates to the Neo-Confucian understanding of "transcendence" and "spirituality," the focus of the following section.

Transcendence and Confucian Spirituality

The question is, How does T'oegye's interpretation of sagehood and self-cultivation relate closely to the Confucian notion of transcendence and the Confucian practice of spirituality? This question is significant not only because it represents a subtle and somewhat underdeveloped area of Zhu Xi's Neo-Confucianism, but also because some meaningful answer comes from T'oegye, who endeavored to engage it in his scholarship and moral-spiritual practice. In this regard, we first need to understand T'oegye's insights into the central Neo-Confucian idea of principle (*li*), for Zhu Xi's philosophy of *li* underwent a major transformation of reinterpretation and spiritual revitalization by the former. Zhu Xi's sophisticated philosophy of *li* and *qi* is a well-researched topic in current scholarship, one that need not be rehearsed here.[16] In short, it is rooted in his emphasis on the objective investigation of things and principles as the search for knowledge and wisdom, which was a central part of Neo-Confucian learning involving both rational comprehension and ethical practice.

T'oegye's exposition of *li* is much more than a conceptual or doctrinal matter of seeing *li* simply as the universal, ordering principle of phenomena. He, unlike Zhu Xi, explicitly acknowledged that *li* is not a passive principle of existence but rather has its own dynamic nature. For example, T'oegye emphasized: "If *li* cannot act by itself, there is something wrong with our mind (*xin*), implying that we cannot speak of the self-arriving nature of *li*" (*TC* 18.31a). In other words, principle is an "active" and "self-manifesting" entity, and this dynamic nature of *li* ought to be realized in terms of engaging the self and the world in an ultimate moral-spiritual process. For this reason, T'oegye always maintained that *li* must be distinguished clearly from *qi* not just from a conceptual standpoint but also in a moral-spiritual context, so that one does not misidentify the material, physical, and psychological desires represented by *qi* (which, if uncontrolled, can lead to evil) with Heaven's Principle and moral virtues represented by *li* (which always remain good and pure) (*TC* 16.11a–b).

The totality of T'oegye's ethics and spirituality is rooted in such a profound belief. His reverence for Heaven's Principle and his contemplative-spiritual cultivation correspond to Wm. Theodore de Bary's insight that T'oegye's thought underscores "the moral and transcendent aspects of principle."[17] His reference to the self-manifesting creativity of *li* (identified with Heaven's Principle) extends from metaphysics and ethics to spiritual contemplation and cultivation. His mature works such as the *Sŏnghak sipto* and Four-Seven thesis frequently underscore *li* as something to be realized and preserved through one's self-cultivation. In other words, *li* means not just the principle of being for all ideas and values in the metaphysical and ethical context but also the transcendent reality of all existence and truth in the religious-spiritual context. Otherwise, Heaven's Principle as *li* could not be the focus of transcendence, and its significance for Confucian spirituality would be meaningless or lost. For this reason, T'oegye sees sagehood as the ultimate truth/goodness of human existence, which is thought to be in full unity with Heaven's Principle. This Confucian referent of transcendence is embodied in the moral-spiritual *xin* (*daoxin*), "Heaven-endowed human nature," "original human nature," or "human nature in itself," as he used all of these phrases interchangeably.

As informed by T'oegye, Confucian spirituality helps the effort of realizing the true self. It engages reverential solemnity and spiritual awareness, while the entire self is continuously controlled and united. As T'oegye said, "When my spirit is clear and my *qi* [vital energy involving physical and psychological dispositions] is undisturbed, I am austere and solemn, and my mind-heart [*xin*] naturally holds itself firm without me having to grasp it" (*TC*, v. 4, p. 176). This personal testimony reveals a deeper insight through contemplative attentiveness and spiritual wisdom, which seems to be a religious experience of the enlightened self forming a unity of existence and a harmonious rhythm with all phenomena. The true self is to be discovered in the *daoxin*, an axiological foundation for Confucian spirituality. In other words, the *daoxin* as human nature in itself pertains to what

Mencius called the "great body/substance" (*dati*) of human beings, an ontological being in a cosmic and moral unity with Heaven (*Mencius* 6A:15). In T'oegye's account as well, it refers to Heaven's Principle as the creative spiritual foundation of sagehood. The entire person is not just a rational and physical self in an empirical sense, but, more important, an existential moral and spiritual being. In other words, the practice of self-cultivation means to recollect one's tranquil interiority, to purify the "dispersed self," to cultivate one's inner wisdom, and to realize the transcendent reality of human nature in a state of spiritual contemplation and moral awareness.

In this regard, the classical Confucian notion of transcendence pertains to T'oegye's understanding of Heaven's Principle. As Mou Zongsan pointed out, Confucianism as a whole takes the Mandate of Heaven as cosmic-moral creativity itself.[18] T'oegye's Neo-Confucian spirituality seems to complement Mou's thesis that the foundation of Confucian religiosity pertains to this belief in Heaven. The true existential self—which is to be discovered in self-transcendence and sagehood—shares the same reality with Heaven. In the Mencian context, this spiritual endeavor is to seek the goodness and truth of one's inner nature (*Mencius* 7A:1). Confucius said, "Human beings can make the Dao great; it is not that the Dao makes human beings great" (*Analects* 15:29).[19] As Mencius personally declared, "If you know your nature, you can serve Heaven" (7A:1), and "Seek [it in your *xin*] and you will get it; let go and you will lose it" (7A:3). In other words, as ordinary, contemporary Confucians would agree, the existential human problem of evil is due to one's ignorance or failure to nourish the moral-spiritual *xin*. Human miseries come from our existential neglect of this *xin* and our moral-spiritual failure to nourish it, not from the presence of any active superhuman/supernatural evil force or humanity's original sin in the theistic and ontological contexts. This basic Confucian view of evil, upheld by T'oegye, also corresponds to what the *Doctrine of the Mean* meant by "Heaven-endowed human nature" in the context of emphasizing the innate capacity of human beings for regulating/harmonizing various physical and mental desires and feelings.

From a similar standpoint, Tu Weiming, in his study of the *Doctrine of the Mean*, pointed out that an "ethicoreligious symbolism" of human nature is embedded within "the Confucian anthropocosmic worldview." For Tu, this seemingly "theological flavor" is "the natural outcome of an attempt to understand Confucian humanism religiously."[20] In light of T'oegye's experiences and insights, I believe, however, that it is not really a question of understanding "Confucian humanism religiously," but rather that Confucian transcendence and religiosity constitute the vital core of "Confucian humanism." In my view, the humanistic significance of Confucianism, associated with a generic pattern of describing the tradition, is essentially rooted in and enhanced by Confucian faith in Heaven or Dao, that is, the transcendent referent of human goodness. Moreover, the way of pursuing this faith necessarily requires self-cultivation, which is significant for Confucianism as a whole.

As informed by T'oegye, it profoundly involves a faithful engagement in contemplative, moral and spiritual self-cultivation. To use a comparative religious-theological language here, the ultimate goal of this Confucian path is the attainment of the enlightened self through a moral-spiritual faith in the "binding" relationship (*religio*) of humanity and its transcendent reality, Heaven. T'oegye's spirituality is grounded in such a *religious* vision of the self and its ultimate reality. It reveals a kind of reverential faith (*jing*) in Heaven (or Heaven's Principle). On the whole, we are talking about a profound Confucian commitment to the self-transcending morality and self-enlightening spirituality of human beings. The T'oegye paradigm can offer us certain reflections on Confucian spirituality as well as on its implications for global religion and spirituality. This is the focus of the next, concluding section.

Comparative Reflections

T'oegye generally sought to bring out the spiritual vitality and religious significance of Confucianism in the light of the fundamental legacy of Confucius, Mencius, the *Doctrine of the Mean*, and Cheng-Zhu teachings. Nonetheless, we also need to understand its basic aspects from a cross-cultural standpoint of comparative religion. In addition to the term "religion," this essay has used other common words, including "spirituality," "religiosity," "transcendence," "self-transcendence," and "faith." This concluding section therefore discusses several relevant questions associated with not just T'oegye's Neo-Confucianism but also comparative religion, while presenting my own reflections and ideas.

Over the last two decades, there has been an active renewal of Western scholarship in discussing "Confucianism as religion," "Confucian religiosity," or "the religious dimensions of Confucianism."[21] This renewal made a significant contribution to understanding Confucianism as a relevant religious tradition in terms of sagehood, "self-transcendence," good and evil, "soteriology," "spiritual tradition," and so on.[22] Nonetheless, what we call spirituality certainly varies according to different languages and worldviews and their corresponding religious-cultural traditions. This variety would apply to other related elements of religion, including "faith."[23] In general, the human phenomenon of spirituality has historically existed almost everywhere in connection with biblical/prophetic religions such as Judaism, Christianity, and Islam, as well as with "nonprophetic" religions such as Confucianism, Buddhism, Daoism, Hinduism, and other Eastern traditions (whether institutionalized or not). In addition, it is, to some extent, associated with the Greco-Roman philosophical heritage of humanism and its later developments, many of which commonly deal with metaphysical, ethical, and spiritual ideas and values.

Among many contemporary scholars (including comparative religionists), however, the notion of spirituality still remains ambiguous in the global context of religion (and theology). For example, regarding the Christian tradition, spirituality usually pertains to the theocentric (God-centered), christocentric (Christ-centered), confessional, and congregational dimensions of Christian faith and life. As a special Christian theme/experience of faith in, and worship of, God and Jesus Christ, it signifies spiritual establishment, relating to church, theology, sacraments, and even mystical traditions. Judaism and Islam, two other biblical/prophetic traditions, maintain a number of different expressions of what might be called theistic spirituality. East Asian traditions such as Confucianism, Buddhism, Daoism, and "New Religions" developed other kinds of spirituality, some of which might relate to certain Western ideals and patterns. In the general context of shamanism and other unorganized traditions (including "native spirituality" in North America) as well, the term "spirituality" can also be used to describe what is known as "spiritualism," which involves ritualistic contact with, and religious devotion to, the spirits of the dead and other kinds of spiritual beings.

On the whole, it is therefore paramount to understand "spirituality" from a cross-cultural and interreligious perspective. Spirituality can include various related components, such as faith, transcendence, spiritual dignity and devotion, self-cultivation, contemplative/ritualistic practice, intuitive wisdom and insights, inner self-understanding, some sort of the ultimate goal, and so on. Hence, I am using the notion of spirituality in this broad context, which enables us to talk about the Confucian and other related religious/spiritual traditions.

Confucianism has often been viewed as humanistic, metaphysical, ethical, or secular. Although these kinds of interpretations are useful for specific purposes, they can be narrow categorizations of Confucianism if its spiritual-religious dimensions are ignored or underestimated. According to Tu, it is important to discuss "Confucian religiosity" in terms of the human capability and aspiration for self-transformation.[24] From a comparative Confucian-Christian perspective, Julia Ching called Confucianism/Neo-Confucianism "a lay spirituality"; moreover, its spiritual teaching of sagehood and its way of self-cultivation would be better expressed in its "religious development than in its philosophical treatises."[25] These kinds of insights fit into Confucian spirituality in general and the T'oegye paradigm in particular.

The idea, experience, or expression of transcendence is expressed in various ways.[26] As informed by T'oegye, the Confucian and Neo-Confucian tradition approaches the transcendent reality or "ultimate concern" (to use Paul Tillich's terminology of systematic theology) of human existence from a distinctive standpoint that is not totally uncommon. However, this uniqueness does not eliminate the tradition from the general context of world religions. As Huston Smith, a comparative religionist and spiritual practitioner, correctly pointed out, even if we define "religion" in a specific and narrow sense, as "a concern to align humanity with the transcendental ground of its existence, Confucianism is still a religion, albeit a muted one."[27] Furthermore, de Bary's view of "(Confucian) sagehood as a secular and spiritual ideal" is relevant here.[28] I also emphasize that the moral and spiritual vitality of Confucianism embodies a continuously engaged faith in the binding relationship between human nature and its transcendent reality, which is expressed in terms of sagehood, Heaven (Heaven's Principle), *daoxin* (moral-spiritual mind/heart), and *benti* (human nature in itself as the absolute; literally, "original substance").

The transcendent referent (or whatever we call it) and other related expressions are often conditioned by different religions, worldviews, languages, and cultures. For this inevitable reason, the comparative religionist John Hick, for example, asserted that "religion (or a particular religious tradition) centers upon an awareness of and response to a reality that transcends ourselves and our world, whether the 'direction' of transcendence be *beyond or within or both*."[29] Other scholars have suggested, from similar angles, that it is necessary to develop a reformulated, global/comparative "theology" in such a way as to understand and appreciate the presence of "divine grace (or love)" in the living pluralistic reality of other faiths.[30] However, we have yet to agree on what is meant by "global theology" or "world theology" and its cross-cultural implications for particular religious traditions. The question is, What about something that can incorporate Confucian spirituality in the inclusively nontheological/nontheistic context?

This and related questions can help us to appreciate Confucian spirituality, including T'oegye's case. Undoubtedly, the Western types of theistic/theocentric spirituality (and "christocentric" spirituality for Christians) do not represent T'oegye's spirituality, mainly because the explicit concept of a personal, monotheistic God (divinity) was not important to the Confucian tradition. From a comparative perspective, I mean that it neither demands nor helps one to worship, or pray to, any divine savior for an other-worldly goal of salvation. Confucian spirituality did not develop, and is not concerned with, the organized confessional, pastoral, or monastic types of spirituality. For this reason, therefore, one has to be careful not to over-explain or misrepresent it in terms of the conventional categories of Western religion. Surely, part of our ongoing dilemma in discussing the topic is that the religious, theological, and philosophical languages of the West have no exact equivalents for Confucian terms, experiences, and expressions, including those discussed so far in this essay. In the Eastern context as well, the Confucian way is distinct from the theistic-devotional spirituality of Pure Land Buddhism, as well as from the monastic or mystical paths of Zen Buddhism and Vedantic Hinduism.

In today's world of religious pluralism and interaction, a growing number of people—including most undergraduate students taking a survey course on world religions or Eastern religions—would agree that the spiritual dimension of any given tradition (such as Confucianism) is expressed and practiced in its own ways. In *Religion and Spirituality*, a brief but insightful study, Eliot Deutsch reminds us that there are various spiritual experiences, including "solitude," "contemplative attentiveness," "wisdom," and "divine love." As he points out, "although religious experience of a relational I-Thou sort is surely a kind of spiritual experience, not all spiritual experience is of that sort."[31] Confucian spirituality, as far as T'oegye is concerned, is not about the "almighty" and "wholly-other" Divine Being that completely transcends the world in which people think, moral principles prevail, empirical things and ideas exist, and so on. The "binding" relationship, or *religio* (if we were to call it so), between human nature and the Heavenly Dao rather engages an intellectual insight, a contemplative self-understanding, a moral-spiritual self-cultivation, and a reverential piety (*jing*), all of which are closely associated with T'oegye's teachings on "learning to be a sage," contemplating on "human nature in itself," "overcoming selfish desires," "nourishing the moral-spiritual mind," and so on.

Confucian spirituality may be designated as a way of self-deliverance together with its own awareness of transcendence and its own type of faith. Human beings have the innate capacity to transform the ordinary self into sagehood in unity with the Heavenly Way, the transcendent yet immanent reality of human goodness.[32] As Wilfred Cantwell Smith reminds us, the scriptural and spiritual core of Confucianism, like other traditions, shares the fundamental human wish (faith) that expresses the transcendent reality of immanence, for which reason he uses "the notion 'transcendence' to include immanence."[33] For T'oegye, our ultimate goodness, truth, and wisdom are rooted in the Dao (referred to as Heaven's Principle); accordingly, Confucian spirituality unites the immanent and transcendent realities and experiences of human existence. As Ching pointed out, Confucian self-cultivation offers a "model of self-transcendence" "to identify the transcendent with what is immanent."[34] Confucius said, "Human beings can make the Dao great; it is not that the Dao makes human beings great" (*Analects* 15:29). As Mencius defined it, "If you know your nature, you can serve Heaven" (7A:1). These and other related teachings justify the Confucian self-understanding of Dao (or Heavenly Principle) as something that is innately bestowed on human nature. As T'oegye emphasized, "preserve Heaven's Principle," "transcend the selfish craving," "nourish the *daoxin*," and so on. In other words, it is never up to the Mandate of Heaven to restore the goodness and truth of human nature or to redeem human evil and miseries. Every human being has an ontological and existential *teleo* to fulfill; that is, to realize and extend one's moral and spiritual nature bestowed by the Heavenly Way. Although our essential being is good, it can be distorted by our neglect of it because this condition is subject to various material, physical, psychological, and environmental factors.

T'oegye made a valuable contribution to Neo-Confucian scholarship and spirituality. He was not just a scholar-thinker but also an engaged man of faith and spiritual practice. The T'oegye paradigm of Confucian spirituality embodies a kind of religious "faith"[35] expressed in its own terms. It fits into, for example, W. C. Smith's comparative thesis that faith is "the fundamental human category" and essentially means and engages "the new and rich and enriching sense of *fides humana*, the faith . . . the final truth of humankind."[36] For T'oegye (as well as for contemporary Confucians), Confucian spirituality integrates morality, rationality, and emotionality, requiring a disciplined way of self-understanding and self-transformation. It is not about attaining a superhuman state of being or a divine power/nature; nor is it intended to be a highly ascetic-mystical life detached from the human world of ideas and values. If this point has to be pondered further, the ethicospiritually engaged Confucian would claim that a concern for *ren* (benevolence/compassion) and others, a reverence for Heaven and Earth, the integration of thoughts, emotions, and feelings, and the experience of wisdom and insight are possible through one's contemplation on the Dao and spiritual self-cultivation.

Confucian spirituality, as informed by T'oegye, engages not only an active life of intellectual knowing and moral effort but also a deep contemplative and attentive life of self-awakening. In other words, it is an ongoing, existential process of living in the world. Isn't this what constitutes the heart and soul of his scholarship and spirituality, thereby representing a major Neo-Confucian ideal? Leonard Angel's study *Enlightenment East and West* would be relevant here; that is, a contemporary appreciation of T'oegye's spirituality corresponds to Angel's view that Confucianism offers us a key model of "Enlightenment East vision" within which Enlightenment East and Enlightenment West can meet fruitfully.[37] From a further comparative and cross-cultural standpoint, the Confucian project of ethics and spirituality takes the Heavenly way/image of human nature as the intrinsic foundation of universal goodness, penetrating truth, and illuminating virtue. Accordingly, it would not necessarily contradict or oppose other kinds of human spirituality, including Christian spirituality.[38] For instance, the Christian way of *metanoia* (repentance; transformation of mind-heart) can accommodate the moral-spiritual core of Confucianism. In fact, there seems to be a growing number of Christians of Confucian values both inside and outside East Asia, who assimilate certain mutual aspects of the two traditions. For many decades in the modern time, this has been a common phenomenon among Korean and other East Asian Confucian-Christians, leading to the fruitful integration of these complementary aspects.[39]

The integrated thrust of the T'oegye paradigm and its contemporary relevance represent a fundamentally Confucian and potentially universal model of human spirituality, one that offers a nonexclusive religious faith in the ultimate reality, affirms the fundamental worth of human nature, emphasizes self-understanding and self-cultivation, and revitalizes the creative and contemplative role of the *xin* in one's journey of spiritual fulfillment. For this reason, Confucian faith embodies a teleological and practical vision of encouraging intellectual learning as well. It conveys the transformability of the ordinary self into the undifferentiated, virtuous, and illuminated being. This engaged spirituality seems to point to our universal path of pursuing the mutual goodness and truth of humanity and the world.

In the final reflection, Confucian spirituality offers us relevant philosophical, moral, and spiritual resources for the pluralistic and interacting world of religion and culture. One's better understanding of it can contribute to comparative religion/philosophy in general and interreligious dialogue in particular. To conclude, the T'oegye paradigm is indeed significant not only for a deeper appreciation of Confucian spirituality and its contemporary implication but also for our global understanding of religion and spirituality as a whole in both scholarly and practical contexts.

Notes

A note on style of citation: Korean names and titles are romanized according to the standard McCune-Reischauer system, and Chinese terms according to the Pinyin system. For T'oegye's writings cited, only the Korean titles are given, as this is the standard style. To avoid confusion, all philosophical terms and phrases and the titles of the primary Chinese sources are given in Chinese only.

1. The relevant literature on T'oegye and Korean Neo-Confucianism includes Edward Chung, *The Neo-Confucianism of Yi T'oegye and Yi Yulgok;* Michael Kalton et al., *The Four-Seven Debate;* Michael Kalton, *To Become a Sage; The Rise of Neo-Confucianism in Korea,* ed. Wm. Theodore de Bary and JaHyun Kim Haboush (which contains articles by Tu Weiming, Wing-tsit Chan, Julia Ching, and others).

2. This is because T'oegye maintained himself as a follower of the so-called Cheng-Zhu school, a legacy associated with the Song Chinese thinkers Cheng Yi (1033–1107), Zhu Xi (1130–1200), and their later followers. Also known as the "school of human nature and principle" (*xingli xue*), this tradition served as Neo-Confucian orthodoxy for five centuries in Korea.

3. The bibliography lists current literature on this topic, including works by Chan, de Bary, Ching, Tu, Taylor, Cheng, Graham, Hall and Ames, Gardner, and others. For the Korean tradition, see Chung, Kalton, and Ro.

4. For a full English translation of T'oegye's *Sŏnghak sipto,* see Kalton, *To Become a Sage.* The Four-Seven letters are another mature and magnificent source of T'oegye's thought and scholarship, which presents a sophisticated Neo-Confucian discourse for understanding the relationship between mind, human nature, and feelings, as well as its implications for ethics and spirituality. For this subject, see Chung, *Neo-Confucianism of Yi T'oegye and Yi Yulgok;* Kalton et al., *Four-Seven Debate;* and Tu Weiming, "T'oegye's Perception of Human Nature: A Preliminary Inquiry into the Four-Seven Debate in Korean Neo-Confucianism," in *Rise of Neo-Confucianism in Korea,* ed. de Bary and Haboush.

5. Translation, with slight modification, based on Chung, *Neo-Confucianism of Yi T'oegye and Yi Yulgok,* 137.

6. Ibid.

7. For a good study of Chen, see Wm. Theodore de Bary, *Neo-Confucian Orthodoxy.*

8. This simple yet subtle doctrine is based on the so-called Sixteen Transmissions of the Mind-and-Heart, an obscure passage from the *Book of History:* "The human mind is precarious; the moral mind is subtle. Remain refined and single-minded: Hold fast the Mean." Zhu Xi identified the *daoxin* with the truth of Heaven's Principle, and the *renxin* with the selfishness of physical and psychological desires and feelings. In his other treatises and letters, Heaven's Principle also means the Great Ultimate (*taiji*) or *li* (principle) in itself, conveying not just the universal and metaphysical ground/essence of all existence but also the moral-spiritual truth and goodness of human nature. For this subject, see Chung, *Neo-Confucianism of Yi T'oegye and Yi Yulgok;* Wing-tsit Chan, ed., *Chu Hsi and*

Neo-Confucianism; Wingtsit Chan, trans., *Reflections on Things at Hand;* Wm. Theodore de Bary, ed., *The Unfolding of Neo-Confucianism;* Daniel K. Gardner, *Chu Hsi: Learning to Be a Sage;* and others.

9. See, e.g., *TC* 7.24a, 16.9a–b, 16.32a–b. For my detailed discussion of this topic, see *Neo-Confucianism of Yi T'oegye and Yi Yulgok.*

10. I have discussed this topic in details elsewhere; see *Neo-Confucianism of Yi T'oegye and Yi Yulgok;* and "Yi T'oegye on the Learning of reverential Seriousness," *Korea Journal* 32, no. 1 (Spring 1992): 61–71.

11. Its *loci classici* in the Confucian classics include the *Book of Ritual* and *Analects.* According to the former, "The superior person never lacks reverence (*jing*)" (*Book of Ritual,* "Summary of Ceremonies," SPPY ed., 1:1a). In Confucius's *Analects* (13:19), we also read: "Be reverent and serious (*jing*) in handling affairs."

12. Three translated passages in this paragraph, with slight modification, are from Chung, *Neo-Confucianism of Yi T'oegye and Yi Yulgok,* 134–35.

13. Rodney L. Taylor, *Religious Dimensions of Neo-Confucianism,* 3.

14. The history of Confucian quiet-sitting meditation is as long as that of Neo-Confucianism itself. In Song and Ming China, a number of different perspectives existed not only in the context of addressing various forms of Neo-Confucianism but also in terms of the distinction between the Neo-Confucian, Daoist, and Buddhist methods of learning. Some Neo-Confucians accepted quiet-sitting, whereas others opposed it. In the continued development of Neo-Confucianism in Ming China, it occupied a prominent position among some Chinese Neo-Confucians including Wang Yangming. For this topic, see Taylor, *Religious Dimensions;* and idem, *Confucian Way of Contemplation,* 140–44.

15. Translation, with slight modification, from Chung, *Neo-Confucianism of Yi T'oegye and Yi Yulgok,* 132, 134.

16. *Li* also means the unitary and omnipresent ground of being present in each phenomenon in its fullness of goodness and truth. By contrast, *qi* means "ether," vital energy, or "material force," which is thought to be the actual physical/immanent agent that brings everything into concrete existence; it determines the individuality and transformation of phenomena that may lead to either good or evil. For Zhu Xi's philosophy of *li* and *qi,* see Wing-tsit Chan, trans., *Reflections on Things at Hand;* idem, *Chu Hsi and Neo-Confucianism.*

17. De Bary, *Neo-Confucian Orthodoxy,* 197. De Bary made this important point in comparing T'oegye with the late Song Neo-Confucian Chen Duxiu, although he did not mention any specific examples of T'oegye's writings and his spiritual experiences.

18. Mou Zongsan, *Hsin-t'i yü hsing-t'i;* idem, *Chung-kuo che-hsüeh te t'e-chih.*

19. The appended Neo-Confucian commentary (including Zhu Xi's sayings) on this famous yet subtle doctrine includes the following: "Without human beings, there is no Dao," because "the Dao exists within every and each human self"; and "the Dao is the ground of human existence and the *li* (principle) of human beings" (*Lun-yü chi-chu ta-ch'üan* [Great Compendium of Commentaries on the *Analects*], Kyôngsô, p. 372).

20. Tu Weiming, *Centrality and Commonality*, 102–6, 120.

21. I do not mean that *all* aspects of Confucianism are religious in nature. As generally acknowledged in current scholarship, the Confucian tradition promoted its humanistic values, practical ideas, and cultural concerns (e.g., learning, moral education, sociopolitical guidelines, etc.). A similar claim would apply to other religions as well. In other words, not all aspects of Christianity and Buddhism, for example, are strictly religious only, because most religious traditions (including Confucianism) are commonly concerned with certain secular matters (social, institutional, and political ideas and values). In any case, the topic of Confucianism as religion still depends on what is meant by "religion" and "religious," in relation to various histories, worldviews, cultures, languages, and so on. Moreover, the notion of "religion" in the comparative and cross-cultural context has been a well-researched topic, one that need not be rehearsed here. The relevant literature on this subject includes John B. Cobb, Jr., *Beyond Dialogue;* idem, "The Meaning of Pluralism for Christian Self-Understanding," in *Religious Pluralism*, ed. Rouner; John Hick, *An Interpretation of Religion;* John Hick and Paul F. Knitter, eds., *The Myth of Christian Uniqueness;* David R. Griffin and Huston Smith, *Primordial Truth and Postmodern Theology;* George A. Lindbeck, *The Nature of Doctrine;* Robert C. Neville, *Behind the Masks of God;* idem, *The Tao and the Daimon;* Willard G. Oxtoby, *The Meaning of Other Faiths;* Geoffrey Parrinder, *Encountering World Religions;* Ninian Smart, *Crosscultural Explorations of Human Beliefs;* Wilfred Cantwell Smith, *What Is Scripture;* idem, *Toward a World Theology;* idem, *Faith and Belief;* Frederick Streng, *Ways of Being Religious;* David Tracy, *Dialogue with the Other;* idem, *Plurality and Ambiguity;* etc.

22. Other relevant works include Julia Ching, *Confucianism and Christianity;* eadem, "What Is Confucian Spirituality," in *Confucianism*, ed. Eber; Hans Küng and Julia Ching, *Christianity and Chinese Religions;* Tu Weiming, *Confucian Thought;* Rodney L. Taylor, *Religions Dimensions of Neo-Confucianism;* idem, *The Way of Heaven;* John Berthrong, *All Under Heaven;* Peter K. H. Lee, ed., *Confucian-Christian Encounters;* Robert Eno, *The Confucian Creation of Heaven;* Liu Shu-hsien, "A Critique of Paul Tillich's Doctrine of God and Christology from an Oriental Perspective," in *Religious Issues and Interreligious Dialogues*, ed. Charles Wei-hsun Fu and Gerhard E. Spiegler; idem, "The Confucian Approach to the Problem of Transcendence and Immanence," *Philosophy East and West* 22 (January 1972): 45–52. For the Korean case as well, see Chung, *Neo-Confucianism of Yi T'oe-gye and Yi Yulgok;* Ro Young-chan, *The Neo-Confucianism of Yi Yulgok;* and Michael Kalton, trans., *To Become a Sage.*

23. This topic of "religion" and "faith" in the comparative and cross-cultural context has been a well-researched topic, one that need not be rehearsed here. For its relevant and selected literature, see n. 21.

24. Tu, *Centrality and Commonality.*

25. Julia Ching, *Confucianism and Christianity*, 7–12, esp. 11; eadem, "What Is Confucian Spirituality?"

26. As we know, this variety includes the following central examples: God

(with different names, meanings, and symbols for Christians, Jews, Muslims, and other theistic Western/Eastern believers); Hindu Brahman and Moksha; Buddhist Nirvana, Dharma, and Enlightenment; Daoist/Confucian Dao and sagehood; Daoist *wuwei* (Non-action); and Confucian Heaven or Heaven's Mandate.

27. Huston Smith, *The World's Religions,* 183.

28. De Bary, *Neo-Confucian Orthodoxy;* idem, "Sagehood as a Secular and Spiritual Ideal in Tokugawa Neo-Confucianism," in *Principle and Practicality: Essays in Neo-Confucianism and Practical Learning,* ed. de Bary and Bloom.

29. Hick, *Interpretation of Religion,* 3 (emphasis added).

30. See W. C. Smith, *Toward a World Theology;* Parrinder, *Encountering World Religions;* Neville, *Behind the Masks of God;* Tracy, *Dialogue with the Other;* etc.

31. Deutsch also states: "Indeed, much of the profound spirituality of many non-Western philosophical-religious traditions defies characterization in Western personalistic religious terms" (*Religion and Spirituality,* ix). Although this is not incorrect, it might be a debatable generalization that depends on the specific "non-Western" traditions and their spiritual teachings, symbols, and practices. For example, contemporary Confucian spirituality does not necessarily oppose or disregard the "personalistic" notion of religion. Although the Confucian tradition did not develop a theism of the covenantal "I-Thou" sort, contemporary Christians of Confucian background in Korea, for example, have been able to accommodate certain personalistic elements of Christian theism and spirituality.

32. From a similar angle, Tu Weiming pointed out that the "anthropocosmic worldview" of Confucian religiosity sees the true human nature as something that "lies not in radical transcendence but in immanence with transcendental dimension" (*Centrality and Commonality,* 121). As John Berthrong also asserted in a comparative theological and philosophical context, the fundamental Western task for understanding transcendence-immanence relations is therefore significant "for a Christian appreciation of the Confucian insistence on the unity of transcendence and immanence" (*All Under Heaven,* 47).

33. W. C. Smith, *What Is Scripture?* 10.

34. Ching, *Confucianism and Christianity,* 10, 79.

35. In my view, the global notion of "religious faith" is still open to further discussion. I simply note that the English word "faith" originates from the Latin *fidere,* which literally means a human attitude of "trust" that may not transcend our reason and emotions completely. In this regard Confucians have a common sense of faith in the Confucian spiritual teachings and values.

36. W. C. Smith, *Faith and Belief,* 5–6.

37. Leonard Angel, *Enlightenment East and West,* 85.

38. Hans Küng, a Christian ecumenical theologian, suggested in his comparative study of Confucius and Jesus, that the moral-spiritual core of Confucianism is based on an "anthropocentric" (humanistic) vision with "an entirely religious emphasis" (Küng and Ching, *Christianity and Chinese Religion,* 109), one that is not incompatible with the basic moral-spiritual teaching of the historical Jesus.

39. This integration is possible partly because Confucianism is neither an orga-

nized membership religion nor a pastoral/evangelical tradition. Despite the question of "diffused" Confucian identity, this phenomenon of complementarity and harmony between Confucianism and Christianity is a significant topic that deserves our serious attention. In my view, it is highly relevant to the currently growing field of comparative religion/theology, including Confucian– Christian dialogue. Accordingly, our further research on this topic will shed new light on the methodology and pedagogy of comparative religion.

Bibliography

Primary Sources:
TC. Yi T'oegye. *T'oegye chônsô* [Complete Works of T'oegye], enlarged edition. 5 vols. Seoul: Sônggyun'gwan University Press, 1986.
Kyôngsô [Four Books and Collected Commentaries]. Seoul: Sônggyun'gwan University Press, 1972.

Secondary Sources:
Angel, Leonard. *Enlightenment East and West.* Albany: State University of New York Press, 1994.
Berthrong, John. *All Under Heaven: Transforming Paradigms of Confucian–Christian Dialogue.* Albany: State University of New York Press, 1994.
Chan, Wing-tsit. "How T'oegye Understood Chu Hsi." In *The Rise of Neo-Confucianism in Korea,* edited by Wm. Theodore de Bary and JaHyun Kim Haboush. New York: Columbia University Press, 1985.
Chan, Wing-tsit, ed. *Chu Hsi and Neo-Confucianism.* Honolulu: University of Hawaii Press, 1986.
———, trans. *Reflections on Things at Hand: The Neo-Confucian Anthology by Chu Hsi and Lü Tsu-ch'ien.* New York: Columbia University Press, 1967.
Ching, Julia. "Chu Hsi on Moral Cultivation." In *Chu Hsi and Neo-Confucianism,* edited by Wing-tsit Chan. Honolulu: University of Hawaii Press, 1986.
———. "Confucianism: Ethical Humanism as Religion?" In *Christianity and Chinese Religions,* edited by Hans Küng and Julia Ching. New York: Doubleday, 1989.
———. *Confucianism and Christianity: A Comparative Study.* New York and Tokyo: Kodansha International, 1977.
———. "What is Confucian Spirituality?" In *Confucianism: The Dynamics of Tradition,* edited by I. Eber. New York: Macmillan, 1986.
———. "Yi Yulgok on the Four Beginnings and the Seven Emotions." In *The Rise of Neo-Confucianism in Korea,* edited by Wm. Theodore de Bary and JaHyun Kim Haboush. New York: Columbia University Press, 1985.
Chung, Edward Y. J. "Confucian-Christian Interaction in Contemporary Korea and Its Implications for Confucian-Christian Dialogue." Unpublished conference paper presented at the Annual Meeting of the American Academy of Religion, Chicago, November 18–22, 1994.

————. "Confucian Ethics in Contemporary Korea: A Common National Discourse." *Korean Culture* 16, no. 3 (1995): 13–19. A special issue on ethics in modern Korea.

————. "Confucianism: A Living Religious Tradition in South Korea." *Korean Studies in Canada* 2 (1994): 11–24.

————. "Confucianism and Women in Modern Korea: Continuity, Change and Conflict." In *The Annual Review of Women in World Religions* 3, edited by Arvind Sharma and Katherine Young, 142–88. Albany: State University of New York Press, 1995.

————. *The Neo-Confucianism of Yi T'oegye and Yi Yulgok: A Reappraisal of the Four-Seven Thesis and Its Practical Implications for Self-Cultivation.* Albany: State University of New York Press, 1995.

————. "Yi T'oegye on the Learning of Reverential Seriousness (*Kyŏnghak*)." *Korea Journal* 32, no. 1 (Spring 1992): 61–71.

Cobb, John B., Jr. *Beyond Dialogue: Toward a Mutual Transformation of Christianity and Buddhism.* Philadelphia: Fortress Press, 1982.

————. "The Meaning of Pluralism for Christian Self-Understanding." In *Religious Pluralism*, edited by L. S. Rouner. Notre Dame, Ind.: University of Notre Dame Press, 1984.

de Bary, Wm. Theodore. *Learning for One's Self: Essays on the Individual in Neo-Confucian Thought.* New York: Columbia University Press, 1991.

————. *The Message of the Mind in Neo-Confucianism.* New York: Columbia University Press, 1989.

————. *Neo-Confucian Orthodoxy and the Learning of the Mind-and-Heart.* New York: Columbia University Press, 1981.

————. "Sagehood as a Secular and Spiritual Ideal in Tokugawa Neo-Confucianism." In *Principle and Practicality: Essays in Neo-Confucianism and Practical Learning*, edited by Wm. Theodore de Bary and Irene Bloom. New York: Columbia University Press, 1979.

————. *Trouble with Confucianism.* Cambridge, Mass.: Harvard University Press, 1991.

————, ed. *The Unfolding of Neo-Confucianism.* New York: Columbia University Press, 1975.

————, and JaHyun Kim Haboush, eds. *The Rise of Neo-Confucianism in Korea.* New York: Columbia University Press, 1985.

Deutsch, Eliot. *Religion and Spirituality.* Albany: State University of New York Press, 1995.

Eno, Robert. *The Confucian Creation of Heaven: Philosophy and the Defense of Ritual Mastery.* Albany: State University of New York Press, 1990.

Fingarette, Herbert. *Confucius—The Secular as Sacred.* New York: Harper & Row, 1972.

Gardner, Daniel K. 1990. *Chu Hsi: Learning to Be a Sage.* Berkeley and Los Angeles: University of California Press, 1990.

Graham, Angus. *Studies in Chinese Philosophy and Philosophical Literature*. Albany: State University of New York Press, 1990.

Griffin, David R., and Huston Smith. *Primordial Truth and Postmodern Theology*. Albany: State University of New York Press, 1989.

Hall, David L., and Roger T. Ames. *Thinking through Confucius*. Albany: State University of New York Press, 1987.

Hick, John. *An Interpretation of Religion: Human Responses to the Transcendent*. New Haven: Yale University Press, 1989.

Hick, John, and Paul F. Knitter, eds. *The Myth of Christian Uniqueness: Toward a Pluralistic Theology of Religions*. Maryknoll, N.Y.: Orbis Books, 1987.

Kalton, Michael C., trans. *To Become a Sage: The Ten Diagrams on Sage Learning by Yi T'oegye*. New York: Columbia University Press, 1988.

————, et al. *The Four-Seven Debate: An Annotated Translation of the Most Famous Controversy in Korean Neo-Confucian Thought*. Albany: State University of New York Press, 1994.

Küng, Hans, and Julia Ching. *Christianity and Chinese Religions*. New York: Doubleday, 1989.

Lau, D. C., trans. *Mencius*. New York: Penguin Books, 1970.

————, trans. *Confucius: Analects (Lun yü)*. New York: Penguin Books, 1970.

Lee, Peter K. H., ed. *Confucian-Christian Encounters in Historical and Contemporary Perspective*. Lewiston/Queenstown: Edwin Mellen Press, 1992.

Lindbeck, George A. *The Nature of Doctrine: Religion and Theology in a Postliberal Age*. Philadelphia: Westminster Press, 1984.

Liu, Shu-hsien. "The Confucian Approach to the Problem of Transcendence and Immanence." *Philosophy East and West* 22 (January 1972): 45–52.

————. "A Critique of Paul Tillich's Doctrine of God and Christology from an Oriental Perspective." In *Religious Issues and Interreligious Dialogues*, edited by Charles Wei-hsun Fu and Gerhard E. Spiegler. New York: Greenwood Press, 1989.

Mou, Zongsan [Mou Tsung-san]. *Chung-kuo che-hsüeh te t'e-chih* (The Uniqueness of Chinese Philosophy). Hong Kong: Student Books, 1963.

————. *Hsin-t'i yü hsing-t'i* (Substance of Mind and Substance of Human Nature). 3 vols. Taipei: Cheng-chung shu-ch, 1975.

Neville, Robert C. *Behind the Masks of God: An Essay Toward Comparative Theology*. Albany: State University of New York Press, 1991.

————. *The Tao and the Daimon: Segments of a Religious Inquiry*. Albany: State University of New York Press, 1982.

Oxtoby, Willard G. *The Meaning of Other Faiths*. Philadelphia: Westminster Press, 1983.

Parrinder, Geoffrey. *Encountering World Religions: Questions of Religious Truth*. New York: Crossroad, 1987.

Ro, Young-chan. *The Neo-Confucianism of Yi Yulgok*. Albany: State University of New York Press, 1989.

Smart, Ninian. *Crosscultural Explorations of Human Beliefs*. New York: Charles Scribners, 1983.

Smith, Huston. *The World's Religions* (Completely Revised and Updated Edition of *The Religions of Man*). New York: Harper, 1991.

Smith, Wilfred C. *Faith and Belief*. Princeton, N.J.: Princeton University Press, 1979.

———. *Toward a World Theology: Faith and the Comparative History of Religion*. Philadelphia: Westminster Press, 1981.

———. *What Is Scripture? A Comparative Approach*. Minneapolis: Fortress Press, 1993.

Streng, Frederick. *Ways of Being Religious*. Englewood Cliffs, N.J.: Prentice-Hall, 1973.

Tang Junyi [T'ang Chün-i]. *Chung-kuo che-hsüeh yüan-lun yüan hsing p'ien* (Sources of Chinese Philosophy, section on human nature). Hong Kong: Hsüeh-sheng shu-chü, 1973.

Taylor, Rodney L. *The Confucian Way of Contemplation: Okada Takehiko and the Tradition of Quiet-Sitting*. Columbia: University of South Carolina Press, 1988.

———. *Religious Dimensions of Neo-Confucianism*. Albany: State University of New York Press, 1991.

———. *The Way of Heaven: An Introduction to the Confucian Religious Life*. Leiden: E. J. Brill, 1986.

Tracy, David. *Dialogue with the Other: The Inter-Religious Dialogue*. Louvain: Peeters; Grand Rapids: Eerdmans, 1990.

———. *Plurality and Ambiguity: Hermeneutics, Religion, Hope*. San Francisco: Harper & Row, 1987.

Tu, Weiming. *Centrality and Commonality: An Essay on Confucian Religiousness* [A revised and enlarged edition of *Centrality and Commonality: An Essay on Chung-yung*]. Albany: State University of New York Press, 1989.

———. *Confucian Thought: Selfhood as Creative Self-Transformation*. Albany: State University of New York Press, 1985.

———. "T'oegye's Perception of Human Nature: A Preliminary Inquiry into the Four-Seven Debate in Korean Neo-Confucianism." In *The Rise of Neo-Confucianism in Korea*, edited by Wm. Theodore de Bary and JaHyun Kim Haboush. New York: Columbia University Press, 1985.

Tu, Weiming, M. Hejtmanek, and A. Wachman, eds. *The Confucian World Observed: A Contemporary Discussion of Confucian Humanism in East Asia*. Honolulu: University of Hawaii Press, 1992.

26

Morality, Spirituality, and Spontaneity in Korean Neo-Confucianism

YOUNG-CHAN RO

T HE TERM "CONFUCIAN SPIRITUALITY" might be unfamiliar not only to the general populus but even more so to the scholars and students of Confucian studies. We may, however, know terms such as "Confucian morality" or "Confucian ethics," since the Confucian tradition is known for its strong moral and ethical teachings. Confucianism, unlike other religious traditions such as Christianity and Buddhism, has not been fully appreciated for its "spiritual" dimension. For a proper understanding of Confucian spirituality, we need a method or an approach to explore the unique form of the Confucian experience of spirituality. I would like to investigate the spiritual aspect of Confucianism in connection with "morality" and "spontaneity" in Korean Neo-Confucianism, especially in the thought of Yi Yulgok (1536–1584). Yulgok's way of thinking and his insight in interpreting the Confucian classics, especially the *Great Learning* (*Daxue*) and the *Doctrine of the Mean* (*Zhongyong*) have laid a foundation for understanding the spiritual dimension of Confucian morality.

Since the term "spirituality" has a broad implication when applied to the Confucian tradition, we must understand the meaning of "spirituality" in this context. Confucian and Neo-Confucian ideas or concepts of "spirituality" may require a different mode of thinking from the way we understand "spirituality" in the theistic religious traditions. The Confucian tradition has developed a subtle yet rich resource for "spirituality." My concern here is how to appropriate and appreciate the significance of Neo-Confucian "spirituality" as a *dimension* of life rather than a transcendental reality. Confucian "spirituality" pervades all aspects of our daily life. From the Confucian point of view, "spirituality" is to be understood neither as an independent and isolated experience nor as a separate form of reality from our daily experience in this world. Rather, "spirituality" is a dimension of "depth" as a foundation of our being that is deeply rooted in this world and in our daily life.

I would like to limit my exploration of Confucian spirituality to three distinctive aspects of the human experience: (1) spirituality in relation to the dimension of emotion or feeling, especially the feeling of "awe"; (2) spirituality as an intrinsic part of the process in Confucian "self-cultivation"; (3) spirituality as a "cosmo-anthropic" experience of being in unity and harmony with the universe and human beings.

From the phenomenological point of view there is, of course, a clear distinction between "emotion" or "feeling" and "spirituality," but there is also a close connection between the dimension of "feeling" and the dimension of "spirituality." The experience of spirituality often manifests itself as feeling or emotion. Since the Confucian idea of spirituality is not to be understood as a transcendental reality but rather as the experience of an immanent reality, it would be fruitful to explore "spirituality" in relation to the "feelings." Rudolf Otto, for example, understood "holy" as a specific form of emotion or feeling, "awe," or *"mysterium tremendum."*[1] From the Confucian point of view, however, the feeling of "awe" is neither an isolated "emotion" nor a purely subjective feeling. Rather the feeling of "awe" or "fear" is closely connected to the moral, ethical, and intellectual processes of being a human. Confucian spirituality is fundamentally "moral and intellectual spirituality" which transcends the dichotomy between "immanence" and "transcendence" or between "subject" and "object." Although there is a general tendency to separate the feeling of "holiness" or "awe" from "rationality" and "morality," the feeling of "awe" is not totally detachable from the intellectual and the ethical dimensions of life. A careful study shows that Otto himself was keenly aware of the problem of such separation. The English translator of Otto's *Das Heilige*, John W. Harvey, explained Otto's position clearly in his preface to the second edition of *The Idea of the Holy*:

> He *was*, as has been said, really opposing the subjectivist trend in religious thought: he was definitely not opposing the attempt of reverent minds to interpret the divine nature in rational and ethical categories. He was urging, on the contrary, that the rational and moral is an essential part of the content of what we mean by holy or sacred: only it is not the whole of it. There is an

overplus of meaning which is non-rational, but neither in the sense of being counter to reason on the one hand nor above reason on the other.[2]

The Confucian experience of "awe," though different from Otto's idea of the "holy," provides a unique way of understanding Confucian spirituality. Confucius said, "The superior man stands in awe (*wei*) of three things. He stands in awe of the Mandate of Heaven (*tianming*); he stands in awe of great men; and he stands in awe of the words of the sages" (*Analects* 16:8).[3] From the Confucian point of view, the feeling of "awe" (*wei*) or the sense of "reverent veneration" (*jing*) has a profound spiritual implication. The idea of *jing* is an important Neo-Confucian concept for exploring the spiritual and religious dimensions of Neo-Confucianism. Yi T'oegye (1501–1570), another great Neo-Confucian scholar together with Yi Yulgok, employed the idea of "reverent veneration" (*jing/kyông*) as the key in his intellectual investigation and spiritual practice. To explore T'oegye's idea of "reverent veneration" in connection with the spiritual dimension of Neo-Confucianism would require a separate study. It suffices here to mention that both T'oegye and Yulgok took the spiritual dimension seriously in their intellectual system and in their moral and spiritual practice.

The superior man (*junzi*) is able to *feel* the sense of awe, while "the inferior man" is ignorant of the Mandate of Heaven and does not stand in awe of it. He is disrespectful to treat men and is contemptuous toward the words of the sages" (*Analects* 16:8). The Confucian sense of awe has a profound moral implication. The feeling of awe is generated from moral authority with spiritual force, a moral *charisma*. From the Confucian point of view, authority or power must have a moral ground and an ethical foundation. Power and authority without moral persuasion may produce an artificial fear or a threat, but they cannot generate the feeling of awe or moral *charisma*. The feeling of awe is based on a genuine sense of respect and veneration that contains a *spontaneous* force for inspiration. In this respect moral *charisma* is a moral force based not on an external authority or a coerced power but on a spontaneous inner feeling that generates an unusual sense of awe. For this reason, the experience of moral charisma is a profoundly spiritual experience. Spirituality has an element of spontaneity. The spiritual experience is a profound human experience that is governed by a genuine spontaneous force. The feeling of awe is an irresistible and spontaneous human feeling that has an element of fear. The fear in this case, however, is not a mere threat from an external power or force in physical, political, or economic form, but a feeling generated from within: the spontaneous and irresistible feeling accompanied by moral authority and persuasion, namely, moral charisma. Nonetheless, this spontaneous feeling of awe is not purely a subjective feeling. Rather, it is the feeling of contact with an objective reality that inspires and invokes, not coerces, an inner spontaneous feeling of awe. The feeling of awe is neither subjective nor objective, but is a subject-object feeling.

Confucius clearly delineated three kinds of awe: the Mandate of Heaven, the great men, and the words of sages. The Mandate of Heaven is not to be understood simply in a theistic sense of transcendental deity, but as a certain moral force that relates human beings to Heaven. "Great men" are not merely political and social beings, but are persons of moral profundity and moral charisma. "The words of the sages" means the spoken or written words that contain the moral teachings and intellectual wisdom of sages. There is a profound moral element and spontaneous spiritual awareness in all three instances. Confucius believed that a ruler must rule with this kind of moral charisma: "The master said, he who rules by moral force (de) is like the pole-star, which remains in its place while all the lesser stars do homage to it" (Analects 2:1).[4] The "moral force" has certain magical attraction, pulling his people to follow his direction. This attraction, however, is not a magical power but a moral charisma:

> Chi K'ang-tzu was troubled by burglars. He asked Master K'ung what he should do. Master K'ung replied saying, if only you were free from desire, they would not steal even if you paid them to. (Analects 12:18)

Arthur Waley made an interesting comment on this passage: "This is a rhetorical way of saying that if K'ang-tzu did not accumulate valuables, he would not be robbed. But coupled with this meaning is the suggestion that the ruler's moral force operates directly on the people, as a magic, not merely as an example."[5] In my view, the moral persuasion seen in this passage, beyond magic, is the power coming from a person's moral charisma.

The following remark of Confucius on the "gentleman" (the superior man, or junzi) clearly shows the moral charisma of the "gentleman": "The essence of the gentleman is that of wind, the essence of small people is that of grass. And when a wind passes over the grass, it cannot choose but bend" (Analects 12:19). Although this passage implies that the moral quality of "gentleman" will prevail over the small people, more importantly, it shows the personal moral charisma of the "gentleman" (junzi) over the small people. The moral quality of the gentleman goes beyond morality, for it contains a profound spirituality.

The Confucian idea of the superior man or the "gentleman" must have this awe-inspiring moral-spiritual force. The awe-inspiring feeling is spontaneous and ineffable. In this state of being, moral authority gains a spiritual force. From the Confucian point of view, the relationship between morality and spirituality is not necessarily dualistic; there is no dichotomy between morality and spirituality. Rather, Confucian spirituality is fundamentally a moral spirituality. Confucian spirituality neither negates nor transcends morality. The process of Confucian self-cultivation is a spiritual process, because the moral dimension and the spiritual dimension of life are inseparable. In other words, morality without spirituality is empty and rigid; spirituality without morality is aimless and dangerous. When morality and spirituality integrate with each other, moral practice gains a dynamic force and spirituality gains moral content. When moral practice becomes spiritual practice, it generates a spontaneous feeling of awe.

For this reason, the superior man (*junzi*) has the feeling of awe: standing in awe of the Mandate of Heaven, standing in awe of the great men, standing in awe of the words of sages. The Mandate of Heaven in this context means a moral destiny that goes beyond the human sense of duty or obligation. The Mandate of Heaven, however, is neither a transcendental nor an objective reality but an *awareness* achieved through the process of human interaction with Heaven, which generates a moral charisma or awe. The "great men" are personal manifestations and living examples of this moral charisma. The "words of the sages" are the accumulated form of wisdom that generates awe-inspiring experience when read or heard.

The Confucian idea of awe, however, is not a sudden experience without the process of moral, intellectual, and spiritual cultivation. Rather, the experience of awe is the result of an unceasing process of human self-cultivation. The Mandate of Heaven is not a fixed or a predetermined static reality that exists outside the domain of human affairs: on the contrary, the Mandate of Heaven is a dynamic and changing reality in which the human being discovers the ultimate moral and spiritual destiny. The great men are the personified forms of the Mandate of Heaven, and the words of the sages are the linguistic manifestation or incarnation of the Mandate of Heaven. For this reason, superior men stand in awe in these three.

The Confucian concept of the superior man (*junzi*) is the person who has developed a spiritual and moral sensitivity to relate and respond to the Mandate of Heaven with the feeling of fear and awe. This feeling of awe is a spontaneous feeling that is intrinsic to the superior persons. The feeling of awe or a proper sense of fear is the inner quality for being a superior person. In this respect, we can say that Confucian spirituality is deeply rooted in the moral quality of the human being. Once this moral and spiritual quality of a person is fully realized, it generates the feeling of awe. The person who does not have a proper moral and spiritual quality may not have the feeling of awe, even if that person stands in the Mandate of Heaven, the great men, or the words of the sages.

Thus, Confucian moral charisma requires both the subjective side of the readiness of receiving or recognizing moral authority and the objective side of authority that invokes the moral and spiritual force in human beings. However, the subjective side and the objective side are not two separate realities, but two different sides of the one reality. The Mandate of Heaven, for example, is not a reality detached from the human receptivity of the Mandate of Heaven. The great men are the great men because of the human ability to respect and revere the great men. The words of the sage become the words of the sage because of the human capacity of understanding those words. For this reason, as quoted above, the inferior person does not stand in awe of the Mandate of Heaven because that person is ignorant of it. The inferior person is disrespectful to great men and contemptuous toward the words of the sage. Confucian moral charisma is to be understood not as a magical or mechanical power but as a spiritual force with moral authority and spontaneity. Confucian moral charisma, beyond morality, is related to the intellectual dimension of Confucian self-cultivation, for there is no dichotomy between the intellectual or learning process and the moral process of self-cultivation.

Spirituality and Self-Cultivation

The Confucian ideal for human beings is to realize sagehood through self-cultivation. One of the best ways to understand the process of the Confucian self-cultivation is found in the *Great Learning* (*Daxue*): the eight stages of self-cultivation, which reflect the way of reaching "sagely-inward" and "kingly-outward" (*neisheng waiwang*) and achieving "cultivating-self and governing-others" (*xiuji zhiren*). The Korean Neo-Confucian scholar Yi Yulgok, for example, understood that "sagely learning" was nothing but the "learning of sagely-inward and kingly-outward," which is the summary of the eight-stage cultivation delineated in the *Great Learning*.

The Confucian vision for the fulfillment of one's human destiny both as an individual being and as a social being is fully realized through the eight-stage process of self-cultivation. The Confucian understanding of the human being, or Confucian anthropology, does not assume the dichotomy between individual and collective, personal and social. This does not mean that the Confucian idea of the human being has no distinction between individual human beings and collective humanity. Rather, the Confucian assumption is that the human being, from the ontological point of view, is both an individual and collective or social being at the same time. For this reason, the Confucian conception of "self" is neither individual nor social, but includes individual, social, and cosmic. Tu Weiming has put it aptly:

"Indeed, learning to be human, in the Confucian perspective, entails a broadening and deepening process that acknowledges the interconnectedness of all the modalities of existence defining the human condition."[6] Accordingly, the Confucian idea of "self-cultivation" does not imply the cultivation of an individual human being alone. Although Confucian self-cultivation starts with a single individual, the process and the goal of Confucian self-cultivation are social, universal, and even cosmic. In other words, individual self-cultivation cannot be fully achieved without the fulfillment of the social and the cosmic dimensions of the self-cultivation. Furthermore, the process of Confucian self-cultivation includes the moral, the intellectual, and the spiritual dimensions. The Confucian concept of moral cultivation is a part of learning or an intellectual process, and the intellectual process of self-cultivation is profoundly moral and spiritual:

> The ancients who wished to manifest their clear character to the world would first bring order to their states. Those who wished to bring order to their states would first regulate their families. Those who wished to regulate their family would first cultivate their personal lives. Those who wished to cultivate their personal lives would first rectify their minds. Those who wished to rectify their minds would first make their wills sincere. Those who wished to make their wills sincere would first extend their knowledge. The extension of knowledge consists in the investigation of things. When things are investigated, knowledge is extended; when knowledge is extended, the will becomes sincere; when the will sincere, the mind is rectified; when the mind is rectified, the personal life is cultivated; when the personal life is cultivated, the family will be regulated; when the family is regulated, the state will be in order; and when the state is in order, there will be peace throughout the world. From the son of Heaven down to the common people, all must regard cultivation of the personal life as the root or foundation. (*Great Learning*, ch. 1)[7]

Confucian self-cultivation, as shown in this passage, consists of two aspects or two dimensions: the internal and the external or "sagely-inward" (*neisheng*) and "kingly-outward" (*waiwang*). The internal process, which is called "sagely-inward," consists of rectification of mind, sincerity of will, extension of knowledge, and investigation of thing. The external process, which is called "kingly-outward," consists of regulating family, bringing order to the state, and peace throughout the world. Within the *Great Learning*'s structure of the process of Confucian self-cultivation, cultivation of personal lives or self-cultivation (*xiushen*) is located in the middle of the eight stages of becoming a fully realized human being. The cultivation of personal lives (*xiushen*) is the focal point of the whole process, which has two directions, inward and outward. However, as Yulgok rightly said, these two sides, the "sagely-inward" and the "kingly-outward," are not two separate steps of Confucian self-cultivation, but they are "one yet two" and "two yet one," a nondualistic formulation typical of Yulgok in interpreting many other important Neo-Confucian concepts such as principle (*li*) and material force (*qi*). The kingly-outward cannot be achieved without the sagely-inward, and the sagely-inward becomes empty without the kingly-outward. In this respect, the Confucian idea of self is to be fulfilled through both the inner investigation and the outer extension. According to Yulgok, sagely learning *(shengxue/sônghak)* is nothing but cultivating self and governing others *(xiuji zhiren/sugich'iin)*. The complete achievement of this self-cultivation is found in the state of the unity of Heaven and human. In this state, the way of Heaven and the way of human become one through "sincerity" *(cheng/sông)*.[8]

The *Compendium of Sagely Learning (sônghak chibyo)*, Yulgok's major work, explains the significance of sagely-inward and kingly-outward. This work is intended to expound the way to reach sagehood by combining two important concepts, "abiding in the highest good" in the *Great Learning* and "realizing equilibrium and harmony to the highest degree" in the *Doctrine of the Mean*. Yulgok thought that the *Great Learning* and the *Doctrine of the Mean* were complementary in terms of the sagely learning. Yulgok's hermeneutical strategy was to interpret the *Great Learning* in light of the *Doctrine of the Mean* and the *Doctrine of the Mean* in light of the *Great Learning*. According to the *Great Learning*, the way of learning to be great consists in "manifesting the clear character," "loving (or renovating) the people," and "abiding in the highest good." The *Doctrine of the Mean*, on the other hand, opens its first chapter with a profound vision of the unity of Heaven and human nature and the way to reach that unity through education: "What Heaven (*tian*, Nature) imparts to man is called human nature (*xing*). To follow our nature is called the Way (*dao*). Cultivating the Way is called education" (*Doctrine of the Mean*, ch. 1).[9]

The *Doctrine of the Mean (Zhongyong)* was the most important spiritual cultivation for Yulgok. He understood that the origin of the Way (*dao*) is Heaven. The Way is nothing but to follow human nature. The process of education for Yulgok was the process of integrating with the "substance" (*ti/ch'e*) and "function" (*yong/yong*) of the Way (*dao*). One of the Yulgok's favorite conceptual frameworks for explaining the intricacy of the Way was the *ti/ch'e-yong/yong* or "substance and function" formula. As a nondualistic thinker, Yulgok understood reality in two distinct yet closely related aspects, namely, substance and function or manifestation. The substance of the Way is human nature, because it is from Heaven, and *following* human nature is the Way. The Way in this sense is nothing but what is already given and imparted to us as substance. Human nature, as the substance of the Way, is the state before the feelings are aroused. However, when the feelings are aroused and attain due measure and degree, this is the function of the way.

According to Yulgok, human nature (*xing/sông*) was substance (*ti/ch'e*), while the feelings (*jing/chông*) were the function (*yong/yong*). Education and cultivation, therefore, were concrete ways (as function) to reach human nature *(xing/sông)*. The Way (*dao*) was not an artificial construction but was to follow human *nature*. While the substance of the Way was human nature, the function of the Way was to follow human nature. For Yulgok, human nature (*xing/sông*) as substance was invisible and unknowable, but function was not only the visible and tangible manifestation of the substance; it was also a concrete and practical way to reach back to the state of substance or human nature. Education and cultivation, in this respect, were the function of the Way.[10] Cultivation and education were the process of reaching the Way, but the Way was nothing but to follow nature (*xing/sông*). Once the Way (*dao*) is fully cultivated, it becomes human nature *(xing/sông)*. Here the vital and dynamic process of cultivation aims at the state of the Way, so that the Way (*dao*) becomes human nature *(xing/sông)*. The process of cultivation is to realize what is in human beings as nature, and following this nature is the Way. Once the process of cultivation becomes a part of nature, it becomes *spontaneous*.

In following his hermeneutical strategy, Yulgok interpreted the *Doctrine of the Mean* with the basic assumption of the *Great Learning*. For Yulgok, the "Heaven-endowed human nature" in the *Doctrine of the Mean* is the embodiment of the "clear virtue" in the *Great Learning*. The way of following human nature is the activity of the "clear virtue," the education of cultivating the way is the norms and the regulations of renovating people" (*Chônsô*, vol. 1 kwon 19:18a). According to Yulgok, the "clear virtue" in the *Great Learning* plays a critical hermeneutical role in understanding the opening statement: "What Heaven imparts to man is called nature." The clear virtue is a moral manifestation of the Heaven-endowed human nature. Yulgok's intention to relate the clear virtue to the Heaven-endowed (human) nature was to relate the moral dimension to the spiritual dimension of human nature. "Following the human nature" was a profoundly moral and ethical activity as a concrete form of realizing clear virtue. However, the clear virtue was not a body of moral codes; it was a Heaven-endowed moral force or power that was self-evident in human nature. "Education as cultivation of the way" was to "renovate (or to love) the people." Yulgok understood that education, as a form of cultivating the

Way, was not a metaphysical or an intellectual process alone; it was fundamentally a moral and spiritual process. In other words, Yulgok expounded the spiritual dimension in the *Doctrine of the Mean* in relation to the Confucian social ideal of "abiding in the highest good" in the *Great Learning*. Yulgok took the concepts of "caution," "apprehension" (or "fear"), and "watchful over himself when alone" in the *Doctrine of the Mean* to achieve the state of "abiding in the highest good" in the *Great Learning*:

> "Cautious" (*chieh/kye*) and "fearful" (*chu/ku*) is the state of being in calm and thus it belongs to the "rectification of mind." "Watchful over oneself when alone" (*shentu/sindok*) is an active observation which belongs to "sincerity of will." [When] equilibrium and harmony are realized to the highest degree and all things are flourished, [this is the time when] the "clear virtue" and the "renovation of the people" are reached to the highest good so that the clear virtue is manifested to the world. (*Chônsô*, vol. 1 Kwon 19:18a)

As discussed above, the idea of fear or awe has special significance in understanding Confucian spirituality and morality. Caution and fear have positive psychological and spiritual implications in the process of self-cultivation. Fear in the Confucian tradition is not a threat. Fear is not a negative feeling of losing self-confidence but a positive feeling of gaining self-respect. The Confucian idea of the sage is the one who constantly and spontaneously feels cautious and fearful. The Confucian idea of fear is originated not heteronomously but autonomously. The autonomous fear is a self-imposed or rather self-generated spontaneous fear that comes from caution. The Confucian sense of fear is not a terror generated from the external threat but a feeling generated from inner spontaneity of the sage. By nature, the sage is cautious and fearful.

Understood thus, Confucian morality is profoundly spiritual and Confucian spirituality profoundly moral. When morality and spirituality are totally integrated, it generates the sense of fear or awe. Confucian ideas such as caution and fear are not to be understood in terms of the feelings that are generated from lack of self-esteem, although a sense of self-limitation or humility may be a part of it: rather, caution and fear are positive and dynamic feelings that are essential in self-cultivation. In contrast to the monotheistic traditions, the Confucian sense of fear is neither the fear of God's wrath for sin and guilt nor threat of punishment. Instead, the Confucian concept of fear is to be understood in terms of *care* and *concern*. The Confucian sage must have this sense of fear not for the sake of selfishness but for others as the extension of his own being. The fear here is not concern about individual personal well-being but the well-being of family, society, nation, and the universe as an ever-extending and ever-evolving self.

In this respect, the fear that the Confucian sage has was neither physical nor psychological but fundamentally ontological and spiritual. The Confucian sage deeply *cares* about the well-being of the human community, which goes beyond the human realm and extends to the cosmic realm. For this reason the Confucian sage has to be watchful over himself even if he is physically alone. The Confucian sage can never be alone because his personal self is deeply integrated with society, nature, and the universe. There is an unbroken ontological unity between the sage, Heaven, and earth. The feeling of caution and fear is a continuous emotional force that is a part of the process of self-cultivation. For Yulgok, the feeling of caution and fear is essential in achieving the calm and tranquillity necessary to reach the state of rectification of mind. The feeling of watchful over himself when he is alone (*shentu/sindok*), however, is an active and dynamic process that is essential to the sincerity of will.

The Confucian concepts found in the *Doctrine of the Mean* such as caution, fear, and watchful when alone provide the spiritual foundation for understanding the profound meaning of the *Great Learning*. Yulgok's *Compendium of Sagely Learning* (*sŏnghak chibyo*) was his hermeneutical attempt to bring the two classics, the *Great Learning* and the *Doctrine of the Mean*, together in order to construct a path to sagely learning. In so doing, Yulgok expounded the unique aspect of Confucian moral-spirituality.

Spirituality and Spontaneity in Yulgok

Korean Neo-Confucianism, for example, has developed the idea of spirituality in relation to the universe (cosmological dimension) and our being (ontological dimension). Spirituality, in this respect, is a form of human experience in which we can respond and relate to the cosmos and to our selves in a most profound manner. Furthermore, Confucian and Neo-Confucian spirituality is to be understood in relation to, not in separation from, the moral and intellectual dimensions of our life. Although the experience of spirituality in the Confucian context is not a *transcendental* experience beyond this world, it is profoundly cosmic in relating to the mystery of the universe. Spirituality in this respect is also the experience of an authentic relationship, to Heaven and earth, and to human beings and to the world.

I would also like to explore the significance of spirituality in relation to spontaneity linked to the moral and intellectual dimensions of life. Spontaneity as a form of action allows us to act in the most genuine and authentic way, or act in accordance with nature. In this connection, I would like to investigate the significance of spontaneity in relation to the moral and intellectual process of cultivation. I shall return to spontaneity in the latter part of this essay.

From the Neo-Confucian perspective, as we observed, the moral dimension is not an independent entity but an integral part of the Neo-Confucian worldview. The moral dimension of the human being is intrinsically related to the cosmological and ontological principle such as *yin-yang*, *li* and *qi*, and *taiji*. The physical world is more than a physical entity, for it is the world of a coherent and meaningful system. It has a moral implication and intellectual system in which human beings can have a meaningful relationship with and make a response to the universe and nature. In this respect, the notion of spirituality, in a Neo-Confucian context, is to be understood not as a transcendental force or a superhuman power but as an intrinsic force inseparable from the physical world and the human being. Neo-Confucian spirituality is closely associated with an immanent and physical spirituality: *qi/ki*, in this sense, is neither matter alone nor a detached spirit but a material *force*, an intrinsic energy in physical being. Spirit can be associated with this force or energy. Although human beings and other beings share *qi/ki*, the human being is able to be associated with spirit or *shen*.

According to Yulgok, human being is a castle of "*hun/hon* and *po/paek* or the heavenly aspect of soul and the earthly aspect of soul."[11] The heavenly aspect of soul (*hun/hon*) is the *spirit* of one's vital force that is expressed in one's intelligence and power of breathing, whereas *po/paek* is the *spirit* of one's physical nature that is expressed in bodily movements.[12] In this statement, we notice that the spirit is not entirely detached from the physical aspect of life whether in "breath" or in "intelligence." In this respect, the Confucian idea of spirit is nondualistic. According to Yulgok, "*hun/hon* is the spirit of *qi/ki* (material force) and *po/paek* is the spirit of *jing/chông*, the feelings: while alive, it is *shen/sin* or spirit, when dead, it is *kuei/kwi*" (*Chônsô*, vol. 2, 4:21, p. 540). Spirit has two sides: the living and the dead or *yang* and *yin*. In the Neo-Confucian way of thinking, the idea of spirit is closely related to the physical state of being. In other words, the state of spirit is definitely determined by the state of physical form.

The conception of "spirit" in Neo-Confucianism does not have an independent ontological basis apart from the physical aspect. Spirituality in Neo-Confucianism, thus, is also to be understood in relation to various other dimensions of life such as the moral and intellectual dimensions. Spirituality for Neo-Confucians was a dimension of life or life itself. Neo-Confucian spirituality is deeply embedded in our daily life. In this sense, Neo-Confucian spirituality can be understood in two distinctive ways: spirituality as awareness and a force of interconnectedness of Heaven, earth, and human being, and as the responsiveness to cosmic and human affairs.

Spontaneity and Cultivation

Unlike Daoism, Confucianism may not appear to be sympathetic to the idea of spontaneity. On the surface, one might think that Confucianism is a well-structured and well-planned way of human self-cultivation and a social program that does not leave any room for spontaneity. Confucianism has certainly provided one of the most elaborate and systematic approaches to realizing human potential and offering a social vision for the world and humanity. What I am trying to do in this paper, however, is to show the Confucian concept of spontaneity as the most desirable stage of the process of self-cultivation and human development to become a sage. The Confucian sage reflects this kind of spontaneity. Confucius himself, in his own spiritual autobiography, made the following remark: "At fifteen my mind was set on learning. At thirty my character had been formed. At forty I had no more perplexities. At fifty I knew the Mandate of Heaven (*tianming*). At sixty I was at ease with whatever I heard. At seventy I could follow my hearts desire without transgressing moral principle" (*Analects* 2:4).[13]

The Confucian way of self-cultivation and becoming a true human being involved a lifelong process that included the knowledge of Heaven and the Mandate of Heaven. Confucian self-cultivation, thus, is not limited to the human dimension alone. Furthermore, the Confucian concept of humanity already includes the dimension of Heaven. In this respect, Confucian humanity or Confucian humanism is unique in extending to Heaven. There is no tension, conflict, or dichotomy between the process of becoming human and the process of reaching Heaven, on the one hand, and the duality of immanence and transcendence, on the other. It was a natural and spontaneous process for Confucius to reach the knowledge of the Mandate of Heaven. In this respect, Confucius shows the stage of the total integration of his will and the will of Heaven. There is no radical conversion from human will to the will of Heaven. Rather, the process of cultivation was gradual and continuous, and human will and the will of Heaven must be perfectly compatible with each other. At the age of seventy, Confucius finally reached the point where he could feel absolutely comfortable in following the desire of his heart without transgressing the moral principle. This was the stage where Confucius finally felt and experienced that his personal desire and the moral principle had become integrated and his action had become morally spontaneous. When morality becomes a part of being, it becomes spontaneous. This is what I would call "moral spontaneity." This is the state where morality is no longer defined in terms of action but is a state of being in which morality becomes a spontaneous expression, an extension, and even an explosion. The state of moral spontaneity is the state in which the dichotomy of doing and being or ethics and ontology are totally integrated. In this respect, the Confucian sage is a person who simply acts morally or does things ethically or meets the expectation of moral perfection not in spite of his being but because of his being. The Confucian sage is a state of being in which he acts in accordance with the Way and is able to follow nature, which is given from Heaven. The ideal of Confucian self-cultivation is not to perfect moral behavior but to transform the human being in accordance with the Heaven-endowed nature. The process of cultivation is not a moral or an ethical process, but it is fundamentally an ontological process. The Confucian concept of sagehood is not only ethically constructed but, more importantly, ontologically grounded.

Sincerity (*cheng/sông*)

One of the best ways to explore the idea of spontaneity in Confucianism is to understand "sincerity/authenticity" (*cheng/sông*). Sincerity or authenticity is not only a moral principle but a metaphysical principle and a spiritual force for realizing sagehood. "Sincerity is not just a state of mind, but an active force that is always transforming things and completing things and drawing man and Heaven (*tian*) together in the same current."[14]

Thus, the Way (*dao*) and education are the means of achieving the essential oneness of the human being and Heaven. Accordingly, in the *Doctrine of the Mean* (*Zhongyong*), true human nature can be realized only through the Mandate of Heaven. The ideal goal of the human being, according to Confucian belief, is to become a sage. Confucianism maintains that sagehood is not something only a few people who have special gifts can achieve; on the contrary, sagehood is the goal of every human being, and everyone has the inherent ability to achieve sagehood, which is nothing other than the fullest realization of human nature.

Although there are many aspects of "sincerity" (*cheng/sông*), I would like to focus on spontaneity in connection with the idea of sincerity as the most essential quality of the sage. According to Yulgok, there are two basic qualifications for becoming a sage: (1) the investigation of things and the extension of *knowledge* (*gewu zhizhi/kyôngmul ch'iji*), and (2) sincerity of will and the rectification of the mind (*cheng'i jengxin/sôngûi chôngsim*). These two qualifications of sageliness cannot be achieved without *cheng/sông*. The "investigation of things and the extension of knowledge" are the intellectual realization of *cheng*, whereas the "sincerity of will and the rectification of the mind" are the ethical realization of *cheng/sông*. The former refers to "thought" (*si/sa*), while the latter refers to action or "labor" (*mian/myôn*). Thus "thinking" and "laboring" are the two most essential characteristics of becoming a sage. For Yulgok, there is no other way to achieve sagehood than these two constant processes involving "thinking" and "laboring." The sage, according to Yulgok, is not someone beyond or outside these two unceasing processes.

One of the most striking aspect of Yulgok's understanding of sage is that he relates the process of self-cultivation to idea of "spontaneity." For the sage, the thinking process and the laboring process become totally spontaneous:

> In my opinion, the sage is one who investigates things to their utmost, extends knowledge to its utmost, makes the will its most sincere and the mind its most correct. The "superior man" (*junzi*) is one who investigates things and extends knowledge, and makes the will sincere and corrects the mind, but does not yet reach [these things to their] utmost. Yen-tzu was the one who went beyond being a "superior man" and came nearest to sagehood, but still fell short. The learner is one who has not investigated things and extended knowledge yet desires to investigate things and extend knowledge, who has not made the will sincere and corrected the mind. The sage does not consciously think of labor, yet comes to investigate things and extend knowledge, and make the will sincere and correct the mind spontaneously. Yen-tzu, was not exempt from "thinking" and "laboring," but he did not have to make an effort. The learner, however, cannot avoid the mental pain and extreme effort [of "thinking" and "laboring"]. In general, I consider understanding without thinking to be the utmost knowledge, and being in the right without effort the utmost action. (*Chônsô*, vol. 1, 9:28b, p. 189)[15]

As we have already seen, the "investigation of things" (*gewu/kyôngmul*) and the "extension of knowledge" (*zhizhi/ch'iji*) are the "thinking" aspect of cultivation, while the "sincerity of will" (*cheng'i/sôngûi*) and the "rectification of the mind" (*jengshin/chôngsim*) are the "laboring" aspect of cultivation. The following representation shows the process of cultivation and the degree of achievement of spontaneity:

Sage—No "thinking" and "laboring" at all (*spontaneous*)

Superior man—Thinking and laboring *without effort*

Learner—Thinking and laboring *with painful effort*

The Confucian concept of spontaneity, however, is not an action based on sheer impulse or an arbitrary action but an act in accordance with the Heaven-imparted human nature. Spontaneity and cultivation are not necessarily two incompatible concepts. The Confucian concept of cultivation does not deny or dismiss the idea of spontaneity. On the contrary, cultivation is a way of discovering and revealing nature. Education is the way to cultivate in order to become one with nature. Nature has its origin in Heaven. Spontaneity based on the original human nature is the empirical beginning and the ontological foundation of Confucian moral cultivation. Mencius speaks clearly on this assumption:

> If you let people follow their feelings (original nature), they will be able to do good. . . . The feeling of commiseration is found in all men; the feeling of shame and dislike is found in all men; the feeling of respect and reverence is found in all men; and the feeling of right and wrong is found in all men. The feeling of commiseration is what we call humanity; the feeling of shame and dislike is what we call righteousness; the feeling of respect and reverence is what we call propriety; the feeling of right and wrong is what we call wisdom. Humanity, righteousness, propriety, and wisdom are not drilled into us from outside. We originally have them with us. (*Mencius* 6A:6)[16]

Furthermore, Mencius, on the basis of empirical experience, illustrated that when we act upon human nature it becomes a spontaneous action: "Now, when men suddenly see a child about to fall into a well, they all have a feeling of alarm and distress" (*Mencius* 2A:6). If we act upon an innate moral quality, it becomes a spontaneous action. Although there is an innate moral quality in human nature, cultivation is required to develop this spontaneous feeling to the highest form of morality, spontaneous action. Although all human beings have spontaneous feelings, not all human beings are able to reach spontaneous action due to the lack of cultivation.

Spontaneity, in this sense, is the outcome or the result of an arduous and diligent attempt to pursue the potential perfection within us. Spontaneity is a form of action that is aligned with nature. *Nature* is the "substance" of spontaneity. Spontaneity is the true function and authentic manifestation of nature. From the Confucian point of view cultivation and spontaneity are not two dialectically opposed notions, but they are dialogically engaged in each other. Cultivation is the process of reaching the most authentic form of action, spontaneity. Spontaneity is the result of cultivation and not against cultivation. Cultivation is a way to seek spontaneity in nature.

Sincerity (*cheng/sông*) and Spontaneity

In expounding the *Doctrine of the Mean* (*Zhongyong*), Yulgok aimed at establishing *sincerity/authenticity* as the foundation of Confucian thought.

Yulgok believed that *cheng/sông* is the way to achieve nature and "spontaneity." *Cheng* is the cohesive force binding us to what is "nature." Thus, *cheng* is not only the essence of the cosmological and ontological sense of principle but also the essence of the anthropological principle. In other words, through *cheng* a human being becomes "human" in relation to the universe, the world, and human nature (*xing*), which is imparted from Heaven. *Cheng* is not simply a theoretical concept or a metaphysical notion but a concrete and practical way of Confucian life. In this respect, *cheng* has a profound spiritual implication beyond a moral significance. The *Doctrine of the Mean* (*Zhonyong*) consistently affirms the underlying unity of Heaven and the human being. The unity of Heaven and the human being, however, can be reached through the realization of authentic human nature. The fulfillment of the authenticity of human nature is spontaneity. This way of fulfilling and understanding human nature assumes the fundamental inseparability of the knowledge of Heaven and the knowledge of human being:

> Therefore the ruler must not fail to cultivate his personal life. Wishing to cultivate his personal life, he must not fail to serve his parents. Wishing to serve his parents, he must not fail to know man. Wishing to know man, he must not fail to know Heaven. (*Doctrine of the Mean* 20)

What seems to be a circular argument is, in fact, the most natural process of human self-cultivation. Serving a parent is not a mere moral duty but a spiritual cultivation that requires the knowledge of Heaven and the human being. Once we understand this circular argument, the practice of filial piety is no longer a moral obligation but a spiritual practice that will become in turn a moral spontaneity. Moral spontaneity is not an act of impulse but a manifestation (*yong*) of the substance (*ti*) of the Way. The process of cultivation may be a moral process until one realizes the spiritual foundation of the process: knowledge of Heaven, human being, and their interconnectedness. In the final analysis, there is no separation between the moral sense of cultivation and spiritual sense of cultivation.

How then is the knowledge of Heaven and human possible? The entire process of self-cultivation can best be seen when we understand the meaning of *cheng*. The *Doctrine of the Mean*, in accordance with the Mencian line of thinking, states that *cheng* is the essential unity that enables one to relate to Heaven: "Sincerity (*cheng*) is the way of Heaven. To think how to be sincere is the way of man" (*Doctrine of the Mean* 20). It is through *cheng* that the way of Heaven and the way of human are intrinsically related. In this respect, *cheng* is a medium in which the way of Heaven and the way of human can be integrated. This medium, however, is not an

external entity but an internal force or spiritual power generated spontaneously through the process of cultivation. In this sense, *cheng* is fundamentally a spiritual reality.

Sincerity (*cheng/sông*) as a Spiritual Medium of the Cosmic and Moral Force

One of the most crucial questions regarding *cheng* is how a human being is
able to achieve a meaningful relationship with the universe and society, the
cosmic sense of reality and moral sense of reality. For the Neo-Confucians,
the moral forces of the individual and society were always reflected in cosmic phenomena. The universe was not an amoral physical object for
human beings, but it was the subject with which human beings must make
a meaningful relationship. Thus, for Neo-Confucians, the universe was not
amoral and not completely detached from human society; rather it was a
larger reflection of human society. For this reason, the significance of
morality was not confined to the personal and social dimensions, but
included the cosmic dimension also. This was especially true for Yulgok. In
his thought, *cheng* was extended to embrace a cosmic significance. In Yulgok's view the cosmos becomes meaningful to human beings only when
the full significance of *cheng* is realized. *Cheng* is the essential spiritual force
by which we human beings are related to the cosmos.

According to Yulgok, Heaven and human beings share *cheng/sông*. The
cheng/sông of Heaven is revealed through cosmic phenomena such as the
mutation of seasons, and the *cheng/sông* of humans is recognized in their
moral force and virtue. The *cheng/sông* of the human being and the
cheng/sông of Heaven share the same ontological reality, although they
appear to be different in their functions. According to Yulgok, "*yuan/won,
heng/hyông, li/yi,* and *jen/chông* are the *cheng/sông* of Heaven, and *ren/in,
i/ûi, li/ye, zhi/chi* are the *cheng/sông* of human nature" (*Chônsô*, vol. 2,
6:18a, p. 571). *Ren, yi, li, zhi, or* humanity, righteousness, propriety, and
wisdom, are the so-called four beginnings of human virtue. The terms,
yuan, heng, li, and *ren* are originally found in the first chapter of the *Book of
changes* (*Yijing*), the explanation of the hexagram *chian* (the Creative). The
original meanings of words are "sublimity," "potentiality of success,"
"power to further," and "perseverance."[17]

These four words of the *cheng* (sincerity) of the cosmos are also manifested in the four seasons of spring, summer, autumn, and winter. In this
manner, the *cheng* of Heaven and the *cheng* of human beings correspond to
each other, and the *cheng* of Heaven gains moral significance relating to the
cheng of human beings as manifested in terms of the "four beginnings." The

four attributes of the hexagram *chian* (the Creative) are also related to the four cardinal virtues of human being. "Sublimity" correlates with *ren* (humanity), "succession" with *li* (propriety), "furtherance" with *yi* (righteousness), and "perseverance" with *zhi* (wisdom). The correlation of the four attributes of the hexagram *chian* (the Creative) with the four cardinal human virtues share essentially the same reality. Furthermore, the *Yijing* confirms the ontological unity of the cosmic and the human processes.

How is one able to realize the unity of human beings and the cosmos? Yulgok's understanding of *cheng/sông*, as we have already observed, clearly indicates that the cosmos, as well as human beings, is able neither to exist nor to function without *cheng*. Thus, *cheng* is not only the essential element that enables a thing be what it is—the universe to be the universe, nature to be nature, human beings to be human—but also the essential force that enables human beings to have the "feeling of co-response" (*kanying/kamûng*) with the cosmos:

> The two material forces [*yin* and *yang*] are not able to move without *ch'eng*. [The four seasons are] are not able to follow the alternating process without *ch'eng*. The sun and moon are bright with this [*ch'eng*]. Mountains are high by this [*ch'eng*], rivers and oceans are deep by this. Therefore it is said: "There is no-thing without *ch'eng*." The nature of the sage is this very *ch'eng*, the superior man (*chün-tzu*) returns to this *ch'eng*. Obtaining one piece [of *ch'eng*] is sufficient enough to move Heaven and human being, so what would it be like if someone obtains the totality of *ch'eng*? (*Chônsô*, vol. 2, 6:18a, p. 571)

According to Yulgok, through *cheng/sông* (sincerity), we are able to realize the true principle (*li*) of the universe. This is because the *cheng* of Heaven and the *cheng* of human nature are essentially the same; *cheng* is the concrete channel through which human beings are able to realize their ontological unity with the cosmos. When cosmic phenomena and human phenomena are successfully realized through *cheng*, cosmic affairs and human affairs are harmoniously reflected in each other.

> The Great Ultimate (*Taiji*) in Heaven is *dao*. The character *dao* denotes movement in accord with the order of Heaven, as well as the *dao* of human nature, the *dao* of human being, and the things which ought to be done. The Great Ultimate in human being is nature. Sublimity (*yuan*), succession (*heng*), furtherance (*li*), perseverance (*jen*) are the flow of *dao*, humanity (*ren*), rightness (*yi*), propriety (*li*), wisdom (*zhi*) are the constitution of human nature. Sublimity (*yuan*) is spring in [earth's] season and humanity (*ren*) in human being, succession (*heng*) is summer in season and propriety (*li*) in human, furtherance (*li*) is autumn in season and justice or righteousness (*yi*) in human, perseverance (*jen*) is winter in season and wisdom (*zhi*) in human. Sublimity, succession, furtherance, and perseverance, as the function (*yong*) of the flow

of movement, are order. Humanity, rightness, propriety, and wisdom, as the substance (*ti*) of one in contrast to the other, are the establishment of names. (*Chônsô*, vol. 1, 20:43b, p. 448)

Yulgok understood the relationship between the cosmic flow—the movement of the four seasons—and the four beginnings of human nature as that of "function" and "substance." The orderly succession of the cosmic flow is inextricably related to human nature. According to Yulgok's view, human beings do not have direct control over cosmic phenomena. Nonetheless, cosmic phenomena are the reflection of the state of human nature.

The sage is the one who has achieved this cosmo-anthropic correspondence and is able to relate the *cheng/sông* of Heaven and the *cheng* of human beings. Once this cosmo-anthropic awareness and spirituality are established, the sage feels at ease with the affairs of universe and the affairs of human beings and responds to the affairs of the universe and to human affairs with the sense of *spontaneity*.

Notes

1. Rudolf Otto, for example, tried to isolate the feeling of "holy" from the moral and ethical significance of the word (*The Idea of the Holy* [London: Oxford University Press, 1958), 5.

2. Ibid., xvii.

3. Wing-tsit Chan, *A Source Book in Chinese Philosophy* (Princeton, N.J.: Princeton University Press, 1973), 45.

4. The following quotations from the *Analects* are from Arthur Waley, *The Analects of Confucius* (New York: Random House, Vantage Books, 1938), 88, 167, 168.

5. Ibid., 167.

6. Tu Weiming, "Confucianism," in *Our Religions*, ed. Arvind Sharma (San Francisco: HarperSanFrancisco, 1993), 141.

7. Trans. Wing-tsit Chan, *Source Book*, 86.

8. Yulgok greatly emphasized the significance of "sincerity" (*cheng/sông*) as the medium of Heaven and humans in expounding the passage in the *Doctrine of the Mean*, "Sincerity is the Way of Heaven. To think how to be sincere is the way of man" (20, trans. Wing-tsit Chan, *Source Book*, 107). For Yulgok's general view on this subject, see Choon Yûn Hwang, *Yulgok ch'ôlhakûi ihae* [Understandng of Yulgok's Philosophy] (Seoul: Sôkwangsa, 1995), 19.

9. Quotations from the *Doctrine of the Mean* are taken from Wing-tsit Chan, *Source Book*, 98, 105, 107.

10. Yulgok wrote a commentary on the *Zhongyong*. He used Zhu Xi's commentary extensively, but he also offered his own understanding of the *Zhongyong* in a

line-by-line commentary based on Zhu Xi's commentary. For the details, see *Chônsô*, vol. 2, 19:12b–13ab, p. 424 (quotations from this work are from the edition published by Sung'gyungwan University Press in Seoul in 1971).

11. The detailed explanation of this issue is found in Yulgok's essay *Saseng kwisillon* [The Discussion on Life, Death, and Ghost]; see *Chônsô*, vol. 2, Subyu 4:21b, p. 540.

12. See Wing-tsit Chan, *Source Book*, 12.

13. Trans. Wing-tsit Chan, *Source Book*, 22.

14. Ibid., 96.

15. For English translation, see also Young-chan Ro, *The Korean Neo-Confucianism of Yi Yulgok* (Albany: State University of New York Press, 1989), 98.

16. Translations of the *Mencius* are from Wing-tsit Chan, *Source Book*, 52, 65.

17. For a fuller and more detailed explanation of these terms, see *The I-Ching, or, Book of Changes*, the Richard Wilhelm translation rendered into English by Cary F. Baynes (Princeton, N.J.: Princeton University Press, 1967), 4–6.

1. A yin-yang image and characters for "moon" and "sun" on these temple staffs in the Bao'an Temple in Taipei symbolize cosmological principles common to many religious traditions in China. The temple houses images of hundreds of spirits, Confucius among them. Photo: Deborah Sommer, 1989.

2. One of the oldest extant buildings at the Confucian temple in Qufu, Shandong, this shrine dates to the twelfth or thirteenth century. Original teachings of Confucius were revered in his hometown even as the tradition took new philosophical turns elsewhere. Photo: Deborah Sommer, 2001.

3. Main hall of the Imperial Academy in Beijing, where the emperor participated in discussions of Confucian teachings to show his respect for learning. The institution of the academy—an educational, political, and ritual center—dates to antiquity. Photo: Deborah Sommer, 2001.

4. Main hall of the Confucian temple, Gaoxiong, Taiwan. Nationalist Party flags at this new temple indicate how such buildings are used for political ends in modern times. Photo: Chu Ronguey, 1998.

5. Main gate, Imperial Academy, Beijing. The inscription praises the effects of education. Photo: Deborah Sommer, 2001.

6. Stele for the 900th anniversary of Cheng Yi's work on the *Book of Changes*. Cheng clan temple, Taejon, Korea. Photo: Cheng Dexiang, 2000.

7. Statue and spirit tablets of Zhang Zai, Zhang Zai shrine, Hengqu, Shaanxi. Photo: Deborah Sommer, 2001.

8. Shao Yong's statue and spirit tablet, Shao Yong shrine, Luoyang. His descendants still live in the neighborhood. Photo: Deborah Sommer, 2001.

9. Divinatory diagrams, Shao Yong shrine, Luoyang. Shao Yong was known for his prognostications using the *Book of Changes*. These diagrams of cosmic forces are folk depictions of Shao's arts. Photo: Deborah Sommer, 2001.

10. Newly renovated shrine to Zhang Zai, Hengqu, Shaanxi. Reconstructed in a traditional style, this shrine complex is maintained by Zhang's descendants. Photo: Deborah Sommer, 2001.

11. Zhang Zai's mother takes him before an image of the hero Zhu Geliang to encourage Zhang to model himself after the ancient sages. Women were responsible for educating their children and teaching them ritual practices. Detail of mural at the Zhang Zai shrine, Hengqu, Shaanxi. Photo: Deborah Sommer, 2001.

12. Zhang Zai lectures on the *Book of Changes* to a mixed crowd of literati, Buddhist monks (with shaved heads), and Daoists (wearing topknots). The different traditions shared many ideas in common. Detail of mural at the Zhang Zai shrine, Hengqu, Shaanxi. Photo: Deborah Sommer, 2001.

13. Meditative aspects of reading are illustrated by Zhang Zai, who grasps one book while absorbed by calligraphy on the wall. Detail of mural at the Zhang Zai shrine, Hengqu, Shaanxi. Photo: Deborah Sommer, 2001

14. Ritual at the Cheng clan shrine in Taejon, Korea, commemorating the first arrival of a descendant of the Cheng brothers in Korea in the thirteenth century. Here Korean Chengs and Chinese relatives celebrate their common ancestral origins. Photo: Cheng Dexiang, 1999.

15. Tea ritual at Zhu Xi's grave, Fujian. A delegation from a women's Korean tea association performs their art to commemorate the tradition of literati learning. An offering of food is presented by the Korean Cheng-Zhu Association on the altar to the right. Photo: Cheng Dexiang, 2000.

16. The intentionality of sacrificers outweighs the intrinsic value of their offerings. Thus a simple offering of herbs displays the purity and sincerity of participants at a rite to Confucius in Jiali, Taiwan.
Photo: Chu Ronguey, 1998.

17. Stresses of modern urban life motivate students to place copies of their exam cards under the incense burners of Confucian temples to ask the sages for help passing college entrance exams. Zhanghua Confucian temple, Taiwan. Photo: Deborah Sommer, 1998.

18. Ritual offering by Korean visitors at the grave of Zhu Xi. The fifth gentleman from the left is the retired chancellor of the former Imperial Academy in Seoul; the eighth, a Chinese descendant of Zhu Xi. Food offerings follow ancient conventions. Photo: Cheng Dexiang, 2000.

19. New stele at the grave of Zhu Xi, Fujian. The stele was donated by the head of the Korean Cheng-Zhu Association (second from right). Renovation of historical sites related to Confucian thinkers is a recent trend in China. Photo: Cheng Dexiang, 2000.

20. Women dancers and musicians perform at the rites to commemorate Confucius at the Confucian temple in Seoul. Ancient texts such as the *Book of Rites* document women's roles in rituals of many kinds. Photo: Chu Ronguey, 1995.

21. Entrance to the Confucian temple, Hue, Vietnam. Teachings of the literati tradition were transmitted throughout Southeast Asia. Temples such as this one commemorate both Chinese and Vietnamese figures. Photo: Chu Ronguey, 1998.

22. Ritual usages governing human relationships were memorialized in public spaces. In the Qing dynasty, women who demonstrated devotion to their late husbands by not remarrying were commemorated with arches such as this one in Xinzhu, Taiwan. Photo: Deborah Sommer, 1989.

27

The Adaptation of Confucianism to Japan

MARY EVELYN TUCKER

Religious Naturalism

The history of Confucianism in Japan spans a period of over a millennium and a half and involves a complex process of interaction with indigenous Japanese thought and institutions. While the extent and the implications of the impact of Confucianism in Japan are a source of some debate, it is nonetheless evident that its role was not simply a matter of the transmission of texts. Confucianism affected political institutions, educational curriculum, social structures, family relationships, and modes of self-cultivation. Indeed, it developed particular forms of Confucian spirituality in the Japanese context which I call religious naturalism.

Religious naturalism might be defined here as the interaction of cosmology and ethics such that a special relational resonance is established between humans and the natural world. This resonance creates the means for moral cultivation and spiritual transformation. Religious naturalism in its Confucian forms is characterized by correspondences or analogies of the relation of the human as microcosm to the natural world as macrocosm. The implications of Confucian religious naturalism transcend the goals of individual salvation or even the achievement of personal sagehood. Rather, it is aimed at the mutual transformation of self and society for the betterment of the political order and the enhancement of the natural world. It is thus not a spirituality of salvation or sacrifice as in the Western religious traditions, nor of liberation and transcendence as in the South Asian religious traditions, but rather an experience of immanence in the natural order and creativity in the human order. Some of the forms of religious naturalism will be explored in this paper as Confucianism mingled with Shinto in early modern Japan.

This essay will first briefly discuss the general nature of the adaptation of Confucianism in Japan, highlighting its effect on politics, ethics, and education in the premodern period. It will then focus specifically on three seventeenth-century Neo-Confucian figures and their use of Shinto to accommodate Confucianism. In so doing, we will emphasize that Japanese Confucianism achieved distinctive expressions of religious naturalism through its interactions with Shinto.

Adoption, Adaptation, Accommodation of Confucianism

Before the Meiji Restoration in the late nineteenth century, Confucianism may be examined in three major periods, namely, its introduction, its medieval development, and its early modern phase. The first period, from the fifth to the thirteenth century, has been referred to as the era of the Han and Tang commentators (*Kanto kunko jidai*); the second period, from the thirteenth to the seventeenth century, as the era of Song learning (*Sogaku jidai*); and the third period, from the seventeenth to the middle of the nineteenth century, as the era of the learning of Chinese scholars (*Kangakusha jidai*).[1]

These periods involve complex processes in the "naturalization"[2] of Confucianism as it was imported from China, often by way of Korea. Kate Nakai speaks of this process as an effort by the Japanese to accommodate and universalize Confucianism in the Japanese context. In referring specifically to the Japanese Confucians of the Tokugawa period, she writes:

> As tutors, advisors, teachers it was in their interest to make the way of the sages acceptable to the Japanese outlook and temperament by modifying the more alien elements of Confucianism in its original Chinese forms. At the same time, neutralization of those alien elements ran the danger of negating the very qualities which drew them personally to Confucianism in the first place. In many ways, then, the early Tokugawa Confucians found themselves walking a tightrope. Individual Confucians took often radically different approaches to getting across this tightrope.[3]

Research on the adoption and adaptation of Confucian thought and institutions to the Japanese context is an important area of East Asian studies in the West that still needs further investigation.[4] As such studies emerge, they will shed light on the spread of Confucianism in East Asia and its various forms of naturalization. In particular, they will reinforce our understanding of the adeptness of the Japanese in borrowing from other cultures.[5]

In East Asia the process of adoption and adaptation has repeatedly occurred across national boundaries, between different religious and intellectual traditions and within those traditions themselves. While this is not unique to East Asia, the degree to which such adaptation has taken place can be highlighted in the case of Japan. A study of the naturalization of Confucianism in Japan during various periods provides insight into the way the Japanese have historically borrowed and adapted aspects of Chinese and Korean culture for their own needs. This process involves selectivity, accommodation, and transformation of both foreign and native ideas and institutions. It is an inherently complex process which generated heated debates over the value claims of foreign versus native elements. This balancing of competing value claims is based on ongoing discussions regarding the validity and utility of particular elements to be adopted.

The result of attempts at accommodation of various religions or philosophical traditions has frequently been termed "syncretism." However, for some Western scholars more accustomed to the strict separation of Western religious traditions, the term often has negative connotations of random or idiosyncratic ecclecticism. I will therefore avoid the term and instead will speak of the accommodation of different thought systems in Japan by using Watsuji Tetsuro's idea of "stadiality."

Watsuji developed a useful mode of understanding how the Japanese have held various truth claims in balance, and this he calls the stadial character (*jusosei*) of Japanese culture.[6] He speaks of this as the simultaneous coexistence of several historical and cultural elements without the need for definitive resolution or absolute displacement. He also emphasizes that earlier cultural strata are not displaced by later ones; rather they coexist in a form of essential synchronicity. Such a matrix of creative elements allows for the lattice-like interresonance of a multiplicity of thought systems such as Shinto, Confucianism, and Buddhism in various stages of development. It may also encourage specific linkages between two of these traditions such as Buddhism and Shinto during the Heian period, or Confucianism and Shinto in the Tokugawa period.

Accommodation, then, in the Japanese intellectual context, can be understood less as a dialectical resolution of opposites than as the tensive coexistence of thought variables. One thought system may predominate for a certain time period but not to the complete exclusion of other systems. Within this model there are a number of linkages resulting from both conscious and unconscious efforts at accommodation. There are numerous examples throughout Japanese intellectual and religious history of parallelisms, correspondences, equivalences, identifications, amalgamations, and reconciliations between traditions.

A few examples of accommodation or stadial coexistence of thought systems are Shotoku's Constitution, *honji suijaku*, and Yuiitsu Shinto. During the seventh century both Buddhist and Confucian elements were incorporated into Prince Shotoku's Constitution and used as a rationale for government. Indeed, as Wm. Theodore de Bary has written: "Where the two ideologies did not conflict he adopted both; in cases of conflict Confucianism was considered supreme in secular matters and Buddhism in spiritual ones. Buddhism and Confucianism were able thus to exist side by side in Japan for a thousand years without any serious quarrels."[7] In the Heian period (794–1185) in order to adapt Buddhism to the native Shinto tradition, the Buddhist *honji suijaku* theory maintained that the native Shinto gods were manifestations of the true nature of the Buddhas and bodhisattvas in the Buddhist pantheon.[8] A counterpoint to this position was subsequently developed by Shinto thinkers and was known as Yuiitsu Shinto. In the Kamakura (1185–1333) and Muromachi (1333–1568) periods Confucianism was promoted by the Zen monks, who clearly saw merit in it for its ethical and political teachings. Finally, while Confucianism tended to dominate the Tokugawa period (1600–1868), accommodation with Shinto was an important means of naturalizing this Chinese philosophy.

In each of the periods discussed above Confucianism played a key role in terms of politics, ethics, and education. To see these as interconnected aspects of the influence of Confucianism in Japan is significant, for it provides a sufficiently wide scope for further detailed studies. A brief description of the influence of Confucianism before the Tokugawa period will set the context for discussing the thought of Hayashi Razan (1583–1657), Yamazaki Ansai (1619–1682), and Kaibara Ekken (1630–1714).

Historical Background

In the period of the introduction of Confucianism to Japan during the Nara and Heian periods, ideas of rule by bureaucratic centralized government, the use of historical writings to legitimize authority, selecting officials by merit, and encouraging moral government were readily adapted to the Japanese context. Moreover, strong kinship ties and ethical family relations were regarded as central to an orderly state. Finally, an educational system was established that was designed ideally to help train and select moral officials. Thus, in the realm of politics, ethics, and education, Confucianism was clearly an influence from the sixth century through the twelfth. It should be noted, of course, that between the ideal and the real, Confucianism often fell short of its intended aims. It should also be observed that many of these Confucian ideas coexisted with Buddhist, Shinto, and Daoist thought. Furthermore, Confucianism declined during the latter part of the Heian period with the flourishing of the esoteric Buddhist sects.

During the Kamakura and Muromachi periods, Neo-Confucian thought was introduced into Japan, largely through the Zen monasteries.[9] Again it was found useful for its political, ethical, and educational ideas. Many of the Zen monks served as advisors to the shogunate, and their knowledge of Confucian political theory was deemed invaluable for establishing and maintaining an effective government.[10] Furthermore, the Zen monks were keenly interested in the ethical and religious teachings of Neo-Confucianism, especially with regard to self-cultivation. Views of disciplining the mind and nourishing one's nature were incorporated into the Gozan monks' practice.[11] Moreover, in the area of education, the Zen monasteries became leading centers of Chinese learning involved in both collecting and publishing Chinese books, especially Neo-Confucian ones.[12] In addition, the temple schools (terakoya) used a curriculum largely based on Confucian and Neo-Confucian texts.[13]

In the Tokugawa period, Neo-Confucianism was again significant in the areas of politics, ethics, and education. In moving out of the Zen monasteries, Neo-Confucianism established a close connection with Shinto and became more widespread in the society at large. This was largely due to the adoption by the samurai (and other classes) of Neo-Confucianism as a coherent worldview for establishing their role in the new Tokugawa order. In terms of politics it was, along with Buddhism and Shinto, part of the political discourse that contributed to the rationalization of the legitimacy of shogunal authority.[14] Moreover, with regard to ethical and religious concerns, Neo-Confucianism had a significant impact on ideas of self-cultivation and the encouragement of the practice of virtue. This was partly because of its self-conscious linkage to Shinto by the Neo-Confucian scholars. Finally, in the area of education, Neo-Confucian texts became the basis for the curriculum of the domain schools (hanko) as well as the private schools (shijuku) which spread rapidly in the Tokugawa period.[15]

Before the Tokugawa period, Confucianism coexisted with Shinto and Buddhism and thus accommodated itself to the Japanese context. Perhaps most striking for our discussion are the self-conscious attempts that emerged particularly in the early Tokugawa period to create linkages of Neo-Confucianism with Shinto. By integrating Neo-Confucianism with

Shinto it appeared that the Neo-Confucian scholars hoped to naturalize Neo-Confucianism. It was thus important to separate it from Buddhism, another foreign tradition, and link it with Shinto which had a strong religious and nationalist appeal. Thus, a distinctive form of Japanese Confucian spirituality emerged in conjunction with Shinto.

In doing this, the seventeenth-century Japanese Neo-Confucian scholars emphasized similar points regarding the compatibility of the two traditions, thus establishing new grounds for their stadial coexistence. They based this on the understanding that one principle runs through both. They agreed that Shinto, before the arrival of Buddhism, was comparable to Confucianism as a form of religious naturalism. Indeed, the natural ethical path of Shinto was said by some to be the same as the naturalistic ethical teachings of Confucianism. In theory, then, Shinto and Confucianism were considered one; in practice, however, they were different. Clearly, Confucian customs and practices were distinct from those of Shinto and thus required adaptation to the Japanese context. Sensitivity to time, place, and circumstances was important in adapting Confucianism to Japan. Distinguishing between appropriate and inappropriate rituals for Japan became a significant task for the Tokugawa Confucians. Kate Nakai summarizes the challenge they faced in the adaptaton process:

> Tokugawa Confucians often found themselves at odds with their society, but at the same time, perhaps reflecting the psychological patterns of samurai society, they remained intensely aware of their identity as Japanese and of the foreign origin of the creed to which they adhered. For this reason, too, they were animated by a strong impulse to detach Confucianism from its Chinese context and to establish that the truth inherent in the way of the sages was as relevant to the Japanese geographical and cultural setting as to the Chinese.[16]

One way to do this was to link Shinto and Confucianism, thus creating new expressions of religious naturalism.

The Flourishing of Confucianism in the Early Modern Period

The rise of Confucianism in the Tokugawa period signals an important transition from the coexistence of Buddhism and Confucianism in the medieval period to the amalgamation and coexistence of Shinto and Confucianism in the early modern era. The period is marked in its early seventeenth-century phase by a transition in roles from *juso* to *jusha*, namely, from those who considered themselves to be *juso*, both Buddhist monk and Confucian advisor, to those who saw themselves as *jusha*, Confucian scholar. This transition can be noted in the sharp attacks of both Yamazaki Ansai and Nakae Toju against Hayashi Razan's acceptance of a Buddhist clerical status in serving the Bakufu. Thus, the role of the *jusha* came to be more clearly defined, and the importance of Neo-Confucian education came to be more widely felt. The Tokugawa Confucian scholar and teacher was influential in the areas of education and culture, in addition to ritual, morality, and politics.[17]

What distinguishes Neo-Confucianism in the early Tokugawa period is a movement to extract itself from any easy accommodation with Buddhism. At the same time, the Neo-Confucian scholars were making efforts to find common grounds for integration with Shinto.[18] This was, no doubt, a mutually beneficial process. Neo-Confucianism could be naturalized by its integration with Shinto mythology, ethics, and practices. Moreover, the naturalistic cosmology of Neo-Confucianism was compatible with the emphasis on nature and seasonal cycles in Shinto. The two traditions had complementary forms of religious naturalism, which began to amalgamate. Thus, the religious concepts and ritual practices of Confucianism found counterparts in Shinto. For example, the theistic attitude toward Heaven that is present in some Neo-Confucian thinkers made the acceptance of belief in the Shinto gods a viable path for Japanese Neo-Confucians such as Fujiwara Seika, Hayashi Razan, Yamazaki Ansai, and Kaibara Ekken. Moreover, the concept of abiding in reverence (Chinese *jing;* Japanese *kei*) was seen as comparable to the Shinto idea of reverent mindfulness (*tsutsushimu*) and Neo-Confucian virtues such as authenticity (Chinese *cheng*) were equated with Shinto virtues such as sincerity (Japanese *makoto*). While this conscious identification had begun already in the medieval period, it seems to have reached new levels of sophistication by the Tokugawa period. In addition, the rejection of any association with Buddhism became more pronounced among both the Neo-Confucian and the Shinto scholars.

Just as Neo-Confucianism became naturalized through association with Shinto, Shinto likewise stood to benefit from such an association with Chinese civilization in the form of Neo-Confucianism. The universal discourse of Neo-Confucianism with its sophisticated metaphysics and appeal to a systematic ethics had a definite value for Shinto theologians. Embodying carefully formulated rational argumentation, couched in language that was both humanistic and religious, Confucianism provided Shinto with an invigorated authority and an expanded understanding of the moral role of the human in the universe.[19]

Various individual scholars contributed to this amalgamation of the two traditions. Their efforts to show the similarities between Confucianism and Shinto were at times tortuous and artificial, and yet they represent an important phase in the growing naturalization of Confucianism and in the expanded authority of Shinto. Among the Confucians who sought such an accommodation were Hayashi Razan, Yamazaki Ansai, and Kaibara Ekken, and, from the Shinto perspective, Yoshikawa Koretaru (1616–1694) and Watarai Nobuyoshi (1615–1690). These Neo-Confucian scholars will be discussed in greater detail so as to examine their particular form of accommodation of Neo-Confucianism with Shinto. The stadial coexistence of these thought variables takes different forms with each scholar.

For Hayashi Razan there is an attempt to set up a series of *correspondences* between Neo-Confucianism and Shinto. His emphasis is somewhat more political than that of Ansai or Ekken in that he repeatedly states that the Way of the gods *is* the kingly Way for rule. Yamazaki Ansai, on the other hand, has created an *amalgamation* of Neo-Confucianism and Shinto that tries to fuse the two through somewhat contrived rationalizations. Ansai is concerned more with self-cultivation than with politics in his synthesis. As Herman Ooms notes, "Ansai . . . never attempted to play the politics of ideology as Razan had done."[20] Kaibara Ekken, on the other hand, sets up a *parallelism* between Neo-Confucianism and Shinto that is more broadly and loosely defined. His particular emphasis on the unity of the human way and the Way of the gods allows him to stress the importance of praying to the gods and showing them reverence. All three thinkers maintain that an accommodation of Confucianism with Shinto is possible because they share the same principles of religious naturalism. Thus, in their fundamental essence they can be identified; however, in particular practices they remain distinct. They felt that one must therefore adapt Confucian practices to the different times, places, and circumstances of the Japanese context. This understanding of both difference and identity is what characterized the stadial coexistence of these two traditions.

Razan's *Rito shinchi Shinto*

Hayashi Razan (1583–1657) was one of the leading Neo-Confucians of the early Tokugawa period. He was born in Kyoto, the son of a samurai family recently turned merchants. Although he was initially sent to study to be a Zen priest, he rejected this in favor of Confucianism. In his early twenties he began lecturing on the teachings of the great Chinese Neo-Confucian Zhu Xi (1130–1200). He soon drew the attention of Tokugawa Ieyasu, who in 1605 invited Razan to enter his service. He was required to dress as a Buddhist monk, as had been the custom for advisors to the shoguns in the medieval period. He remained employed by the bakufu for more than half a century until his death in 1657.

Although Razan's employment by Ieyasu has often been taken as a sign of the establishment of Neo-Confucian orthodoxy by the bakufu, recent scholarship has shown this to be something of a distortion.[21] Razan's erudition was useful to the shogunate for such tasks as carrying on diplomatic correspondence with foreign rulers, drafting legislation, and compiling genealogical records.

As a Confucian scholar he did found a private school and shrine in Edo, which eventually received shogunal support. Although he did not establish a distinct branch of Confucianism, as did Yamazaki Ansai, Razan was noted for his broad scholarship and writings on Zhu Xi's thought. He attacked both Christianity and Buddhism as lacking moral principles but saw Shinto and Confucianism as intrinsically compatible.

He was especially influenced by the teachings of the Yoshida school of Shinto, although he disagreed with Kanetomo's easy syncretism with Buddhism. He wrote two major works dealing with Shinto, one called *Honcho jinja ko* (*On Shrines in Japan*, written between 1638 and 1640) and the other called *Shinto denju* (*Shinto Initiation*, written from 1644 to 1648).[22] The first involves a historical survey of shrines in Japan, and the second represents his ideas on the essential correspondence of Shinto and Confucianism. His system was known as *Rito shinchi Shinto* (*Shinto where Principle Corresponds to the Heart-Mind*).[23]

Razan felt that in the medieval period Shinto and Buddhism had come to be too closely joined and that this caused a decline in Confucianism and a distortion of Shinto. He called for the separation of Shinto from Buddhism and the revival of the Confucian Way of the Kings through association with Shinto. Following Yoshida Shinto he insisted that the Way of the gods (Shinto) *is* the Kingly Way (*Odo*). Thus he accepted and promoted an essential correspondence between Shinto and Confucianism. He did this through a series of analogies and identifications of the macrocosm of nature with the microcosm of humans on which he builds his arguments for a synthetic religious naturalism. These involve discussions of cosmology, ethics, and government in which he draws on both Chinese and Japanese sources. As David Dilworth has noted, this "repossession" and "synchronistic inter-resonance" of earlier strata of values from China and Japan is a "vivid example of the stadial character of Japanese culture."[24]

With regard to cosmology, for example, Razan posits a similarity between Chinese cosmologies of the *Yijing* (*The Book of Changes*) or the *Taijitu shuo* (*The Diagram of the Great Ultimate*) and Shinto cosmologies in the *Nihon shoki*. The primeval chaos (*konton*) of the universe is the original material force (Chinese *qi;* Japanese *ki*) before it divides. The god Kuni-tokotachi is identified with the original *ki* of the universe and is considered the first of the heavenly gods.[25] This original *ki* divides into *yin* and *yang*, which are identified with Izanagi and Izanami. They, in turn, produce Heaven and Earth and the five elements. These give rise to plants, animals, humans, and all things. Indeed, all of these receive the *ki* of the original god, Kunitokotachi (NST 39:26). Razan also sets up a series of macrocosm–microcosm correspondences derived from Chinese Han cosmology which include the five elements, virtues, colors, seasons, directions, senses, parts of the body, and so on (NST 39:16).

Razan's Shinto-Confucian cosmology is developed as a background to his understanding of the role of the human in the universe. From the opening passages of *Shinto denju,* Razan's religious and ethical concerns are clearly stated in relation to the gods and the human heart-mind: "The kami are the soul of heaven and earth. The heart-mind is the home of the kami" (NST 39:12). He uses the analogy of a home to illustrate the immanent and indwelling quality of the kami: "The body is like a house, the mind is like the master and the kami are the soul of the master" (ibid.). Thus he suggests a person's heart-mind should be directed and guided by the divine presence within. This lends clarity to one's choice between appropriate and inappropriate action: "To do good, for example, implies following the kami of one's heart-mind and thus being in accord with the way of Heaven. To do evil means to go against the kami of one's heart and thus invites retribution" (ibid.).

The closeness of the gods and humans is attested to by the fact that they share a common principle: "The same principle [*li*] underlies both the kami [in nature] and the kami of the human heart-mind" (NST 39:12). This indwelling of the kami in the heart-mind is compared to the clarity of a mirror and the brightness of the mind is likened to a divine light (ibid. 39:19, 22). To maintain this purity is the goal of ethical behavior and the means to following the way of Heaven. Thus, the Song Neo-Confucian idea of principle is linked with the kami in nature and in humans to enrich the macrocosm–microcosm correspondences.

This Shinto–Confucian correspondence of cosmology and ethics is possible because Razan maintains repeatedly that "the Way of the gods (Shinto) *is* the Way of the kings (*Odo*)" (NST 39:12–13, 19, 21). Thus, the Japanese native Way and the Chinese Confucian Way are seen as sharing similar worldviews of religious naturalism. The principles that unite the two are the same according to Razan; only the practices are different. Shinto, he believes, is a teaching that relies on the language of nature, and it existed in Japan prior to a written language. His particular form of accommodation has implications not only for individual ethics, but for government as well. Thus, for Razan the political ideas of Confucianism as formulated in the Kingly Way can be seen as the same as Shinto political theories. He states that the conduct of government reflects the virtue of the gods and ruling the country reflects their strength.[26] This has been transmitted from Amaterasu down to all the ruling emperors of Japan (NST 39:19).

From the outset of *Shinto denju,* Razan establishes correspondences between the three regalia of Shinto (the mirror, the sword, and the jewel), the Confucian virtues, and the elements in nature (NST 39:12–13). Thus, they come to embody important aspects of both the natural and human orders. The mirror is likened to wisdom and to the sun. The jewel is equated with humaneness and with the moon, and the sword is compared with courage and the stars.[27]

Razan feels that by nurturing these virtues in one's heart one can clarify the Way in the world. Through such virtues one can extend goodness from oneself to one's family and to the country, as has been taught in the *Great Learning.* He feels that this is where the Way of the gods and the Way of the kings are not different. Kate Nakai describes Razan's purpose in this: "the equation between Chinese theory and Japanese practice was not an end in itself, not solely a means of providing an added affirmation of the existing order; it was also the means to set the stage for an infusion of the way of the sages into contemporary Japanese life by showing that such an infusion would be no more than restoration of what was identical with Shinto in the latter's original form."[28]

Thus, in terms of cosmology, ethics, and politics, Razan attempts to create coherent correspondences between Shinto and Neo-Confucian teachings. He relies on elaborate macrocosm–microcosm analogies which distinguish his form of religious naturalism. While originally influenced by Fujiwara Seika and the ideas of Ise and Yoshida Shinto, he nonetheless formulated his own unique synthesis, which in turn influenced later Tokugawa Neo-Confucians.

Ansai's Suika Shinto

Yamazaki Ansai (1619–1682), the son of a samurai, initially studied Zen Buddhism. In his twenties he discovered Zhu Xi's writings and was deeply affected by Zhu's critique of Buddhism. He left the monastery and began an earnest exploration of Confucianism. Through his lectures, which were in a colloquial style, he began to attract a large number of followers. Many of his ideas have been transmitted in the form of lecture notes recorded by his followers. He was instrumental in spreading Confucian ideas in the early Tokugawa period, especially among the samurai class. He stressed the importance of loyalty between the samurai and his lord and also emphasized the virtue of reverence.

Ansai was particularly interested in linking Confucianism with Shinto, and he thus created his own form of religious naturalism. He studied with Yoshikawa Koretaru while he and Yoshikawa were in the service of Hoshina Masayuki, Tokugawa Iemitsu's brother. Indeed, Koretaru initiated both Masayuki and Ansai into the secret traditions of Yoshida Shinto. It was from Koretaru that Ansai received the initiation name of "Suika," by which his school of Shinto became known. The impact of that school was not insignificant. Herman Ooms claims:

> Suika Shinto was the most dynamic force in the world of Shinto theology until the second half of the eighteenth century, when it had to make room for Motoori Norinaga. Even then, Suika Shinto did not leave the field to Norinaga's "pure" Shinto. Its tenets and ideological impact can be detected in Hirata Atsutane (1776–1843), Motoori's successor. It also played an important role in modern times. In the 1930s and 1940s, Suika Shinto was appropriated for the construction of an ultranationalist ideology.[29]

In addition to receiving the secret teachings of Yoshida Shinto from Yoshikawa Koretaru, Ansai studied Ise Shinto in some depth. He visited Ise six times and was able to receive access to the Nakatomi purification rituals and Ise's secret traditions from Watarai Nobuyoshi. Ansai's personal association with Shinto was further strengthened by his marriage to the daughter of a Shinto priest from the Kamo shrine in Kyoto.

Along with his passionate interest in Shinto, Ansai was a devoted follower of the Chinese Neo-Confucian thinker Zhu Xi. His religious-like respect for Zhu and his desire to make Zhu's teachings understood in Japan occasionally led him to somewhat doctrinaire extremes. He stressed the importance of reverence, loyalty, duty, practice, and self-realization (*jitoku*). He especially stressed Zhu Xi's idea of preserving the mind by "reverence to straighten the internal life and righteousness to square the external life."[30] He reduced the Neo-Confucian corpus to six texts (the *Elementary Learning, Reflections on Things at Hand,* and the *Four Books*) and clung to a strict sense of orthodoxy regarding their interpretation. His severity and his doctrinaire attitude toward Confucianism were rejected by other Confucians, such as Kaibara Ekken, who regarded this as incompatible with the more balanced and broad approach of Zhu Xi. Moreover, Ansai was vehement in denouncing Buddhism, which he had studied in his youth. His attack on Buddhism, *Hekii* (*Heresies Refuted*), was published in 1647 and drew extensively on earlier Neo-Confucian arguments against Buddhism.

In sharp contrast to this, Ansai claimed that the teachings of Confucianism and Shinto were one, for they had the same principle: "In the universe there is only One Principle, [although] either Gods or Sages come forth depending on whether it concerns the country where the sun rises [Japan] or the country where the sun sets [China]. The [two] Ways [of Shinto and Confucianism] are, however, naturally and mysteriously the same (*onozukara myokei suru*)."[31] He also believed, as did other Confucians, that early Shinto, prior to the arrival of Buddhism in Japan, was identical with Confucianism.[32]

Ansai developed a series of analogues and comparisons in his amalgamation of Shinto and Confucianism which have been described as tortuous rationalizations[33] and etymological manipulations.[34] Indeed, some of his followers were highly critical of Ansai's interest in Shinto. These included Asami Keisai, Sato Naokata, and Miyake Shosai. Nonetheless, as Okada Takehiko observes, "Ansai's involvement with Shinto can be seen as a natural outcome of the thoroughgoing manner in which he pursued the substance of Chu Hsi's [Zhu Xi] teaching, which inevitably led him back to traditional Japanese thought itself. The religious intensity with which he had committed himself to Chu Hsi was already one manifestation of this."[35]

Herman Ooms maintains that the long-lasting impact of Ansai's thought was not due to his religious intensity, his focus on practice, or even the particular content of his teachings. Rather, he suggests that Ansai's thought had a significant impact because it was systematic in its own terms and did indeed achieve "ideological closure."[36] Ooms makes a useful comparison between Ansai's method and the four types of interpretations used by Western medieval scholastics for explaining scripture. These four levels of interpretation are the literal, the allegorical, the moral, and the anagogical. Ooms asserts that "together *and simultaneously,* these four levels of interpretation induce an ideological transformation of the textual heritage of Japan's indigenous tradition. Ansai's systematic textual intervention can be summed up by saying that he constructed a new overall allegorical system that nevertheless preserved the literality of the original texts."[37]

Ooms argues that Ansai accepted the literal truth of the Shinto scriptures as establishing the real "historical" beginning of creation and that this set him apart from other Shinto scholars. Second, with regard to allegory, "he worked out a comprehensive and systematic articulation of all core tenets of the Chinese [ethico-political teachings] with the Japanese tradition." Third, on the moral level "he stressed more intensely than others the imperative of ethical practice," and, fourth, using the anagogical level, he emphasized Japan's privileged position and thus "laid the groundwork for a full development of the 'nationalistic' dimension" of Japan as superior to other countries.[38]

With these interpretive categories it is easier to examine Ansai's Shinto–Confucian amalgamation. As with other Neo-Confucians, central to his writings is his concern with both cosmology and ethics, where he establishes direct parallels between the Way of the kings and the Way of the gods. With regard to cosmology, for example, reflecting the influence of Yoshida Shinto, Ansai cited Kunitokotachi as the first of seven generations of gods. This evolved to the Five Elements and ended with Izanagi and Izanami, namely, *yin* and *yang*. Izanagi and Izanami are the links between Heaven and Earth. They produce the physical world and the earthly gods, of which Amaterasu is the most prominent.[39] He writes that Izanagi and Izanami "followed the divination teachings of the Heavenly Gods, obeyed yin and yang, and thus correctly established the beginnings of ethical teachings."[40] Ansai suggests that the gods also gave rise to proper ethical behavior for humans.

Because humans are part of this creation process, human affairs take on a sacred, mythical character.[41] Indeed, ethics becomes central to the role of the human in the universe. In this form of religious naturalism Ansai links the key Confucian virtue of reverence to an intricate process of natural transformation of earth into metal. This rather unusual analogy of relating reverence in the human order to an intensification of natural processes is an important feature of Ansai's thought and reflects his constant effort to show the profound interaction of cosmology and ethics. Thus, he claims that the hardening of earth (*tsuchi o shimuru*) is in fact comparable to abiding in reverence (*tsutsushimu*).[42] Ansai's thrust in this discussion is to ground his religious concerns in both natural cosmic processes and human affairs.

Ansai's Suika Shinto is an amalgamation of various ideas from Shinto and Confucianism with the apparent intention of creating a more comprehensive, unified, and compelling system of thought. This is what we would call his own unique form of religious naturalism. Although Ooms feels that Ansai does have a systematic structure,[43] his success is somewhat mixed, as becomes clear in the choices of his followers. There arose a split between those who embraced Suika Shinto and those who were loyal to the Kimon school of Neo-Confucianism. Most of Ansai's followers were unable to accept completely his dogmatic personal synthesis. Yet, like Ekken, he was passionately interested in the implications of his thought for self-cultivation and practice. This was not simply an abstract synthesis of ideas. It was an intricately conceived amalgamation of two traditions, resulting in a stadial coexistence and suggesting a unified view of truth and practice. While the task itself was too large to succeed completely, aspects of his method and spirit continued in the schools of his followers.[44]

Ekken's Parallelism of Shinto and Confucianism

Kaibara Ekken (1630–1714), like Hayashai Razan and Yamazaki Ansai, was one of the leading Neo-Confucian thinkers of seventeenth-century Japan. Born in Fukuoka in Kyushu to a lower-class samurai family, he was initially educated in the Confucian classics by his father and his elder brother, Sonzai. He spent several years as a masterless samurai (*ronin*) until the Kuroda han lord recognized his talents and sent him to Kyoto, where he studied for seven years. There he came in contact with many of the leading scholars of his day including Matsunaga Sekigo, Kinoshita Jun'an, and Ito Jinsai.

Toward the end of his stay in Kyoto he began lecturing on the Confucian classics and Zhu Xi's *Reflections on Things at Hand*. Ekken continued to lecture for the han *daimyo* (lord) and high ranking samurai after he returned to Kyushu. In addition, he tutored the han daimyo's heir and frequently accompanied the lord on his trips to Edo. Through such trips to Edo and also visits to Kyoto, Ekken was able to maintain a wide circle of intellectual contacts. He was, no doubt, inspired in these contacts by his own broad interests to pursue an astonishing range of practical learning (*jitsugaku*) along with his Chinese philosophical studies.

Ekken's writings on Neo-Confucianism range from complex philosophical arguments regarding the monism of *qi* to popular treatises on Confucian ethics. His *Taigiroku* (*Record of Great Doubts*) is an important philosophical statement of his disagreements with Zhu Xi regarding the relationship of principle (Chinese *li,* Japanese *ri*) and material force (Chinese *qi;* Japanese *ki*).[45] He also wrote numerous instructional essays (*kunmono*) for various groups in the society, including the daimyo, the samurai, families, women, and children. In addition, he wrote essays on learning and literature, on calligraphy, and, one of the most popular, on health care (*Yojokun*).[46] Besides these various writing projects, Ekken punctuated and commented on the Confucian classics and Zhu Xi's *Reflections on Things at Hand,* so they could be read and appreciated by a wider audience in Japan.

One of the most interesting aspects of Ekken's thought is his concern to demonstrate the parallelism of Confucian and Shinto teachings. Indeed, he feels that these are essentially the same Way and have one principle running through both. In his works *Precepts Concerning the Gods* (*Jingikun*) and the *Parallelism of Shinto and Confucianism* (*Shinju heiko fuso hairon*)[47] Ekken says emphatically: "Between Heaven and Earth there is one Way. Thus the Way of humans is the Way of the gods; the Way of the gods is the Way of Heaven. They are not two different things."[48] He sees an essential

identity between Confucianism and Shinto which he repeats like a constant refrain throughout these writings. He accepts this premise as nearly
axiomatic, and yet he realizes that it requires detailed explanation. In his
form of religious naturalism Shinto and Confucianism are one because he
believes that there is one principle running through nature and human life
(3:641). Indeed, China and Japan have the same principle because principle
is not divided between Heaven, Earth, and the natural Way of the gods.
Ekken makes an important distinction, however, in his attempt to show
the basic coincidence of Shinto and Confucianism. He maintains that while
the Way (*Dao*) is the same in both China and Japan, the laws (*ho*) or customs of each country are different. Thus, while there is an essential similarity between the Way of the sages and the Way of the gods (3:642–43), there
are necessarily differences in terms of practice.

Ekken particularly criticizes Buddhism and expresses regret that even
the noteworthy seventh-century ruler of Japan, Shotoku Taishi, was so
favorable to Buddhism. Shinto, he feels, was eclipsed by Buddhism, and the
natural way of human relations must reemerge through understanding the
essential parallels between Shinto and Confucianism.

Natural Virtue: Sincerity without Words

Shinto, Ekken maintains, is a way of elemental simplicity. He constantly
assures his readers that Shinto is "easy to know and easy to practice"
(3:647). It is a teaching without words that people can follow naturally.
Indeed, in many respects he feels it is innate within the human heart. That
is because the practice of Shinto involves what is close at hand, not what is
distant or difficult. Shinto is rooted in an intuitive understanding called sincerity (*makoto*). Sincerity is nothing other than responding to people and
to the gods (ibid.). Thus Shinto takes human feelings as its base, and the
constant effort to purify one's heart is crucial to Shinto (ibid.). One must
thus cleanse impurities and avoid deceitfulness.

Ekken speaks of the importance of the inherent "good knowing" (*ryochi*)
within people. Because people have an innate ability to know and to act
appropriately, it is easy for them to respond correctly. Thus he says, "The
Way is practiced naturally." He uses the analogy with the four seasons:
"The heavenly way is wordless, the four seasons come into being and the
myriad things grow. Summer and fall, autumn and winter, rain and thunder need not be taught, and even the way of earth is without words and the
myriad things grow" (3:646). Elsewhere he writes, following the *Doctrine of
the Mean*, "The sincerity of the heavenly way is ceaseless" (3:645).

Reverence for the Kami

One of the most interesting aspects of Ekken's attempt to show the parallels between Shinto and Confucianism is his reference to the kami. The overt religiosity of Shinto with regard to reverence for the kami appears to be somewhat incompatible with Confucianism's humanistic and rational emphasis. Yet for Ekken, the abstract philosophical dimensions of his philosophy of *qi* most likely were made more concrete and comprehensible by his discussion of the kami in *Jingiken*.

As Chikao Fujisawa has defined kami, we can note the similarity with *qi* or "material force." He writes, "It will be relevant to construe kami as the deification of life-force which pervades all beings animate and inanimate. Kami is the invisible power which unites spirit and matter into a dynamic whole, while it gives birth to all things without exception."[49] While *qi* remains a philosophical concept describing the vital force of the universe, kami are experienced in the Japanese context as numinous forces in the natural world.

Similarly for Ekken, the kami are closely associated with the transformative life force of *qi*. He compares the way of the heavenly gods to the vitality of the four seasons. He writes: "We can see the transformation of yin and yang in the activity of the four seasons. In spring it is warm and things grow, in summer it is hot and things flourish, in fall it is cool and they contract, and in winter it is cold and they are dormant" (3:643).

Within this process, he maintains, there is the change and movement of the kami. Both constancy and change reflect the Way of the gods. Indeed, in the flow of water, in burning fire, in vegetation and in stones one can see the gods. Thus, when Ekken says we must revere the gods, he is suggesting that it is the vital force of the natural world with which we should be in harmony. This is the essence of his form of religious naturalism.

Ekken frequently refers to the gods in his discussion. He opens *Jingikun* by suggesting a mutual complementarity of humans and kami, namely, "The gods rely on the reverence of the people to increase their dignity (authority) and the people rely on the help of the gods to be free from harm" (3:641).

Thus, the role of the human is considered vital to maintaining the effectiveness of the kami. Elsewhere he writes, "The gods rely on the good and evil (actions) of humans. The movement of Heaven and Earth and the feelings of the gods depend on (our having) reverence and sincerity" (3:681). For humans to be reverent and sincere is not simply for their own personal sake; it is to allow the gods to be operative in human affairs.

Ekken repeatedly emphasizes the need for reverence and respect toward the gods. He urges people to pray to them with sincerity, not flattery. He assures his readers that if they pray correctly they will have good fortune and will experience a divine response (3:648–49, 662, 656). Ultimately there will be no separation between human beings and the gods. He writes:

> Always being reverent and serving the gods is making the heart correct. Purifying it, not doing evil, we should not pollute it. If we do this responding to the heart of the gods, there will be no separation between gods and humans, there will be resonance and good fortune. Thus the responses of the gods are actions relying on humans. (3:681)

Ekken observes that Japan has traditionally been a country of the gods, and he divides the numerous gods into certain categories and ranks (3:679). He notes that first there are *yin* and *yang* of Heaven and Earth, then the gods of creation, of the sun and moon, of mountains and rivers, and all the gods of Heaven and Earth. Next are the gods of the important ancestors of Japan and the gods of the shrines. Third, there are the ancestral gods.

He urges people to worship the gods appropriately according to their rank and not to flatter the gods or defile them. Humans should fear the gods and not act carelessly toward them. Ekken speaks specifically concerning various gods, citing prayers and festivals of earth and of grain as particularly important (3:678, 654). Recognizing the significance of the agricultural life of the people, he calls for special celebrations in the spring and fall to mark the planting and harvest of rice and other crops.

He cites the key role of the Ise shrine as the center of Shinto rituals but notes also that local shrines are vital protectors of the land and its inhabitants. Thus, the gods of mountains, rivers, and fields should be worshiped. Furthermore, as climate is an important factor in agricultural societies, Ekken urges appropriate prayers to the gods of the sun, the moon, and the stars. He observes that people should similarly have respect for clouds and rain, thunder and storms (3:655, 659).

Above all, in worshiping the gods, sincerity is most important. He writes: "To follow Heaven we need reverence, to love the people we need humaneness, to worship the gods we need sincerity." In this regard Ekken feels that "heavenly changes, earthly disasters, and human failings are the admonishments of heaven." Thus, if people do not respect the heavenly Way, disasters will result. He continually comments that good will be rewarded and evil will be punished (3:679, 657, 660, 680).

Essential to Shinto is purification. Indeed, Ekken writes, "Shinto takes cleansing as essential" (3:649). He notes that the human heart is originally directed by emotions and desires and there is thus a need for purification both externally and internally. Through fasting and cleansing a person will develop reverence without; through ceasing from anger and desires people will purify their heart and nurture reverence within.

He notes that continually purifying both inner and outer is like receiving the gods and being reverent and pure. This, he reiterates, is the essence of Shinto. The rituals of purification exemplify this aspect of Shinto. *Misogi,* for example, means to cleanse oneself and *harai* means to purify wickedness. Ekken speaks frequently about ancient Japan as a country of the gods where the rulers of old "respected Heaven, served Earth, and honored the gods." He idealizes people of old as having "a pristine simplicity and sincerity" (3:649, 651, 641).

Thus, the *yoki* of Heaven and Earth which Japan has received is mild and pure and the people were originally gentle and sincere, brave and loving. Because this *yoki* flourished in Japan, people are naturally respectful and have an appropriate sense of ritual propriety. People are warm and cooperative and not violent or disorderly (3:677). They naturally follow the five virtues and five relations, although there are no words for these concepts. Thus, even without sages or teachers like Confucius and Mencius, the five virtues and five relations passed down through the generations, and there are numerous examples in Japanese history of loyal retainers, filial children, and honorable women. He especially believes that by comparison with other countries the Japanese faithfully practiced the five virtues. Thus, he argues that Japan is superior to other countries.

Ekken's particular method of showing the parallels between Shinto and Confucianism reflects concerns similar to Ansai's, namely, encouraging reverence and self-cultivation. In addition, his thought, like Ansai's, is not politically motivated. Rather, his religious concerns are primary, along with his interest in naturalizing Confucianism. Shinto, it appears, is the ideal soil in which to transplant Neo-Confucian ideas of nature and virtue. For Ekken, this is not an all-encompassing systematic endeavor, as it was for Yamazaki Ansai. Instead, the parallels between Shinto and Neo-Confucianism are natural and axiomatic. This sense of the innate, intuitive goodness of human nature is emphasized by both Shinto and Neo-Confucianism. In particular, Ekken wishes to encourage a kind of religious reverence toward the Shinto gods as an important aspect of Neo-Confucian practice in Japan. He also makes a close connection between the rhythms of the natural world celebrated by both Shinto and Neo-Confucianism with an appreciation of the fecundity of the life processes. Ultimately Ekken is paralleling the Confucian ideas of nature and virtue with those of Shinto. A testimony to his success and those of other Neo-Confucians in developing particular expressions of religious naturalism is the fact that many of these patterns of nature, virtue, and self-cultivation have been carried down to the present century and have found new life in several of the new religions in Japan.[50]

Conclusion

In their attempts to reconcile Confucianism and Shinto, Hayashi Razan, Yamazaki Ansai, and Kaibara Ekken represent three examples of the stadial character of Japanese culture. The reconciliation they proposed varied in emphasis with each of these thinkers, but they held in common a desire to plant Confucianism firmly in Japanese soil and thus to naturalize it. They all rejected Buddhism as having an insufficient metaphysical basis for establishing moral principles for action in the world. Instead, they felt that Confucianism spoke to the needs of Tokugawa society, especially because of its humanistic and educational concerns as well as its political and social teachings. Through uniting it with Shinto they were able to bring out the religious dimensions of Confucianism along with its keen desire to promote harmony with nature and reverence for all living things. This can be seen in their distinctive forms of religious naturalism.

The particular methods of demonstrating the inter-resonance of these two systems are different with each thinker, yet their goals are similar. Thus, Razan establishes a series of correspondences; Ansai attempts an amalgamation; and Ekken sets up parallels between Shinto and Confucianism. This helped to promote the adaptation and naturalization of Confucianism during the early Tokugawa period. It demonstrates the stadial coexistence of thought variables so characteristic of Japanese culture. Further study of this naturalization process would add greatly not only to our understanding of Confucianism in Japan but also to the way the Japanese have adapted foreign elements throughout their history.

Indeed, the history of Confucianism in Japan spanning a period of over fifteen hundred years is clearly complex and merits further study. The particular function of Confucianism in different periods is multifaceted, especially as it coexists with other thought systems such as Buddhism and Shinto. Its enduring impact on Japanese society is as significant as its accommodation and indigenization in that society. It has served, then, to transform as well as be transformed by its encounter with Japanese thought, traditions, and institutions. Its expressions of religious naturalism bear further study especially in relation to the search in our own time for more comprehensive modes of human–earth relations.[51]

Notes

1. For general discussion of the history of Confucianism in Japan, see Muraoka Tsunetsugu, *Nihon shisoshi gaisetsu,* Nihon shisoshi kenkyu 4 (Tokyo: Sobunsha, 1961); Sagara Toru, *Kinsei Nihon ni okeru Jukyo undo no keifu* (Tokyo: Risosha, 1965); Takada Shinji, *Nihon Jugakushi* (Tokyo: Chinin shokan, 1941); Wajima Yoshio, *Chusei no Jugaku,* Nihon rekishi sosho 11 (Tokyo: Yoshikawa kobunkan, 1965).

2. Kate Wildman Nakai makes effective use of this term in her article "The Naturalization of Confucianism in Tokugawa Japan: The Problem of Sinocentrism," *Harvard Journal of Asiatic Studies* 40 (June 1980): 157–99.

3. Ibid., 159.

4. The work of Okada Takehiko, Minamoto Ryoen, Watanabe Hiroshi, Maruyama Masao in Japan and Wm. Theodore de Bary, Irene Bloom, Herman Ooms, Kate Nakai, Peter Nosco, Samuel Yamashita, Barry Steben, John Tucker, Janine Sawada in the West has been critical to establishing Japanese Confucianism as an emerging field of study.

5. This area of borrowing is a significant topic of investigation for contemporary scholars of world history who are interested in tracing the larger patterns of cultural diffusion. Historians such as William McNeill, Leftan Stavrianos, Philip Curtin, Alfred Crosby, Linda Shaffer, and Ross Dunn have made significant contributions in this area.

6. See "Nihon bunka no jusosei" [The Stadial Character of Japanese Culture], in *Watsuji Tetsuro zenshu,* 20 vols. (Tokyo: Iwanami shoten, 1963), 17:377–86. David A. Dilworth has utilized Watsuji's heuristic model in his essay "'Jitsugaku' as an Ontological Conception: Continuities and Discontinuities in Early and Mid-Tokugawa Thought," in *Principle and Practicality: Essays in Neo-Confucianism and Practical Learning,* ed. Wm. Theodore de Bary and Irene Bloom (New York: Columbia University Press, 1979), 471–513.

7. In *Sources of Japanese Tradition,* ed. Ryusaku Tsunoda, Wm. Theodore de Bary, and Donald Keene (New York: Columbia University Press, 1958), 1:36.

8. See Alicia Matsunaga, *The Buddhist Philosophy of Assimilation: The Historical Development of the Honji-Suijaku Theory* (Tokyo: Sophia University; Rutland, Vt.: Charles Tuttle, 1969).

9. For a discussion of medieval Confucianism, see Wajima Yoshio, *Chusei non Jugaku;* and Yuiki Rikuro, "Kamakura jidai no gakumon," *Rekishi kyoiku* 18, no. 5 (1970): 25–30.

10. Two of the leading examples of this are Gen'e (1279–1350) and Muso Soseki (1275–1351).

11. A detailed discussion of this can be found in Joseph Parker, *Zen Buddhist Landscape Arts of Early Muromachi Japan* (Albany: State University of New York Press, 1999).

12. Some important collections of Confucian texts in Japan are in Zen monasteries such as Tofukuji in Kyoto.

13. See R. P. Dore, *Education in Tokugawa Japan* (Ann Arbor: Center for Japanese Studies, 1984), esp. 279–80.

14. This is the thesis of Herman Ooms's book *Tokugawa Ideology: Early Constructs 1570–1680* (Princeton, N.J.: Princeton University Press, 1985).

15. Dore, *Education in Tokugawa Japan;* Richard Rubinger, *Private Academies of Tokugawa Japan* (Princeton, N.J.: Princeton University Press, 1982).

16. Nakai, "Naturalization of Confucianism," 162.

17. See John W. Hall, "The Confucian Teacher in Tokugawa Japan," in *Confucianism in Action,* ed. David Nivision and Arthur Wright (Stanford: Stanford University Press, 1959), 268–301.

18. See Uida Yoshiko, "Juke Shinto," in *Shinto no shiso* (Tokyo: Yuzankaku, 1974), 142–99.

19. Herman Ooms has expressed this view in a paper titled "The Syncretism of Neo-Confucianism in Shinto," delivered at the annual meeting of the American Academy of Religion, November 25, 1986. Joseph Kitagawa also notes that Confucian activism was "injected, through the Confucian-Shinto alliance, into the veins of Shinto which became rejuvenated and began to be more self-conscious about its own unique heritage" (*On Understanding Japanese Religion* [Princeton, N.J.: Princeton University Press, 1987], 163).

20. Ooms, *Tokugawa Ideology,* 227.

21. Ibid., 72–80.

22. For Razan's texts, see *Kinsei Shinto-ron; zenki Kokugaku,* ed. Taira Shigemichi and Abe Akio, Nihon shiso taikei 39 (Tokyo: Iwanami shoten, 1972) (hereafter abbreviated NST in references).

For a discussion of Hayashi's form of Shinto, see Iwahashi Koyata, *Shintoshi sosetsu* (Tokyo: Yoshikawa kobunkan, 1941), 227–50; and Takahashi Miyuki, "Hayashi Razan no Shinto shiso," *Kikan Nihon shisoshi* 5 (1977): 106–21.

I am indebted to the discussions of Razan's thought by Herman Ooms in *Tokugawa Ideology* (pp. 86–93) and Peter Nosco in "Masuho Zanko (1655–1742): A Shinto Popularizer Between Native Learning and National Learning," in *Confucianism and Tokugawa Culture* (Princeton, N.J.: Princeton University Press, 1984), 170–72. (Ooms translates *Shinto denju* as *Shinto Initiation,* while Nosco translates it as *Traditions of Shinto.*)

23. I am following Peter Nosco's translation of the phrase *Rito shinchi Shinto* in "Masuho Zanko," 171. I have used "heart-mind," however, instead of simply "mind."

24. Dilworth, "'Jitsugaku' as an Ontological Conception," 487.

25. This cosmogony is described by Ooms in *Tokugawa Ideology,* 87; see also NST 39:33.

26. See Peter Nosco's translation of this phrase in "Mashuo Zanko," 172.

27. These correspondences are used by other Neo-Confucians such as Yamazaki Ansai in similar attempts to naturalize Confucian teachings for the Japanese.

28. Nakai, "Naturalization of Confucianism," 161.

29. Ooms, *Tokugawa Ideology,* 195.

30. Trans. Wing-tsit Chan in *A Source Book in Chinese Philosophy* (Princeton, N.J.: Princeton University Press, 1963), 604.

31. *Zoku Yamazaki Ansai zenshu* (Tokyo: Nihon koten gakkai, 1937), 2:236–37. Trans. Ooms, *Tokugawa Ideology*, 234.

32. Ooms, *Tokugawa Ideology*, 221.

33. See *Sources of Japanese Tradition*, ed. Ryusaku Tsunoda, de Bary, and Keene, 354.

34. Ooms, *Tokugawa Ideology*, 264.

35. Okada Takehiko, "Practical Learning in the Chu Hsi School: Yamazaki Ansai and Kaibara Ekken," in *Principle and Practicality*, ed. de Bary and Bloom, 249.

36. Ooms, *Tokugawa Ideology*, 282. I am indebted to Ooms for his interpretation of Ansai's thought in this section.

37. Ibid., 283–84.

38. Ibid., 285.

39. This cosmology is described by Nosco ("Mashu Zanko," 177) and by Ooms (*Tokugawa Ideology*, 250).

40. Ooms, *Tokugawa Ideology*, 234.

41. Ibid., 250; see also NST 39:151, 156, 171.

42. Ooms, *Tokugawa Ideology*, 259.

43. Ibid., 282.

44. It should be noted again that aspects of Suika Shinto were also appropriated for the formation of a Shinto nationalist ideology in the twentieth century.

45. For *Taigiroku*, see *Ekken zenshu* (Tokyo: Ekken zenshu kankobu, 1910–11), 2:149–75; and *Kaibara Ekken, Muro Kyuso*, ed. Inoue Tadashi and Araku Kengo, Nihon shiso taikei 34 (Tokyo: Iwanami shoten, 1970), 34:10–64.

46. For his *kunmono*, see *Ekken zenshu*, vol. 3.

47. *Jingikun* is in *Ekken zenshu*, 3:641–85. References to this work in the following paragraphs will give the volume and page number in parentheses. *Shinju heiko fuso hairon* is in Komoguchi Isao and Okada Takehiko, *Ando Seian; Kaibara Ekken* (Tokyo: Meitoku shuppansha, 1985), 220–21.

48. These are the two opening lines of *Shinju heiko fuso hairon* (in *Ando Seian; Kaibara Ekken*, 220). For a discussion of this piece, see Aoki Yoshinori, "Kaibara Ekken no shinju heiko fuso hairon," *Shigaku zasshi* 50, no. 1 (January 1939): 223–39.

49. Jean Herbert, *Shinto: At the Fountainhead of Japan* (New York: Stein & Day, 1967), 25.

50. See a discussion of this in Helen Hardacre, *Kurozumikyo* (Princeton, N.J.: Princeton University Press, 1986), esp. 10–28.

51. See Mary Evelyn Tucker and John Berthrong, eds., *Confucianism and Ecology* (Cambridge, Mass.: Harvard Center for the Study of World Religions, 1998); and Harvard Forum on Religion and Ecology, http://environment.harvard.edu/religion.

28

The Confucian Linguistic Community in Late Tokugawa Japan

JANINE ANDERSON SAWADA

C ONFUCIAN MODES OF THOUGHT were long mediated by particular texts (as well as by rituals and patterns of behavior) and the language of these texts in turn helped shape the "grammar" of traditional East Asian thought. Classical Confucian discourse functioned in this sense as both a benchmark and a limiting factor for the shifting meanings imposed on the "Way" over time by its spokespersons and critics. The boundaries of Confucianism were in fact constantly renegotiated in reference to certain core texts, across both national contexts and different subcultures within the same country.

This essay concerns the multiple uses to which Confucian textual language was put within one particular sociohistorical context—early-nineteenth-century Japan. I will address the issue of the Japanese reinterpretation of Confucian thought by concentrating on the ways in which religious leaders of this period used common language patterns to represent different doctrines and praxes. "The paradox of communication," Pierre Bourdieu notes, "is that it presupposes a common medium, but one which works . . . only by eliciting and reviving singular, and therefore socially marked, experiences."[1] People in any differentiated society bring a range of cultural, economic, and political interests to their engagement with a common language, and in the process they place various, sometimes contrasting, claims on the same words. A shared vocabulary accordingly takes on quite different, even conflicting, meanings within the same "linguistic community" or social group that shares a common language.[2] This multiplication of meanings is particularly evident in the case of philosophical or religious discourse, which often exploits the plurality of denotations afforded by the conventional language of a particular society. Religious language often "manages to speak to all groups and all groups speak it . . . ."[3] Confucian language in Tokugawa Japan (1600–1868) was exceptionally flexible in this regard. It was appropriated and reinterpreted in numerous ways by the wide spectrum of groups that constituted the "Confucian linguistic community"—that is, the sector of society whose members were versed (albeit to varying degrees) in the vocabulary and phraseology of the classical Confucian texts and their commentaries.

The spokespersons discussed below do not represent the entire range of religious discourses in early nineteenth-century Japan; they are simply an arbitrary sampling of individuals who belonged to the Confucian linguistic community of the time. However, the examples I have selected, when taken together, show that people of diverse religious perspectives commonly took advantage of the polysemy of Confucian language, often in the interests of critiquing professional Confucian scholars' preoccupation with that very same language (particularly in its written form), and of establishing their own claims to a transverbal source of religious truth. We shall find that members of this linguistic community, despite their different religious identities, used Confucian vocabulary to enunciate their arguments for extratextual sources of religious authority, whether they conceived of these as located primarily in the mind or in the gods. In order to clarify the immediate impetus for this shared anxiety over the limitations of the written word, however, a few preliminary remarks about the late Tokugawa Confucian world are in order.

Textual Studies and Eclecticism

Confucian studies in the early nineteenth century exhibited two interrelated trends: textualist-eclectic perspectives, and preoccupation with the inner self (mind, heart, kokoro).[4] Modern scholars usually depict the former phenomenon as two distinct schools, but, for the most part, the same scholars participated in both the "textualist" and "eclectic" movements.[5] The first wave of these thinkers appeared in the mid-eighteenth century, partly in response to the rise of the Ancient Learning (Kogaku) schools—Kogigaku, founded by Itô Jinsai (1627–1705), and especially Kobunjigaku, associated with Ogyû Sorai (1666–1728). The textualists and eclectics were generally critical of Sorai's ideas, but their own emphases on philologically correct readings of ancient Chinese texts were often indebted to his approach. Indeed, Confucian scholars in the late Tokugawa virtually all acknowledged the value of close study of the classical texts. Particularly from the early eighteenth century, numerous editions of the primary

Confucian works were imported to Japan; and by the late Tokugawa, scholars could also make use of Japanese renditions of the classics written earlier in the period. These later scholars, who no longer focused simply on the Four Books and other Song compilations, produced many commentaries on the Five Classics and other ancient Chinese texts. Several, notably Minagawa Kien (1734–1807) and Ota Kinjô (1765–1825), put out their own comprehensive, annotated editions of the classics. For its part, the shogunal college in Edo (Shôheikô) sponsored publication of about two hundred classical texts from the beginning of the nineteenth century until the Meiji Restoration; the domains were ordered to publish their own official versions of the Chinese classics.[6]

The heightened concern with books and book learning, particularly the study of ancient Chinese books, was closely related to the rise of "eclectic studies" or "eclecticism" (Setchûgaku), an approach that might more accurately be described as one of reconciliation.[7] The literal meaning of *setchû* is to decide the mean or middle between phenomena that are perceived as excessive or deficient, particularly different theoretical points of view. In practice, the Setchûgaku approach was not a random grouping of unrelated ideas but a process of choice based on the individual scholar's particular criteria. Scholars associated with this trend purported to rectify the defects of Ancient Learning (as well as of the Zhu Xi and Wang Yangming schools) on the basis of their own distinctive philological methods. Through these methods, they advocated, one could make a judicious selection of the best insights from all the commentarial traditions, regardless of school, and in this way could establish the most accurate interpretation of the ancient texts. In his *Keigi setchû* (A Reconciliation of Interpretations of the Classics, 1764), usually cited as the inaugural work in this movement, Inoue Kinga (1739–1784) accordingly proposes his own views after comparing and selecting ideas from the works of Zhu Xi, Wang Yangming, Itô Jinsai, and Ogyû Sorai.

The idea of reconciling the contrasting textual interpretations of the time seemed to offer late Tokugawa students a method for coping with the proliferating Confucian discourses. In the final analysis, of course, the criteria for selecting and reconciling existing interpretations were necessarily subjective and idiosyncratic. But by undergoing the process of surveying the field and developing a critical perspective on each school's proposal, the eclectics were forced to come to terms with opposing positions and to articulate their own thinking on the matter. These scholars were thus under less pressure to exhibit loyalty to school lineages; their constant comparing, selecting, and borrowing paradoxically allowed them the freedom to establish relatively independent positions.[8]

Most of the eighteenth- and early-nineteenth-century textualist-eclectics served as domain school teachers or ran their own academies. Some of their schools became quite popular and attracted many members of the next generation of Confucian scholars, who taught similar approaches in their own academies during the last decades of the Tokugawa period. In those years, the number of so-called eclectic schools steadily increased—a well-known example is the Kangien academy, established by Hirose Tansô (1782–1856), which attracted over four thousand students between 1801 and 1871. Tansô himself testified to the popularity of the eclectic approach in the early nineteenth century, remarking that at the time, "among well-known Confucian scholars, seven or eight out of ten were [proponents of] Setchûgaku."[9]

Reading Wordless Books

The tendency to borrow and select from a variety of interpretations of the Confucian canon was not peculiar to eclectic and textualist scholars; it was common among Japanese Confucian scholars during this time. A great deal of interchange took place across school lines in the Confucian community of the late Tokugawa. In the aftermath of Ancient Learning, followers of both Wang Yangming and Zhu Xi found it easier to acknowledge their common concern with personal cultivation, even though they still disagreed sharply on several issues. Many of these inclusivist Neo-Confucians studied under the shogunal school director in Edo, Satô Issai (1772–1859), who "never accepted the notion of a single lineage or school," and is said to have advocated the ideas of Wang Yangming privately, while publicly professing Zhu Xi learning.[10]

Issai and his students best illustrate another characteristic feature of late Tokugawa Confucian thought—the concern with personal cultivation, especially mind-discipline. Their approach to Confucian studies was, in effect, a revival of the "learning of the mind-and-heart" (Japanese *shingaku;* Chinese *xinxue*) developed by Neo-Confucian scholars in Song and Ming China, Yi Korea, and earlier Tokugawa Japan. Whether they identified themselves primarily with the ideas of Zhu or Wang, these thinkers all gave high priority to *shugyô,* personal discipline or religious practice. True to their continental predecessors, they conceived of this not only in terms of particular praxes, such as quiet-sitting, but as an overall self-discipline to be carried out in the context of everyday life. In this regard, Confucian-influenced figures who became famous for their political activism (Oshio Heihachirô, Sakuma Shôzan, and Yoshida Shôin) were not representative of nineteenth-century Japanese Neo-Confucian trends. Most Zhu Xi and Wang Yangming scholars of this time believed that self-cultivation should be the first step in bringing order to society, and they tended to look askance at their activist colleagues.

The renewed interest in the inner life of the mind has been interpreted as an escapist response to the sociopolitical disorder of the Bakumatsu period.[11] There may be truth in this assessment. However, the focus on the inner self was also part of a dialectic within the contemporary Confucian community, which included, as we have seen, numerous academicians imbued with a keen post-Sorai awareness of the limitations of Song- and Ming-style mind-cultivation. Unlike earlier Tokugawa mind-learning, the late Tokugawa emphasis on the spiritual authority of the subject defined itself in relation to a recent wave of encyclopedic analyses of ancient classical texts. Amid the diverse Confucian perspectives that circulated (not to mention the abundance of Nativist, Western learning, and other intellectual proposals that accompanied the gradual dissolution of the shogunal order), the deliberate return by some scholars to the well-worn language of mind-cultivation was an attempt, not unlike others at the time, to maintain a plausible system of meaning within the growing plurality of positions generated by the Ancient Learning and textualist-eclectic schools.

Several scholars thus chose to reiterate familiar Neo-Confucian cautions against overemphasis on textual studies (and its associated evil, academic disputation) and to depict these tendencies as threats to the personal dimension of the way. Yômeigaku (Wang Yangming) scholar Yoshimura Shûyô (1797–1866) suggested three guidelines for reading books that pinpoint these concerns exactly:

(1) Do not fall into the pettiness of textual exegesis.

(2) Do not establish school views.

(3) Do not rely on the minute details of intellectual understanding.[12]

Yoshimura believed that a concentrated discipline of reflection and quiet-sitting was required to counterbalance the contemporary preoccupation with books. He spoke of this discipline in terms of maintaining a serious, reverent attitude (Japanese *kei;* Chinese *jing*), reflecting upon oneself, and transcending the self's sense of separation from the external world of objects. An inner-directed discipline of this kind would naturally lead to improved enactment of virtues such as filial piety and deference.[13] The same mode of thought, particularly the critical attitude toward intellectualizing activities, was enunciated by Yoshimura's teacher, the aforementioned Satô Issai, doyen of Confucian studies at the time. "People today read books containing words with their eyes. As a result they are held back by the words and are incapable of proceeding beyond them. What they should do is read wordless books with their hearts. Then their self-understanding will be [as deep as] as a cave."[14]

In his youth, Issai had studied under the creative textualist scholar Minagawa Kien, among others; he was not necessarily out of tune with the philological interests of his time. His statement about "wordless books" is not a denial of the value of book learning, but simply a reaffirmation of the priority of the inner dimension of learning. He proposed reading the classics as a means of dispelling erroneous thoughts and advocated writing as a method of self-reflection. Ultimately, however, Issai argued for a Confucianism that was *beyond* words. In his life work, *Genshi shiroku* (A Statement of My Aspirations: Four Records), Issai repeatedly takes up the subjective dimension of Confucian life and the value of the individual. He argues that one needs to respect oneself—which implied, for him, making oneself into an authentic human being. Issai echoes earlier Neo-Confucians when he speaks of "studying for the sake of oneself" rather than for the sake of impressing others, but he pushes the argument for individuality a bit further, insisting that a man who is committed to learning should rely entirely on himself, not on the power of others.[15] This perspective was partly a critique of contemporary trends in Confucian scholarship. "This learning is to be carried out for the sake of oneself . . . . Do not adorn yourself with a motley assortment of knowledge. The learning of recent times is nearly all what is called making wedding costumes for the sake of [impressing] others" (Satô, 171). Issai goes so far as to claim that, in the end, one cannot really rely on anything external in the process of authenticating oneself. "Our discipline consists in seeking on one's own and reflecting on one's own" (Satô, 109).

The ultimate aim of this self-reliance was understood, of course, in terms of its larger physical and social effects. Issai speaks in *Genshi shiroku* of the intimate relation between physical and mental health. In the face of external inducements, he advises, one needs to hold one's spirit in reserve and prevent its energy from becoming dissipated through the gratification of one's desires.[16] If one could "store one's life energy" internally in this way, one's mind and body would both remain healthy (Satô, 27). The progress of affairs in society and in the external world also depended on one's internal condition. "If you lose your self," Issai warned, "then you lose people. If you lose people, then you lose things" (Satô, 30). This kind of language is a hallmark of the mode of thought recorded in such Neo-Confucian canons as the *Great Learning*. We shall see below how similar Confucian locutions, taken to imply the priority of an internal realm of cultivation that transcends the limits of written discourse, were "exploited" by persons who spoke for non-Confucian groups.

Confucius beyond Words

The well-known Zen Buddhist saying, "separately transmitted outside the teachings, without setting up words" (*kyôge betsuden furyû monji*), posits that the truth cannot be contained in words—or, more broadly, intellectual discourse—and that in order to grasp it, one must ultimately forgo reliance on the authority of any text. When the young Confucian scholar who would later become known as Imakita Kôsen (1816–1892) first encountered this saying, he felt it was precisely the perspective he had been seeking, and soon afterwards he became a Zen monk. But Kôsen's concern with words had commenced long before he discovered Zen texts. He was no stranger to the debates and divisions among the Confucian schools of the early nineteenth century.

Educated in his youth by a follower of Ogyû Sorai, Kôsen later rejected Sorai's approach to Chinese studies and embarked on an exploration of Shushigaku (Zhu Xi Learning) and other systems that were being elaborated in the Confucian academies of Osaka and Kyoto. For five years, Kôsen ran his own Confucian school in Osaka, where he is said to have propagated his particular "eclectic" synthesis (Setchûgaku). By the time he decided to take the tonsure in 1840, Kôsen had been exposed to a wide range of Confucian scholarly approaches and in the process had developed a rather dim view of the contemporary Confucian world. Some years later, he wrote that Confucian scholars of the day all emphasized literary activities and failed to enact the morality of humaneness and rightness. He felt that these scholars were incapable of moving beyond their trivializing, unrealistic exegetical methods and that as a result their teachings would never satisfy people. Furthermore, he perceived Confucians of his time to be hopelessly divided; they merely built up their own theories and were intolerant of those with whom they disagreed.[17]

Where did Japanese Confucian scholars go wrong? Not unlike Satô Issai, Kôsen felt that Confucian learning had declined in Japan since the time of Nakae Tôju (1608–1648) and Fujiwara Seika (1561–1619). In particular, with the emergence of Itô Jinsai, Itô Tôgai (1670–1738), and Ogyû Sorai, Kôsen felt, "the learning of the art of the mind (*shinjutsu no gaku*) had become obsolete and rote learning developed." Lost in superficial and frivolous matters (textual exegesis and literary composition), scholars had grown proud and self-indulgent, and no longer bothered to cultivate their own moral qualities, much less edify others. In short, the priorities of contemporary Confucian scholars were simply erudition and literary skill;

they offered no program of personal cultivation to back up these external types of study (Imakita, 170).

The Zen master expressed these views of the Confucian world and proffered a solution in his best-known work, *Zenkai ichiran* (One Wave in the Zen Sea), a Buddhist apologetic addressed to the Confucian-oriented daimyo and samurai officials of Iwakuni domain. The book, written in 1862, is a concerted effort to translate Kôsen's version of Buddhism into Confucian language. He complains in it that scholars and exegetes influenced by Sorai had lost appreciation, both aesthetic and spiritual, of the transverbal truth that he claimed was at the heart of Confucius's message. He cites a passage of the *Analects* (11:26) in which one of the Sage's disciples reveals an aspect of the Confucian path that is often overlooked:

> [Dian said:] "In late spring, after the spring clothes have been newly made, I should like, together with five or six adults and six or seven boys, to go bathing in the River Yi and enjoy the breeze on the Rain Altar, and then to go home chanting poetry."
> The Master sighed and said, "I am all in favour of Dian."[18]

For Kôsen, this anecdote was evidence that an ineffable, delightful realm of truth was accessible through an advanced Confucian mode of being as well as through Zen practice (Imakita, 239–40). In response to a rhetorical questioner who asks why Kôsen downplayed the Confucian emphasis on "relying on [book] learning and enjoying the arts," the Zen master ventures that these activities are merely one aspect of the "elementary stage" of the path (to attain Buddhahood). He directs the questioner's attention to what he sees as the nondiscursive dimension of Confucian learning: "The most profound teaching of the Confucian school is illuminating the virtuous nature. Therefore, its true meaning does not lie in books" (Imakita, 202). Authentic Confucianism, in other words, was necessarily beyond the world of textual analysis.

Kôsen's interpretation of Confucius's message is confirmed, paradoxically, by the texts. For example, Confucius's admission that he was not "the kind of man who learns widely and retains what he has learned in his mind," but simply possessed "a single thread binding it all together" is proof, according to Kôsen, that the Confucians, like the Zen Buddhists, have a "separate transmission outside the teachings" (Imakita, 202).[19] Kôsen's creative rereading of Confucius culminates in the Zen master's gloss on *Analects* 17:19 (Lau, p. 146) in the closing lines of *Zenkai ichiran*:

> The Master said, "I am thinking of giving up speech." Zigong said, "If you did not speak, what would there be for us, your disciples, to transmit?" The

Master said, "What does Heaven ever say? Yet there are four seasons going round and there are the hundred things coming into being. What does Heaven ever say?"

Kôsen argues that this passage conveys the gist of Confucius's teaching: that the truth, in the end, transcends verbal discourse (Imakita, 271–72). Just as Confucius's "single thread" was not merely an oblique reference to the essential virtues of the Way, his impulse to "give up speech" was not simply a reverent acknowledgment of the efficacy of the natural order. The Zen master depicts these and other famous Confucian expressions as signposts to a religious truth that is free of all linguistic restrictions.

Kôsen implies that the Zen message could be a critical life-saver for the community of scholars who, in the aftermath of the Sorai school's textualist and ritualist extravagances, had lost sight of the true Confucius. In his critiques of late Tokugawa Confucian trends, Kôsen in fact presents himself less as a Buddhist than as a true Confucian who aims to revive a nearly moribund system of spirituality. He takes it upon himself to shore up the deteriorating Confucian world with Zen Buddhism and documents his qualification for this salvific role by means of his own biography. Having found his own first inspiration in the Confucian way, he avows, he could not bear to sit back and watch the Confucian "system of the mind" fall out of use in the world (Imakita, 175). In a gloss on a passage from the *Doctrine of the Mean*, he uses an anecdote about his early Zen training to pinpoint the key role that Confucian texts play in the Zen life of faith:

> The Master said, "Men all say, 'We are wise'; but being driven forward and taken in a net, a trap, or a pitfall, they know not how to escape. Men all say, 'We are wise'; but happening to choose the course of the Mean, they are not able to keep it for a round month."[20]

> Master [Daisetsu Jôen, 1797–1855] asked me, "If suddenly an enormously powerful demon-king caught you from behind and threw you into a fire-hole that was erupting in flames, how would you get yourself out?" I could not answer, and the sweat from my shame ran down my back. I agonized over this for many days. One day, all of a sudden, I recalled the [above] words, "net, trap, or pitfall," and had a tremendous insight. It was like drinking sweet nectar. Then I entered Master's room and presented my understanding. The Master laughed quietly and rested. At that point, I understood privately that the Sage had helped me along my path of learning. (Imakita, 257)

Even so, Kôsen adds, he did not fully understand the above passage from the *Mean* until he completed several more years of Zen practice—only then did he realize that Confucius's words were "not easy" to grasp (Imakita,

173–74). The implication of his testimony is that Zen practice is a clearing-house for genuine engagement with the words of Confucius. In order to understand the full meaning of Confucius's words, one needs to undergo a regimen of meditation and consultation with a Zen master.

Given his view that contemporary Confucian scholars "let their minds become drunk with ornate words and make their living from perusing lit-erature" and that these exegetes and literati were, in effect, bringing down the Confucian school from within, Kôsen ostensibly felt compelled to affirm a realm of truth that was not susceptible to linguistic analysis (Imakita, 173–74). In the face of the textualist-eclectic currents that domi-nated several Confucian schools in the early nineteenth century, scholars of diverse religious identities thus sought to establish a source of spiritual authority that transcended the limitations of the exegetical and literary enterprise. Professional Confucian scholars like Satô Issai, inextricably associated with the Tokugawa government's educational policies, necessar-ily promoted an orthodox course of book learning, but wrote profusely about the ultimate authority of the individual human spirit. Imakita Kôsen, also steeped in Confucian textual learning, proclaimed that a trans-verbal "separate transmission" was the only hope for the survival of authentic Confucianism.

Not only academy teachers and learned Buddhist priests displayed an ennui with the preoccupations of Chinese learning during this period, however. Many lower-ranking samurai, rural notables, successful mer-chants and artisans, physicians, and Shinto priests had learned to "read off" the Four Books and Zhu Xi's commentaries in domain, local, or private schools, and (especially if they attended private academies) had become aware, even if cursorily, of Ancient Learning, textualist, and eclectic approaches to the classics. A number of the religious subworlds that emerged or revived in the late Tokugawa (Confucian-oriented groups such as Sekimon Shingaku, Nativist movements, and new religions such as Kurozumikyô and Misogikyô) were produced by members of these mid-level social groups. The spokespersons of their religious associations thus also belonged to the Confucian linguistic community, even if only to its periphery, and their discourses drew on common Neo-Confucian ideas. In particular, the notion that social harmony and national security depended on cultivating one's mind or heart was virtually undisputed in this semied-ucated social milieu, though diverse interests ensured contrasting interpre-tations of the paradigm. To be sure, some claims of identity with the Neo-Confucian cultivation program were almost nominal: the paradigm was used as a politically correct rubric for agenda that, in reality, defined themselves in reaction to Confucian learning. The remainder of this essay outlines a system of religious practice that exploited the polysemy of Neo-Confucian language in this manner.

Ritual Purification and the Grammar of Self-Cultivation

A religious group that later became known as Misogikyô appeared in the Edo area about the same time that Kôsen determined to take the tonsure (1840).[21] Like all new religious developments, this system was heavily indebted to existing practices and ideas. The samurai-born founder, Inoue Masakane (1790–1849), had spent several years traveling through Japan and studying under various Buddhist, Confucian, Shinto, and Chinese-medicine teachers. In its final form, his teaching especially emphasized breath regulation, which he referred to as *Nagayo no den* (the Eternal Tradition). This exercise involved inhaling deeply through the nose while directing the breath to the abdominal area below the navel and exhaling slowly through the mouth. Masakane advised his followers to practice *Nagayo* "in front of the gods" every day for the amount of time it took to burn one stick of incense.[22] This discipline of exorcising or purifying oneself (*harae shugyô*) focused on a prayer formula that was commonly used in the *sanshu no harae* (Triple Purification), an important ritual ceremony practiced in the main Shinto schools of the Tokugawa era.

Masakane advised his followers to carry out the discipline of purification by repeating the prayer, *To ho kami emi tame, harai tamai kiyome tamau,* in conjunction with rhythmic breathing.[23] The practitioners' exhalations represented a "blowing away" of their accumulated defects, offenses, and impurities. After a prolonged period of intensive chanting/breathing of these syllables, they would reach a turning point, usually marked by feelings of joy, serenity, and gratitude.[24] Masakane implies in his writings that repeated enunciation of the sacred formula activates *kotodama* (the mysterious spiritual power believed to inhere in Japanese words), expels impurities, and allows the gods to endow the individual with the true "mind of faith (*shinjin*)" (Inoue, 77).

In addition to the central purification practice, Masakane developed other rituals for specific purposes and occasions, though they also tended to center on the prayer formula. Like the Pure Land Buddhist chant, *Namu Amida Butsu*, the words of the Misogi formula were not only an invocation of the deity and an articulation of divine power, but a device for mental concentration and a magical code that was believed to effect changes in the physical world. Not unlike Satô Issai, but in a far more detailed and practical way, Masakane identified personal or religious discipline with health care. His program of cultivation required self-restraint with regard to food, drink, and general lifestyle. In essence, however, the discipline of purification itself was all that one needed to maintain good health and, by implication, long life (Inoue, 87). Masakane's promotion of breathing and purification practices as the best treatment for any illness is well documented in his letters to followers who were suffering from various emotional or physical ailments. Whether they were afflicted by scabies, a short temper, or fear of thunder, Masakane invariably advised his correspondents to concentrate on chanting the formula and breathing properly (Inoue, 100, 105). This regimen would allow them to transcend intellectual processes and simply entrust themselves to the power of the gods—an approach guaranteed to destroy the very root of illness (Inoue, 98). The ritual chant was, in short, the centerpiece of Masakane's entire religious and healing system.

Masakane usually did not encourage his followers to seek others' help in curing their ailments, but emphasized their own responsibility in the matter. He expected them to grasp the "foundation of medicine" for themselves and to learn to apply it (Inoue, 108). Because proper breathing was the key to the health of the individual's entire psychophysical complex, the power of healing was accessible to any follower, given the requisite amount of effort. As long as one were diligent in the breathing and purification practices, there would be little need to visit a professional healer or physician. To be sure, in his writings Masakane emphasized that healing ultimately depended on the grace of the gods, not on one's own power—but the gods' grace was in turn activated by the initiative of the practitioner. Misogikyô was presented to the members as a method for healing themselves, rather than primarily as a form of faith healing.

Although further details of Inoue Masakane's program are beyond the scope of this discussion, taken together they provide a bird's-eye view of the plethora of religious, intellectual, and medical discourses that were circulating during his time. Pure Land Buddhism, Shirakawa Shinto, medical-cosmological theories, Nativism, a touch of Zen, and various folk traditions all seem to have played a part in Masakane's world of meaning. Of particular interest for our purposes is his penchant for organizing these systems of knowledge under the rubric of Neo-Confucian self-cultivation. He carries out this identification process on more than one level in his writings. Masakane's use of Confucian analogies and identifications in his major work, *Shintô yuiitsu mondô sho* (Questions and Answers about Primal Shinto), which he wrote with the express aim of defusing the Tokugawa shogunate's charges of heteropraxy against him, may be read as an apolo-

getic demonstration that his ideas were within the bounds of accepted ideologies of self-cultivation of the time. Of course, the interspersing of allusions to classical texts was an expected feature of popular didactic literature
and no doubt came to Masakane naturally, given his own Confucian education. But specific Neo-Confucian conceptions also play a key role in the
general structuring of Masakane's system.

It was precisely during the late Tokugawa, when the various Confucian
scholarly proposals, elaborated and reelaborated, seemed to be losing their
plausibility, that the fundamental premises of the original Song synthesis
imbued popular Japanese thought most profoundly.[25] For many educated
members of late Tokugawa society, whether samurai or privileged commoners, the premise that personal cultivation was the basis of social well-
being was virtually built into the structure of thinking. Inoue Masakane
typifies this mentality. He was not a scholar in the style of either Satô Issai
or Imakita Kôsen, but he was familiar, at the very least, with Zhu Xi's
selection of the classics and was also conscious of the contemporary surplus
of Confucian school interpretations (if not of their detailed content). It
seemed to him, in fact, that "the learning of China" had degenerated from
the time of Confucius into a fragmented spectrum of conflicting proposi-
tions—he notes in his writings that it had splintered into Ancient Learning,
the teachings of the Cheng brothers and Zhu Xi, and the teachings of Wang
Yangming, among others. Nevertheless, Masakane avowed, "they are all
the teachings of the Sage, the precious teachings of cultivating the person
and regulating the family" (Inoue, 5).

It was this pithy rendition of Neo-Confucian spirituality that informed
the Misogi teacher's program most effectively. His entire religious-medical
teaching was subsumed under the structure of the steps of the *Great Learning:* internal rectification, personal cultivation, family order, and social/
national security. This grand project was presented as the overarching aim
of all Misogi rituals, prayers, breathing exercises, and healing practices.
Indeed, Masakane identifies the purpose of his "teaching of the gods" in
terms of this paradigm so repeatedly throughout his writings that reference
to it functions not simply as a statement of doctrine but as a regular feature
of his rhetorical style—a kind of flourish that gives added meaning to all the
details that have gone before. The following example typifies the Misogi
founder's "translation" of his Shinto perspective into the dominant cultural
language of his time.

> As the great land of Japan is a country that originated in the gods, if one sim-
> ply worships these gods, one's person will be cultivated, one's family regu-
> lated and the country governed . . . . Those who wish to cultivate their

persons and regulate their families should first respect the power of the great
goddess Amaterasu and worship her every morning and evening. (Inoue, 50)

In letters to disciples, Masakane reiterates that the teaching of the gods is to
attain peace and well-being in one's body, mind, and family (e.g., Inoue,
102). Citing the *Doctrine of the Mean* to the effect that sincerity (*makoto;*
Chinese *cheng*) is the Way of Heaven and that the path of human beings is
to fulfill this Way, Masakane simply equates the classical process of personal authentication with the practice of *harae shugyô*—intensive chanting
of the prayer formula reinforced by rhythmic breathing (Inoue, 3, 68).

The goals of cultivating one's person, putting one's family in order, and
governing the nation are thus repeatedly identified as the aim of Misogikyô. But even while advocating the conventional order of Neo-Confucian
learning, Masakane subverts it. The key to the efficacy of the purification
ritual, he claims, is the "transmission of the mind of faith," an endowment
that originates in the mind of the Shinto gods. If one simply follows the
program of cultivation outlined, for example, in the *Great Learning*, one
will tend to make strenuous efforts to reform oneself and one's relations
with others. One will proceed on the assumption that one can rely on
one's own wisdom to put everything in order. But in the process of striving
to improve oneself, Masakane warns, one will forget the power of the gods
and in fact confound and obscure it. He accordingly advises that the proce-
dure envisioned in the Neo-Confucian texts (which assumes the initiative
of the self as agent) be bypassed long before one reaches this stage by
entrusting the entire project to the gods through worship and ritual disciplines (Inoue, 82).

The Shinto leader reveals this skepticism about the workability of the
Confucian program in several writings. Referring again to the *Doctrine of
the Mean*, he warns that "the Chinese say to 'take hold of the Mean'; but if
you wish to take hold of that Mean, you will become deluded in various
ways, things will multiply, and you won't be able to do so . . ." (Inoue, 69).
Masakane's purification and breathing disciplines, on the other hand, could
definitely be put into action—Shinto, as Masakane conceived it, was emi-
nently more practicable than the path of the sages (Inoue, 24). It was precisely at the level of application, then, that Masakane parted ways with the
Neo-Confucian vision of personal cultivation. In a similar vein, he remarks
in a letter that in both China and Japan people have engaged in the "study
of principles" *rigaku* (Song Confucianism), but that few have succeeded in
embodying those principles. In fact, those who possess intellectual knowledge of these principles often labor under the illusion that they have mastered this form of learning, but since they do not put the principles into

practice, their understanding remains superficial. In Misogikyô, in contrast, one is encouraged to "abandon the study of principles, not rely on the wise or on the foolish, and learn the law of the gods" (Inoue, 180). Masakane accordingly advocated *not* knowing the Neo-Confucian principles until after one had practiced Misogi purification disciplines for some time. Otherwise, the knowledge itself would block the fulfillment of one's religious quest. "If one knows the principles in advance, one obscures the power of the gods, and the power of one's own person becomes weak" (Inoue, 180). In short, if one became familiar with the various doctrines contained in the Chinese textual corpus, one would remain stuck in an abstract, intellectualized realm and would not be able to enact the sacred teaching in the natural, spontaneous way that the gods intended.

The Misogikyô leader's ambivalence toward the Neo-Confucian system was partly fueled by his Nativist sentiments. He rejected the idea of teaching Confucian moral ideas (such as the Five Constant Virtues) in "Chinese" fashion, "by means of words and books" (Inoue, 8). According to Masakane, Confucian virtues, laws for governing the nation, and indeed all Chinese formulations were encompassed within the sacred teachings that Amaterasu transmitted to the Japanese people. These traditions of knowledge were articulated, not in words and books, but through Shinto rituals of worship and musical performances (*kagura*). It was best, then, not to rely on the Confucian textual canon or, for that matter, on any other (foreign) systems of knowledge (Inoue, 9). In this way, one could gain direct access to the truth, which was beyond the limitations of Confucian textual discourse (an ideal that oddly parallels Imakita Kôsen's transmission beyond words).[26] The gods would bestow whatever insight one might require to fulfill one's moral obligations; one had only to follow the dictates of one's divinely endowed "mind of faith." Moreover, as long as one kept this faith, the power of the gods would ensure the success of one's affairs in the world, without any particular effort on one's own part (Inoue, 98). The simplicity of the system, compared to contemporary Confucian textual extrapolations, was disarming. One could achieve the respected Neo-Confucian aims of personal health, peace of mind, and family harmony simply by practicing the purification disciplines and having faith in the gods.

In the context of his times, Masakane felt compelled to demonstrate the universal relevance of his novel teachings, and he did this by casting the broad aims of Misogikyô in Confucian terms. He was able to exploit the Neo-Confucian phraseology of personal cultivation effectively, even while cautioning his followers not to lapse into a Neo-Confucian–style "self-power" mentality, precisely because he relied on this language for a grammatical outline rather than for any specific content. In his view, the outline badly needed filling up with concrete, practical details. It was the very generality of Neo-Confucian language that allowed the Misogi leader, like others of his milieu, to use it as code that would legitimate his message within the Confucian linguistic community.

Our sampling of religious proposals in late Tokugawa Japan brings two points into relief. First, spokespersons of diverse religious groups utilized a common vocabulary and phraseology, composed of words taken from the Confucian textual corpus, in order to enunciate their distinctive programs. Issai's scholarly ruminations in *Genshi shiroku*, Kôsen's apologetical legerdemains in *Zenkai ichiran*, and Masakane's constant reliance on the mental grammar of the *Great Learning* signify these individuals' continuing respect for the power of Confucian language in their time. Second, these spokespersons iterated their views on the ultimate source of religious authority partly in response to contemporary trends in some segments of the Confucian scholarly community—especially to what they perceived as an obsession with philological and literary minutiae to the neglect of the inner self. Their proposals, on one level, simply carried forward the conventional arguments of Neo-Confucian mind-learning, Zen Buddhism, and Shinto/Nativism concerning the limitations of the written word. However, these elaborations were also part of a shared "discussion" that was taking place within the late Tokugawa Confucian linguistic community. In the early nineteenth century, natural disasters, economic stresses, peasant rebellions, and the threat of foreign incursions all contributed to the perception of dissonance and instability in the existing social order. The religious arguments I have discussed were singular articulations of this perception—variations on a theme performed (albeit unwittingly) in a kind of counterpoint. The similarity of these proposals seems to illustrate the "cultural overdetermination" of this period—that is, the appearance in the late Tokugawa of multiple discourses "whereby the same elements appear time and again in different form."[27] Specifically, the rejection of the utility of the Confucian language of "words and books" (often, paradoxically, articulated in that very language) and the concomitant proclamation of the ultimate authority of the inner self (or, as the case may be, of the gods who "grant" the self) signaled a growing ambivalence within the Confucian linguistic community toward its own raison d'être. These religious proposals marked an anxiety over the meaningfulness of the Confucian language itself—a language that was closely associated with the deteriorating sociopolitical order.

As Japan moved into the Meiji period, the educational institutions that had previously instilled knowledge of the Confucian texts in members of the middle and upper levels of society were dismantled, and although Chinese learning did not disappear, the intelligentsia no longer relied on it as a cultural lingua franca. The Confucian linguistic community that had been constituted by religious spokespersons of disparate interests and perspectives—people such as Satô Issai, Imakita Kôsen, and Inoue Masakane—gradually dispersed as new idioms began to compete for dominance in the Meiji world. Confucian modes of thought and behavior nevertheless lived on, and many would argue that they remain a vital dimension of the Japanese life-world today. For the most part, however, residual Confucian influences in modern Japan are not mediated by the language of the classical texts; the boundaries of Confucianism are now so porous that they no longer demand negotiation in reference to specific texts.

Notes

1. Pierre Bourdieu, *Language and Symbolic Power*, trans. G. Raymond and M. Adamson (Oxford: Polity Press, 1991), 39.

2. The notion that language is embedded in a particular community goes back at least to Ferdinand de Saussure, who emphasized that "language is not complete in any speaker, but exists fully only in a collectivity" (cited in Fred Dallmayr, *Language and Politics* [Notre Dame, Ind.: University of Notre Dame Press, 1984], 58).

3. Bourdieu, *Language*, 40.

4. See Nakamura's seminal essay, "Kinsei kôki jugakkai no dôkô," in *Kinsei kôki Juka shû*, ed. Nakamura Yukihiko and Okada Takehiko, Nihon shisô taikei 47 (Tokyo: Iwanami shoten, 1972), 479–98, for a typology of late Tokugawa Confucian studies that includes these and other trends.

5. Here I use the terms "textualism" and "textual studies" broadly to include the whole range of Japanese Confucian scholarship of this time that, in the aftermath of Ancient Learning (Kogaku), emphasized close analysis of primary texts. The textualist schools thus include both Ancient Commentary Studies (Kochûgaku), which advocated reevaluation of pre-Song Confucian commentaries, and Evidential Studies (Kôshôgaku), a broader intellectual movement that had roots in late Ming and early Qing scholarship.

6. For the above details on the textualist movement, see Nakamura, "Kinsei kôki jugakkai no dôkô," esp. 483–87.

7. Though evidently first inspired by Inoue Kinga's early usage (see below), "Setchûgaku" became a retrospective category used by modern Japanese scholars to refer to Tokugawa thinkers who seemed to advocate this approach to Confucian textual studies. This later use of the term is based on the premise that all scholars belong to formal master–disciple lineages and that these lineages define the parameters of exclusive schools of thought. Much like "eclecticism" in English-language discussions of thought, "Setchûgaku" is to some extent a catchall term for

phenomena that do not seem to fit easily under the main Tokugawa Confucian rubrics (Shushigaku, Yômeigaku, Kogaku, Kobunjigaku, and Kôshôgaku).

8. Takehiko Okada, "Neo-Confucianism in Nineteenth-Century Japan," in *Confucianism and Tokugawa Culture*, ed. Nosco, 218; I have drawn heavily from Okada in this and the following paragraph.

9. Cited in Nakamura, "Kinsei kôki jugakkai no dôkô," 487.

10. Satô Issai, *Genshi shiroku*, in *Satô Issai, Oshio Chûsai*, ed. Sagara Tôru et al., Nihon shisô taikei 46 (Tokyo: Iwanami shoten, 1980), 12, 111, 121.

11. Nakamura, "Kinsei kôki jugakkai no dôkô," 493.

12. Cited in ibid., 492.

13. Ibid., 492–93.

14. Translation in Okada, "Neo-Confucianism," 230.

15. Sagara Tôru, "*Genshi shiroku to Senshindô sakki*," in *Satô Issai, Oshio Chûsai*, ed. Sagara et al., 710. My use of the word "man" here reflects Issai's term *shi*, which denotes a samurai, male leader, or scholar.

16. He speaks of this, following the Song masters, as "gathering in the spirit" (*seishin no shûren*). Sagara, "*Genshi shiroku*," 716. See also Satô, *Genshi shiroku*, 12.

17. Imakita Kôsen, *Zenkai ichiran*, ed. Morinaga Sôkô (Tokyo: Hakujusha, 1987), 151, 240.

18. Quotations from the *Analects* are from the translation by D. C. Lau (New York: Penguin Books, 1979), with orthographic modifications. For this quotation, see p. 111.

19. See *Analects* 15:2 (Lau, p. 13), for the passage about the "single thread."

20. Trans. James Legge, *Confucian Analects, the Great Learning, the Doctrine of the Mean* (New York: Dover Publications, 1972), 388.

21. From 1872 to 1876 the group was called Tohokami-kô, and only later adopted the name "Misogikyô," but in the interests of clarity, I use "Misogikyô" or "Misogi" to refer to the group and its teachings.

22. See, e.g., Inoue Masakane, in *Shoka Shintô* 2, Shintô taikei 28, Ronsetsu hen (Tokyo: Shintô Taikei Hensankai, 1983), 64, 98.

23. One version of the formula's meaning is "Distant gods, please bless us; exorcise [evil from us], purify us." But cf. H. D. Harootunian, *Things Seen and Unseen* (Chicago: University of Chicago Press, 1988), 337–40; and Tahara Tsuguo et al., eds., *Hirata Atsutane, Ban Nobutomo, Okuni Takamasa*, Nihon shisô taikei 50 (Tokyo: Iwanami shoten, 1973), 410 n. 549b, on the Nativist Ōkuni Takamasa's (1792–1871) distinctive interpretation of the five words of the formula.

24. For details on contemporary practices, I have consulted Matsuno Junkô, *Shin shûkyô jiten* (Tokyo: Tôkyôdô Shuppan, 1984), 409–10; and Ogihara Minori, "Misogikyô no gyōhō," typescript of a talk presented at the Fifty-fifth Meeting of the Nihon Shûkyô Gakkai, Kokugakuin Daigaku, Sept. 21, 1996.

25. See Sagara Tôru, *Kinsei Nihon Jukyô undô no keifu* (Tokyo: Kôbundô, 1955), Preface, 6.

26. Kôsen, of course, did not polemicize against Chinese discourse in particular, as does Masakane. Still, there are resonances here with Zen cultivation systems in

which direct insight into the mind is purportedly given precedence over textual learning. Masakane (who may have practiced Zen meditation in his youth) viewed Shinto teachings as centrally concerned with the state of the human mind. He agreed that one could not really trust the vicissitudes of one's own mental processes, but, unlike Kôsen, he framed the solution in theistic terms rather than in the language of "enlightenment." Masakane almost seems to echo Shinran when he indicates that we cannot attain the "true mind" by means of our own power, and should rejoice over the gods' sacred pledge on our behalf (Inoue, 66).

27. H. D. Harootunian, "Late Tokugawa Culture and Thought," in *Cambridge History of Japan*, vol. 5, *The Nineteenth Century*, ed. Jansen, 253.

Suggested Readings

Harootunian, H. D. "Late Tokugawa Culture and Thought." In *The Cambridge History of Japan*. Volume 5, *The Nineteenth Century*, edited by Marius Jansen, 168–258. Cambridge: Cambridge University Press, 1989.

Nosco, Peter, ed. *Confucianism and Tokugawa Culture*. Princeton, N.J.: Princeton University Press, 1984.

————. *The Religions Dimension of Confucianism in Japan*. Philosophy East and West 48, no. 1, special issue (January 1988).

Okada, Takehiko. "Neo-Confucianism in Nineteenth-Century Japan." In *Confucianism and Tokugawa Culture*, edited by Peter Nosco, 215–50. Princeton, N.J.: Princeton University Press, 1984.

Tu Weiming, ed. *Confucian Traditions in East Asian Modernity: Moral Education and Economic Culture in Japan and the Four Mini-Dragons*. Cambridge, Mass.: Harvard University Press, 1996.

29

An Exploration of Vietnamese Confucian Spirituality: The Idea of the Unity of the Three Teachings (*tam giao dong nguyen*)

DUNG N. DUONG

WHEN DISCUSSING VIETNAMESE CONFUCIANISM, O. W. Wolters's cautionary advice immediately comes to mind: think twice before using the term "Confucianism" in Vietnamese cultural history.[1] Wolters has pointed out the ambiguity of the term "Confucianism" in the context of Vietnamese traditional culture. The word might refer to the general study of Chinese texts, which were mostly Confucian classics, in preparation for state examinations and might not refer to Confucianism as a consciously adopted system of sociopolitical ethics. In traditional Vietnam, a scholar was generally called a "Confucian" (*nha nho*) regardless of his philosophical persuasion. Chinese characters were called "Confucian writing" (*chu nho*), and students were referred to as "Confucian disciples" (*nho sinh*), which means, among other things, that in the Vietnamese perception then, Chinese culture and civilization were identifiable with Confucianism itself.

The objective of this essay is not to attempt to reconstruct the development of Confucianism in Vietnam along historical lines, but to make a tentative effort to explore what might be called "Vietnamese Confucian spirituality," that is, the spiritual dimension of Vietnamese moral and religious consciousness, which has once been referred to by Tu Weiming as "the ontological grounding of the Neo-Confucian project on the learning of the heart-and-mind."[2] The essay will move from an introductory investigation of the meaning of Confucianism as reflected in the popular image of Confucian scholars and the role of spirituality in Vietnamese traditional culture, to the conclusion that Confucianism, understood as a way of life and thinking, has become an integral part of Vietnamese culture (sharing its influence with Buddhism) as the principal expression of Vietnamese religiosity. Moreover, this spiritual syncretism, conceptually referred to as "the Unity of the Three Teachings," has found perfect expression in King Tran Thai Tong's *Essays on Emptiness* (*Khoa Hu Luc*), *Biographies of Eminent Chan Masters* (*Thien Uyen Tap Anh*), and Nguyen Du's *The Tale of Kieu* (*Kim Van Kieu* or *Doan Truong Tan Thanh*). These works, though different in genre, share the same universe of meaning, that is, an espousal of the view that ultimate spiritual reality could be inclusively approached from many different orientations,[3] and these different orientations could be unified under one unique cognitive-affective function called "heart-mind" (*tam*).

The Image of Confucian *literati* (*nha nho*) and the Meaning of Confucian Spirituality in Vietnamese Traditional Context

Although the study of Vietnamese Confucian spirituality as an academic discipline has received scant attention, it can be initially argued that a tradition of Confucian spirituality existed and shaped the Vietnamese people's moral consciousness for a very long time. To start the discussion of Confucian spirituality in the context of traditional Vietnamese culture, however, both the terms "Confucianism" and "spirituality" require explanations. From the Vietnamese perspective, the connotation of Confucianism involves many different, and even contradictory, images simultaneously. Confucianism might evoke the image of a poverty-stricken village scholar who accepted a "pure and clean" (*trong sach*) or "pure and poor" (*thanh ban*) life for the sake of maintaining a system of social ethics that had been considered to consist of immutable truths concerning human interpersonal relationships. Confucianism might also conjure up an image of a quite opposite sort: a successful candidate who had passed the royal examination, returning to his hometown in full glory, prepared to participate in the government of people. This image was usually negative; that is, that scholar-official might be viewed with suspicion now that he was going to participate in the general exploitation of his own people for his own self-centered interests. The Confucian system of morality, in the second case, would be interpreted as a discourse of power that made use of the ideas of "loyalty" (*trung*), "filial piety" (*hieu*), "humaneness" (*nhan*), and "righteousness" (*nghia*) to cover up the will to control and exploit people. These two opposing images constitute the whole structure of Confucian *imaginaire* in the history of Vietnamese culture; that is, a heroic village scholar who failed in the exams and lived among the common people to teach and counsel them about the way to become paragons of morality, or a successful scholar-official who might be suspected, with good reason, to have abandoned Confucius's True Way (*chanh dao*) to follow the false way of "greedy officials and corrupt clerks" (*tham quan o lai*).[4] Grasping the significance of this *imaginaire* is making a long step toward understanding Vietnamese Confucianism.

In the context of Vietnamese culture, "spirituality" (*doi song tam linh*) plays an important role that bears an ambiguous relationship to society and religion. Most Vietnamese people, especially the intellectual elites, looked upon the term "religion" (*ton giao*) with disfavor and usually identified religion with superstitious beliefs (*me tin di doan*). Few have ever used the term "religion" (*ton giao*), preferring the term "the Way" (*dao*), which can be interpreted as the primary image of Vietnamese spirituality. Vietnamese people, for example, usually refer to Buddhism, Daoism, and Confucianism respectively as "the Way of the Buddha" (*dao Phat*), "the Way of Laozi" (*dao Lao*), and "the Way of Confucius" (*dao Khong*). The Way in this case is synonymous with "a spiritual life" (*doi song tam linh*), which is supposed to exist independently of one's social life. In other words, Vietnamese people consider their spiritual life in terms of its opposition to their social life. In theological language, both transcendent and immanent aspects of Vietnamese life are always in a tense and dialectical relationship which tends to privilege the former over the latter. This relationship has given rise to a paradoxical situation that puzzles Western scholars when they try to understand Vietnamese culture and ways of thinking. On the one hand, they recognize that Vietnamese people can be pragmatic and "anti-intellectual," as evidenced in the fact that they produced no philosophical or theoretical works of great stature; on the other hand, scholars can find innumerable literary works that praise the development of an inner spiritual life in terms of its separateness from all socially oriented activities.

This uncomfortable relationship between spirituality and society was one of the inevitable results of the role of Confucianism in Vietnamese traditional culture and society. The idea, for example, that a supporter of Confucius's Way (*dao Khong*) must live in poverty, loneliness, and usually under the state's suspicion and persecution has been beautifully summarized in the following stanza, written by Nguyen Trai (1380–1442), the greatest Confucian scholar in the fifteenth century:

> Of old and now you've followed your lone path.
> On duty's path you've struggled and you fought.
> The Way exists in heaven and on earth.
> Righteousness will outlast both stone and bronze.[5]

The image of a lonely heroic figure who tried to save his own chaotic society is hauntingly present in the whole corpus of Nguyen Trai's poetical works:

> The past's beyond recapture—time's so fleet!
> I'm yet to serve my country—age is woe!
> I've nursed a statesman's purpose all my life—
> all night I'm sitting, hugging my cold wrap.[6]

Comparisons between Chinese and Vietnamese Confucianism

In contrast to Confucian colleagues in China, who usually considered society to be the center of their activities, Nguyen Trai and many other Vietnamese Confucian scholars articulated a strong contempt of the social world in which the game of power dominated interpersonal transactions, and they advocated a life of inner spirituality that had a strong Daoist flavor:

> You dread the world of men, their nets and toils.
> Lie down in wilderness and feel at home.
> Bamboos and plums don't fail a gentleman.
> Gibbons and cranes befriend a poor recluse.[7]

A rebellious and arrogant Confucian scholar, Cao Ba Quat (?–1854),[8] who lived under the Nguyen dynasty, most clearly represented an extremely skeptical attitude toward socially oriented activities, which were regarded as the arena of stupid yet power-hungry officials clustering around the king:

> The self must hide from wind and dust—
> the door is always tightly shut.
> I strive to nurse a simple soul,
> open to images of yore.[9]

Cao Ba Quat's contempt and suspicion of a social life that took the royal court to be its center has been reflected in his refusal to have any relationships with the outside world, claiming that his attention now was focused on the nursing of a "simple soul."

Nguyen Binh Khiem (1491–1587), a well-known Confucian scholar respectfully known as Doctor Trinh (*Trang Trinh*), also shared the idea that a wise person should stay away from sociopolitical arenas, where misfortune could strike at any moment and where one could not distinguish truth from falsity:

> From the realms of glory and renown let us stay aloof, with arms folded.
> Already time and again have I escaped from the disaster that strikes without warning.
> The plum-blossom gleams silver in the moonlight;
> The shadows of the bamboos stirring in the wind are like lace.
> It is not that I forget the old feelings of patriotism and devotion to the Prince,
> But in matters of today I shrink from deciding between true and false.
> I have traveled over all the mountains and rivers:
> How many perilous places there are in the world![10]

Differences between Chinese and Vietnamese Confucian attitudes toward the social world, however, need not be overemphasized. In Neo-Confucian texts, passages can also be found urging the maintenance of personal integrity against a corrupt social system:

> Master Ch'eng's commentary says, "If one is not at ease with his usual poverty and humble station, his advance will be motivated by greed and solicitous desire. When the great man is obstructed, he upholds his integrity and does not mix with bad people. Although he is obstructed from attaining his proper station, the Way flourishes.

> What the superior man regards as adornment, popular society regards as shame, but what popular society regards as honorable, the superior man regards as lowly. Therefore it is said, "One adorns his feet. He discards a carriage and walks on foot."[11]

Distinctive Features of Vietnamese Confucianism

One of the most distinctive features of Vietnamese spirituality is that it expressed itself most fully in poetry. While Confucian scholars in China, Korea, and Japan were busy writing commentaries on Confucian classics, Vietnamese Confucians dedicated their intellectual energy to the articulation of their innermost spirituality in poetic language.[12] Therefore, the study of the "simple soul," another expression of the Vietnamese people's inner spirituality, inevitably involves the study of traditional Vietnamese poetry itself. When discussing Chan Buddhism in medieval Vietnam, Cuong Tu Nguyen also comments on this characteristic feature in negative terms:

> In Vietnam it is the romantic and heroic atmosphere in Zen literature that appears to be the most attractive element. As I have mentioned above, most learned Vietnamese monks at some point would emulate the Chinese Zen patriarchs and compose Zen poetry or sayings to express their romantic expressions.[13]

Another distinctive feature of Vietnamese Confucian spirituality is that it has always been a multivocal phenomenon, that is, a voice that made no distinction among Confucianism, Buddhism, and Daoism. In 1760, on the occasion of renovating a Buddhist temple in village Kim Bang, appropriately called the Temple of the Three Teachings (*chua Tam Giao*), Ngo Thoi Si (1726–1780), a Confucian scholar, wrote a stele inscription expressing the unity of Confucian ethics of humanity and social obligations, Buddhist doctrine of compassion, and Daoist notions of purity:

> The Buddha preaches compassion, Taoists advocate purity and quietude, and Confucians use humaneness, righteousness, loyalty, and integrity to help people understand the cosmic cardinal principles and thereby enable them to establish a human order. It is essential to integrate the world of phenomena (*van huu*) into the world of unified emptiness (*nhat hu*) and synthesize all varieties into a unity.[14]

For the Vietnamese, there were no contradictions among religions in general and among the Three Teachings in particular. All spiritual teachings were considered different roads leading to inner self-transformation. Being a Confucian sage (*thanh*), a Buddha (*Phat*), or a Daoist immortal (*tien*), required a purification of heart and mind, which had been hitherto wallowing in the muds of excessive lust, hatred, and ignorance, and a transformation from ordinary humanity (*pham nhan*) into spiritually pure beings (*nhung ca the tam linh trong sach*). Self-cultivation in the Confucian tradition, as Tu Weiming has pointed out, is predicated on the perfectibility of human nature.[15] The Vietnamese completely endorse this position. However, while Chinese Confucianism emphasized that this Confucian project of self-cultivation can be implemented only in a predominantly social context (family, state, society),[16] Vietnamese Confucianism was committed to the view that such a project should be realized in conjunction with Buddhism and Daoism, which were basically oriented to the individual rather than the larger society. In other words, the Confucian project in the Vietnamese context might be, and usually was, implemented independently of socialized conventional norms.[17]

A further explanation is necessary to clarify this seemingly paradoxical idea. Applying the distinctions made by Ferdinand Tonnies (1855–1936) between the concept of "society" (*Gesellschaft*) and that of "community" (*Gemeinschaft*) to the case of Vietnamese spirituality,[18] I would argue that the Vietnamese people were basically committed to their communally shared interests (*Gemeinschaft*) but usually indifferent to socially sanctioned norms of behavior (*Gesellschaft*). Tu Weiming, when he was attending a Confucian workshop in Vietnam in 1997, was surprised to discover that the concept of "ritualized behavior" (*li*), the main pillar of the Confucian structure, played no role at all in the Vietnamese system of ethical reasoning. Ho Chi Minh changed the five cardinal Confucian virtues (humanness, righteousness, ritualized behavior, knowledge, and trustworthiness) into humaneness (*nhan*), righteousness (*nghia*), knowledge (*tri*), bravery (*dung*), and honesty (*liem*).[19] From the Vietnamese perspective, which might be influenced by neighboring Southeast Asian cultures, rites (*li*) usually were seen in a negative light. *Li* was interpreted as a set of mechanically performed behaviors for form's sake only, not as expressions of sincere respect for communally sanctioned moral standards. Objections to this meaning of rites did not mean that the Vietnamese people did not possess a moral consciousness; they just revealed the fact that the Vietnamese did not wholeheartedly embrace the Chinese ideal of rites.[20] Mouzi, a Confucian scholar who took refuge in Vietnam at the end of the second century and may have been influenced by Vietnamese culture, also offered a critical view of Confucian rites by pointing out cases in which Confucian sages did not observe "the right thing to do." He emphasized that flexibility must be the essence of human action:

> According to the Five Classics the proper thing to do is to take the eldest son of the legal wife as heir. Yet King T'ai, seeing Ch'ang's firmness of character, made the youngest son heir. Thus he completed the work of the Duke of Chou and brought about peace. The right thing to do when taking a wife is to inform one's parents. Yet Shun married without telling [his parents] and established the great relationship [of husband and wife]. An upright scholar must be invited to serve. An illustrious minister waits to be summoned. Yet Yi Yin sought to attend T'ang with his pots, and Ning Ch'i knocked on the horns [of his ox] to get the attention of the Duke of Ch'i. As a result T'ang won the throne and the Duke of Ch'i gained hegemony. According to the proprieties there should be no intimate contact between men and women. But if one's sister-in-law is drowning, to grab her by the hand is to act with discretion in accord with the exigency of the moment. If you see the whole,

you would not be trapped in the minutiae. How could a great man be bound by the ordinary rules?[21]

Two other Confucian concepts, humaneness and righteousness, however, played a significant role in shaping Vietnamese moral discourse. For Nguyen Trai, the idea of humaneness was concretized into the love of one's own country (*long ai quoc*). The concept of righteousness, in Nguyen Trai's view, was transformed into the idea that some action should be done in a specific situation and the question of appropriate moral action should be completely determined by oneself, not by an external set of moral rules or norms. In a specific context, such as war, righteousness meant struggle to protect one's own country and defeat invaders.[22] A historian, Tran Van Giau, asserts that Confucianism in Vietnam might be simply interpreted as patriotism.[23] The identification of Confucianism and patriotism not only reveals a fundamentally political agenda but also distorts the whole substance of Vietnamese moral sense.[24] Nguyen Ngoc Huy correctly points out that Nguyen Trai's ideas of humaneness (*nhan*) and righteousness (*nghia*) were "not seriously at variance with the ethic of Buddhism which had been so much a part of Vietnamese culture up to that point."[25] Le Manh That, in a study of Mouzi, convincingly argues that the Confucian concept of humaneness in the Vietnamese cultural context was interpreted as love and care, not only for one's own family, but also for everyone, an idea strongly reminiscent of the Buddhist concept of compassion (*karuna*).[26]

Tran Van Giau also lists several important differences between Chinese and Vietnamese Confucianism: (1) Chinese Confucianism did not preach patriotism, while Vietnamese Confucianism inherited a patriotic tradition from the time of Hung kings; (2) Vietnamese Confucianism glorified the virtue of bravery so much that five Confucian virtues were reduced to four, namely, humaneness (which was synonymous with love of common people), righteousness (which was identified with patriotism), knowledge, and bravery; (3) Vietnamese Confucianism did not adopt the idea of "universal peace" (*ping tianxia*) as expressed in the *Great Learning*; (4) Chinese Confucianism emphasized the idea of the Mandate of Heaven, but Vietnamese Confucianism downplayed this idea and emphasized the determining factor of human power.[27]

Differences between Chinese and Vietnamese Confucianism were not as sharp as Tran Van Giau has claimed. The idea of heroic bravery, for example, runs through *Mencius* and embodies itself in the image of the "great hero" (*da zhangfu*), whom "wealth cannot corrupt, poverty cannot change, and force cannot subdue" (*fu gui bu neng yin, pin jian bu neng yi, wei wu bu neng qu*) (*Mencius* 3:2). The phrase "bringing about universal peace" (*ping tian xia*) was not removed from the text of the *Great Learning* as used in Vietnam's traditional examination system, which means that no Confucian scholar intentionally set up a different ideology from Chinese Confucianism.[28] The view that Vietnamese Confucianism emphasized human power at the expense of the Mandate of Heaven (which was erroneously interpreted by Tran Van Giau as a form of fatalism) should be relied on with caution. Le Quy Don (1726–1784), the greatest Confucian scholar in the eighteenth century, asserted:

> Heavenly affairs, though quiet and calm, take place prominently. Heaven's mandates are infrequent, but things small and big are all predetermined. Fatalism has been mentioned by ancient sages. Those which we have read in Classics and Histories about kings and commoners, whether in terms of dreams, divinations, or children's songs show that they seem at first blush mysterious but effective in the end, because fate is also principle.[29]

It should be emphasized in this connection that, although the Vietnamese people were successful in escaping from Chinese domination and protecting their own self-identity, the intellectual elites usually looked up to China as a cultural model. History books, literary works, legal institutions, religious ideas, all were modeled after Chinese counterparts. The most important differences between the two worldviews, Chinese and Vietnamese, were reflected not in the realm of the written signs (*van tu*) but in the realm of inner spirituality (*tam linh*). Here all the factors of Confucianism, Buddhism, and Daoism came into play and blended into a syncretic attitude toward transcendent reality and one's day-to-day activities in the world.

Kim Dinh has summarized the main features of Vietnamese Confucianism as follows: (1) the centrality of spirituality in intellectual life; (2) an ontology founded on the continuity of Heaven, Man, and Earth (*tam tai*); (3) a philosophy of life grounded in anthropocracy (*nhan chu*), that is, a middle way between theocracy (*thien chu*) and democracy (*dia chu*); (4) ancestor worship as the foundation of religious feeling; (5) a social philosophy built on the basis of family.[30] In close examination, however, we cannot detect any feature that had not also figured prominently in Chinese Confucianism. Kim Dinh's insistence on the centrality of spirituality in Vietnamese intellectual life, however, has underscored an important feature of both Vietnamese and Chinese Confucianism. His idea of Confucian-oriented anthropocracy, which is admittedly very intriguing, should have been developed on the basis of a detailed investigation of the Confucian self, an undertaking that would clarify better the deficiencies both in a theocratic state and a democratic society.

The Heart-mind (tam) in Vietnamese Confucianism

When using the binome *tam linh* (literally, "heart-mind and spirit") to refer to their own inner spirituality, the Vietnamese have underlined a close linkage between human cognitive-affective faculty (*tam*) and a transcendent reality (*linh*).[31] This transcendent reality exists independently of mundane realities and can be accessed only by a special cognitive-affective ability called "*tam.*" *Tam* is a word whose meaning has been culturally rooted in the syncretism of Confucianism, Buddhism, and Daoism and has played an important role in Vietnamese moral consciousness. Nguyen Du (1765–1820), the greatest poet of Vietnam, concludes his well-known story with the following line:

> The root of goodness has been implanted in our heart-mind (*long*). One's heart-mind (*tam*) is three times more valuable than one's talent (*Thien can o tai long ta. Chu tam kia moi bang ba chu tai*).[32]

Nguyen Du, like most Vietnamese intellectuals, looked at the human heart-mind as something completely subjective and internalized, a view that was akin to Lu Xiangshan's idea that "the universe is my mind" (*yu zhou bian shi wu xin*).[33] Nguyen Du's idealist position on moral issues reflected the fact that in the Vietnamese traditional discourse, socially sanctioned norms of behavior and intellectual pursuits did not earn high respect. "Talent" (*tai*) in Vietnamese discourse might have a broad range of meaning, but it basically referred to success in mastering academic or intellectual learning. Kieu, in this story, was a well-educated woman who mastered the four basic skills of traditional learning, namely, music (*cam*) chess (*ky*), poetry (*thi*), and painting (*hoa*). However, circumstances had reduced her to the status of a prostitute. Nguyen Du, thus, meant to say that on the basis of her heart-mind (*tam*) Kieu was still a pure and morally perfect woman. From an external point of view she was at the lowest rung of the social ladder; but from an internal self-understanding she deserved respect for her unsullied heart-mind. All her intellectual skills did not lend her any assistance. On the contrary, it is those skills, coupled with her charming beauty, that forced her to go through the ordeal of prostitution. The emphasis on intellectual learning, as advocated by Zhu Xi,[34] was totally rejected by Nguyen Du in favor of a Buddhist-oriented cognitive-affective function (*tam*) that was established as a transsocial and deep-rooted sense of spirituality.

It is interesting and appropriate in this connection to return to the question of poetic predominance in the East Asian tradition in general and in the Vietnamese cultural heritage in particular. Kim Dinh, the late professor of Confucian philosophy at Saigon Faculty of Letters (before 1975), defended this love of poetry in the Confucian tradition on the grounds that only the voice of poetry could succeed in expressing human nature, which is essentially rooted in emotion rather than rationality. He also argued that poetry was the favorite form of philosophical discourse in the East Asian tradition, whose essence was simplicity and practicality, in contrast to the argumentative form of Western philosophy, which abounded in complexities and abstractions.[35] Kim Dinh's observation can be supported by the fact that the Western form of philosophical discourse was almost nonexistent in the East Asian tradition. The fact that such a form did not exist or figure prominently in East Asian cultures does not imply that East Asian peoples did not possess a philosophical sense or awareness. The argument, however, that human nature was grounded in emotions, which was usually understood as a subjective state from which rational cognition was completely excluded, should be abandoned for a better understanding of the role of poetry in the Vietnamese tradition. Robert Solomon has argued that emotions are in fact normative judgments; that is, they are not completely irrational and are also liable to rational evaluations.[36] Nguyen Du used the term *tam* in this sense, that is, a spiritual faculty that could produce perfectly correct normative judgments in specific tension-riddled situations. The best means that could be used to talk about such a faculty was poetry, which fictionalized a situation so that it could philosophize about it in its distinctive way. "The choice of fantasy fiction as a way of making truth claims," says Francisca Cho Bantly, "inherently recognizes that the truth-value of fiction does not lie in its referentiality to external realities."[37] Nguyen Du's poeticized truth claims, in this view, can be objectively validated not by their reference to external facts but by an inner self-examination to discover the "root of goodness implanted in one's heart-mind."

It is also in this literary masterpiece that a reversal of Confucian-oriented ritualized behavior (*li*) was presented as something natural and morally acceptable. Thuy Kieu, the heroine of the story, was a beautiful, talented, and well-educated woman who fell in love with Kim Trong, a Confucian scholar, at their first meeting. She then came to see him in his studio, an action that both she and Kim Trong found completely natural. Kieu went so far as to agree in the next meeting to be Kim Trong's wife without consulting her parents. This natural impulsiveness had an unsettling impact on many Confucian scholars, such as Huynh Thuc Khang and Ngo Duc Ke, who regarded Thuy Kieu's behavior as completely counter to the established norms of morality. The redeeming feature in Kieu's character was her *tam*, which was described as compassionate, sympathetic understanding, and just simply love.[38] Nguyen Du has emphasized the value of this cognitive-affective function at the expense of ritualized moral behavior.

This story illustrates the fact that the downplaying of the value of ritualized behavior was not Ho Chi Minh's creation in his attempt to establish a Vietnamese ethical system on a new basis; it had been around for a long time before it was formulated in his thoughts. Moreover, great Chinese Neo-Confucian thinkers also objected to sets of ritualized behavior performed mechanically for form's sake only. They insisted that rites be observed in full sincerity. Zhu Xi (1130–1200) quoted his master, Cheng Hao (1032–1085), as saying, "Let one reduce his concern with external matters. If he only understands the good and advances in his sincerity, even if he does not hit the mark of ceremonies and institutions, he will not be far from it."[39] It seems, however, that in practice few Confucian scholar-officials paid heed to Zhu Xi's and his master's giving priority to sincerity (*cheng*) over mechanically ritualized behavior (*li*).[40]

The Unity of the Three Teachings
(*tam giao dong nguyen*)

The idea of *tam giao dong nguyen* (literally, "three teachings are of the same original source) was a long-established cultural construct in Vietnamese intellectual-spiritual history. It was really embodied in the religious doctrine of Caodaism, a syncretistic religion established in South Vietnam in 1926.[41] As a matter of fact, the idea that all roads to ultimate enlightenment as expressed in Confucianism, Buddhism, and Daoism were equally valid also came from China, perhaps under the Yuan dynasty (thirteenth century). The difference from the Chinese synthesis is that Daoism in Vietnam was usually identified with folk-religion professionals (geomancers, thaumaturges, diviners, fortune-tellers, astrologers, physiognomists, and so on). Laozi's ideas and Zhuangzi's deconstructive philosophy were usually assimilated to the Buddhist ontology of emptiness (*sunyata*) and thus did not receive a serious separate treatment like Confucianism. In China, Buddhism had to wear the Daoist garb and speak Daoist language for a long time to be accepted by Chinese society. In Japan, Buddhism had to do the same thing with Shinto to earn the right to coexist.

In Vietnam, however, the situation was quite the opposite: Daoism and even Confucianism had to accommodate themselves to Buddhism. Though never an official state ideology, Buddhism, with its doctrine of *karma*, *samsara*, *nirvana*, and *sunyata*, became a preexisting fabric into which the threads of Daoism and Confucianism were woven. Two key Confucian concepts, humaneness and righteousness, which were identified with the Buddhist doctrine of universal compassion, have come to play a significant role in the shaping of Vietnamese moral consciousness and spiritual development. Another concept, which was philosophically more sophisticated, was the cognitive-affective function called *tam*. *Tam* is the meeting point of the Three Teachings. Laozi spoke of "the heart-mind of a newborn baby" (*chi zi zhi xin*). Confucianism emphasized the "rectification of the heart-mind" (*zhengxin*). Buddhism preached "the cultivation of the mind" (*xinxue*). All seemed to converge on the idea that the heart-mind symbolizes an inborn nature that was originally pure and good but needed to be nurtured with care and cultivated with diligence for its full blossoming. If clouded and overlaid by self-centered desires, this heart-mind cannot function properly. Lo Qinshun (1465–1547), a Neo-Confucian scholar, offered an appropriate definition of the human heart-mind that would be totally endorsed by all Vietnamese Confucians:

> The human mind has pure spirituality as its substance. Originally it is all-compassing. It is only that it is blinded by the selfishness of egotism and thus it is clear about what is near at hand and vague about what is distant.[42]

This emphasis on the role of the heart-mind might be the result of the influence of Chinese Neo-Confucianism on fifteenth-century Vietnamese culture. We know that although Confucianism was introduced very early to Vietnam (between the first and the second century C.E.), it became a dominant discourse and ideology only under the Le dynasty (fifteenth century), and the form of Confucianism that was officially adopted by the state then was Neo-Confucianism.[43] Zhu Xi's emphasis, however, on intellectual and rational investigation of things did not meet with enthusiasm among the intellectual elites, who seemed to embrace, unbeknownst to themselves, Lu Xiangshan's and Wang Yangming's (1472–1529) idealist position[44] that the source of ultimate spiritual reality and moral consciousness should be sought not in the external world of objectivities but in the inner world of subjectivity. This moral idealism was espoused mainly because of the impact of Chan Buddhism on all aspects of Vietnamese spiritual and intellectual life.

It is appropriate in this context to introduce the most important historical record of Vietnamese Chan Buddhism in the fourteen century, *Thien Uyen Tap Anh*.[45] One of the key themes of the *Thien Uyen Tap Anh* (Biographies of Eminent Chan Masters) is the peaceful and mutually beneficial relationship between Buddhism, understood as a religion transcending all worldly concerns, and Confucianism, seen as the best system of social ethics, personal cultivation, and political science of control. This relationship was most explicitly expressed in the biographies of Van Hanh, Khuong Viet, and Vien Thong. Van Hanh (?–1025), in the role of a prophet, helped with the birth of a new dynasty (Ly dynasty). Khuong Viet (933–1011), as national preceptor to King Dinh Tien Hoang, contributed significantly to the defeat of a Song invasion. In addition, he assisted in the peaceful diplomatic relations between China (under the Song dynasty) and Vietnam (under the Dinh dynasty). Vien Thong (1080–1151), as national preceptor to King Ly Nhan Tong, outlined the whole project of government on the basis of Confucian ethics. He said:

> Peace or disorder all depends on people. If officials could win the people's heart, there would be peace. If they lose the people's heart, there would be disorder. Having observed all the previous reigns, I venture to say that no reign that did not use *junzi* (*quan tu* = good people) could be successful, no reign that did not use *xiaoren* (*tieu nhan* = bad people) could decline and fall. The cause of prosperity or decline was not immediate but has been latent so far from the beginning. Like the weather, it cannot immediately turn cold or hot; it has to go gradually from spring to fall and so on. A king cannot make his empire prosper or decline overnight. This should happen gradually, from day to day, depending on the accumulation of his good or bad karma. Kings in ancient times realized this, so they followed the Way of Heaven to cultivate themselves incessantly and followed the Way of Earth to promote virtue so that people could be in peace.[46] Self-cultivation must be carefully conducted like walking on thin ice. Control of people must be respectfully conducted like riding a horse with a set of worn-out reins. (*TUTA* 68b 5)

In this advice to the king, Vien Thong skillfully wove together the three threads of the Buddhist theory of karmic rewards and retributions, the Confucian art of governing people, and the *Book of Change*'s metaphysics of the Triad (Heaven, Earth, and Humans). Good kings should model themselves after Heaven and Earth in their governance of people because ontologically they are in the same status as Heaven and Earth.[47] They should not be so shortsighted that only immediate causes of prosperity or decline are attended to. These causes have been planted a long time before, even in numerous previous lives. The seminal causes might be good or bad. If they were good, the king's empire would prosper; if they were bad, his empire would go down. This is, however, not fatalism. The king could improve the situation by his own self-cultivation and authentic love for his people. The Buddhist theory of *karma*, which was used in this case to account for the empire's prosperity or decline, was connected to the Confucian practice-oriented ethics of self-transformation by virtue. Love for people in Vien Thong's thought was nothing more than the Buddhist compassion that had been contextualized.

Nguyen Lang comments on the syncretism of the Three Teachings during the Ly and Tran dynasties as follows:

> Zen Masters under the Lû dynasty not only supported the harmonious unity of the Three teachings (*tam giao hoa hop*) but also encouraged the Ly leadership to follow this path. All the Ly kings were Buddhists. The educational system under the Ly dynasty, guided by such a spirit, created many intellectual generations whose mind was open and undogmatic. The first examination in the Three Teachings was held in the Ly age. Under the Tran dynasty, those kings who were well-versed in Buddhism like Tran Thai Tong and Tran Thanh Tong continued to espouse this liberal attitude, expanding the influence of Confucianism. Thai Tong proposed the idea of "the division of labor on the basis of mutual co-operation between the Buddha and the Sage" (*Phat Thanh phan cong hop tac*). The king had the statue of Zhou Gong, Confucius, and Mencius built for worship and the National Learning Institute (*Quoc Hoc Vien*) set up in the capital for the indoctrination of Confucianism. Tran Ich Tac, Thanh Tong's brother, also encouraged the establishment of schools for the instruction of Confucianism [. . .]. In 1227, that is, less than two years after his coming to the throne, King Thai Tong had the examination in the Three Teachings organized for the first time under the dynasty.[48]

Chan Master Huong Hai, the author of *Su ly dung thong* [The Interpenetration of Principle and Practicality], composed the following poem to express the unity of the Three Teachings:

> As regards the most outstanding teachings, there are three.
> Confucianism supports the state, rectifies the family, and rules people.
> Taoism helps nurture the vital energy and stabilize the spirit.
> Buddhism saves sentient beings from three ways of suffering.[49]

As a matter of fact, although all Chan Masters in the *Biographies* without exception promoted the idea of the syncretism of the Three Teachings, they always made a hierarchical distinction: the ultimate way of salvation must be Buddhism. Confucianism was perceived as the embodiment of Buddhist philosophy in the realm of practice-oriented social ethics.[50] Some Chinese thinkers, while they upheld the idea of syncretism, reversed the order of priority. Jiao Hong (1541–1620) said: "The Buddhist texts are commentaries on Confucianism. The contents of Buddhism are the flowers of Confucianism."[51] Tri Thien, a Chan master who passed the highest royal examination and was appointed to a high-ranking position, after listening to a lecture on the *Diamond Sutra*, sighed and said:

The Buddha's teaching must certainly be not empty words. All worldly phenomena are just illusory and unreal. Only the Way is real. What else do I wish for? While Confucianism talks about the Way of the king and his subjects, the Way of father and son, Buddhism talks about the merits of Sravakas and Bodhisattvas. Two religions, though different, can be traced back to the same source. But if one really wants to transcend the suffering of birth and death and overcome the attachment either to being or non-being, only Buddhism can help one achieve that. (*TUTA* 63b 7)

One of the most popular sutras that Buddhist monks in China, Japan, and Vietnam enjoyed quoting when they wanted to specify the relationships between Confucianism and Buddhism was *Renwang jing* (The Sutra for Benevolent Kings).[52] Chan master Minh Tri specialized in lecturing on this sutra (*TUTA* 26b 3). The sutra describes the Buddha's giving some advice to benevolent kings who wished to protect their kingdoms in the Apocalypse of Buddhist Dharma, so the intended audience of this sutra was not monks and nuns but kings, especially "benevolent kings" (*renwang*), a specifically Confucian concept. In this scripture a king is in a cooperative relationship with *arhats* and *bodhisattvas*.[53] In the Buddhist view, the secular realm of Confucianism-based kingship would belong to the realm of conventional reality, which must be transcended to achieve the highest level of spiritual transformation: enlightenment and becoming the Buddha.

The final work to be discussed is King Tran Thai Tong's *Essays on Emptiness* (*Khoa Hu Luc*). This work, in the Vietnamese traditional estimation, has been unanimously regarded as the masterpiece of Buddhist philosophy. Its important position in both Vietnamese Buddhism and Vietnamese culture has never been questioned by any scholar.[54] From a historical perspective, it symbolizes the climax of a long evolution of Buddhist philosophy in Vietnam and coincides with a golden age of political unity, peace, and security (the Tran dynasty, 1225–1400). From a cultural point of view, it gives an unambiguous presentation of syncretic tendencies that began with Mouzi's *Removing Doubts* (*Lihuolun*) and have dominated Vietnam's religious-intellectual discourse ever since. The syncretism in Mouzi's *Removing Doubts* was still hierarchically represented: religious Daoism (understood as the techniques of immortality) was dismissed outright, philosophical Daoism (Laozi's ideas) was equated with Buddhism, and Confucianism functioned in a secondary role compared with philosophical Daoism and Buddhism. Syncretic ideas or pronouncements were presented in *Biographies of Eminent Zen Masters* (*Thien Uyen Tap Anh*) in an unsystematic manner and focused on similarities between Confucianism (understood as a system of social ethics) and Buddhism (understood as a theory and technique of enlightenment in Chan sense). Daoism was rarely mentioned. Only in *Essays on Emptiness* do Vietnamese syncretic tendencies find their clearest expression. Syncretism here refers not only to the harmonization of the Three Teachings (Daoism, Confucianism, and Buddhism) but also to the cooperation and compatibility of Chan and Pure Land practices.

The Buddhist-Confucian Syncretism of Tran Thai Tong

The most famous treatise included in the *Essays* is *Preface to a Guide to Chan Buddhism* (*Thien Tong Chi Nam Tu*). This is the best introduction to an in-depth understanding not only of Tran Thai Tong's syncretic ideas but also of the traditional Vietnamese stance toward Buddhism and Confucianism. Because of its importance as this unique document to enable us to grasp King Tran Thai Tong's religious motivation, I will quote at length from the *Preface*:[55]

I think that Buddha-Nature is universal [lit., Buddha-Nature is neither Southern nor Northern, *Phat vo Nam Bac*] so everyone can gain access to it by self-cultivation. As regards human nature, there are people who are born smart, there are people who are born stupid, but all of them are capable of enlightenment. Therefore, the Buddha's teaching is both the means to enlighten sentient beings laboring under illusions, and to point out the way to liberation [lit., to make clear the ways of life and death, *minh sinh tơ chi tiîp kinh gia*]. The former sages' serious responsibility is regulating [affairs] for posterity and offering a role model to future generations. Therefore, the Six Patriarch said: "Former great sages are not different from great [Chan] masters" (*tien dai thanh nhan du dai su vo biet*). Obviously, the Buddha's teaching must rely on [the teachings of Confucian] former sages to be transmitted throughout generations. So, why don't I, as a king, shoulder the responsibility of former sages and propagate the Buddha's teaching? [Lit., Why is it not possible that I take former sages' responsibility to be my responsibility, take the Buddha's teaching to be my teaching? *tram yen kha bat di tien thanh chi nham vi ky chi nham, nga Phat chi giao vi ky chi giao tai?*]

Since, as a child, I began to have understanding of some sort, whenever listening to a Chan master's lecture, I always purified my thoughts and stopped [random] ideas, and deep down felt very calm. I have since then been interested in the Buddha's teaching [lit., the inner teachings, *noi giao*][56] and the study of Chan Buddhism, so I have dedicated myself to the search of a master, being a devoted and honest admirer of the Way. Although the wish to become a Buddhist was latent from the beginning, the real motivation that pushed me to do so [lit., the machine of emotions, *xuc cam chi co*] was not available.

When I was sixteen, my mother passed away [lit., sick of the world, *yem the*], I went into a deep mourning [lit., lying on thatch and using dirt as a pillow, *tam thiem cham tho*], cried so much that blood came oozing from my eyes, and my heart was broken [*khap huyet toi tam*].[57] During this period of mourning, I did not have stomach for anything else. Only a few years later, my father also left the world [lit: continued the death of an empress, *ke nhi yen gia*]. No sooner had suffering for my mother's death not been alleviated than pain for the loss of my father came. I felt confused and sick of everything. I think parental love of children, [as expressed in] nursing, embracing, feeding, caring, is really unlimited and incomparable. Children, even if they tried their best [lit., even if they grind their bones into powder and break their body into small pieces, *phan cot toai than*] can by no means repay a small fraction of this huge debt. Moreover, my father, as the first king of the Tran dynasty, overcame innumerable difficulties to establish the foundation of the dynasty. What is more important is his wise regulation of the country [*king bang*] and salvation of the people [from suffering, *te the*].

Since my father entrusted the throne to me [lit., entrusted the great instrument to me, *di dai khi thu du*] when I was so young, I have always been worried and never felt at ease at all. I told myself: Up above there are no parents to rely on, so I am incapable of meeting the aspirations of those down below. What could I do then? I tried and tried to figure a way out. Would it be best to retreat into the woods and mountains, seeking the teachings of the Buddha so as to understand the secrets of life and death and to repay the debt of my parents' love? My determination was then settled. In 1245, on the night of April 3rd, I got dressed and went to the palace gate, telling the guards that I wanted to go out to investigate public opinion [lit., stealthily overhearing the people's words, *tiem thinh dan ngon*] and observe people's aspirations so that I could understand their suffering. Then there were only a few bodyguards who followed me out. When crossing the river and going towards the west, I told them my true intention. They were all taken back and started crying. The following day, at the time of *mao*, I came to the Dai Than ferry post, close to Mount Pha Lai. Afraid that someone might recognize me, I covered my face with the sleeve when I crossed the river. Then I took a shortcut to go to the mountain. At night I took a rest in Giac Hanh pagoda. At daybreak I continued my journey. After much hardship enroute, my horse refused to advance forward. I left the horse there and walked on, leaning on the cliff. At the time of *mui*, I arrived at Mount Yen Tu. The next morning I climbed up to the top and presented myself to the National Preceptor of Bamboo Groves (*Quoc Su Truc Lam*) who was a great monk residing in that temple.

At the sight of me, the National Preceptor was very happy. He leisurely said: "As an old monk, I've lived in this wilderness for a long time, [so] my bones get hardened and my appearance looks so gaunt, [because] my food is only vegetables and chestnuts, and I drink only spring water, wandering in the woods, my heart floating like a cloud, following the wind to get here. Now Your Majesty leaves the emperor's throne and drops by this wild and rustic place [lit., thinks about the poverty of this wilderness, *tu lam da chi tien*]. "May I know the purpose of your visit?" Hearing his question, I burst into tears, saying, "I am still too young, but my parents hurried to leave the world [lit., suddenly buried the two parents, *kich tang song than*]. As a king, I feel very lonely [lit., Lonely I stand above scholars and people, *co lap si dan chi thuong*], and I do not know where to seek support. Looking back to the royal career of my ancestors and its vicissitudes [lit., rising and declining are not permanent, *hung phe bat thuong*], I decided to come over to this place. My only wish is to become a Buddha. I don't want anything else." The National Preceptor replied: "In the mountains there is no Buddha. The Buddha is in the Mind. If the Mind is calm and wise, it is the real Buddha. Now if Your Majesty is awakened to this Mind, you become a Buddha right away. You don't have to look for [the Buddha] in the external world.[58]

It is interesting to note some similarities between Sakyamuni's religious motivation and Tran Thai Tang's. Sakyamuni was a prince and a future king, and he left his royal palace at night on his horse, accompanied only by a loyal servant. He did not inform the servant of his true intention until the last minute. Tran Thai Tong did the same thing, or he might try to frame his story in the same model: a king leaving his throne for some lofty purpose or in pursuit of intellectual liberation. Tran Thai Tong implied in this self-presentation that, like the founder of Buddhism, he was also born with the special gift of religious sympathy and understanding. He explicitly said that as a child whenever he listened to a Chan master he immediately "purified his thoughts and stopped all random ideas" [*trung tu tuc lu*]. This was an ability that few practitioners of meditation could master even after a long time of devoted practice. Sakyamuni left his palace basically because of his perception of the fact that existence had been rooted in suffering as expressed in limit-situations (Karl Jaspers's terms) such as birth, senility, sickness, and death. Tran Thai Tong left his throne also because of his confusion at the mystery of death. The similarity, however, ended there. We should pay special attention to Tran Thai Tong's conscious motivation that pushed him on the way to seek religious liberation: he would like to repay the huge debt of love that he owed his parents. His motivation to become a Buddhist monk sprang from Confucian roots (filial piety). He said: "Would it be best to retreat into the woods and the mountains, to seek the teachings of the Buddha so as to understand the secrets of life and death and to repay the debt of parental love?" (*Bat nhu thoai xu son lam, bang cau Phat Giao, di minh sinh tu chi dai su, huu di bao cu lao chi duc, bat diec my tai?*)

The connection between Confucianism and Buddhism, in point of fact, has been established from the beginning of the *Preface*. Tran Thai Tong asserted: "The Buddha's teachings must rely on the former [Confucian] sages' [teachings] to be transmitted throughout generations" (*nga Phat chi giao, huu gia tien thanh di truyen u the da*). In this case, Tran Thai Tong assigned two different functions to two teachings. Buddhism served as a kind of metaphysics that helped to clarify the mystery of life and death or a technique that enabled ignorant people to become enlightened. Confucianism served as a kind of social ethics that established norms and standards for subsequent generations to use as a model. After making clear the two different functions of Buddhism and Confucianism, Tran Thai Tong took a step further, claiming that he himself was the embodiment of the two teachings. His responsibility as a king required him to adopt Confucian ethics, but his religious motivation urged him to take Buddhism as a philosophy of life and death. Yet he wanted to make sure there was no contradiction between metaphysics and social ethics, so he gave an additional reason for the adoption of Buddhism, namely, to carry out a Confucian ethical obligation (filial piety).

Like all Confucian scholars in China, Tran Thai Tong would face the same objection usually raised against Buddhism, namely, that Buddhism was an antifamilial and antisocial religion that was diametrically opposed to Confucianism, which was basically family-oriented.[59] Bernard Faure observes:

> From a Chinese perspective in particular, the apparent lack of filial piety of the Buddha raised serious issues. In response to this criticism, Chinese Buddhists worked hard to assert a typically Buddhist form of filial piety: the Buddha even went to heaven, we are told, to preach the Dharma to his mother. He also took good care of his father: tradition has it that when King Suddhodana died, the Buddha and his half-brother Nanda were at his pillow, and Ananda and Rahula were at his feet. At the time of the funeral, the Buddha is said to have shouldered his father's coffin.[60]

Mouzi, in his defense of Buddhism, chooses to broaden the concept of filial piety. He feels that universal compassion and love of all sentient beings are the best way to repay the debt of parental love. This is because the blessings accumulated from such an excellent action would be more than enough to compensate for what the parents have done on behalf of their children. Tran Thai Tong engaged himself in a similar line of reasoning. He felt that leaving his family and becoming a monk was the best way to meet the demands of filial obligation. Viewed from this perspective, the issue of accommodation turns out to be not a defense of Buddhism but ultimately a defense of Confucianism itself. Even Lin Zhaoen, the Ming thinker advocating the Unity of Three Teachings, "revealed a Confucian commitment in his *Sanjiao heyi dazhi* (the Meaning of Uniting the Three Teachings), when he stated that he used the concept of *sanjiao heyi* 'to Confucianize the Daoists and Buddhists, and broaden Confucianism to its fullest extent'; or as he said further on, 'to cause the Daoists and Buddhists to return to Confucianism.'"[61] King Tran Thai Tong in his *Preface* did the same thing as Lin Zhaoen, namely, "broaden Confucianism to its fullest extent" to include Buddhism and eliminate all discrepancies between "a theory of life and death" and a "social ethics of norms and standards."

Tran Thai Tong's hermeneutics of relations between Confucianism and Buddhism, however, advanced to a more sophisticated level than Mouzi's. Inheriting a long-established tradition of Chan Buddhism, Tran Thai Tong could resolve intellectual or moral contradictions between the two teachings by resorting to Chan theory of Mind as expressed in his national preceptor's advice: "There is no Buddha in the mountains. The Buddha is in the Mind" (*son ban vo Phat duy ton ho tam*). In other words, it is not, theoretically and practically, necessary for a person to lead a monk's life in a monastic context to be enlightened and become a Buddha. The duties and responsibilities of kingship would not prevent him from reaching for Buddhahood and enlightenment, because he was already a Buddha, at least potentially. The idea that everyone was born with Buddha-nature, therefore, played an important role in shaping Tran Thai Tong's hermeneutical solution of the tensions between Confucianism and Buddhism.[62]

Discussing Chinese Buddhism from a Freudian perspective, Alan Cole offers a very interesting thesis on the Chinese Buddhist concept of filial piety. He argues that, if Confucian ethics of filial piety is father-centered, the Buddhist conceptualization of filial obligation is mother-based:

> The traditional version of filial piety, as found in the Confucian canon, took the father-son dyad as the primary relationship in the family. While the son owed a debt of care and respect to both parents, his identity and his primary allegiances were to be formed around his father. Thus, for the Confucians, a son's sense of self-origin was tied to his father and his patrilineal ancestors, with little mention of his connection to his mother. Buddhist writers challenged this arrangement by redefining filial piety so that it reflected the importance of the mother-son relationship.[63]

On the basis of this interpretation, I argue that Tran Thai Tong shows his father-centered ethics of filial repayment very clearly in the way he was worried about how to continue his father's royal career.[64] He mourned the death of both his parents, but all his attention was focused on how to maintain the inheritance from his father. In Cole's words, "his identity and his primary allegiances were formed around his father."[65] To construct an identity of kingship was Tran Thai Tong's primary concern. In terms of his own interpretation, this was the religious motivation that forced him into a search for enlightenment and illumination from Buddhism. This kind of Buddhism, however, was, also in his own interpretation, not true Buddhism, because true Buddhism was Chan Buddhism, which claimed that "the Buddha is not in the mountains, but in the Mind." His religious motivation sprang from a practical Confucian father-centered discourse on the ethics of filial obligation that shapes the construction of his own identity as a king. After saying that "there is no Buddha in the mountains," the national preceptor, a Buddhist monk, went on to give a lecture that is completely Confucian in orientation and language:

> Being a king, basically, means taking people's wish to be one's own wish and taking people's mind to be one's own mind (*Pham vi nhan quan gia, di thien ha chi duc vi duc, di thien ha chi tam vi tam*).

At the end of the *Preface* Tran Thai Tong made it clear that the purpose of his writing this *Guide to Chan Buddhism* was "not only instrumental in pointing out the illusions on behalf of future generations" (*phi dac di vi hau the chi me*) but also in "continuing and expanding the works of former [Confucian] sages" (*cai duc ke tien dai thanh nhan chi cong, nhi quang chi da*). The *Preface* ended with such a perfect blend of the two teachings and on such a note of striking modesty. In another essay, *Encouragement for the Rise of Mind* (*Khuyen phat tam van*), the idea of syncretism was repeated in unambiguous terms: "Only deluded people stick to the separation of the Three Teachings; radical enlightenment can help see that they all come from the same Mind" (*Vi minh nhan vong phan tam giao, lieu dac de ngo dong nhat tam* [KHL: 46]).

The combination of Confucianism and Buddhism for the creation of a holistic religious and sociopolitical vision continued to be a great theme of interest in the following ages. Under the Le dynasty, for example, Ngo Thoi Nhiem (1746–1803), a Confucian scholar-official, cooperated with two other Buddhist monks, Hai Au and Hai Hoa, to author a work entitled *Truc Lam Tong Chi Nguyen Thanh* (The Original Sound of the Truc Lam Chan School's Essential Teaching), which proposed the unity of Neo-Confucianism (*Ly hoc*) and Chan Buddhism. Hai Hoa wrote: "Elucidation of the deep meaning of Principle (*Ly*) and opening the gate to the Mind (*tam*) are a Zen student's first obligations."[66] Ngo Thoi Nhiem felt strongly that the Buddhist idea of nonattachment (*vo chap/pha chap*) was the primary *sine qua non* for the application of the Neo-Confucian theory of principle.[67]

Conclusion

The evolution of Confucianism in Vietnamese culture was a long and tortuous process. Although it was introduced by Chinese ruling officials between the first and second centuries, Confucianism did not play any significant role in the shaping of Vietnamese spiritual identity until the fifteenth century, when it was officially espoused by the government as the orthodox ideology. During the whole process, Confucianism had to carry out an extensive dialogue with Buddhism, a religion long-established in the Vietnamese tradition, and to accommodate itself to some prominent Buddhist concepts. Daoism, which arrived in Vietnam at nearly the same time as Confucianism and Buddhism, performed a special function in contrast to that of Confucianism. It was the loser's philosophy in traditional Vietnam. Whenever a Confucian official was dismissed, justly or unjustly, from his position in the governing system, he would turn to Daoism as a spiritual consolation. Laozi's and Zhuangzi's philosophy, expressed in Vietnamese traditional poetry as love of nature and freedom from worldly concerns and constraints, became then a spiritual resource from which those who failed in the Confucian-oriented system could draw an inner strength and construct a new orientation to the world, their own self, and the surrounding society. Buddhism provided the Vietnamese people with a basic ontological structure to think about the world in terms of karmic retribution and eternal cycles of rebirth. This was so that people might prepare themselves for the next life by purifying their heart-mind and performing morally good deeds. Confucianism, in addition to being a way to social advancement through intellectual training, provided a practical ethics of interpersonal relationships that has gradually become, in conjunction with Buddhism, an integral part of Vietnamese moral-spiritual identity. Neo-Confucian theory of the heart-mind also enabled the intellectuals to handle, to a great extent, relationships between Buddhist philosophy and Confucian ethics and to effect a synthesis of the Three Teachings. Recent discussions and studies in Vietnam[68] have shown a marked attention to the role of Confucianism in Vietnamese traditional culture, but they are still in the stage of explorative attempts that mainly focus on the historical dimension of Confucianism, not on its role as a spiritual resource of self-transformation or a moral way of life facing the challenge of interpersonal transactions. This essay is an attempt to fill that gap.

My argument is that Confucianism was not separable from Buddhism and Daoism as constituent elements of Vietnamese spirituality. In other words, Vietnamese spirituality was continually nurtured by these three spiritual resources. This Vietnamese spirituality expressed its philosophical ideas through poetic language and manifested itself in the day-to-day practical handling of things and relations. Thus, a historical and textual-based study of this spirituality could hardly reveal anything distinctive about it. A future phenomenological investigation of Vietnamese moral-spiritual consciousness, deeply rooted in the inner subjectivity of the heart-mind, might be the key to a fuller understanding of the multiform nature of Vietnamese spirituality.

Notes

1. O. W. Wolters, "Le Van Huu's Treatment of Ly Than Tong's Reign (1127–1137)," in *Southeast Asian History and Historiography: Essays Presented to D. G. S. Hall,* ed. C. D. Cowan and O. W. Wolters (Ithaca, N.Y.: Cornell University Press, 1976), 203–26.

2. Tu Weiming, "Beyond the Enlightenment Mentality," in *Confucianism and Ecology: The Interrelation of Heaven, Earth, and Humans,* ed. Mary Evelyn Tucker and John Berthrong (Cambridge, Mass.: Harvard University Press, 1998), 15. Tu Weiming has correctly pointed out that Enlightenment mentality should not be identified with the West alone: "The rise of industrial East Asia symbolizes the instrumental rationality of the Enlightenment heritage with a vengeance" (ibid., 7).

3. I take this cue from Robert C. Neville. He suggests the use of orientations as Weberian ideal types in the study of East Asian traditions: "I propose the reconstruction of some parts of the East Asian tradition, especially a certain line of Confucian thinking, so as to define the habitual or ritual part of the self in terms of how the self 1) is oriented towards various orders of reality and 2) integrated those orientations. In this way of thinking, to be a person is to have, as constituent elements of the self, orientations, well or badly formed, to ecological matters as well as to all the other orders of 'ten thousand things'" (Robert C. Neville, "Orientation, Self, and Ecological Posture," in *Confucianism and Ecology,* ed. Tucker and Berthrong, 265).

4. This idea, *imaginaire,* has been taken from Bernard Faure, *Visions of Power: Imagining Medieval Japanese Buddhism* (Princeton, N.J.: Princeton University Press, 2000), 10–11. Faure took this idea from Jacques LeGoff, *The Medieval Imagination,* trans. Arthur Goldhammer (Chicago: University of Chicago Press, 1988). In a nutshell, those scholars who emphasize the primacy of images in their study of a culture engage in the investigation of its *imaginaire.* Those images do not necessarily reflect a preestablished reality. They reflect, however, the way people in a culture look at society, life, the world, etc. Images are neither purely fictive nor completely built on external units of reality.

5. Huynh Sanh Thong, trans. and ed., *The Heritage of Vietnamese Poetry* (New Haven/London: Yale University Press, 1979), 78.

6. Ibid., 73.

7. Ibid., 76.

8. Cao Ba Quat was famous for his arrogance. According to one anecdote, he was said to boast that if there were four baskets of knowledge in the whole world, he had taken two of them. He considered his talent and learning to be superior to those of Confucius, Mencius, the Cheng brothers, and Zhu Xi.

9. Huynh Sanh Thong, *Heritage*, 56.

10. Maurice M. Durand and Nguyen Tran Huan, *An Introduction to Vietnamese Literature*, trans. D. M. Hawke (New York: Columbia University Press, 1985), 72.

11. Zhu Xi and Lu Zuqian, *Reflections on Things at Hand: The Neo-Confucian Anthology*, trans. Wing-Tsit Chan (New York/London: Columbia University Press, 1967), 184–85.

12. Robert C. Neville correctly observed that "East Asian culture has an extraordinarily aesthetic approach to life" ("Orientation, Self, and Ecological Posture," 267). This "aesthetic approach," however, was defined almost exclusively in terms of poetry and, to a lesser extent, painting in China and Japan—almost never in music. The reason might be that, in the Confucian tradition, *The Book of Poetry* (*Shijing*) was one of the classics that was both admired and loved by Vietnamese scholars. Confucius also placed the *Book of Poetry* in high esteem: "Why don't you study poetry? Poetry can elevate one's soul, observe things, assemble people, and express one's resentment" (*Lunyu* 7:9). Truong Tuu, an eminent author in the 1960s, even wrote a book titled *Kinh Thi Viet Nam* (Vietnam's Book of Poetry) to show that Vietnamese identity was mostly shaped by folk songs. He argued, in Shawn McHale's words, that "Confucianism stimulated (*kich thich*) Vietnamese to develop their character" ("Censorship, Memory, and the Reconstruction of the Vietnamese Past, 1920–1945," a paper presented at the meeting of the Association for Asian Studies, Boston, March 1994, p. 14).

13. Cuong Tu Nguyen, *Zen in Medieval Vietnam: A Study and Translation of the Thien Uyen Tap Anh* (Honolulu: University of Hawaii Press, 1997), 98.

14. Le Anh Dung, *Conéng Tam GiỸo VietNam* [The Vietnamese Way of the Three Teachings] (Ho Chi Minh City: Ho Chi Minh City Publishers, 1994), 93–94.

15. This idea can be found in any of Tu Weiming's works. For a brief account of it, see Tu Weiming, "The Confucian Tradition," in *Heritage of China: Contemporary Perspectives on Chinese Civilization*, ed. Paul S. Ropp (Berkeley: University of California Press, 1990), 112–37.

16. Tu Weiming points out that this view was fundamentally shaped by Xunzi: "The Confucian project, as shaped by Hsun Tzu, defines learning as socialization. . . . A cultured person is by definition a fully socialized participant in the human community who has for the public good successfully sublimated his instinctual demands" ("The Confucian Tradition," 121). The Vietnamese Confucian scholar tended to endorse Mencius's view that in bad times the scholar-gentleman (*junzi*) should "walk alone following his Way" (*du xing qi dao*). Xunzi's views did not have any influence on Vietnamese moral and spiritual life.

17. Nguyen Ngoc Huy, relying on John K. Whitmore, writes: "Ming Neo-Confucian scholars also disparaged the Vietnamese when they attempted to colonize the country after the end of the Tran dynasty. One Ming Chinese commentator referred to the Vietnamese as "worthless and cruel," people "who knew neither the rites (*li*) nor righteousness (*i*)" ("The Tradition of Human Rights in Vietnam," *Vietnam Review* 3 [1997]: 35).

18. Ferdinand Tonnies, *Community and Society*, trans. Charles P. Loomis (New York: Harper & Row, 1963).

19. Vu Khieu, *Nho Giao va Phat Trien o Viet Nam* [Confucianism and Development in Vietnam] (Hanoi: Social Sciences Publishers, 1997), 182.

20. John K. Whitmore mentions the fact that Ming Confucian scholars were shocked by the absence of correct rites among the Vietnamese people ("Chiao-chih and Neo-Confucianism: The Ming Attempt to Transform Vietnam," *Ming Studies* [1977]).

21. John P. Keenan, *How Master Mou Removes Our Doubts: A Reader-Response Study and Translation of the Mou-tzu Li-huo-lun* (Albany: State University of New York Press, 1994), 106. Mouzi, though an ex-Confucianist, answered the challenge by distorting the true spirit of Confucian ethics which always emphasized flexibility of action and had never advocated a rigid observance of moral prescriptive rules. Heiner Roetz correctly points out: "To take into account the specificity of situations neither justifies nor necessitates abandoning principles. A principled ethic that knows about responsibility will not only acknowledge that flexibility is needed in the concrete application of its norms, but will even admit the possibility of dramatical circumstances in which certain principles may not be applicable at all" (*Confucian Ethics of the Axial Age* [Albany: State University of New York Press, 1993], 188).

22. Nguyen Hung Hau, "Buoc dau thu dat van de ve dac diem Nho Giao o Viet Nam" [Preliminary Explorations of Vietnamese Confucian Salient Features], *Tap San Khoa Hoc Xa Hoi va Nhan Van* 3 (1997): 118.

23. Tran Van Giau, "Luan cuong ve Nho Giao o Vietnam" [A Treatise on Vietnamese Confucianism], *Tap San Khoa Hoc Xa Hoi va Nhan Van*, 5.

24. Even the idea that patriotism was a distinctive feature of Vietnamese Confucianism is also mistaken and shows a superficial knowledge of Chinese Confucian culture, which did not lack a large body of literary writings devoted to patriotic themes. Wen Tianxiang's *Zhengqi ge* [The Song of Righteousness] in the Song dynasty is one of the most well known examples of Confucian patriotic literature.

25. Nguyen Ngoc Huy, "Tradition of Human Rights," 36.

26. Le Manh That, *Nghien Cuu ve Mau Tu* [A Study of Mouzi] (Ho Chi Minh City: Van Hanh Publishers, 1982), 382–89. Le Manh That also argues that Vietnamese people in Han times deliberately contrasted their "virtue" (*hanh*) with Chinese rites (*li*). This virtue, according to That, was defined completely in Buddhist terms: compassion for everyone.

27. Tran Van Giau, "Luan cuong," 7. The sources for all these ideas, unfortunately, are not provided.

28. In modern times, however, there were some attempts to construct the identity of Vietnamese Confucianism. Truong Tuu, a Northern author, tried to defend the position that the Vietnamese people possessed their own form of Confucianism as embodied in folk songs. See his *Kinh Thi Viet Nam* [Vietnam's Book of Poetry] (Hanoi: Han Thuyen, 1945). Kim Dinh, a professor of Confucian philosophy in Saigon before 1975, boldly asserted that early Confucianism was originally a Vietnamese creation, later adopted and modified by Chinese ideologues. See his *Cua Khong- Nho Giao Nguyen Thuy* [Introduction to Original Confucianism] (Saigon: Ca Dao, 1969).

29. Le Quy Don, *Van Dai Loai Ngu* [A Confucian Encyclopedia], trans. into modern Vietnamese by Pham Vu and Le Hien (Saigon: Mien Nam, 1973), 54.

30. Kim Dinh, *Tinh hoa ngu dien* [The Essentials of the Five Classics] (Saigon: Nguon Sang, 1973), 172.

31. Truong Quoc Dung (1797–1864), a Confucian scholar-official, wrote that spirits were the manifestations of the two generative-transformative forces of *yin* and *yang*. This view had been around for a long time before it was adopted by Vietnamese Confucian scholars in their cosmological explanations.

32. The way Huynh Sanh Thong translates these lines into English does not bring out the prominent role of the heart-mind: "Inside ourselves there lies the root of good: the heart outweighs all the talents on this earth" (Nguyen Du, *The Tale of Kieu*, trans. Huynh Sanh Thong [New Haven: Yale University Press, 1983], 167).

33. For a discussion of Lu Xiangshan's theory of mind, see Tang Junyi, *Zhongguo zhexue yuanlun yuanxing pian* (Hong Kong: New Asia Institute, 1968), 538–52.

34. Zhu Xi was well known for his educational emphasis on the intellectual study of Confucian classics as the primary condition for moral self-cultivation. For a discussion of this theme, see Ying-shih Yó, "Morality and Knowledge in Chu Hsi's Philosophical System," in *Chu Hsi and Neo-Confucianism*, ed. Wing-tsit Chan (Honolulu: University of Hawaii Press, 1986), 228–54.

35. Kim Dinh, *Cua Khong* [Introduction to Confucianism] (Saigon: Tu Sach Ra Khoi Nhan Ai, 1965), 149–74. This book is a collection of the author's lectures at Saigon Faculty of Letters (*Dai hoc Van Khoa Saigon*) in the 1960s.

36. Robert C. Solomon, "The Cross-Cultural Comparison of Emotion," in *Emotions in Asian Thought: A Dialogue in Comparative Philosophy*, ed. Joel Marks and Roger T. Ames (Albany: State University of New York Press, 1995), 253–94.

37. Francisca C. Bantly, *Embracing Illusion: Truth and Fiction in the Dream of the Nine Clouds* (Albany: State University of New York Press, 1996), 152.

38. "*Tam*" is the Sino-Vietnamese equivalent of "*long*," "*noi long*," or "*tam long*."

39. Zhu Xi and Lu Zuqian, *Reflections on Things at Hand*, 49.

40. The question of observing rites was closely tied to relationships that Confucian scholars tried to clarify between "standard" (*jing*) and "expedient" (*quan*). See Wei Cheng-t'ung for a very instructive discussion of this issue, "Chu Hsi on the Standard and the Expedient," in *Chu Hsi and Neo-Confucianism*, ed. Wing-tsit Chan, 255–72.

41. Le Anh Dung, *Lich Su Dao Cao Dai Thoi Ky Tiem An 1920–1926* [The Early History of Caodaism 1920–1926] (Hue: Thuan Hoa Publishers, 1996).

42. Lo Ch'in-shun, *Knowledge Painfully Acquired*, trans. Irene Bloom (New York: Columbia University Press, 1987), 53.

43. See John K. Whitmore, "Chiao-chih and Neo-Confucianism: The Ming Attempt to Transform Vietnam," *Ming Studies* (1977); Nguyen Ngoc Huy, "The Confucian Incursion into Vietnam," in *Confucianism and the Family*, ed. Walter H. Slote and George A. Devos (Albany: State University of New York Press, 1998), 91–102; R. B. Smith, "The Cycle of Confucianization in Vietnam," in *Aspects of Vietnamese History*, ed. Walter F. Vella (Honolulu: University of Hawaii Press, 1973), 1–30.

44. For a discussion of Wang Yangming's idealism, see David S. Nivison, "The Philosophy of Wang Yangming," in *The Ways of Confucianism: Investigations in Chinese Philosophy*, ed. Bryan W. Van Norden (Chicago/La Salle, Ill.: Open Court, 1996), 217–47.

45. This has been translated and studied by Cuong Tu Nguyen, *Zen in Medieval Vietnam*. This work will be cited in the text as *TUTA*.

46. Robert Eno has discussed "Xunzi's theory that ritual social forms, *li*, are, at root, merely extensions of principles of nature, *li*, which govern every aspect of the cosmos. In this theory, Nature or T'ien-as-Nature, is tied to the normative dimensions of ritual social behavior" (*The Confucian Creation of Heaven* [Albany: State University of New York Press, 1990], 163). That is to say, Vien Thong spoke like an orthodox Confucian, who theorized on the Trinity of Heaven, Man, and Earth.

47. Julia Ching has pointed out: "Indeed, as Son of Heaven, the ruler considers it one of his most important tasks to understand the intentions and feelings of Heaven above, in order to be able to act upon such an understanding. And 'Heaven,' as we said, refers not merely to the supreme Lord-on-High, but also the firmament, which is his visible realm—to use Mircea Eliade's term, his 'hierophany'. The belief was that all heavenly phenomena had earthly effects, and served as signs of Heaven's pleasure or displeasure regarding the government of men" (*Mysticism and Kingship in China* [Cambridge: Cambridge University Press, 1997], 49).

48. Nguyen Lang, *Viet Nam Phat Giao Su Luan*, vol. 2 (Paris: La Boi Society, 1977), 257–58.

49. Ibid., 260.

50. The situation of Buddhism in Korean history, in terms of its doctrinal relation to Confucianism, was nearly the same. Robert E. Buswell, Jr., in his study of Hyujong, an eminent Chan master (Sosan) of the Choson dynasty (1392–1910), writes: "Hyujong sought to demonstrate the fundamental agreement between Buddhism and Confucianism—and eventually with Daoism as well—by revealing how all creeds and religions were alternative statements of a unitary reality that vivified them all" (Robert E. Buswell, Jr., "Buddhism under Confucian Domination: The Synthetic Vision of Sosan Hyujong," in *Culture and the State in Late Choson Korea*,

ed. Jahyun Kim Haboush and Martina Deuchler [Cambridge, Mass.: Harvard University Press, 1999], 148–49).

51. *Jiaoshi pi cheng zu ji.* Quoted from *The Unfolding of Neo-Confucianism,* ed. Wm. Theodore de Bary (New York: Columbia University Press, 1975), 47.

52. The original title is *Ren wang hu guo panruo boluomi jing* (The *Prajn a pa ramita* Sutra for Benevolent Kings Who Want to Protect their Kingdoms), *Taisho* 8:246. For a discussion of the text, see M. W. De Visser, *Ancient Buddhism in Japan: Sutras and Ceremonies in Use in the Seventh and Eighth Centuries A.D. and Their History in Later Times,* 2 vols. (Leiden: E. J. Brill, 1935), 1:116–42.

53. Charles D. Orzech writes: "The success of the scripture lay in its promotion of a Samgha-state partnership in which monks and rulers could understand their relationship both in similar and in different terms" (*Politics and Transcendent Wisdom: The Scripture for Humane Kings in the Creation of Chinese Buddhism* [University Park: Pennsylvania State University Press, 1998], 136). Orzech also informs us that "in marked contrast to the mystery surrounding the origin of the first version of the *Scripture for Humane Kings,* the second version was produced on imperial order by the monk Pu-k'ung (Sanskrit: Amoghavajra) with the aid of his disciples Liang-pi, Fei-his, Yuan-chao, and others in 765-66, and we have an imperial preface for the text as well" (p. 135).

54. Nguyen Dang Thuc, in his introduction to Bhiksu Thich Thanh Kiem's translation of *Khoa Hu Luc* [*KHL*], praised the work as a "world masterpiece of religious philosophy" (Thich Thanh Kiem, *Khoa Hu Luc* [Thanh Hoi Phat Giao Thanh Pho Ho Chi Minh an hanh, 1992]). As a point of reference, it should be noted that, according to Robert C. Neville "philosophy of religion is an invention of modern Western philosophy. The modern period opened with the theme of deep skepticism. Instead of asking the medieval question of whether God's existence can be proved, without doubting for a moment the divine existence, the early modern philosophers sought to prove God precisely because they doubted. Philosophy of religion arose with the assumption that philosophy needs an integrity of its own irrespective of the outcome of reflections about God" ("The Chinese Case in a Philosophy of World Religions," in *Understanding the Chinese Mind: The Philosophical Roots,* ed. Robert E. Allinson [Oxford: Oxford University Press, 1989], 48–49).

55. Thich Thien An, in cooperation with Carol Smith, produced a translation of this *Preface* in the former's *Buddhism and Zen in Vietnam in Relation to the Development of Buddhism in Asia* (Los Angeles: College of Oriental Studies, 1975), 205–9, which is basically a free version of the original and contains a lot of mistakes.

56. Like the Tibetans, who refer to Buddhism as *nang chos* or *nang kyi chos* [the inner teachings].

57. All these expressions are Chinese stereotyped clichés to describe extreme suffering. They are so familiar and conventional that they almost elicit no emotional reaction from any Vietnamese or Chinese reader.

58. My translation is based on the Chinese text provided in Nguyen Dang

Thuc's version, *Khoa Hu Luc* (Saigon: Khuong Viet Publishers, 1972). Thòc's Chinese text is based on *Dai Nam Phat Dien Tung San* [Vietnam's Collection of Buddhist Works], published by Bac Ky Phat Giao Tong Hoi [Northern Buddhist Association]. Thich Thien An also provided a Chinese text in his translation (pp. 197–99). I have also consulted Thich Thanh Kiem's translation into modern Vietnamese (pp. 52–54).

59. It is unlucky that Chinese Buddhists were not aware of a Sanskrit source, *Sanghabhedavastu* section of *Mulasarva stiva da Vinaya*, which makes clear, in John S. Strong's words, that "the night of the Great Departure marks not the birth but the conception of the Buddha's son, for far from not waking his wife on his way out the door, the Bodhisattva decides to make love to her. The *Sanghabhedavastu* is explicit about this: 'Lest others say that the prince Sakyamuni was not a man (*apuman*, a eunuch) and that he wandered forth without paying attention to Yasodhara, Gopika, Mrgaja, and his other sixty thousand wives, the Buddha entered his bedchamber, and thinking let me now pay attention to Yasodhara, he did so, and Yasodhara became pregnant" (John S. Strong, "A Family Quest: The Buddha, Yasodhara, and Rahula in the *Mulasarva stiva da Vinaya*," in *Sacred Biography in the Buddhist Traditions of South and South-East Asia*, ed. Juliane Schober [Honolulu: University of Hawaii's Press, 1997], 114–15).

60. Bernard Faure, *The Red Thread: Buddhist Approach to Sexuality* (Princeton, N.J.: Princeton University Press, 1998), 24.

61. Timothy Brook, *Praying for Power: Buddhism and the Formation of Gentry Society in Late-Ming China* (Cambridge, Mass.: Harvard University Press, 1993), 79.

62. Nguyen Dang Thuc, in an article on Vietnamese humanism, gives a different interpretation, which I think is based on his misreading and mistranslation of Tran Thai Tong's *Essays on Emptiness*. He writes: "According to the above preface, the king did not think, as did the Sixth Patriarch of Zen, that Buddhism and Confucianism were alike, but he pointed out the strong and weak points of these two important systems of thought in Asia" ("Vietnamese Humanism," *Philosophy East and West* [January 1960]). In point of fact, Huineng does not think that Confucianism and Buddhism are alike and Tran Thai Tong does not "point out" any "strong and weak points" of the two systems, as my translation and analysis of the *Preface* have shown. Anyway, Thòc's article should be welcomed as the first interpretive essay in English on Tran Thai Tong's work.

63. Alan Cole, *Mothers and Sons in Chinese Buddhism* (Stanford: Stanford University Press, 1998), 2.

64. Stephen B. Young correctly pointed out that "the Vietnamese disposition to believe strongly in individual destiny reinforces adherence to a conformist social ethic. If individuals are perceived to be driven by the beyond, then their conformity to social codes is a necessary means of placing them under some control. Conformity to role engenders the trust necessary for social intercourse" ("The Orthodox Chinese Confucian Social Paradigm Versus Vietnamese Individualism," in *Confucianism and the Family*, ed. Walter H. Slote and George A. Devos [Albany:

State University of New York Press, 1998], 154). Seen in this perspective, King Tran Thai Tong's religious anxiety also involves an element of role-conformity concern.

65. Cole, *Mothers and Sons*, 2.

66. Nguyen Lang, *Viet Nam Phat Giao Su Luan*, 2:281.

67. Ibid., 2:279. It should be cautioned, however, that basically the Le kings tended to be more Confucianism-oriented than syncretic. John K. Whitmore observed: "Only in this Le period did contemporary Chinese Neo-Confucianism begin to have a major impact on the people at large across Vietnam. Before the fifteenth century, Mahayana Buddhism and the spirit cults were the main forms of popular belief; later, the nineteenth century saw the height of Neo-Confucian orthodoxy in the country's history. During the Le dynasty, the ruling elite, particularly under Le Thanh Tong (1460–97), adopted Neo-Confucianism as the state ideology and moved to encourage its dicta among the people via the sinic bureaucratic system brought into use at the same time" ("Social Organization and Confucian Thought in Vietnam," *Journal of Southeast Asian Studies* 15, no. 2 [1984]: 296–306).

68. See, e.g., Cao Tu Thanh, *Nho Giao o Gia Dinh* [Confucianism in Gia Dinh] (Ho Chi Minh City: Nha Xuat Ban Thanh Pho Ho Chi Minh, 1996); Dao Phan, *Dao Khong trong Tho Van bac Ho* [Confucianism in Ho Chi Minh's Literary Writings] (Hanoi: Nha Xuat Ban Van Hoa Thong Tin, 1996); Vu Khieu, *Nho Giao va Dao Duc* [Confucianism and Morality] (Hanoi: Nha Xuat Ban Khoa Hoc Xa Hoi, 1995); *Nho Giao va Phat Trien o Viet Nam* [Confucianism and Development in Vietnam] (Hanoi: Nha Xuat Ban Khoa Hoc Xa Hoi, 1997); Nguyen Tai Thu, "Nho Giao- Nhung Tranh Luan va Nhung Van De Dat Ra" [Confucianism-Debates and Issues], *Triet Hoc* [Journal of Philosophy] 1 (1992): 44–48; Ha Van Thu, "Nho Giao voi Gia Dinh Viet Nam" [Confucianism and Vietnamese Family], *Dan Toc va Thoi Dai* [People and Times Magazine] 1 (1995); Tran Hong Thuy, "Nuoc trong Hoc Thuyet Khong Manh va Chu Nghia Yeu Nuoc Truyen Thong Viet Nam" [The Concept of Nation in Confucian and Mencian Doctrines and Vietnamese Traditional Patriotism], *Triet Hoc* [Journal of Philosophy] 2 (1996): 45–47.

Part Five

THE THIRD EPOCH OF CONFUCIAN HUMANISM IN THE GLOBAL COMMUNITY

30

Mou Zongsan's Spiritual Vision: How Is *Summum Bonum* Possible?

L IN T ONGQI

T
HIRTY YEARS AGO, Joseph Levenson (1920–1969), author of the influential *Confucian China and Its Modern Fate: A Trilogy* (Berkeley: University of California Press, 1968), regretfully asserted that Confucianism was incompatible with the march of modernization and Westernization and that therefore its fate was sealed. It might still find a place in the "museum without walls," but it could never reemerge as a dynamic intellectual force in the twentieth century. Levenson's verdict echoed the view of a great majority, if not the virtual consensus, of scholars of Confucianism of his days. Yet, at about the same time, Mou Zongsan (1909–1995), then a professor of philosophy at a Hong Kong college and now widely acknowledged as the most profound Confucian thinker of the twentieth century, propounded a completely different reading of the future of Confucianism.

Mou noted that in the past two millennia and a half there were two high points in the development of Confucian thinking: the classical pre-Qin period, from Confucius's time (551–479 B.C.E.) to the end of the Zhou dynasty (221 B.C.E.) and the Neo-Confucianism of the Song-Ming period from the eleventh to the sixteenth century. Now, he asserted, we were on the eve of a third upsurge of Confucianism—the emergence of a new interpretation of Confucianism that could meet the challenges of contemporary life. Mou's voice was almost prophetic. In the past fifteen years or so, his idea of a new wave of Confucianism, vigorously advocated by Tu Weiming as "the third epoch of Confucian humanism" is reflected in a revival of Confucian study.[1] A contemporary school of Confucian thinking known as *xinrujia* (New Confucian School) has picked up momentum visibly not only in Taiwan and on the Chinese mainland but also in the United States and even in Europe.[2] It seems reasonable to assume that the emergence of the third epoch of Confucianism is no longer a dim dream of a few visionaries.

In fact, *xinrujia* as a philosophic discourse originated in China as early as seventy years ago in the famous May Fourth movement (1919-1923). Although it was primarily a reaction to this predominantly Western-oriented reform and renewal movement, it was also an attempt to meet the moral and spiritual crisis that developed in China at the turn of the century. Like the Westernizers of the May Fourth movement, these Confucian thinkers too were attracted by such Western core values as science and democracy. Therefore, they did not advocate a simple return to the past. Instead, they tried to renew and reform the main thrust of the Confucian spiritual orientation while tapping into the symbolic resources of other cultural heritages.

Xinrujia in its more inclusive sense covers several strands. Its development can be seen as the sustained effort of three generations of scholars. The first generation were pioneers: Liang Shuming (1889-1947), Zhang Junmai (Carson Chang) (1886-1969), Xiong Shili (1885-1968), Qian Mu (1895-1990), and Feng Youlan (1895-1991). The second generation emerged in Taiwan and Hong Kong after the Communist takeover in 1949 and ended with the death of Mou Zongsan in 1995. They built up a solid foundation for future development of Confucianism in terms of both scholarship and education of scholars. The most prominent among them were Tang Junyi (1909-1978), Mou Zongsan (1909-1995), Xu Fuguan (1903-1982), and Fang Tungmei (1899-1976). The third generation, most of whom were trained in prestigious universities in the United States, tried to spread the influence of *xinrujia* across the world. The major scholars of that generation include Tu Weiming (b. 1940), Liu Shuxian (b. 1934), Yu Yingshi (b. 1930), and Cheng Zhongying (b. 1935). With the vigorous revival of Confucian study in China and in the West, we can reasonably expect the emergence of the fourth generation of *xinrujia*.

Of the variegated efforts of three generations, Mou's endeavor was definitely the most systematic, sophisticated, and articulate. He spent his whole life studying Confucianism as a philosophy with deep moral-spiritual implications and also teaching and writing about it. He published over twenty books and hundreds of articles, ranging from logic and political thought to intellectual history and metaphysics. His insightful interpretations of Chinese spiritual traditions encompass Confucianism, Buddhism, and Daoism. He also translated single-handedly the three monumental *Critiques* by Immanuel Kant, studied Bertrand Russell and Ludwig Wittgenstein intensely, and translated some sections of Heidegger's works into Chinese with critical comments. Many critics of Confucianism believe that his death in 1995 marked the end of a period in the development of New Confucianism.

The Concept of *Summum Bonum* and How the Question Is Raised?

Mou calls the philosophical system he constructs "moral metaphysics." Since metaphysics deals essentially with the problem of ultimate reality and its nature, which is also the central concern of great spiritual traditions, Mou's exposition of spirituality can be found almost throughout his major writings. Like other major forms of spirituality, Mou's spiritual vision involves many issues and dimensions that cannot be covered in a short essay such as this.

However, in his 1985 book entitled *On Summum Bonum*, Mou gives a highly focused exposition of what he believes to be the essence of Confucian spiritual vision. In that book he declares conclusively that the highest standard of aspiration for human beings, the peak of their spiritual achievement, is the realization or fulfillment of *summum bonum*. Mou borrows the Latin term *summun bonum* directly from Kant and subscribes basically to his definition of the term. The term is generally translated into English as the "highest good." Mou, however, chooses to render it as the "perfect good" in English and *yuanshan* (literally, the "round good") in Chinese. (To avoid misleading, hereafter in this article instead of the "highest good," either the original Latin *summum bonum* or "the perfect good" is used.)

Summun bonum is defined by Kant briefly as "the proper proportion between virtue and happiness." Or, to borrow from Alasdair MacIntyre, it is "the individual's moral perfection crowned by the happiness which it merits."[3] Kant, however, further specifies the term in two important ways. First, he specifies that each of the two concepts in *summum bonum*, that is, virtue and happiness, must not be logically derivable from each other. We are not supposed to analyze the concept of happiness from that of virtue, as the Greek Stoics did, who said that to be conscious of one's virtue *is* happiness; nor are we supposed to analyze the concept of virtue from that of happiness as the Greek Epicureans did, who said that to be conscious of one's conducts as leading to happiness *is* virtue. Virtue and happiness, Kant insists, are two heterogeneous concepts. They exist independently of each other. Second, Mou specifies that the connection between virtue and happiness must be understood as *necessary* rather than *accidental*. In other words, the two elements, although heterogeneous, are thought of as *necessarily* combined so that one cannot be assumed without the other belonging to it.

Kant's exaltation of *summum bonum* reflects the high spiritual aspiration of a moral idealist. But, given the grim reality of life in this world, it is obvious that the connection between happiness and virtue is at best *accidental*. It has never been *necessary*. Common sense seems to suggest that *summum bonum*, as it is defined by Kant and accepted by Mou, never exists in this world. It is a mere illusion, an unattainable mirage constructed by some visionary minds. Both Kant and Mou therefore faced up to the difficult question: How is *summum bonum* possible? The two philosophers approach the question in different ways. While Kant does it through his moral theology, postulating the existence of God and the immortality of the soul, Mou does it by his moral metaphysics, demonstrating first of all the existence of what he calls "the infinite mind" (*wuxiangxin*).

This essay will explain how Mou solves the problem by justifying the possibility of *summun bonum* and revealing it as the consummation of a spiritual pilgrimage based on his moral metaphysics. It will focus on the following topics: (1) Mou's concept of the infinite mind and his bilevel ontology; (2) his concept of "attachment" (*zhi*) as the self-negation of the infinite mind; (3) his specification of the Confucian infinite mind; (4) his definition of "intellectual intuition" as the self-illumination of the Confucian infinite mind; (5) his concept of "perfect teaching"; and finally (6) his final justification of *summum bonum*, both theoretically and practically.

The Infinite Mind and Mou's Bilevel Ontology

The confirmation of "the infinite mind" is the first and ultimate principle of Mou's moral metaphysics. At the formal rather than the substantive level, Mou takes Kant's transcendental distinction between the phenomenal and the noumenal world as his basic theoretical scaffoldings. Mou's concept of the infinite mind can be best understood through his interpretation of Kant, an interpretation that in some cases is close to being idiosyncratic. For one thing, Kantian scholars usually believe that Kant's noumenal world consists solely of things-in-themselves, which Kant sometimes calls "intelligible entities," meaning entities that can never be thought of as objects of our sensibility but can only be thought of as things-in-themselves by pure understanding unmixed with sensuous intuition. But Mou insists that in Kant's noumenal world there are two types of intelligible entities, in which things-in-themselves represent only one of them. The other type, Mou contends, includes God, the immortality of the soul, and the freedom of the will.

Unsatisfied with the scattered and loose picture of Kant's noumenal world as he defines it, Mou advocates, in accordance with the "three

Chinese teachings" of Confucianism, Daoism, and Buddhism, a focused and monistic picture of the noumenal world. He declares in his *Phenomenon and Thing-in-Itself*:

> [My intention of writing the book] is to display the one single "noumenal reality" in a concentrated and substantiated way and call it "the infinite mind" (*wuxianxin*) in order to justify the existence of things-in-themselves. Here, however, things-in-themselves (to which all [the Kantian] "intelligible entities" are assigned) obtained not only a passive but also a positive significance. But at the same time I also intend to disclose and bring forth from this single noumenal reality, i.e., the infinite mind, and that in a dialectical way— "dialectical" is used here not in its Kantian but in its Hegelian sense—the cognitive subject [or the cognitive mind] in order to justify the existence of the "phenomenal world."[4]

The infinite mind as the single ultimate reality is here specified as the source from which the cognitive mind is derived. In contrast with the infinite mind, which functions only in connection with the noumenal world, the cognitive mind functions in the daily life of the phenomenal world. Based on this dual character of the human mind, Mou contends that a complete ontology must consist of two levels: the ontology of phenomena and the ontology of noumena. In constructing his bilevel ontology, Mou draws his inspiration not only from Kant but also from certain schools of Mahayana Buddhism. In fact, Mou's theory of bilevel ontology can be seen as a product of the critique of the former by the latter. But it is Kant's rigorously constructed and systematically reasoned theory of the distinction of the two worlds that provides much of the theoretical justification of Mou's bilevel ontology.

However, Mou argues again in a singular way that, according to Kant, noumena and phenomena, though appearing to us as two distinctive worlds, are actually two representations of one and the same thing. In other words, whatever we find or do in our daily life possesses a dual character. Things disclose themselves either as things-in-themselves or as phenomena, depending on how one's mind functions. The distinction, Mou argues, is therefore not an objective but a subjective one. It is subjective in the sense that the distinction is brought about or caused by the distinctive functioning of the infinite and the cognitive mind. That which the infinite mind reveals to us is things-in-themselves and that which the cognitive mind reveals to us is the empirical world of phenomena. The latter constitutes the content of his ontology of phenomena or, to borrow a term from Buddhism, the "attached" ontology. The former, that is, things-in-themselves, constitutes the content of Mou's ontology of noumena or, to use a term Mou coined, the "non-attached ontology." Thus, Mou transforms Kant's theory of two worlds—phenomenal and noumenal—into his theory of bilevel ontology. Kant's contribution, Mou says, lies mainly in the sphere of attached ontology. His own contribution, he believes, consists of the construction of a non-attached ontology.

In Kant's metaphysics, Mou stresses, things-in-themselves can only have a negative or passive significance because their characteristic function is to set a limit to empirical knowledge and disclaim any possible knowledge about things-in-themselves. This assertion by Kant is usually understood as suggesting that things-in-themselves represent the factual prototype of which phenomena are only their inaccurate and distorted copy. But Mou argues that, if Kant is to be consistent, things-in-themselves could not and should not be understood merely as a factual concept. They should be understood as a concept that signifies something that possesses value significance. Otherwise, Mou argues, the *qualitative* difference between phenomena and things-in-themselves would disappear and we would have no standard to establish a valid demarcation line between the two. Indeed, we would be compelled to admit that the human mind could gradually approach and eventually reveal the "true face" of things-in-themselves. Our sensibility and understanding would accordingly be allowed to encroach upon the territory of noumena, thereby inadvertently nullifying the distinction of phenomena and noumena, a distinction Kant himself had tried so laboriously to establish. Mou's singular interpretation can actually be seen as a drastic transformation of Kant's concept of things-in-themselves. Things-in-themselves no longer constitute a factual prototype of the phenomenal world. They signify primarily a spiritual world charged with and empowered by value significance. This transformation has a far-reaching significance for Mou's construction of his moral metaphysics.

"Attachment" as Self-negation of the Infinite Mind

One question, however, remains to be answered: If an ontology has two levels, how are they to be connected or mutually related to form a coherently structured ontology? There are, according to Mou, two ways to achieve this, both of which are merely self-activities of the infinite mind: (1) through what he calls the self-negation (*ziwokanxian*) of the infinite mind, or "attachment" as used by the Buddhists, and (2) through the self-illumination of the infinite mind, or "intellectual intuition" as Kant calls it. The former might be called the "descending" way, the path from sagehood to humanhood; the latter the "ascending" way, the journey from humanhood to sagehood. We will leave the ascending way, namely, the issue of intellectual intuition, for later discussion and focus first on the descending way, namely, the self-negation of the infinite mind.

Since, according to Mou, whatever the infinite mind discloses to us are things-in-themselves and since things-in-themselves "withdraw totally into themselves and never disclose themselves to us,"[5] they reside exclusively in themselves. As a result, no bifurcation of subject and object is at all possible. In other words, the infinite mind, though capable of disclosing to us things-in-themselves, could do nothing to help enhance our knowledge of the empirical world. However, empirical knowledge, Mou emphasizes, is indispensable for the solution of problems that are specific to us as human beings. Without the solution of these problems, none of us can claim to have completely fulfilled the ideal of a perfect humanhood, which is another name for sagehood. As a result, the development of the infinite mind, the culmination of which is sagehood, would also be obstructed. Therefore, to implement and realize itself fully, the infinite mind must negate and transform itself into the cognitive mind—consciously and willingly. To explain the process of self-negation two points needs clarification.

First, the infinite mind, as will be shown later, typically moves and generates ceaselessly in a wondrous and unfathomable way and yet, being absolute and unrelated to anything else and dwelling completely in its own identity, it could only be said to move "without any forms of moving." Yet, once it starts to negate itself, it would immediately "stop," so to speak. In doing so, it immediately turns itself into the cognitive mind. At the same time it also "pushes" things-in-themselves revealed by the infinite mind "out there to the other side," turning them into external objects for the cognitive mind to observe and study.

Second, that process is accompanied by the cognitive mind's "imposing" its innate "constructs," typically the Kantian a priori forms of time and space and categories, onto the things-in-themselves, turning them into a world of differentiated forms, a world of the myriad things, each manifesting what Kant calls "universal characteristics," such as quantity, quality, substance, causality. Mou believes that when Kant talks about "the synthesis of apprehension in intuition," "the synthesis of reproduction in imagination," and "the synthesis of recognition in concepts," or about the synthesizing function of apperception he is actually talking about the Buddhist "attachment"—only without himself realizing it. This is because, Mou argues, no synthesizing is possible without "holding (something) together," thereby giving some kind of unity to the manifold. Therefore, both the Kantian "synthesizing" and the Buddhist "attachment" produce the same result. While Kant calls the result "universal characteristics," the

Buddhist calls it the "arising of [determined] "forms" (i.e., *xiang* in Chinese or *lakashana* in Sanskrit).[6] In Kantian terms, this is the arising of the world of phenomena. Conversely, the world of phenomena, once shed of the "forms" determined by pure forms of time and space and categories a priori, would immediately return to things-in-themselves, which in Buddhist terms is called True Suchness (*zhenru*).

The Confucian Infinite Mind

Mou believes that we can find the concept of the infinite mind in Buddhism, Daoism, and Confucianism, known as the Three Teachings in China. The Confucian infinite mind has developed both historically and philosophically its own emphases and content and has assumed its own names. It began with Confucius's concept of *ren*, which is variously translated as humanity, benevolence, altruism, love, perfect virtue, and so on. First of all, Mou maintains that Confucius's own teaching consists of two basic components: humanity (*ren*) and Heaven (*tian*). The concept of Heaven is much older than Confucius. In the early Zhou dynasty (1063–221 B.C.E.), it was tied closely to the destiny of a dynasty, since Heaven's Mandate was then believed to belong only to the ruling king who is truly virtuous. One of Confucius's historic achievements, Mou notes, was to "liberate the concept of Heaven from the dynastic concern of the ruling king"[7] and expand it into a concern for the destiny of civilization, morality, and even the cosmos itself. But, Mou emphasizes, Confucius's greatest contribution lay not in the liberation of Heaven but in the initiation of a spiritual vision based on the concept of *ren*. By introducing the concept of *ren*, Mou stresses, Confucius opened up a new dimension of spiritual life— the vast realm of human subjectivity scarcely explored before. However, given the momentous role Heaven played in Confucius's time and based on what the master said about Heaven in the *Analects*, it is reasonable to assume that Confucius's understanding of *ren* is accompanied by a deep-rooted, though seldom clearly articulated, yearning for Heaven as the transcendent. Heaven certainly formed the backdrop that loomed large in his quest for the vision of *ren*. "Confucius," Mou argues forcefully, "is indeed using *ren* to achieve the verification [in one's heart/mind] of Heaven's way or Heaven's Mandate."[8]

Ren as introduced by Confucius in the *Analects* is a term loaded with fruitful ambiguity. The master mentions *ren* over a hundred times in the *Analects* and yet never gives it a clear-cut definition. He seemed to prefer a heuristic or contextual strategy to any rigid definition in explaining the concept. However, what is clear, Mou maintains, is that *ren*, unlike what many scholars assume, does not refer to a specific virtue. Nor can its significance be exhausted by such terms as "general virtue" or "perfect virtue" that embraces all virtues, as some scholars suggest. Indeed, *ren*, Mou insists, is not something that is or could be limited to virtues, although each virtue points back to *ren*. *Ren* is, in fact, the ultimate source of all virtues, the essence of being human. Broadly speaking, what the master intended, Mou contends, was to reveal the very fountainhead of life that keeps bubbling and welling up in the mind/heart of human beings. Specifically speaking, it points to the capability that enables human beings to feel "uneasy" or "unsatisfied" when encountering certain "pitiful" or regrettable situations, a capability endowed by Heaven and, rooted in human nature. It is revealed typically in the feeling of sympathy and commiseration, which in turn signifies a vitality that surges up spontaneously or even irresistibly (*Analects* 6:28; 7:8; 7:26; 10:17; 12:12; 14:45; 15:23; 17:11; 17:21; *Mencius* 6A:6). Thus Mou elaborates:

> As I was wont to say, *ren* possesses two defining characteristics: one is sensitivity or keen awareness (*jue*) [as opposed to numbness or insensitivity], the other is robustness or a vitality to flourish (*jian*) [as opposed to stagnancy or inertia]. Robustness is implied in sensitivity. It refers here to the robust growth of one's spiritual life, not his physical life. Sensitivity indicates a quick-responding and all-penetrating and -pervading capability (*gantong*) and a keen awareness that soothes and anoints wherever it goes. It is to be sensed through a feeling of uneasiness, unbearableness, and compassion. It signifies the overflowing of life, the instilling of warmth just like the soothing effect of a timely rain. Therefore, the term "soothing sensitivity" (*juerung*) is used—a sensitivity that, once awakened, soothes wherever it goes and brings life to whatever it touches and makes it grow. . . . This is why "soothing sensitivity" is creativity itself that has been triggered and why I also say that "*ren* takes responsiveness and all-penetrating power as its nature and things-soothing as its function."[9]

The concept of the infinite mind, initially expressed by *ren*, has been constantly worked on by Confucian thinkers since Confucius's time. It has assumed different names in different contexts, each adding some new significance to the concept. For example, it is known as Heaven's Principle (*tianli*) in terms of its being "principle" (*li*) in its most general and encompassing sense. It can be called Heaven's Way (*tiandao*) in terms of its natural running course, or Heaven's Mandate (*tianming*) in terms of its possessing a profoundly determined direction and ceaseless bestowing. It can be called the Great Ultimate (*taiji*) in terms of its ultimate consummation to which nothing more could be added, or the Great Vacuity (*taixu*) in terms of its being soundless and odorless, transparent and free of any obstruction and restriction. It can be called *ren*-in-itself (*renti*) in terms of its moral creativity and quick responding and things-soothing capability. It can also be called nature-in-itself (*xingti*) in terms of its constituting individually the transcendent ground of the individual's moral creativity and enabling Heaven and Earth and myriad things to possess, each and all, their own self-nature, or mind-in-itself (*xinti*) in terms of its possessing an autonomy of will and capability of formulating an existential moral decision for oneself. In short, Mou says: "Being perfectly still and non-active all at and yet responding and going forth and penetrating everything, it is the [ultimate] reality that creates and generates, responds and soothes—the 'mystery-in-itself, (*oati*), which is 'Ah, profound and without end!'"[10]

Given the complexity of concept of the infinite mind thus specified, one problem arises: How can we know the mind which is so elaborately conceived and is called "mystery-in-itself"? This leads us to the problem of the possibility of intellectual intuition, the "ascending" way that connects the two worlds of phenomena and noumena.

Intellectual Intuition as Self-illumination of the Infinite Mind

Mou borrows the term "intellectual intuition" from Kant. Kant believes that to know the world of noumena, one must possess the faculty of intellectual intuition, which, however, he denies to humans but reserves for God only. Intellectual intuition, as Kant defines it, refers to an ability to understand without the mediation of concepts and to intuit without appealing to senses. More important, unlike sensibility, the objects of which are always given and which therefore always remains receptive and passive, intellectual intuition gives its own objects. In this sense, its activities are always objectless. They are, as Mou argues, always self-activities and can therefore be regarded as creativity itself. Mou embraces essentially Kant's definition of intellectual intuition but gives it an interpretation based on his theory of the infinite mind: he defines intellectual intuition as the self-illumination of the infinite mind.

The justification of intellectual intuition as a human faculty, Mou argues, is of vital importance to all of the three Chinese spiritual traditions—Confucianism, Daoism, and Buddhism. He believes that each of them has its own understanding of the infinite mind and hence its own interpretation of intellectual intuition. "If humans really did not possess intellectual intuition," Mou asserts, "then the whole of Chinese philosophy would totally collapse and all the painstaking effort of the past thousands of years would have been made in vain and turned out to be merely idle dreams."[11] It is the human possession of intellectual intuition too that in the first place makes *summum bonum* an attainable and meaningful goal for human aspiration.

As mentioned earlier, there are in Chinese intellectual history various formulations of the Confucian infinite mind. Mou is known for his intellectual affinity to Wang Yangming (1472–1529), the most important Confucian master of the Ming dynasty. He chooses to base his formulation on that of Wang, namely, *the innate-knowing-in-itself as the illuminating sensitivity (zhitimingjue)*, or briefly *knowing-in-itself* (*zhiti*). For brevity's sake we will simply use *zhiti* hereafter in this article to stand for the longer term. To understand the meaning of *zhiti*, however, an explanation of each element in the longer term is required.

"Knowing" (*zhi*) here does not refer to the cognitive knowing process in its ordinary sense. It refers, on the one hand, to the innate ability of knowing good and evil, which makes morality subjectively possible. On the other hand, it also refers to or implies the innate capability to determine (or choose) a universally applicable moral law for one to follow, which makes morality objectively possible. It is therefore totally different from knowing in its ordinary sense with its dichotomy of subject and object and should be understood in terms of moral practice as a process of self-cultivation. Moreover, like the metaphysical *ren* explained earlier, innate-knowing, in Yangming's philosophy, should be understood both subjectively as the innermost and indestructible essence of the individual person and objectively as the single ultimate noumenal reality that is universal and absolute and independent of anything else. Hence, the use of the suffix in-itself (*ti*) when it is translated into English as "knowing-in-itself."

"Illuminating" (*ming*) suggests that *zhiti* is capable of sharp awareness or penetrative insight, not discursively by using concepts but by "shedding light," as it were, onto the ultimate reality directly and revealing it as things-in-themselves. "Sensitivity" (*jue*) is used as mentioned earlier to imply a capability of responding instantly when confronted with certain "pitiful" or regrettable situations, typically with compassion, warmth, and an all-pervasive soothing power. Therefore, *zhiti* (more commonly known as *liangzhi*) and *renti*, which has already been explained, actually refer to the same thing. The all-penetrating and all-pervasive soothing sensibility of *renti* is also the "wondrously affecting and responding" capability of the illuminating sensibility of *zhiti*. The content of *liangzhi*, therefore, is more than an ability to tell good from evil. It is even more than a moral or metaphysical principle. It is also a sensitivity that enables us to feel pitiful and saddened, to sympathize and commiserate with others. It is not merely an abstract principle that applies universally but also a concrete heart/mind that can feel and is always active. The following is how Mou explains the concept of intellectual intuition in terms of the self-activity of *zhiti* so understood:

> How do we know *zhiti* itself? The answer is: *zhiti* could present itself anytime. For example, we all have a feeling of commiseration when we suddenly see a baby about to fall into a well. This feeling is in fact *zhiti*'s self-shocking, which in turn alarms and awakens us and so we can, through a process of "retractive feeling" (*nijue*) or tracing it backward to its origin, come to know *zhiti* itself. However, the way in which *zhiti*'s self-shocking awakens us is like a red sun that emerges radiantly right from the bottom of the sea, but shedding itself of all elements of sensibility. The process of the so-called "retractive feeling" through which we know *zhiti* refers to nothing else but the fact that the light issued by *zhiti* is thrown back onto *zhiti* itself. . . . Therefore "retractive feeling" is purely intellectual and not at all passive as in the case of the sensible intuition. . . . Thus, the very self-illuminating of the infinite mind is intellectual intuition.[12]

There are several points in this passage that need to be clarified and made explicit. First, lest he be misunderstood, Mou hastens to warn us that, strictly speaking, to say "alarms and awakens us" is not exactly true and can even be misleading. What actually happens is that *zhiti* as the infinite mind, at the sight of a baby about to fall into a well, instantly alarms and awakens itself. The sight serves merely as an occasion. The feeling of commiseration that wells up at the sight, however, is only one form of the function of *zhiti*. By means of the light it is shedding, *zhiti* traces the feeling of commiseration aroused by the sight backward to *zhiti* itself, and comes to find, "Nay," says Mou, "comes to identify itself with the [infinite] mind and thus claims to know it." The occasion belongs to our sensibility and understanding. But the presentation of *zhiti* as a feeling of commiseration accompanied by an unconditional commitment to action is not. It is the self-activity of the infinite mind. All the while, what is happening is that the infinite mind, being the single ultimate noumenal reality, relies solely on its own resources, illuminating and self-illuminating, all independently, "just like a red sun that emerges radiantly right from the bottom of the sea."

Second, Mou stresses that the infinite mind can *present* or show itself anytime. For him, the infinite mind is not something abstract and merely theoretically assumed. It is a lived experience, something we all palpably feel because it is constantly active and could present itself to us anytime in our daily life. Yangming describes it in one of his most famous passages. The alarm and commiseration, the pity and regret could range from the pitiful feelings welling up at the sight of a baby about to fall into a well, to similar responses to the pitiful cries of a bird or animal about to be slaughtered, or to a plant suddenly broken and destroyed, and even to a tile or stone suddenly shattered and crushed. Herein lies a fundamental difference between Mou and Kant. Kant contends that God, the immortality of the soul, and the freedom of the will—which three, when combined, can be regarded as the Kantian counterpart of Mou's Confucian infinite mind—are mere postulates necessitated by the possible realization of moral laws and *summum bonum*. Mou, on the other hand, argues that the infinite mind is a vivid and palpable presentation made possible by the function of intellectual intuition as the self-activity of the infinite mind, or *zhiti* in our case.

Third, as we can see, intellectual intuition so defined is neither understanding nor intuition in either of its typically Kantian senses. It is an understanding that is nonconceptual and an intuition that is nonsensible. Yet, according to Mou, we can still claim that we "know" *zhiti*. Obviously, "knowing," as mentioned earlier, is not used in its ordinary sense of cognition with its bifurcation of subject and object. It means the subject's "tracing the feeling (of alarm and commiseration etc.) back to its root [i.e., *zhiti* in this case], and existentially verifying and embodying it." This process of "retracting one's feeling and verifying by embodiment (*nijuetizhen*) is, Mou repeatedly emphasizes, an important form of intuition and an essential way of self-cultivation in Confucianism.

The Concept of the Perfect Teaching

From the perspective of spiritual aspiration rather than consummation, we can provisionally visualize the philosophical edifice Mou constructs as a two-story structure with a Gothic cathedral on top, pointing toward the infinite firmament. If the first floor represents his attached ontology of phenomena and the second floor his non-attached ontology of noumena, the Gothic cathedral can be properly regarded as his theory of "the perfect teaching" on the pedestal of which *summun bonum* as a theory and practice is mounted.

As mentioned earlier, the concept of *summum bonum* includes both virtue and happiness. While virtue belongs to freedom of the will and hence totally amenable to us, happiness depends much on external conditions in the empirical world which we cannot totally control. These conditions in their entirety and their most generalized sense are referred to as "being (or beings)" by Mou.

All individual beings, Mou affirms, are ends in themselves. They are entitled to happiness because happiness is simply the nurturing and growth of one's being, namely, the specific condition one's own body and mind are in. Without being, Mou argues, happiness would, as it were, have nothing to "hang on." Indeed, happiness can be properly regarded as the improvement on the condition of one's being. But unfortunately, being is not completely amenable to us. In fact, much of it is hopelessly beyond the individual's control, a condition designated as "fate or destiny" (*ming*) in Confucianism. Fate as a serious concern in Confucian thought is defined by Mou as the "inherent constraints imposed on an individual's life as a result of its congruity or incongruity with the infinite quantity and complexity of vital force (*qi*) the cosmos possesses."[13] We can say after Confucius: "Lo, there comes *ren* so long as I desire it!" (*Analects* 7:29); but we can never say so with regard to happiness. To justify that the connection between virtue and happiness is a necessary one, which is what *summum bonum* amounts to, Mou has to justify that the connection between virtue and being is a necessary one. This justification constitutes the core of Mou's theory of the "perfect teaching."

But *summum bonum*, as Mou defines it, is not only a theory; it is primarily a practice to "purify or sanctify one's life to attain the highest, ideal spiritual realm."[14] In Confucian terms, it is a moral practice known as self-cultivation. In this section we will first explain the meaning of the perfect teaching and then focus on the self-cultivation process that leads to the attainment of *summum bonum* as the pinnacle of Confucian spiritual aspiration.

"Perfect teaching" is a term initially used in connection with a Buddhist discourse known as "critique of teachings" (*panjia*), which means a critical examination of the teachings of the major Buddhist schools and arranging them in the order of their theoretical and spiritual achievements. The perfect teaching is supposed to represent the most encompassing or inclusive of all Buddhist teachings. It is considered to be the height of the development of Buddhist thinking and the most faithful presentation of the real intention of the Buddha himself.

Mou emphasizes that a perfect teaching does not mean that the ideal it offers, for example, Plato's idea, the Christian God, or the Buddhist Nirvana, is perfect. Nor does it mean that the system it constructs is completely consistent and hence logically perfect, because Mou contends that any system once constructed, no matter how logically perfect it is, must imply the existence of alternative systems. A perfect system, he specifies, must be perfect (or "round") in two ways: functionally perfect and ontologically perfect.

To be functionally perfect means the teaching must enable one's mind to function in a perfectly unobstructed and all-penetrating way. This is best illustrated by the character of the Buddhist wisdom known as *prajna*. The function of *prajna* as a mode of thinking and expression, Mou maintains, is not to positively assert the ontological existence of something but to remove all our "attachments" to everything, namely, to dismantle all boundaries and restrictions among all phenomena in order to return to the absolute, fundamental reality, or the Buddhist True Suchness. It has to be noted, however, that *prajna* does not abolish one single phenomenon or dharma, to use a Buddhist term. What it does abolish are attachments to dharmas and all boundaries and restrictions that obstruct one's free access to the ultimate reality. In order to truly accomplish this, *prajna* when functioning has to dispense totally with the ordinary analytical mode of thinking and expression, because no analysis is possible without using concepts, and concepts by their own nature always imply limitations. Concepts can at best be used as clues, or heuristic guides to reach ultimate reality. Ultimate reality as a spiritual vision is simply not an object for conceptual analysis and theoretical speculation. It is as such a self-disclosure, a vivid presentation to be existentially experienced. In other words, it can be reached only through the exercise of intellectual intuition.

Therefore, a nonanalytical, or a dialectically paradoxical mode of thinking and expression has to be used. For example, when defining *prajna*, the Buddha said, "*prajna* but not *prajna* is called *prajna*," he was using the nonanalytical mode of expression. When he said: "I have been teaching for forty-nine years, and yet I've got nothing to teach," he was using the analytical expression in the first part of the sentence and the nonanalytical one in the second part. In short, since the perfect teaching has to convey an absolute and totally undifferentiated whole, the nonanalytical mode of expression is its indelible hallmark.

To be ontologically perfect means that the teaching must be perfectly complete in its inclusion of each and all beings, primary and secondary, good and evil, past, present, and future. This is best illustrated by what is called the "Buddha-nature (or character)" (*Buddhata*). The ultimate goal of a Buddhist is to achieve Buddhahood. But each of the many Buddhist schools has its own way to achieve Buddhahood. The result is a variety of interpretations of the concept of Buddha's nature. Some advocate a narrow interpretation of Buddha's nature, others a broader and more inclusive one. The Hinayana school, for example, is described as seeking only personal salvation. It does not take other beings into the Buddha's nature, thereby narrowing its concept of Buddhist-nature. The Mahayana school, on the other hand, advocates universal salvation and claims that personal salvation is impossible without the salvation of all living beings. As a result, it incorporates and absorbs into the Buddha-nature all living beings, making it more inclusive.

Of all Buddhist schools, the *Tiantai* school, Mou maintains, has the most inclusive Buddha's nature. This is because it insists that Buddhahood can only be achieved by having oneself identified with, or "dwelling in" the entirety of dharmas, a doctrine known as "the three thousand worlds [i.e., the totality of manifested reality] immanent in just one instance of thought."[15] In other words, to attain Buddhahood, one simply cannot afford to ignore one single dharma (or being) in the universe, past, present, and future. This implies that to achieve Buddhahood one even has to dwell in hells and identify oneself with hungry ghosts, since hells and hungry ghosts are also considered to be an integral part of Buddha's nature. Indeed, given the Buddha's boundless compassion, it is his real and ultimate intention, Mou emphasizes, to realize his own nature not by cutting himself off from any one dharma but by identifying itself with them all. Although all attachments are removed, not one single dharma is left out. In other words, the realization of Buddha's nature, which is the supreme Buddhist virtue, is tantamount to the preservation of all beings, and these beings each and all are preserved in a blissful state of emancipation. To put it in Kantian terms, all beings "return" to their status as things-in-themselves and become ends in themselves. The necessary connection between virtue and happiness is thus established and justified. It is also the *Tiantai* school, Mou contends, that is best in its usage of nonanalytical mode of thinking and expression. It does not reject the teachings of any other schools. What it does is "dig through the expediencies that mark all other teachings and reveals the ultimate reality or the True Suchness hidden in them."[16]

However, Mou emphasizes, it is not the *prajna*-like function of one's mind, but the preservation of all beings that constitutes the core of a perfect teaching. Ontological perfection, therefore, is more crucial than functional perfection as a defining characteristic of a perfect teaching. For example, functional perfection in the form of *prajna* is shared by all Buddhist schools, but ontological perfection in the form an all-inclusive Buddha's nature, Mou claims, is possessed by the *Tiantai* school only. It is the Buddhist theory of the perfect teaching, especially that of *Tiantai* school, that inspires Mou to formulate his Confucian theory of perfect teaching. One of the best ways to understand this theory together with Mou's Confucian interpretation of *summum bonum* is to understand the process of moral practice known as self-cultivation in Confucianism.

Self-cultivation and Spiritual Vision: Doctrines of *Siyu* and *Siwu*

Self-cultivation begins with the rectification of one's moral misconduct. To give an example Wang Yangming often cited: at the sight of one's parents, one's intention is instantly activated as to whether to serve them or not.

Liangzhi (or *zhiti*) can tell automatically which intention is right or wrong. If the intention is wrong, say, intending to totally ignore their needs, then the action that follows will certainly be wrong. Therefore, the first step in self-cultivation, according to the *Great Learning*, an important Confucian cannon, is the "rectification of actions." (Many Confucian masters, for example Zhu Xi [1130–1200], have a quite different interpretation of the original text, and hence it is often translated as "investigation of things" in English.) This step, in turn, requires the "extension of *liangzhi*," which means the extension of the application of the Heaven's Principle (*tianli*) (or "universal moral laws," to use a Kantian term) inherent in one's *liangzhi* to the rectification of one's misconduct. The extension of *liangzhi* in turn requires one to make sure that one's intention to comply with the demand of *liangzhi* is genuine and without any self-deception, which is called "sincerity of intentions." If one's intention is sincere, then one's mind, which has run astray because of the evil intentions, will be restored to its original state of supreme good, namely, the original mind (i.e., the infinite mind or mind-in-itself). This process is known as "rectification of mind." Starting with external "actions" (or "things"), going through "knowing" and then "intention" and ending in the "mind," self-cultivation is conceived as a process that digs into one's subjectivity step by step with an ever-increasing depth. Yangming explains pithily his understanding of the four root concepts (or items) involved in self-cultivation (i.e., mind, intention, *liangzhi*, and action or thing), in his famous Four-Sentence Teaching:

> That which has neither good nor evil is the mind-in-itself;
> That which has good and evil is the activation of intentions;
> That which knows good and evil is *liangzhi*;
> That which performs good and removes evil is the rectification of
>   actions.[17]

Mou contends that of the four root concepts in self-cultivation, intention is the central link, because the other three are all connected to it directly in one way or another. First, *liangzhi* and the mind, Mou points out, actually refer to one and the same thing. They are called by different names simply because they are connected to intentions in different ways. Our intentions, Mou notes, are invariably "activated" by the intervention of the activities of our sensibility as used by Kant, that is, by our "human, all too human flesh." At the very moment our intentions are activated, the differentiation of good and evil occurs. This differentiation simultaneously calls for, or simply presumes, the existence of a transcendental standard according to which the activated intentions are to be judged as either good or evil. That standard is nothing less than the mind-in-itself, which as a standard in itself must be "beyond good and evil." At the same time, a faculty, as distinct from a standard, is also required that can tell good intentions from evil ones according to the standard. This faculty is *liangzhi*, which literally means "innate knowing." *Liangzhi*, as explained earlier, is not knowing in its cognitive sense. It refers to the illuminating sensitivity, meaning a sharp, keen awareness that the mind-in-itself exhibits when it is functioning (*lingming* or *mingjue*). As for the fourth concept, that is, action (or "things," as the term is used by many other Confucian masters), it is motivated by intentions and can therefore be properly conceptualized as "where intentions direct." Mou also reminds us importantly that, while the mind and *liangzhi* belong to the noumenal world (or the transcendent level), intentions and things belong to the phenomenal world (or the empirical level). It is this distinction of two levels, he stresses, that makes moral practice necessary and possible.

However, Mou argues that Yangming's Four-Sentence Teaching is not the Confucian perfect teaching. It is merely the preparatory stage, the first step that paves the way to the perfect teaching. The Confucian perfect teaching was made explicitly by Wang Lungxi (1489–1583), known as the most brilliant and innovative disciple of Yangming. Lungxi's theory is pithily called the doctrine of "Fourfold Non-being" (*siwu*) in contrast to Yangming's Four Sentence Teaching, which is known as the doctrine of "Fourfold Being" (*siyu*). Since Lungxi's position was fully endorsed by his master, the doctrine of *siwu* is sometimes regarded as an innovative interpretation of the doctrine of *siyu*. However, the distinction between the two positions is crucial to the comprehension of Mou's theory of the Confucian perfect teaching.

It is important to note that here the terms "being" and "non-being" are ad hoc English translations of the Chinese *yu* and *wu*. "Being" here, as Mou interprets it, means "having forms," and "non-being" means "having no forms." "Form," as explained earlier, is used by Mou in its Kantian sense to denote "universal characteristics" or "determined forms," namely, forms determined by the Kantian categories a priori. This usage coincides, according to Mou, basically with its Buddhist usage of "form" (*xiang* in Chinese; *lakshana* in Sanskrit), meaning describable characteristics or appearance of things manifested. In Buddhist terms, "form" is related to "nature" (*svabhava*) just as phenomenon is to noumenon.[18]

In the doctrine of *siyu*, which is implied in Yangming's Four-Sentence Teaching, Mou observes, the four items involved are all in a state of "being" (*yu*), which means that they are all differentiated, separate entities, each with its own describable characteristics and manifesting itself in concrete forms. In this connection, these forms are referred to by Mou as "forms of identity" (*zitixiang*), meaning forms that can identify one object as distinct from another. Lungxi's doctrine of *siwu*, on the other hand, tries to show that "if we truly realize that the mind-in-itself is beyond good and evil," then the four items should all be conceived as in the state of non-being. They are all devoid of any forms of identity and merge into one single process of self-presentation, or, as Mou puts it, "a ceaseless self-so flow" (*ziranliuxing*) of *liangzhi*, which is totally undifferentiated and without any specific or even specifiable forms or characteristics. The four items are, accordingly, all beyond good and evil. The following quotation from Lungxi is particularly illustrative of his *siwu* position:

> The Master [i.e., Yangming] sets up his teaching in response to contingent situations. This is called expediencies (*quanfa*). We must not be rigidly attached to its fixed formulations. Substance and function, manifestations and [hidden] subtleties, are all simply one and the same incipience (*ji*). The mind, the intention, the knowing [of *liangzhi*], and the thing are all simply one and the same event. If we truly realize [or fully appreciate] that the mind is the mind without good and evil, then the intention is the intention without good and evil, the knowing [of *liangzhi*] is the knowing without good and evil, and the thing is the thing without good and evil. For the mind without [the form of] a mind is to be concealed in its profundity, the intention without [the form of] an intention is to be round and perfect in its response, and the knowing without [the form of] knowing is to be tranquil in its substance, and the thing without [the form of] a thing is to be unfathomable in its function.[19]

In order to understand the meaning or import of the state of non-being (*wu*), or "without the form of [its own identity]" in this passage, we need first to understand in what sense the four items in the theory of *siyu* are said to be in a state of being (*yu*), that is, "having its form of identity."

As mentioned above, the beingness (*yu*) of the four items in *siyu*, according to Mou, starts as soon as one's intention is activated by the participation of one's sensibility. The activation immediately brings about the differentiation of the empirical and the transcendent level, with intentions and things belonging to the empirical level and the mind and *liangzhi* to the transcendent level. It is this distinction, Mou notes, that initially causes each item to have its own form of identity. This can be readily inferred from the differentiation that is implied in the Four-Sentence Teaching: the form of identity of the intention lies in its being either good or evil; that of *liangzhi* in its ability to tell good from evil; that of things—action—in its being either rectified or not rectified. As for the mind, Mou argues, its form of identity lies in its absolute purity without any form of good and evil.

It could be puzzling to the reader that the mind, being absolute and completely self-sufficient, is still said to have its own form of identity distinct from those of others. But Mou would argue that, since the mind now serves as the transcendent standard of moral judgment, it is implied that the mind is set against an empirical object to which the standard is to be applied. The differentiation of standard of judgment and object of judgment shows that the mind is already relativized or contextualized. Only when completely decontextualized, can mind-in-itself be regarded as having no form of identity.

It could be more difficult to explain the meaning of "without its form of identity" in the doctrine of *siwu*. However, before going further, it must be noted that Mou makes an important distinction between two dimensions of Confucian metaphysics: the ontological and the functional. The ontological dimension concerns itself with the essence of ontological being understood as an objective entity and focuses on the question: What is being? The functional dimension, on the other hand, concerns itself not with the objective entity of being but with the subjective state of the mind. The question it addresses is not *what* being is but *how* to attain an ideal and lofty spiritual realm through moral/spiritual practice. Since spiritual attainment hinges primarily on the function of the subjective mind, it belongs to the functional rather than the ontological dimension of metaphysics. The distinction of two dimensions in metaphysics is of vital importance to the understanding of Mou's interpretation of the doctrine of *siwu*.

When Lungxi says "the mind without [the form of] a mind" or "the intention without [the form of] an intention," Mou argues, he is talking not about the ontological status of mind and intention but about the manner or the mode in which the mind and intention function. Actually, the message Lungxi intends to deliver is that mind and intention are both *functioning* in such a wondrous manner that they do not have any trace of mindfulness or intentness. The following quotation from Cheng Hao would aptly illustrate this point:

> The Norm of Heaven and Earth is for its mind to pervade completely
>   the myriad things and hence without a mind;
> The Norm of the Sage is for his feelings to traverse all along with the
>   myriad things and hence without any feelings.[20]

Obviously, the ontological existence of both the mind and the feelings is presumed when Cheng Hao uses "its mind" and "his feelings" in the first part of each sentence. But the main thrust of the couplet is not about the ontological status of mind and feelings but about the manner in which they *function*. Although ontologically asserted, the mind and feelings are, functionally speaking, thoroughly removed to attain a spiritual realm not only free of any conscious effort but also absolutely independent and totally undifferentiated. The same is the case with "intention [without the form of] an intention." Quoting from Liu Zongzhou (1578–1645), the last towering Confucian master of the Ming dynasty, Mou says that this means "to transform and dissolve intention and have it incorporated back with the [infinite] mind," thereby functionally purging intention of any forms of identity.[21]

As for "knowing without [the form of] knowing," Mou says it means that *liangzhi* as knowing, unlike what it is in the state of being, now has neither intentions nor things against which it is set as a standard of judgment or a subject of judgment. Being objectless, knowing is, as explained earlier, in effect *liangzhi*'s (or *zhiti*'s) "throwing back onto itself the light it emanates." It becomes the self-activity of the infinite mind and as such is known as intellectual intuition. The oneness of *liangzhi* and the mind is restored, and the need to call *liangzhi* and the mind by separate names simply disappears.

"The thing without the form of a thing," Mou explains, means that the thing, unlike what it is in the state of being, no longer assumes the form of an object set against *liangzhi* as the subject. Nor has it the form of being good or evil. This is because things in their state of non-being should no longer be conceived of as moral actions "[that come into being] where [activated] intentions direct" and therefore belonging to the world of phenomena. They should be conceived of as "[those which come into being] where *liangzhi* wondrously affects and responds," and therefore as things-in-themselves in the noumenal world. The de-linking of things with activated intentions and their re-linking with *liangzhi* purge them of any form of good and evil.

Lungxi further describes the state of non-being of the four items of mind, intention, knowing, and thing respectively as "concealed in its profundity," "perfect in its response," "tranquil in its substance," and "unfathomable in its function." These epithets, although each laden with subtleties typical of Chinese spiritual traditions, are actually applicable to each other. They all merge into "one and the same event" and point to a spiritual vision which Mou sums up in accordance with Lungxi's doctrine of *siwu*:

> The four items of mind, intention, knowing and thing become simply the "ceaseless self-so flow" (*ziran liuxing*), or the "ceaseless as-such presentation" (*ruru chengxian*) of the Heavenly endowed nature, which is purely and supremely good and cannot help manifest itself and flow ceaselessly.[22]

In other words, the spiritual realm Mou visualizes is the "ceaseless self-so flow" of the infinite mind, undifferentiated, unobstructed, and free of all attachments. It is the spontaneous and ongoing self-disclosure of the infinite mind-in-itself or, in Buddhist terms, the self-disclosure of the True Suchness itself. This line of thinking is vividly explained as Yangming describes *liangzhi* in terms of the concept of the Great Vacuity (*taixu*):

> Indeed, only those who have appropriated the Way can truly realize that his *liangzhi,* luminously enlightening and sensitive as spirit, all-dissolving and all-penetrating, is so vast and tranquil as to dwell squarely in the Great Vacuity itself and become one with it. Is there anything you could imagine that the Great Vacuity does not contain? Yet, not one single thing could ever hamper it and be its obstruction. . . . Therefore for those who have appropriated the Way, to be rich or poor, to be powerful or lowly, to gain or to lose, to love or to hate, these are all "forms" (*xiang*) just like fleeting winds and floating clouds that come and go, change and transform across the Great Vacuity. And yet the Great-Vacuity-in-itself always remains the same: vast and tranquil and free of all obstructions.[23]

As mentioned earlier, the Great Vacuity, according to Mou, is another way to characterize the Confucian ultimate reality. The message is abundantly clear: Just as not one single phenomenon (i.e., being or dharma) needs to be removed from the Great Vacuity, none of the four items needs to be removed from *liangzhi*. But all attachments in the form of "obstructions" or "sojourns" should be removed to make way for the "ceaseless self-so flow" of the infinite mind.

Ontological Perfection

However, a closer scrutiny shows that the main thrust of both Cheng Hao's couplet and Yangming's metaphor concerns what Mou calls "functional perfection," which is particularly suggestive of the Daoist or even Buddhist approach. To be fully qualified for a Confucian perfect teaching, "ontological perfection," as mentioned earlier, is even more essential and must be added. In other words, Mou has to show how the Confucian infinite mind (or *liangzhi* in this case) can create not only a moral world but also an ontological world, a world that is not only functionally perfect but also ontologically perfect.

The message of ontological perfection is contained in one of Yangming's important theses mentioned earlier: his conceptualization of "things as [those which come into being] where the illuminating sensitivity [of *zhiti*] affects and responds." The thesis is important because it demonstrates succinctly Yangming's view about the relationship between virtue and being, the crux of *summun bonum*. Some brief explanation is in order.

"Illuminating sensitivity," as explained earlier, refers to *zhiti*'s capability to respond instantly to a pitiful situation with an all-penetrating and all-soothing power and simultaneously to reveal the ultimate reality as if by shedding light onto it. It is important to bear in mind that the whole discussion here is conducted on the transcendent level. Therefore, strictly speaking, when Yangming conceptualizes things as "where the illuminating sensitivity affects and responds," he does not, Mou stresses, mean to say that *zhiti*'s illuminating sensitivity is affecting and responding to something external to itself and already in existence out there, because this line of interpretation would relativize *liangzhi* and turn it into a passive faculty like our sensibility and forfeit its ontological status as being creativity itself. As mentioned earlier, external conditions (say, the sight of a baby about to fall into a well) serve merely as an occasion that "triggers off" *liangzhi*'s awareness. The occasion itself belongs to the empirical level and is therefore always conditioned and limited. But what it triggers, namely, *zhiti*, belongs to the transcendent level and is unconditioned and unlimited. Once triggered, *liangzhi*, as creativity itself cultivated through "retracting verification," would extend until it pervades and penetrates the myriad things. The very process of pervading and penetrating is the process of creating. In this sense, *zhiti* is actually self-affecting and self-responding. It is creating in the sense that while it discloses and presents itself spontaneously and ceaselessly, "things"—or rather things-in-themselves—simultaneously emerge or come into being.

Now it is obvious that there are two ways in which Yangming conceptualizes "things": things as "[what came into being] where the intentions direct," as in his Four-Sentence Teaching, or the doctrine of *siyu*, and things as "[what came into being] where illuminating sensitivity affects and responds," as in his endorsement of Lungxi's doctrine of *siwu*. In the former, "things" refers to moral actions in the process of self-cultivation. In the latter, "things" refers to things-in-themselves, which, according to Mou, are beings bathing in and nurtured by the soothing and life-giving spring of *liangzhi* or *ren*. They represent the ultimate spiritual realm to which Mou aspires and which he believes is humanly attainable through moral cultivation. The "things" in the former case belong to the phenomenal world, a world of facts, which he deals with in his attached ontology. The "things" in the latter case, belong to the noumenal world, a world of value, which he deals with in his non-attached ontology.

In this connection, it is interesting and illuminating to note how Mou interprets in Kantian terms the famous thesis of Yangming that "the great man regards Heaven and Earth and the myriad things as one body":

Zhiti as illuminating sensitivity is the infinite mind. But it is not an infinite mind that suspends abstractly up in the empty air. It is the infinite mind that "dwells in and co-exists with" (*ziyu*) the being of the actual things-in-them-selves. As a result, the being of things-in-themselves also becomes infinite and eternal. "Regarding Heaven and Earth and the myriad things as one body" simply means taking the being of all things-in-themselves as the content of the being of myself as thing-in-itself while keeping intact the independent infinity and eternality of each individual thing-in-itself in Heaven and Earth and the myriad things. In short, each and every thing is in-itself, and each and every thing-in-itself is an independent individual "substance."[24]

However, Mou cautions that Lungxi's theory of *siwu*, strictly speaking, is still flawed in the sense that it could lead to an "isolated perfect teaching," as in the case of the teaching of the Buddhist *Huayen* school when compared with the truly perfect teaching of *Tiantai* school. "The teaching of *Huayen* school is too high and lofty to be perfect. It is just like the rising sun, which can shine only on the high mountain but cannot reach the deep valley."[25] The truly perfect teaching in Confucianism, Mou believes, is best represented by Cheng Hao. Many Confucian masters tend to say "experiencing the transforming and nourishing process of Heaven and Earth." But according to him, the word "experiencing" is superfluous. This is because "this [infinite mind of ours] is by itself alone already the transforming process of Heaven and Earth. There could never be a transforming process of Heaven and Earth apart from this [mind]."[26] "This," Mou explains, refers here to the ceaseless moral creation of the infinite mind. Nothing exists beyond the infinite mind, whose transforming and nourishing capability is all-penetrating and all-pervasive. Not one single phenomenon is left out under its all-encompassing aura. The infinite dwells in the finite and vice versa. The phenomenal and the noumenal world collapse into one, each dwelling in and co-existent with the other. As Lou Rufang (1514–1588), a Confucian master of the Ming Dynasty, puts it:

> Even a lifting of one's head and a sighting of one's eyes are all actualization of *zhiti*; even the minute acts of uttering a word and expressing some feelings in one's face are all the radiation of *zhiti*.[27]

All beings, including the slightest ones, bathing in and emerging from the benevolent and generative radiance of *zhiti*, are bestowed with a blissful-ness that is unconditional and necessary.

Thus, ontological perfection and functional perfection combine to round up the Confucian perfect teaching. Together they point to a spiritual realm in which not only everything—or rather every thing-in-itself—is an end in itself, but each and all find a proper niche, a true home in the "ceaseless self-so flow" of the infinite mind. Happiness appears wherever virtue goes because being or things emerge wherever the infinite mind or *liangzhi* penetrates with its all-soothing and all-anointing creative capability. *Summum bonum* as "moral perfection crowned by the happiness it merits" is thus theoretically justified.

Gongfu: "Retractive Verification" and "Vigilant Solitariness"

To Mou, however, *summum bonum* is not an abstract idea or a postulate in the Kantian sense but a spiritual realm to be existentially experienced and even embodied. Theoretical justification is at best a clue to the way moral-spiritual practice is to proceed and at worst could prove to be a hindrance. "The major part of a teaching," Mou asserts, "is the purification of one's life through practice in accordance with reason. . . . Practice," he stresses, "is a tough fighting that definitely calls for an endeavor."[28] This moral practice is called *gongfu* in all of the three major Chinese spiritual traditions. The final goal of *gongfu* is to appropriate the ultimate universal truth and attain an experiential state of mind initially known in Buddhism as "enlightenment" (*wu*).

There are two approaches in characterizing *gongfu* as the effort to achieve enlightenment: sudden enlightenment and gradual enlightenment. The former believes in the possibility of attaining the ultimate truth in an instantaneous, direct, and complete way, which can be exemplified by Wang Lungxi's advocating a sort of quantum leap, so to speak, into the realm of *siwu*. The latter believes that the ultimate goal can be reached only step by step, in a piecemeal, incremental way. For example, Zhu Xi tends to insist that "investigating things" on a daily basis should constitute the central piece of self-cultivation. Mou, while rejecting Zhu Xi's gradual enlightenment as "thoroughly *a posteriori* learning," also criticizes Wang Lungxi's position as "imprudent and negligent."[29]

Mou maintains that the primary ground for enlightenment cannot be sought, as Zhu Xi tends to advocate, outwardly in investigating external things. It must be sought first of all inwardly in the extension of one's *liangzhi*. "Once *liangzhi* is fully extended, all problems will be solved," he says. The extension of *liangzhi*, Mou contends, depends on *liangzhi* itself. The extension is made possible, as explained earlier, only by the self-activity of *liangzhi*, that is, by the functioning of intellectual intuition when one "retraces one's feeling of commiseration, etc. back to its root of *zhiti* and existentially verifying and embodying it," namely, by "retractive verification." Both the gradual and the sudden enlightenment, Mou argues, must turn inward and take *liangzhi* as their transcendent ground and practice "retractive verification." Otherwise, no enlightenment is possible, sudden or gradual.

The difference between the two approaches, Mou maintains, is caused not by the presence or absence of "retractive verification" but by that of moral cultivation. Gradual enlightenment is intended for people with ordinary inherence, whose *liangzhi* is inevitably beclouded by their sensibility. They need moral cultivation and therefore have to start with the state of *siyu* and proceed in a graduated way. Sudden enlightenment is suitable only for people of superb inherence (i.e., people with little or no selfish desires but not necessarily with high intelligence). They need little—or, in a few exceptional cases, even no—moral cultivation and therefore can easily or even automatically be initiated into the state of *siwu* and be enlightened. However, Mou stresses, since moral cultivation, although empirically activated by sensibility, is transcendently grounded in *liangzhi*, gradual enlightenment also possesses the ground for sudden enlightenment. The two types of enlightenment are not totally severed from each other. Commenting on Lungxi's remark that "sudden enlightenment" as a kind of a priori learning makes extension of *liangzhi* "simple and easy," Mou stresses: "Sudden enlightenment is far from being easy. Neither is it the way everyone can follow; even men with superb inherence are not completely free from impurities of worldly passions and desires, although for them these impurities are comparatively slight and relatively easy to be transformed. Man is, after all, a finite being, a being with sensibility." Since we all possess intellectual intuition, sudden enlightenment is potentially possible for each of us. Lungxi's rigid dichotomy of the sudden and the gradual enlightenment, Mou cautions, could lead to "wandering in the [Buddhist] realm of void."[30]

It is noteworthy that Mou assigns a pivotal position to a method of self-cultivation known as *shendu*. The term is often translated as "to be watchful over oneself when alone," but is better rendered as "vigilant solitariness" by Tu Weiming. The concept appeared as early as in the pre-Qin Confucian cannons of *Great Learning* and *Commonality and Centrality* (usually translated as *The Doctrine of the Mean*) but was later developed by Liu Zhongzhou. Liu tried to avoid the fallacies of the later developments of Wang Yangming's teaching and attempted to pinpoint human weakness at the deepest stratum of one's motivational structure. He is suspicious of the claim that the mind, by the knowing of *liangzhi* alone, can directly bring about an effective self-cultivation and self-transformation. He chooses to give intention (or will) rather than the knowing of *liangzhi* top priority in moral cultivation. This is reflected in his unique characterization of sincerity of intention: "The root of intention is the subtlest; sincerity-in-itself lies originally in Heaven."[31] Liu's message seems to be: Dig into the subtlest root of your intention and there you will find yourself becoming one with Heaven.

Mou, accordingly, stresses that there is a deep message in Liu's emphasis on intention: Constant practice in "vigilant solitariness" can bring about a complete fusion of the phenomenal with the noumenal, the experiential with the ontological and can achieve the ceaseless self-so flow of the presentation of the infinite mind. In other words, although humans are finite beings experientially, they can become infinite ontologically. This is because the gap between the experiential and the ontological world, caused by the interference of sensibility, can be bridged by moral practice. Given the moral-spiritual depth "vigilant solitariness" seeks to probe and the holistic vision it tries to embrace, Mou regards it as the pivotal link that enables the infinite mind to present itself fully through one's own practice.

Summum bonum as "the proper proportion between happiness and virtue" is thus both theoretically justified and practically vindicated. It is valid primarily because "beings emerge [or things-in-themselves come into being] wherever the infinite mind directs." *Summum bonum* is, thus, guaranteed not through the existence of God and the immortality of the soul, as Kant has it, but through the attainment of a spiritual realm by human self-effort. In Confucian terms, the realm can be encapsulated in terms of Yangming's conceptualization of "things [i.e., things-in-themselves] as where the illuminating sensitivity [of *zhiti*] wondrously affects and responds." However, this transcendent world of things-in-themselves, instead of being separate from the mundane world, dwells squarely and directly in it. This is a realm where all theoretical analyses and explanations are irrelevant and hence completely abolished. The elaborate philosophical edifice Mou has painstakingly constructed is also leveled down: "The meaning having been appropriated, the language is forgotten." The cumulative tradition of religious dogmas, rituals, and institutions disappears. Even the boundaries among major spiritual traditions are also blurred, if not totally erased. What remains is the "ceaseless self-so" flow of the infinite mind. As a concluding remark, Mou's following thought-provoking observation is particularly revealing in understanding his spiritual vision:

> Infinity is always manifested through a finite path, an actual life (the life of an individual), but at the same time it is also limited by the path. This is an inevitable paradox. Therefore there must exist a dialectical process that can break through the limit. Having realized that each teaching is only one path among many, one should not merely assert one's own teaching to the exclu-

sion of others, and this implies that although limited, one is not to be restricted by the limitation and therefore is actually not limited. Only by way of the resulting unobstructed, unrestricted and mutually penetrating capability can the infinite mind truly and fully disclose and present itself. Once fully disclosed, the infinite mind would contain infinite meanings and infinite virtues, all of which would mutually inter-fuse and inter-penetrate and never mutually exclude. Therefore, although it is understood that the one path of a teaching expresses only one meaning, the meaning it expresses will not limit itself simply because of the limitation of that teaching. This means that there is no sticking to one meaning to the exclusion of others, because otherwise the mind would not be the infinite mind. Not only does this one meaning not exclude other meanings, but actually it inter-penetrates and conflows with the entirety of meanings and even subsumes them all in itself. This is the so-called "Great Inter-Penetration" (*datong*) of each and all perfect teachings. But it should be noted that "Great Inter-Penetration" is not a teaching at all. It is merely the mutual penetration and sharing of all perfect teachings. At this point, no teaching has any form of a teaching. The meaning having been appropriated, the teaching is forgotten. All we have is simply an authentic life doing what it ought to do, an infinite mind in its "ceaseless self-so flow." This "doing what ought to be done," this "ceaseless self-so flow"—I really don't know whether it belongs to Confucianism, Buddhism, Daoism, or even Christianity.[32]

Notes

1. Tu Weiming, *Humanity and Self-Cultivation: Essays in Confucian Thought* (Berkeley: Asian Humanities Press, 1979), 3–22.

2. Liu Shu-hsien, "A Critical Review of Contemporary Neo-Confucian Thought with a View to Modernization," in *The Triadic Chord*, ed. Tu Weiming (Singapore: Institute of East Asian Philosophies, 1991), 377–96.

3. Alasdair MacIntyre, *After Virtue* (Notre Dame, Ind.: University of Notre Dame Press, 1984), 44.

4. Mou Zongsan, *Xianxiang yu wuzishen* [Phenomenon and Thing-in-itself] (Taipei: Xuesen shuju, 1975), 44–45.

5. Mou Zongsan, *Zhongsi zhexue zhi huitong shisi jiang* [Fourteen Lectures on the Confluence of Chinese and Western Philosophy] (Taipei: Xuesen shuju, 1990), 181.

6. Wing-tsit Chan, *A Source Book in Chinese Philosophy* (Princeton, N.J.: Princeton University Press, 1969), 786; Mou Zongsan, *Yuanshan lun* [On *summum bonum*] (Taipei: Xuesen shuju, 1985), 318.

7. Mou Zongsan, *Zhongguo zhexue de tezhi* [The Unique Characteristics of Chinese Philosophy] (Taipei: Xuesen shuju, 1974), 21.

8. Ibid., 44.

9. Mou, *Yuanshan lun*, 260–61.

10. Mou Zongsan, *Mou Zongsan de zhexue yu zhuzuo* [The Philosophy and Works of Mr. Mou Zongsan] (Taipei: Xuesen shuju, 1978), 639–40.

11. Mou, *Xianxiang yu wuzishen*, 3.

12. Ibid., 100–101.

13. Mou, *Yuanshan lun*, 142.

14. Ibid., 306.

15. Chan, *Source Book*, 397.

16. Mou Zhongsan, *Zhongguo zhexue shijui jiang* [Nineteen Lectures on Chinese Philosophy] (Taipei: Xuesen shuju, 1983), 360.

17. Mou, *Yuanshan lun*, 313.

18. Chan, *Source Book*, 789.

19. Mou, *Yuanshan lun*, 316. The translation is based on Tu Weiming's version (*Humanity and Self-Cultivation*, 163–64); the author's insertion of "the form of" in his translation is based on Mou's own interpretation. This will be soon become clear.

20. Ibid., 317.

21. Ibid., 318.

22. Mou, *Xianxiang yu wuzishen*, 319.

23. Chen Lai, *Yu wu zhi jing: Wang Yangming zhexue de jingsheng* [The Spiritual Realm of Being and Non-being: The Spirit of Wang Yangming's Philosophy] (Beijing: renmin chubanshe, 1991), 208.

24. Mou, *Xianxiang yu wuzishen*, 118.

25. Mou, *Yuanshan lun*, 272.

26. Ibid., 137.

27. Mou, *Xianxiang yu wuzishen*, 118.

28. Mou, *Yuanshan lun*, 267, 270.

29. Mou Zongsan, "The Immediate Successor of Wang Yangming: Wang Lung-hsi and His Theory of Ssi-wu," *Philosophy East and West* 23 (January–April 1973): 115.

30. Ibid.

31. Mou Zongsan, *Xinti yu xingti* [Mind-in-self and Human-nature-in-self] (Taipei: Zhengzhong shuzhu, 1968–69), 1:394.

32. Mou, *Xianxiang yu wuzishen*, 454–55.

Suggested Readings

Berthrong, John. *All Under Heaven: Transforming Paradigms in Confucian–Christian Dialogue.* Albany: State University of New York Press, 1991.

Ching, Julia. *Confucianism and Christianity: A Comparative Study.* Tokyo: Kodansha International, 1977.

Cheng, Chung-ying. *New Dimensions of Confucianism and Neo-Confucianism.* Albany: State University of New York Press, 1991.

De Bary, Wm. Theodore. *Learning for One's Self: Essays on the Individual in Neo-Confucian Thought* (New York: Columbia University Press, 1991).

Fingarette, Herbert. *Confucius: The Secular as Sacred.* New York: Harper & Row, 1972.

Hall, David, and Roger Ames. *Anticipating China.* Albany: State University of New York Press, 1995.

Liu, Shu-hsien. "The Religious Import of Confucian Philosophy: Its Tradition Outlook and Contemporary Significance." *Philosophy East and West* 21 (April 1971).

———. "Some Reflections on the Sung-Ming Understanding of Mind, Nature, and Reason." *Journal of the Institute of Chinese Studies of the Chinese University of Hong Kong* 21 (1990).

Schwartz, Benjamin. *The World of Thought in Ancient China.* Cambridge, Mass.: Belknap Press of Harvard University, 1985.

Taylor, Rodney. *The Religious Dimensions of Neo-Confucianism.* Albany: State University of New York Press, 1991.

Tu, Weiming. *Centrality and Commonality: An Essay on Confucian Religiousness.* Albany: State University of New York Press, 1989.

Yu, Ying-shi. "Cong jiazhi xitong kan zhongguo wenhua de xiandai yiyi." *Wen-hua: shijie yu zhongguo* [Culture: The World and China], no. 1 (1987).

31

Contemporary Neo-Confucian Philosophy

SHU-HSIEN LIU

T HE SCOPE OF THE SO-CALLED New Confucianism is not clearly defined. It may include scholars with varied backgrounds, such as the scholar-thinker Liang Souming (Shu-ming; 1893–1988), the historian Qian Mu (Ch'ien Mu; 1895–1990), the scholar-statesman Zhang Junmai (Carsun Chang; 1887–1969), and Xu Fuguan (Hsü Fu-kuan; 1903–1982), a leading intellectual historian and also a political commentator. For philosophical reasons, however, I have chosen to discuss only the following five scholars: Feng Youlan (Fung Yu-lan; 1895–1990), Xiong Shili (Hsiung Shih-li; 1885–1968), Thomé H. Fang (1899–1977), Tang Junyi (T'ang Chün-i; 1909–1978), and Mou Zongsan (Mou Tsung-san; 1909–1995). And I prefer to use the more restrictive term "contemporary Neo-Confucian philosophy," in order to show the connection between the vital philosophical movement today and that of Song-Ming Neo-Confucianism except in the case of Thomé Fang.[1] From the perspective of contemporary Neo-Confucianism, there are three epochs in Confucian philosophy: First, Confucius (551–479 B.C.E.) and Mencius (371–289 B.C.E. [?]) established the spiritual foundation of Confucian philosophy. Second, Song-Ming Neo-Confucian philosophers developed a new philosophy in order to answer the challenges from Buddhism and Neo-Daoism. Third, it is the mission of contemporary Neo-Confucian philosophers to develop a radically new philosophy to answer the challenges from the unprecedented impacts from the West.[2] There are obviously both novelty and continuity, and the emphasis of my discussions will be on spiritual Confucianism, not on politicized Confucianism, which served as the ideological ground for the dynasties since it was adopted as the state doctrine in 136 B.C.E. by Emperor

Han Wu, or popular Confucianism, beliefs and customs of the people blended with Daoist and Buddhist traditions and other folkways that still thrive today.[3] In the following I can provide only a few clues for the emergence of the movement.

The challenge the Chinese culture has faced in the last two hundred years is far more stringent than in the other two epochs. It has always been the mother culture in the Far East and has never faced a culture that is superior or even equal to its own. Suddenly, however, Chinese culture was under the onslaught of a superior modern Western civilization, and Confucianism was thought to be something dead that could be found only in the museums.[4] In the late Qing period, Kang Youwei (1858–1927) pushed for radical reform within the Confucian framework but failed miserably in the attempt, and finally the last dynasty fell in 1912 and was replaced by the Republic of China. In the early twentieth century it was usual to blame the Confucian tradition for this. During the New Culture movement symbolized by May Fourth (1919), the slogans were: "Down with the Confucian shop!" "Throw the stitched volumes into the toilet!"[5]

Western learning came to the fore, and the intellectual leader in those days, Hu Shi (1891–1962), the famous disciple of John Dewey, advocated wholesale Westernization or modernization. But even his ideas of gradual reform were cast aside, as China had to face both serious internal problems and also domination of foreign powers culminating in the Japanese invasion. The Chinese tended to adopt more and more radical means for China's survival. Eventually all these led to the establishment of the People's Republic of China in 1949 under the leadership of Chairman Mao Zedong (1893– 1976), and the official ideology became Marxism-Leninism-Maoism. Under the direction of Mao and the Gang of Four, the anti-Confucian campaign reached its climax during the disastrous Cultural Revolution from 1966 to 1977. It was only after the death of Mao that China returned to a more moderate policy, and Confucius's fortunes have gradually changed in recent years.

From the above we can see clearly that Confucianism certainly does not belong in the mainstream Chinese thought in the present century. But this does not mean that it can be uprooted altogether. Not only have some of its ideas and practices become long-standing habits of the Chinese that have inadvertently produced beneficial as well as harmful consequences, but some leading intellectuals still refuse to abandon the Confucian cause. Although they do not advocate returning to the traditional ways, they realize the extent of the impact from the West and feel that wholesale Westernization may not be the best course for us to follow.

The first thinker who reflected on the problems of culture in depth was undoubtedly Liang Souming. Liang did not come from a conservative family; he was open to new ideas, and as a young scholar he believed that only Buddhism could provide the ultimate answer for life. After he was invited to teach Buddhism at Peking University in 1917, he was under pressure to think hard on problems of culture. In 1920 he began to give his public lectures on Eastern and Western cultures and their philosophies, which were published in 1921 and 1922.[6] His ideas may appear simplistic from today's perspectives, but they were provocative in those days.

Liang took a comparative approach and found that the Western, the Chinese, and the Indian cultures have opted for three different directions of life. According to him, the guiding spirit for the Western culture is that the will always strives forward. Characteristics of this culture are conquest of nature, scientific method, and democracy. The guiding spirit for the Chinese culture, on the other hand, is that the will aims at achieving harmony and equilibrium. Characteristics of this culture are contentment, adjustment to the environment, and acceptance of authority. Such a culture would not invent steamships and trains or democracy. Finally, the guiding spirit of the Indian culture is that the will looks backward. The only things it cares for are religious aspiration and liberation from worldly cares. Western culture values material gratification; the Chinese society, life; and the Indian, transcendence.

After examining these three directions of life, Liang felt he was ready to answer the question, What are the attitudes we should adopt today? Apparently Liang changed his mind and deviated from his earlier views; he found that the Indian and Chinese cultures were premature and failed to fully develop their potentialities. His conclusions at that time were that (1) because the Indian attitude looks backward, it must be totally excluded; (2) Western achievements must be taken over without any reservation, but the Western attitude of only striving forward must be changed, so that undesirable consequences of Western civilization can be avoided; finally (3) the middle way of the Chinese culture, which looks both forward and backward, should be revived from a critical point of view.

Confucius's strength lies in that he finds resources in life itself, and both traditional shortcomings and modern diseases should be overcome in the future. Liang, of course, never showed how such a synthesis could actually be achieved, but he did suggest the revival of the Confucian spirit as a way for us to face the situation today. Clearly Liang should never be accused of being a conservative who rejected science and democracy, but he saw the limitations of the Western culture. Even though he commited himself as an activist to reviving the Confucian spirit, he never saw Confucianism as his ultimate goal. Thus, Guy Alitto was shocked to find that Liang rejected the label "the last Confucian" for himself. Not only was he not the last Confucian, but he still looked beyond Confucianism to find messages for liberation from Buddhism.[7]

After World War I, Liang Qichao (Ch'i-ch'ao; 1873–1929) led a team to study Europe and wrote about his impressions of the European tour.[8] Even though Liang had always enthusiastically introduced things from the West, this time his observations led him to conclude that we must not blindly follow the model of the West. Two members of his team, Zhang Junmai and Ding Wenjiang later engaged in the famous debates between metaphysics and science.[9] After Zhang gave a talk on views of life in which he attacked on the undesirable consequences that resulted from a one-sided emphasis on science and technology, Ding gave a rebuttal, pointing out that as there is still not a solid foundation for science to be developed in China, a revival of the so-called metaphysical ghost would be harmful for the future. Zhang responded, and many scholars were drawn into the debate. In retrospect, the debates then were not of very high quality, but full of emotional overtones. Zhang was a follower of Rudolf Eucken and Henri Bergson, who put so much emphasis on intuition, which appeared to be too subjective to be acceptable. Ding was a follower of Ernst Mach and Karl Pearson, who advocated a scientism rather than science. At that time it seemed that most scholars were on the side of science over metaphysics, but a closer examination showed that this was largely a strawman attack, as Zhang was by no means against science. What he really intended was to point out the limitations of a one-sided emphasis on science and technology.

Now in the twenty-first century, such a reservation would make a lot of sense not only to the Chinese but to the whole world as well. But ideologies usually draw a line between the modernists and the conservatives. As a rule, contemporary Neo-Confucian philosophers are usually put in the camp of the so-called conservatives.[10] In fact, none of them are against science and technology or democracy; what they want is only to put them in the proper perspectives. They urge us to conserve traditional insights and to reinterpret or reconstruct them so that they may have vital meanings for us today. In the following I shall introduce thoughts of five representative contemporary Neo-Confucian philosophers.

Feng Youlan

Feng Youlan (Fung Yu-lan) was only a few years younger than Hu Shi and Liang Souming, who taught at Peking University. Feng was a student there and was influenced by both Hu Shi and Liang Souming. In some ways Feng seems to have followed in the footsteps of Hu Shi. He studied under John Dewey, earned his Ph.D. from Columbia University, and returned to China to work on his *History of Chinese Philosophy*. He parted ways with Hu Shi, who advocated wholesale Westernization or modernization, while Feng developed his own philosophy based on new interpretations of traditional Neo-Confucian insights. Feng was familiar with the debates on science and culture at that time. In fact, the first article he published in English, while he was still a graduate student at Columbia, was "Why China Has No Science: An Interpretation of the History and Consequences of Chinese Philosophy."[11] He tried to answer the question from a cultural perspective. His dissertation was entitled "A Comparative Study of Life Ideals: The Way of Decrease and Increase with Interpretations and Illustration from the Philosophies of the East and West," in which Confucianism, Daoism, Mohism, and Buddhism were placed alongside major Western schools of philosophy. He was sympathetic to Liang Souming's ideas expressed in *Eastern and Western Cultures and their Philosophies*, but had reservations about the intuition that Liang espoused.

Feng wrote his *History of Chinese Philosophy* after he had benefitted from reading Hu Shi's *Outlines of a History of Chinese Philosophy*. Feng's first volume was published in 1931, and the second in 1934.[12] The complete history exerted far greater influence than Hu Shi's incomplete project. After Feng's disciple Derk Bodde translated the book into English in the early 1950s, it became a standard text and is still used today.[13]

Not satisfied with being only a historian of philosophy, Feng developed his own philosophy, incorporating what he had learned from the West into a new interpretation of Neo-Confucian philosophy inherited from the Chinese tradition. During wartime in 1939 he published the first of six books which he called a "series written at *a time of national rebirth*,"[14] the *Hsin li-hsüeh* (New Treatise on Neo-Confucian Philosophy). This was followed in 1940 by three more volumes: the *Hsin shih-lun* (New Treatise on Practical Affairs), the *Hsin shih hsün* (New Treatise on the Way of Life), and the *Hsin yüan-jen* (New Treatise on the Nature of Man). In 1944 the *Hsin yüan-tao* (The Spirit of Chinese Philosophy) appeared and in 1946 the *Hsin chih-yen* (New Treatise on the Methodology of Metaphysics). These works were supplementary and complementary to one another.

Feng's originality lay in that he borrowed certain concepts from Neo-Realism to reinterpret Zhu Xi's philosophy of *li* (principle) and *qi* (material force) in response to challenges against metaphysics from logical positivism. He made the attempt to transform some Neo-Confucian ideas into what he understood as logical concepts; as a result he transformed the fundamental character of Neo-Confucian philosophy, shifting the emphasis from *xin-xing* (mind-heart and nature) discipline to logical, philosophical analysis. His thoughts were novel and ingenious, but problematic as well.

There are four main metaphysical concepts in his philosophy, namely, principle (*li*), material force (*qi*), the substance of Dao (*daoti*), and the Great Whole (*daquan*). The first concept—principle—is derived from the proposition that "as there are things, there must be their specific principles." In the Cheng-Zhu school, principle was considered to be self-existent, absolute, and eternal. It is a universal as understood in Western philosophy. In itself it does not enter into any temporal or spatial relationship. A thing has to follow principle, but principle does not have to be actualized in a thing. It belongs to the realm of reality but not actuality. The sum total of principle is the Great Ultimate (*taiji*).

The second concept—material force—is derived from the proposition that "if there is principle, there must be material force." The Cheng-Zhu school maintained that if a thing is to exist, there must be material force by which it can exist. This is comparable to matter in Western philosophy. Being the material of actualization, *qi* appears to have the characteristics of existence but itself does not exist either in principle or in the actual world. In this sense it is only a formal logical concept like principle.

The third concept is the substance of Dao. It is derived from the Neo-Confucian proposition of "the Ultimate of Non-being and also the Great Ultimate."[15] This means that the universe is a "great functioning" through the processes of "daily renewal" and incessant change. This concept shows the relation between principle and material force.

The fourth concept—the Great Whole—is the equivalent of Dao, or Heaven. According to Buddhism and Neo-Confucianism, one is all and all is one. This is a formal concept, because it is the general name for all and not an assertion about the actual world. It is comparable to the Absolute in Western philosophy, just as the concepts of principle, material force, and the substance of Dao may be compared to the concepts of being, non-being, and becoming, respectively.

Such abstract philosophical analysis may be applied to practical affairs. Since, according to Feng, only universals are transferable, they transcend the difference between ancient and modern, East and West. Particulars, however, are confined to specific times and places, and there is no need to demand conformity on this level.

Feng also developed his interesting theory of four realms or spheres in his *Xin yuanren*.[16] A person may be nothing more than a creature of unquestioning natural instincts. Unreflectively, one follows one's natural tendency. This sphere of human life is the sphere of human innocence.

Next, one may be aware of oneself as distinct from other persons and may seek exclusively one's own greatest advantage. This sphere of human life is that of egoistic "profit." Next, it is possible for one to be aware of something above oneself, namely, society, and to be aware that society is a whole of which one is a part. The person is bound by moral duty to serve the society. This sphere of human life is the "moral" sphere. Lastly, it is possible for an individual to be aware of something above society, namely, the universe. One will devote oneself to the Great Whole, rejoicing in its joy, transcending all sorrows. This sphere of human life is the "transcendent" sphere.

By this series of books Feng believed that he had given new meanings to the old and had tried to establish a "new tradition" that would help China recover from her lowest fortunes to find a bright prospect in the future.

In 1947 Feng was visiting in America, but he decided to go back to China against the advice of his friends. After a short time of elation for the establishment of People's Republic of China in 1949, however, the Chinese intellectuals very quickly had to face the harsh reality of living under the strict control of thought by the Communist regime.[17] Feng was an obvious target. He was forced to write one confession after another after 1950 and to denounce his own philosophy completely. When the disastrous Cultural Revolution started in 1966, the situation became even worse. It was under such circumstances that the Anti-Confucius Campaign was launched in 1973. This time Feng turned around and decided to side with the "people." He denounced Confucius in newspapers and was endorsed by the top authorities and invited to serve as an adviser to a team writing under the guidance of the notorious Gang of Four. This was the black spot in his life. After the fall of the Gang of Four, Feng was under investigation for several years. In 1982 he was allowed to go to Hawaii to participate in an international conference on Zhu Xi. At that time he openly confessed that he had not been true to himself during the Cultural Revolution. Now his thought reverted to the philosophy he developed during the war.[18] For a decade Feng devoted himself to rewriting his *History of Chinese Philosophy*, published in seven volumes from 1982 to 1992.[19] This history was written principally from a Marxist viewpoint but included some "strange" thoughts of his own. He paid tribute to Mao Zedong, but criticized Mao in his later years, turning to radical leftist ideologies without paying attention to the actual state of affairs.[20] In the concluding chapter of the seventh volume, Feng pointed out that while Mao's guiding principle is strife, for Neo-Confucian philosophy it is harmony.[21]

From this brief summary of Feng's thought, one can see that it is indeed a very ingenious system that purports to combine ancient and modern,

Western and Chinese ideas. However, it neither solves any contemporary Western philosophical issues nor captures the most important insights of Neo-Confucian philosophy.[22] Feng seemed to understand what is empty as what is not actual. Thus, for him, principles are merely empty logical concepts that have great metaphysical import. He claimed to have combined the methods of analysis and intuition. For logical positivists, however, it is the formal logical or mathematical operations, tautologies without any empirical or factual relevance, that are empty.[23] Obviously Feng's thought was on a totally different track from theirs. Furthermore, Feng's interpretation of Zhu Xi's *li* as merely universals or that which has subsistence also failed to capture the primary concern of Neo-Confucian philosophy. Zhu Xi's search for true understanding of *xin* (mind-heart) and *xing* (nature) was for self-discipline to solve his existential problems, and in this sense these concepts are much more than formal ideas. Metaphysical and cosmological reflections were only by-products of his thought, and they were certainly not just tautologies as understood by the logical positivists. To his credit, however, Feng was indeed the first to develop a philosophical system that helps to call attention to the contemporary significance of Neo-Confucian philosophy.

Xiong Shili

Xiong Shili (Hsiung Shih-li) was ten years older than Feng Youlan, but he achieved fame much later than Feng and was known only in a small circle of scholars. Ironically, however, although Feng did not inspire any important figures to become followers of his philosophy, Xiong is commonly regarded as the founder of contemporary Neo-Confucianism in Hong Kong, Taiwan, and overseas. Among his disciples were Tang Junyi, Mou Zongsan, and Xu Fuguan. Even though they were not faithful followers of his philosophy, they all admitted that they were greatly inspired by their teacher. Xiong was raised in a poor family. When he was young, he was engaged in revolutionary activities against the Manchu dynasty. In his middle age, he was puzzled by the problem of life and experienced a spiritual crisis. Following the advice of Liang Souming, he entered the Institute of Buddhism at Nanking to study *Weishi* (Consciousness-Only) Buddhism under Ou-yang Jingwu (1871–1944).

When Liang resigned from Peking University, he recommended Xiong to teach Buddhism in his place. But Xiong soon became dissatisfied with the Consciousness-Only doctrine, as he felt that, in its cosmology, the realm of origination and destruction was cut off from the realm that transcends origination and destruction. He liked Nagarjuna's dialectics, which destroys the illusions that result from our natural tendency to cling to something substantially real that remains constant amidst changes, and realizes that everything is *shunya* (emptiness). However, Xiong found that even though nothing remains constant in the world, this is nevertheless a creative universe, which cannot be accounted for by Buddhist philosophy. Hence he returned to the insights of a philosophy of creativity implied in the *Yijing* (*Book of Changes*) and developed a "New Consciousness-Only doctrine" that opened up a new direction for contemporary Neo-Confucian philosophy.

The new doctrine was a challenge to the old theory, and it created a big stir in Buddhist circles. The Institute of Buddhism quickly published a book to refute Xiong's new doctrine, but he countered by writing a refutation of the refutation of the new doctrine. When the colloquial version of his book was published in 1944, it was easily recognized as the most original work of philosophy at that time. A number of young talents were attracted to his circle, and he was recognized as one who "has influenced more young Chinese philosophers than any other contemporary Chinese philosopher."[24] After the Communist takeover of the Chinese mainland in 1949, Xiong continued to publish books in small circulation. Although there had been a transformation of his thought, he never accepted materialism or used any Marxist clichés in his writing. In epistemology and metaphysics, apart from subtle changes, he maintained his philosophical outlook for the most part. In social and political philosophy, however, his thought underwent radical changes, which he claimed were based on his new understanding of Confucius. He appeared to be the only one who did not write a single confession to criticize himself. Nevertheless, he was abused by the Red Guard during the Cultural Revolution and died under miserable conditions.

Xiong was a prolific writer, and his publications can be divided into two groups—before 1949 and after. Included in the first group are his *magnum opus, Hsin wei-shih lun* (New Consciousness-Only Doctrine) and *Shih-li yü-yao* (Important Sayings by Hsiung Shih-li, four volumes [1947]). Among the publications after 1949, *Yüan-ju* (An Inquiry on Confucianism) came out first, in 1956, followed by *T'i-yung lun* (A Treatise on Substance and Function) in 1958, *Ming-hsin p'ien* (On Enlightenment of the Mind) in 1959, and *Ch'ien-k'un yen* (An Explication of the Meanings of Hexagrams Ch'ien and K'un) in 1961. Although Xiong felt that his earlier writings should be replaced by his later writings, the quality of the latter is no match for the former. Thus, for his metaphysical and epistemological thought, it is better to rely on his earlier publications, while for his social and political thought, there is no choice but to use his later publications.

Although Xiong meant to write a treatise on epistemology and methodology, he was not able to accomplish the task. However, his epistemology and his metaphysics are inseparable from each other. He followed the lead of Indian logic to study *liang* (means of knowledge). According to Nyaya, there are four means of knowledge: perception, inference, analogy, and testimony. The Buddhist tradition never trusts perception and inference, because they start from something phenomenal and can never get to the bottom of things. Analogy is helpful but never accurate; only testimony from an enlightened person can guide us to follow the right ways. Without any doubt Xiong was in this tradition, which presupposed that there is a higher source of knowledge than empirical knowledge built on sense perception and logical inference. He told us that throughout his career he never opposed the intellect, but felt deeply that, apart from the pursuit of external knowledge, there is a world to which one can gain access only in terms of meditation beyond thought and self-realization beyond words. Thus, he endorsed the Buddhist distinction between the so-called two levels of truth: worldly truth (*laukikasatya*), the common or relative truth that things exist provisionally as dependent beings or temporary names; and absolute truth (*paramarthasatya*), which surpasses language expression and conceptualization. Xiong appreciated the Buddhist wisdom about being delivered from evil consequences of clinging to the usual fabrications of consciousnesses, but he refused to see absolute truth as *sunyata* (emptiness), as taught by the Buddhists.

From Xiong's perspective, even though the world does not stand still even for an instant, it is not something we need to escape from. Actually it is an ever-creative universe, the message of which can be realizable by digging deep in our own being. Thus, Xiong returned to the Confucian tradition, as the opening statements of the *Doctrine of the Mean* declared: "What Heaven imparts to man is called human nature. To follow our nature is called the Way. Cultivating the Way is called education."[25] Xiong believed that Heaven is the ultimate creative metaphysical principle that works incessantly in the universe, and that we are endowed with the kind of nature we have through the decree of Heaven. In order to understand the message of Heaven, there is no need to make a quest from external sources. If we can realize the creativity within ourselves, then we can also realize the creativity of Heaven. There is a correlation between microcosm and macrocosm. The metaphor Xiong loved to use was the waves and the ocean. When you taste a drop of water in the ocean, you taste the whole ocean. Thus, Xiong made a crucial distinction between what he called *liangzhi* (measuring wisdom) and *xingzhi* (original wisdom). From the former is derived knowledge by measurement, and from the latter knowledge by nature.[26] *Liangzhi* refers to the function of measurement through inference. It differentiates between the principles of things and evaluates our experiences. It may be called "reason" or "the intellect." On this level empirical sciences can be established, but it will be futile to construct a metaphysical theory from conjectures through logical reasoning and empirical generalization. Furthermore, because *liangzhi* has to depend on senses to manifest its function, there is a chance that the senses could mislead one into assuming that external objects are metaphysically real. In contrast, *xingzhi* refers to a kind of illumination through self-realization. There is no need of justification for *xingzhi*, as it is originally with us. Only when the waves assume a separate identity from the ocean, or when we are misled by senses to chase after external objects, then we become victims of our own delusions. But there is a dialectical relationship between *xingzhi* and *liangzhi*. In the final analysis, *liangzhi* has no source other than *xingzhi*, but *xingzhi* has to manifest itself through *liangzhi*. Unfortunately, however, sometimes the slave tends to usurp the position of the master, and then we have to pay the heavy price. But the Buddhists tend to put too great an emphasis on the negative side of life caused by suffering through deep-seated ignorance (*avidya*), while the Confucians choose to emphasize the affirmative side of life.

Another pair of related concepts are *benxin* (the original mind) and *xixin* (the habitual mind). The latter always directs its attention outward. It marks the self off from things and makes the distinction between what is internal and what is external. The original mind is empty, because it is not identified with any concrete forms. And yet it is illuminating, as it realizes the creative power of the Way as inexhaustible and is the origin of all genuine knowledge. The original mind should not be seen as the opposite of matter; it is the habitual mind that is the opposite of matter and the correlate with matter. This explains why Xiong rejected both materialism and idealism, since both matter and mind are manifestations or functions of the metaphysical principle of creativity. Creativity has to manifest as matter and through matter, but it is not to be dominated by matter. In this sense it is the absolute. It is only through the realization of the original mind that we can establish any metaphysical knowledge at all.

Xiong was firmly in the Confucian tradition; he cared not only for *neisheng* (inward sageliness), which emphasized personal cultivation, but also for *waiwang* (outward kingliness), which aimed at achieving a just social and political order. For Xiong, the socialist ideals were proposed by Confucius some two thousand years ago. In *Yüan-ju* he advanced the bold thesis that the six classics were the works of Confucius in his later years, but that after the death of the great master these texts were revised by what he called slave-scholars in order to support the rule of emperors. Only by recovering the great meanings (*dayi*) hidden in the subtle words (*weiyan*) of the Sage can the Way of Confucius be made manifest. He believed that *Spring and Autumn Annals* pointed to Confucius's ideal of Great Unity (*dadong*), which favors a socialist democracy in place of monarchy, the ideal of Small Peace (*xiaokang*); and *Chou Rituals* had designed the best goverment system ever conceived by humankind. Such views stirred up controversies. But Xiong's scholarship was highly questionable and his ideas impractical; not even his closest disciples could support his views. Hence this aspect of his philosophy has largely been ignored by scholars who have studied his thought in recent years.[27]

As Feng Youlan and Xiong Shili chose to remain on Mainland China, Thomé H. Fang, Mou Zongsan, and Xu Fuguan chose to flee to Taiwan, and Qian Mu and Tang Junyi decided to start New Asia College in Hong Kong. These thinkers have exerted profound influence over the next generations of scholars in these areas and overseas.

Thomé H. Fang

Thomé H. Fang came from an illustrious family in Tongcheng, Anhwei, with an excellent background in classical studies. After studying at the University of Nanking, he went abroad to study Western philosophy. He had been attracted by American pragmatism for some time, but then there was a turnaround. During the Second World War, his national spirit was awakened. As an intellectual, he followed the example of Johann Gottlieb Fichte from an earlier time, giving public lectures to stir up morale against the Japanese invasion. He felt strongly that the profound wisdom of traditional Chinese philosophy should not be allowed to die, and he committed himself to uncovering the meanings and values in this tradition. After moving to Taiwan in 1948, he became totally disillusioned with national politics and devoted himself to philosophical speculation and scholarly studies. Most of his important works were published after that time, including books in English: *The Chinese View of Life* (1956); *Creativity in Man and Nature* (1980), a collection of essays, and *Chinese Philosophy: Its Spirit and Its Development* (1981), both published posthumously after his death in 1977.[28]

Although Thomé Fang identified the spirit of what he called Primordial Confucianism as the most healthy one, he never excluded other traditions such as Daoism and Mohism, or Western and Indian philosophies. He recognized their contributions to world philosophy and culture, and he never considered Chinese philosophy apart from its cultural context. In his insightful article "Three Types of Philosophical Wisdom: Greek, European, and Chinese" (1937), he showed that each type of wisdom had its own achievements as well as its own limitations, and he was convinced that each should be complemented by the others. Fang maintained this outlook in the later stage of his thought, although expanding his scheme even further to include another type of philosophical wisdom—Indian. He had already formed his ideas and also accumulated vast amounts of material. Unfortunately however, he was unable to finish his final project. Only an outline was left, which was published as an appendix to his *Chinese Philosophy: Its Spirit and Its Development*: "Outline of 'Prolegomena to a Comparative Philosophy of Life'—Ideals of Life and Patterns of Culture."[29] In this outline Fang adopted a fourfold, tripartite division, as follows:

(a) Greek: (1) Appollonian, (2) Dionysian, (3) Olympian

(b) Modern European: (1) Renaissance, (2) Baroque, (3) Rococo

(c) Indian: (1) Upanishadic, (2) Buddhist, (3) Bhagavadgitaic

(d) Chinese: (1) Taoist, (2) Confucian, (3) Mohist

It is impossible here to discuss in detail his observations on various cultures; instead I will attempt to summarize his presuppositions.

1. In the vast universe there is a tremendous creative force incessantly at work that gives rise to various species of life. On this earth, however, only humans have the ability to develop the great potentiality of seeds of wisdom within themselves and to find expression in the achievement of variegated patterns of culture. As intelligence must not be cut off from wisdom, reason and emotion should be consonant with each other. The ultimate commitment of a philosopher is to enlightenment based on intelligence and wisdom, and the great disaster for humans is the loss of wisdom and the fall into *avidya* (ignorance).

2. The kind of wisdom achieved by individuals on the basis of extensive learning, reflective thinking, and the effort of self-discipline is individual wisdom, whereas the kind of wisdom found in the spirit of a cultural race is common wisdom. Common wisdom relies on the genius of a cultural race, and individual wisdom is dependent on the genius of an individual. Individual wisdom is derived from common wisdom, and common wisdom is the result of the accumulation of individual geniuses. Common wisdom is the root, whereas individual wisdom is the branch.

3. It is possible for humans to develop into different types. To study various types of human beings is the job of philosophical anthropology. There is a correlation between the different types of people and the different types of worlds they live in. It is owing to the different worldviews and life views that we live in the context of different meaning structures, even though, from another perspective, we may still be said to live in a common world.

4. The problem of existence and the problem of value should be kept distinct but not totally apart from each other. Humans' concept of value cannot be separated from their concept of existence. As a matter of fact, their choice of the world they live in corresponds to their choice of the course of development of a culture.

5. Different cultures have developed different kinds of wisdom, and different worldviews, life views, and concepts of value have been formulated. First, we need to have an objective understanding of the implications of such views and concepts, and then we need to give an evaluation and make a judgment about their merits and demerits. From a philosophical point of view, there are four great traditions in the world: Greek, Modern European, Indian, and Chinese. Each tradition has its great achievements and also shows its specific limitations. But the most healthy sentiment of life is that which has been developed in the Chinese culture: the spirit of creative creativity and comprehensive harmony.

6. After studying the merits and demerits of various cultural traditions, we must look forward to the future and make an attempt to accomplish an even greater synthesis surpassing all existing achievements. Under the guidance of wisdom, a person's search for truth, self-discipline, and practice according to moral principles; aspiration toward greater political ideals; and creative work in the world of art each would receive its proper attention. We may strive for an ideal of life that will give satisfaction in answer to the demands of both human reason and emotion.[30]

As we can see, Fang has a macrocosmic view of things, and he definitely does not belong in the school of contemporary Neo-Confucianism in the narrower sense initiated by Xiong Shili, since he had a rather low opinion of Song-Ming Neo-Confucianism, which turned inward and lost the healthy sentiment of life of Primordial Confucianism. Still, there is no denying that Fang's ultimate concern was certainly Confucianism more than anything else.

Tang Junyi

Tang Junyi, who drafted the famous manifesto on Chinese culture signed by four scholars on the New Year's day in 1958 that marked the official birthday of contemporary Neo-Confucianism in Hong Kong, Taiwan, and overseas,[31] had studied under both Xiong Shili and Thomé Fang in Nanking. He graduated from National Central University and taught there for many years. He left for Hong Kong in 1949, and, along with Qian Mu and other refugee scholars, founded New Asia College. This was the undisputed center as well as symbol of contemporary Neo-Confucianism for two decades, until it became one of the three foundation colleges for the Chinese University of Hong Kong. Most of Tang's important works were published after he came to Hong Kong.[32]

Tang shared with Fang an interest in comparative philosophy and culture, but he only reached a proper understanding of the fundamental insights in Chinese philosophy through Xiong, and he found his closest ally in Mou Zongsan. Together they formed the core of contemporary Neo-Confucian philosophy, and, along with Zhang Junmai and Xu Fuguan, they issued the "Manifesto for a Re-appraisal of Sinology and Reconstruction of Chinese Culture." They urged Sinologists to study Chinese culture not just through the eyes of missionaries, archaeologists, or political strategists, but with a sense of reverence and sympathetic understanding of that culture. According to Tang and his colleagues, the wisdom of Chinese philosophy is crystallized in its philosophy of mind and nature, an unmistakable reference to Neo-Confucianism. Although recognizing the need for the Chinese culture to learn from the West by absorbing its achievements in science and democracy, Neo-Confucianism claims that there is something invaluable in the Chinese tradition that should not be overlooked simply because of the weakness of China as a nation. It suggests that the West may learn from Eastern thought in the following five areas:

1. The spirit asserting what is here and now and letting everything go [in order for nature to take its own course]

2. All-around and all-embracing understanding or wisdom

3. A feeling of warmth and compassion

4. The wisdom of how to perpetuate the culture

5. The attitude that the whole world is like a family.

Surely this is not to suggest that the West has totally lacked such elements, only that they have been particularly emphasized in Oriental thought without being equally emphasized in the West. It may be argued that Tang has painted an idealized picture of the East, but surely the ideals to which a people are committed do make a significant difference in practice. A change in the way of thinking would produce a profound difference in the future.

In his later years Tang devoted himself to tracing the origins of insights in traditional Chinese philosophy, publishing six volumes on the subject. The last work he published was a comprehensive system of the philosophy he conceived during his lifetime. According to him, the function of the mind can reach nine worlds, each of which has distinct characteristics. His disciple Tu Li has given us a succinct summary statement of the system:

> The book deals with the whole existence of man, tries to understand the different activities of the mind. Owing to the different activities of the mind, there are different views of things. These views may be horizontal, straightforward, or vertical. Correlating to these views, there are objects of the views of the mind. These objects may be represented as either substance, or form, or function. And they may be regarded as either the objective existents grasped by the mind, or the subjective activities of the mind, or the aspired ideals of the mind that transcend both the subject and the object. When these are combined together, there are nine worlds of the activities of the mind. They are:
>
> (1) the world of discrete things;
>
> (2) the world of species and genus in terms of empirical generalization;
>
> (3) the world of functional operation;
>
> (4) the world of perceptions interpenetrating with one another;
>
> (5) the world of contemplation of what is transcendent and vacuous;
>
> (6) the world of moral practice;
>
> (7) the world of aspiration toward God;
>
> (8) the world of *shunya* of both the self and the *dharmas*;
>
> (9) the world of the embodiment of heavenly virtues.

As these worlds are manifested by the views of the mind, they are encompassed by the mind. The first three worlds are the worlds of the object. World (1) is formed by the correlation of the mind to substances; world (2) is formed by the correlation of the mind to forms; and world (3) is formed by the correlation of the mind to functions. The next three worlds are the worlds of the subject. World (4) is formed when the mind reflects on its perceptual activities; world (5) is formed when the mind reflects on the manifestation of the subjective forms; and world (6) is formed when the mind reflects on the function of the activities of the subject. The last three worlds are the worlds which transcend both the subject and the object. World (7) is formed when the mind aspires toward the transcendent substance; world (8) is formed when the mind aspires toward the transcendent form; and world (9) is formed when the mind aspires toward the transcendent function.[33]

Obviously, Tang's formulation of his philosophical system had been influenced by Hegel, but Tang had avoided using a deductive model that would force empirical data into his system in a rigid fashion. We can see that Tang tried hard to find a proper place for the insights discovered in the Indian and Western civilizations. But the world he admired most was still the world discovered in the Confucian philosophy of humanity and creativity.

Mou Zongsan

Mou Zongsan was a graduate of Peking University, but he felt alienated from dominant figures there like Hu Shi, who advocated wholesale Westernization or modernization. The one teacher who influenced him most was Xiong Shili, but Xiong did not offer courses on a regular basis at Peking University. Mou reported a story that explains to us why he was so attracted to Xiong in his student years:

> Once Professor Feng Youlan paid a visit to Professor Xiong, . . . [and they had a discussion on the problem of *liangzhi* (innate knowledge of what is morally good)]. Professor Xiong said, "You said that *liangzhi* is a postulate, but how can *liangzhi* be merely a postulate? It is really real, moreover, it is a presence. It needs self-consciousness here and now, affirmation here and now." . . . This gave a great shock, and helped to raise the consciousness to the level of that realized by Song-Ming Neo-Confucian philosophers.[34]

Mou's study of Song-Ming Neo-Confucianism far surpassed that of his teacher; he was the first to bring conceptual accuracy to the field. Mou also opened up new vistas to contemporary Neo-Confucian philosophy, and he was, without any doubt, the most original and the most influential thinker in his generation.[35]

Mou's early interest lay in logic and epistemology. He studied Bertrand Russell and Alfred North Whitehead's *Principia Mathematica,* reflecting on the foundation of logic and mathematics. As he was dissatisfied with the contemporary approaches, he turned to Kant and made a thorough study of the transcendental approach of *Critique of Pure Reason.* His effort in this regard culminated in the publication of *A Critique of the Cognitive Mind* in two volumes (1956–57). After he absorbed the insights and found the shortcomings of Kant's *Critique of Practical Reason,* he returned to the great tradition of Chinese philosophy. Most of Mou's important works were published after he left Mainland China in 1949. These publications may be divided into the following three stages:

1. After he was forty years old—objective concern and concrete understanding: *Philosophy of History* (1955), *Moral Idealism* (1959), *The Way of Politics and the Way of Government* (1961)

2. After he was fifty years old—intensive classical studies: *Physical Nature and Speculative Reason* (1963), *The Substance of the Mind and the Substance of the Nature* (three volumes, 1968–69). Actually he continued to do this type of work in his sixties, and the fourth volume of the work was published under a different name: *From Lu Hsiang-shan to Liu Ch'i-shan* (1979), and finally, *The Buddha Nature and Prajna* (two volumes, 1977).

3. After he was sixty years old—development of new insights: *Intellectual Intuition and Chinese Philosophy* (1971), *Phenomenon and the Thing-in-itself* (1975), *On Summum Bonum* (1985).[36]

In the first stage, Mou felt that this was the moment Chinese culture faced its life or death crisis; this required a deep reflection on the origins of the value of this culture and a search for a way to open up new vistas in the future. In *Moral Idealism* he formulated the doctrine of three traditions:

1. The assertion of *daotong* (the tradition of the Way): We must assert the value of morality and religion, jealously guarding the fountainhead of the universe and human life as realized by Confucius and Mencius through a revitalization of the learning of the mind and the nature.

2. The development of *xuetong* (the tradition of learning): We must expand our cultural life and further develop the learning subject to absorb the Western tradition of formal sciences such as logic and mathematics on the one hand and empirical sciences on the other.

3. The continuation of and expansion of *zhengtong* (the tradition of politics): We must recognize the necessity of adopting the democratic system of government as developed in the West in order to fulfill truly the political ideals of the sages and worthies in the past.[37]

In the second stage Mou returned to tradition and devoted himself to scholarly studies of Daoism, Confucianism, and Buddhism in order to grasp the principles of the Chinese philosophy of mind and nature.

Although Mou dug deeply into his own tradition, his thought has never lacked a comparative perspective, which was brought into focus in the latest stage of the development of his thought. In *Intellectual Intuition and Chinese Philosophy,* he pointed out that the major difference between Chinese and Western philosophies lies in the fact that the three major Chinese traditions—Daoism, Buddhism, and Confucianism—all believe in the possibility of intellectual intuition, whereas major Western traditions deny that there is such a possibility.[38] Mou used Kant as his point of departure, since Kant believed that all human knowledge must depend on sensible intuition and only God has intellectual intuition. Hence, Kant could develop only a metaphysics of morals, not a moral metaphysics. Owing to his Christian background, he could only hope to formulate a moral theology. Consequently, freedom of the will for Kant can only be a postulate of practical reason; the same is true for immortality of the soul and the existence of God.

For the major Chinese traditions, however, even though it is clearly recognized that humans are finite beings, they have been endowed with the ability to have a firm grasp of the Way as both transcendent and immanent, regardless of whether the Way is understood to be Daoist, Buddhist, or Confucian. Since the Chinese believe that they have the ability to penetrate reality, there is no longer the wide gap between the phenomenon and noumenon. It is in this sense that Mou insisted that intellectual intuition must not be excluded from humans, who are capable of participating in the Way through personal realization. But Mou readily admitted that the Chinese were short in purely theoretical pursuits; in this regard they have a great deal to learn from the Western tradition. Although the West has been plagued by the duality of the supernatural and the natural, phenomenon and noumenon, going beyond Kant's position would help the West to appreciate the insights of the Chinese philosophical tradition. Confucianism in particular offers a truly humanistic philosophy that transmits the message of the earth. Mou criticized Martin Heidegger's attempt to reconstruct metaphysics as being inadequate and misguided, because it loses sight of the true meaning of transcendence. Only the Confucian philosophy of humanity and creativity has been able to take care of the perspectives of both the transcendent (Heaven) and the immanent (humans).[39]

In *Phenomenon and the Thing-in-itself,* Mou made a distinction between what he called "ontology with adherence" and "ontology without adherence." The former has been highly developed in the Western traditions, and the latter has been elaborately formulated in the Oriental traditions. When the infinite mind puts restrictions on itself, the knowing subject is formed; this is the result of a dialectical process. The adherence of the knowing mind and the realization of the infinite mind actually share the same origin. It is here that we can find a foundation for the unity of the two perspectives.

Mou's last work was *On Summum Bonum*. Again he used Kant as the point of departure to explicate meanings implicit in Chinese philosophies: Confucian, Daoist, and Buddhist. Kant envisaged that this world is imperfect, for *summum bonum* (the highest good) to be realized, it can only be in the kingdom of God. But the Chinese tradition is a thoroughly this-worldly tradition; there is no need to look up to the other world. Kant's problem was not really solved in Chinese philosophy, as only God's omnipotence can bring about the unity of happiness and good. The Chinese also know only too well that in real life happiness and good rarely go together, but one can always find fulfillment in nonfulfillment. *Summon bonum* is realized here and now, there is no need to hope for a kingdom of God in the other world.[40]

I have summarized the thoughts of five prominent Contemporary Neo-Confucian philosophers. They shared something in common, in that they all showed a sense of urgency to revitalize the insights implicit in the Confucian tradition before they became extinct under the domination of current ideas imported into China by the Western powers. They were not reactionary fundamentalists resisting change or modernization at all costs. They had tried their best to learn from the West, but they were not convinced that wholesale Westernization was necessary or that things traditional were all bad. They did not treat the traditional ideas as burdens or stumbling blocks that would prevent China from joining the modern world. Feng and Xiong flourished during the Second World War. They did not find much room for further development by choosing to remain on the Mainland after the Communist takeover in 1949. Fang, Tang, and Mou became refugee scholars who fled to Taiwan and Hong Kong and worked under most difficult circumstances. As China fought the Korean War, Taiwan miraculously survived. Living on borrowed time, they turned to scholarly research, devoted to teaching. Half a century later, contemporary Neo-Confucianism was developed into a trend that can no longer be ignored either overseas or on Mainland China.[41]

Needless to say, their writings appeared to be somewhat apologetic and at times defensive, and they tended to contrast the East and the West. At the same time, however, they realized that cultures are always in the making, and what is achieved in one culture can be learned by another culture. When Tang and his colleagues published their manifesto in 1958, no one paid any attention to what was said by a few refugee scholars. But now the situation is totally changed. With the success of Japan and the four mini-dragons—all of them have shared similar Confucian heritage—the interest in Confucianism has greatly increased. Even Mainland China designated contemporary Neo-Confucianism as a national study program in 1986. Many studies on the subject have been published since then. If we take Xiong Shili as the first generation, Tang Junyi and Mou Zongsan as the second generation, then their disciples such as Tu Weiming at Harvard, being the third generation, are facing very different problems. Some of them went abroad to study and made their careers overseas. They are concerned much less with China as a nation than with the so-called cultural China, which not only survives in Mainland China and on Taiwan but also overseas. Confucianism is no longer seen as an orthodoxy, but one of the spiritual traditions in a pluralistic setting. As the world has turned into a global village, how it is possible for different peoples and cultures to live harmoniously together on the same earth becomes a pressing issue. Certainly the Confucian idea of *zhonghe* (equilibrium and harmony) would have a role to play, and the Neo-Confucian dictum: *liyifenshu* (one principle, many manifestations), which steers a middle course between universalism and particularism would have its contemporary significance.[42] It is in this sense that some of the insights conserved in Confucianism as a spiritual tradition need to be revitalized and further developed as humankind marches into the twenty-first century.

Notes

1. See Shu-hsien Liu, "Postwar Neo-Confucian Philosophy: Its Development and Issues," in *Religious Issues and Interreligious Dialogues,* ed. Charles Wei-hsun Fu and E. Spiegler (Westport, Conn.: Greenwood Press, 1989), 277–302.

2. The view of three epochs in Confucian philosophy was first initiated by Mou Zongsan and was later spread to the world by Tu Weiming. See his article "Confucianism," in *Our Religions,* ed. Arvind Sharma (New York: HarperCollins, 1993).

3. For the distinction of three meanings of Confucianism, see Shu-hsien Liu, *Understanding Confucian Philosophy: Classical and Sung-Ming* (Westport, Conn.: Greenwood Press, 1998), 13–14.

4. Joseph R. Levenson, *Confucian China and Its Modern Fate: A Trilogy,* vol. 3 (Berkeley: University of California Press, 1968).

5. Chow Tse-tsung, *The May Fourth Movement: Intellectual Revolution in Modern China* (Cambridge, Mass.: Harvard University Press, 1960).

6. Liang Souming, *Dongxi wenhua ji qi zhexue* [East-West Cultures and Their Philosophies] (Shanghai: Commercial Press, 1922).

7. Alitto first saw Liang in 1980, and he gave a report on his impressions in "On

the Elements and the Characteristics of the Formation of the Chinese Culture," in the collection of essays: *Wen-hua te ch'ung-tu yü yung-ho* (The Conflicts and Coalition of Cultures) (Beijing: Peking University Press, 1997), 270–95.

8. See D. W. Y. Kwok, *Scientism in Chinese Thought, 1900–1950* (New Haven, Conn.: Yale University Press, 1965), 136–39.

9. Ibid., 135–60.

10. See Charlotte Furth, ed., *The Limits of Change: Conservative Alternatives in Republican China* (Cambridge, Mass.: Harvard University Press, 1976).

11. Fung Yu-lan [Feng Youlan], "Why China Has No Science: An Interpretation of the History and Consequences of Chinese Philosophy," *International Journal of Ethics* 31, no. 3 (April 1922): 237–63.

12. Feng Youlan, *Zhongguo zhe xue shi* [A History of Chinese Philosophy], 2 vols. (Shanghai: Commercial Press, 1934).

13. Fung Yu-lan [Feng Youlan], *A History of Chinese Philosophy*, 2 vols. (Princeton, N.J.: Princeton University Press, 1952, 1953).

14. These were the so-called *Zhen yuan liu shu* [Six Books from Chen to Yüan]. Feng's ideas were taken from the *Book of Changes, Chen* is the last and *Yüan* the first of the four heavenly virtues. After descending to the lowest point, there will be hope for ascendancy in the future. The situation is not unlike seasonal changes: after a severe winter, spring will come. That was why in the darkest moments of the Second World War, Feng saw the glimpses of hope for national rebirth in the future.

15. This is the very first statement in Zhou Dunyi's (1017–1073) famous essay "An Explanation of the Diagram of the Great Ultimate." See Wing-tsit Chan, *A Source Book in Chinese Philosophy* (Princeton, N.J.: Princeton University Press, 1963), 463.

16. Fung Yu-lan [Feng Youlan], *The Spirit of Chinese Philosophy*, trans. E. R. Hughes (London: Kegan Paul, 1947).

17. See his autobiographical essay "The Period of People's Republic of China," in the first volume of *San song tang quan ji* [The Collected Works at the Hall of Three Pines, or The Collected Works of Feng Youlan] (Chengzhou: Henan People's Publications, 1985), 1:122–83.

18. In a personal conversation with me at Honolulu.

19. Feng Youlan, *Zhongguo zhe xue shi xin bian* [New Edition of a History of Chinese Philosophy]. Six volumes were published by Beijing People's publications from 1982 to 1989. The seventh volume was never published on Mainland China, but was published in Hong Kong with the title *Chung-kuo hsien-tai che-hsüeh-shih* [A History of Contemporary Chinese Philosophy] by Zhong-ua shuju in 1992, hereafter cited as Feng, *Contemporary Chinese Philsophy*. The seventh volume was also published in 1991 in Taipei by Lan-teng wen-hua shu-ye ku-fen co.

20. Feng, *Contemporary Chinese Philosophy*, 144–78.

21. Ibid., 256–62.

22. For a useful reference for studies of Feng's thought in English, see "Selected

Papers of the International Research Seminar on the Thought of Feng Youlan," *Journal of Chinese Philosophy,* vol. 21, nos. 3/4, special issue, ed. Diane B. Oberchain (September–December 1994). Feng's Collected Works were published in fifteen volumes by Henan People's Publications, 1985–2000.

23. A. J. Ayer, *Language, Truth and Logic,* rev. ed. (London: Gollancz, 1946); see also A. J. Ayer, ed., *Logical Positivism* (Glencoe, Ill.: Free Press, 1959).

24. Chan, *Source Book,* 765. For Xiong's life and works, see Quo Qiyong [Kuo Chi-yung], *Xiandai xin ru xue de genji* [The Foundation of Contemporary Neo-Confucianism]—Selective Papers by Xiong Shili (Beijing: China Broadcasting and Television Pub. Co., 1996) (hereafter cited as Quo, *Xiong Shili*). Xiong's Collected Works were published in ten volumes by Hubei Educational Publications in 2001.

25. Chan, *Source Book,* 98, with slight modification.

26. The transliteration of the term *liangzhi* (knowledge by measurement) can be misleading, as it is the same as the transliteration of *liangzhi* (innate knowledge of what is morally good) in Wang Yangming's philosophy. In Chinese, however, *liang* as measurement and *liang* as original or good are two different characters. Actually Wang's *liangzhi* is the equivalent of Xiong's *xingzhi* (knowledge by nature), which is in contrast to knowledge by measurement. See Shu-hsien Liu, "The Contemporary Development of a Neo-Confucian Epistemology," *Inquiry* 14 (1971): 23–24. This article was later republished as a chapter in *Invitation to Chinese Philosophy,* ed. Arne Naess and Alastair Hannay (Oslo/Bergen/Tromso: Universitetsforlaget, 1972), 19–40.

27. See Quo, *Xiong Shili,* 14–28.

28. For Thomé Fang's life and works, see his *Chinese Philosophy: Its Spirit and Its Development* (Taipei: Linking Pub. Co., 1981), 525–33.

29. Ibid., 535–38.

30. See Shu-hsien Liu, "A Review of Thomé Fang's *Sheng-sheng-chih-te* and *Creativity in Man and Nature,*" *Journal of Chinese Philosophy* 10, no. 4 (December 1983): 420–22.

31. The manifesto was first published in Chinese in *Democratic Review* 9, no. 1 (January 1958) in Hong Kong. It was later translated into English and published as an appendix in Carsun Chang, *The Development of Neo-Confucian Thought,* 2 vols. (New York: Bookman Associates, 1957, 1962), 2:455–83.

32. *Tang Junyi quan ji* [The Collected Works of Tang Junyi], rev. ed., 30 vols., were published by Xuesheng shuju from 1984 to 1991.

33. Tu Li, *Tang Junyi xiansheng de zhexue* [The Philosophy of Master Tang Junyi] (Taipei: Xuesheng shuju, 1982), 59 (translation mine).

34. Mou Zongsan, *Shengming de xuewen* [The Learning of Life] (Taipei: Sanming shuju, 1970), 136 (translation mine).

35. Mou's collected works were published in thirty-two volumes by Linking Pub. Co. in Taipei in 2003.

36. This classification is based on that adopted in Tsai Jen-hou, Shu-hsien Liu, et

al., *Mou Zongsan Xiansheng de zhexue yu zhuzuo* [Master Mou Tsung-san's Philosophy and Works] (Taipei: Xuesheng shuju, 1978), 12–13. Only *On Summum Bonum* was added to the list. According to this classification, before these three stages, there were still two earlier stages: in the first stage, Mou was interested in the philosophy of change and cosmology; in the second stage, logic and epistemology. For Mou's epistemology, see Liu, "Contemporary Neo-Confucian Epistemology," 27–36.

37. Mou Zongsan [Mou Tsung-san], *Dao de li xiang zhu yi* [Moral Idealism], rev. ed. (Taipei: Xuesheng shuju, 1982), 260–62.

38. Mou Zongsan [Mou Tsung-san], *Zhi de zhijiao yu zhongguo zhexue* [Intellectual Intuition and Chinese Philosophy] (Taipei: Commercial Press, 1971).

39. Mou Zongsan, *Xianxiang yu wuzesheng* [Phenomenon and the Thing-in-itself] (Taipei: Xuesheng shuju, 1975).

40. Mou Zongsan [Mou Tsung-san], *Yuan shan lun* [On Summum Bonum] (Taipei: Xuesheng shuju, 1985).

41. See Lin Tongqi et al., "Chinese Philosophy: A Philosophical Essay on 'State-of-the-Art,'" *Journal of Asian Studies* 54, no. 3 (August 1995): 735–37; Tu Weiming, ed., *Confucian Traditions in East Asian Modernity* (Cambridge, Mass.: Harvard University Press, 1996); and Shu-hsien Liu, *Essentials of Contemporary Neo-Confucian Philosophy* (Westport, Conn./London: Praeger Publishers, 2003).

42. See Shu-hsien Liu, "Reflections on World Peace through Peace among Religions—A Confucian Perspective," *Journal of Chinese Philosophy* 22, no. 2 (June 1995): 193–213. More recently, UNESCO organized the first meeting of the Universal Ethics Project, which was held March 26–28, 1997, in Paris. Twelve philosophers representing different theories and traditions participated in the meeting to discuss definitions, content, approach, justification, and diversity. I was invited to speak and engage in the interchange of ideas from a Confucian perspective. About thirty philosophers participated in the second meeting of the Universal Ethics Project, which was held December 1–4, 1997, in Naples, Italy. Tu Weiming and I spoke from a Confucian perspective. My paper, entitled "Reflections on Approaches to Universal Ethics from a Contemporary Neo-Confucian Perspective," appears in *For All Life: Toward a Universal Declaration of a Global Ethic,* ed. Leonard Swidler (Ashland, Ore.: White Cloud Press, 1999).

32

Tang Junyi's Spirituality: Reflections on Its Foundation and Possible Contemporary Relevance

WILLIAM YAU-NANG NG

TANG JUNYI (1909–1978) is one of the most important contemporary Neo-Confucian scholars. This paper aims to examine the foundation and possible contemporary relevance of Tang's spirituality.

Before moving to the main part of this paper, a word on "spirituality" seems to be necessary.[1] The term "spirituality" can have many different meanings, and it would be hard to find a universally acceptable definition.[2] That different criteria have been employed in the definition has made the task even more difficult. For instance, spirituality may or may not relate to the divine. Accordingly, we have, on the one hand, religious spirituality, involving an explicit reference to the divine, and, on the other hand, a spirituality that is completely secular in character. However, two definitions have been most important for me. Joann Wolski Conn understands spirituality in terms of the capacity for self-transcendence, while John Macquarrie defines the term as "becoming a person in the fullest sense."[3] Based on their ideas, I think that "spirituality," broadly defined, can be understood as the quest for ultimate value through efforts at self-transformation.[4] It relates to our ability to transcend beyond ourselves with the aim of achieving perfection. It should be clear, however, that I am not attempting to offer a "standard" definition acceptable to all. My explanation aims merely at clarifying how I understand the word and the way I use it. Let it suffice.

In what follows, I shall first examine Tang's conception of the transcendent consciousness (*chaoyue yishi*), the foundation and dynamics in Tang's spirituality. Two aspects—the epistemological aspect and the axiological aspect—will be examined. Tang's understanding of this kind of consciousness is related to his notion of human nature, an issue I will examine in the next section. What is important is that Tang's analysis of the authentic self is also a transformation of our existential selves. The function of philosophical exposition here lies mainly, if not solely, in rekindling the transformative power of the authentic self. The dynamics of such a process include two interrelated notions: detachment from the existential self; and pursuit of the authentic self. All these involve a process of self-cultivation, the actualization of the transcendent consciousness. We shall continue our discussion with a review of Tang's ideas of self-cultivation, and lastly I shall conclude by showing the possible contemporary relevance of this topic in the light of comparison between East Asian and Western spirituality.

The Transcendent Consciousness

The transcendent consciousness is the foundation and dynamics of Tang's spirituality. It is the inner force that enables human beings to transcend their existential situation and reach the transcendent dimension. Since it can also be perceived as a self which transcends the existential self, it is also known in Tang's works as the transcendent self (*chaoyue ziwo*), or simply the spiritual self (*jingshen ziwo*).[5]

The Epistemological Aspect

Consciousness, for Tang, cannot be adequately explained by taking an epiphenomenal position, that is, by reducing it to mere biological and neurological structures. It has several levels of meaning, and the biological-neurological level is just one among them.[6] For Tang, consciousness has both subjective and objective sides.[7] It is a response to contact with the external world and is always intentionally directed toward it. Tang used the idea of *gantong* to explain this. *Gantong* refers to one's ability to feel and know an object or a situation and to penetrate it with one's empathetic response.[8] In the framework of *gantong*, there exists not just an experiencing mind-heart but also the object (world) of experience. This is why, despite the overriding idealism observed in Tang's system of philosophy, the objective element (world) never loses its place by being reduced to a mere manifestation of the subjective consciousness.[9] Thus, to label Tang a Hegelian philosopher is at best a partial truth. Tang's major disagreement with Hegel lies precisely in his preservation of individual identity. That is to say, for him, individual consciousness is not merely a part of the Absolute, but has its own identity. However, it is also wrong to view our consciousness as a self-contained entity, since it is always a consciousness of something, and it should not be seen as a closed monad as Gottfried Wilhelm Leibniz (1646–1716) suggested.[10] Rather, it is a bridge that links our mind and the external world. Such an understanding of our consciousness reveals the epistemological relationship between human minds and the external world. It points to the cognitive structure of our consciousness. I term this the epistemological aspect of the consciousness.

The Axiological Aspect

Tang's even-handedness toward the subjective and objective aspects of human consciousness does not represent the whole picture, because when he talked about moral (or transcendent) consciousness, he concentrated on the subjective realm, the inner structure of our consciousness instead of the world that is presented to human cognition. The question of the relation between the mind and its surrounding world is thus suspended, and one's attention is directed solely to consciousness itself.[11] In this sense, what Tang was talking about was actually self-consciousness, which can be called pure consciousness, in the sense that it is devoid of the external world. One may wonder how such a concept of consciousness without an object (e.g., world) reconciles with the notion that consciousness is always the consciousness of something. However, this is not a meaningful question. The epistemological structure of consciousness remains unchanged. The main difference is that the object of the consciousness has shifted from the external world to the immanent world of the subject. In fact, even when we talk about the external world within the epistemological structure of the consciousness, we are always referring to the external world as experienced and grasped by the knowing subject instead of the external world as such. Such a consciousness is a reflective consciousness.

In such a reflective endeavor, consciousness splits into two modes: consciousness as a knowing subject and consciousness as an observed object. In this process, the perceiving mode of our consciousness treats our own consciousness as an object under observation. In this sense, it no longer attaches to consciousness under observation and thus can be said to have transcended the existing mode of our consciousness and entered a reflective order. This is a reflection on the activity of our consciousness, and such a kind of reflective activity can go on in like manner. That is to say, we can also reflect on our reflection. In Tang's words, it is the "activities of reflection upon reflection" (juejuezhihuodong).[12] One of the key characteristics of this kind of activity is that one is able to transcend the existing mode of consciousness. For this reason, I term this aspect of our consciousness as the transcendent aspect of our consciousness. However, it is important to note that this transcendent aspect of our consciousness is not limited to the epistemological function of reflecting upon and knowing itself, but also generates dynamics to transform the present mode of existence of an individual.

Thus, the transcendent aspect also refers to the function of self-transformation, which enables one to transcend one's original limits and become a better person in a moral sense. It is here that one can most easily detect the Confucian in Tang. Unlike other philosophers, who stop at describing the epistemological structure of our consciousness, Tang pointed to an axiological aspect, its moral dynamics, which enable one to move from the existential stage to a higher, moral stage of existence. Such a transcendent consciousness is not a mere knowing faculty but also a transformative inner force. In traditional Confucian terminology, it is the conscience (*liangzhi*),[13] or the original mind-heart (*benxin*).[14]

Two questions have to be addressed here: (1) Why does the cognitive aspect of consciousness relate to the transformative aspect? (2) What is meant by the original goodness of our pure consciousness?

Let us turn to the first question. Tang asserted the attainability of the knowledge of the true self. Even if one is illiterate, s/he is able to know and become an authentic human being.[15] In fact, we are not free to decide if we want to attain the knowledge of our self or not. For Tang, one necessarily possesses a certain degree of such knowledge; in other words, the abilities to know oneself and be oneself are both intrinsic to human beings.

What is more important, however, is that knowing the true self is not equal to knowledge of an external object. The latter may allow us to set apart the knowing subject and the object under observation and, crucially, to isolate the former from any resultant influences. Thus, for example, one's knowledge of a car may not change one's personality. However, in a process of self-understanding, not only are subject and object not apart, but the process of being and knowing are one as well. A knowledge of who one is is actually a force that turns one toward a true self and eventually transforms one into a better human being.[16] In fact, there is no opportunity for us to wipe out this knowledge. One can ignore it for a while, but it will come back from time to time as the "call" of our conscience. This knowledge is capable of shaping the existential self into a true self or authentic self. This is a ceaseless process of transformation through which humanity is fully and concretely realized. In sum, the knowledge of the object, in this case ourselves, shapes and affects its subjects, which is why such self-knowledge is transformative knowledge. Such a transformative knowledge is a fundamental dynamic which calls not only for acknowledgment of the true self but also for detachment from the existential self. Thus, the cognitive aspect and the transformative aspect of the transcendent consciousness are simultaneous; we can even say that they belong to a single continuum.

This points to another important aspect of Tang's notion of the transcendent consciousness. The essence of the transcendent consciousness is not shaped by a posteriori experience, let alone nourished by the external world. It is the "original" mind-heart—that is to say, it is a priori and innately good. This is exactly the issue of human nature in the Mencian tradition and the question I posted above, which I must answer now.

Tang's Notion of Human Nature
The Moral Self and Existential Self

The debate on human nature is an ancient one, dating as far back as the pre-Qin period (pre-221 B.C.E.). In fact, even as late as the Tang dynasty (618–907), there was not a single predominant notion of human nature. For example, the famous Tang literary figure and Confucian Han Yu (768–824), criticized Mencius's idea of human nature,[17] which became orthodox with the rise of Neo-Confucianism during the Song dynasty period (960–1279).[18]

Following Neo-Confucianism, Tang centered his philosophical system on the notion of human nature. He believed that human nature is innately good, and he called the essence of human nature the *daode ziwo*, which can be translated as the "moral self." However, Tang used different terms for it in different contexts: the *chaoyue ziwo* (transcendent self), the *jingshen ziwo* (spiritual self), the *daode lixing* (moral reason), and the *xingshang ziwo* (metaphysical self). He wrote:

> By *lixing*, we mean the nature or the faculty (*xing*)[19] of manifesting and following the Principle (*xianli shunli*). We can also say that the Principle is that faculty. Reason is what Chinese Confucians termed as *xingli*, that is, what we call our "moral self," "spiritual self," or the essence or subsistence that constitute the moral self, the spiritual self, or the transcendent self.[20]

It should be noted that Tang pointed to the fact that *lixing* is the ability to manifest as well as to follow. The character *shun* can mean *shuncong* ("be obedient to"), *shunying* ("comply with"), or *shundao* ("guide along its proper course"). Thus, *shunli* means to follow the reason or to follow the principle.

It is obvious that Tang's argument is heavily influenced by the so-called

School of Mind or the School of Lu-Wang, a school of Neo-Confucianism named after its founder, Lu Xiangshan (1139–1193) and its best-known thinker, Wang Yangming (1472–1529). Following the Lu-Wang school, Tang saw the mind, or better the moral mind, as identical with that of the Principle. Thus, to say that the moral self shows or follows the Principle is not to mean that one has to follow any norm that is imposed upon or learned from without. Rather, it is the manifestation of the moral self or one's innate goodness within. Thus, to follow the Principle is not to conform oneself to external rule or social norms but to follow the "call" of one's own conscience.

However, for the so-called school of Cheng-Zhu, which was named after the founders, the Cheng brothers[21] and Zhu Xi (1130–1200),[22] the principle is not identical with the mind. According to this school, the relation between the mind and the principle is best summarized by Zhu Xi's famous maxim, *bujibuli,* which can be translated as "not identical, [but] not separate [either]." Such a view is drastically different from seeing the moral mind and the principle as one and the same thing.

Tang did not naively believe that everyone in reality is morally perfect. He contrasted the notion of the moral self with that of the existential self. This is certainly in line with the tradition of the *Book of History,*[23] which differentiates the moral mind (*daoxin*) from the human mind (*renxin*).[24] However, instead of viewing the moral self and the existential self as two separate entities, Tang regarded the latter as the fallen stage of the former. The use of the two terms is only to suggest two stages of the same self/mind, not two independent entities. Both stages are realities of human experience, which belong to the one human nature.

For Tang, the existential self is not a true self. The moral self alone is the true self. Why? It is because the existential self is a self that presents itself here and now. In other words, it presents itself within a temporal and spatial framework and is a physical self. In it, everything is changing and nothing is eternal. And, for Tang, if a thing is ever changing, it is illusory and therefore unreal. For one thing, then, the existential self exists in time, an ever-changing sequence where one can find nothing permanent. Naturally, such a self can only be illusory and untrue. In contrast, the moral self is a self that transcends temporal limitation and thus is real. For another, the existential self presents itself in a spatial framework; and since anything that exists in a spatial framework is particular, the existential self cannot be universal and thus is not real.

Therefore, Tang thought that such a self, which exists in the empirical world, could never be real. As he wrote in his *Establishment of the Moral Self,*

When I go to the graveyard, I think about those lying inside the tombs. They used to be lovely children or healthy youngsters. When I see lovely children and healthy youngsters, I think about their eventual scatter among the graves in the fields. . . . Time is cruel. Everything is illusion and all must return to extinction.[25]

However, even if we believe that the existential self is unreal, there still remains a question waiting to be answered: How to prove the moral self as real? According to Tang, the moral self is transtemporal. It is transtemporal not because it is eternal but because one can always link the past and the future by remembering the former and imagining the latter. In this way, one can be said to be able to break the limitations of time. Second, the existential self is also a physical self which occupies a particular space. Since anything that exists in a particular space can only be a finite being, the physical self cannot be a universal existence. Unlike the physical self, which can only exist in a particular space, the mind can speculate about visiting anywhere and thus, for Tang, has no spatial limitation. Therefore, Tang believed that neither space nor time binds the moral self. It is in this particular sense that one can say that the moral self enjoys a transtemporal-spatial existence, which is why it is a true self.

Although Tang's arguments are loose and inconclusive, they do reflect his own understanding and use of the term *zhen,* which can be rendered as "true," "authentic," or "real."[26] For Tang, a self is *zhen* if and only if it is not bound by space and time. Tang's arguments, despite their naivete, do reveal his criteria of an authentic self or a true self (*zhenwo*): (1) It must be permanent, and (2) it must be universal. I think the reason for Tang to establish a self or consciousness that is free from the limitations of space and time is that he wanted to establish the "transcendental" character of morality. By transcendental, we mean universal and necessary. That is to say, moral commands, on the one hand, do not discriminate between the individuals they bind. They apply to all, and thus are universal. On the other hand, they allow neither exceptions nor alternatives, and thus are necessary.[27]

Tang also applied his criteria for the moral, or true, self to his judgment of an "authentic life" (*zhenshi rensheng*) or a "moral life" (*daode rensheng*). An authentic life for him is a life dedicated to the pursuit of virtue, and it contrasts with a life devoted to pleasure, wealth, and fame, which can be anything but authentic. I termed this latter kind of life a materialistic life (*wuzhi rensheng*).

What is wrong with a materialistic life? First, the attainment of material ends relies heavily on external circumstances, which are almost wholly beyond one's control. No one can be secure in his/her possessions. Satisfaction will be short-lived. Note, however, that Tang did not actually oppose material possessions.[28] Rather, he admitted that they are important and even necessary for realizing some of our moral actions. After all, a moral achievement such as building a school—something close to Tang's heart—requires not only a morally good intention but also material things (such as financial support). Having said that, for Tang it is not right to have a materialistic mentality or, in Tang's words, "be attached to material things" (*xianni yuwu*).

An authentic life or a moral life is a life of autonomy, where one can be the master of oneself.[29] A materialist mentality dehumanizes us, for it always makes us the slaves of material possessions, never their masters. After all, it is difficult for us to command pleasure, wealth, or fame, which depends mostly, if not totally, on external circumstances.[30] But we have a better command of our own hopes and fears, our desires and aversions that are within us. Tang did not think that all desires are bad and should be condemned. Neither did he believe that pleasure, wealth, and fame are all intrinsically evil. He realized that in order to carry out noble plans, material possessions could be very helpful.[31] The important thing is to make sure that one has the right intention. Thus, one cannot refuse the reputation resulting from a good deed. But the same deed could never be counted as moral if had been done for the sake of achieving a good reputation. This again points to the question of the purity of our heart-and-mind.

The Essence of Human Nature: The benxin benxing

Given the assertion of what is the real self, Tang went on to explain what is the essence of the real self, the moral mind. For Tang, the real essence is the innate goodness of human nature. He even asserted that the moral self is the *benxinbenxing*, which can be literally translated as "the original heart-and-mind," and "original nature." To put it in a simplistic way, the characters *xin* and *xing*[32] refer to human nature, while the character *ben* is an adjective that means not only "original" but something more. It means "originally good" in the sense Mencius understood the nature of human being.[33]

In this regard, Tang was following closely in the footsteps of Mencius and Wang Yangming. Mencius has always been recognized as an important source of inspiration in Neo-Confucian teaching, which asserted that human nature is innately good, because human beings possess the so-called *siduan* (Four Indications), which include the heart of compassion, the heart of shame, the heart of dutifulness (the heart of courtesy and modesty), the heart of observance of the rites, and the heart of right and wrong (the heart of wisdom) (*Mencius* 2A:6). These Four Indications correspond to the four Confucian "cardinal virtues" of benevolence (*ren*), dutifulness (*yi*), observance of the rites (*li*), wisdom (*zhi*) (*Mencius* 6A:6). And since all are rooted in one's mind-and-heart, the nature of such a mind-and-heart must be good, and from them follows the doctrine of the innate goodness of human nature.

Mencius used the character *duan* in the sense of *duanni* or *duanxu*. Here, *duan* refers to "indications" of the presence or the "beginnings" (*kaiduan*) of the unfolding of conscience. To use a metaphor, *duan* is a piece of ice protruding above the sea: it indicates the presence of an iceberg, it is part of the iceberg, but it is not the whole iceberg. Similarly, the *siduan* "indicate" the presence of conscience, or the starting points, *kaiduan,* of the disclosure of conscience. There is no doubt that the Chinese character *duan* denotes the sense of a beginning of a process of change. But we must emphasize that this process of change is not qualitative, in the sense of a change from evil nature to good nature. Human beings have, from the beginning, only one nature: good. Our conscience has always been there. We just somehow become indifferent or deaf to its admonitions. When we speak of moral cultivation, therefore, we mean essentially a return to what we truly are. For Tang, this begins with the reaffirmation of our belief in the innate goodness of human nature, the foundation without which moral cultivation is impossible. Tang wrote:

> We must believe in the goodness of human nature. Only then can goodness be cultivated without ceasing. We must [first] believe in the goodness of human nature, then we understand the nobility and the dignity of human beings, and gain devout reverence towards them. We must believe in the goodness of human nature, then we can have confidence in the bright future of humanity. We must [first] believe in the goodness of human nature, then believe in humanity's unceasing realization of all the goodness that human nature possesses, thus making the present world better, more and more perfect, and precious.[34]

This, of course, is more a wish than an argument. From it, we can easily discern an important religious element—faith. Even if there is disagreement over the line between religion and philosophy, it is commonly agreed that faith belongs more, if not solely, to the realm of religion, while reason is the cornerstone of philosophy. Tang said,

> However, the Confucian must, at the very outset, positively and enthusiastically affirm the sublimity and existence of moral value, and the possibility of the existence of Sages. . . . All these beliefs can directly be rooted and nur-

tured in the human mind/heart. They need not undergo rational and philosophical justification. They are simply beliefs that arise by themselves.[35]

If we agree with the use of the words "philosophy" and "religion," in the
above senses, then it is clear that at least one important religious element,
faith, is present in Tang's thought.

Self-cultivation

It is easy to criticize the previous statements as ignoring the role of the
external environment in the formation of the mind-heart. Studies in developmental psychology show clearly that the interaction with the external
world is important for the growth of the human mind. However, Tang
would certainly agree with this view without finding any possible conflict
with his belief in the original goodness of human nature. To say that there
"is" a moral consciousness (or moral self) is a matter of ontology. That is to
say, we are asking (1) if there exists a moral self or not; and (2) if there is a
self, if it is innately good or not. It may have nothing to do with the question of cultivation and growth. Indeed, an innately good moral self still
needs cultivation. This is the issue we must now examine.

Self-awakening and Self-illumination

Tang saw our inner moral life as a constant struggle between the "moral
self" and the "existential self." He believed that the dialectical interplay of
good and evil must be understood if we are to understand human nature.
Human beings are usually reluctant to acknowledge the commands of the
moral self within themselves. Rather, they are inclined to act according to
the drives of the existential selves, which seem to promise pleasure and promote self-interest—if not in the long run, then at least in the present
moment. That is why self-cultivation is important for success in our spiritual pursuit. Tang pointed out one of the most important notions of cultivation, the so-called *yinian zijue,* which literally means "moment of
self-realization."

> . . . from a single moment, one can open a world of moral existence. A turn
> and one can recreate a totally new life. In a moment of self-realization, one
> comprehends/apprehends the totality of all moral value and the inex-
> haustible moral meaning. In a moment of self-realization, one grasps the wis-
> dom of all morality.
>   If one day, in a moment of self-realization, you realize your transcendent
> self or the original nature of your mind-heart. . . . then the unfolding of your

moral life should have a boundless future—that is, you should have absolute self-confidence.

On these matters, we will have no further discussion. We can only appeal to your deep intuition and enlightened vision resulting from your efforts/practice. They are more profound and lasting than what all languages can attain.[36]

Tang also pointed out that,

The great wisdom which moves the universe [meaning: a complete change of mind-set] is nothing but this moment of self-realization. If we truly have such self-realization, we can by ourselves find answers to doubts and difficulties within us through self-reflection. Everything I mentioned above is not meant to tell others [what to do]. All I have said is meant only to inspire others to pursue self-realization and self-understanding.[37]

Yinian zijue, therefore, is a kind of self-awakening that marks a fundamental choice for the pursuit of goodness. In this context, the Chinese characters *zijue* are significant. *Jue* can mean two things: *juezhi* and *juexing*. The former can be translated as "being conscious/aware of," which has a cognitive connotation; literally, the latter means "to awaken from," which has an axiological meaning. I think Tang meant both. *Juezhi* suggests that one is aware of the existential situation and the moral direction to follow. *Juexing* suggests not only that one has awakened from the slumber of ignorance; it also implies the capability to detach and transcend the existential situation. These two interrelated dimensions echo the above-mentioned structures of our consciousness.

Zi is significant because it emphasizes the fact that the process of awakening is a self-driven effort. It is self-driven in the sense that no external agency, such as "God" or "gods," is involved. For Tang, the inner self is a self-correcting, self-directing faculty capable of generating the inner dynamic of moral transcendence.[38]

This points to the very nature of the moral self as a self-generating and self-energizing moral faculty. We might also call it "conscience." This might manifest itself as self-reproach, or self-restraint. No matter what, it is a kind of regulating force that moves one toward a morally right direction.

To Establish One's Aspiration

For Tang, one of the most important directions, or the starting point of cultivation, is *lizhi*.[39] This term, *lizhi*, is a verb that has several levels of meaning. First, etymologically speaking, the character *zhi* means the direction or goal of one's mind-heart (*xinzhisuozhi*). It should not be confused with the will in a psychological sense, for *zhi* has an axiological connotation while the will in a psychological sense does not. In other words, *zhi* has to be either good or bad, right or wrong, and so on.

To *lizhi* means, literally, to establish one's aspiration and will.[40] It refers to a personal commitment and, in particular, the setting of one's mind toward moral and spiritual pursuit. This is a fundamental choice regarding what one ought to be as a human being, and it involves refusing any form of temptation for pleasure that would dehumanize oneself. Mencius's contrast between human beings and beasts is one of the most frequently quoted metaphors in the Neo-Confucian tradition. In a sense, to learn to establish one's aspiration is to learn for the sake of oneself (*Analects* 14:24). Thus, the establishing of one's aspiration is a fundamental choice to fulfill oneself, to complete oneself, or better to authenticate oneself.

But *lizhi* also has another level of meaning. Since it is a personal commitment which aims at transforming oneself, it has to be done by one's own effort. In this sense, *zhi* has to be individualistic. This characteristic of *zhi* is especially unique if we compare it with an ideal. First, the concept of *zhi* differed from the meaning of an ideal (*lixiang*), since, for Tang, an ideal is something external to strive for while *zhi* come from the "calls" from within.[41] Tang wrote, "*zhi* is a real existence within myself, and it comes out profoundly from one mind-and-heart."[42] Therefore, we can ask others to fulfill our ideals, if we discontinue our pursuit for different reasons (e.g., death). However, in the realization of one's *zhi*, which is inseparable from one's own inner life, only one's own self can help. There follows the second difference between *zhi* and ideal. An ideal can be an object presented to a cognitive mind, and thus can be conceptualized as a universal. But *zhi* must be particular, for it arises from and targets one's individual inner life. Tang termed this characteristic the uniqueness (*dutexing*) and irreplaceability (*burong tidaixing*) of *zhi*.[43] No matter how we are going to term it, the individualistic character is clear. After all, Confucianism, especially Neo-Confucianism, is well known for its emphasis on the aspect of learning for one's own sake.[44]

However, we should be careful not to confuse this with individualism. A clarification on this issue leads us to a better understanding of Tang's notion of transcendence. Tu Weiming is certainly right in reminding us that one's learning for the sake of oneself should not be mistaken as a quest for one's individuality.[45] According to such an understanding of human nature, the ultimate foundation of one's moral perfection lies in the very innate structure of being human, that is, the conscience. Human beings are capable of becoming what they ought to be solely through the process of transformation. No external agency plays any role in such a process. Thus, it is a process of self-transformation or, in traditional Chinese philosophical terminology, self-illumination (*ziming*).

Self-transformation can be seen as an unceasing process of self-appropriation. We adjust our existential selves to follow the command of our consciences instead of blindly following external social norms or divine laws. If one is to liken our life situation to living in complete darkness, we might say that the light comes not from sources without but from the rekindling of the candle which we always possess within but usually forget about. The thought that our selves are the sole source for us to rely on is comparable to Wang Yangming's assertion of the "self-sufficiency of our human nature" (*wuxing zizu*). The main reason why we are capable of self-illumination lies precisely in the innate goodness of human nature. According to such an understanding of self-illumination, moral cultivation, in an ultimate sense, aims not at the acquisition of something new from without but at self-discovery from within. Thus, to discuss ways of moral cultivation in terms of internalization is not in accordance with the main current of Confucianism.

The Origin of Evil

The need for cultivation is another way of recognizing the existence of evil, and a comprehensive analysis of Tang's idea of humanity requires an exposition of it. Tang was well aware of the fallibility of human beings and the possibility that even the best of us would lapse into moral weakness. In fact, he was perhaps the only one among the various contemporary Neo-Confucian philosophers who paid the most attention to the problem of evil. He was also clear about the fact that our moral motivation can easily turn impure when it becomes partly sustained by prudential interests. However, he did not see this as an indication of the fact that a person is morally evil. Rather he saw it as a lack of virtue.

Indeed, Tang's explanation of the existence of evil is a continuation of the school of Lu-Wang, which is based mainly on Mencius, who believed in the original goodness of human nature and maintained that evil results from a loss of one's original nature, that is, conscience (*Mencius* 6A:7). Following Mencius, Tang also used the concept of *xianni*, which is composed of two Chinese characters that may be translated respectively as "capitulate to" and "obsessed with." Tang wrote:

> Why do human beings have evil [in them]? Where does evil comes from? We say:
>> Evil originated from the moment of human being's fall. The moment one

becomes obsessed with the good taste of food and drink, he/she continues to seek good taste, thus becoming a glutton. The moment one becomes obsessed with sexual pleasure, he/she becomes a lascivious person. The moment one becomes obsessed with the praise and approval of others, he/she becomes hungry for fame and power. With obsessive desires, one proceeds to chase insatiably after external things and fight with others for wealth, sex, fame, and power.[46]

If one chases constantly after materialistic ends, all that matters is one's desires. If anyone stands between one and one's desires, one will always be prepared to sacrifice other human beings to materialistic ends, because they are now more highly valued than other human beings. This kind of attitude naturally results in one's being indifferent to, separate from, and unconcerned with others. And this, in turn, results in not acknowledging the value of human beings as persons. One thus shows no compassion or respect for anything that hinders him in achieving his materialistic ends. However, a person who has no true respect and love for others will eventually lose respect for his own value as well. In other words, he will dehumanize himself as well as other human beings.

A true humanity is necessarily a humanity that stands against any tendency of dehumanization. A true human can stand with a strong moral will against any temptation. One of the real challenges is vice, that is, a moral failing or an immoral habit. Vice is a result of embracing self-love as one's absolute principle, adopting the disposition to transgress the command of one's conscience whenever it conflicts with the possibility of pleasures one wants. We normally resist the disclosure of the true meaning of our authentic mode of being, ren. The choice of our existence or, better, our freedom, is fundamental to the authenticity of human existence. To borrow the existentialist's terms, one can say that the fundamental ontological characteristics of everyday beings are existentiality and facticity. We engage in idle talk, where we enter the given view of the world entertained by others. This is a state of inauthentic being, since our own innermost potential for being human is hidden from us. By turning away from our true self, we commit evildoings and experience anxiety. Our conscience keeps on telling us the truth and blaming us for our wrongdoings with an aim of transforming us into a better person. The attempts to control or to eliminate evils and have a better hold of our lives are the process of self-transformation.

Self-transformation

Indeed, our greatest potential is to be free to take hold of our lives and choose who we are. Our potential unfolds itself in life so that we are oriented to what we can become: ren, a true human being. To realize our potential we must also become absorbed in concern for the world. We have concern for our fellow human beings and in turn we care about our "brothers and sisters within the four seas," and love all beings under Heaven. Tang lamented that people submerse themselves into materialistic waves and lose their true selves. He labeled those who care for no one but themselves as selfish. Thus, an important part of cultivation is to train one's will to follow the command of one's conscience. That is to say, to let our conscience be the master of our selves. However, to become human is not merely an individual matter; it has a social dimension as well. Such an incorporation of a social dimension is perhaps best illustrated in the Confucian notion of learning.

Learning here means learning to be human, and this understanding is self-understanding. That is why it is called the learning of being human.[47] The common sense of learning is based on acquiring knowledge from without. Our attention is directed externally; however, learning to become an authentic human being brings our attention to an inner pursuit. This is mainly a matter of developing one's own self, but, more importantly, it is not limited to one's self alone. Indeed, Tang's philosophy is ultimately based on an intuition of the circumstances of the human condition, humanity itself and its relation to the world. It is a kind of auto-archaeological process which digs deeply to uncover a person's true self. For Tang, however, it is not just a deepening process; it is also a broadening process.[48] It concerns not merely one's own benefit, moral or spiritual, but also the well-being of others. This contributes to the social dimension of becoming human. This kind of view is a continuation of the tradition of the *Great Learning.*

The perfection of oneself is not only a process of fulfilling one's self (*chengji*); it is, for Tang, also a process of fulfilling others (*chengren*), and things (*chengwu*).[49] This is based on the assumption that the separation between one's own self and the selves of others is artificial and illusive, indeed impossible, for the mind that draws the dividing line is a mind aware of both the realm of one's own and that of the other. One must be able to see both oneself and others before one can separate the two. This primordial oneness of the self and all others is the foundation for any possible separation that follows. This can be understood as the nature of mind-heart, which never envelops itself in itself but remains open to all others.[50]

To sum up, the transformation of one's own self and concern for the transformation of the selves of others both point to detachment from the existential self. That is to say, it transcends not only the existential self but also the existential situation which causes present suffering. Such a transcending process points to a better way of life, or a higher stage of existence. This is what Tang called "the horizon of transcendence."[51]

Concluding Remarks

Comparative religious studies between East and West are very demanding, as they require familiarity with more than one religious tradition. My remarks here should be taken only as suggestions instead of as the answer. Moreover, considering the quantity and depth of Tang's publications, these pages are indicative rather than exhaustive of his spirituality. Let me turn to my remarks now.

Spiritual writers often discuss the drive toward transcendence and the drive toward accomplishment in this world as isolated topics, suggesting that we put our emphasis on one at the expense of the other.[52] This is related to a special idea of human nature. Western thought, J. J. Clarke suggests, is rooted in essentialism and traditionally inclined to postulate human nature as a fixed essence that distinguishes humans from nature and to believe in a concept of self that is a permanent and stable seat of power and cognition.[53] However, the essence of human nature, according to Tang, is a dynamic that constantly drives one toward growth and fulfillment through interactions with the actual world. In other words, human nature is dynamic and transformative, not stable and permanent. Human nature, understood this way, points to the primordial link of one's mind with people's lives and the life of society, as well as to the earthly realities connected with them. Thus, instead of idly speculating on the abstract idea of the essence of human nature, Tang's spirituality points to the dynamic growth of human nature in the world where one is not in competition with the other but relies on the other for support and growth. Introspective self-illumination and the establishment of one's aspiration are not the ultimate stage of one's spiritual cultivation. Rather, they are the beginning stages for the development of personal awareness, the ultimate goal of which is social action.

In Tang's own career he devoted a lot of effort to concrete actions aimed at fulfilling his humanistic ideal for the revitalization of Chinese culture and the improvement of humanity. His strong commitment to Chinese culture moved him to work with some other scholars to establish the New Asia College, which later became the center of contemporary Neo-Confucianism. What is worth mentioning in particular is how the college got started. It was organized at a time when the people and the economy had not yet recovered from either the Second World War or the Civil War that ensued, and its foundation and survival testify to Tang's and his colleagues' commitment to the Confucian ideal of education. In the beginning most faculty members were volunteers. As homeless refugees in Hong Kong, they often slept in the classrooms. Many of the students who had lost their families lived in the college as well, and those who could not afford the tuition fee were welcomed on the condition that they help with cleaning the school. Tang and his colleagues were not content with merely preaching Neo-Confucianism; they actually lived according to its principles and served as models for several generations of future scholars. Such a kind of learning and practice reviews a continuation of the spiritual tradition of Wang Yangming, which emphasizes the unity of knowledge and action.

Naturally, in Tang, we see no divergence between the two drives mentioned above. A true Confucian, according to Tang, should never put aside concern for this world in his/her quest for transcendence. One has to commune with oneself, one's family, other human beings, and ultimately Heaven. In other words, the fulfillment of one's humanity involves not only the personal realm but also the social realm. In fact, it is precisely in and through the world that one grows in one's humanity. Tang's spirituality is thus not enveloped in the pursuit of inner life but points to concern for and participation in the struggle for the improvement of humanity. Viewed from this perspective, spirituality is not a merely personal matter; it is communal in character. In this regard, Tang's position reflects a continuation of the tradition of Confucian spirituality, which, as suggested by Julia Ching, "is a spirituality which unites inner sageliness and outer kingliness, a life of contemplation and a life of activity."[54] However, it sharply contradicts the *contemptus mundi* that has so often characterized Catholic spirituality. Actually, even though contemporary currents and perspectives emphasize more holistic and integrative approaches to the Christian life, the common perception is still that spirituality is primarily concerned with the interior life. Nowadays, the tendency to equate the spiritual life with the interior life is particularly popular. Knowing God thus means an ever deeper journey inward. An unchecked pursuit of a personal spirituality can easily amount to narcissism and indifference to the actual world. Social and political responsibilities, in particular, are not taken to be essential to Christian spiritual growth.[55] Understanding these shortcomings, new orientations in Christian spirituality especially after the Second Vatican Council have brought these "earthy" issues back to the tradition.[56]

What I want to emphasize here is that Tang's evenhanded spirituality, rooted in his notions of consciousness and human nature, shows a balance between pursuit of inner life and accomplishment in the world. It reveals an affirmation of the complementarity of human and spiritual development. This not only can be a supplemental resource for some new orientations in Christian spirituality in recent decades, especially those inspired by the spirit of Second Vatican Council, but also should be seriously considered as a foundation for the future development of world spirituality. Will we welcome the gift from East Asia, which Tang offers the West, a gift of humanity?

Notes

1. My understanding of spirituality here has greatly benefitted from John Macquarrie, *Paths in Spirituality* (New York: Harper & Row, 1972); and Michael Downey, *Understanding Christian Spirituality* (Mahwah, N.J.: Paulist Press, 1997).

2. See Walter Principle, "Toward Defining Spirituality," *Studies in Religion* 12, no. 2 (1983): 127–41.

3. Joann Wolski Conn, ed., *Women's Spirituality: Resources for Christian Development* (Mahwah, N.J.: Paulist Press, 1986), 3; Macquarrie, *Paths in Spirituality*, 40.

4. Donald Evans has pointed out three elements of spirituality: a psychological motivation, a transformative process, and a mystical core. He refers to "spiritualism" as "the process by which we stop resisting the reality of spirit." See his *Spirituality and Human Nature* (Albany: State University of New York Press, 1993), 1–3. I have some reservations about his use of this word, because it usually refers to a faith centering on communication with spirits of the dead.

5. Tang used many other terms to refer to the consciousness of transcendence, such as the moral self, spiritual self, metaphysical self, moral reason, mind-heart, etc. See my discussion later in this essay. Tang was not very careful in defining these terms, but the central idea is the ability to transform ourselves and to transcend the existential situation. I also notice that Tang was inclined to use the word "self" to refer to this foundation of goodness or the dynamics of self-transformation in his earlier years, but the word "consciousness" was used more frequently in his later writings (e.g., *Wenhua yishi yu daode lixing* [Cultural Consciousness and Moral Reason], in *Tangjunyi quanji* [The Complete Works of Tang Junyi] (Taipei: Xuesheng shuju, 1986), vol. 20. I have found no explanation for such a change, but I suspect it is because the concept of "self" is difficult to define, especially when one is talking about moral consciousness as a self within another self.

6. Tang also discussed other levels of human consciousness, and among them the moral consciousness and the religious consciousness are more relevant to our present discussion. See his *Wenhua yishih yu daode lixing*, esp. chs. 7 and 8, pp. 462–514 and pp. 515–83 respectively.

7. Tang's idea of the world is best examined by Lau Kwok-keung. Lau concluded that Tang asserted "the existence of the material world and the mind." See Lau's *Creativity and Unity*, ch. 5, pp. 114–56; quotation from p. 135.

8. A more detailed discussion of the notion of *gantong* and its relations with the horizons of the mind-heart can be found in my "Tang Chun-I on Transcen-

dence: Foundation of a New-Confucian Religious Humanism," *Monumenta Serica* 46 (1998).

9. See Lau, *Creativity and Unity,* 129–32.

10. Tang's discussion of Leibniz can be found in his *Life, Existence, and the Horizons of Mind-heart* [*Shengming cunzai yu xinling jingjie*] (Taipei: Xuesheng shuju, 1986), 2:53–60.

11. See Tang, *Zhexue gailun* (Introduction to Philosophy) (Taipei: Xuesheng shuju, 1982), 1:202. Tang called this "transcendental reflection" (*chaoyue fansheng*).

12. Tang, *Daode ziwo zhijianli* (The Establishment of the Moral Self) (hereafter *Moral Self*), in *The Complete Works,* 1:106.

13. The notion of *liangzhi* can be traced back at least to Mencius in the Confucian tradition, and is the central concept of Wang Yangming's (1472–1529) philosophy. *Liangzhi* is very rich in meanings, and Julia Ching has especially reminded us of the danger of translating *liangzhi* in any single way such as "innate knowledge" or "innate moral intuition." While careful consideration should be paid to render Chinese philosophical terms, and very often transliterations should be preferred, it is the author's intention to avoid as many transliterations as possible. Thus, *liangzhi* is rendered here as "conscience," though this translation is far from satisfactory. However, I must also remind the reader to bear in mind that "conscience" in this essay refers to the Chinese term *liangzhi* and should be understood in the context of Chinese philosophy. Julia Ching has provided a very useful interpretation of the concept: "it is that in man which enables him to discern between right and wrong, an inborn capacity to know and do the good, a capacity to be developed as well as a goal to be attained, since the perfect development of *liang-chih* [*liangzhi*] signifies sagehood." She also pointed out that *liangzhi* can be referred to as the "Absolute" and thus have "certain metaphysical importance." See her *To Acquire Wisdom: The Way of Wang Yangming* (New York/London: Columbia University Press, 1976), xv, 267–68.

14. Tang also referred to it as the *xinzhi benti*. See Tang, *Moral Self,* 101–10. However, Tang usually used "*xinzhi benti*" to refer to the *liangzhi* of many individuals instead of one single individual.

15. This is in line with the Neo-Confucian thought of Lu Xiangshan. Tang expressed this idea in many of his works; see "Rendi xuewen yu rendi cuncai," in *Zhonghua renwen yu dangjin shijie* [Chinese Humanities and Contemporary World] (Taipei: Xuesheng shuju, 1988), vol. 1; in *Complete Works,* 7:77–121.

16. Tang, *Zhonghua renwen yu dangjin shijie,* 1:91–93.

17. Han Yu's idea can best be found in "An Inquiry on Human Nature." See Wing-tsit Chan, *A Source Book in Chinese Philosophy* (Princeton, N.J.: Princeton University Press, 1963), 451–54. Han wrote, "In discussing human nature, Mencius said, 'Man's nature is good.' . . . [This] is to mention only the medium grade and leave the superior and inferior grades out of account and to take care of one case but to lose sight of the other two" (p. 452).

18. Regarding discussions on the rise of Mencius, see Huang Junjie, "The Rise of Mencius" (Ph.D. diss., University of Washington, 1978).

19. The character *xing* is rich in meaning, and it is difficult to maintain consistency in rendering the term. I translated it here as "faculty" because Tang emphasizes the innate knowing capacity of humans.

20. Tang, *Wenhua yishi yu daode lixing*, 19.

21. Cheng Hao (also called Cheng Mingdao [1032–1085]) and Cheng Yi (also called Cheng Yichuan [1033–1107]).

22. It is also known as the School of the Principle (*lixuepai*).

23. The *locus classicus* of this pair is the *Shujing*, which says that "the *jen-hsin* is precarious; the *tao-hsin* is subtle. Remain refined and single-minded. Hold fast to the Mean." See J. Legge, trans., *The Chinese Classics*, 5 vols. (Hong Kong: Hong Kong University Press, 1960), 3:61.

24. See Wm. Theodore de Bary, *The Message of the Mind in Neo-Confucianism* (New York: Columbia University Press, 1989), 9–11.

25. Tang, *Moral Self*, 99.

26. I use these three different translations of *zhen* interchangeably in this essay.

27. This reveals a particular position in moral philosophies, that is, the Kantian understanding of "transcendental." A brief but authoritative introduction to I. Kant may be found in *The Cambridge Companion to Kant*, ed. Paul Guyer (Cambridge: Cambridge University Press, 1992). See also Roger Sullivan, *An Introduction to Kant's Ethics* (Cambridge: Cambridge University Press, 1994).

28. Tang, *Rensheng zhi tiyan xubian* (Supplement to the Life Experience) (Taipei: Xuesheng shuju, 1984), 83.

29. See Tang, *Moral Self*, 37–43.

30. Tang, *Rensheng zhi tiyan xubian*, 64–65.

31. Ibid, 79–80.

32. Tang followed Mencius closely in seeing morality as a full realization of the *xing* (nature) of human beings, which is inborn and is indicated by moral inclination of the *xin* (mind/heart). However, the meanings of the *xin* and the *xing* are very complex and include spiritual, moral, cosmological, anthropological, and ontological implications. For a brief exposition of the meaning of *xin*, see Julia Ching, *To Acquire Wisdom: The Way of Wang Yang-ming* (New York: Columbia University Press, 1976), 267 and 55–61.

33. Tang, *Moral Self*, 30.

34. Ibid., 153.

35. See Tang, *Rujia zhixue yujiao zhi shuli ji zongjiao fenzhen zhi genjue* (The Establishment of Confucian Teaching and Religion and the Ending of Religious Competition), in Tang, *Zhonghua renwen yu dangjin shijie*, vol. 2, in *Complete Works*, 8:75.

36. See Tang, *Moral Self*, 92.

37. See Tang, *Huagou piaoling yu linggen zizhi* (The Separation of Flowers and Fruits and the Replanting of the Spiritual Roots), in Tang, *Zhonghua renwen yu dangjin shijie*, 1:65.

38. Scholars have suggested the creative power of the self in the Confucian tradition. However, the word "create" might suggest a certain sense of bringing into

being from nothingness. Therefore, I think it is better to use self-correcting and self-directing instead.

39. See Tang, *Rensheng zhi tiyan xubian*, ch. 4, pp. 75–95.

40. Cf. Tu Weiming, *Confucian Thought: Selfhood as Creative Transformation* (Albany: State University of New York Press, 1985), esp. 31.

41. Tang, *Rensheng zhi tiyan xubian*, 79–80.

42. Ibid, 81.

43. Ibid, 80.

44. The works of Wm. Theodore de Bary and Tu Weiming, in particular, have contributed much to the exploration of this aspect. See de Bary's *Learning for One's Self* (New York: Columbia University Press, 1991) and *The Liberal Tradition in China* (New York: Columbia University Press, 1983). In true Confucian tradition, therefore, "learning for one's own sake" does not suggest that the pursuit of knowledge be directed solely to pure pleasure.

45. Tu writes, "Self, in the classical Confucian sense, referred to a center of relationships, a communal quality which was never conceived of as an isolated or isolable entity." See his "A Confucian Perspective on Learning to be Human," in his Confucian Thought: Selfhood as Creative Transformation (Albany: State University of New York Press, 1985), 53.

46. Tang, *Moral Self,* 155.

47. Tu Weiming has rightly pointed out that the Confucian proposition that human beings are perfectible is based on, in his terms, two interrelated ideas, the ontological postulate and the experiential assertion: "(1) The uniqueness of being human is an ethico-religious question which cannot be properly answered if it is reduced to biological, psychological or sociological considerations; and (2) the actual process of self-development, far from being a quest for pure morality or spirituality, necessarily involves the biological, psychological and sociological realities of human life." See Tu, "The Moral Universal from the Perspectives of East Asian Thought," in *Confucian Thought: Selfhood as Creative Transformation,* 19. Tang's discussion of the learning of being human (*renxue*) can be found in his *"renxue"* in *Bingliqiankun* (The World within Sickness) (Taipei: Ehu chubanshe, 1984), 141–51.

48. Tu Weiming uses the words "deepening" and "broadening" to describe the philosophy of the *Great Learning*. See his "The Confucian Sage: Exemplar of Personal Knowledge," in his *Way, Learning and Politics: Essays on the Confucian Intellectual* (Albany: State University of New York Press, 1993), 29–44.

49. Tang, *Rensheng zhi tiyan xubian*, 127.

50. Ibid, 127.

51. See my "Tang Chun-I on Transcendence: Foundation of a New-Confucian Religious Humanism," *Monumenta Serica* 46 (1998).

52. Such a trend was greatly influenced by St. Augustine. Michael Downey writes, "whether Augustine intended it or not, his version of contemplation and ascent to God through decent into the self muted the relational and communitarian dimensions of the Christian life. He believed that the structure of the individ-

ual human soul was a mirror image of the Trinity. By knowing oneself, one would know God." See Downey, *Understanding Christian Spirituality,* 106.

53. J. J. Clarke, *Oriental Enlightenment: The Encounter Between Asian and Western Thought* (London & New York: Routledge, 1997), 214.

54. Julia Ching, "What Is Confucian spirituality?" in *Confucianism: The Dynamics of Tradition,* 80.

55. See Downey, *Understanding Christian Spirituality,* 106.

56. Ibid, pp. 75–87. For a brief introduction to the ecclesiology of Vatican II, see Richard P. McBrien, *Catholicism,* new ed. (New York: HarperCollins, 1994), 683–89.

Suggested Readings

Primary Source

Tang, Junyi. *Tangjunyi quanji* [The Complete Works of Tang Junyi]. 30 vols. Taipei: Xuesheng shuju, 1986–1990. There are no English versions of any of Tang's major works. However, a handful of his articles have been translated into English, especially his contributions to international conferences. They have been collected and reproduced as volume 19 of *Complete Works.*

Western Sources

Alitto, Guy S. *The Last Confucian: Liang Shu-ming and the Chinese Dilemma of Modernity.* Berkeley: University of California Press, 1979.

Berthrong, John. *All Under Heaven: Transforming Paradigms in Confucian–Christian Dialogue.* Albany: State University of New York Press, 1994.

———. *Transformation of the Confucian Way.* Boulder, Colo.: Westview Press, 1998.

Chan, Wing-tsit. *Religious Trends in Modern China.* 1953. Reprint, New York: Octagon Books, 1969.

Chang Hao. "New Confucianism and Contemporary China." In *The Limits of Change,* edited by Charlotte Furth, 276–302. Cambridge, Mass.: Harvard University Press, 1976.

Ching, Julia. "What Is Confucian Spirituality?" In *Confucianism: The Dynamics of Tradition,* edited by Irene Eber, 63–80. New York: Macmillan, 1986.

Levenson, Joseph R. *Confucian China and Its Modern Fate: A Trilogy.* Berkeley/Los Angeles: University of California Press, 1972.

Metzger, T. *Escape from Predicament: Neo-Confucianism and China's Evolving Political Culture.* New York: Columbia University Press, 1977.

———. "The Thought of Tang Chun-i (1909–1978): A Preliminary Response." In Huo Taohui et al., *Tang Chun-i sixiang guoji huiyi lunwenji,* 1:165–98. Hong Kong: Fazhu chubanshe, 1992.

Taylor, Rodney L. *The Religious Dimensions of Confucianism.* Albany: State University of New York Press, 1990.

Tu Weiming, ed. *The Triadic Chord: Confucian Ethics, Industrial East Asia and Max Weber.* Singapore: Institute of East Asian Philosophies, 1991.

33

Interpreting Confucian Spirituality in Postwar Taiwan: The New Confucians and Their Critics

CHRISTIAN JOCHIM

PERHAPS THE FIRST MAJOR REAPPRAISALS of Confucianism since the debate between liberals and conservatives of the May Fourth era have occurred in postwar Taiwan, presaging the current reappraisal by intellectuals in the People's Republic of China (PRC). Postwar Taiwan provided a lively interpretive environment for efforts to revive as well as to criticize Confucianism. Elements of this interpretive environment included hegemonic government sponsorship of the study of Confucianism, the need of interpreters in Taiwan to distinguish their views of Confucianism from those of its official PRC detractors, the presence of certain self-styled "New Confucians" (*xinrujia*) living in exile from the PRC, the continuation of the May Fourth frame of mind among liberal intellectuals, and the efforts of Chinese Catholics to reconcile Christian beliefs with their Confucian heritage.

Because so few post–May Fourth intellectuals dared to embrace Confucianism, the New Confucians became heroes for some but, more often, a lightning rod for the tradition's critics. On the one hand, these scholars (notably Mou Zongsan and Xu Fuguan) attracted devoted students, many of whom teach in departments of Chinese, history, and philosophy in Taiwan's universities today. On the other hand, they attracted the criticism of liberal opponents such as Yin Haiguang, Wei Zhengtong, and their students. In recent years, PRC liberals such as Bao Zunxin have joined the fray. Moreover, certain younger-generation New Confucians, such as Liu Shu-hsien (Liu Shuxian) and Tu Weiming (Du Weiming), have provided a more self-critical perspective on modern Confucian thought.[1]

In what follows, we will look at each of the perspectives mentioned above, with the exception of official interpretations. These were promulgated through units of the government, such as the Ministry of Education, and certain semi-governmental organizations, including the Confucius-Mencius Scholarly Society, which was led by Chen Lifu, chief architect of official interpretations. Although Chen and other interpreters in the government camp were clearly adversaries of the New Confucians, the tensions between them did not produce genuine philosophical debates.[2] After summarizing the various New Confucian views that have been considered controversial by their critics, I will cover criticisms in an order that leads from anti-traditionalist to pro-traditionalist perspectives and, finally, to New Confucian self-criticism.

New Confucianism:
The Category and the Controversies

Here I will not attempt a general introduction to New Confucian thought. Essays published in this volume and elsewhere come closer to serving this purpose.[3] In particular, I will concern myself with elements of New Confucian thought that have been controversial among its critics in postwar Taiwan, ignoring for the most part ideas that New Confucians share with these critics and aspects of their thought that the critics have never or rarely discussed. But, before introducing any of their ideas, let us confront the question: Who are the New Confucians?

In 1982, a conference was held in Taipei on the topic of New Confucianism and Chinese modernization, sponsored by China Forum, which published the results in its journal, *Zhongguo luntan* (China Forum). Several of the participants are featured in this essay, including one representative of New Confucianism, Liu Shu-hsien. Among the critics who participated, Wei Zhengtong, in a paper titled "The Mentality of Contemporary New Confucians," offered a list of seven New Confucians and a list of seven common characteristics that define New Confucianism.[4] He listed Xiong Shili (1885–1968), Carson Chang (Zhang Junmai, 1887–1969), Liang Shuming (1893–1988), Qian Mu (1895–1990), Xu Fuguan (1903–1982), Tang Junyi (1909–1978), and Mou Zongsan (1909–1995). This is identical to the list in the introduction to New Confucianism by Chang Hao (Zhang Hao),[5] except for the inclusion of Qian Mu, who may not belong on the list for reasons to be considered later in this essay. However, neither list includes any younger (third-generation) New Confucians.

Liang Shuming, his friend Xiong Shili, and Carson Chang are clearly the thinkers who gave birth to the movement through their response to May-Fourth era attacks on Confucianism. While Liang and Xiong stayed in the PRC after 1949, the second generation of Xu, Tang, and Mou (all Xiong's students) went to Hong Kong and Taiwan, where they had considerable scholarly influence. Chang, as leader of the Democratic Socialist opposition party, sought exile in the United States, fearing that he would be persecuted in either the Communist PRC or the Nationalist Republic of China (ROC) on Taiwan. He should be included because he joined Xu, Tang, and Mou as signatories of a famous 1958 New Confucian manifesto[6] as well as because he was the inspiration for certain key ideas of these second-generation New Confucians. Of course, because of Chang's choice, he was not as much of an influence on members of the third generation of New Confucians, such as Liu Shu-hsien and Tu Weiming, who were schooled in Taiwan. Perhaps partly as a result of this, their interests are moral and spiritual but rarely political.

The seven common characteristics of New Confucian thought listed by Wei are as follows: (1) They see Confucianism as the orthodoxy and main pillar of Chinese culture, and they stress the learning of the mind and nature (*xin-xing zhi xue*) within Confucianism. (2) They see China's historical culture as a spiritual entity, and its course as this spiritual entity's progressive manifestation. (3) They see the tradition of the Way (*daotong*) as the root for establishing the nation and the source of cultural creation. (4) They stress that one must employ respect and sympathy in understanding historical culture. (5) With their esteem for roots, they stress the uniqueness, or one-rootedness, of Chinese culture. (6) They have a very deep consciousness of cultural crisis, considering the main cause of the crisis to be Chinese people's lack of self-confidence. (7) With their esteem for religious piety, they have a sense of mission about reviving Chinese culture.[7]

Certain aspects of Wei's summary need elaboration because of their importance for what follows here. For example, when Wei mentions that, within Confucian thought, New Confucians stress the learning of the mind and nature, this raises metaphysical concerns from the perspective of intellectuals who have a secular outlook as well as those who do not, such as Roman Catholic scholars. In their 1958 manifesto, the New Confucians strove to distinguish their view of *xin-xing* (the mind and nature) from both the Western psychological tradition's view of human nature as a locus of biological instincts and the Western religious tradition's view of human nature as sinful and alienated from God.[8] In their view, one can understand *xin-xing* only through practice—the learning (or discipline) of the mind and nature—and in doing so one can understand Heaven (*tian*) as something fully revealed in *xin-xing*. This led to an understanding of *xin-xing* within a theory of the self-sufficient moral mind, which Mou Zongsan derived from Kantian moral theology. For secular intellectuals, this gives Confucian ethics a far too theological grounding. For Catholic scholars, by contrast, it reduces Heaven's role in Confucian ethics and, thereby, endangers the basis for Confucian–Christian rapprochement.

As for the second common characteristic, the New Confucians' appeal to a spiritual entity underlying the development of China's historical culture reveals their bent toward philosophical idealism, which has roots in both German idealism and Xiong Shili's understanding of Yogacara Buddhism. In certain instances (especially in the case of Tang Junyi), the emphasis is on a Hegelian unfolding of the Spirit. Moreover, as this implies, there is a timeless and universal quality to essential Confucianism, which transcends the historical plane on which it has unfolded. Chang Hao, in his survey of New Confucianism, distinguishes the New Confucians from certain other modern Chinese conservatives, such as those of the National Essence school, not only because of their emphasis on the Confucian tradition within Chinese culture but also because of the universal value they claim for it. In his words:

> Unlike the broad trend generally known as the School of National Essence (*guocui xuepai*) whose adherents tended to define the Chinese national identity in terms of general cultural or racial traits, the New Confucians were inclined to identify Chinese civilization with one particular trend, namely, Confucianism. Further, while the National Essence school was distinguished mainly by a particularistic striving to seek China's national identity in certain historical cultural-racial traits, the New Confucianism was characterized by a universalistic claim that Chinese civilization features something of a transcultural intrinsic worth in Confucianism.[9]

With the third generation of New Confucians, we see even more clearly the results of this emphasis on Confucianism as a spiritual tradition of universal significance. Liu Shu-hsien and Tu Weiming are quite content to view the tradition as one among several "world religions" and have entered into dialogue with representatives of other religions to explore mutual enrichment.[10]

Wei's third common characteristic also requires elaboration for two key reasons. First of all, the New Confucians' stress on *daotong*, "tradition of the (Confucian) Way," signifies the revival of an idea from Song (960–1279) and Ming (1368–1644) period Confucianism as well as a general revival of Song-Ming Confucianism after a hiatus of several hundred years. Qing-period (1644–1911) Confucians, including late Qing reformers, such as Kang Youwei (1858–1927) and Liang Qichao (1873–1929), generally bypassed their Song-Ming predecessors in seeking an understanding of early Confucian scriptures. In other words, New Confucianism is not only a movement to restore Confucianism in general; it is also a movement to reestablish a version of Confucian orthodoxy that had been rejected or ignored for centuries. This fact is of utmost significance for understanding the New Confucians as well as their critics, many of whom either lack knowledge of Song-Ming Confucian hermeneutics or purposely ignore it in favor of other interpretations of early Confucian teachings. The New Confucians have seen themselves, in both their general sense of mission and in their specific interpretations, as seeking to reestablish the true Confucian Way in the image of Song-Ming Confucians.

Second, the New Confucians' use of the concept of the "tradition of the Way" lies at the heart of their efforts to modernize Confucianism and, thus, at the heart of the controversy over whether or not they have succeeded in doing so. Mou Zongsan has most clearly articulated the need for a modern reestablishment of the tradition of the Way as part of his controversial three traditions derivation doctrine (*santong kaichu shuo*). This is explained by Liu Shu-hsien, with a translation of relevant material, as follows:

> In the first stage [of his postwar publications] Mou thought that this was the moment traditional Chinese culture faced its life or death crisis, requiring a deep reflection on the origins of the value of Chinese culture and seeking a way to open up new vistas in the future. In *Moral Idealism* [1959] he formulated the doctrine of three traditions.
>
> 1. The assertion of *daotong* (the tradition of the Way): We must assert the value of morality and religion, jealously guarding the fountainhead of the universe and human life as realized by Confucius and Mencius.
>
> 2. The development of *xuetong* (the tradition of learning): We must expand our cultural life and further develop the knowing subject to absorb the Western tradition, so that learning would gain its independent status.
>
> 3. The continuation of *zhengtong* (the tradition of politics): We must recognize the necessity of adopting the democratic system of government to fulfill truly the political ideals of the sages and worthies in the past.[11]

This doctrine becomes the basis for Confucian guidance of Chinese modernization when one understands the relationships among the three traditions. While the Western contribution to the traditions of (scientific) learning and (democratic) politics must be acknowledged, the Chinese contribution—the tradition of the Way—is most essential for Chinese modernization. For one thing, it is Chinese; for another, modern science and politics can go astray without needed moral guidance. For these same reasons, the New Confucian doctrine of the "new outer kingliness" (*xinwaiwang*) presents a revision of the traditional ideal, "sage within, king without" (*neisheng waiwang*), giving the inner sage priority while insisting on a commitment to Western-style democracy in outer kingliness.

What needs to be said here about the fourth common characteristic of New Confucian thought is closely related to the issue of the relationship between the tradition of the Way and the tradition of learning. New Confucians emphasize the need for respect and sympathy in studying traditional culture so as to avoid an excessively cold scientific orientation in scholarly work. In studying the history of Confucian thought, for example, one needs to do more than just describe the contextual development of specific texts and ideas. One needs to understand how, in history, the tradition of the Way was embodied and how, in the future, it can be further developed as a living tradition.

Regarding the seventh common characteristic, we must address the sense in which the New Confucians acknowledge the Confucian tradition's religiousness. This has become a controversial issue. For example, secular scholars such as Yü ying-shih (Yu Yingshi) consider them too theological (see below), while others, such as Roman Catholics, chastise them for being atheistic in their humanism. Speaking for themselves, New Confucians acknowledge that Confucianism has had a religious function or a religious import.[12] Their point is that, whether considered a "religion" or not, the tradition can serve the individual and society in all those essential ways, as have the major world religions (e.g., Buddhism, Christianity, Hinduism, Islam, Judaism). Indeed, as already noted, leading New Confucians today have put themselves in dialogue with representatives of certain world religions.

Nonetheless, many of their critics have expressed little interest in New Confucian thought as a way of life for individuals in the modern world and have focused mainly on its alleged role in Chinese modernization. This is natural in that the task of saving the nation (*jiuguo*) has preoccupied most Chinese intellectuals for at least a century. However, it is also unfortunate, since it means that critics have scrutinized one isolated aspect of New Confucianism but, for the most part, have not evaluated the whole project. In beginning our survey of its critics with Bao Zunxin, we will see the extent to which this can be true.

Bao Zunxin: A Pro-Democracy
but Anti-Confucian PRC Intellectual

Bao Zunxin is thoroughly anti-Confucian in the mold of May Fourth movement intellectuals. He is the antipode to the New Confucians in almost every way. He is anti-traditional and leans toward historicism, Marxism, and existentialism. They support tradition and are more ahistorical, anti-Marxist, and, in key ways, essentialistic. In stressing the ahistorical and essentialistic elements in the thought of New Confucians, especially Mou Zongsan and Tang Junyi, Bao simplifies their ideas to a degree and exaggerates their theological tendencies. Bao does not call them theologians directly, but his chief criticism is that they treat the Confucian "Constant Way" (changdao) as a kind of eternal truth.[13] They should see that it was the product of specific historical conditions and that it belonged to a social value system that was distinctly different from the modern one. In fact, in Bao's view, the two-value systems are polar opposites. Thus, he challenges the New Confucian belief that *Chinese* modernization necessarily requires the contributions of traditional *Chinese* thought. In his view, no such thing is necessary. Chinese modernization will go where it is led by the practical experience of Chinese life in the modern world. The contributions of traditional thought will be whatever the Chinese people decide through specific historical choices.[14]

Owing to Bao's view that Confucian thought was wedded to the socio-historical context that produced it, he is skeptical about New Confucian efforts to pull the ideas of science, democracy, human rights, and freedom out of traditional Confucianism, in his words, "like a magician pulling rabbits from his pocket."[15] He feels that it is implausible that the "new outer kingliness," which consists of science and democracy, can in any sense be derived from inner sageliness, which is rooted in the "tradition of the Way." It is the failure of New Confucians to understand the historically conditioned nature of their tradition that makes it possible for them to believe in such a facile explanation of the tradition's contribution to modernization.

For similar reasons, Bao is unimpressed by the claim of Mou Zongsan, for example, that science and democracy are like the Buddhist "*dharma* common to all ages" (gongfa). In his view, just as Confucian thought was the product of its unique historical circumstances, so were Western science and democracy. In any case, he feels that it is contradictory to praise science and democracy as the common property of all humankind, while promoting Confucian thought as a uniquely Chinese set of ideas that can save the Chinese people from excessive or monolithic adaptations of Western scientific and political practice.[16]

For all their claims of newness, says Bao, New Confucians have not rid themselves of the basic flaws of traditional Confucianism. He asserts that they share a "moral-centrism" according to which all social problems are moral problems, and all dimensions of human personhood are subordinated to morality. He sees this kind of subordination in the New Confucian argument that the moral conscience can, through a special process (literally, its "self-entrapment" in worldly affairs), bring forth a modern cognitive subject that can guide scientific developments without being excessively scientistic. For Bao, this is just a new version of the old nineteenth-century *tiyong* formula, in which Chinese learning constitutes the substance (*ti*) and Western learning provides the means (*yong*), that is, the methods to achieve goals defined by Chinese thought. Another example of this lies in the subordination of the "tradition of politics" and the "tradition of learning" to the "tradition of the Way." Thus, although the New Confucians speak of the "new outer kingliness," they hold onto a traditional model of the relation between inner sageliness and outer kingliness that privileges the role of traditional morality.[17]

Finally, there is the issue of New Confucian claims that today people need a system of meaning beyond the scientific worldview held by May Fourth intellectuals, among others. As a representative of May Fourth intellectualism, Bao resents the implication that his worldview lacks meaning and values and, therefore, needs Confucianism to fill the gap. For him, New Confucians' thinking in this regard is another instance of their inability to understand that every worldview is embedded in a socially constructed system of values. The worldview of modernity and science is itself a system of meaning and values, not something devoid of these qualities and needing help from traditional culture.[18] In any case, because the worldview of traditional Confucianism was itself a distinct social construction—not a set of timeless truths—Bao sees no reason to believe that it can provide much help for modern China.

Liberal Critiques

Not only in the PRC but also in Taiwan, it is easy to see the influence of intellectuals who are still committed to certain political and intellectual ideals of the May Fourth movement. Such scholars, while not as adamantly antitraditional as Bao Zunxin, are deeply skeptical about the project of finding a major role for traditional thought in modern Chinese societies generally or in Taiwan specifically. For these reasons I call them "liberals."[19] To represent them, I choose Wei Zhengtong and two of Yin Haiguang's students who are well established scholars in both Taiwan and the United States: Chang Hao and Lin Yü-sheng (Lin Yusheng). In a 1968 preface to Wei's work *Rujia yu xiandaihua* (Confucianism and Modernization), he reports on the profound personal experiences whereby he gave up his unquestioned acceptance of traditional culture. After a period of intellectual chaos, he began to reflect critically on the flaws of traditional Chinese moral thought, especially its overdependence on the ancients' simplistic solution to the problem of evil acts in human life.[20] He ultimately came to see that their views on virtuous government offered little to those seeking to establish a modern democratic state. Beyond this, he felt compelled not only to look at the political potential of Confucian thought today, or at its historical alliance with an authoritarian state, but also to investigate whether or not it had any role among the causes of the democratization of politics in Taiwan. In an essay on Confucianism and Taiwan's democratic movements, he seeks the real causes of democratization, finding no evidence that Confucians or Confucianism played any significant role. This is explained, he said, by the fact that the main problem for Taiwan was how to move from "rule by men" to "rule by law." Not only was the so-called Confucian system of the premodern state one of rule by men, so also was the system of virtuous government advocated by ancient Confucian thought.[21]

As for the New Confucians in particular, in Wei's aforementioned essay on the mentality of New Confucianism, he acknowledges the value of their efforts to counter the extreme rejection of Chinese tradition by May Fourth intellectuals. However, he notes their inadequate grasp of the pluralistic nature of modern academic as well as political life.[22] He feels that their claims regarding the special status of traditional Chinese culture as an expression of humanity's heart-mind of compassion (*renxin*) or regarding the unique spirit of sacred heroes in Confucian history is out of line with the requirements of modern scholarship. Similarly, he doubts that New Confucian views on government can fit into the modern political arena, in which contending forces compete on an equal basis. Instead he praises the alternative view of Charles Fu. Fu's view is well expressed in an essay he has written on postwar Confucianism and Western democracy:

> If we can distinguish *minima moralia* and *maxima moralia* as two categories of human morality, then Confucian morality belongs in the second category. Although *minima moralia* only concerns the individual's minimal fulfillment of moral duties or obligations in human society, such as observing law and order, promotion of human rights, moral reciprocity (in Confucius' own

words, "Do not do to others what you would not want them to do to you"),
social justice, and so on, without emphasizing the constant moral perfecting
of man and society, Confucian morality as a typical representative of *maxima
moralia* insists on the ethical necessity to realize *ren* as the way of both inner
sagehood and outer kingship. But the constitutional democracy which contemporary Confucianists advocate only requires *minima moralia* in the legal
form. Thus, without being able to see the distinction between *minima
moralia* and *maxima moralia* in their attempts to absorb Western democracy
into the Confucian tradition, contemporary Confucianists have not successfully shown us why and how the traditional way of inner sagehood can still
serve as the moral basis of constitutional democracy in China today and in
the future.[23]

Regarding the pluralistic world of modern scholarship, Wei finds New
Confucians similarly out of sync. He notes that Tang Junyi and Mou
Zongsan rejected a strictly objective approach to China's historical culture,
in which it is treated as a dead fossil, and that they have advocated the use
of sympathy and respect. But he suspects that, while the approach they
advocate may build people's self-esteem and give solace to conservatives, it
is merely a subjective orientation that stands in the way of good historical
research.[24] By placing the Confucian tradition on a pedestal, Wei concludes, one cannot attain the ideal in which modernity and tradition stand
on an equal footing in mutual criticism of each other. In addition to praising Charles Fu for coming closer to this ideal, he also mentions the two figures to whom we now turn: Chang Hao and Lin Yü-sheng.

The English publications of Lin and Chang have a more strictly objective tone that belies their involvement in Taiwan's intellectual debates
between cultural conservatives and liberals. To demonstrate their critical
approach to New Confucianism, I will report on their role in the previously mentioned 1982 conference on this topic sponsored by *China Forum*.

Lin Yü-sheng understands that New Confucians have addressed issues of
individual life as well as those related to Chinese modernization. However,
his own interests are clearly in the latter area. In fact, he says that the primary concern of any modern Chinese intellectual should be China's
future: to devise methods whereby we can improve the structure of Chinese government, economy, society, and culture so that Chinese people
can have more rational, more prosperous, and more respected lives. On the
basis of this singular criterion, he ranks the three New Confucians that he
discusses, putting Xu Fuguan first, Mou Zongsan next, and Tang Junyi
last.[25]

According to Lin, Tang's problems begin with his choice of philosophies
on which to base his methodology: Hegelian thought and Huayan Bud-

dhism. Since neither is compatible with Confucianism, Tang's thought is "chaotic" at the level of method. The Confucian tradition is worldly, Huayan is otherworldly. Hegel's thought is bound up with nationalism, especially German nationalism and fascism, which cannot be reconciled with Tang's stress on a Confucian philosophy of benevolence (*ren*) that transcends national interests. For Lin, it seems obvious that Tang threw Hegelian and Confucian thought together without much critical reflection. Three major problems stem from this: (1) Chinese culture is not treated critically but rather as if every element has some positive, rational significance; (2) Tang cannot connect "tradition" and "future" in any meaningful way since he is not able to separate the good from the bad in China's past and apply it to the future; (3) Tang loves to make East–West comparisons (as in characterizing ancient Greece as rational, and ancient China as affective), but these are mostly the result of wishful thinking rather than any rigorous use of the comparative method.

As for Mou, Lin considers him a first-rate student of Chinese philosophy, while criticizing his comparative work for its inexact use of concepts of foreign origin, such as "freedom" and "democracy." For example, Mou is well known for saying that traditional China had a strong "way of rulership" (*zhidao*) rather than a modern "way of politics" (*zhengdao*). When Mou builds on this to argue that premodern China had a "way of rulership (style of) democracy," Lin feels he is using the concept of "democracy" in a very questionable manner.

As for Xu, Lin believes that he left the best resources for facing China's future concerns precisely because he applied the most *critical* reflection toward traditional attitudes. Without such a rigorous use of the critical spirit, there is no way to grasp the essential elements of traditional culture while discarding the dross. Nonetheless, Xu did not realize the results of his application of a critical spirit because, for example, he had an inadequate understanding of the actual nature of freedom and science and, therefore, criticized mere caricatures of them. Lin's own idea of creative transformation leaves no role for a self-comforting mentality that makes one feel better but does not help concretely to create a better future. It also avoids the other extreme—wholesale rejection of tradition in the manner of the May Fourth radicals—which allows no way to identify the healthy, life-giving elements of tradition and to link them to future needs.[26]

Turning to Chang Hao, he has been interested primarily in understanding the motivations and search for meaning of New Confucians. He cautions us against seeing their thought simply as an emotional or even intellectual response to modernization. He says they were involved in a search for meaning motivated not only by "modernization" (defined as the result of the modern Western belief in social change through the mastery of the world) but also by the spread of Christianity, the revival of Chinese Mahayana Buddhism, and, in particular, "the worldwide crisis of understanding provoked by the propagation of Western positivism."[27]

In addition to this objective assessment, Chang also has certain critical views. Like Lin, he stresses the need for a middle way between self-comforting adulation of Chinese tradition and May Fourth–style vilification of it. Indeed, he is quite appreciative of the New Confucians for providing one angle from which to see not only the excesses of May Fourth radicals but also the potential flaws in the whole project of modernization. His main complaint with them is that their attitude toward traditional Confucianism is not critical enough. For one thing, they fail to see how wide the gap is between modern democratic (*minzhu*) self-rule and traditional "people-based" (*minben*) paternalistic rule. For another, they tend to ignore the topic of Confucian cosmology and thus to overlook a whole dimension of the tradition that serves to support conservative sociopolitical conventions (*gangchang mingjiao*).[28]

Yü Ying-shih: My Teacher Is Not a New Confucian

Yü Ying-shih is among those who have given thought to the definition of the term "New Confucian." He has opted for the narrowest possible definition, according to which only the four signatories of the 1958 manifesto would be included. He is not without vested interests in making his decision. In fact, he intends specifically to counter others' tendency to include his teacher, Qian Mu, on their list of New Confucians. As he points out, Qian Mu was a historian, not a philosopher, let alone one with leanings toward German idealism or even the idealistic wing of Song-Ming Confucianism.[29] However, one gets the impression that Yü's main motivation is to distance his teacher from a group of thinkers whose style of thought he dislikes. He considers the New Confucians a kind of religious sect, in contrast to his teacher, who avoided sects or factions, as have all the great "consummate Confucians" (*tong ru*) through the centuries. Yü states: "Qian himself was indeed a consummate Confucian of the twentieth century, deeply penetrating every area of study: classics, histories, philosophical works, and literary collections."[30]

Yü feels that the New Confucians made poor choices in basing their interpretation of Confucian tradition on German idealism and the idealist wing of the Confucian tradition itself, which he associates with the school of Lu Xiangshan and Wang Yangming. He is relentless in his criticism of the results. As evidence of the sectarian religious nature of the New Confucians, he cites their emphasis on *xin-xing* and the need to know it by intuition, to have a kind of religious experience. In Yü's view, because of this emphasis, the New Confucians' understanding of the Confucian Way is available only to a select few, not to all those willing to exert the effort to study Confucian history.[31] He develops this general criticism with attacks on two specific aspects of New Confucian thought: (1) the theory that the tradition of the Way must be used to bring forth and guide the traditions of modern politics and scientific learning; and (2) the psychological structure of New Confucian thought.

Because the tradition of the Way is given priority over the other two traditions, Yü sees here an example of the New Confucians' tendency to avow a superior intuitive awareness that is not accessible to others. Only one who has found the tradition of the Way through inner sageliness will be able to make pronouncements on the Confucian contribution to the development of modern Chinese political and scholarly traditions. Moreover, Yü feels that the New Confucian claim that one can derive democracy and science from the Confucian Way has little merit. It is but a transparent attempt to avoid embarrassment for China's having to import science and democracy from the West.[32]

In discussing the psychological structure of New Confucian thought, Yü seeks to bolster his claim that the New Confucianism is theological and sectarian in nature. In this instance, he focuses on New Confucian use of the traditional concept of the innate moral mind (*liangzhi*). Because access to this level of human awareness is the *sine qua non* for being the kind of inner sage that can properly guide political and scientific development, we once again see New Confucian elitism. According to Yü, a pyramidal psychological structure thus remains in place, even as New Confucians await reconstruction of the pyramidal social structure approved by traditional Confucianism. Yü sees a deeper contradiction in the New Confucians' attack on the epistemology of science, sometimes called its "epistemological conceit," while they have their own "conceit of the moral mind." By claiming special access to an even higher level of understanding than that of the scientific method, they reject the modern notion of a common public quest for knowledge and adopt a method more like that of medieval theology. They seek to establish a kind of supreme "religion" rather than a knowledge-based scholarly tradition.

Taiwan's Catholics and the New Confucians

If Yü well represents secular scholars who have a distaste for the New Confucians' religiousness, Taiwan's Catholic scholars best exemplify those who find them too atheistic in their interpretation of the Confucian teachings. These scholars either have connections to Fu Jen Catholic University or have been prominent figures there, such as university president and archbishop Luo Guang and his predecessor, Cardinal Yü Pin (Yu Bin). Tu Weiming has described the relationship of this group to the New Confucians as follows:

> The acrimonious exchange between Mou Zongsan and Luo Guang is more than episodic in this intriguing struggle for orthodoxy in Confucian discourse. While the New Confucians accuse the Catholics (a few of them are former Jesuit priests) of Christianizing the tradition, the Christian interpreters condemn Mou and his followers for couching the tradition in German idealism. Their scholarly debates are as much about hermeneutics in Western philosophy as about exegesis in Confucian thought.[33]

Considering the importance of the Confucian tradition as a badge of Chineseness, it is not surprising that each side impugns the other for spoiling the tradition by introducing foreign ideas.

While Tu is surely right to see this as a central issue, there are also several other major points on which the two groups disagree. First, while New Confucians see the Confucian tradition as a full functional equivalent of religion, some Catholic scholars still subscribe to the old Jesuit fulfillment theory, according to which Confucianism needs the religious dimension provided by Christianity in order that it may serve the whole person and contribute to one's salvation. As indicated previously, each generation of New Confucians has emphasized the religious role Confucianism can play in a person's life. Mou, for example, explained that Confucianism can serve *as* a religion, even though it lacks such typical elements of religion as prayer and God. He wrote:

> The emotional cry for help is to be found in every people, and in every individual. Christianity is simply the religion in which it is most clearly expressed. Thus, Christianity is the religion which most thoroughly preserves the primitive religious spirit. The emotional cry for help never developed into formalized religious prayer in Confucianism, and consequently, objectively, the concept of God was never prominent. The Confucian emphasis was never on God and prayer.[34]

Of course, Mou's characterization of Christianity is matched by Catholic scholars' equally simplistic portrait of New Confucianism as atheistic and anthropocentric, which brings us to a second point of disagreement.

Peter Kun-Yu Woo (Wu Kunru) is one Taiwanese Catholic scholar who tells us that New Confucians employ an anthropocentric interpretation of Confucianism and explains that foreign atheistic influence is behind such a wrongheaded interpretation. For example, he states: "It is well known and very widely advertised in Chinese academic circles that the representatives of the Xinya school of Neo-Confucianism, such as Tang Junyi, Mou Zongsan, Lao Siguang, etc., interpret Confucian theory as strictly anthropocentric."[35] He prefers Catholic scholars' metaphysical reinterpretation of Confucian philosophy in which God, as the equivalent of Heaven (*tian*), is the ultimate source of Confucian morality. This reinterpretation is necessary because the Confucian tradition has long been subject to anthropocentric, nontheistic foreign influences. Indeed, Western materialism is only the latest negative influence. Prior to it, Buddhism had led Song- and Ming-period Confucians away from the correct understanding of early Confucian teachings.

This brings us to a third Catholic criticism: New Confucians are not truly in touch with early Confucian teachings because they see these teachings through the distorted vision of Song-Ming Confucianism. While Catholic scholars are not alone in their preference for early Confucianism,[36] their preference is unusually strong and deeply rooted. From the time of Matteo Ricci (1552–1610) Catholics in China have disliked the views of Song-Ming Confucians, or "Neo-Confucians," as they are often called. Peter Woo's statement on the subject, as follows, is unusually strong yet typical of the basic Chinese Catholic perspective. "The Neo-Confucians from Song and Ming dynasties onward rejected the transcendental and personal God and held human nature to be absolute and eternal. This resulted in the deification of man, and the inner moral postulate became the ultimate foundation of all ethical affairs."[37] Moreover, he leaves no doubt that, in his view, foreign influence is at fault today as it was in Song and Ming times. He states: "It is not unreasonable to suspect that the anthropocentric humanism of the Song and Ming dynasties was influenced by Buddhism, and that the same theory in circulation today is affected by the western materialism, atheism, or anti-theism."[38]

The final and, perhaps, most important Catholic criticism is that Heaven (*tian*) has lost its proper role in Confucian teachings as presented by the New Confucians. Back to the time of Matteo Ricci, Catholics have equated the Confucian "Heaven" with the Christian "God." This trend has been especially strong in postwar Taiwan under the influence of Yu Bin and Luo Guang. On one occasion, Yu wrote:

> People in ancient China said that all things have their origin in Heaven. This is precisely the theologians' concept of creation and of a lord of creation. . . . But when the influence of Europe and America began to be felt in China, Chinese were afraid to admit this kind of theory, or sought to give other explanations for the meaning of the Way of Heaven. . . . There is, of course,

no question that theism was a part of Confucian thought, and that Confucianism is therefore wholly opposed to materialism and atheism.[39]

This interpretation of Heaven as personal deity has become the basis for criticizing the New Confucian view of the self-sufficient moral mind as the basis for Confucian ethics. The criticism hangs on the assumption that Confucius and Mencius never doubted the essential role of Heaven in the creation of moral principles, despite their interest in the human mind and nature. From this comes the charge that the New Confucian doctrine of a self-sufficient moral mind is a product of Western, and in Mou Zongsan's case, Kantian, influence. This, of course, brings us back full circle to Tu Weiming's comment about Catholic scholars chastising New Confucians for introducing the pernicious influence of German idealism into modern Confucian hermeneutics. Thus, let us now turn from external criticism of New Confucianism to self-criticisms penned by Tu and his fellow younger generation New Confucian, Liu Shu-hsien.

New Confucian Self-Criticism

The third generation of New Confucians grew to adulthood and practiced their careers in far more stable circumstances than did their predecessors, who survived war and revolution, became exiled from their homeland, and developed a deeply emotional as well as intellectual sense of cultural crisis. Moreover, Tu Weiming and Liu Shu-hsien, for example, had the opportunity to study and teach at leading American universities, exposing themselves to recent trends in Western thought as well as developing ways to present Chinese thought to Western audiences. While still deeply involved in Taiwanese scholarly debates, they have also established themselves in new geographical as well as intellectual "locations." As a result, their comparative work has become more sophisticated than that of first- or second-generation New Confucians, and they have been able to combine scholarly distance with religious commitment in their approach to Confucian studies. With greater scholarly distance, they have been able to employ a more self-critical stance toward New Confucianism.

Although Tu takes the New Confucian project in many new directions through his dialogue with Western thought, he is less explicitly critical of the previous generation than Liu can be. Nonetheless, on occasion he hints at their shortcomings. For example, at the end of his celebrated essay "Towards a Third Epoch of Confucian Humanism," he writes:

> There is no way to predict the future direction of the Confucian humanism envisioned by Tang, Xu, and Mou. Given the fruitful indications to date,

however, we can suggest the steps by which such a project can be further developed. If the well-being of humanity is its central concern, Confucian humanism in the third epoch cannot afford to be confined to East Asian cultures. A global perspective is needed to universalize its concerns. Confucians can benefit from dialogue with Jewish, Christian, and Islamic theologians, with Buddhists, with Marxists, and with Freudian and post-Freudian psychologists. The attempt to analyze Confucian ideas in terms of Kantian and Hegelian categories, an attempt that has yielded impressive results, will have to be broadened to accommodate new philosophical insights in the twentieth century.[40]

One cannot help but feel that Tu is speaking of directions in which his predecessors were unable or unwilling to go, while he has begun to do so. In particular, he has engaged in interreligious dialogue, looked to contemporary Western religious thinkers for inspiration, and sought to redefine "religion" as a category which is not foreign to Confucian spirituality. This activity, more than any explicitly self-critical New Confucian writings, is a demonstration of his different "location," when compared to his teachers.

Liu's activities have exhibited a similar change in "location." However, perhaps because he has been closer to the world of Taiwan's intellectuals (at least geographically), he seems more aware of others' criticisms of New Confucianism and more willing to state his own. Indeed, two of his seminal overviews of New Confucian thought give substantial space to his critical reflections, including evaluations of specific thinkers as well as general criticisms. In "Postwar Neo-Confucian Philosophy: Its Development and Issues," he evaluates the thought of Mou and Tang, of their teacher, Xiong Shili, and of his own teacher, Thomé Fang (Fang Dongmei, 1899–1977, who never claimed to be a New Confucian). Xiong is the only one whose scholarship Liu criticizes, pointing out that the work in question was written after Xiong had lived for years under PRC influence. He criticizes Fang and Tang for going too far in harmonizing various forms of thought, Eastern and Western, without taking account of deep-seated differences. He also notes that, in Tang's case, the problem was exacerbated by a tendency to present a highly idealized view of traditional Chinese culture. As for Mou, he is criticized (as is Fang) for speaking of unity of theory and action, without explaining concrete ways in which to put theory into practice.[41]

Like these comments, the four general criticisms that Liu presents elsewhere,[42] are reminiscent of certain views I have surveyed in this essay, although his criticisms are embedded in a very positive appreciation of New Confucian thought, especially as represented by the 1958 manifesto signed by Chang, Mou, Tang, and Xu. First, says Liu, although their thought appealed to us at the level of ideals, it had problems in the area of *praxis*. Liu wonders whether or not they thought through what it means to say that philosophical efforts to uncover the truth of the Way take priority over scientific thought. Practically speaking, it sounds as if a true Confucian would never pursue a scientific career. Such an attitude surely will not aid Chinese modernization. In this context, he states: "A nostalgic feeling toward the past which puts more emphasis on humanistic values will not help to solve our problems."[43] Second, in the area of cultural development, earlier New Confucians were slow to offer concrete solutions for the flaws they saw in modern Western culture, from personal alienation to the erosion of social morality. While not naive enough to believe humanity can return to premodern values as such, "they have not the slightest idea how to implement their lofty ideals in the real world."[44] Third, their political views are the most problematic. While committed to democracy as a vague ideal, New Confucians did not answer even some of the most basic questions: Is minimum or maximum government more desirable? Since traditional Confucianism's weakest link is in the political area, exactly what can it contribute to the "new outer kingliness"? When a state permits free economic activity, how does it prevent the un-Confucian scenario of having a country's wealth in the hands of a few capitalists? Fourth, and most important, says Liu, New Confucians did not show us how we can square the traditional monistic approach to religious or philosophical truth with the modern pluralistic approach. According to him, it is indeed possible for a modern Confucian thinker to show this, for example, through a new interpretation of the traditional Confucian idea that "principle is one, but the manifestations are many."[45]

Conclusion

Although they continue to respond to the critics of New Confucianism, younger-generation representatives are not isolated "conservatives" in a largely anti-Confucian intellectual milieu. In looking at Liu and Tu, it is hard to see how one could level at them the complaint of Yü Ying-shih, for example, that New Confucian thinkers are unwilling to enter into the public marketplace of ideas without claiming a privileged status for their own tradition. In postwar Taiwan, the movement has evolved along with its milieu. Even social scientists with an erstwhile commitment to the intellectual values of the May Fourth era have championed Confucianism for its alleged contribution to Taiwan's economic development.[46]

Leaving aside Chinese Catholics, whose commitment to a Western religion complicates the picture, the debate between New Confucians and their critics is unlike that between fundamentalists and modernists in the

United States, the Middle East, or India, for example. Not only Liu and Tu, but even New Confucians of their teachers' generation were "modernists" in the cross-cultural sense. Thus, while Tu wrote about them under the auspices of the American Academy of Arts and Sciences Fundamentalism Project, he acknowledged that he could not properly label their Confucian revival "fundamentalist."[47] Their goal was to modernize traditional Confucianism, not to revive it in order to reimpose its premodern social and political forms on modern society. Indeed, in postwar Taiwan, the debate was not about whether or not to modernize Confucianism. It was about *how* to modernize it and about whether or not *even* a modernized Confucian tradition could contribute anything to Taiwan's economic, political, and social development. The traditionalists in the debate were Confucian modernists: self-professed *New* Confucians.

Nonetheless, the debate over Confucianism in postwar Taiwan has been as emotionally charged as debates between traditionalists and their critics elsewhere in the world. In many ways, intellectuals there remain as polarized as their May Fourth–era predecessors, and it hard to find one who does not have some opinion about Confucianism. How are we to explain this? Elie Wiesel, a leading modern Jewish intellectual, once said that post-Holocaust Jews can be for God or against God, but they cannot be without God. Perhaps modern Chinese intellectuals are in a comparable situation: They can be for Confucianism or against Confucianism. But they cannot be neutral.

Notes

1. Pinyin Romanization is used, except for the names of persons for whom there is a well known English spelling. In these cases, Pinyin Romanization is given in parentheses at the first mention of the name.

2. On this tension, see Tu Weiming, "The Search for Roots in Industrial East Asia: The Case of Confucian Revival," in *Fundamentalisms Observed*, ed. Marty and Appleby, 771.

3. In addition to the other chapters in this volume, there are good overviews in Umberto Bresciani, *Reinventing Confucianism: The New Confucian Movement;* Chang Hao, "New Confucianism and the Intellectual Crisis of Contemporary China," in *The Limits of Change*, ed. Furth; Liu Shu-hsien, "Postwar Neo-Confucian Philosophy: Its Development and Issues," in *Religious Issues and Interreligious Dialogues*, ed. Fu and Spiegler, 277–302; idem, "Confucian Ideals and the Real World: A Critical Review of Contemporary Neo-Confucian Thought," in *Confucian Traditions in East Asian Modernity*, ed. Tu; and John Makeham, ed., *New Confucianism: A Critical Examination*. For New Confucianism in the context of other postwar trends in Taiwan, see Huang Chün-chieh, "Confucianism in Postwar Taiwan," in *Proceedings of the National Science Council, ROC*, 2, no. 2 (1992):

218–33; Christian Jochim, "Carrying Confucianism into the Modern World: The Taiwan Case," in *Religion in Modern Taiwan,* ed. Clart and Jones; and Thomas A. Metzger, "The Chinese Reconciliation of Moral-Sacred Values with Modern Pluralism," in *Two Societies in Opposition,* 3–56. For New Confucianism as a dimension of Confucian revival in modern East Asia, see Tu, "Search for Roots in Industrial East Asia."

4. Wei Zhengtong, "Dangdai xinrujiade xintai," 44. Here and elsewhere in this essay, when quoting text with Romanization other than Pinyin in the original text, this is converted to Pinyin for the sake of consistency.

5. Chang, "New Confucianism and the Intellectual Crisis of Contemporary China."

6. Carson Chang et al., "A Manifesto for a Re-appraisal of Sinology and Reconstruction of Chinese Culture," 455–83.

7. Wei, "Dangdai xinrujiade xintai," 44.

8. Carson Chang et al., "Manifesto," 461–64.

9. Chang Hao, "New Confucianism and the Intellectual Crisis of Contemporary China," 277.

10. On this, see the essay by Berthrong in this volume as well as John Berthrong, *All Under Heaven;* and Christian Jochim, "The Contemporary Confucian-Christian Encounter."

11. Liu, "Postwar Neo-Confucian Philosophy," 289.

12. See Mou Zongsan, "Confucianism as Religion," in *Chinese Essays on Religion and Faith;* Liu Shu-hsien, "The Religious Import of Confucian Philosophy." For a survey of approaches to Confucian religiousness, see John Berthrong, "Trends in Interpretation of Confucian Religiosity," in *Confucian–Christian Encounters in Historical and Contemporary Perspective,* ed. Lee.

13. Bao Zunxin, *Piping yu qiming,* 2.

14. Ibid., 12, 27, 3–4.

15. Ibid., 4–5.

16. Ibid., 15–17.

17. Ibid., 11–13.

18. Ibid., 19–20.

19. On the place of liberalism in the larger intellectual scene, see Metzger, "Chinese Reconciliation of Moral-Sacred Values," which lists "Chinese liberalism" among five political outlooks in postwar Taiwan, filling out his list with official state doctrine, a petit bourgeois outlook, modern Chinese humanism, and Taiwan independence. He deals with the New Confucians under "modern Confucian humanism."

20. Wei Zhengtong, *Rujia yu xiandaihua,* 2–4.

21. Wei Zhengtong, "Rujia yu Taiwande minzhu yundong," in *Lishi zhuanbandiande fanxing.*

22. Wei Zhengtong, "Dangdai xinrujiade xintai," *Zhongguo luntan* 169 (October 10, 1982): 44–50.

23. Charles Wei-hsun Fu, "Postwar Confucianism and Western Democracy," in *Movements and Issues in World Religions,* ed. Fu and Spiegler, 193. Thomas A.

Metzger levels this criticism at a whole range of intellectuals in Taiwanese politics, including liberals. He argues that liberals and Confucian humanists alike have utopian tendencies that contrast with "the Western Millsian tradition," in which "democracy is more a procedural, constitutional form maximizing equality and freedom rather than a system necessarily putting a morally and intellectually enlightened elite in control of the government" (Metzger, "Chinese Reconciliation of Moral-Sacred Values," 36).

24. Wei, "Dangdai xinrujiade xintai," 45–47.

25. Lin Yü-sheng, "Miandui weilaide zhongji guanhuai," *Zhongguo luntan* 169 (October 10, 1982): 22.

26. Ibid., 24.

27. Chang Hao, "New Confucianism and the Intellectual Crisis of Contemporary China," 301.

28. Chang Hao, "Xinrujia yu zhongguo wenhua weiji," *Zhongguo luntan* 169 (October 10, 1982): 24–25.

29. Yü Ying-shih, *You ji feng chui shuishang lin*, 67–68.

30. Ibid., 33.

31. Ibid., 71–72, 79.

32. Ibid., 82.

33. Tu, "Search for Roots in Industrial East Asia," 772.

34. Mou, "Confucianism as Religion," 34–35.

35. Peter Kun-Yu Woo, "The Metaphysical Foundations of Traditional Chinese Moral Education," in *Chinese Foundations for Moral Education and Character Development*, ed. Tran Van Doan et al., 17 n. 1.

36. One key example is Thomé Fang (Fang Dongmei), an influential interpreter of Confucianism in postwar Taiwan, who has been designated as a New Confucian by some observers, including his student Liu Shu-hsien. On this proclivity of his teacher, see Liu, "Postwar Neo-Confucian Philosophy," 277.

37. Woo, "Metaphysical Foundations," 13.

38. Ibid., 16.

39. Yu Bin, "Roman Catholicism and Confucianism," in *Chinese Essays on Religion and Faith*, 160–61.

40. Tu Weiming, "Towards a Third Epoch of Confucian Humanism," in *Way, Learning, and Politics*, 158–59.

41. Liu, "Postwar Neo-Confucian Philosophy," 294–97.

42. Liu Shu-hsien, "Confucian Ideals and the Real World: A Critical Review of Contemporary Neo-Confucian Thought," in *Confucian Traditions in East Asian Modernity*, ed. Tu, 105–11.

43. Ibid., 107.

44. Ibid.

45. Ibid., 108.

46. Christian Jochim, "Confucius and Capitalism: Views of Confucianism in Works on Confucianism and Economic Development," *Journal of Chinese Religions* 20 (1992): 135–71.

47. Tu, "Search for Roots in Industrial East Asia," 745.

Bibliography

Bao, Zunxin. *Piping yu qiming* [Criticism and Enlightenment]. Taibei: Lianjing, 1989.

Berthrong, John. "Trends in Interpretation of Confucian Religiosity." In *Confucian–Christian Encounters in Historical and Contemporary Perspective*, edited by P. K. H. Lee, 226–54. Lewiston, N.Y.: Edwin Mellen Press, 1991.

———. *All Under Heaven: Transforming Paradigms in Confucian-Christian Dialogue*. Albany: State University of New York Press, 1994.

Bresciani, Umberto. *Reinventing Confucianism: The New Confucian Movement*. Taipei: Taipei Ricci Institute, 2001.

Chang, Carson, et al. "A Manifesto for a Re-appraisal of Sinology and Reconstruction of Chinese Culture." Appendix in *The Development of Neo-Confucian Thought*, 2:455–83. New York: Bookman Associates, 1962.

Chang, Hao. "New Confucianism and the Intellectual Crisis of Contemporary China." In *The Limits of Change: Essays on Conservative Alternatives in Republican China*, edited by C. Furth, 276–302. Cambridge, Mass.: Harvard University Press, 1976.

——— (Zhang Hao). "Xinrujia yu zhongguo wenhua weiji" [The New Confucians and China's Cultural Crisis]. *Zhongguo luntan* [China Forum] 169 (October 10, 1982): 24–27.

Fu, Charles Wei-hsun. "Postwar Confucianism and Western Democracy." In *Movements and Issues in World Religions*, edited by C. W. Fu and G. E. Spiegler, 177–96. New York: Greenwood Press, 1987.

Huang Chün-chieh. "Confucianism in Postwar Taiwan." In *Proceedings of the National Science Council, ROC, Part C, Humanities and Social Sciences* 2, no. 2 (1992): 218–33.

Jochim, Christian. "Carrying Confucianism into the Modern World: The Taiwan Case." In *Religion in Modern Taiwan: Tradition and Innovation in a Changing Society*, edited by Philip Clart and Charles Jones, 48–83. Honolulu: University of Hawaii Press, 2003.

———. "Confucius and Capitalism: Views of Confucianism in Works on Confucianism and Economic Development." *Journal of Chinese Religions* 20 (1992): 135–71.

———. "The Contemporary Confucian-Christian Encounter: Interreligious or Intrareligious Dialogue?" *Journal of Ecumenical Studies* 32, no. 1 (Winter 1995): 35–62.

Lin, Yü-sheng (Lin Yusheng). "Miandui weilaide zhongji guanhuai" [Facing Ultimate Concerns of the Future]. *Zhongguo luntan* [China Forum] 169 (October 10, 1982): 21–24.

Liu Shu-hsien. "The Religious Import of Confucian Philosophy: Its Traditional Outlook and Contemporary Significance." *Philosophy East and West* 21, no. 2 (April 1971): 157–75.

———. "Postwar Neo-Confucian Philosophy: Its Development and Issues." In

Religious Issues and Interreligious Dialogues: An Analysis and Sourcebook of Developments Since 1945, edited by C. W. Fu and G. E. Spiegler, 277–302. New York: Greenwood Press, 1989.

————. "Confucian Ideals and the Real World: A Critical Review of Contemporary Neo-Confucian Thought." In *Confucian Traditions in East Asian Modernity*, edited by Tu Weiming, 92–111. Cambridge, Mass.: Harvard University Press, 1996.

Makeham, John, ed., *New Confucianism: A Critical Examination*. New York: Palgrave Macmillan, 2003.

Metzger, Thomas A. "The Chinese Reconciliation of Moral-Sacred Values with Modern Pluralism: Political Discourse in the ROC, 1949–1989." In *Two Societies in Opposition: The Republic of China and the People's Republic of China After Forty Years*, 3–56. Stanford: Hoover Institution Press, 1991.

Mou Tsung-san (Mou Zongsan). "Confucianism as Religion." In *Chinese Essays on Religion and Faith*, trans. D. Lancashire, 21–43. San Francisco: Chinese Materials Center, 1981 (from *Zhongguo zhexuede tezhi*, 1963).

Tu Weiming. "The Search for Roots in Industrial East Asia: The Case of Confucian Revival." In *Fundamentalisms Observed*, edited by M. Marty and S. Appleby, 740–81. Chicago: University of Chicago Press, 1991.

————. "Towards a Third Epoch of Confucian Humanism." In *Way, Learning, and Politics*, 141–59. Albany: State University of New York Press, 1993.

Wei Zhengtong. "Dangdai xinrujiade xintai" [The Mentality of Contemporary Neo-Confucians], *Zhongguo luntan* [China Forum] 169 (October 10, 1982): 44–50.

————. *Rujia yu xiandaihua* [Confucianism and Modernization]. Taibei: Shuiniu, 1989.

————. "Rujia yu Taiwande minzhu yundong" [Confucianism and Taiwan's Democratic Movements]. In *Lishi zhuanbandiande fanxing* [Reflections on a Turning Point in History]. Taibei: Dongda, 1989.

Woo, Peter Kun-Yu. "The Metaphysical Foundations of Traditional Chinese Moral Education." In *Chinese Foundations for Moral Education and Character Development*, ed. Tran Van Doan et al., 7–18 Washington, D.C.: Council for Research in Values and Philosophy, 1991.

Yü Pin. "Roman Catholicism and Confucianism." In *Chinese Essays on Religion and Faith*, trans. D. Lancashire, 160–66. San Francisco: Chinese Materials Center, 1981.

Yü Ying-shih (Yu Yingshi). *You ji feng chui shuishang lin: Qian Mu yu Zhongguo xiandai xueshu* [Still Remembering Wind Blowing Ripples on the Water: Qian Mu and China's Modern Scholarship]. Taibei: Sanmin, 1991.

34

New Confucian Spirituality in Interreligious Dialogue

JOHN BERTHRONG

T HE AIM OF THIS ESSAY is to address the question of the range of dialogues engaged in by the modern movement called New Confucianism. The term "New Confucianism" will be further defined below, as will the extent of the dialogical connections of the Confucian tradition with other intellectual and religious movements. The focus will be on the modern period, that is to say, from the mid-nineteenth century to the present. While the majority of cases of interreligious exchange are drawn from Chinese history, it is also important to remember that Confucianism is an international tradition that has played an important role in the lives of Chinese, Korean, Japanese, and Vietnamese peoples for thousands of years. For instance, it would be illuminating to review the interaction of Confucianism and Buddhism in Korea and the exchange of Shinto and Confucian scholars in medieval and early modern Japan. There have even been times, especially in the sixteenth, seventeenth, and eighteenth centuries when it is fair to argue that the most creative work in the development of the Confucian Way was being done in Korea and Japan. In terms of the modern engagement of Confucianism with other religions, Korea and Japan would have a great deal to offer a more extensive study of the dialogical history of Confucianism. However, we will be able to provide only the merest outline of this rich history in order to provide a background for the Confucian dialogue with the religious, spiritual, and intellectual forces of the modern world.

The great Canadian historian of religion Wilfred Cantwell Smith has repeatedly made the point that humanity has one religious history, however variegated its manifestations have been.[1] The examination of how

New Confucianism has entered into interreligious dialogue at the end of the twentieth century should be enough to convince even the most skeptical scholar of the viability of Smith's hypothesis. New Confucianism designates a group of modern Chinese scholars who sought to rescue, reinterpret, and reform the whole of the Confucian tradition from the 1920s to the present. This was a lonely task because the Confucian tradition has been under intense criticism as an outworn vestige of the feudal past after the great intellectual reform movement of May 1919. These New Confucian scholars developed a sophisticated series of research programs aimed at the hermeneutic retrieval not just of tradition but of a tradition useful for modern women and men.

W. C. Smith has shown that there is a great deal more interaction between and among religious communities than has been commonly recognized or accepted. While some traditions acknowledge their connections to other religions such as the sharing of common themes among Judaism, Christianity, and Islam and between Buddhism and Hinduism, the more common reaction is to disavow any such substantive relationship. Religious communities angrily deny that they are eclectic or syncretistic. In a negative sense, syncretism has been defined as the attempt to combine two or more historically divergent religious traditions into a new, third kind of religion. Yet religions have borrowed from each other from the dawn of time even if none of them is particularly keen on being labeled syncretistic.

What has changed in the modern period is that religionists have become more aware of the fact of borrowing and mutual stimulation and the modern media and telecommunications have documented more fully than before the wanderings of religious seekers. There is simply more transparency about commerce that is going on today. For instance, a strong case could be made for the fact that the phenomenon of the New Age religious movement is an example of something that has gone on before, such as in the late Hellenistic world, but is unique perhaps because of its self-conscious eclecticism or syncretism. Of course, the guardians of official orthodoxy in any and all of the axial-age religions are displeased to see religions becoming items in a global supermarket of spirituality. In short, most representatives of the major and minor axial-age religions (the great historic traditions that arose from the sixth century B.C.E. in west, south, and east Asia such as Judaism, Christianity, Islam, Buddhism, and Hinduism) and the primal traditions have decidedly mixed feelings about all the exchanges going on today. For instance, the Native peoples of North America find it ironic that the same dominant Anglo-American culture that has persistently tried to destroy, convert, and criminalize their religious traditions now is full of "wanna-be" Native elders. The traditional elders are outraged that Anglo-

Americans, sometimes on the basis of a weekend experience, will set themselves up, for a fee, to conduct the sacred pipe or sweat lodge ceremonies.

Nonetheless, the Confucian tradition, as other essays will attest, has always been a movement in dialogue. The traditional biography of Confucius chronicled his visits to other scholars in order to learn about their traditions. While it is true that Confucius was seeking the authentic rituals and teachings of the ancient sages and of his beloved Zhou dynasty, the picture illustrates someone open to conversation with others, including proto-Daoist hermits. This dialogical relationship with other traditions was sharpened through the encounters of Mencius (fl. 371–298 B.C.E.) and Xunzi (fl. 310–210 B.C.E.) with the exponents of the Hundred Schools of thought in the late Zhou. Nor did these need to be pleasant exchanges; Mencius definitely did not like debating the Mohists and Yangists of his day. From Mencius's point of view, the Mohists were interested only in pragmatic success and not true virtue, whereas Yangists were the worst sort of hedonists. The buzzing, exuberant world of Warring States China was full of heated exchanges of basic concepts and philosophic techniques.

Xunzi is another example of a Confucian who engaged in extended conversations and debates with followers of other schools. The Confucian line, followed by Xunzi, was that this situation was to be deplored. Just like Mencius, Xunzi tried to persuade his partners in dialogue of the error of their ways. Nonetheless, as modern scholarship has shown, Xunzi was indebted to other philosophic traditions. For instance, his theory of the mind-heart and its proper cultivation owed an immense debt to Zhuangzi; his whole theory of disputation would have been unthinkable without tutelage by the Neo-Mohists.

The Confucian Encounter with Buddhism

The greatest example of mutual stimulation, borrowing, and dialogue is the Confucian–Buddhist interchange begun in the second century of the Common Era. It is impossible to imagine Confucian spirituality without considering the rich history of Buddhism in China. It is much easier to think of Chinese thought without too much concern for dialogue with other religious traditions such as Islam or Christianity. There have been sporadic dialogues concerning spirituality with Muslims and Christians over the centuries, but these exchanges have not yet transformed the Chinese religious landscape the way Buddhism modified everything it touched. It was with Buddhism that Confucianism has had its significant dialogue about spiritual matters until the arrival of the modern West and its relentless modernization process. Except for Buddhism, the only dialogue that has actually transformed Confucianism has been its agonizing encounter with the imperial Western powers from the middle of the nineteenth century.

The exchange between Buddhists and Confucians was multifaceted in the extreme. At the one end of the spectrum was the confrontation of two vastly divergent sets of cultural sensibilities. The Chinese have always had a sturdy respect for the reality of the world and the place of human beings in it. The Buddhists challenged these assumptions and suggested that the world was ultimately illusion or, even worse, empty of any substantial being. Furthermore, the Buddhists provided a completely new image of the religious virtuoso, the celibate monk or nun. Because Confucian thought always gives pride of place to images of the extended family, for Buddhism to affirm that the family was not the proper place for religious life, was shocking in the extreme. Chinese metaphysical values and family values were assaulted at the same time, all in the name of a higher vision of reality.

The great Buddhist translation projects that went on from the second to the sixth centuries of the Common Era forced Confucian intellectuals to dialogue in a way that they had not had to do since the end of the Warring States period and the foundation of the Han dynasty (206 B.C.E.). The precision with which the Buddhists went about their metaphysical analysis of the world was almost revelatory to the Chinese. The Chinese even created their own great philosophic schools such as Tientai, Huayan, and Chan, better know in the West by its Japanese name, Zen, in order to synthesize their own Buddhist philosophies. All these Buddhist schools asked Chinese intellectuals to try to comprehend how the phenomenal world of the senses is linked to the realm of absolute nothingness. Or, even better, how could the mundane mind-heart grasp and conform itself to the nonduality of nirvana? In the midst of the great debates, the Buddhists taught the Confucians how to think about how the abstract, metaphysical aspects of reality were related to the concrete things we take for granted in our daily lives.

One of the best examples of this Confucian–Buddhist spiritual exchange revolves around the Neo-Confucian practice of quiet-sitting as the preferred form of meditation. Very few scholars hold that quiet-sitting owes nothing to Buddhist influence. The only other alternative would be Daoist meditation practices, and by the Song period when quiet-sitting had become a recommended feature of Confucian spiritual formation, the point can be made that the Daoists themselves had borrowed many of their meditational practices from the Buddhists. A dispassionate historian of religion also has to wonder about how much Neo-Confucian self-cultivation praxis owed to Buddhist stimulus and models. However, the Confucians were correct to point out that Mencius and other late Zhou Confucians, such as the author of the *Doctrine of the Mean*, had been passionately concerned with the spiritual edification of the moral mind-heart.

Modern Engagements

Because we are primarily concerned with the dialogue of the New Confucians with the modern world, we need to move forward a number of centuries, to the beginning of the twentieth century, when the dominance of Confucianism was challenged throughout East Asia. As Mark Elvin has argued so eloquently, no other great axial-age tradition has suffered as much damage as Confucianism in the twentieth century.[2] Elvin's stark conclusion is that no large social group in East Asia now studies the Confucian canon as a comprehensive guide for the conduct of life. The destruction visited upon key Confucian social institutions caused Joseph Levenson to surmise that, for all practical measurements, the Confucian Way was dead. If it were to have a life, it would be in the museum of history. Levenson's metaphor was powerful: Confucians, who had made history in East Asia for more than twenty-five hundred years, were now reduced to mere historical curiosities. What had been a living tradition was only a skeleton of its former self. Actually, Levenson's prediction now appears premature. There has been a slow but persistent reinvigoration of Confucianism going on since the pioneering work of scholars such as Xiong Shili (1885–1968), Liang Shuming (1893–1988), Qian Mu (1895–1990), Xu Fuguan (1903–1982), Tang Juni (1909–1978) and Mou Zongsan (1909–1994), and others, since the 1920s.

The Confucian revival is called New Confucianism in order to distinguish it from earlier forms such as the classical Confucianism of the late Zhou and Han dynasties and the Neo-Confucianism of the Song, Ming, and Qing dynasties. New Confucianism has continued to grow owing to the efforts of a second and third generation of scholars such as Tu Weiming, Liu Shu-hsien (Liu Shuxian), Cheng Zhongying, Cai Renhou, and Julia Ching. It is often thematized as the third epoch or wave of Confucian humanism. It too has a great dialogue partner, and that is the modern West.

Nonetheless, the destructive changes chronicled by Elvin and Wm. Theodore de Bary for Confucians as they tried to cope with the modern West from the middle of the nineteenth century were immense. As de Bary has noted, prior to 1905, when the civil service examinations were suspended in China, Confucians had controlled the civil service through the examination system, education through private academies that provided the education needed to pass the examinations, and family life and ritual through manuals such as Zhu Xi's *Family Rituals*. None of these potent social institutions remained after the 1920s.

Working with a fractured tradition from the 1920s, the New Confucians have engaged in a process of hermeneutic retrieval. Hermeneutics is the science of the systematic interpretation of texts. In the Neo-Confucian tradition it would have been called *dushu*, or the art of reading. The New Confucians are in search of a usable past. For instance, all of the New Confucians recognize that they will have to pay careful attention to feminist critiques of the role of women in Confucian history. Allied to the feminist thinkers are other radical social critics—the Marxists being the most powerful but not the only ones—who have wondered if Confucianism can ever become something more than the ideology of a powerful and educated elite. Can there ever be a more egalitarian, democratic form of Confucianism? Physical and social scientists wonder if Confucianism can adapt itself to modern cosmologies and empirical research programs? In short, can New Confucianism find its feet and a place in the life of modern East Asia? Can it take its place among the dialogue of the axial age religions?

The major effort of New Confucianism has been to describe, explain, understand and commend the tradition. The first moment of this process of hermeneutical retrieval is to frame an accurate, adequate, and comprehensive description of the tradition. This is a historical moment. The second phase is to explain the nature of the tradition, to seek its religious or secular roots. This is the moment of the self-conscious translation of the material from the past to the present. The stage of explanation often makes use of contemporary religious, historical, and social-scientific methodologies in its search for a usable past. The third phase is to seek to understand what was uncovered in and by description and explanation. Understanding attempts to order the retrieved materials for modern usage. The fourth phase is normative in that it commends what has been described, explained, and understood. It is highly theoretical because it projects into the future possible outcomes based on a cumulative hermeneutics of retrieval. If one had to hazard a guess, a great deal of the New Confucian project is historical in nature and is involved in the first two phases of description and explanation.

For instance, the reformation in Confucian studies since the 1960s has been primarily historical in nature. The reasons for this are pragmatic, though in different ways. Scholars identified with the massive research project spearheaded by Wing-tsit Chan and Wm. Theodore de Bary at Columbia University have been primarily cultural and religious historians in terms of inclination and methodology. In China, especially during the last decade, scholars, motivated by a sense of prudence in the face of various drastic and dangerous changes in the Chinese political scene since 1949, have also gravitated to the historical exploration of the Confucian tradition. It would be unwise to move too quickly to commend a classical tradition that is still politically suspect in China. However, these historical studies have transformed our image of the tradition. We have moved from a vision of an unchanging "Confucian China" to the recognition of a radically diverse and contentious Confucian world that mutates before our eyes from century to century and from country to country.

Confucian spirituality in dialogue with other traditions is nested within the larger historical program of hermeneutical retrieval. Tu Weiming argues that although Confucianism is not an organized religion on the model of the West Asian religions, it does possess a distinctive religious dimension. This religious sensibility is just as real as any other of the sociological and intellectual elements of the tradition. In his widely quoted definition of Confucian religiosity Tu stipulates that the Confucian religious process is one of "learning to be fully human."[3] In fact, a number of New Confucians define their reformed tradition as an inclusive humanism. Thus, public intellectuals such as Tu, Liu Shu-hsien and Cheng Zongying define the tradition as a form of inclusive humanism with a distinctive religious dimension. As Tu writes, "We can define the Confucian way of being religious as *ultimate self-transformation as a communal act and as a faithful dialogical response to the transcendent.*"[4] This is a highly suggestive definition of the religious element because, as Tu adds, the notion of ultimate self-transformation "implies that the process of learning to be human never ends (even though the Confucians do not subscribe to the "existentialist" belief that since our existence precedes our essence we can shape our nature according to our own independent action through conscious living)."[5]

Rather like some modern analysts of Judaism, New Confucians describe the tradition as including religious elements but not being limited just to those dimensions. Confucianism is more than its religious element, but it would not be what it is without the religious dimension helping to shape its whole civilizational complex. In fact, perhaps the best way to define Confucianism (as for Judaism) is to say that it is a way of life, a set of metaphors that define an entire approach to civilized life. A civilization is an amalgam of various domains, metaphors, or sets of cultural interests, including art, morality, religion, science, and philosophy.[6] Some civilizations emphasize or develop one interest more rigorously than others and sometimes even refine one interest in different ways. For instance, both Judaism and Confucianism emphasize the social dimensions of ethics and pay more attention to analogical or correlative thinking and the power of metaphor than would be the case in the strictly logical enterprise of modern Western philosophy. For the New Confucians, specific cases matter and cannot always by subsumed under some larger rational theory about the way the world ultimately is or is not. For instance, the Confucians were inordinately interested in how ethics was applied to imperial governance, whereas rabbinic Judaism elaborated its understanding of divine covenant and injunctions. However, the main point is that neither tradition can be confined entirely to what medieval or early modern Christian (or Jewish and Muslim) theologians would consider theological or religious concerns.

There is yet another dimension of New Confucian spiritual dialogue that must be recognized. While not always named, one crucial, if not dominant, partner in ecumenical spiritual dialogues is the modern Western Enlightenment project. Contemporary deconstructionists and postmodernists may argue all they want, but it is as close to a fact as any social reality can be that the European modernist and Enlightenment project is the most powerful and expansive philosophic vision ever devised by human beings. It does not matter whether you live in Moscow, Delhi, Cairo, Teheran, Singapore, New York, Tokyo, Taipei, or Beijing, the pattern of modern discourse is governed by positive or negative reactions to the agenda of the Enlightenment: questions of human rights, market economy and justice, democracy, the role of science, the emancipation of women, the equality of all people, and so on. The list can be expanded to include a variety of other civilizational semantics as well, such as the role of technical rationalism as the sole point of access for the use of human wisdom.

The New Confucians are heirs of the European Enlightenment, and here again it does not matter whether this inheritance comes from the liberal, democratic side of the tradition or from the more authoritarian Marxist version. Just like the Japanese Kyoto school philosophers famous for their modern Buddhist philosophy, New Confucians read Plato, Aristotle, Thomas, Descartes, Leibniz, Kant, Hegel, Peirce, Dewey, Derrida, and Rorty along with Confucius, Mencius, Xunzi, Dong Zongshu (fl. 179–104 B.C.E.), Han Yu (768–824), the northern Song masters, Zhu Xi, Wang Yangming (1472–1529), Wang Fuzhi (1619–1692) and Dai Zhen (1723–1777), just to list some of the major Chinese figures. The Enlightenment project has always been nervous about how closely to embrace the religious dimension of human life. On the one hand, the Enlightenment thinkers, especially in the Romantic phase, did not want to reject any part of human life. On the other hand, many Enlightenment thinkers believed themselves to be locked into a profound struggle with the Christian churches for the souls and minds of their peoples. The New Confucians did not inherit this European struggle to find a place for the secular beyond the control of religious authorities, but they do share an ingrained Confucian suspicion about popular religious practice.

The New Confucians, therefore, have brought a sense of dual cultural heritage to the exploration of spirituality. One pragmatic way to discover the range of New Confucian spiritual concerns is to review certain key topics of dialogue in the recent set of renewed Confucian–Christian dialogues begun in the 1980s and 1990s.

The story of how the dialogues were invented tells volumes about the complicated connections of interreligious relations in the late twentieth century. The possibility of the first Confucian–Christian dialogue was first discussed at an international Buddhist–Christian dialogue in Hawaii in 1984. It struck a number of participants in the dialogue that an understanding of Buddhism in East Asia was impossible without considering the relationship of Buddhism and Confucianism. It was decided that Confucian–Christian dialogue would be intrinsically a good thing and that it would serve to sharpen Buddhist–Christian understanding as well.

Participation and Reference

Two questions have dominated the discussion of Confucian spirituality in modern Confucian–Christian dialogue. The first has to do with the reciprocal question of the relationship of transcendence and immanence. It goes to the heart of how the New Confucians construe the world; it correlates how the various elements of Confucian "worldmaking" come together.[7] Many religiously minded New Confucians frame their description and understanding of the Confucian Dao based on an explanation of some ultimate reference point. This point of ultimate reference has been given different names depending on the philosopher or school in question. Some of the more common designations are Dao, the Mandate of Heaven, the Dao of Heaven, or the Supreme Ultimate. In all these cases, the New Confucians maintain that Confucian spirituality is a form of immanent transcendence. Moreover, this ultimate referent is always and everywhere balanced against and with the way of humanity in a unity that can never be severed.

According to the New Confucians, the canonical origin of the notion of immanent transcendence, at least since the Song Neo-Confucian revival, is traced to the *Doctrine of the Mean*. Zhu Xi always maintained that a student should read the *Doctrine of the Mean* as the last of the Four Books because it encapsulated the most sublime, ultimate reflections of the Confucian Way. The first aspect of the characteristic Confucian sense of the unity of humanity and the ultimate reference is warranted by the first line of ch. 1, which says "The *xing* (human nature) is what Heaven has called into existence within us through its mandate."[8] The text immediately informs us in no uncertain terms that the Dao can never be left even for a moment. Furthermore, the specific spiritual dimensions of the human response to the Dao as immanent or embodied human nature is linked to the cultivation of the states of equilibrium and harmony. Equilibrium and harmony are characterized as the roots of the cosmos and the way the cosmos ought to function when things are in proper balance.

In ch. 22, the *Mean* explains the ultimate goal a person can reach if and only if she or he is in tune with human nature and the Dao. First, the person must achieve *cheng*/self-realization as the outcome of the cultivation of their human nature. *Cheng*/self-realization references the achievement of a balance of the emotions, what ch. 1 called the unity of equilibrium and harmony. Once realizing *cheng*, the person "can participate in the production-by-transformation of Heaven and Earth. If he can participate in the production-by-transformation of Heaven and Earth, then he can form a trine with Heaven and Earth" (trans. Moran, 229). It was this passage, as interpreted by Zhu Xi, that caused great alarm to the Jesuit and early Protestant missionaries because it implied much too great an unbroken and uncorrupted link between human nature (without any infusion of grace beyond its original mandating by the Dao) and the ultimate referent of the world. Not only did the Neo-Confucians not have a doctrine of original sin and the concomitant corruption of human nature, but they believed that humanity could reform the mind-heart through appropriate ethical effort.

When the religious dimension of the Confucian tradition is linked to the idea of immanent transcendence, more modern alarm bells are sounded. For instance, David L. Hall and Roger T. Ames (1987; 1995) have stoutly denied the existence in early Chinese culture of anything like the classical Western sense of transcendence, either in its Greek philosophic commitment to dialectical reason as the principle of the cosmos or in its Judaic and Christian monotheistic narrative of a volitional divinity bringing order out of chaos.[9] When Hall and Ames uncover discussions of transcendence in Chinese philosophy, they posit that these discussions are either derived from later material, that is, material influenced by Indian or Western thought, or are theories propounded by New Confucians who have imbibed transcendental themes from their ecumenical reading of world philosophy and theology.

I mention the controversial work of Hall and Ames not to debunk their claims. Many of their warnings about moving from the categoric system of one philosophic culture to another are extremely well taken. But Hall and

Ames protest too much, especially once Confucianism went through the grand transformation known as the Neo-Confucian revival in the Song dynasty. Mou Zongsan would confirm at least one of Hall and Ames's suspicions. Mou has argued at length that Zhu Xi hijacked the Song Confucian revival because of his excessive commitment to the use of reason and the exploration of the cosmos in terms of principle. Mou, although respecting the place of reason within the Confucian project, construes the main form of Confucian cognitive engagement with the world as being intellectual intuition as a reformed version of analogical or correlative insight. For Mou, intuition includes reason, but reason is only a part of intuition.

Whatever their understanding of the relationship of reason and intuition, the Neo-Confucians and the New Confucians had a robust encounter with ultimate referents, either in their mind-hearts or in contact with the principle of the object-events of the world. Whether or not the Western notion of strict theistic transcendence does justice to the Neo- and New Confucian spirituality is a tricky question that goes to the heart of what makes for a good cross-cultural comparison. Besides, traditions are living entities and have every right to change their minds even about fundamental issues and to borrow new ideas wherever and whenever they choose. It is for the tradition to define its own boundaries; it is for scholars to argue about whether or not this borrowing is in line with previous theory and praxis.

Actually, much of the argument between Hall and Ames and New Confucians such as Tu Weiming, Liu Shu-hsien and Cheng Zhongying might be semantic. The point that the New Confucians are arguing is rather like what Hall and Ames say when they define classical Chinese philosophic discourse as an example of analogical or correlative discourse. If I understand both parties correctly, they are all defending the notion that there is no purely transcendental (monotheistic) thinking in early China and that all things are correlative in nature. Hall and Ames define their comparative methodology as interpretive pluralism, whereas the New Confucians feel more comfortable calling their version of the Confucian Dao an inclusive humanism.

The root of the problem lies in the fact that the New Confucians mean something very different by transcendence from what Jewish, Christian, and Muslim theologians (and Enlightenment philosophers such as Kant) intend. Their point, one solidly grounded in Confucian discourse, is that we human beings have a capacity to compare and contrast what is with what is not. Along with its moral details, this is what Mencius pointed out in his discussion of the four seeds of humanity. We learn, as Whitehead argued, by the method of difference. We notice things like elephants (one of Whitehead's favorite examples of something that humans do tend to notice when they amble into view) when present and then absent. Much of human creativity resides in our ability to hold in memory and consciousness the negative judgment that something is missing from a pattern that had been there before or ought to be there in order to ensure harmony.

The New Confucians argue that we have an ability, based on negative judgment, to recognize ethical and religious patterns along with other kinds of patterns. We collectively compare our actions in terms of good and bad. This is how we can transcend (i.e., creatively transform for the better) our present imperfect states of conduct. Actually, Mou Zongsan uses the language of vertical and horizontal to describe our spiritual connection to ultimate referents. Mou holds that we relate to the world of things by horizontal regularities. However, there are moments of spiritual creativity when human beings can overcome the strictures of purely instrumental reality and can achieve a vertical breakthrough to something new. Our moral intuition of the vertical dimension allows us to compare what has been with what ought to be.

Confucian masters have held before us images of what we ought to be and not just what we are. This is the basis for all the complex forms of Confucian spiritual self-cultivation. Confucian transcendence is really a form of cultivational creativity based on either Mencius's four seeds of human character or Xunzi's socially defined morality based on correct ritual action. Virtue, defined as the wisdom of the sages, is used to compare what is with what should be. Confucian immanent transcendence focuses on the human ability to move beyond, to transcend our ordinary lives in search of something better. As Yan Hui, Confucius's favorite student and a patron saint for the Neo-Confucians, said about Confucius in the *Analects*, the master lures you by means of moral example and then never lets you rest in any specific achieved state because the world always presents you with some new venture needing moral excellence.

Another point that emerges again and again in modern Confucian–Christian dialogues on spirituality revolves around what it means to participate in a religious or philosophic tradition. This is a question of identity and community. Of course, the debate is caused by the Western Christian conviction that a person can faithfully participate in only one religion at a time. The classical theological corollary was that because the Christian faith was God's final and supreme revelation, the only truly faithful religious participation ought to be in the Christian movement. Needless to say, this strong form of religious exclusivism is deemed excessive by many East Asian thinkers. Exclusivism means that Christian theologians hold that only Christianity is a true and fully revealed religion; all other communities of faith do not measure up, and if one is to be sure of salvation, then only a formal profession of Christian faith is worthy of interest. On the other hand, some Confucians, especially those identified with Zhu Xi's school, have argued that Confucianism is the best way for humanity, but this rarely has caused them to affirm that it is the only way of human excellence or that all other ways are completely pernicious.

The East Asian religious sensibility has generally been to recognize a number of viable religious spiritualities.[10] Sometimes they are ranked according to the lights of the tradition, such that Confucians are less disconcerted by philosophic Daoists and Buddhists than by popular religions, which seem highly superstitious to them. Other times it is theorized that different religions are divergent ways to bring the person to realization. Hence different religious spiritualities relate to different levels of human ability and inclination. There are even respectable schools of thought in China and Japan that argued for the acceptability of multiple religious participation.

Because of the complexity of the sources of modern religious life, New Confucians ask, Is it possible to conceive of a Confucian Christian or a Christian Confucian? The answer, from the Confucian side, is that it is entirely possible to conceive of a person faithfully and creatively participating in both traditions at once. Besides, no New Confucian is untouched in a profound way by Western philosophy and religious discourse, traditions massively informed by Christian history, themes, and motifs. The Enlightenment program evolved within the world of Christian symbolic discourse. The highest ideals of modern European thought owe their virtues and vices to their Christian (and Jewish and Muslim) past.

From the Confucian perspective, there are elements in Christianity that might make sense to New Confucians of a religious inclination. For instance, the role of theism is a case in question. New Confucians find some forms of contemporary philosophic theology, such as the process movement derived from the speculative metaphysics of Whitehead, to be appealing. Whitehead's reflections on the primordial and consequent natures of God speaks the language of immanent transcendence dear to the habits of the Confucian mind-heart. In fact, such a reformed or globally expanded theism may prove to be a bridge between the religious sensibilities of the two communities. Just as their Ming ancestors did, the New Confucians begin their reflection on ultimate things with a doctrine of God before commenting on other aspects of the Christian tradition.

The reason for this is that deity qua ultimate reference plays a role in the early classical period, and there are many references to *tian* or *shangdi* in the classical literature. The later Confucians did not make very much of these suggestive passages, but they are still available to a hermeneutics of retrieval as something to stimulate thinking about ultimate things. From the Western point of view, the Confucian tradition is best described as agnostic when Confucians consider the divinity of the ultimate referent. New Confucians, like Confucius, do not deny the existence of God; they merely suggest that human intellectual effort is better spent in dealing with the problems of the mundane world. However, there is nothing that would forbid a New Confucian from embracing a theistic reading of the cosmos because the crucial mind-heart of the tradition lies elsewhere. To be a theist would not demand abandoning or contravening any major Confucian intellectual or social commitment.

One gets the distinct impression that we are witnessing the generation of a new group of New Confucians, who see nothing wrong with participating in the intellectual and symbolic worlds of different traditions. Of course, there is ample precedent for such a symbiosis in the history of Japanese Tokugawa Confucianism. Some respected Confucians were Buddhists and others followed Shinto. In the current period, Okada Takehiko has demonstrated the continuing role for Confucian contemplation in dealing with modern issues such as animal rights, medical ethics, and the technological society.[11]

This is a perfect example of what Judith Berling and I have labeled "multiple religious participation." This means that individuals involved in the interreligious dialogue come to a point when their own religious practice is modified. For instance, sustained contact with Confucians, Daoists, and Buddhists can cause Christians to modify their exclusivist theologies. For their part, Confucians become fascinated with the richness of Christian images and concepts of God, thinking that this might help them make sense of parts of their own tradition. Buddhists watch Christians battle for social justice and develop what is now called a socially "engaged Buddhist" practice. The very idea of the Dao moves from East Asia into modern North Atlantic religious life as a new expression of the divine reality.

Multiple religious practice is not syncretism. As the Buddhists often say about human consciousness after enlightenment, Confucians remain Confucians and Christians remain Christians. But the contours of the faith of individuals have been modified. In a very intriguing sense, Confucian ideas then begin to play a role in the development of Christianity. On the other hand, the ideals and problems of the Enlightenment such as freedom, equality, and fraternity have become interwoven with modern Confucian reforms. Some Christians even begin to wonder if these patterns of multiple religious participation as witnessed in East Asia might not just be the wave of the future of religious life for all people. This is a form of religious practice that goes beyond mere tolerance but yet continues to respect the existence of many communities of faith.

The term "New Confucian" usually designates a group of modern Chinese public intellectuals who are committed to preserving and reviving the Confucian tradition. However, the case of Korean Christianity is a potent current example of a religious tradition struggling to come to terms with its Confucian past.[12] Both Catholic and Protestant theologians such as Kim Sung-Hae and Kim Heup Young are carrying out complicated versions of the interreligious dialogue with East Asian Confucians and the inner dialogue of intellectuals who recognize that they participate, by culture, birth, and education, in diverse religious worlds. The Koreans are attacking the problem of multiple religious spiritualities by examining the foundations of the Confucian and Christian traditions as well as by framing their own modern constructive and speculative natural and systematic theologies.

What makes the Korean case particularly intriguing is that the Koreans, compared to their Chinese and Japanese cousins, place a great deal of stock in embracing orthodoxy. This Korean inclination to define and perfect the one true teaching makes the Korean Confucian–Christian dialogue an utterly serious business. If the Korean theologians, Confucian and Christian alike, are successful in showing how multiple religious participation is not only possible but to be embraced, they will make a dramatic contribution to the emerging world of modern Confucian spirituality.

It might be the case that Christian theism will provide a useful methodology for Confucian reflection on ultimate things. Although Zhu Xi was not a theist, he was certainly concerned with ultimate things and believed that these ultimate things mattered. If that were not the case, why would one worry about conforming the mind of humanity, which is prone to error, to the mind of Heaven, the ultimate source of proper values? The intersection of modern theology and the emerging New Confucian spirituality is a fruitful one. It joins the traditional Confucian sensibility to combine what are, in the post-Enlightenment West, judged to be the distinct domains of philosophy (critical reason) and theology (faith, myth, and emotion).

Furthermore, the growing Christian presence in East Asia and the Asian Diaspora might also provide an institutional base for a renewed Confucian spirituality within a growing and vital Christian movement. In terms of contemporary theology, most Asian Christians carry on an inner dialogue about their relationship to the Confucian past. More and more younger theologians are eager to explore what Confucianism has to contribute to the Asian church in the twenty-first century and are less and less intimidated by Western theologians eager to defend a pristine view of fidelity to only one transmission of the truth.

Prophecy in religious matters is difficult if not silly. The spirit blows where it will and creates something new. Religion is certainly not more of the same. Confucianism will change in the modern world. It will change because of its encounters with the Enlightenment project. It will surely change because of its dialogue with Christianity and the other religions of the world. Its habits of the heart-mind will again become part of a new world of Confucian spirituality to be shared with the entire world.[13]

Notes

1. See Wilfred Cantwell Smith, *Towards a World Theology: Faith and the History of Religion* (Philadelphia: Westminster Press, 1981), *passim*, for his most suggestive account of the history of religion.

2. Mark Elvin, *Another History: Essays on China from a European Perspective.*

3. Tu Weiming, *Centrality and Commonality*, 94.

4. Ibid.

5. Ibid., 95.

6. In defining the scope of civilization, I have followed David L. Hall, *The Civilization of Experience: A Whiteheadian Theory of Culture* (New York: Fordham University Press, 1973). I have chosen Hall's definition of civilization because he, along with Roger Ames, has become such a trenchant critic of any theory of transcendence in Chinese culture. Of course, religion need not a priori demand a transcendent element. In David L. Hall and Roger T. Ames, *Anticipating China: Thinking Through the Narratives of Chinese and Western Culture* (Albany: State University of New York Press, 1995), the collaborators slightly modify their view of civilization. They argue that the five areas of interest they outline are properly distinctive of Western civilization because of its commitment to reason (qua dialectical argumentation and logic) rather than correlation as a means of adjusting the varieties of interest in a culture dominated by technical rationality. However, because of the links between New Confucianism and ecumenical modern thinking—not to mention reflection on the Song achievement—the range of cultural interests is still a useful taxonomy.

7. I have borrowed Nelson Goodman's term to express how the New Confucians view their world. It is a vague category of world construal that does not commit the comparative project to an immediate taxonomy of metaphysics, ontology, and cosmology as the only way a high culture such as China describes, explains, understands, and commends its worldview. See Nelson Goodman, *Ways of Worldmaking* (Indianapolis, Ind.: Hackett Publishing, 1978).

8. Patrick Edwin Moran, *Three Smaller Wisdom Books*, 201. I have followed Moran's translation because he thoughtfully includes the Chinese text and because

he follows Zhu Xi's interpretation of the text. There are, of course, other excellent renditions of the *Doctrine of the Mean*. Nonetheless, Moran's translation takes into account the spiritual dimension of the defining Confucian classic.

9. David L. Hall and Roger T. Ames, *Thinking Through Confucius;* eidem, *Anticipating China.*

10. Judith A. Berling has written eloquently on just what this means for modern intercultural religious practice. See Judith A. Berling, *A Pilgrim in Chinese Culture.*

11. Rodney L. Taylor, *The Confucian Way of Contemplation.*

12. Various conversations with Prof. Kim Sung-Hae, Prof. Kim Heup Young, and Prof. Chung Chai-sik have given me what little insight I have into the Korean situation. The present Korean theological scene is passionately committed to working on the question of dialogue. I also want to thank my former student Prof. Kim Sung-wan and current student Rev. Oh Jung Sun, for inviting me on their adventures in comparative speculative theology. Mr. Oh has pointed out that the question of Confucian–Christian relations has been on the agenda of the Christian church in Korea for decades.

13. After this essay was completed, six important books were published about the history of Confucian thought that discuss the questions raised here about Confucianism in dialogue with other traditions and the definition of the religious dimension of the Confucian movement. These are Cheng Chung-ying and Nicholas Bunnin, eds., *Contemporary Chinese Philosophy* (Oxford: Blackwell, 2002); Yao Xinzhong, ed., *RoutledgeCurzon Encyclopedia of Confucianism,* 2 vols. (London/New York: RoutledgeCurzon, 2003); John Makeham, ed., *New Confucianism: A Critical Examination* (New York: Palgrave Macmillan, 2003); Umberto Bresciani, *Reinventing Confucianism: The New Confucian Movement* (Taipei: Taipei Ricci Institute for Chinese Studies, 2001); Liu Shu-hsien, *Essentials of Contemporary Neo-Confucian Philosophy* (New York: Praeger, 2003) and Antonio S. Cua, ed., *Encyclopedia of Chinese Philosophy* (New York: Routledge, 2003).

Bibliography

Berling, Judith A. *A Pilgrim in Chinese Culture: Negotiating Religious Diversity.* Maryknoll, N.Y.: Orbis Books, 1997.

Berthrong, John H. *All Under Heaven: Changing Paradigms in Confucian-Christian Dialogue.* Albany: State University of New York Press, 1994.

Cheng Chung-ying. *New Dimensions of Confucian and Neo-Confucian Philosophy.* Albany: State University of New York Press, 1991.

Ching, Julia. *Confucianism and Christianity: A Comparative Study.* Tokyo: Kodansha International, 1977.

de Bary, Wm. Theodore. *East Asian Civilizations: A Dialogue in Five Stages.* Cambridge, Mass.: Harvard University Press, 1988.

————. *The Trouble with Confucianism.* Cambridge, Mass.: Harvard University Press, 1991.

Elvin, Mark. *Another History: Essays on China form a European Perspective*. Canberra: Wild Peony, 1996.

Hall, David L. *The Civilization of Experience: A Whitehead Theory of Culture*. New York: Fordham University Press, 1973.

Hall, David L., and Roger T. Ames. *Anticipating China: Thinking Through the Narratives of Chinese and Western Culture*. Albany: State University of New York Press, 1995.

————. *Thinking Through Confucius*. Albany: State University of New York Press, 1987.

Kim, Sung-Hae. "Liberation through Humanization: With a Focus on Korean Confucianism." *Ching Feng* 33, nos. 1 & 2 (April 1990): 20–46.

————. *The Righteous and the Sage: A Comparative Study of the Ideal Images of Man in Biblical Israel and Classical China*. Seoul: Sogang University Press, 1985.

Kim, Heup Young. *Wang Yang-ming and Karl Barth: A Confucian–Christian Dialogue*. Lanham, Md.: University Press of America, 1996.

Lee, Peter K. H., *Confucian–Christian Encounters in Historical and Contemporary Perspective*. Lewiston, N.Y.: Edwin Mellen Press, 1991.

Levenson, Joseph R. *Confucian China and Its Modern Fate*. 3 vols. Berkeley: University of California Press, 1968.

Moran, Patrick Edwin. *Three Smaller Wisdom Books: Lao Zi's Dao De Jin, The Great Learning (Da Xue) and the Doctrine of the Mean (Zhong Yong)*. Lanham, Md./New York: University Press of America, 1993.

Prazniak, Roxann. *Dialogues Across Civilizations: Sketches in World History from the Chinese and European Experiences*. Boulder, Colo.: Westview Press, 1996.

Rozman, Gilbert, ed., *The East Asian Region: Confucian Heritage and Its Modern Adaptation*. Princeton, N.J.: Princeton University Press, 1991.

Second International Confucian–Christian Conference, Graduate Theological Union, Berkeley, California, July 7–11, 1991. Papers. *Pacific Theological Review* 25–26 (1992–93): 18–94.

Sharma, Arvind, ed., *Our Religions*. San Francisco: HarperSanFrancisco, 1993.

Smith, Wilfred Cantwell. *Towards a World Theology: Faith and the History of Religion*. Philadelphia: Westminster Press, 1981.

Taylor, Rodney. *The Confucian Way of Contemplation: Okada Takehiko and the Tradition of Quiet-Sitting*. Columbia: University of South Carolina Press, 1988.

Tu, Weiming. *Centrality and Commonality: An Essay on Confucian Religiousness*. Albany: State University of New York Press, 1989.

35

Contemporary Confucian Spirituality and Multiple Religious Identity

R O B E R T   C U M M I N G S   N E V I L L E

I APPROACH THIS ESSAY from the perspective of a practicing religious Confucian who is also a practicing religious Christian, not from the perspective of an expert historical scholar of either tradition. Religions contain more than their spiritual elements, for instance, conceptual elements from mythos to metaphysics and ritual elements from magic to masses, as well as ministry and management. Although these and other elements are interconnected, the spiritual elements will be focused in this essay and the others treated insofar as they bear upon the spiritual.

The argument here begins with reflections on the nature of spirituality in connection with some other elements of religion, and on the special characteristics of viable contemporary spirituality. It then moves to consider some particulars of Confucian spirituality as it might meet the needs of the contemporary situation. Of special importance is the ability of Confucian spirituality to meet the needs of different cultures in our global society. The argument is then complicated by the consideration of multiple religious identities, that is, Confucian plus something else. In my case, those are Confucianism and Christianity, although Confucianism has long been associated with Daoism and Buddhism in China, and with those plus shamanism and Christianity in Korea.

Contemporary Spirituality

Spirituality has meant a great many things in the history of religions, affected by different conceptions of the human, the transcendent, and the world as susceptible to a spiritual dimension. The prefaces to the volumes in this Encyclopedia of World Spirituality contain a characterizing statement that is likely to become normative, for the time being, because of the monumental scale of the series and its legitimation of the disciplined notion of spirituality:

> The series focuses on that inner dimension of the person called by certain traditions "the spirit." This spiritual core is the deepest center of the person. It is here that the person is open to the transcendent dimension; it is here that the person experiences ultimate reality. The series explores the discovery of this core, the dynamics of its development, and its journey to the ultimate goal. It deals with prayer, spiritual direction, the various maps of the spiritual journey, and the methods of advancement in the spiritual ascent.

That statement calls up the metaphors of a *core* of the human person, a *transcendent dimension* or *ultimate reality* to which that core has access, *experience* as the mode of access, the *transformations* of the core by means of its experience of the transcendent, and the *journeys* according to which the transformations are understood for individual persons.

Spirituality is usually associated with religion in a broader sense that includes founding persons, core texts and motifs, institutions for the ritual practice and transmission of traditions, conceptualities for understanding the human relation to the transcendent, and even organizations with membership in several senses of that term.[1] Nevertheless, spirituality need not be closely associated with religions, as evidenced by the volume in the World Spirituality series entitled *Spirituality and the Secular Quest*.[2] Whereas it is unlikely that anyone could have much of a spiritual life without leaning heavily on one or several religious traditions, it is very possible these days to have a spiritual life with no positive allegiance to a religious community or commitment to the authority of a text or tradition. The major religious traditions themselves, it should be noted, differ widely in the importance they attach to membership and allegiance, with Islam being an extreme case insisting on self-conscious attachment and Confucianism paying much more attention to competence in the Confucian Way than to membership or denominational commitment.[3]

I shall propose here a more specific hypothesis about spirituality that makes precise general sense of the intuitions about the core human being, ultimate reality, experience, transformation, and journeys noted above. The hypothesis consists of an essential subhypothesis and several conditional subhypotheses that relate the essential one to various aspects of life and religion. Spirituality is not the essential subhypothesis alone but the harmony of that one with the rest, situating spirituality in a larger context.

Moreover, the explication of the essential subhypothesis is by means of elaborating several of the conditional ones.[4]

The essential subhypothesis about spirituality is that it is *the deliberate effort to improve the human process of engaging ultimate reality truthfully by means of practices that shape the engagement with signs or religious symbols, that discern improved religious symbols for this purpose, that increase competence in the use of the symbols for engagement, and that foster the transformations of soul derivative from the engaging of ultimate reality with the symbols.* This essential subhypothesis differs from the prefatory statement in several rhetorical ways, so as to attain both greater tolerance for various spiritualities and greater precision in characterizing them. So, for instance, it substitutes *engagement* for *experience* in order to suggest the give-and-take of living with ultimate reality and the things that bear it and to avoid the overly subjective connotations of *religious experience* that have been rightly criticized.[5] The subhypothesis does not suppose a natural "core" of the human person but suggests that some special integration might be the outcome of spiritual growth. It stresses the importance of religious symbols to shape the engagement and thus places the philosophy of spirituality within philosophical semiotics. It suggests that spiritual development or transformation can be a function of at least two things: improved or deeper symbols, and changes in the person's capacity to employ the symbols in engaging the ultimate. These and other elements of the subhypothesis require brief comments that introduce some of the appropriate conditional subhypotheses.

To face the most controversial element first, it is necessary to justify reference to ultimate reality in a hypothesis about spirituality. The Kantian subjectivism of much contemporary philosophy of religion would prefer to treat spirituality wholly as an anthropological topic without ultimate references. The cautiousness of some contemporary Confucians about reference to transcendence, limiting it to "immanent transcendence," reinforces the anthropological circumscription of the topic.[6] But I believe that the attempt to characterize spirituality without reference to the ultimate is finally reductive and self-defeating; it would not be recognized by spiritual people. Therefore I shall offer a conditional subhypothesis about ultimate reality.

The conditional subhypothesis about ultimate reality in relation to spirituality is that it consists in a finite–infinite contrast.[7] A finite–infinite contrast is anything a culture's or person's semiotic system takes to be a founding element of what is religiously important in the culture or person's world. The contrast both is what it is as merely finite and grounds or orients some crucial elements in the rest of the world, defining "world-ness."

The finite side of the contrast is some thing or process without which the world would not be in some important religious respect. Cosmological existence, the ontological question, the coming into being of the world, is an obvious candidate and may well be universal among religions. The opening of Zhou Dunyi's *Explanation of the Diagram of the Great Ultimate* is a classic Confucian example:

> The Ultimate of Non-being and also the Great Ultimate (*taiji*)! The Great Ultimate through movement generates *yang*. When its activity reaches its limit, it becomes tranquil. Through tranquillity the Great Ultimate generates *yin*. When tranquillity reaches its limit, activity begins again. So movement and tranquillity alternate and become the root of each other, giving rise to the distinction of *yin* and *yang*, and the two modes are thus established.[8]

Yin and *yang* form the five elements or agents that in turn form the ten thousand things at which point the world exists in its familiar temporal process. The Ultimate of Non-being and the Great Ultimate in their process of generating diversity in unity constitute the finite side of a Confucian finite–infinite contrast. Another Confucian example is the beginning of Zhang-zai's *Western Inscription*: "Heaven is my father and Earth is my mother, and even such a small creature as I finds an intimate place in their midst."[9] Here the conjunction of Heaven and Earth is the foundation of the intimacy of human belonging in the universe, a major Confucian religious theme. Yet another finite element in a Confucian finite–infinite contrast is the beginning of the *Doctrine of the Mean*: "What Heaven (*tian*, nature) imparts to man is called human nature. To follow our nature is called the Way (*Dao*). Cultivating the Way is called education. The Way cannot be separated from us for a moment. What can be separated from us is not the Way."[10] Here the finite element in the finite–infinite contrast is not so much the process of cosmic grounding, though it is that too, or a cosmic character that gives human beings an intimate place, though it is also that, but rather the founding of the human capacity to follow the Dao, which is to be truly human and which derives from the ontological reality of heaven and is its gift.

In all these examples there is something that is finite at least in the sense that it can be described or symbolized. Moreover, without that finite thing or process, the world and human life would lack something extraordinarily important. Yet the finite thing or process cannot be taken by itself in any positivist fashion. For its religious significance is its contrast with what would be if it were not there. So, without the process of the Great Ultimate generating *yang* and *yin*, there would be only the Ultimate of Non-being, that is, nothing determinate or finite at all, a completely empty infinite. Zhou is explicit about the connection of Non-being and the Great Ultimate (*wuji, taiji*) in his finite–infinite contrast. In the case of Zhang-zai, it is the spousal embrace of Heaven and Earth in parenting that gives human life its cosmic intimacy. Without that, with no cosmic origins that could be symbolized in terms of sexual cooperation and mutual fit, the human place would not be intimate; consider the alienating metaphoric impact of the notion that the cosmos is only matter in motion, or atoms in the void. The infinite side of the contrast for Zhang-zai would be an inhumane habitation, supposing that human beings arise some other way. In the case of the *Mean*, the infinite side would be the failure of heaven to impart its basic character to human beings, with the result that human powers would not be able to accommodate life to what is most basic in reality; at best they would be conventional fabrications.

In all these examples, and others from Confucianism and other traditions, the finite side is religiously or spiritually important only in connection with the infinite side, the condition that would obtain if the finite side were not a founding element of the world. There is thus a kind of apophatic element built into the notion of a religious object as a finite–infinite contrast. The process of grounding the cosmos is not religiously important except in light of what would be the case (if that language could be used) were that process not to be real. Similarly with the ontological harmony of elements in the cosmos as the ground of human cosmic intimacy, and with the human possession of the Dao. *Of course* the generation of *yin* and *yang* (or the Big Bang) is not what we mean as ultimate except in consideration of its contrast with the alternative; *of course* the cosmic harmony of Heaven and Earth is just another fact and not ultimate except in consideration of its contrast with what its denial would mean for the cosmic harmony of human life; *of course* Heaven's imparting the Dao to human beings is not more ultimate than the presence of elements from the periodic table in the human body except in consideration of what the alternative would mean to the human capacity to attain cosmic attunement. The finite sides are not ultimate except in contrast or conjunction with the infinite side in each case: the world would not exist, or would lack some religiously crucial feature, if the finite condition did not obtain. Some theistic religious theories give a kind of positive force to the infinite side, saying that it creates the finite side; perhaps Zhou would agree.[11] But there is no need to say that all finite–infinite contrasts construe the relation between the finite and infinite elements this way.

Sociology of knowledge is involved in this subhypothesis about the ultimate insofar as it proposes that one of the main functions of religious symbols, myths, cosmologies, and so forth is to provide what Peter Berger calls a "sacred canopy" defining the limits and meaning of the world.[12] The symbols are foundational for what counts as real and important in the world, and thus are not to be taken only at face value but also in their founding roles. Without the legitimating viability of the symbols in the sacred canopy, the culture whose canopy it is supposed to be is confused and disoriented about what is real and important. That a culture's symbols of the ultimate are viable and functionally legitimate its worldview does not mean that they are true and refer correctly to what really is ultimate. But if they are not viable and lead to disorientation, this shows that they are false in at least some respects; and if they are viable, this shows that in at least some respects they keep the culture successfully oriented to what is genuinely real. This subhypothesis about ultimate reality as finite–infinite contrasts locates spirituality's reference to the ultimate or transcendent squarely within semiotics, a theory of symbolism.

A crucial moral for the contemporary Confucian discussion should be drawn from the discussion so far, namely, that Confucian reference to ultimate reality is far more substantial and important than might be supposed from limitations of the discussion to the immanent transcendent or to anthropocosmic unity, the apparently ultimate references of Tu Weiming, surely the most forward proponent of Confucian religiousness and spirituality. Rather, Confucians need to pay direct attention to such notions as the Dao, the Great Ultimate, Heaven and Earth, principle and material force, and other metaphysical or ontological conceptions that have been so richly articulated in the tradition, and which Tu also thematizes in various places. If the direct ontological significance of these notions is not explored as the essential foundation of spirituality, then it will be impossible to give Confucian spirituality a seriousness required for any full-blown spiritual tradition. And, of course, those transcendent elements are pervasive in the Confucian tradition. Only when "transcendence" is taken to mean only something that is separate and real apart from the world, as some Christians believe about God, could it be said that Confucianism does not have transcendence in the sense of ultimate realities as finite–infinite contrasts. And for many monotheists, God is not to be construed as separate and real apart from the world; consider Aquinas's conception of God as Act of Esse, or Paul Tillich's as Ground of Being. That the ontological considerations are important for contemporary Confucian spirituality means that their contemporary viability needs to be assessed, just as the Christian conception of God needs contemporary viability. The next section will return to this topic.

The conception of the self or soul in the above essential subhypothesis about spirituality is vaguer than the Western metaphor of "core." All that is supposed is that a self can engage finite–infinite contrasts by means of symbol systems and be transformed in the process. Another conditional subhypothesis, this one about the self, can make this clear: a self or soul consists of a person's engagements with realities, ultimate and otherwise, and its structures have to do with how the person is poised with reference to the realities and integrates the different structures of poise. Thus, the self is always defined in reference to its orientations to things so as to engage them, and in reference to how it puts its orientations together. Minimal engagement with ultimate realities as finite–infinite contrasts is simply to exist as shaped by the contrasts—for instance, as a materially existing thing, intimately placed in the cosmos, capable of acting in cosmic harmony. Persons unaware of this engagement are likely to act in ways contrary to their founding conditions, and hence to be in some alienation from themselves and their world. To engage interpretively with the finite–infinite contrasts is to be spiritual and to attempt to be oriented properly to them. This hypothesis is vague enough to allow for Aristotelian conceptions of substantial cores for human beings. But it is also vague enough to allow for Buddhist rejections of the self—the no-self doctrine—and to sustain only the claim that persons can be properly oriented to what is real (for instance, suchness as empty). Of course, it also allows for the Confucian conception of the self as described in the *Mean* and elsewhere which stresses the structural integration of principle or Dao as resident in the perspective of one's body with the persons, institutions, and natural surroundings that constitute the ten thousand things to which the mean relates.[13]

An epistemological conditional subhypothesis about spirituality is that the truth of our engagements with ultimate realities consists in the *carry-over* of the value in those realities (finite–infinite contrasts) into the interpreters' lives in the respects in which the engagements interpret the realities, and as qualified by the biological, cultural, semiotic, and intentional characters of the interpreters.[14] Two interesting deviations from customary epistemologies should be noted in this hypothesis, namely, its orientation to causation and its orientation to value.

To claim that truth is a causal matter—a relation of accurate transmission from object to subject—is to subvert much of the modern European mind/body distinction. It is also to buy into the claim that Confucianism is a naturalism in philosophy, and it does so by linking Confucianism to American pragmatism, from which the semiotics employed here derives. Enormous complexities lie in the way of calibrating the causal mechanism to carry over something real and external into the interpreter. The crucial conceptual tool is a semiotic theory that analyzes (1) how signs refer to objects outside the semiotic system (not just to other signs within that system of things outside), (2) how meanings evolve culturally and also devolve, and (3) how communities and persons interpret realities by means of signs which are taken to stand for the realities in certain respects.[15] The defense of the claim that a semiotic system and interpretive mental behavior are natural parts of human life is somewhat difficult in a Kantian environment which supposes that only science speaks authoritatively about nature and that philosophy is limited to philosophy of science. Nevertheless, it can be shown that the Kantian project is as limited as the Enlightenment project now subject to so much criticism. Moreover, there is a contemporary alternative theory of nature that demonstrates how knowing is a part of natural life and not a transcendental (supernaturalistic) commentary.[16] Confucianism from its ancient sources onward should flourish in such a naturalistic epistemological environment.

The other peculiar part of the hypothesis about truth is that it is the carryover of *value*. Aristotle, who also had a causal theory of truth as touch, believed that the carryover was of form: for Aristotle, the form of the object, minus its material substrate, is to be carried over into the substance of the mind to be (part of) its form. We now see this to be implausible for at least two reasons. The form of an inert material object such as the fortress-city at Mycenae simply does not fit into a meat-brain interpreter such as Agamemnon. To get the "same thing" into Agamemnon's mind it is necessary to "change" the material form as might be analyzed by a positivist physicist into the visual-auditory-olfactory-touch-kinesthetic signs of the human body, into the respects of interpretation that reflect what Mycenaean culture thinks is important, into the signs of its specific semiotic systems, which allow for interactive interpretation, and into the interests directing interpretation that come from its society and Agamemnon's personal intentions.[17] Far better is it to get what is *important* in the object, its value, into the interpreters so that they can intentionally comport themselves toward it well, especially as such comportment might require a different form. To be sure, there is no *mirroring*, for that is a formal metaphor. Interpreting something addresses what it is only in the respect in which the sign interprets the object. There is much more to the object than the interpretation picks up. But the interpretation is better or worse insofar as it picks up on what is valuable in the object and makes it important or significant in the interpreter who intends to interpret the object in a certain respect. The fact–value distinction of the early European renaissance Enlightenment project is a false lead and needs to be repudiated in terms of a naturalistic theory of the carryover of value that can render not only scientific hypotheses about what the forms of things are but also ethical, political, and aesthetic hypotheses, all as subject to correction as the scientific.

That truth is the carryover of value means that the soul or self needs to be ready to receive and embody the value as the object is interpreted in the proper respect. Neurophysiological development of the ordinary sort determines that we can interpret ordinary physical objects. Ordinary maturation in physical and social terms determines that we can interpret complex phenomena such as the perceptions required for driving a car or whether the mood at a gathering is happy or hostile. Specialized training cultivates the sensibilities of musicians to hear more in music than most of us can, of scientists to have more discriminating taste with respect to experiments than is common, of parents to discern the special moods of their children, and of religious people to engage ultimate realities with sophistication most of us lack. As mentioned earlier, spiritual progress can be made in at least two ways. First, one can learn better, more profound symbols for engaging ultimate realities. Second, one can become better at the employment of those symbols so as to affect engagement more thoroughly and directly (direct but not immediate, because the signs always mediate).

Philosophy and theology are the critical disciplines charged with the improvement of symbols. In addition, however, are the spiritual practices that transform the soul to be more adept at engaging the ultimate realities with the symbols. The East Asian traditions have emphasized the importance of yoga as the discipline of working through and reading life under the interpretive guidance of texts and gurus with founding spiritual symbols. The more profound spiritual symbols require the development of just as much unordinary capacity as the more complex musical symbols.

This leads to yet another conditional subhypothesis, this time concerning the psychology of transformation: the soul is both shaped and developed by acquiring the capacities to employ symbols so as to engage the world in ever more accurate and true appropriations of the values of things. Human personal and social identities are formed by the individuation of relations toward things in symbolically rich interactions, a prominent Confucian theme. Spirituality, which deals with the transformations of soul occasioned by engagement with the ultimate, thus supposes from the outset that selves are malleable and that spiritual life will change the self. The purpose in the long run is to transform the self so that it becomes able to embody and bring into its constitution and behavior the values of the religious objects. This means conforming one's life to the bearing of the finite–infinite contrasts upon it, becoming holy as Christianity would put it, or "manifesting the clear character" as Confucianism would.

Embodying the value of ultimate realities has immense practical effects. Confucianism is clear that this involves continued pursuit of personal transformation so as to become more and more sagelike: sages are the ones attuned most thoroughly to the Dao, the existential intimacy, and the contingency of ontological flourishing arising from Non-being and the Great Ultimate. But more than what some Christians might suppose is a merely individualistic rendition of transformation, the Confucians would emphasize the communal aspect. If the self consists in the relations it individuates with the persons, institutions, and natural elements around it, then personal transformation requires transforming one's neighborhood, a point as familiar to John Wesley as to Wang Yang-ming. Tu Weiming brilliantly expresses this point by saying that one relates to transcendent things only through first participating in the fiduciary community.[18] From the Christian side the social connection is equally important, if problematic. H. Richard Niebuhr explored several models of personal-social transformation in *Christ and Culture*.[19]

This section has expressed a complex hypothesis about spirituality, consisting of an essential subhypothesis that says that spirituality is the engagement of ultimate reality by means of signs, and several conditional subhypotheses that interpret ultimate reality, the self, transformation, truth, and interpretation. The implication of this section is the displacement of purely anthropological and immanent approaches to spirituality in favor of one essentially referring to ultimacy and conditionally related to several other disciplines. At this point the crucial thesis to remember is that spiritual discernment aims to be true, and that spiritual development aims to embody with increasing fullness and exactitude what is real and relevant to human life. Spirituality is fundamentally practical: its goal is the deepening of one's engagement with ultimate reality, and it does so by means of specific practices that include prayer and meditation but also action in the world.

Now the discussion turns to the challenges of spirituality for contemporary Confucianism, although the topics have been adumbrated in what has been said already.

Confucian Spirituality in a Global Society

Like any axial-age religion at the end of the twentieth century, Confucianism faces three major problems for which its traditional roots, core texts, and motifs do not provide immediate satisfaction. These are, first, coming to terms with the cosmos as understood by modern science; second, envisioning a global social ethic that can interpret distributive justice now that we have the global economic and political means to do something about oppression and inequalities; and third, articulating the moral structure of human beings' relations with the natural environment now that science has shown us something of the complexity of the vast web of interconnectedness and the hitherto hidden consequences of human modifications of our niche. Contemporary Confucianism is very well positioned to make helpful responses to these problems, although those answers will require creative transformations of the tradition.

The topic here is not the challenge to religion in general but to spirituality, and with regard to this topic contemporary Confucianism has variations on these special issues. I shall discuss three, reflective of the general challenges to religion; only the first will be discussed in detail.

First, contemporary Confucian spirituality requires a conception of Confucian ultimate realities adequate to the world of modern science yet expressing the dominant motifs of the Confucian tradition that can be used to guide spiritual engagement. The ancient picture of Heaven above and Earth below cannot by itself provide resonance to strike the heart of contemporary Confucians, and therefore it cannot function at face value to guide our engagements. That picture must be reconstructed and its ancient motifs reinterpreted as symbols that say something other than what they seem to say if interpreted as scientific claims. It would be disastrous for contemporary Confucian spirituality to retreat to "mere humanism" in order to avoid the challenge of modern science, for there is nothing ultimate about human nature, according to the Confucian conception, unless it is indeed connected to the ultimate Dao, given an intimate place in the cosmos, and construed as the self-conscious perceiving outcome of the onto-genesis process as Zhou described it.[20] This is to say that Confucian spirituality, in contrast to a blander Confucian humanism of moral striving, needs to relate human life to the ultimate and therefore needs symbols of the ultimate that resonate with the vastness and impersonality of what we now understand the world to be.

Like the great monotheistic spiritual traditions, and several of those of India, Confucianism has thematized ultimacy in terms of the foundation of the physical-spiritual cosmos which I called onto-genesis. How these onto-genesis Confucian themes can be reconstructed to accord with modern physical theory, say the Big Bang cosmology, is not so much different from the similar reconstructions required of monotheistic creation theories or Brahman-Isvara-world theories.[21] For all such onto-genesis concerns, a contemporary theory and resultant set of symbols needs to be developed that, on the one hand, points to the grounding act or process without making that one more thing to be grounded and, on the other hand, represents the world as determinate in a sufficiently vague sense that can allow for whatever science discovers empirically that the world is.[22] Such an ontology can be employed to give contemporary meaning to the core texts and motifs of each of the world's great spiritual traditions, or at least those with ancient onto-genesis themes.[23]

The special focus of Confucian onto-genesis, however, is less the grounding of physical existence than the grounding of real value that existence bears and the very definition of the human as the value-seeker. This positive axiological commitment is expressed in the general Chinese sensibility that the world and human life are good, in the sense that human beings are intimately, rightly, fitly placed in the cosmos relative to the ultimate (Zhang-zai, and the notion that the human forms a trinity with Heaven and Earth), in the motif that the human is given the Dao as part of its essential nature (the *Mean*) and, as the Neo-Confucians put it, that the one principle is manifested in every thing and especially in the human character. Both the Cheng-Zhu and the Lu-Wang schools agree that principle in the heart anticipates and is responsive to principle in things and requires a cultivated expression in personal and social life so as to constitute sagely virtue. Like all moral traditions, Confucianism has recognized from the beginning that, in the human case, existence and optimal value do not go together automatically but require deliberate discernment of the ideal relative to the actual and possible and then controlled and disciplined behavior to accomplish that ideal. The Neo-Confucian conception of principle, say in the Cheng brothers, as that which would harmonize anything that needs harmonization, and which is a ready cognitive impulse in human nature, is as sophisticated a theory of moral realism as has been developed in any tradition.

Modern science, however, poses an extraordinary obstacle to the Confucian claim that ultimate reality is good, that it can be known as good expressed throughout nature, and that human moral striving is possible as a realistic way of relating to ultimate reality, that is, that moral behavior can have a spiritual dimension. The obstacle is not so much in the science itself as in the conception of knowledge associated with science in modern European philosophy. Although the European Christian tradition had long maintained that the creation is good and that moral behavior is part of holiness, the fact-value split adopted by much early modern European philosophy undermined that. Facts are the province of science and alone are objects of cognition; values cannot be known but are somehow functions of human subjectivity, projection, or contract. The story of the development of the fact–value split is extremely complex, beginning with Descartes and Hobbes. By the beginning of the twentieth century, however, it was manifested in science as conceived by positivism and in value-theory as a function of Nietzschean will to power. Even most critics of scientific positivism who insist that all theories and observations are value-laden suppose that the values are functions of interest and power rather than cognition of the worths of things. The dimension of Confucian spirituality that relates to the ultimate as grounding value and human value-discernment is simply impossible for contemporary persons whose sensibilities are deeply formed by the fact–value dichotomy suppositions of the theory of knowledge usually associated with modern science.

Therefore, contemporary Confucianism needs to develop a comprehensive conception of knowledge expressive of its core motifs of value and valuation, a kind of axiology of thinking. On the one hand, this axiology needs to be compatible with science and in fact to provide accounts of fallibility in both science and morals and of the justification of the interests that guide science, as well as guide moral and political (as well as aesthetic) life. In this respect, fact- and theory-oriented science needs to be represented as an abstraction from a richer, value-laden concrete reality which can also be known in appreciative and evaluative ways. On the other hand, the axiology of thinking needs to reconstruct the valuative elements of the Confucian tradition's symbols, from Mencius's four beginnings to Mou Zongsan's moral metaphysics. Confucian spiritual engagement as grounding value is impossible without a reconstruction of the Confucian symbols in terms that address and circumvent the value-subjectivizing ideology of modern science.

A successful axiology would have to address four families of thinking. One has to do with *imagination*, from the elementary forms of cognitive synthesis by which we transform physical stimuli into an experiential field through the religious images of worldliness to the spiritual images of connection with the ultimate. The central axiological claim about imagination is that it consists in valuation, and that form is a function of valuation rather than the other way around (as in Aristotelianism). Imagination is not true or false, only the forms by which we engage reality. *Interpretation* is true or false, and it employs imagination to make claims or suppositions about reality. An axiological theory of interpretation needs, on the one hand, to show how interpretation is a part of natural process, representing intentionality, judgment, discernment, and the like as special functions within nature, a project congenial to Confucianism. On the other hand, it needs to show how real values in nature—natural things as valuable to human beings and able to be evaluated by them—are known in interpretation. The axiological formula for the latter condition is that interpretive truth is the carryover of value from the object interpreted into the interpreter in the respects in which the object is interpreted, qualified by the biology, culture, semiotics, and purposes of the interpreter, a formula familiar from the earlier discussion. Interpretations are cognitive engagements with specific objects, connected by the semiotic systems providing the interpretive signs. *Theories* are self-conscious cognitive constructions of how interpretations hang together and are vulnerable to criticism, one of another. The axiological problem for theorizing is to prevent the values resident in the forms of theories—whether will-to-power interests, value-biases of form as such, or private evaluations—to prejudice what is valuable or important in the phenomena encompassed within the theory. Therefore, an axiological theory of theories needs to show how good theories are vulnerable to correction by engagements with the phenomena. How we imagine, interpret, and theoretically situate ourselves in reality are all ways of thinking that affect what we do. But the *pursuit of responsibility*, as a Confucian might put it, or practical reason, is a family of thought processes issuing in actions that define moral identity. An axiological approach to responsibility needs to be able to show how the real values of things make a difference to what should be done and thus define obligation; it needs to show how general obligation can fall to individuals as their own responsibility; it needs to show how nearly all actions are not merely individual but conjoint and social, reflecting cultural valuations and embodied in social rituals that frame conjoint behavior; it needs finally to account for how different cultures define obligation and human nature differently and yet should accept obligations to normatively good intercultural social interaction (something better than the "clash of civilizations"). Imagination, interpretation, theorizing, and the pursuit of responsibility are the four families of kinds of thought that need an axiological interpretation if the Confucian emphasis on the ultimacy of goodness and its demands is to be a viable system of symbols for spirituality.[24] Developing a reconstructed set of Confucian symbols of the ultimate that embody Confucianism's concern for the grounding of value in the world and true valuation and practice in the human being is the most essential cognitive task for contemporary Confucian spirituality, without which such spirituality is but wishful thinking. Only this will allow Confucian spirituality to let the ultimate be carried over into persons with the sensibility of modern science in the contemporary world. This is "manifesting the clear character."

Confucian spirituality is not only the direct engagement of what is ultimate but also the playing out of this engagement with the rest of life, especially in our relations with other people and with nature as our home in the cosmos. Whereas the engagement of the ultimate is the essence of spirituality, connecting this with people and nature is its condition. Together the essence and the conditions constitute the harmony of things in which spirituality consists. From this follow my second and third points about contemporary Confucian spirituality, briefly considered.

The second point is that we live in a changed moral situation from that obtaining during most of Confucian thinking. There are two important changes. The first, mentioned earlier, is that because of the development of the social sciences we can now envision global social structures and global social engineering. This gives a point to questions of structural oppression and unjust economic inequalities. Before the twentieth century, Confucianism thought only rarely about structural issues of justice on a global scale, though, of course, it has focused on how China can keep its soul in the modern world. To some extent, the globalization of structural issues of justice runs in tension with Confucianism's focus on attending first to what is close to home based on the person-to-person genesis of moral character in filiality, a major theme of Tu's *Centrality and Commonality*.

The second change in the moral situation is the increasingly widespread appreciation of the double value of democratic equality with meritocratic rewards on the one hand and respect for personal and cultural otherness, pluralism, on the other. Neither democracy nor pluralism is native to the Confucian moral tradition. Both developed from the European Enlightenment. Yet in their Enlightenment forms, democratic equality and meritocracy can be given empty procedural meanings; and otherness and pluralism can be so privatized as to be trivial and alienating. The Confucian emphasis on the need to cultivate concrete content to individuating relationships is a fine counterweight to Enlightenment abstraction. Moreover, the Confucian insistence on attending to the institutions of human interaction, from family to state, as more determinative of effects on human beings than isolated face-to-face interactions, is a fine counterweight to the rather thin Enlightenment view of institutions as reduced to public procedures and private rituals.

Without claiming that Confucianism has only one contribution to make to the changed moral situation, I do want to suggest that its most important contribution would be a reconstruction of its theory of ritual, especially as anciently framed by Xunzi. For Xunzi, rituals are the invented and learned general social habits that constitute the frameworks within which specific civilized human interactions can take place. Without rituals of greeting, greetings are impossible. In a ritual, all the players are brought into a conjoint action. Now with respect to global structural injustices, the problem lies not so much with specific policies or actions as with the social habits, often bought into by all parties, that constitute an unjust ritual dance. Social classes, for instance, are people grouped by different roles in structured habitual interactions. A Confucian ritual analysis of global structural problems of injustice would locate the problems in the generalities of the habits rather than specific acts and policies, and would be able to show why even those who suffer seem often to accept the roles they play. The Confucian moral solution would be to criticize the current global rituals and invent improved ones, and then to administer the changes in specific acts and policies that would establish the new rituals. The Secretary General of the United Nations should be a Confucian Ritual Master.

A similar point can be made about giving humanizing concreteness to democratic equality and meritocracy and to cultural and personal pluralism. Although these particular values have not been prominent in the Confucian tradition, what is a Confucian ritual except a complicated social dance form in which all can participate (democracy) and yet can play roles that recognize their vast differences from one another (pluralism)? Contemporary Confucians should develop rituals that allow all persons to participate equally with regard to political power and be rewarded with placement and wealth according to their merit, and that allow persons to interact respectfully and concretely with people very different from themselves: the key is rituals that require affirming ritual participation without necessarily agreeing to affirm the character and values of those importantly different from oneself (except to respect them in the ritually defined social construction).

Contemporary Confucian spirituality requires a practical orientation to moral action, which in turn requires moral programs that address the changed moral situation of issues of global justice and the combination of democracy and pluralism. Without those new Confucian programs, Confucian morals will be parochial and disconnected from spiritual life. The Confucian spiritual life will be vital when Confucianism has a program that addresses the most important questions of contemporary morality. This is "renovating the people."

The third issue for contemporary Confucian spirituality is the redefinition of our orientation to the universe in light of the new knowledge deriving from ecology. Partly this is a moral matter, and Confucians should let ecological awareness shape the rituals developed for habitual social interaction. What I want to stress here, however, is less the moral dimension than that of orientation. Here the Confucian tradition is far more advanced than most others in grasping the contemporary problem. Xunzi said in his treatise on Heaven or Nature that we are oriented one way to the regular processes we cannot affect, such as the rotation of the heavens; that orientation involves wonder and appreciation, perhaps ritual celebration.[25] We are oriented another way to the rotation of the seasons, to which we need to respond adroitly to avoid starvation and disaster; this orientation requires the kind of social habits passed down from generation to generation in peasant culture, and now in more technologically advanced forms. We are oriented in yet a third way, said Xunzi, toward irregular events for which preparation should be made, for instance, floods and droughts and the appearance of the barbarians over the hill; this orientation requires political organization to provide for relief, storage ahead, and military readiness. Taking Xunzi's analysis as a clue, we note that we have orientations toward our families that differ from those toward the workplace; toward our universities that differ from those toward our professional public; toward our neighborhood that differ from those toward our country; toward our gardens that differ from those toward the wilderness, and so on. Ecological knowledge of nature has forced upon us issues of orientation toward many facets of our habitation that previously we more or less ignored. An orientation is not an action, but the general habit or behavioral and interpretive context within which an action toward the object of orientation is shaped, much the way a ritual is a context for social interaction.

One of the geniuses of Confucianism has been to recognize that our lives require orientations to many different things and that what is required does not easily fit together. To balance out our orientations is to have poise, to keep one's balance in the constant shift of attention required for responsiveness. A person's poise is structured, and the structure of one's poise determines much of one's personal identity. That identity also includes what goes on specifically with regard to each of the things to which the person is oriented; but the person's character out of which the actions spring lies in the structure of poise with regard to orientations. I can now say that the Confucian Way of specifying the vague notion of self is neither to claim that it has a core nor that it is wholly to be negated in terms of relations but that it is a structure of poised balancing of orientations to the ten thousand things. The poise issues from the ready responsiveness of principle within each person and from the attunement, such as it is, of our various orientations to the principle or worth in the things to which we are oriented. Righteousness is getting our orientations right. Humanity is the poise to keep them in balance.

Ecology has shown us a new domain of things with respect to which we should be oriented and whose integration into family-, economic-, and political life-orientations will require new forms of poise. Confucian spirituality is well placed to develop new forms of life-poise and new humane orientations that situate us more accurately in respect of what we now know to be of very great value in the cosmos. This is "abiding in the highest good."

My argument in this section has been that contemporary Confucian spiritual practice needs to be guided by realistic signs and symbols, first, toward the ultimate in order to be spiritual at all, and then toward the expression of our engagement of the ultimate in moral behavior and comportment toward life. In each case, the traditional symbols of Confucianism, its core texts and motifs, have firm commitments that are needed in the contemporary situation, but that also need to be reconstructed in light of the plausibility conditions and objects of attention of the late modern world. Spirituality, of course, is practice for which theory is a support. If my discussion of the contemporary problems has focused too much on the intellectual issues and too little on setting the intellectual solutions to work, perhaps that can be excused by the fact that my own practice is the ritual management of theory construction.

Multiple Religious Identity[26]

One more condition of contemporary Confucian spirituality needs to be examined at this point, namely, that because Confucianism has permeated a global society, some of its practitioners will come from non–East Asian traditions and will combine Confucianism with spiritual identities from elsewhere. How can one person be a Confucian and something else, say, a Christian?

A socially significant but spiritually superficial way to address the question is through the issue of religious membership. A person is a member of a spiritual tradition if membership is self-consciously affirmed and the person's spiritual practice is guided by the symbols and terms of the core texts and motifs of the tradition, however reconstituted for contemporary viability; it helps also if the person's membership is recognized by other members of the tradition, although isolation and heresy (a form of membership) are not uncommon.

With regard to traditions' attitudes toward multiple membership, the situation is diverse. Exclusivistic Christians who say that all other religions are wrong or merely disguised forms of Christianity would not permit or take the time for the cultivation of Confucian spiritualty. But nonexclusivist Christians look for spiritual sustenance wherever it might be found, and Confucianism is a good source. Christian identity is maintained by self-conscious participation in the Christian movement of reconciliation and worship begun by Jesus with his disciples and continuing down to practicing Christians today.

From the Confucian side, the whole issue of membership is just not very important. True, there was an existentialist theme in some Neo-Confucians who emphasized the importance of a defining decision to pursue the path of the sage; in our time, Tu Weiming has defended this position.[27] But even here the point is turning the self to the effort of spiritual perfection, not so much joining up to do it in a Confucian way, though that is supposed too. Efforts of the Song and Ming Neo-Confucians to distinguish their school from Buddhism and Daoism did indeed reflect a self-consciousness about a reconstituted Confucian school; but their main criticisms of the other schools had more to do with their failures to support adequate practice in personal, family, and public life than with primary doctrinal differences. The Confucian stress is not on whether one is in or out of the movement, although that is a question, but whether one is any good at it. Given the practical intentionality of Confucianism, the practical effort and accomplishment are more important than labels. Tai Chen (1723–1777) would have thought John Wesley (1703–1791) a profound Confucian sage if Wesley had been able to talk with him about the *Analects*. On the social level of membership, there is no difficulty being a member of the Confucian and Christian movements at once so long as they do not interfere conceptually and their practices reinforce and complement one another; only the limits of time and energy need inhibit the efforts needed to practice both spiritualities where they are different from one another.

On a spiritually profound level, of course, the issue is more complicated. The essential feature of spirituality is to engage the ultimate, and this requires both appropriate symbols and competence in using the symbols to engage. The symbols of Confucianism and Christianity are quite different. Perhaps we can show clear similarities and differences at the intellectual level. But when the symbols are functioning within the soul in meditation and practice they have very different imaginative structures. The Confucian symbols, such as those quoted in the first section above, have only faint reminiscences of intentionality, little stronger that "the Mandate of Heaven," for instance. By contrast, Christian symbols of the ultimate are redolent with intentionality even when the underlying metaphysical conception puts that aside apophatically (as in Thomas Aquinas or Paul Tillich). The imaginative functioning of the different symbol systems in meditation, quiet-sitting, communal liturgies, and spiritually directed practices must be quite different: though both spiritual traditions emphasize self-examination, Confucians do not pray to anybody, and Christians do not focus much reverence on ancestors.

There are several ways to understand the difference between spiritually significant symbologies. First, the traditions might simply be oriented to different ultimates, and it might be possible to defend a plurality of ultimates; in this case one can be a Confucian for some ultimate matters, a

Christian for others. Second, the traditions might be oriented to the same thing as ultimate but interpret it in different respects, the Confucian picking up on the nonintentional aspects, for instance, and the Christian on the intentional ones; in this case multiple religious identity is a positive asset for a richer spiritual life. Or third, and most problematically, suppose the traditions might agree on the ultimate orientation and interpret it in the same respect: do their different symbols for engaging that mean that they disagree in their interpretations, or that they are saying much the same thing in different ways? That is a serious scholarly question to which there is no full answer now because we lack clear and publicly justified comparative categories. But any person affirming multiple religious identities has to be ready to defend at least the compatibility if not the agreement and complementarity of the multiple traditions' symbols when they are about the same thing.[28]

Now the defense of the consistency of a spiritual life lived actively through two or more spiritual traditions is not just an antiquarian project, merely examining the compatibility of traditional spiritual texts. All the great spiritual traditions are facing the challenges of late modernity, at least those posed by science, global morals, and ecology. Every religion needs to be reconstructed, or creatively extended, to address those challenges, and each would have to be reconstructed even if it were alone in facing those challenges. But they are not alone. The global interaction of religious traditions is yet another novelty of late modernity, a challenge in itself to religious identity.[29] The practical tests for the compatibility of spiritualities lie in the struggles they have together to call upon their traditional resources to address contemporary challenges. Highly intentional anthropomorphic Christian conceptions of God are just as much in need of decontruction and reconstruction as Confucian conceptions of Heaven above and the Earth below. Modern science, the global moral situation, and ecology set a common agenda that differentially challenges the various traditions but unites them in the task of presenting symbols for spiritual engagement.

None of this guarantees in advance that the traditions are indeed compatible and that multiple religious identity might not be schizophrenic. Moreover, any reconstructive effort, even within a single tradition, is open to the charge that the reconstruction leaves out the most important parts of the tradition. But the proof of compatibility and illustration of its limitations come only in concrete lives, developed in conversation that is serious in the Confucian sense, and that is justified philosophically by reflection tolerably faithful to all sides. Like the Christian who replied to the question whether he believed in infant baptism, "Believe it? Why I've seen it!," I can say that in observing and participating in the creative transformations of Confucianism in Boston, I have seen multiple religious identities in many forms, much to the benefit of contemporary Confucian spirituality.

Notes

1. I have argued that "religion" might be characterized helpfully as consisting in the rituals, conceptualities, and spiritual practices by which people relate to the fact of their existence, their ground or transcendent context; see my *Soldier, Sage, Saint* (New York: Fordham University Press, 1974).

2. *Spirituality and the Secular Quest,* ed. Peter H. Van Ness, Encyclopedia of World Spirituality 22 (New York: Crossroad, 1996).

3. Some say that Confucianism is not a religion at all, and hence the language of denominational membership and allegiance is inappropriate. Not to join that issue here, I shall assume that it is a religion, as has been argued by so many, for instance, Tu Weiming (*Centrality and Commonality: An Essay on Confucian Religiousness,* rev. and enlarged ed. [Albany: State University of New York Press, 1989]) and Rodney L. Taylor (*The Religious Dimensions of Confucianism* [Albany: State University of New York Press, 1990]).

4. The distinction between essential and conditional subhypotheses is not philosophically innocent. It reflects a general thesis that to be a thing is to be a harmony of essential and conditional features, the conditional ones constituting the thing as related to other things which condition it and the essential ones expressing the principles of its own being. I take it that this conception of things as harmonies, especially as applied to changing things, is a contemporary reconstruction of the Neo-Confucian theme of harmony. For a succinct expression, see my "Sketch of a System" in *New Essays in Metaphysics*, ed. Robert C. Neville (Albany: State University of New York Press, 1987). Following the lead of this notion, concepts should be defined by tracing out the harmony of conditional and essential features, and phenomena should be described that way too. In this sense, there are no "boundaries" to definitions, but harmonic structures; that's the way to get around nasty essentialism.

5. See, e.g., Wayne Proudfoot, *Religious Experience* (Berkeley: University of California Press, 1985). On the other side, John E. Smith has defended what I would call an engagement theory of experience, deriving from pragmatism and its critique of British empiricism, that gets around the criticisms. See his *Experience and God* (New York: Oxford University Press, 1968).

6. See, e.g., Tu Weiming's contribution to this volume, chapter 22.

7. This is defined at much greater length in my *Truth of Broken Symbols* (Albany: State University of New York Press, 1996), ch. 2. The subhypothesis derives from the bearing of both sociology of knowledge and ontology or metaphysics on the understanding of religious or spiritual symbolism, and is conditional in this sense.

8. Wing-tsit Chan's translation in his *Source Book in Chinese Philosophy* (Princeton, N.J.: Princeton University Press, 1963), 463.

9. Ibid., 497.

10. Ibid., 98.

11. There is scholarly debate as to whether in Zhou's line the Great Ultimate is supposed to proceed from the Ultimate of Non-being in some ontological sense, or just be reciprocal. I discuss this in *Behind the Masks of God* (Albany: State University of New York Press, 1991), ch. 4.

12. See Peter Berger, *The Sacred Canopy: Elements of a Sociological Theory of Religion* (Garden City, N.Y.: Doubleday, 1967).

13. I have developed this interpretation of the Confucian conception in *Behind the Masks of God*, ch. 8, and in "A Confucian Construction of a Self-Deceivable Self," in *Self and Deception: A Cross-Cultural Philosophical Enquiry*, ed. Roger T. Ames and Wimal Dissanayake (Albany: State University of New York Press, 1996).

14. This large claim is the thesis of my *Recovery of the Measure: Interpretation and Nature* (Albany: State University of New York Press, 1989). It is defended with respect to religious objects in *Truth of Broken Symbols*, ch. 7.

15. See my *Truth of Broken Symbols*, chs. 2–4.

16. See my *Recovery of the Measure*. The entire pragmatic tradition, as well as that of process philosophy, supports a philosophy of nature that represents mentality as part of natural processes.

17. These qualifications are analyzed in detail in my *Recovery of the Measure*, ch. 4.

18. This is the main thesis of Tu, *Centrality and Commonality*.

19. See H. Richard Niebuhr, *Christ and Culture* (New York: Harper and Brothers, 1951).

20. Zhou says:

It is man alone who receives (the five Agents) in their highest excellence, and therefore he is most intelligent. His physical form appears, and his spirit develops consciousness. The five moral principles of his nature (humanity or *ren*, righteousness, propriety, wisdom, and faithfulness) are aroused by, and react to, the external world and engage in activity; good and evil are distinguished; and human affairs take place. The sage settles these affairs by the principles of the Mean, correctness, humanity, and righteousness. . . , regarding tranquillity as fundamental. . . . Thus he establishes himself as the ultimate standard for man. Hence the character of the sage is "identical with that of Heaven and Earth; . . . The superior man cultivates these moral qualities and enjoys good fortune, whereas the inferior man violates them and suffers evil fortune. (Chan, *Source Book*, 463–64)

21. For a sophisticated discussion of the theme of ontology in reference to the reconstruction of Christian theology, with attendant epistemological considerations that would apply to any religious tradition, see *Religion and Science: History, Method, Dialogue*, ed. W. Mark Richardson and Wesley J. Wildman (New York: Routledge, 1996), Part 3: Dialogue. This text deals with the theological challenges of physical cosmology (Big Bang theory), chaos theory, quantum complementarity, information theory, molecular biology, and social genetics.

22. I have developed such a science-tolerant ontology, with a correlative episte-mology and religious applications in *God the Creator: On the Transcendence and Presence of God* (Chicago: University of Chicago Press, 1968; new ed., Albany: State University of New York Press, 1992).

23. This has been argued in schematic fashion in my *The Tao and the Daimon* (Albany: State University of New York Press, 1982), especially ch. 6, "The Empir-ical Cases of World Religions." See also ch. 7, "The Notion of Creation in Chinese Thought." The varying ways by which a contemporary ontology can reconstruct Christian and Confucian traditional symbols respectively is a major theme of my *Behind the Masks of God*, especially chs. 3, 4, 8, and 9.

24. By pure chance (according to the European scientific conception of think-ing) or *tianming* (according to the Confucian), I have written a three-volume series called *The Axiology of Thinking: Reconstruction of Thinking* (Albany: State Univer-sity of New York Press, 1981), which gives an extended critical analysis of the European scientific fact–value distinction and its alternatives and presents a theory of imagination. *Recovery of the Measure* provides a theory of interpretation set in the context of a philosophy of nature according to which the values of things can be rendered. *Normative Cultures* provides theories of theorizing and of the pursuit of responsibility or practical reason; it attends especially to the social or cultural elements of responsibility and develops a new Confucian theory of ritual as nor-mative conjoint action.

25. Xunzi's text is ch. 17 in John Knoblock's *Xunzi: A Translation and Study of the Complete Works*, vol. 3 (Stanford: Stanford University Press, 1994). See also Edward J. Machle, *Nature and Heaven in the Xunzi: A Study of the Tian Lun* (Albany: State University of New York Press, 1993), whose interpretation I follow here.

26. I owe the phrase "multiple religious identity" to John Berthrong; see his *All Under Heaven: Transforming Paradigms in Confucian–Christian Dialogue* (Albany: State University of New York Press, 1994), especially ch. 6.

27. See Tu Weiming's early *Humanity and Self-Cultivation: Essays in Confucian Thought* (Berkeley: Asian Humanities Press, 1979), especially chs. 6–11.

28. I have attempted this with regard to certain topics in "Some Confucian-Christian Comparisons," *Journal of Chinese Philosophy* 22 (1995): 379–400.

29. See John Berthrong's contribution to this volume.

36

Treacherous Terrain: Mapping Feminine Spirituality in Confucian Worlds

VIVIAN-LEE NYITRAY

T HIS ESSAY IS AN INVITATION. Specifically, it is an invitation to engage in a classic Confucian activity, *gewu*, "the investigation of things," wherein "things" refers to aspects of Confucian feminine spirituality. In the spirit of the *Great Learning*, which observed that "things have their roots and branches," this paper examines some of the canonical Confucian "roots" for apprehending spiritual paths for women, and then looks to their later historical branches and burgeoning offshoots in women's lives today.[1] Prior to embarking on this investigation, however, several points of clarification must be made. First, "Confucian worlds" refers here to those societies or local cultures—"cultural China," Korea, Japan, portions of Southeast Asia, and an efflorescence of global diasporic communities—in which some institutional and/or practical legacy of an authoritative Confucian canonical tradition is discernible, however disparately interpreted by local scholars or differentially adopted or legislated. Second, in these worlds, Confucian ideologies were, and overwhelmingly still are, products of male and masculine subjectivities; as such, they have never been either objective or inclusively "human." Ideal attitudes and behaviors in the canonical literature are decidedly gendered, and the female subject position is subordinate to that of the male. Traversing the largely uncharted "treacherous terrain" of Confucian worlds to map the contours of feminine spirituality, then, requires patience and, at times, the donning of particular sorts of interpretive lenses.

Finally, for the purposes of this essay, the tradition here termed "Confucianism" is understood to be a multifaceted religious (and spiritual) enterprise wherein the seemingly "natural" power of its values was traditionally promoted through standardized education and the "natural" power of its deeply rooted symbolic structures—reinforced by both the state-sponsored cult and civil bureaucratic rewards for appropriate conduct—is historically observable in the osmotic spread of rhetoric, imagery, and, owing to its linguistic basis, imagination itself. Thus, despite conceptual change over time, regional variation in practice, competing intellectual lineages, and a tendency toward accommodation or syncretic appropriation of other traditions, what any given generation of ru or "Confucian" scholars understood as "Confucianism" was for them an explanation of the way the world had been (whether in a real or mythic past), the way the world of their own time ought to be, and the way the world ought to proceed in the future.

This last point regarding the posited continuity and validity of Confucian truth(s) highlights the paradoxically atemporal character of Confucianism. It is a tradition that not only sees in the past the roots of the present but also sees the past as a rationale for the future, a reading that may be either prescriptive or proscriptive in nature but which is rarely merely descriptive. Past, present, and future are thus subtly confused, conflated. Han dynasty support for the Five Classics as embodying orthodoxy and suggesting orthopraxy was later taken together with the Song dynasty elevation of the Four Books to create an ahistorical core of state-invested tradition, variously interpreted but always accepted as comprising what was real and true. These texts and their agglomerated commentaries became the basic substrata of a Confucian scholar's worldview.

As every text or canon entrains readers in its own fashion, Confucian texts, through a gradual, accumulative process, taught Confucians to "read out" meaning from their narratives and, eventually, to anticipate meaning as they moved from text to text. What was "read out" from one text was then "read into" the next. Confucian structures of textual meaning are thus analogical, obsessed with history as moral guide yet oddly ahistorical, perceived as deeply "natural," foundationally true, and, through the circular confirmation of redaction and commentary, they prove ultimately to be self-evident. In Chinese Confucian worlds, the final vision of womanly (and thus feminine) virtue and spiritual potential—sex and gender being closely identified in the Confucian system—was constructed in the Qing dynasty (1644–1911), so that restrictive emphases on chastity, modesty, and actual or symbolic confinement to the inner quarters appear to be the tradition's last words on the subject, an assumption confirmed by the early-twentieth-century May Fourth and New Culture feminist attacks on Confucian patriarchy.

But perhaps it need not be so. As with any other world religious tradition engaged in the reimagining of its particular configurations of human spirituality, the tasks of locating and then encompassing those who were previously overlooked or marginalized by the tradition are primary. Looking for "feminine spirituality" within the closed hermeneutical circle of the Confucian tradition, one finds possibility in both its roots and branches, that is, in the *re-reading* of canonical and commentarial texts with an eye toward separating the prescriptive from the descriptive; in the *dis-covery* of the realities of women's lives in their historical and regional particularities by way of *re-membering* women into a textual tradition that did not foreground them; and in the *re-thinking* and *re-cognition* of Confucianism as a historically contentious, innovative, and intellectually responsive tradition.[2]

Confucius himself had virtually nothing to say about women—merely describing them and others who were "of low birth" as "difficult to deal with" (*Analects* 17:25), presumably because their relative lack of education in matters of ritual and the cultivation of virtue left them unable to negotiate social relations with grace. There is little in the early texts of the school to deny women access to the education that would make them virtuous and ritually refined. In the *Book of Changes*, women are considered to be the human manifestation of the *yin* cosmic principle; as such, they are identified with the hexagram *kun*, "the receptive, the earth," notable for the yielding devotion and quiet perseverance understood to characterize the Earth, in contrast to the activity of Heaven. This is not to say that women had no active religious role or spiritual path; rather, the key image was one of overarching complementarity of male and female, albeit with women in the yielding or deferential position. In terms of specific religious duties, women were to assist with the preparation of sacrificial altars by setting up the requisite ritual implements; they were to prepare the liquors, sauces, and preserved foods used in the rites; they were to observe the ceremonies; and in participating in these ways, their performance was understood to mirror and thereby complete the actions of male participants (*Book of Rites*, ch. 12). Women, just as men and in concert with them, were to find spiritual fulfillment in the performance of ritual activities and in the cultivation of harmonious relations among members of the family and in social interactions beyond the family sphere; in this way, according to the Han text of the *Doctrine of the Mean*, they would assist in the transforming powers of Heaven and Earth (ch. 22).

It was with the grafting of popular cosmological speculation, especially *yin-yang* theories, onto the core of Confucian ideas during the Han dynasty (206 B.C.E.–220 C.E.) that gender hierarchies proliferated within the tradition.[3] Han cosmology required a hierarchy of traits, perhaps to underscore the qualities of the *yang* ruler over the *yin* ruled. The unfortunate consequence was that *yang* (strength, growth, light, life) was given primacy over its complement, *yin* (weakness, decay, darkness, death). Although the human heart-mind was seen to have both rational *yang* and emotional *yin* qualities, the latter was thought to cause disorder and error; *yang* was accordingly more highly regarded and was ultimately seen as morally superior. Pre-Confucian notions of patrilineality and patrilocality thereby fused with the Confucian directive to educate, cultivate, and control the self—to the detriment of traits and persons associated with *yin*. Women were not perceived as without potential for either virtue or knowledge, but the essentializing tendency to associate women with *yin* served to undermine their accomplishments or to valorize them principally as they were displayed in the service of larger family or state needs.

As the focus of the present volume is on Confucian spirituality, this essay cannot begin to offer a full treatment of women's history in China, nor can it address alternative religious paths for women found in Daoist, Buddhist, local shamanic traditions, or combinations thereof. What follows can only suggest that the ambivalent regard for women's capabilities and the circumscribing of their spiritual potentialities varied greatly according to historical epoch: expanding and contracting in response to state ideology, male scholarly anxiety, and the vicissitudes of economic trends and literacy rates.

During the Han dynasty, while *yin-yang* theories were gradually accreting onto Confucian moral teachings, Liu Xiang (77–6 B.C.E.) compiled his *Biographies of Exemplary Women*, offering models of virtuous women who exemplify filiality, loyalty, or other core Confucian virtues, and who adeptly criticize their husbands, sons, and even their rulers for failure to heed good advice or otherwise shoulder their responsibilities.[4] Women are repeatedly portrayed as the virtuous equals (if not superiors) of male family members, their domestic example crucial for the development of a family's moral standards and its public stature. Indeed, the *Biographies* opens with a collection of lives of virtuous mothers, underscoring the crucial role women play as primary educators of the young. A mother's didactic responsibility was shown to extend even to instruction *in utero*: the expectant mother should appreciate her body's function as conduit and expose the fetus only to uplifting sights and sounds (ch. 1.6). The most famous maternal exemplar is Mother Meng, Mencius's widowed mother, who, foreshadowing her son's later emphasis on the crucial role of environment in the cultivation of innate moral potential, moved their residence three times in search of the most edifying influences: their first home abutted a cemetery (where young Mencius and his friends played at conducting burials); their second house was in the vicinity of the marketplace (where Mencius played shopkeeper and cultivated cunning methods of enhancing his profits); but their third adjoined an academy (so that Mencius played at performing sacrificial rites and emulating scholarly etiquette). In other incidents, Mother Meng sternly reminds her son of the gravity of industriousness when she rips up her own weaving—the source of their livelihood; later, when he threatens to divorce his wife for lack of decorum (he entered her chambers to find her less than fully dressed), his mother makes clear the fact that any fault was his for having gone in unbidden and unexpectedly (ch. 1.11).

Complementing this collection of exemplary biographies was the first of what would be a long line of didactic texts for women, Ban Zhao's (ca. 48–ca. 120) *Instructions for Women*. Such texts, in reinforcing images of female subordination drawn from classic texts such as the *Book of Odes* and the *Book of Rites*, symbolically consigned women to the domestic sphere, where they had but limited access to spiritual teachings that would enable them thoughtfully to cultivate virtue beyond that defined as "womanly." Thus, even though Ban Zhao, herself a prominent scholar, decried the trend in her own day to neglect women's education beyond an elementary level, she promulgated an unambiguous view of women's primary duty as "humbling herself before others" (*Instructions for Women*, ch. 1). Moreover, Ban Zhao's call for education stemmed not from a belief in the ability of women to progress toward sageliness or moral nobility but rather from her belief that, unless women were educated, the efficacious performance of family rites would be jeopardized.[5]

Throughout the Six Dynasties period of disunion (420–589) and on into the Sui-Tang dynasties (589–907), exemplary biographies emphasized filiality for both men and women, acknowledging the emotional ties that bind women to their natal families. This extended concept of family was reflected in the Tang legal code, in which even married daughters could inherit property in certain circumstances. Although subject to "Thrice Following" (*san cong*), that is, following the dictates of father, husband, and eldest son over the course of life, women were again elevated to the position of "moral custodian" of the household. This understanding was illustrated in the early-eighth-century *Classic of Filial Piety for Women*, wherein the narrator, in the voice of Ban Zhao, enjoins women to lead their fathers, husbands, and sons to improve their character with their own modeling of respect, filiality, affection, virtue, and modesty, and through their artful use of ritual and music (ch. 2:17).

With the revitalization of Confucianism in the Song (960–1279) and its incorporation of interior spiritual techniques borrowed from Buddhism and Daoism, increasing emphasis was placed on the elimination of distraction and on the quelling of passion as crucial to the success of meditation and other forms of quiet-sitting. Not surprisingly, then, ambivalence toward women increased; as essentialized representations of *yin*, they required regulation and restriction lest they instigate male passion. The full force of this suspicion was not felt, however, until Song Confucianism was enshrined as state orthodoxy in the later Yuan (1280–1368) and Ming (1368–1644) dynasties. Close reading of Song documents, especially the manuals of "family instruction" favored by scholars, yields a sense of a tradition straining to reconcile appreciation for womanly talent with the need to constrain female sexuality by advocating such concepts as "chastity" (*jie*) for both the unmarried and the widowed. In his *Rules for Social Life*, Yuan Cai (late twelfth century) acknowledged that there were women with stupid, unworthy, or inept husbands who could somehow manage the family on their own, keeping the accounts and not allowing others to take advantage of them. There were even some "whose husbands had died when sons were young [who] can nourish and teach their sons, stay on good terms with inner and outer affinal kin, perform household chores and even bring the family to prosperity." He concluded that "All of these are wise and worthy women."[6] It was regrettable when women had to assume public duties; however, Yuan Cai admitted that if a woman's husband and sons were reckless wanderers or gamblers and the woman was unmindful, the consequences for the family would be grave and unacceptable.

Similarly, in recording Master Cheng Yi's saying, "To starve to death is a very small matter; to lose one's integrity, however, is a grave matter," Zhu Xi (1130–1200) was not describing the prevalence of chastity in his time; rather, he reproduced this dictum precisely because remarriage by widows was a popular practice in the Song, even among those of the upper class (*Reflections on Things at Hand* 6:3a). In terms of education, Zhu Xi, who emphasized functional differentiation between men and women, nonetheless affirmed the fact that women could not perform their own crucial function within the home unless they took part in the higher culture the family system strove to maintain.[7]

By the Ming dynasty, household instructions and regulations proliferated. The number of stipulations on women exceeded Song times by far, with restrictions on women in family instructions becoming ever more tedious and severe. For example, by the age of eight, a daughter was expected to learn the *Instructions for Women* and *Biographies of Exemplary Women* by rote "so that she knows a woman's way; she must not be allowed to be skilled in the writing brush or write poetry," for "a wife's job is to prepare food and wine; she should be knowledgeable in matters of rice and salt, but must not step away from the stove."[8] Ban Zhao's call for women's education centuries earlier was thus ironically realized in the promotion of her narrowly written *Instructions for Women*; instead of clarifying and promoting regard for women's status, however, her words justified the diminution of their roles, and her *Instructions* (or any of nearly fifty similar didactic texts) were often their sole curriculum. Illustrated and easy to read, these primers became extremely popular, even among commoners.[9] That these texts were multivocal, however, is attested by the work of the scholar Lü Kun (1536–1618), advocate of complementarity rather than hierarchy as the defining characteristic of the marital relationship, who updated the Han text of *Biographies of Exemplary Women* in an effort to augment increasingly prominent images of decorous maidens and chaste widows by resuscitating earlier images of wise wives and mothers.[10]

The definition of womanly virtue in terms of wifely fidelity or chastity (*jie*) advanced through the Ming and into the early to mid Qing dynasty (through the mid-nineteenth century). Once again a period of Confucian intellectual dominance, the Qing evidenced interest in "Han learning" that differed from earlier revivals in that its reach extended down to the commoner class and was focused less on the personal cultivation of sageliness than on discerning the contours of ideal family life. State-supported "Han learning" promoted the reexamination of classical texts to discern and define these ideals, with chastity becoming the most vaunted moral quality for women. Elementary texts for the education of males were mirrored in the publication of the *Four Books for Women*, all of which stressed female receptivity to regulation: Ban Zhao's *Instructions for Women*; the Tang text of *Analects for Women* by Song Rohua; and two Ming compilations, the *Training for the Inner Quarters* by Ren Xiaowen (Empress Xu, second empress of the Ming) and *An Outline of Rules for Women* by Mme. Wang, a text that substituted for the earlier *Classic of Filial Piety for Women*.

Yet even in this more repressive era, discordant notes were sounded. The otherwise conservative text of the *Training for the Inner Quarters* upheld the Neo-Confucian claim that all people can become sages, here extending the notion to include women, urging them to keep watch on their thoughts and to cultivate sageliness, a jewel more precious than pearls or jade (3:22).[11] The foundational value of the mother as primary educator of the young was reinforced by scholars such as Chen Hongmou, whose preface to his *Registry of Rules for Women's Education* states that "the process of kingly transformation . . . begins in the women's quarters."[12] And Yü Zhengxie (1775–1840), a prominent critic of footbinding and widow chastity, invoked a classic Han-dynasty text, *Discourses in the White Tiger Hall*, to support his refutation of women's subordination in marriage.[13]

Scholarly efforts notwithstanding, it is the image of the obedient daughter-in-law and chaste widow that prevailed, and against which feminist and socialist reformers have railed for nearly a century. Despite historical variation in degree of valorization or particulars of practice, the portraits of women cutting their flesh to feed their in-laws and of chaste young widows languishing in the deep recesses of the inner quarters (or committing suicide rather than be forced into remarriage) remain deeply rooted in modern imagination, the product of continuous oral transmission throughout Confucian worlds as well as their reproduction in almanacs, popular morality books, and primers.

In the daunting landscape of Confucian history, however, are hidden the traces of women whose fates allowed them to be born to some privilege in periods of historical toleration. Beyond "womanly virtue," such talented women (*cainü*) cultivated intelligence, literary and artistic talents, and even martial courage. Slowly, the underrepresentation of research into women's experiences is being redressed, especially for the Ming-Qing period but reaching farther back as well. Evidence from earlier periods, although less ample and documenting only the lives of elite women of influential clans, still details the stories of women whose drive to immerse themselves fully in a moral life of relationship proved unrestrainable. The turbulent social transitions of the Wei-Jin era (220–420), for example, produced a great many women who were wealthy, politically and philosophically savvy, and/or accomplished in literary arts.

A case in point has been offered by Lily Xiao-hung Lee in her analysis of the life of Xie Daoyun (fl. mid-fourth century C.E.), a woman whose biography is the longest of those found in the *History of the Jin Dynasty*. Born into the Xie clan, renowned for its superlative traditions of Confucian scholarship and literary arts, she was said from youth to have excelled in philosophical argumentation; she was skillful in playing literary games and in writing both prose and poetry—even to commenting on the *Analects*. Xie Daoyun's most astonishing abilities were displayed when, following the murder of her husband, a lackluster commandery administrator, and at least two of their sons during a religiously-inspired military uprising led by Sun En in 399, "she conducted herself as usual."

> She ordered her maids to carry her out of her quarters in a sedan chair, and she went out with drawn sword. Soon insurgent soldiers arrived. She managed to kill several of them before she was taken prisoner. Her maternal grandson, Liu Tao, was only a few years old, and the bandits wanted to kill him as well. Xie Daoyun said, "This is a matter concerning the Wang clan; what has it to do with his family? If you must kill the child, I insist that you kill me first!" Sun En was ruthless and cruel, but her words moved him and

he did not kill Liu Tao. (*History of the Jin Dynasty* 96; Lily Xiao-hung Lee's translation)

Nor did he kill Xie Daoyun. She lived to be at least sixty, a chaste and respected widow who is said to have run her household efficiently and to have conversed with men—even those not of her family—about philosophical matters of state and society. At least two volumes of her poetry, essays, odes, and eulogies survived her, as did glowing peer estimates of her abilities.

In accounting for Xie Daoyun's individualism and personal courage, Lee suggests that it stems from Xie's commitment to Daoism, with its focus on individual freedom and its equating of life and death. I would argue that the life can also be read in Confucian terms as portraying a woman of erudition and ability, fulfilling the demands of her many relationships and obediently accepting, if not entirely liking, a husband whose talents were in no way equal to her own. Neither reading, however, is entirely accurate, for it is almost never tenable to characterize any one life as exclusively or even predominantly "Confucian" or "Daoist"; neither of these religious traditions was practiced in isolation from the other or from other religious and philosophical traditions, notably Buddhism. Nor does any life unfold in isolation from a welter of social factors, not the least of which are the dictates of local history and the differing appropriation of religious ideals occasioned by class. For example, the notion of "valuing boys and slighting girls" held by the common people has always differed from the concept of "male superior and female inferior" held by the educated upper classes and promoted by elite Confucian culture. Rural families rely on female as well as male labor for productivity, and their expectations of women's behavior have always been tempered by practical concerns. From Song times onward, the concepts of "thrice following" and "four virtues" (proper virtue, speech, carriage, and work, as outlined in the *Book of Rites*, ch. 44) were doubtless widely known and accepted, but such ideals were always, and of necessity, honored more in the breach than in the promise.

In circumstances where women were clearly restricted, whether by historical epoch, class, or regional custom, the fact remains that the number of women who somehow managed to overcome such strictures was extremely small. Historian Susan Mann has estimated that the talented women of the Qing dynasty whom she studies "comprise at best a thousandth of one percent of women in the Lower Yangtze region, where nearly 75 percent of [such women] were concentrated."[14]

This observation at last brings us to consider the contemporary situation. Both canonical and historical sources make clear that "distinctions

[are] to be observed between man and woman" (*Book of Rites* ch. 41), and yet, particularly in terms of current realities, we should not rush to posit an unbridgeable gulf between men's and women's potential for spiritual fulfillment. For both men and women in Confucian worlds today, the cultivation of authentic "humanity" is predicated on negotiating the redefinition of familial relations wrought by the forces of industrialization, urbanization, education, and population growth policies. As diagrammed in the *Great Learning*, the fruits of Confucian self-cultivation radiate outward in ever-widening circles of influence. The family—locus of the father–son, husband–wife, and older brother–younger brother relationships—is where one first learns ritual interaction and is the first recipient of one's cultivated virtue as well. Thus, far from being merely a political or economic unit, in Confucianism the family is a profoundly religious unit, a venue for self-transformation and the springboard to public application of virtuous action.

For all who would create new Confucian spiritual modes, the paramount tasks are dual in nature: *redefining* familial relationships and responsibilities, and *reconfiguring* traditional spiritual goals, images, and practices in ways that strip away centuries of social convention to expose what is theologically necessary and do so in gender-sensitive ways. This last point bears some discussion. Some feminist scholars familiar with the Confucian tradition, especially in the West, may weary of the revisiting of "Mencius's mother" as valorized exemplar and/or may find any positive emphasis on the paradigms of the virtuous wife and good mother to be overdetermined or embedded in a "victim script" for women which serves only as an apologetic for Confucian patriarchy.[15] However, we would do well to bear in mind that even in the post-Enlightenment and postmodern West, feminism, particularly in religious terms, is an epistemological continuum that stretches to embrace orthodox Jewish women such as Blu Greenberg as well as self-styled "postchristian feminist freethinkers" such as Mary Daly.

Furthermore, it is a grave mistake to assume that feminism in Confucian cultures is the product of encounter with Western feminism(s), whether recent or in the so-called first wave of the nineteenth and early twentieth centuries. In refuting this too-common assumption, the contemporary Japanese feminist Saito Chiyo has observed, "Information is a transferable commodity. Information about feminism can, of course, be both exported and imported, and this trade may influence the various local feminisms. However, it is not so simple for a foreign feminism to take root as the basic ideology of a movement in another country."[16] Thus it is that in the political arena, feminist movements in Confucian worlds often not only refer to their own earlier "first waves" of feminism but also contest the perceived

Western devotion to terms such as "equality," asserting instead the acceptability of gender segregation. Once again turning to the historically Confucianized Japanese context—and without suggesting that all "Confucian" cultures similarly value women's experience—the concept of "equality with protection" has been pronounced an acceptable feminist position by at least one noted feminist, Ueno Chizuko.[17]

At this juncture, although it may seem as though we have strayed from our journey into feminine "spirituality," it must be remembered that in the Confucian context, the path toward human perfectibility is an inward endeavor which leads ineluctably to outward application. An interesting consequence of this underlying and socially encompassing ideology is that, despite the identification of the individual as the starting point for social and even cosmic transformation, the primacy of individual experience that generally characterizes Western feminisms and spirituality movements is not upheld. In Confucian worlds today, educationally and economically successful women increasingly face the necessity of creating spiritual resources and practices for themselves as alone (and not just "when alone," as in the formulation in the *Doctrine of the Mean*), but it is still the vision of relationality, expressed chiefly in kinship terms, that overwhelmingly informs Confucian spiritual ideals and practices.[18] The remainder of this essay will briefly survey such creative alterations in feminine spiritual ideals as are already occurring in Confucian worlds.

Always a hallmark of Confucian virtue, filiality remains a principal starting point for self-cultivation. Moreover, owing to the increasing prevalence of nuclear rather than extended families, and economic developments that facilitate the maintenance of natal ties, filial daughters as well as sons are once again prominent. Educational billboards on the subject of population growth which exhort expectant parents to believe that "Girl or Boy, either is fine!" recall the words of Yuan Cai, reminding his audience that some sons are incapable of fulfilling their responsibilities: "[Some people] have to depend on their daughters' families for support, even their burials and sacrifices falling to their daughters. So how can people say that having daughters is not comparable to having sons?"[19] Throughout Confucian worlds, the past decade has increasingly witnessed daughters assuming wider or longer-term responsibilities for their parents as well as parents-in-law, if they are married, and the younger siblings of their natal family; filiality now extends far beyond a woman's "maiden years."

In the work of redefining the complementarity, or perhaps the mutuality, of the marital bond, passages such as that describing the marriage rite from the *Book of Rites* may prove instrumental and are certainly in accord with now-familiar egalitarian images thought to characterize non-Confucian marriages: "They eat together of the same animal, and join in drinking from cups made of the same gourd, in this way showing they now form one body of equal rank, pledged to mutual affection" (ch. 41).[20] Elsewhere in the *Rites*, passing mention is made of the fact that "except at sacrifices and funerals, they should not hand vessels to one another" (ch. 10). If the Confucian spiritual life entails extending the proprieties of ritual to all endeavors, that is, to conduct all of one's business in ritual fashion, then might not the reaching out of hands for vessels be metaphorically extended to forming "one body of equal rank" in all matters pertaining to the central religious unit of the family?

Throughout Confucian history, the role of the good or wise mother has represented the apex of feminine achievement. As primary educators in a religious culture that values learning, women were lauded for their attention to the young and for their role as lifelong educators within their home. Today, women in Confucian worlds are increasingly politically active in educational and consumer affairs (and the antinuclear movement in Japan), all of which have come to be seen as extensions of their concerns at home. Western feminisms have long maintained that "the personal is political," but within the context of Confucianism, one might say that an emergent spiritual insight for women is that, as has always been the case for men, the personal is the public.

As we have highlighted throughout this volume, Confucians posit a conscious and artful relationality as a unique aspect of being human. No individual exists in isolation; all are grounded in relationships which, except for that of friends, are not characterized as existing between equals but are clearly hierarchical in nature. The five relationships—ruler–subject, parent–child, husband–wife, older–younger [brother], and that of peers—offers no images of women in relation except that within the mother–daughter bond, traditionally valued most highly in its altered form of mother and daughter-in-law. "Sisterhood" is not natural to this system, and the bond of "friends" for women was historically fragile and often fleeting, dependent for maintenance on factors beyond their control. In general, hierarchy rather than lateral ties characterize women's relations with each other.

This being so, it is not surprising that the record of women's activism on issues that elsewhere appear to concern women as a class—for example, regulation of the sex trade for the protection of minors—has been hampered in part by the lack of emphasis on women's relation to each other as peers, equals, or "sisters"; moreover, with regard to prostitution, there is also a long-standing tacit appreciation that it in fact works to uphold the same Confucian family system which benefits "virtuous wives and good mothers." In Confucian worlds, "women" as a category of analysis separate from class or kinship is a recent construct. Thus, Japanese women have only recently begun to speak out against the sexual exploitation of foreign women, whether in Japan or abroad, and both mainland Chinese and Taiwanese women in Taiwan only slowly rallied to the cause of aboriginal girls sold into the domestic sex trade.[21] Once inaugurated, however, the growth of "women's consciousness" is unlikely to recede, as women increasingly gain spiritual sustenance from one another in a group as well as deriving it from traditional individual roles of daughter, wife, and mother.

"Confucian spirituality" is deeply amenable to reason and suggestive of a profound engagement of a coherent self with reality in all of its dimensions—in all of its rational, irrational, and superrational complexity. Thus, with the recovery of women's history (and nonelite history), the reconfiguration of the family, and a global consciousness that no longer permits the easy location of a principal cultural center, the resulting "extension of knowledge" opens vast new avenues for Confucian spirituality. Universal suffrage has visibly expanded women's activities into the "ruler–subject" relation, and an emergent environmental awareness has begun to impel women's involvement in transnational ecofeminist concerns.

The present enhancement of traditional views of female roles and the expansion of women's participation into all five of the core relationships seem fitting extensions of Confucian principles, as do their incorporation and reappropriation within non-Confucian traditions. A striking example of such reappropriation can be drawn from the Buddhist Compassion Relief Tzu Chi Foundation, a predominantly female lay organization established in 1966 in Hualien, Taiwan, by Dharma Master Cheng Yen, a nun who preaches a "Just do it!" brand of "Buddhist" activism. Now claiming four million (mostly ethnic Chinese) followers in thirty-two countries, Master Cheng Yen upholds a traditional yet positive image of women. As presented in Master Cheng Yen's collected talks, *Still Thoughts*, women are domestic moral custodians whose influence naturally extends to the society as a whole:

> Every religious woman should cultivate her mind and body so she is like the moonlight, tender and soft. She should broaden her mind and shine the light of her wisdom. She should let her whole family, or everyone who comes in contact with her, feel like they were bathing in cool, refreshing moonlight. This way, she loves everyone and everyone loves her. She will attain the real meaning of love and improve her character. (*Still Thoughts* 1:38)

A loving, merciful, compassionate heart is the mark of a woman. It is a wife's duty to guide her husband in the right direction, and it is a mother's duty to do things that are beneficial to others. (*Still Thoughts* 2:26)

When a husband has more than enough to eat and wear, his wife should encourage him to do good things for others and be considerate for the poor. It is also a wife's duty to be thoughtful towards her aged father-in-law and mother-in-law, so that her husband will be able to relate to his parents without friction. (*Still Thoughts* 2:90)

A society's stability stems from its family education. Family education is based on personal moral cultivation. If we do a good job in moral cultivation, then we will create a peaceful society. (*Still Thoughts* 2:36)

If we maintain pure hearts, we will enjoy a pure world. We should protect our minds from the poisons of greed, anger and delusion. We should actively protect the world from disasters and pollution and keep the world free from violence. (*Still Thoughts* 2:85)

Studying family relationships among Tzu Chi Foundation members, anthropologist Lu Hwei-syin has found a lessening of gendered allocations of domestic chores, with men (typically brought into the foundation by their wives or sisters) gradually assuming a greater share of the tasks of child care and food preparation. In building on familiar images of family structure, stability, and nurturance, Master Cheng Yen has expanded the purview of women's spiritual activities to include medical social work at all levels, participation in labor reform and trash recycling movements, and, in a clear break from Confucian traditions concerning the filial preservation of the body, the organization and administration of international bone marrow and organ donation registries.

One way of interpreting the history of Christianity is to see it as a successive and ongoing dismantling of the disparities between Jew and Gentile, free person and slave, and male and female. In terms of Confucianism, might it be said that its history has progressively engaged in the dismantling of distinctions between the noble of birth and the noble of character, innate ability and acquired skill, and now male and female? Confucius was indeed a Janus-headed figure, always looking to the past in order to identify efficacious paths for the future. Following his lead, creators of new Confucian spiritual modalities can embrace all these: traditional and canonical visions of complementarity; the mutuality (or yielding/alternating hierarchy) of the relationship between friends; difference as well as the blurring/overlap/redrawing of certain boundaries in the marital bond; the blending of personal and public cultivation; and the syncretic practice of engaged Buddhism (or Daoism). In this multiple fashion, women may find it possible to scout the terrain of Confucian spiritual practice and chart new paths toward the goal of authentic female humanity, accomplished as much beyond as within the walls of "the inner quarters" of Confucian worlds.

Notes

1. This essay was originally presented at the conference on Confucian spirituality held at Harvard University July 30–August 3, 1997. I would like to thank Deborah Sommer and Mary Evelyn Tucker for their useful comments on the work as it progressed.

2. This technique of word breaking is borrowed from self-described post-Christian feminist thealogian Mary Daly, whose use of what she calls "labrys words" (i.e., words that are broken open in order to break open a feminist consciousness for the reader) has been influential for this author. See Daly's many works, including *Beyond God the Father: Toward a Philosophy of Women's Liberation* (1973); *Pure Lust: Elemental Feminist Philosophy* (1984); and *Webster's First New Intergalactic Wickedary of the English Language* (1987), all published by Beacon Press, Boston.

3. See Alison Black, "Gender and Cosmology in Chinese Correlative Thinking," in *Gender and Religion: On the Complexity of Symbols,* ed. Caroline Walker Bynum et al. (Boston: Beacon Press, 1986), 166–95; and Daniel L. Overmyer, "Women in Chinese Religions: Submission, Struggle, Transcendence," in *From Benares to Beijing: Essays on Buddhism and Chinese Religion,* ed. Koichi Shinohara and Gregory Schopen (New York: Mosaic Press, 1992), 91–120.

4. For an extended study of the *Biographies,* see Lisa Raphals, *Sharing the Light,* and "Gendered Virtue Reconsidered," in *The Sage and the Second Sex,* ed. Li.

5. Paul Rakita Goldin offers a nuanced discussion of female obedience within the context of emergent Confucianism in *The Culture of Sex in Ancient China* (Honolulu: University of Hawaii Press, 2002), 99–104.

6. Patricia Ebrey, "Women in the Kinship System of the Southern Song Upper Class," in *Women in China,* ed. Guisso and Johannesen, 115–16.

7. Bettine Birge, "Chu Hsi and Women's Education," in *Neo-Confucian Education,* ed. de Bary and Chaffee, 357.

8. Details on Ming instructions are from Zang Jian, "Women in the Song Dynasty and Confucian Culture" (unpublished paper prepared for the conference entitled Women in Confucian Cultures in Premodern China, Korea and Japan, held in La Jolla, California, June 28–July 1, 1996.

9. Katherine Carlitz, "Desire, Danger and the Body: Stories of Women's Virtue in Late Ming China," in *Engendering China;* Ann Waltner, "Widows and Remarriage in Ming and Early Qing China," in *Women in China,* ed. Guisso and Johannesen.

10. Joanna F. Handlin, "Lü K'un's New Audience: The Influence of Women's

Literacy on Sixteenth-Century Thought," in *Women in Chinese Society*, ed. Wolf and Witke; Susan Mann, "Grooming a Daughter for Marriage: Brides and Wives in the Mid-Qing Period," in *Marriage and Inequality in Chinese Society*, ed. Watson and Ebrey.

11. Theresa Kelleher, "Confucianism," in *Women in World Religions*, ed. Sharma, 157.

12. Mann, "Grooming a Daughter," 214.

13. Ibid., 211; see also Paul Ropp, *Dissent in Early Modern China*, 144ff.

14. Susan Mann, "The Feminist Turn in Confucian History," 9.

15. Charlotte Furth, "The Patriarch's Legacy: Household Instructions and the Transmission of Orthodox Values," in *Orthodoxy in Late Imperial China*, ed. Kwang-ching Liu; Mann, "The Feminist Turn in Confucian History"; T'ien Ju-kang, *Male Anxiety and Female Chastity*.

16. Sandra Buckley, *Broken Silence*, 257.

17. Ibid., 280.

18. While fuller discussion is beyond the scope of the present paper, it should be noted that while Confucian traditions indeed may be able to accommodate most feminist concerns, lesbians (and all other non-heterosexual individuals, for that matter) may well find themselves unable to break the hermeneutical circle of canonical Confucian constructions of the family. To my mind, the greatest challenge to new Confucianism will come from those wishing to establish nontraditional family groupings.

19. Ebrey, "Women in the Kinship System," 115.

20. Trans. James Legge, *The Chinese Classics*, 5 vols. (Hong Kong: Hong Kong University Press, 1960).

21. The cynical may attribute some of the newfound activism surrounding the sexual exploitation of women in Asia to rising and self-centered fears about HIV/AIDS; while I do not discount this as a contributing factor, my conversations with women in Taiwan and Hong Kong in 1995 and 1997 persuade me that the belated publicity surrounding the maltreatment and neglect of World War II "comfort women" has been instrumental in furthering women's consciousness of their commonalities.

Bibliography

Birge, Bettine. "Chu Hsi and Women's Education." In *Neo-Confucian Education: The Formative Stage*, edited by Wm. Theodore de Bary and John W. Chaffee, 325–67. New York: Columbia University Press, 1989.

Buckley, Sandra. *Broken Silence: Voices of Japanese Feminism*. Berkeley: University of California Press, 1997.

Carlitz, Katherine. "Desire, Danger and the Body: Stories of Women's Virtue in Late Ming China." In *Engendering China: Women, Culture, and the State*, 101–24. Cambridge, Mass.: Harvard University Press, 1994.

Chan, Wing-tsit. *Reflections on Things at Hand: The Neo-Confucian Anthology Compiled by Chu Hsi and Lü Tsu-ch'ien.* New York: Columbia University Press, 1967.

Ebrey, Patricia. "Women in the Kinship System of the Southern Song Upper Class." In *Women in China: Current Directions in Historical Scholarship,* edited by Richard W. Guisso and Stanley Johannesen, 113–28. Youngstown, N.Y.: Philo Press, 1981.

Furth, Charlotte. "Androgynous Males and Deficient Females: Biology and Gender Boundaries in Sixteenth- and Seventeenth Century China." *Late Imperial China* 9, no. 2 (December 1988): 1–31.

————. "The Patriarch's Legacy: Household Instructions and the Transmission of Orthodox Values." In *Orthodoxy in Late Imperial China,* ed. Kwang-ching Liu. Berkeley: University of California Press, 1990.

Handlin, Joanna F. "Lü K'un's New Audience: The Influence of Women's Literacy on Sixteenth-Century Thought." In *Women in Chinese Society,* edited by Margery Wolf and Roxane Witke. Stanford, Calif.: Stanford University Press, 1975.

Kelleher, Theresa. "Confucianism." In *Women in World Religions,* edited by Arvind K. Sharma, 135–59. Albany: State University of New York Press, 1987.

The I Ching or Book of Changes. Translated by Richard Wilhelm. Rendered into English by Cary F. Baynes. 2nd ed. Princeton, N.J.: Princeton University Press, 1967.

Lu Hwei-syin. "Fei guan nan nü" [Taking No Notice of Male and Female]. *Tzu Chi Monthly* (March 1997): 35.

Mann, Susan. "The Feminist Turn in Confucian History." Unpublished paper presented at the seminar entitled "Rethinking Chinese Women's History," held at University of California at Los Angeles, November 13, 1993.

————. "Grooming a Daughter for Marriage: Brides and Wives in the Mid-Qing Period." In *Marriage and Inequality in Chinese Society,* edited by Rubie Watson and Patricia Ebrey, 204–30. Berkeley: University of California Press, 1991.

Raphals, Lisa. "Gendered Virtue Reconsidered: Notes from the Warring States and Han." In *The Sage and the Second Sex: Confucianism, Ethics, and Gender,* edited by Chenyang Li, 223–47. Chicago: Open Court, 2000.

————. *Sharing the Light: Representations of Women and Virtue in Early China.* Albany: State University of New York Press, 1998.

Ropp, Paul. *Dissent in Early Modern China: Ju-lin Wai-shih and Ch'ing Social Criticism.* Ann Arbor: University of Michigan Press, 1981.

Swann, Nancy Lee. *Pan Chao: Foremost Woman Scholar of China.* 1932. Reprint, New York: Russell & Russell, 1968.

T'ien Ju-kang. *Male Anxiety and Female Chastity: A Comparative Study of Chinese Ethical Values in Ming-Ch'ing Times.* Leiden: E. J. Brill, 1988.

Waltner, Ann. "Widows and Remarriage in Ming and Early Qing China." In *Women in China: Current Directions in Historical Scholarship,* edited by Richard W. Guisso and Stanley Johannesen. Youngstown, N.Y.: Philo Press, 1981.

The Ecological Turn in New Confucian Humanism: Implications for China and the World

Tu Weiming

A N INTRIGUING PHENOMENON has occurred in Cultural China in the last twenty-five years. Three leading Confucian thinkers in Taiwan, mainland China, and Hong Kong independently concluded that the most significant contribution that the Confucian tradition, indeed Chinese culture in general, can offer to the global community is the idea of the "unity of Heaven and humanity" (*tianrenheyi*). Qian Mu in Taiwan characterized his understanding of this precept as the mutuality between the human heart-and-mind and the Way of Heaven.[1] Tang Junyi of Hong Kong emphasized "immanent transcendence," meaning that since Heaven confers our nature, we can apprehend the Mandate of Heaven by understanding our heart-and-mind. Thus, the transcendence of Heaven is immanently present in the communal and critical self-consciousness of human beings as a whole.[2] Similarly, Feng Youlan of Beijing rejected his previous commitment to the Marxist notion of struggle and underscored the value of harmony not only in the human world but also in the human–nature relationship.[3] Since all three of them articulated these positions toward the end of their lives, the unity of Heaven and Earth symbolizes the wisdom of the elders in the Sinic world. I would like to suggest that this ecological turn in contemporary New Confucianism is profoundly meaningful for China and the world.

An Ecological Turn

Qian Mu characterized this new realization as a major breakthrough in his thinking. When his wife and students raised doubts about the originality of this insight because the idea of the unity between Heaven and humanity is centuries old, Qian, already in his nineties, emphatically noted that his understanding was not a reiteration of conventional wisdom but a personal enlightenment, thoroughly original and totally novel.[4] Qian, as a cultural historian, is noted for his sympathetic appraisal of Chinese political thought and institutions as the unfolding of a rational humanist vision. Although liberal thinkers have criticized him as an apologist for traditional authoritarianism, he received much critical acclaim for his scholarly contribution to the chronology of classical Chinese philosophy, Chinese intellectual history of the last three centuries, and Zhu Xi's (1130–1200) thought. However, since he never showed any strong interest in Confucian metaphysics, his fascination with the idea of mutuality between the human heart-and-mind and the Way of Heaven and his assertion that this idea is a unique Chinese contribution to the world attracted a great deal of attention in Cultural China.[5]

Tang Junyi, on the other hand, presented his view from a comparative civilizational perspective. He contrasted Confucian self-cultivation with Greek, Christian, and Buddhist spiritual exercises, concluding that Confucianism's commitment to the world, combined with its profound reverence for Heaven, offered a unique contribution to human flourishing in the modern world. The Confucian worldview, rooted in earth, body, family, and community, is not "adjustment to the world,"[6] submission to the status quo, or passive acceptance of the physical, biological, social, and political constraints of the human condition. Rather, it is dictated by an ethic of responsibility informed by a transcendent vision. We become "spiritual" not by departing from or transcending our earth, body, family, and community but by working through them. Indeed, our daily life is not merely secular but is a response to a cosmological decree. Since the Mandate of Heaven that enjoins us to take part in the great enterprise of cosmic transformation is immanent in our nature, we are Heaven's partners. Life has purpose. In Tang's graphic description, the ultimate meaning of being human is to enable the "Heavenly virtue" (tiande) to flow through us. Therefore, Tang's project of reconstructing the humanist spirit is predicated on an anthropocosmic vision.[7]

Feng's radical reversal of his earlier position was an implicit critique of Mao Zedong's thought on struggle and the human capacity to conquer nature. His return to Zhang Zai's (1020–1077) philosophy of harmony signaled a departure from his Marxist phase and a re-presentation of his Confucian ideas prior to the founding of the People's Republic of China in 1949. The opening lines in Zhang Zai's Western Inscription state:

Heaven is my father and Earth is my mother, and even such a small creature
   as I finds an intimate place in their midst.
Therefore that which fills the universe I regard as my body and that which
   directs the universe I consider as my nature.
All people are my brothers and sisters, and all things are my companions.[8]

This idea of "forming one body with Heaven, Earth, and myriad things" is
a variation on the theme of the unity of Heaven and humanity. Accordingly, Feng characterizes the highest stage of human self-realization as the
embodiment of the "spirit of Heaven and Earth."[9]

   On the surface, the ecological turns of Qian, Tang, and Feng were
attempts to make the "local knowledge" of New Confucian humanism universally significant by retrieving the spiritual resources of the classical and
Neo-Confucian heritage. Their efforts to employ Confucian ideas to enunciate their final positions seem no more than personal choices for their own
distinctive styles of philosophizing. Yet they were obviously convinced
that their cherished tradition had a message for the emerging global village,
and they delivered it in the most appropriate way they knew. Their use of a
prophetic voice suggests that their Confucian message was addressed not
only to a Chinese audience but also to the human community as a whole.
They wished not merely to honor their ancestors but also to show that
they cared for the well-being of future generations.

   What was the ethos of Cultural China when they encountered the ecological issue? Were they even conscious of the ecological implications of
their final positions? Surely, Taiwan, Hong Kong, and, later, mainland
China were all involved in the restless march toward a Western-style
modernity. Modernization was the most powerful ideology in Cultural
China. The brave new world of industrialization so seriously challenged
China's traditional agriculture-based economy, family-centered social
structure, and paternalist government that the fate of the Confucian world
was thought to have been sealed in the early twentieth century.[10] Perhaps
Qian, Tang, and Feng were nostalgic for the kind of "universal brother-
hood" or "unity of all things" that Max Weber and others have long cri-
tiqued as being outmoded in our disenchanted modern world. Traces of
romantic sentiment can be seen in their writings. However, although long-
ing for a lost world, they discovered a new vitality and a new persuasive
power in the tradition. Qian's fascination with a seemingly age-old idea is
understandable. An appreciation of this renewed sense of intellectual
creativity merits a historical reminder.

Holistic Humanism

Prior to the impact of the modern West, Confucian humanism was the defining characteristic of the political ideology, social ethics, and family values in East Asia. Since the East Asian educated elite were all seasoned in Confucian classics, what the three contemporary thinkers advocated as a unique Confucian contribution to the human community was, in fact, the shared spiritual orientation of scholars and officials as well as the populace of China, Vietnam, Korea, and Japan. Of course, specifying the salient features of this shared spiritual orientation is not a simple matter. Region, class, gender, and ethnic differences have led to conflicts of interpretation not unlike those of the world's major religions (Hinduism, Buddhism, Judaism, Christianity, and Islam). Suffice it to present the famous "eight steps" in the first chapter of *The Great Learning* as a glimpse of what Confucian humanism purported to be:

> The ancients who wished to illuminate "illuminating virtue" all under Heaven first governed their states. Wishing to govern their states, they first regulated their families. Wishing to regulate their families, they first cultivated their personal lives. Wishing to cultivate their personal lives, they first rectified their hearts and minds. Wishing to rectify their hearts and minds, they first authenticated their intentions. Wishing to authenticate their intentions, they first refined their knowledge. The refinement of knowledge lay in the study of things. For only when things are studied is knowledge refined; only when knowledge is refined are intentions authentic; only when intentions are authentic are hearts and minds rectified; only when hearts and minds are rectified are personal lives cultivated; only when personal lives are cultivated are families regulated; only when families are regulated are states governed; only when states are governed is there peace all under Heaven. Therefore, from the Son of Heaven to the common people, all, without exception, must take self-cultivation as the root.[11]

Speaking directly to this passage, Wm. Theodore de Bary observed, "Chinese and Confucian culture, traditionally, was about settled communities living on the land, nourishing themselves and the land. It is this natural, organic process that Confucian self-cultivation draws upon for all its analogies and metaphors."[12] He further observed that the American Confucian/Christian farmer poet Wendell Berry's *Unsettling America* "makes the Confucian point":

> [H]ome and family are central, and we cannot hope to do anything about the environment that does not first establish the home—not just the self and family—as the home base for our efforts.

If we have to live in a much larger world, because ecological problems can only be managed on a global scale, the infrastructure between home locality and state (national or international) is also vital. But without home, we have nothing for the infrastructure, much less the superstructure, to rest on. This is the message of Wendell Berry; and also the lesson of Confucian and Chinese history.[13]

Underlying this project of human flourishing, from self-cultivation to universal peace, is a worldview that entails an overall vision of the proper niche of the human in the cosmos. The idea of home, in this sense, is expanded beyond the world. The human, so conceived, is an active participant in the cosmic process with responsibility of stewardship for the environment. A statement in the *Doctrine of the Mean* succinctly captures the essence of this line of thinking:

> Only those who are the most sincere (authentic, true, and real) can fully realize their own nature. If they can fully realize their own nature, they can fully realize human nature. If they can fully realize human nature, they can fully realize the nature of things. If they can fully realize the nature of things, they can take part in the transforming and nourishing process of Heaven and Earth. If they can take part in the transforming and nourishing process of Heaven and Earth, they can form a trinity with Heaven and Earth. (22)[14]

Obviously, this idea of the interrelation of Heaven, Earth, and humans was precisely what the three thinkers had in mind when they stressed the centrality of the precept of "the unity of Heaven and humanity," after it had been totally relegated to the background as a sort of archaic irrelevance for more than a century in Cultural China. The excitement of rediscovery of this central Confucian precept was a poignant reminder of how much had already been lost and how difficult it was to retrieve the elements that remained significant. What actually happened?

Secularization of Confucian Humanism

Although the fate of Confucian China since the Opium War of 1839 has been well documented, the story of the modern transformation of Confucian humanism has yet to be told. In the period between the Opium War and the founding of the People's Republic of China in 1949, Chinese society was inflicted with a major destructive event at least every decade: the Taiping Rebellion, the unequal treaties, the Western encroachment, the Sino-Japanese War of 1895, the Boxer Uprising, the 1911 Revolution, the internecine conflicts among the warlords, Japanese aggression, and the struggle between the Communists and the Nationalists. From 1949 until the "reform and opening" policy was put into practice in 1979, Chinese society was subjected to profoundly disruptive campaigns every five years or so: the Korean War, the Great Leap Forward, collectivization, and the Cultural Revolution, just to mention a few.

The highly politicized and ideologized master narrative about modern China's restless landscape is the story of the decline of the Middle Kingdom, principally due to Western imperialism, and of the Chinese people's struggle, against overwhelming odds, to regain their independence. It is the story of China's tortuous road toward modernization. The introduction of Marxism-Leninism, the emergence of the Chinese Communist Party, and the rise of Mao Zedong as the revolutionary leader are integral parts of the narrative. For Confucian humanism, the single most critical event was the intellectual effervescence of the 1919 May Fourth Movement. The iconoclastic attack on Confucianism, an aspect of the May Fourth ethos, was explained in simplistic utilitarian terms: to save the nation, it is imperative that we transcend our "feudal past" to learn from the modern West. The sole criterion for judging the value of Confucianism was its compatibility with modernization as defined in Western values. It was the modernist turn that definitively restructured Confucian humanism. Certainly ecological concerns were not on the agenda.

Some scholars have noticed the paradox in the May Fourth approach to national crisis. The intellectuals' totalistic rejection of the Confucian tradition and the thorough commitment to the well-being of China as a civilization-state compelled them to find a new cultural identity and to reject the mainstream thought that, for centuries, had defined Chinese polity and society.[15] Although a group of sophisticated intellectuals tried to tap the rich resources of non-Confucian traditions, such as Mohism, Legalism, Daoism, and folk religions, to formulate new visions of being Chinese, the scholarly community's general tendency was to equate modernization with Westernization. As a result, Confucian humanism lost much of its persuasive power. The courage to transcend the "feudal past" was considered imperative for China to emerge as an independent nation. Ironically, nationalism was the motivating force for China's intellectual elite to replace Confucian humanism and adopt the Enlightenment values of the modern West. Although wholesale Westernization was no more than a radical slogan, the Chinese perception of the Western source of wealth and power became the guiding principle for action.

Science and democracy were widely accepted as the most effective Western formulas for transforming China into a modern nation. It was not the search for truth or the dignity of the individual that prompted Chinese intellectuals to embrace them. Intent on making China wealthy and strong, scientism and populism were promoted as instruments of nation-building. They were techniques for the mass mobilization of material and human resources for China to rise again as a unified nation. The overall ethos was shaped by materialism, progressivism, utilitarianism, and instrumentalism. The Enlightenment mentality, as a form of secular humanism, was primarily an ideology for survival.

Under the shadow of the "feudal past," the New Confucians of the May Fourth generation stringently criticized Confucian practices deemed contradictory to the modern spirit. The Confucian ideology that asserted the authority of ruler over minister, father over son, and husband over wife (the so-called "three bonds") was demolished. Instead, the five-relationships based on mutual exhortation—affection between parent and child, rightness between ruler and minister, orderliness between older and younger siblings, division of labor between husband and wife, and trust among friends—were critically analyzed in a new context. Although the need for differentiation was obvious, social ethics predicated on hierarchy, status, gender, and age were severely scrutinized. Even family values were thoroughly reexamined. The naive belief that family is always congenial to wholesome self-development was seriously questioned. Arbitrary authority based on age, gender, and status was rejected. Any assertion, including statements in the classics, that evoked sentiments of authoritarianism, male chauvinism, or hierarchical mechanisms of control, was denounced. The viciousness with which Chinese intellectuals, including the New Confucians, deconstructed the Confucian heritage was unprecedented in Chinese history.

However, even at the height of the May Fourth generation's obsession with modernization as Westernization, some of the most original-minded New Confucians had already begun to question the worldview and ethics implicit in the Enlightenment project. Their views were profoundly meaningful for the Confucian ecological turn. Xiong Shili (1885–1968) reconfigured Confucian metaphysics through a critical analysis of the basic motifs of the Consciousness-Only school in Buddhism. Xiong insisted that the Confucian idea of the "great transformation" is predicated on the participation of the human in the cosmic process, rather than the imposition of human will on nature. He further observed that as a continuously evolving species, human beings are not created apart from nature but they emerge as an integral part of the primordial forces of production and reproduction. The vitality that engenders human creativity is the same energy that gives rise to mountains, rivers, and the great earth. Consanguinity exists between us and Heaven, Earth, and the myriad things. Since his philosophy is based on the *Book of Change*, the ethics of forming one body with nature looms large in his moral idealism.[16]

Liang Shuming (1893–1988) characterized the Confucian life-orientation as a balance between detachment from and aggression toward nature. Although he conceded that China had to learn from the West to enhance its fitness for competition for the sake of national survival, he prophesied that, in the long run, the Indian spirit of renunciation would prevail.[17] Liang may have anticipated Arnold Toynbee's ethical recommendation toward the end of his life:

> According to Toynbee, the twentieth century's intoxication with technology has led to the poisoning of our environment and has created the possibility that humanity may destroy itself. He believes that any solution to the current crisis depends on self-control. Mastery of the self, however, cannot be achieved through either extreme self-indulgence or extreme asceticism. The people of the twentieth-first century must learn to walk the middle path, the way of moderation.[18]

Although Liang did not develop a philosophy of his own, his comparative civilizational inquiry generated a strong current in reevaluating and revitalizing Confucianism at the time when Westernization dominated the intellectual scene.

Nevertheless, the modernist trajectory was so powerful that Confucian humanism was profoundly reconfigured. Neither Xiong nor Liang was able to sustain an argument in favor of a nonanthropocentric, not to mention eco-friendly, ethic. The rules of the game determining the relevance of Confucianism to China's modern transformation were changed so remarkably that attempts to present a Confucian idea for its own sake were largely ignored except for a small coterie of ivory-tower academicians. Under the ethos of saving the nation, the repertoire of modern Western ideas was relatively narrow. Even values of liberty and human rights became problematic because their contribution to nation-building, according to a restricted rational calculation, was considered neither direct nor urgent. The triumph of science and democracy was the result of a utilitarian consideration rather than a true commitment to Western values.

In a deeper sense, had China's modernist project followed the ideal of building democratic societies that are "just, participatory, sustainable, and peaceful,"[19] it could have had a salutary effect on China's overall conception of development. Issues of "eradicat[ing] poverty as an ethical, social, and environmental imperative," promoting human flourishing as well as material progress, "uphold[ing] the right of all, without discrimination, to a natural and social environment supportive of human dignity, bodily health, and spiritual well-being," "affirm[ing] gender equality and equity as prerequisites to sustainable development," and "ensur[ing] universal access to education, health care, and economic opportunity" would have been put on the national agenda for discussion. A Confucian sense of economic equality, social conscience, and political responsibility could have been relevant to and significant for debate and conversation on these vitally important matters. The cost of the secularization of Confucian humanism was high. As China turned its back on its indigenous resources for self-realization, it embarked on a course of action detrimental to its soul and its long-term self-interest.

Confucian Revival as a Modernist Ideology

The revival of Confucianism since the end of the Second World War, first in industrial East Asia and, more recently, in socialist East Asia, seems to suggest, on the surface, that the tradition has been successfully modernized. Actually, some of the most brilliant Confucian thinkers were instrumental in transforming the tradition from an agrarian mode of thinking to an ethics congenial to an industrial, cosmopolitan society. When China was going through major turmoil during the last five decades, the neighboring countries were not adversely affected. Moreover, industrial East Asia (Japan and the Four Mini-Dragons) achieved spectacular economic growth. For years, Confucianism enjoyed state sponsorship in Taiwan, South Korea, and Singapore. If Confucianism has survived as a political ideology in industrial East Asia, it seems to have transcended its "feudal past" and become a viable tradition shaping East Asian modernity.[20]

Mainland China, under the influence of Maoism, was openly hostile to Confucian theory and practice. Yet Confucian ideals manifested as habits of the heart have been pervasive in all walks of life, especially among the workers, farmers, and soldiers, in the People's Republic. Recently, socialist East Asia (China, Vietnam, and North Korea), challenged by industrial East Asia, has taken a more positive attitude toward its Confucian roots. North Korea has thoroughly politicized Confucian ideas for its cult of personality and family values. Vietnam has begun to retrieve its Confucian cultural resources. The Beijing government is now actively promoting Confucian ethics. Unfortunately, the Confucian Way that has been revitalized is at best a mixed blessing.

The Confucian ethics that has emerged in socialist East Asia, under the influence of the modernist ethos, is often a confirmation, rather than a critique, of the Enlightenment mentality. Because it takes instrumental rationality as its modus operandi, its precepts can be easily co-opted by social engineering as a mechanism of control. Scientism is the basic life orientation, and religion is equated with backwardness. This rationalist and scientistic ethos is thoroughly anthropocentric. Successful nation-building requires the accumulation of economic capital, enhancement of technical competence, upgrading of cognitive intelligence, and improvement of material conditions. On the other hand, little attention is paid to the long-term significance of "social capital," cultural competence, ethical intelligence, and spiritual values. The strong preference for technological solutions to well-defined problems and the pervasive influence of the technocratic mind-set mean that nonquantifiable issues are often totally ignored or inadequately managed. As a result, ecology and religion are seriously misunderstood. The gigantic hydraulic project of the Three Gorges Dam is an obvious example. The promotion of Confucianism as secular humanism is unfortunate because its rich resources for developing a truly ecumenical worldview and global ethics will not be tapped. Instead, a narrowly defined notion of progress, rather than a broad agenda for human flourishing, will be underscored.

Confucian humanism is not secular humanism; as an anthropocosmic vision, it emphatically rejects anthropocentrism as an impoverished idea of humanity. However, Confucians insist that we begin our journey of self-realization with the acknowledgment that we are concrete living human beings embedded in the world here and now. Although this positive attitude toward the world enables us to appreciate our natural and social environment as an inseparable dimension of our humanity, it also predisposes us to accept the status quo as intrinsically reasonable. The danger of abusing the reconstructed Confucian values as a neo-authoritarian justification for domination is a case in point.

Asian (Confucian) values have been enthusiastically promoted as positive factors in economic growth, political stability, and social cohesiveness. Self-discipline, duty-consciousness, diligence, frugality, networking, cooperation, consensus-formation, and harmony are identified as salient features of Confucian economic and political culture. At this critical juncture of Chinese history, these values might be considered more relevant for nation-building than exclusive concerns for liberty, rights, and individual autonomy. The discussion of Asian values, as a critique of the rhetoric of human rights, is itself a reflection of the Enlightenment mentality: anthropocentrism, social engineering, progressivism, scientism, and instrumental rationality. As long as the reconstructed Confucian humanism is incorporated into the discourse on modernity, its anthropocosmic insight is lost and its possibility of promoting "a holistic, non-anthropocentric, egalitarian, eco-friendly worldview respectful of nature and compassionate to all forms of life"[21] is also diminished.

Humanity as Sensitivity, Sympathy, and Empathy

What Qian Mu, Tang Junyi, and Feng Youlan offered is a new horizon, a re-presentation of Confucian humanism. Whether or not they conscientiously propounded their thoughts as a critique of the Enlightenment mentality and, by implication, the discourse on modernity, their new horizon extended beyond aggressive anthropocentrism and instrumental rationality. Furthermore, they presented an inclusive humanist vision by transcending the "either-or" mode of thinking.

The exclusive dichotomies—spirit/matter, mind/body, sacred/profane, and subject/object—characteristic of modern consciousness working directly out of the Enlightenment are in sharp contrast to the Confucian preference for the "nuanced between"[22] in interconnected binary structures. In the Confucian tradition, such categories as root/branch, surface/depth, former/latter, above/below, beginning/end, part/whole, and inner/outer are employed to indicate interaction, interchange, interdependence, and mutuality. The earth–human relationship, viewed in this perspective, is organically intertwined. Earth is not a material object "out there"; rather, it is our proper home. For spiritual self-realization, the human should become the steward, guardian, and protector of nature in an aesthetic, ethical, and religious sense.

How can we "respect Earth and life in all its diversity," "care for the community of life with understanding, compassion, and love," and "secure Earth's bounty and beauty for present and future generations"?[23] For one thing, we must transcend the view that earth is a profane matter, a soulless object, and a spiritless body. Rather, there is consanguinity between earth and us because we have evolved from the same vital energy that makes stones, plants, and animals integral parts of the cosmic transformation. We live with reverence and a sense of awe for the fecundity and creativity of nature as we open our eyes to what is near at hand:

> The heaven now before us is only this bright, shining mass; but when viewed in its unlimited extent, the sun, moon, stars, and constellations are suspended in it and all things are covered by it. The earth before us is but a handful of soil; but in its breadth and depth, it sustains mountains like Hua and Yüeh without feeling their weight, contains the rivers and seas without letting them leak away, and sustains all things. The mountain before us is only a fist-ful of straw; but in all the vastness of its size, grass and trees grow upon it, birds and beasts dwell on it, and stores of precious things (minerals) are dis-

covered in it. The water before us is but a spoonful of liquid, but in all its unfathomable depth, the monsters, dragons, fishes, and turtles are produced in them, and wealth becomes abundant because of it. (*Doctrine of the Mean* 26:9)[24]

This magnificent display of fecundity and creativity in nature is readily visible, but only through depth of self-knowledge can we fully appreciate our place in it and our learned capacity to establish a "spiritual communion" with it.

The recognition that earth, our home, is alive and dynamically evolving encourages us to protect "Earth's vitality, diversity, and beauty" as "a sacred trust."[25] However, our ability to build global security as a basis for a wholesome human–earth relationship has been significantly undermined by the dominant patterns of development in the world today. Despite quantifiable economic progress, injustice, inequality, poverty, and violence remain widespread. China, burdened by its huge population, is particularly concerned about diminishing natural resources for future consumption. How can China become a responsible member of the Earth community without losing sight of the basic needs of local communities.

China, in its quest for modernity, is aware of the need to embrace Enlightenment values, such as liberty, rationality, rule of law, human rights, and dignity of the individual. However, it is imperative that China mine its indigenous resources to strengthen salient features of Confucian ethics: distributive justice, sympathy, civility, responsibility, and human-relatedness. Otherwise, it will be difficult for China to enter the dialogue among civilizations and actively participate in exploring the possibilities of "a global civil society."[26] Fundamental changes in behavior, attitudes, and beliefs, conditioned by instrumental rationality and anthropocentrism, are required before China can make a positive contribution to "a shared vision of basic values to provide an ethical foundation for emerging world community."[27] For China to develop a sound environmental ethic, the nurturing of a culture of peace and the promotion of social and economic justice are essential.

Strictly speaking, Qian, Tang, and Feng were not ecological thinkers. However, implicit in their concern for the future of China as a civilization rooted in the spirituality of the Confucian humanist tradition is a cultural message with ethical and religious implications that are profoundly meaningful for the human–earth relationship. Concretely, they advocated the idea of humanity primarily as sensitivity, sympathy, and empathy. A unique feature of being human is the ability to commiserate with all modalities of being in the universe through loving care. Qian believed that this

tender-minded approach, a kind of soft power delicately maintaining balance and equilibrium in polity and society, was instrumental for China's
longevity as a civilization.[28] Tang, in his exploration of the core values in
Chinese philosophy, suggested that the Confucian focus on humanity,
which entails a warm heart and a brilliant mind rather than the exclusive
concern for rationality, may have helped to develop an all-encompassing
humanist vision.[29] Feng was particularly fascinated by Zhang Zai's four-
sentence articulation of the Confucian ideal of human responsibility:

> To establish the heart for Heaven and Earth
> To establish the destiny for all people
> To transmit the interrupted learning of the former sages
> To bring about peace and harmony for ten-thousand generations.[30]

The heart of Heaven and Earth, the destiny of all people, sagely learning,
and perpetual universal peace constitute, in time and space, the full distinctiveness of being human. In Feng's words, "the spirit of Heaven and Earth"
symbolizes the highest human aspiration.[31]

Surely, the myth of China as a culture of peace has been thoroughly
deconstructed, and the story that Sinicization implies acculturation and
moral persuasion is heatedly contested in the scholarly community. China,
as one of the longest continuous civilizations, has experienced more dramatic ruptures in thought and institutions than most other civilizations in
recent history. Collective amnesia, rather than historical consciousness, is
prevalent in modern Chinese intellectual discourse. China may evoke
images of longevity, stability, enduring patterns, and even unchanging per-
manence, but in reality, it is a restless landscape, constantly changing,
reconfiguring, and restructuring. Nevertheless, as Tang noted, the New
Confucian reconstruction of the humanist spirit as a response to the contemporary scene is not an attempt to mythologize China's past but an
effort to imagine what China can become in the future.[32] They believed
that humanity as sensitivity, sympathy, and empathy is not merely a Confucian ideal but also a moral imperative for the global community.

Wang Yangming's (1472–1529) "Inquiry on the Great Learning" offers
an elegantly simple interpretation of this idea in Neo-Confucian thought:

> The great man regards Heaven and Earth and the myriad things as one body.
> He regards the world as one family and the country as one person. As to
> those who make a cleavage between objects and distinguish between self and
> others, they are small men. That the great man can regard Heaven, Earth, and
> the myriad things as one body is not because he deliberately wants to do so,
> but because it is natural to the humane nature of his mind that he do so.[33]

By emphasizing the "humane nature of his mind" as the reason that the great person can embody the universe in his sensitivity, Wang made the ontological assertion that the ability to strike a sympathetic resonance with Heaven, Earth, and the myriad things is a defining characteristic of being human. Even ordinary people are capable of realizing such a seemingly lofty ideal. Inherent in the human mind (since the Chinese word *xin* entails both the cognitive and affective dimensions, it is often rendered as "heart" or, better, "heart-and-mind") is this limitless sensitivity that enables us to be receptive and responsive to all modalities of being in the universe (i.e., a blade of grass or a distant star). The great person who possesses this magnificently expansive sense of interconnectedness does not achieve it through deliberate action. Moreover, our limited capacity to achieve it is primarily the result of our negligence of our endowed nature.

To demonstrate that this is indeed the case, Wang offered a series of concrete examples:

> . . . when he sees a child about to fall into a well, he cannot help a feeling of alarm and commiseration. This shows that our humanity (*ren*) forms one body with the child. It may be objected that the child belongs to the same species. Again, when he observes the pitiful cries and frightened appearances of birds and animals about to be slaughtered, he cannot help feeling an "inability to bear" their suffering. This shows that his humanity forms one body with birds and animals. It may be objected that birds and animals are sentient beings as he is. But when he sees plants broken and destroyed, he cannot help a feeling of pity. This shows that his humanity forms one body with plants. It may be said that plants are living things as he is. Yet even when we see tiles and stones shattered and crushed, he cannot help a feeling of regret. This shows that his humanity forms one body with tiles and stones.[34]

These examples clearly indicate that "forming one body" is not a romantic idea about unity but a highly differentiated sense of interconnectedness. However, "forming one body" as the unlimited sensitivity of our heart-and-mind is rooted in our Heavenly-endowed nature.

Wang further observed that a realistic understanding of the human condition must also account for our inability to make any meaningful connections with anyone or anything:

> When it [our mind] is aroused by desires and obscured by selfishness, compelled by greed for gain and fear of harm, and stirred by anger, he will destroy things, kill members of his own species, and will do everything. In extreme cases, he will even slaughter his own brothers, and the humanity that forms one body will disappear completely.[35]

The ecological implications are obvious. We are capable of either creating a great harmony in the universe through building meaningful connections with humans and the cosmos or destroying the most intimate relationships at home because of desires, selfishness, greed, fear, and anger.

This deceptively simple notion of moral choice is predicated on a firm belief that human beings, as co-creators of the cosmic order, are responsible not only for themselves but also for Heaven, Earth, and the myriad things. The more we are able to move beyond our self-centeredness, the more we are empowered to realize ourselves. Yet we are rooted in the world as our proper home. We do not create a spiritual sanctuary outside the earth, body, family, and community. Our embeddedness in them allows us to form one body with children, birds, animals, plants, tiles, and stones; it is the reason that we embody others in our sensitivity. Moving beyond selfishness in an ever-expanding network of relationships enables us to realize the full potential of our humanity, for our self-realization is personal and communal rather than egoistically private.

As Heaven's partners, we are individually and communally entrusted with a sacred mission. To borrow Herbert Fingarette's felicitous phrase, our mission is to recognize "the secular as sacred."[36] Indeed, it is "to transform our earth, body, family, and community into the emanations of Heaven's inner virtue (de) which is creative vitality or simply creativity in itself."[37] Our recognition of the sanctity of the earth, the divinity of the body, the holiness of the family, and the sacredness of the community is the first step in transforming our sense of the outside world as "a collection of objects" into a "communion of subjects."[38] This holistic vision of the human is predicated on the idea of mutual responsiveness between Heaven and Humanity; the idea of "unity," far from being a static relationship, is the attainment of an ever-renewing dynamic process.

We in the modern world are acutely aware that we have seriously polluted our home, substantially depleted the unrenewable energy available to us, endangered numerous species, and gravely threatened our own existence. Obviously, we need to rethink the human–earth relationship. Since virtually all developing nations consider economic growth and the eradication of poverty the highest priorities, the development strategy directed by a modernist ideology has shoved environmental concerns to the side. The strong commitment to development as a positive good clearly outweighs the fear of ecological degradation. The urgency of the environmental crisis is often relegated to the background.

One of the most depressing scenarios of the human condition is that with increasing clarity we know what we ought to do so that environmental degradation will not seriously threaten the viability of our species; and yet, for structural, mental, conceptual, and other reasons we are moving ever closer to a point of no return. For those who have helped us scientifically, economically, politically, culturally, and religiously to see the self-destructive trajectory of development, it must be agonizing to realize that, despite all the effort and energy, the crying in the wilderness has not yet made a significant enough impact to turn the tide. Understandably, the revival of Confucian humanism is often attributed to its contribution to the work ethic, a necessary ingredient for development. Against this background, the advocacy of the precept of the unity between Humanity and Heaven is a countercurrent philosophical position, a cultural criticism—indeed, a vision of the future rather than nostalgic attachment to the past.

Confucian Humanism as an Anthropocosmic Vision

Qian, Tang, and Feng saw the possibility for Confucian humanism to occupy a new niche in comparative civilizational studies. As a partner in dialogue among civilizations, what message can Confucians deliver to other faith communities and to the global village as a whole? To put it simply, can Confucian humanism informed by an anthropocosmic vision deepen the conversation on religion and ecology? Specifically, can Confucian self-cultivation philosophy inspire a new constellation of family values, social ethics, and political ideology that will help Cultural China develop a sense of responsibility for the global community, both for its own benefit and for the improvement of the state of the world? Indeed, can Confucian thinkers enrich the spiritual resources and broaden the Enlightenment project's scope so that it can embrace religion and ecology?

The idea of the unity of Heaven and humanity implies four inseparable dimensions of the human condition: self, community, nature, and Heaven. The full distinctiveness of each enhances, rather than impedes, a thorough integration of the four. Self as a center of relationships establishes its identity by interacting with community variously understood, from the family to the global village and beyond. A sustainable harmonious relationship between the human species and nature is not only an abstract ideal but also a concrete guide for practical living. Mutual responsiveness between the human heart-and-mind and the Way of Heaven is the ultimate path for human flourishing. The following three salient features constitute the substance of the New Confucian ecological turn.

Fruitful Interaction between Self and Community

As Theodore de Bary has noted, "we cannot hope to do anything about the environment that does not first establish the home—not just the self and family—as the home base for our efforts."[39] Since the community as home must be extended to the "global village" and beyond, the self in fruitful interaction with community must transcend not only egoism and parochialism but also nationalism and anthropocentrism.

In practical ethical terms, self-cultivation, reminiscent of Toynbee's idea of self-mastery, is vital to the workability of this holistic humanist vision. Specifically, it involves a process of continuous self-transcendence, always keeping sight of one's solid ground on earth, body, family, and community. Through self-cultivation, the human heart-and-mind "expands in concentric circles that begin with oneself and spread from there to include successively one's family, one's face-to-face community, one's nation, and finally all humanity."[40]

> In shifting the center of one's empathic concern from oneself to one's family, one transcends selfishness. The move from family to community transcends nepotism. The move from community to nation overcomes parochialism, and the move to all humanity counters chauvinistic nationalism.[41]

While "[t]he project of becoming fully human involves transcending, sequentially, egoism, nepotism, parochialism, ethnocentrism, and chauvinist nationalism," it cannot stop at "isolating, self-sufficient humanism."[42]

A Sustainable Harmonious Relationship between the Human Species and Nature

The problem with secular humanism is its self-imposed limitation. Under its influence, our obsession with power and mastery over the environment to the exclusion of the spiritual and the natural realms has made us autistic to ecological concerns.[43] This de-spirited and de-natured version of the human has seriously undermined humanity's aesthetic, ethical, and religious significance. As a result, arrogant and aggressive anthropocentrism with little concern for religion and ecology has become the unstated worldview of scientism and materialism. Confucians, under the influence of modern discourse, are deeply concerned about improving material conditions through science and technology and promoting democracy as the surest way to attain an egalitarian society. Yet their preoccupation with nation-building, through the art of "managing the world" (*jingshi*), has overshadowed the spiritual and naturalist dimensions of their inclusive humanism.

Therefore, an ecological focus is a necessary corrective to the modernist discourse that has reduced the Confucian worldview to a limited and limiting secular humanism. Confucianism, appropriated by the modernist mind-set, has been misused as a justification for authoritarian polity. Only by fully incorporating the religious and naturalist dimensions into New Confucianism can the Confucian world avoid the danger of underscoring social engineering, instrumental rationality, linear progression, economic development, and technocratic management at the expense of a holistic anthropocosmic vision.

For the human species' continued existence, in principle and practice, a fundamental reformulation of our relationship to nature is critical. Confucianism must free itself from the modernist mind-set of economic development at all costs and reexamine its relationship to authoritarian polity as a precondition for its own creative transformation. The facilitation of sustainable and harmonious human–earth communication is a return to its own home base rather than a departure from its source. Indeed, the best way for the Confucians to attain the new is to reanimate the old so that the digression to secular humanism, under the influence of the modern West, is not a permanent diversion.

Mutual Responsiveness between the Human Heart-and-Mind and the Way of Heaven

In the appeal of scientists at the Global Forum Conference in Moscow in 1990, religious and spiritual leaders were challenged to envision the human–earth relationship in a new light:

> As scientists, many of us have had profound experiences of awe and reverence before the universe. We understand that what is regarded as sacred is more likely to be treated with care and respect. Our planetary home should be so regarded. Efforts to safeguard and cherish the environment need to be infused with a vision of the sacred.[44]

Obviously, the ecological question compels all religious traditions to reexamine their presuppositions with regard to the earth. It is not enough that one's spiritual tradition makes limited adjustments to accommodate the ecological dimension. The need is none other than the sacralization of nature. This may require a fundamental restructuring of the basic theology by taking the sanctity of the earth as a given. Implicit in the scientists' appeal is the necessity for a new theological thinking involving nature in the largely God–human relationship.

For the New Confucians, the critical issue is to underscore the spiritual dimension in the harmony with nature. Wing-tsit Chan notes in his celebrated *Source Book in Chinese Philosophy:*

> If one word could characterize the entire history of Chinese philosophy, that word would be *humanism*—not the humanism that denies or slights a

Supreme Power, but one that professes the unity of man and Heaven. In this sense, humanism has dominated Chinese thought from the dawn of its history.[45]

The "humanism that professes the unity of man and Heaven" is neither secular nor anthropocentric. Although it fully acknowledges that we are embedded in earth, body, family, and community, it never denies that we are in tune with the cosmic order. To infuse our earthly, bodily, familial, and communal existence with a transcendent significance is not only a lofty Confucian ideal but also a basic Confucian practice. In traditional China, under the influence of Confucian ritual and folk belief, the imperial court, the capital city, the literary temple, ancestral halls, official residences, schools, and private houses were all designed according to the "wind and water" principles. Although these principles, based on geomancy, can be manipulated to enhance one's fortune, they align human designs with the environment by enhancing intimacy with nature.

Confucians believe that Heaven confers our human nature and that the Way of Heaven is accessible to us through our self-knowledge. They also believe that to appreciate the Mandate of Heaven we must continuously cultivate ourselves. Nature, as an unending process of transformation rather than a static presence, is a source of inspiration for us to understand Heaven's dynamism. As the first hexagram in the *Book of Change* symbolizes, Heaven's vitality and creativity are incessant: Heaven always proceeds vigorously. The lesson for the human is obvious: we emulate the constancy and sustainability of Heaven's vitality and creativity by participating in human flourishing through "ceaseless effort of self-strengthening."[46] The sense of awe and reverence before the universe is prompted by our aspiration to respond to the ultimate reality that makes our life purposeful and meaningful. From either a creationist or an evolutionist perspective, we are indebted to Heaven, Earth, and the myriad things for our existence.

Mencius succinctly articulated this human attitude toward Heaven as self-knowledge, service, and steadfastness of purpose:

> When a man has given full realization to his heart, he will understand his own nature. A man who knows his own nature will know Heaven. By retaining his heart and nurturing his nature he is serving Heaven. Whether he is going to die young or to live to a ripe old age makes no difference to his steadfastness of purpose. It is through awaiting whatever is to befall him with a perfected character that he stands firm on his proper destiny. (*Mencius* 7A:1)[47]

Self-realization, in an ultimate sense, depends on knowing and serving Heaven. The mutuality of the human heart-and-mind and the Way of

Heaven is mediated through a harmonious relationship with nature. This sense of mutuality is a far cry from the imposition of the human will on Heaven and the human desire to conquer nature.

The Ecological Turn from a Global Perspective

Ironically, at the time Wing-tsit Chan made his extraordinary assertion about humanism, very much in the spirit of the ecological turn characterized by Qian, Tang, and Feng, the ethos of Cultural China, especially the People's Republic, was overwhelmed by secular humanism. On the occasion of the Stockholm Conference on the Environment in 1972, the Chinese delegation refused to sign the preamble rejecting limitations on economic growth and parameters restricting advances in science and technology. The obsession with development and faith in human ingenuity made the Chinese oblivious to environmental concerns.

The situation has improved somewhat, but the ethos of scientism and materialism still persists. Since the "reform and opening" policy of 1979 Beijing has transformed itself into a developmental state, thoroughly embracing the market mechanism as a strategy of globalization. At first blush, commercialism, mercantilism, and international competitiveness are characteristic of the current Chinese mentality. China as a growing economic, political, and military power is one of the most important players in the construction of a new world order. Prior to the "reform and opening" policy, China endured many travails on its long march toward modernization. For decades, however, its externally inflicted and self-imposed isolation prevented the internal calamities from having a major impact on the security and stability of the neighboring countries or on the Asia-Pacific region in general. The current situation is totally different. The Chinese economy and polity are such an integral part of the larger world that whither China is a local and national issue with profound regional and global implications. If secular humanism, whether socialist or Confucian, remains the ruling ideology in China, its adverse influence on the wholesome growth of Cultural China and the rest of the world, let alone the environment, will be tremendous.

The ecological turn, as an alternative vision, is particularly significant in this regard. To make it sustainable and, eventually, consequential in formulating policies, the need for public-spiritedness among intellectuals is urgent. The emergence of a public space in Cultural China provides a glimpse of hope. Although full-fledged civil societies in the Chinese cultural universe are found only in Taiwan and Hong Kong, the horizontal communication among public intellectuals in several sectors of society in the People's Republic has generated a new dynamism unprecedented in modern Chinese history. If we define public intellectuals as those who are politically concerned, socially engaged, and culturally sensitive (in the present context, we should add "religiously musical and ecologically conscientious"), they are already readily visible and audible on the political scene. Indeed, public intellectuals in academia, government, mass media, business, and social movements have the great potential of articulating a cultural message inherent in the rise of China as a civilization-state.

China has been victimized for more than one hundred and fifty years. As a victim, survivability has been its primary concern. China is no longer a victim but a rising power. What kind of psychology will guide the leadership as China enters the global community? If retaliation is not a viable option and sharing power has only a limited appeal for encouraging China to be a responsible player, what other motivations are relevant for China's new identity? Is China comfortable with the thought that its aspirations may depend on the persistent misery of the less fortunate areas of the world? Can China help to change the international rules of the game to make the world more equitable and humane? Will China decide to help facilitate a new world order that is, in theory and practice, nonhegemonic? How can China move beyond the mind-set of development defined exclusively in terms of wealth and power?

The first difficult step is to broaden the frame of reference for China's quest for modernization. So far, the obsession with the modern West (North America and Western Europe) has blinded China to many of its indigenous resources. I have been advocating, albeit with only limited success, that the Chinese intellectual community take India as a reference society and Indic civilization as a reference culture for China's future development. Certainly, China would do well to avoid negative examples in India's economic strategies, political arrangements, and social practices; the rise of militant Hindu nationalism and communal conflicts are obvious cases. Yet India as the most populous democracy, with millions of English-speaking intellectuals, bureaucrats, entrepreneurs, and social activists, has a great deal to offer for China's self-reflexivity. In the present context, India's most valuable asset is its richly textured spiritual landscape. As spiritual matters go, India is a major exporting civilization. Liang Shuming predicted in 1923 that the Indian way of life would eventually prevail, even though he strongly urged China to learn from the West.[48] China's iconoclastic attack on tradition is in sharp contrast to India's continuous reaffirmation of her spiritual roots. What lessons can Chinese intellectuals learn from the Indian experience?

If China takes India seriously as a reference society and culture, she will begin to appreciate her indigenous Mahayana Buddhist heritage. Anti-religious humanism, vividly captured by Hu Shi's reflection on the Indianization of Sinic civilization, can be substantially transformed.[49] Already, in Taiwan, Hong Kong, and the Chinese Diaspora, Humanist Buddhism is the most powerful religious movement.[50] Its impact on economic culture, social ethics, political behavior, moral education, and, above all, environmental ethics has been considerable. If Mahayana Buddhism reemerges in China as a major spiritual force, religious Daoism may have a chance to flourish, and Confucian humanism that professes the unity of Heaven and humanity, rather than secular humanism, will prosper.

Since Tibet regards India as its spiritual source, the Chinese political authority and intellectual elite could better appreciate Tibet as a culture if India were to reenter the Chinese mind as a reference. Beijing could deepen its understanding and not deal with the Tibet question simply as a political issue threatening national unity. As a result, the ethnic conflicts, laden with religious import, between Han Chinese and the nationalities (Uighurs and Mongols as well as Tibetans) could be handled with more cultural sophistication and ethical intelligence. An added benefit of this value-orientation is that new religions will be better assessed and their possible contribution to social solidarity better recognized. Assuming that religion will be a powerful force shaping the cultural landscape of the new China, a fundamental change in the social constructivist approach to nation-building will be unavoidable. If the Chinese political authority and intellectual elite become more attuned to spiritual matters, they will develop a more reverential attitude toward their own indigenous traditions, and consequently they will become more sensitive to ecological concerns.

Still, even if China is able to broaden her frame of reference to include non-Western experiences in her modernization strategy, notably the Indian experiment, her participation as an active contributor and a responsible member of the international community depends primarily on interaction with the West, particularly the United States. With a view toward the cultivation of what U.N. Secretary General Kofi Annan has advocated as a culture of peace, the Sino–American relationship is perhaps the single most important bilateral relationship in the world today. Unfortunately, the asymmetry between China's obsession with the United States and the American inattention to China has made the relationship extremely complex and difficult. Since the Tiananmen tragedy in 1989, China has often been portrayed in the American media as a pariah state. Issues of human rights, religious freedom, Tibet, Taiwan, and trade have made China the target of criticism from the radical left to the Christian right. This unusual alliance in American politics has significantly tarnished the image of China as a responsible member of the international community in the eyes of the general public. Yet the United States is in a unique position to offer an alternative model for China's modernization.

It should be noted that cooperation between American and Chinese scientists in dealing with the environment has been cordial and productive. Realistically, however, this kind of collaboration, under the strict protocol of scientific exchanges, cannot be easily broadened to include critical ideological issues on the agenda. Yet it seems obvious that involving China's active participation in international projects dealing with environmental degradation, such as global warming, is critical from a long-term perspective.[51]

In a broader picture, how the Chinese leadership deals with domestic affairs, such as political dissent, religious cults, freedom of speech, and the cultural expressions of its minorities, will be taken seriously by the international community concerned with human rights. This, in turn, will have a major impact on China's acceptability by the American general public. On the other hand, from the Chinese perspective, the United States, as the only superpower, ought to be more obligated to play an active and constructive role in improving the state of the world. Given that only 5 percent of the world's population produces 22 percent of the globe's greenhouse gasses[52] and that the average American standard of living is beyond the wildest imagining of the overwhelming majority of the Chinese people, questions of fairness and distributive justice must be raised. It is not surprising that China criticizes America's use of national interest as its guiding principle in foreign policy and as a pretext for acting contrary to the well-being of the international community; it is a clear sign that the United States is not willing to assume global moral leadership.

Even so, a wholesome Sino–American relationship based on a series of fruitful dialogues on religion and ecology, as well as human rights, trade, education, science, and technology, is possible, desirable, and necessary. On the Chinese side, social Darwinian competitiveness will have to be replaced by a much broader vision of human flourishing. If China widens her frame of reference, which seems inevitable, she will find her niche in an increasingly interdependent pluralistic world, rather than in the narrow trajectory of linear progression. In addition to India, many other non-Western societies, such as Southeast Asia, Latin America, the Islamic Middle East, and Africa, will become relevant to China's intellectual and spiritual self-definition. For the United States, the need to transform herself from a teaching civilization into a learning culture is obvious. As a great immigrant society, the United States has been a vibrant learning culture oriented toward Europe for centuries. Since the end of the Second

World War, the American self-image as a tutor of Confucian East Asia has been so much ingrained in the public consciousness that the teacher–disciple relationship, as in the case of John Dewey and Hu Shi/Feng Youlan, has been accepted as the norm. It is now time to work at a new equilibrium of mutual learning and appreciation.

The Copenhagen Social Summit in 1995 identified poverty, unemployment, and social disintegration as three serious threats to the solidarity of the human community. Globalization enhances localization. Our community compressed into a "village," far from being integrated, blatantly exhibits difference, differentiation, and outright discrimination. For the Southern Hemisphere to appreciate the environmental movements of the Northern Hemisphere, the perceived contradiction between ecological and developmental imperatives will have to be resolved. The North's advocacy of elegant simplicity as an alternative lifestyle is not persuasive, if the South considers development, in the basic material sense, a necessary condition for survival. China as a developing society has been thoroughly seasoned in the Southern mentality. If her sense of responsibility is not simply confined to nation-building, China can become a constructive partner on global environmental issues. She can be encouraged to become so if the North, especially the United States, demonstrates moral leadership. But without encouragement and reciprocal respect from the developed countries, it is unlikely that China will independently embark on such a path. Actually, on a limited scale, mutually beneficial dialogues on religion and ecology, as well as human rights, trade, education, science, and technology, between China and the United States, on the one hand, and the European Union, on the other, have already begun.

Given the current political ethos in China, religion is a particularly delicate matter. However, religion as a vibrant social force is widely recognized by public intellectuals in government, the academy, business, and the mass media. Whether or not religion will play an active role in shaping China's development strategy is perhaps the single most important indicator for assessing China's new cultural identity. The possibility of a sound environmental ethic depends heavily on China's ability to transcend secular humanist nationalism. In a broader context, for religious and spiritual leaders to play a significant role on the global scene in articulating a shared approach to environmental degradation, they must assume the responsibility of public intellectuals. As the Millennium Conference at the United Nations in September 2000 clearly showed, unless religious and spiritual leaders can rise above their faith communities to address global issues as public intellectuals, their messages will be misread, distorted, or ignored. Notwithstanding the demands for recognition and representation, identity politics is detrimental to fostering a global ethic for human survival and flourishing.

Religious and spiritual leaders should develop, as William Vendley suggests, in addition to their primary language of faith, a secondary language (which, I think, may very well be an emerging universal language) to facilitate their engagement in nurturing a culture of peace in our conflict-ridden pluralistic societies.[53] The Confucians seem to have developed a secondary language as the basic cultural competence of an engaged scholar. In fact, their primary language has been so integrated in their secondary language that they have difficulty making the distinction between them. Assuming that the role of the public intellectual has become a defining characteristic of being a Confucian may explain why the term "Confucian" has often been used in interreligious dialogues as an adjective to describe the political concern, social engagement, and cultural sensitivity of Christians, Buddhists, and Muslims. Thus a Confucian Christian, Buddhist, or Muslim must aspire to the role of the public intellectual. A priest whose ultimate concern is the Kingdom yet to come would not choose to be a Confucian; nor would a monk who is totally devoted to the journey to the other shore or a Sufi who is primarily involved in the purification of the soul. However, socially committed Christians and Muslims, not to mention Humanist Buddhists, can identify themselves as Confucians also.

Toward a New Worldview and Global Ethic

The New Confucian ecological turn clearly shows that an inseparable aspect of a sustainable human–earth relationship is the creation of harmonious societies and benevolent governments through the self-cultivation of all members of the human community. At the same time, Confucians insist that being attuned to the changing patterns in nature is essential for harmonizing human relationships, formulating family ethics, and establishing a responsive and responsible government. As Mary Evelyn Tucker notes:

> The whole Confucian triad of heaven, earth, and humans rests on a seamless yet dynamic intersection between each of these realms. Without harmony with nature and its myriad changes, human society and government is threatened.[54]

Since each person's self-cultivation is essential for social and political order, the public intellectual is not an elitist but an active participant in the daily affairs of the life world. The Confucian idea of a concerned scholar, rather than the philosopher, prophet, priest, monk, or guru, seems the most appropriate model. The Confucians remind us that, in order to foster a wholesome worldview and a healthy ecological ethic, we need to combine our aspiration for a harmonious relationship with nature with a concerted effort to build a just society.

Political leadership in China is in an advantageous position to "promote a culture of tolerance, nonviolence, and peace."[55] Chinese people are well disposed by Mahayana Buddhism and religious Daoism as well as by inclusive Confucian humanism to "treat all living beings with respect and consideration." An increasing number of public intellectuals in the academic community have already forcefully articulated the wish to "integrate into formal education and life-long learning the knowledge, values, and skills needed for a sustainable way of life." The major challenge is democratization at all levels, which must begin with greater transparency and accountability in governance at the top. As rule of law rather than rule by law is widely accepted as the legitimate way to provide access to justice for all, the ideal of "inclusive participation in decision making" will no longer be unimaginable.

New Confucians fully acknowledge that in their march toward modernization in the cause of nation-building, their primary language has been so fundamentally reconstructed that it is no longer a language of faith but a language of instrumental rationality, economic efficiency, political expediency, and social engineering. But they are now recovering from that modernist malaise. Through their own creative transformation, their re-presentation of the Confucian anthropocosmic vision will provide sources of inspiration for a new worldview and a new ethic. The New Confucian ecological turn has great significance for China's spiritual self-definition, for it urges China to return to its home base and rediscover its own soul. This, in turn, will be beneficial to the sustainable future of the global community.

Notes

1. Qian Mu's last essay, "Zhongguo wenhua dui renlei weilai keyou de gongxian" [The Possible Contribution of Chinese Culture to the Future of Humankind], first appeared as a newspaper article in the *United News* in Taiwan (September 26, 1990). It was reprinted, with a lengthy commentary from his widow, Hu Meiqi, in *Zhongguo wenhua* [Chinese Culture], no. 4 (August 1991): 93–96.

2. For an elaborate discussion of this, see Tang Junyi, *Shengming cunzai yu xinling jingjie* [Life Existence and the Spiritual Realms] (Taipei: Xuesheng Book Co., 1977), 872–88.

3. Feng Youlan, *Zhongguo xiandai zhexueshi* [History of Modern Chinese Philosophy] (Guangzhou: Guangdong People's Publishers, 1999), 251–54.

4. See Hu Meiqi's commentary (n. 1 above).

5. For example, Ji Xianlin of Peking University, Li Shenzhi of the Chinese Academy of Social Sciences, Cai Shangsi of Fudan University, and a number of other senior scholars all enthusiastically responded to Qian's article. My short reflection appeared in *Zhonghua wenhua* [Chinese Culture], no. 10 (August 1994): 218–19.

6. Max Weber, *The Religion of China: Confucianism and Taoism*, trans. Hans H. Gerth (Glencoe, Ill.: Free Press, 1951), 235.

7. Tang Junyi, *Shengming cunzai yu xinling jingjie*, 833–930.

8. Chang Tsai [Zhang Zai], "The Western Inscription," in Wing-tsit Chan, trans., *A Source Book in Chinese Philosophy* (Princeton, N.J.: Princeton University Press, 1963), 497.

9. Feng Youlan, *Xin yuanren* [New Origins of Humanity], in *Zhenyuan liushu* [Six Books of Feng Youlan in the 1930s and 1940s] (Shanghai: East China Normal University Press, 1996), 2:626–49.

10. Joseph Levenson, *Confucian China and Its Modern Fate: A Trilogy* (Berkeley: University of California Press, 1968).

11. "The Text" of *The Great Learning*; see Chan, *Source Book*, 86. My translation.

12. Wm. Theodore de Bary, "'Think Globally, Act Locally,' and the Contested Ground Between," in *Confucianism and Ecology*, edited by Mary Evelyn Tucker and John Berthrong (Cambridge, Mass.: Harvard University, Center for the Study of World Religions, 1998), 32.

13. Ibid., 32–33.

14. See Tu Wei-ming, *Centrality and Commonality: An Essay on Confucian Religiousness* (Albany: State University of New York Press, 1989), 77. This translation is slightly different.

15. See Lin Yu-sheng, *The Crisis of Chinese Consciousness: Radical Antitraditionalism in the May Fourth Era* (Madison: University of Wisconsin Press, 1979); and Vera Schwarcz, *The Chinese Enlightenment: Intellectuals and the Legacy of the May Fourth Movement of 1919* (Berkeley: University of California Press, 1986).

16. Xiong Shili, *Xin weishilun* [New Theory on Consciousness-only] (reprint, Taipei: Guangwen Publishers, 1962), vol. 1, chap. 4, pp. 49–92.

17. Liang Shuming, *Dongxi wenhua jiqi zhexue* [Eastern and Western Cultures and Their Philosophies] (reprint, Taipei: Wenxue Publishers, 1979), 200–201.

18. Daisaku Ikeda, *A New Humanism* (New York: Weatherhill, 1996), 120.

19. For quotations in this paragraph, see The Earth Charter, at www.earth charter.org.

20. See Tu Wei-ming, ed., *Confucian Traditions in East Asian Modernity: Moral Education and Economic Culture in Japan and the Four Mini-Dragons* (Cambridge, Mass.: Harvard University Press, 1996).

21. Donald K. Swearer, "Principles and Poetry, Places and Stories: The Resources of Buddhist Ecology," *Daedalus* 130, no. 4 (Fall 2001): 225–41.

22. I am indebted to Benjamin Schwartz for this idea.

23. The Earth Charter (n. 19 above).

24. Trans. Wing-tsit Chan, *Source Book*, 109.

25. The Earth Charter.

26. Ibid.

27. Ibid.

28. Qian Mu, *Cong Zhongguo lishi laikan Zhongguo minzuxing ji Zhongguo wenhua* [Chinese National Character and Chinese Culture from the Perspective of Chinese History] (Hong Kong: Chinese University Press, 1979).

29. Tang Junyi, "Chinese Culture and the World," in *Zhonghua wenhua yu dangjin shijie* [Chinese Culture and the World Today] (Taipei: Xuesheng Publishers, 1975), 865–929.

30. Feng Youlan, *Zhongguo xiandai zhexueshi*, 245–49.

31. Ibid.

32. Tang Junyi, *Renwen jingshen zhi chongjian* [The Reconstruction of the Humanist Spirit] (Taipei: Xuesheng Book Co., 1991).

33. Wang Yangming, "Inquiry on the Great Learning," in Chan, *Source Book*, 659.

34. Ibid., 659–60. Since Wang Yangming wishes to demonstrate that even the mind of the small man can form one body with all things, he uses "he" rather than "we" in the text.

35. Ibid., 660.

36. Herbert Fingarette, *Confucius: The Secular as Sacred* (New York: Harper & Row, 1972).

37. Tu Weiming, "Crisis and Creativity: A Confucian Response to the Second Axial Age," in *Doors of Understanding: Conversations in Global Spirituality in Honor of Ewert Cousins*, ed. Steven L. Chase (Quincy, Ill.: Franciscan Press, 1997), 414.

38. Thomas Berry, "Ethics and Ecology" (a paper delivered to the Harvard Seminar on Environmental Values, Harvard University, April 9, 1996), 2.

39. De Bary, "'Think Globally and Act Locally.'"

40. Huston Smith, *The World's Religions* (San Francisco: HarperSan Francisco, 1991), 182.

41. Ibid.

42. Ibid., 186–87.

43. For his reference to this "autism," see Berry, "Ethics and Ecology," 5.

44. Quoted in Mary Evelyn Tucker, "The Emerging Alliance of Religion and Ecology," in *Doors of Understanding*, ed. Chase, 111.

45. Chan, *Source Book*, 3.

46. *Yijing* (*Book of Change*), *jianqua* (hexagram 1), *xiang* (image).

47. See D. C. Lau, trans., *Mencius* (Harmondsworth: Penguin, 1970), 182. The first line is my translation.

48. Liang Shuming, *Dongxi wenhua jiqi zhexue*, 199–201.

49. Hu Shi, "The Indianization of China," in *Harvard Tercentenary Conference of Arts and Sciences, Independence, Convergence and Borrowing in Institutions, Thought and Art* (New York: Russell & Russell, 1964).

50. For a thorough discussion of one of the prominent movements, see Stuart Chandler, "Establishing a Pure Land on Earth: The *Foguang* Buddhist Perspective on Modernization and Globalization" (Ph.D. diss. Committee on the Study of Religion, Harvard University, June 2000).

51. Michael B. McElroy notes that the future of controlling global emissions of carbon dioxide "will depend in large measure on what happens in large developing countries such as China, India and Indonesia" (see "Perspectives on Environmental Change: A Basis for Action," *Daedalus* 130, no. 4 [Fall 2001]: 16).

52. Ibid.

53. William Vendley, "The Multireligious Engagement of Civil Society: The Need for Bilingualism," in *Toward A Global Civilization? The Contribution of Religions*, ed. Patricia M. Mische and Melissa Merkling (New York: Peter Lang, 2001).

54. Tucker, "Emerging Alliance of Religion and Ecology," 120.

55. Quotations in this paragraph are from The Earth Charter.

Glossary

報　Ben/pao—reciprocity, mutuality, mutual regard, reciprocal relations

本　Ben/pen—root, fundamental, essential

本體　Benti/pen-t'i—the essential or fundamental root

本心　Benxin/pen-hsin—fundamental heart-mind

變　Bian/pian—to change gradually across time

不仁　Buren/pu-jen—insensitive, dead, without human feeling

誠　Cheng/ch'eng—sincere, integrity, self-realization, actualization of the true creative potential of human affairs, even of the cosmos

成　Cheng/ch'eng—to complete an action or process; something which is complete

道　Dao/tao—The Way, a path, way of proper conduct, to lead through, matrix of all the things and events of the cosmos

大同　Datong/ta-t'ung—the Great Harmony (political), perfected state of affairs

德　De/te—virtue, potency, excellence, the power of virtue; that which has ethical power

法　Fa—law; also means *dharma* in Buddhism

改　Gai/kai—to correct, reform, improve

感應　Ganying/kan-ying—activity and response; stimulus and response; correlative action and response; often cited as the foundation for correlative cosmology

格物　Gewu/ko-wu—examination of things and events

公　Gong/kung—public good, the public sphere of activity

工夫　Gongfu/kung-fu—effort, action, activity

鬼神　Guishen/kuei-shen—spiritual forces of the cosmos; positive and negative spiritual powers or forces; also related to the heavenly and earthly aspects of the human soul; shen is positive and kuei is the negative force of spirit

和   He—harmony of a situation or person

化   Hua—to transform utterly such that A becomes B

幾   Ji/chi—the subtle, incipient

教   Jiao/chiao—teaching or instruction, education

敬   Jing/ching—reverence, respect, reverence, the concentration of
        reverence on the moral path

君子 Junzi/chün-tzu—gentleman or exemplary person; originally
        meant the son of a prince or a nobleman; second in virtue only
        to the sage

理   Li—principle that orders all things, persons, and events, form, pat-
        tern, norm, the defining pattern or principle of the cosmos

禮   Li—ritual, civility, proper social order, customs, etiquette, ritual
        propriety

立   Li—to establish, set up, to make firm (in virtue and conduct)

良知 Liangzhi/liang-chih—innate good knowledge

理一分殊
        Liyi fenshu/li-yi fen-shu—principle (pattern, norm) is one, the
        manifestations are many

立志 Lizhi/li-chih—establish the will, make the will secure

明   Ming—brightness, brilliant, clarity (or person, purpose, or action)

明德 Mingde/ming-te—clear character or virtue, illustrious virtue

明明德 Ming mingde/ming-ming-te—manifesting the clear character or
        virtue

命   Ming—mandate, command, order, destiny, fate

末   Mo—branch (of a plant), something that branches off from the
        root of a thing, person, event or situation

內外 Neiwai—inner and outer

氣   Qi/ch'i—vital force, vital energy, matter-energy, vapor, the
        dynamic element of all that is

器   Qi/ch'in—concrete thing, something of substance

遷   Qian/ch'ien—to change from one place to another

親   Qin/ch'in—relatives or kin

情   Qing/ch'ing—emotions, feelings, desires, the developed nature of
        a person; the vital force of a person or thing

仁   Ren/jen—humaneness, humanity, human-heartedness, benevo-
        lence, first of the Confucian virtues, love

人欲 Renyu/jen-yu—human emotion, human passions, passionate
        human feelings or emotions

儒   Ru/ju—scholar, ritual specialist, Chinese term for what is called a
        Confucian

善　Shan—good, perfect, excellent, felicity

善人　Shanren/shan-jen—good, adept person, someone who achieves the good, excellent, or perfect

神　Shen—spirit, spiritual beings, deities, immortals, souls

聖人　Shengren/sheng-jen—sage, the perfected person

詩　Shi/shih—poetry

士　Shi/shih—scholar, literati, official, member of the gentry

恕　Shu—altruism, reciprocity, empathy, to extend feelings to others

私　Si/ssu—private, personal

四端　Siduan/ssu-tuan—four roots or seeds of virtue

太極　Taiji/t'ai-chi—the Supreme Polarity or the Supreme Ultimate

天　Tian/t'ien—Heaven; sky, the blue sky, the High God of the Zhou people

天下　Tiangxia/t'ien-hsia—All under Heaven, everyone and everything

天理　Tianli/t'ien-li—Heavenly principle, ultimate principle or norm of the good or perfect

天命　Tianming/t'ien-ming—Mandate of Heaven

體認　Tiren/t'i-jen—realization through personal experience

體用　Tiyong/t'i-yung—substance and function

未發　Weifa/wei-fa—not yet manifested

文　Wen—culture, what the sage and worthies seek to create for human society

無　Wu—nonbeing, nothingness

五常倫　Wuchang lun/wu-ch'ang lun—five constant virtues: humaneness, righteousness, ritual/civility, wisdom or discernment, and faithfulness

無極　Wuji/wu-chi—the Ultimate of Non-polarity, the infinite

物事　Wushi/wu-shih—things and events

無爲　Wuwei—/wu-wei—uncontrived action; non-action

五行　Wuxing/wu-hsing—five phases of the vital force and yin-yang modalities; air, wood, fire, earth, and metal

孝　Xiao/hsiao—filial piety, filiality, deference, respect

信　Xin/hsin—faithfulness, honesty, integrity of thought, word, and action; virtue of friendship, credibility

心　Xin/hsin—heart-mind; seat of the intelligence; most refined aspect of the vital force

性　Xing/hsing—human nature, natural tendencies, nature as principle, norm or pattern

形而上
    Xingershang/Hsing-er-shang—what is above (shape); incorporeal
形而下
    Xingerxia/hsing-er-hsia—what is below (shape); corporeal
形名 Xingming/hsing-ming—actuality and name
修身 Xiushen/hsiu-shen—self-cultivation of the mind-heart of the person
虚 Xu/hsü—vacuous, blank, empty
玄 Xuan/hsüan—profound, mysterious, deep
學 Xue/hsüeh—study; the study or cultivation of the Dao is education
易 Yi/i—change or transformation, processive
意 Yi/i—intentions, motivations
義 Yi/i—righteousness, moral, appropriateness, second of the cardinal virtues
已發 Yifa/I-fa—already manifested (as certain qualities or objects and events)
陰陽 Yin-yang—yin-yang forces; positive and negative, light and dark, male and female
有 You/yu—being present, having, existing, to have certain qualities, being in a certain state
欲 Yu/yü—desire, passion, emotion
正 Zheng/cheng—rectification, to make correct, to bring order
正心 Zhengxin/cheng-hsin—established or rectified mind-heart
政 Zheng/cheng—government, politics, the public realm
志 Zhi/chih—will, fortitude of character
至 Zhi/chih—fully develop, cultivate, to reach a goal
知 Zhi/chih—knowledge, intelligence, to realize, discernment, wisdom
至知 Zhizhi/chih-chih—the extension of knowledge or capacity to know
中 Zhong/Chung—centrality, focus, equilibrium, being centered in proper virtue
忠 Zhong/chung—loyalty, being completely committed
忠恕 Zhongshu/chung-shu—conscientiousness and altruism
中庸 Zhongyong/Chung-yung—Centrality and Commonality, locus for achieving harmony; title of one of the Four Books
自然 Ziran/tzu-jan—spontaneity, uncontrived action, complete freedom

General Bibliography

General Reference Works:
Asian and Chinese Thought

Ames, Roger T., Wimal Dissanayke, Thomas P. Kasulis, eds.
  1994   *Self as Person in Asian Theory and Practice*. Albany: State University of New York Press.

Chan, Wing-tsit
  1953   *Religious Trends in Modern China*. New York: Columbia University Press; Octagon Books, reprint 1969.
  1963   *A Source Book in Chinese Philosophy*. Princeton, N.J.: Princeton University Press.

Chang, Kang-I, and Huan Saussy, eds.
  1999   *Women Writers of Traditional China: An Anthology of Poetry and Criticism*. Stanford, Calif.: Stanford University Press.

Ch'en, Kenneth K. S.
  1964   *Buddhism in China: A Historical Survey*. Princeton, N.J.: Princeton University Press.
  1973   *The Chinese Transformation of Buddhism*. Princeton, N.J.: Princeton University Press.

Ching, Julia
  1993   *Chinese Religions*. Maryknoll, N.Y.: Orbis Books.

de Bary, Wm. Theodore, et al., eds.
  1999,   *Sources of Chinese Tradition*. 2 vols. 2nd ed. New York: Columbia
  2000   University Press.
  2001   *Sources of Japanese Tradition*. 2 vols. 2nd ed. New York: Columbia University Press.

Fung, Yu-lan
  1947   *The Spirit of Chinese Philosophy*. Translated by E. R. Hughes. Boston: Beacon Press.
  1952,   *A History of Chinese Philosophy*. 2 vols. Translated by Derk Bodde.
  1953   Princeton, N.J.: Princeton University Press.

Jochim, Christian
  1986   *Chinese Religions: A Cultural Perspective*. Englewood Cliffs, N.Y.: Prentice-Hall, Inc.

513

Lee, Peter H.
   1997,   *Sourcebook of Korean Civilization.* 2 vols. New York: Columbia
   2000   University Press.
Liu, Shu-hsien, and Robert E. Allinson, eds.
   1988   *Harmony and Strife: Contemporary Perspectives, East & West.* Hong
                Kong: Chinese University Press.
Loewe, Michael
   1993   *Early Chinese Texts: A Bibliographic Guide.* Early China Special
                Monograph Series 2. Berkeley, Calif.: Institute of East Asian Studies.
Lopez, Donald S., Jr.
   1996   *Religions of China in Practice.* Princeton, N.J.: Princeton University
                Press.
Martinson, Paul Varo
   1987   *A Theology of World Religions: Interpreting God, Self, and World in
                Semitic, Indian, and Chinese Thought.* Minneapolis, Minn.: Augsburg
                Publishing House.
Moore, Charles A.
   1967   *The Chinese Mind: Essentials of Chinese Philosophy and Culture.* Hon-
                olulu: University of Hawaii Press.
Mote, Frederick W.
   1989   *Intellectual Foundations of China.* 2nd ed. New York: McGraw-Hill
                Publishing Company.
Nakamura, Hajime
   1965   *Ways of Thinking of Eastern Peoples: India, China, Tibet, and Japan.*
                Honolulu: East-West Center Press.
   1975   *Parallel Developments: A Comparative History of Ideas.* Tokyo:
                Kodansha.
Overmeyer, Daniel L.
   1986   *Religions of China: The World as Living System.* San Francisco: Harper
                & Row.
Schirokauer, Conrad
   1990   *A Brief History of Chinese Civilization.* 2nd ed. Fort Worth, Tex.:
                Harcourt Brace Publishers.
   1993   *A Brief History of Japanese Civilization.* 2nd ed. Fort Worth, Tex.:
                Harcourt Brace Publishers.
Shahar, Meir, and Robert P. Weller
   1996   *Unruly Gods: Divinity and Society in China.* Honolulu: University of
                Hawaii Press.
Smith, Jonathan Z., ed.
   1995   *The HarperCollins Dictionary of Religion.* William Scott Green, Asso-
                ciate Editor with the American Academy of Religion. San Francisco:
                HarperCollins.
Sommer, Deborah, ed.
   1995   *Chinese Religion: An Anthology of Sources.* New York and Oxford:
                Oxford University Press.

Thompson, Laurence
    1989   *Chinese Religion.* 4th ed. Belmont, Calif.: Wadsworth Publishing.
Tsunoda, Ryusaku, ed.
    1958   *Sources of the Japanese Tradition.* New York: Columbia University
              Press.
Tu Weiming, ed.
    1996   *Confucian Traditions in East Asian Modernity: Moral Education and
              Economic Culture in Japan and the Four Mini-Dragons.* Cambridge,
              Mass.: Harvard University Press.
Tucker, Mary Evelyn, and John Berthrong, eds.
    1998   *Confucianism and Ecology: The Interrelationship of Heaven, Earth, and
              Humans.* Cambridge, Mass.: Harvard University Center for the
              Study of World Religions.
Weller, Robert P.
    1987   *Unities and Diversities in Chinese Religion.* Seattle: University of
              Washington Press.
Yang, C. K.
    1967   *Religion in Chinese Society.* Berkeley: University of California Press.
Yao, Xinzhong
    2000   *An Introduction to Confucianism.* Cambridge: Cambridge University
              Press.

Monographs: China

Allan, Sarah
    1991   *The Shape of the Turtle: Myth, Art, and Cosmos in Early China.* Albany:
              State University of New York Press.
    1997   *The Way of Water and the Sprouts of Virtue.* Albany: State University
              of New York Press.
Alitto, Guy S.
    1979   *The Last Confucian: Liang Shu-ming and the Chinese Dilemma of
              Modernity.* Berkeley: University of California Press.
Ames, Roger, and David L. Hall
    2001   *Focusing the Familiar: A Translation and Philosophical Interpretation of
              the Zhongyong.* Honolulu: University of Hawaii Press.
Barrett, T. H.
    1992   *Li Ao: Buddhist, Taoist, or Neo-Confucian?* Oxford: Oxford Univer-
              sity Press.
Bauer, Wolfgang
    1976   *China and the Search for Happiness: Recurring Themes in Four Thou-
              sand Years of Chinese Cultural History.* Translated by Michael Shaw.
              New York: Seabury Press.
Berling, Judith A.
    1980   *The Syncretic Religion of Lin Chao-en.* New York: Columbia Univer-
              sity Press.

Berthrong, John H.
1994   *All under Heaven: Transforming Paradigms in Confucian-Christian Dialogue.* Albany: State University of New York Press.
1998   *Transformations of the Confucian Way.* Boulder, Colo.: Westview Press.
———, and Evelyn Nagai Berthrong
2000   *Confucianism: A Short Introduction.* Oxford: Oneworld.
Birdwhistell, Anne D.
1989   *Transition to Neo-Confucianism: Shao Yung on Knowledge and Symbols of Reality.* Stanford, Calif.: Stanford University Press.
1996   *Li Yong (1627–1705) and Epistemological Dimensions of Confucian Philosophy.* Stanford, Calif.: Stanford University Press.
Black, Alison Harley
1989   *Man and Nature in the Philosophical Thought of Wang Fu-chih.* Seattle: University of Washington Press.
Bloom, Irene
1987   *Knowledge Painfully Acquired: The K'un-chih chi by Lo Ch'in-shun.* New York: Columbia University Press.
———, and Joshua A. Fogel, eds.
1997   *Meetings of Minds: Intellectual and Religious Interaction in East Asian Traditions of Thought.* New York: Columbia University Press.
Bodde, Derk
1981   *Essays on Chinese Civilization.* Edited by Charles Le Blanc and Dorothy Borei. Princeton, N.J.: Princeton University Press.
Bol, Peter K.
1992   *"This Culture of Ours": Intellectual Transition in T'ang and Sung China.* Stanford, Calif.: Stanford University Press.
Bruce, J. Percy
1973   *Chu Hsi and His Masters: An Introduction to Chu Hsi and the Sung School of Chinese Philosophy.* London: Probsthain & Co., 1923; New York: AMS Press Edition.
Chan, Alan K. L.
1991   *Two Visions of the Way: A Study of Wang Pi and the Ho-shang Kung Commentaries on the Lao Tzu.* Albany: State University of New York Press.
Chan, Hok-lam, and Wm. Theodore de Bary, eds.
1982   *Yüan Thought: Chinese Thought and Religion under the Mongols.* New York: Columbia University Press.
Chan, Wing-tsit
1986   *Chu Hsi and Neo-Confucianism.* Honolulu: University of Hawaii Press.
1987   *Chu Hsi: Life and Thought.* Hong Kong: Chinese University Press.
1989   *Chu Hsi: New Studies.* Honolulu: University of Hawaii Press.
1986   *Neo-Confucian Terms Explained (The Pei-hsi tzu-i) by Ch'en Ch'un, 1159–1223.* New York: Columbia University Press.

Chang, Carsun
1957,   *The Development of Neo-Confucian Thought.* 2 vols. New York:
1962   Bookman Associates.
1970   *Wang Yang-ming: Idealist Philosopher of Sixteenth-Century China.*
        New York: St. John's University Press.
Chang, Hao
1971   *Liang Ch'i-ch'ao and Intellectual Transition in China (1890–1907).*
        Cambridge, Mass.: Harvard University Press.
Chaves, Jonathan
1993   *Sing of the Source: Nature and Gospel in the Poetry of the Chinese Painter Wu Li.* Honolulu: SHAPS Library of Translations, University of Hawaii Press.
Chen, Charles K. H., compiler
1969   *Neo-Confucianism, Etc.: Essays by Wing-tsit Chan.* Hanover, N.H.: Oriental Society.
Chen, Jo-shui
1992   *Liu Tsung-yüan and Intellectual Change in T'ang China, 773–819.* Cambridge: Cambridge University Press.
Chen, Li-Fu
1948   *Philosophy of Life.* New York: Philosophical Library.
1972   *The Confucian Way: A New and Systematic Study of the "Four Books."* Translated by Liu Shih Shun. Taipei: Commercial Press.
Cheng, Chung-ying, trans.
1971   *Tai Chen's Inquiry into Goodness.* Honolulu: East-West Center Press.
1991   *New Dimensions of Confucian and Neo-Confucian Philosophy.* Albany: State University of New York Press.
Ch'ien, Edward T.
1986   *Chiao Hung and the Restructuring of Neo-Confucianism in the Late Ming.* New York: Columbia University Press.
Chin, Ann-ping, and Mansfield Freedman
1990   *Tai Chen on Mencius: Explorations in Words and Meaning.* New Haven, Conn.: Yale University Press.
Ching, Julia, trans.
1972   *The Philosophical Letters of Wang Yang-ming.* Columbia: University of South Carolina Press.
1976   *To Acquire Wisdom: The Way of Wang Yang-ming.* New York: Columbia University Press.
1977   *Confucianism and Christianity: A Comparative Study.* Tokyo: Kodansha International.
1990   *Probing China's Soul: Religion, Politics, and Protest in the People's Republic.* San Francisco: Harper & Row.
1997   *Mysticism and Kingship in China: The Heart of Chinese Wisdom.* Cambridge: Cambridge University Press.
2000   *The Religious Thought of Chu Hsi.* Oxford and New York: Oxford University Press.

———, and Hans Küng.

1989   *Christianity and Chinese Religion.* New York: Doubleday.

Chow, Kai-wing

1995   *The Rise of Confucian Ritualism in Late Imperial China: Ethics, Classics, and Lineage Discourse.* Stanford, Calif.: Stanford University Press.

Chow, Kai-wing, On-cho Ng, and John B. Henderson, eds.

1999   *Imagining Boundaries: Changing Confucian Doctrines, Texts, and Hermeneutics.* Albany: State University of New York Press.

Chu Hsi

1973   *The Philosophy of Human Nature.* Translated by J. Percy Bruce. London: Probsthain & Co., 1922; New York: AMS Press Edition.

1991   *Chu Hsi's Family Rituals: A Twelfth-Century Chinese Manual for the Performance of Cappings, Weddings, Funerals, and Ancestral Rites.* Translated and edited by Patricia Buckley Ebrey. Princeton, N.J.: Princeton University Press.

———, and Lü Tsu-ch'ien

1967   *Reflections on Things at Hand: The Neo-Confucian Anthology.* Translated by Wing-tsit Chan. New York: Columbia University Press.

Clarke, J. J.

1997   *Oriental Enlightenment: The Encounter Between Asian and Western Thought.* London: Routledge.

2000   *The Tao of the West: Western Transformations of Taoist Thought.* London: Routledge.

Confucius

1992   *Confucius: The Analects (Lun yü).* Translated by D. C. Lau. Hong Kong: Chinese University Press.

Creel, H. G.

1949   *Confucius and the Chinese Way.* New York: Harper & Row.

1970   *What Is Taoism? And Other Studies in Chinese Cultural History.* Chicago: University of Chicago Press.

Cua, A. S.

1982   *The Unity of Knowledge and Action: A Study of Wang Yang-ming's Moral Psychology.* Honolulu: University Press of Hawaii.

1985   *Ethical Argumentation: A Study in Hsün Tzu's Moral Epistemology.* Honolulu: University Press of Hawaii.

1998   *Moral Vision and Tradition: Essays in Chinese Ethics.* Washington, D.C.: Catholic University of America Press.

———, ed.

2003   *Encyclopedia of Chinese Philosophy.* New York and London: Routledge.

Dardess, John W.

1973   *Conquerors and Confucians: Aspects of Political Change in Late Yüan China.* New York: Columbia University Press.

1983   *Confucianism and Autocracy: Professional Elites in the Founding of the Ming Dynasty.* Berkeley: University of California Press.

1996   *A Ming Society: T'ai-ho Country, Kiangsi, Fourteenth to Seventeenth Centuries.* Berkeley: University of California Press.

de Bary, Wm. Theodore

1981   *Neo-Confucian Orthodoxy and the Learning of the Mind-and-Heart.* New York: Columbia University Press.

1983   *The Liberal Tradition in China.* New York: Columbia University Press.

1988   *East Asian Civilizations: A Dialogue in Five Stages.* Cambridge: Harvard University Press.

1989   *The Message of the Mind in Neo-Confucianism.* New York: Columbia University Press.

1991a   *The Trouble with Confucianism.* Cambridge, Mass.: Harvard University Press.

1991b   *Learning for One's Self: Essays on the Individual in Neo-Confucian Thought.* New York: Columbia University Press.

——, ed.

1970   *Self and Society in Ming Thought.* New York: Columbia University Press.

1975   *The Unfolding of Neo-Confucianism.* New York: Columbia University Press.

——, trans.

1993   *Waiting for the Dawn: A Plan for the Prince-Huang Tsung-hsi's Ming-i-tai-fang lu.* New York: Columbia University Press.

——, and John Chaffee, eds.

1989   *Neo-Confucian Education: The Formative Stage.* Berkeley: University of California Press.

Dimberg, Ronald G.

1974   *The Sage and Society: The Life and Thought of Ho Hsin-yin.* Honolulu: University of Hawaii Press.

Eber, Irene, ed.

1986   *Confucianism: The Dynamics of Tradition.* New York: Macmillan.

Ebrey, Patricia Buckley.

1991   *Confucianism and Family Rituals in Imperial China: A Social History of Writing about Rites.* Princeton, N.J.: Princeton University Press.

1993   *The Inner Quarters: Marriage and the Lives of Chinese Women in the Sung Period.* Berkeley: University of California Press.

Elman, Benjamin A.

1984   *From Philosophy to Philosophy: Intellectual and Social Aspects of Change in Late Imperial China.* Cambridge, Mass.: Harvard University Press.

1990   *Classicism, Politics and Kinship: The Ch'ang-Chou School of New Test Confucianism in Later Imperial China.* Berkeley: University of California Press.

Eno, Robert

1990   *The Confucian Creation of Heaven: Philosophy and the Defense of Ritual Mastery.* Albany: State University of New York Press.

Fairbank, John K., ed.
1957	*Chinese Thought and Institutions*. Chicago: University of Chicago Press.

Fang, Thome H.
n.d.	*The Chinese View of Life: The Philosophy of Comprehensive Harmony*. Hong Kong: Union Press.

Fingarette, Herbert
1972	*Confucius—The Secular as Sacred*. New York: Harper & Row, Publishers.

Gardner, Daniel K.
1986	*Chu Hsi and the Ta-hsüeh: Neo-Confucian Reflection the Confucian Canon*. Cambridge: Harvard University Press.
2003	*Zhu Xi's Reading of the Analects*. New York: Columbia University Press.

———, trans.
1990	*Learning to Be a Sage: Selections from the Conversations of Master Chu, Arranged Topically*. Berkeley: University of California Press.

Geaney, Jane
2002	*On the Epistemology of the Senses in Early Chinese Philosophy*. Honolulu: University of Hawaii Press.

Gernet, Jacques
1985	*China and the Christian Impact*. Translated by Janet Lloyd. Cambridge: Cambridge University Press.

Graham, A. C.
1986a	*Studies in Chinese Philosophy and Philosophical Literature*. Singapore: Institute for East Asian Philosophy.
1986b	*Yin-yang and the Nature of Correlative Thinking*. Singapore: The Institute of East Asian Philosophy.
1989	*Disputers of the Tao: Philosophical Argument in Ancient China*. La Salle, Ill.: Open Court.
1992	*Two Chinese Philosophers: The Metaphysics of the Brothers Ch'eng*. La Salle, Ill.: Open Court.

Granet, Marcel
1968	*La pensée Chinoise*. Paris: Editions Albin Michel.
1975	*The Religion of the Chinese People*. Translated by Maurice Freedman. New York: Harper & Row.

Grant, Beata
1994	*Mount Lu Revisited: Buddhism in the Life of Su Shih*. Honolulu: University of Hawaii Press.

Gregory, Peter N.
1991	*Tsung-mi and the Sinification of Buddhism*. Princeton, N.J.: Princeton University Press.

———, trans.
1995	*Inquiry in the Origin of Humanity: An Annotated Translation of Tsung-*

mi's Yüan jen lun with a Modern Commentary. Honolulu: University of Hawaii Press.

Hall, David L., and Roger T. Ames
1987   *Thinking Through Confucius*. Albany: State University of New York Press.
1995   *Anticipating China: Thinking Through the Narratives of Chinese and Western Culture*. Albany: State University of New York Press.
1998   *Thinking from the Han: Self, Truth and Transcendence in Chinese and Western Culture*. Albany: State University of New York Press.

Handlin, Joanna
1983   *Action in Late Ming Thought: The Reorientation of Lu K'un and Other Scholar-Officials*. Berkeley: University of California Press.

Hansen, Chad
1992   *A Daoist Theory of Chinese Thought: A Philosophic Interpretation*. Oxford: Oxford University Press.

Hartman, Charles
1986   *Han Yü and the T'ang Search for Unity*. Princeton, N.J.: Princeton University Press.

Henderson, John B.
1984   *The Development and Decline of Chinese Cosmology*. New York: Columbia University Press.
1991   *Scripture, Canon, and Commentary: A Comparison of Confucian and Western Exegesis*. Princeton, N.J.: Princeton University Press.
1998   *The Construction of Orthodoxy and Heresy: Neo-Confucian, Islamic, Jewish, and Early Christian Patterns*. Albany: State University of New York Press.

Henke, Frederick Goodrich
1964   *The Philosophy of Wang Yang-ming*. 2nd ed. New York: Paragon Boo Reprint Co.

Hoobler, Thomas, and Dorothy Hoobler
1993   *Confucianism: World Religions*. New York: Facts On File, Inc.

Hocking, William Ernest
1936   "Chu Hsi's Theory of Knowledge." *Harvard Journal of Asiatic Studies* 1 (1936): 109–27.

Hsiao, Kung-chuan
1975   *A Modern China and New World: K'ang Yu-wei, Reformer and Utopian, 1854–1927*. Seattle: University of Washington Press.
1979   *A History of Chinese Political Thought*. Vol. I: *From the Beginnings to the Sixth Century A.D.* Translated by F. W. Mote. Princeton, N.J.: Princeton University Press.

Hsieh, Shan-yuan
1979   *The Life and Thought of Li Kou (1009–1069)*. San Francisco: Chinese Materials Center.

Huang, Chin-shing
1995   *Philosophy, Philology, and Politics in Eighteenth-Century China: Li Fu*

and the Lu-Wang School Under the Ch'ing. Cambridge: Cambridge University Press.

Huang, Chun-chieh
2001   *Mencian Hermeneutics: A History of Interpretations in China.* New Brunswick and London: Transaction Publishers.

Huang, Siu-chi
1968   "Chang Tsai's Concept of *Ch'i.*" *Philosophy East & West* 18 (October 1968): 247–60.
1971   "The Moral Point of View of Chang Tsai." *Philosophy East & West* 21 (April 1971): 141–56.
1977   *Lu Hsiang-shan: A Twelfth Century Chinese Idealist Philosophy.* Westport, CT: Hyperion Press.

Huang Tsung-hsi
1987   *The Records of Ming Scholars.* Edited by Julia Ching with the collaboration of Chaoying Fang. Honolulu: University of Hawaii Press.

Ivanhoe, Philip J.
1990   *Ethics in the Confucian Tradition: The Thought of Mencius and Wang Yang-ming.* Atlanta: Scholars Press.
1991   "A Happy Symmetry: Xunzi's Ethical Thought." *Journal of the American Academy of Religions* 59.2 (Summer): 309–22.
2000   *Confucian Moral Self Cultivation.* 2nd ed. Indianapolis: Hackett Publishing Company.

——, ed.
1996   *Chinese Language, Thought, and Culture: Nivison and His Critics.* Chicago, Ill.: Open Court.

——, and Bryan Van Nordon, eds.
2001   *Readings in Classical Chinese Philosophy.* New York: Seven Bridges Press.

——, and Xiusheng Liu, eds.
2002   *Essays in the Moral Philosophy of Mengzi.* Indianapolis: Hackett Publishing Company.

Jensen, Lionel M.
1997   *Manufacturing Confucianism: Chinese Traditions and Universal Civilizations.* Durham, N.C.: Duke University Press.

Jiang, Paul Yun-Ming
1980   *The Search for Mind: Ch'ien Pai-sha, Philosopher-Poet.* Singapore: Singapore University Press, 1980.

Kasoff, Ira E.
1984   *The Thought of Chang Tsai.* Cambridge: Cambridge University Press.

Kim, Sung-Hae
1985   *The Righteous and the Sage: A Comparative Study on the Ideal Images of Man in Biblical Israel and Classical China.* Seoul: Sogang University Press.

Kim, Yung Sik
2000   *The Natural Philosophy of Chu Hsi (1130–1200).* Philadelphia: American Philosophical Society.

Knoblock, John
   1988–   *Xunzi: A Translation and Study of the Complete Works.* 3 vols.
   1994   Stanford, Calif.: Stanford University Press.
Ko, Dorothy
   1994   *Teachers of the Inner Chambers: Women and Culture in Seventeenth-Century China.* Stanford, Calif.: Stanford University Press.
Kohn, Livia
   1991   *Early Chinese Mysticism: Philosophy and Soteriology in the Taoist Tradition.* Princeton, N.J.: Princeton University Press.
   1995   *Laughing at the Tao: Debates among Buddhists and Taoists in Medieval China.* Princeton, N.J.: Princeton University Press.
Kuhn, Philip A.
   1990   *Soulstealers: The Chinese Sorcery Scare of 1768.* Cambridge, Mass.: Harvard University Press.
Lee, Peter K. H., ed.
   1991   *Confucian-Christian Encounter in Historical and Contemporary Perspective.* Lewiston, N.Y.: Edwin Mellen Press.
Lee, Thomas H. C.
   1985   *Government Education and Examinations in Sung China.* Hong Kong: Chinese University Press.
Legge, James, trans.
   1960   *The Chinese Classics.* 5 vols. Hong Kong: Hong Kong University Press.
   1968   *The Li Ki.* 2 vols. Delhi: Motilal Barnarsidass.
Leibniz, Gottfried Wilhelm
   1977   *Discourse on the Natural Theology of the Chinese.* Translated by Henry Rosemont and Daniel J. Cook. Honolulu: University of Hawaii Press.
   1994   *Writings on China.* Translated by Daniel J. Cook and Henry Rosemont, Jr. Chicago: Open Court.
Levenson, Joseph R.
   1968   *Confucian China and Its Modern Faith: A Trilogy.* 3 vols. Berkeley: University of California Press.
Lewis, Mark Edward
   1990   *Sanctioned Violence in Early China.* Albany: State University of New York Press.
Leys, Simon, trans.
   1997   *The Analects of Confucius.* New York: W. W. Norton & Company.
Liang Ch'i-ch'ao
   1959   *Intellectual Trends in the Ch'ing Period.* Translated by Immanuel C. Y. Hsü. Cambridge, Mass.: Harvard University Press.
Liu, James T. C.
   1959   *Reform in Sung China: Wang An-shih (1021–1086) and His New Policies.* Cambridge, Mass.: Harvard University Press.
   1967   *Ou-yang Hsiu: An Eleventh-Century Neo-Confucianist.* Palo Alto, Calif.: Stanford University Press.

1988   *China Turning Inward: Intellectual Changes in the Early Twelfth Century*. Cambridge, Mass.: Harvard University Press.

Liu, Shu-hsien
1971   "The Religious Import of Confucian Philosophy: Its Traditional Outlook and Contemporary Significance." *Philosophy East & West* 21 (April 1971): 157–75.
1978   "The Functions of the Mind in Chu Hsi's Philosophy." *Journal of Chinese Philosophy* 5 (1978): 204.
1989   "Postwar Neo-Confucian Philosophy: Its Development and Issues." In *Religious Issues and Interreligious Dialogues*. Edited by Charles Wei-hsun Fu and Gerhard E. Spiegler. New York: Greenwood Press.
1990   "Some Reflections on the Sung-Ming Understanding of Mind, Nature, and Reason." *The Journal of the Institute of Chinese Studies of the Chinese University of Hong Kong* 21 (1990): 331–43.
1998   *Understanding Confucian Philosophy: Classical and Sung-Ming*. Westport, Conn.: Praeger.

Lo, Winston Wan
1974   *The Life and Thought of Yeh Shih*. Hong Kong: Chinese University of Hong Kong.

Loden, Torbjon, trans.
1988   "Dai Zhen's Evidential Commentary on the Meaning of the Words of Mencius." *Bulletin of the Museum of Far Eastern Antiquities* [Stockholm] no. 60 (1988): 165–313.

Loewe, Michael
1979   *Ways to Paradise: The Chinese Quest for Immortality*. London: George Allen & Unwin Ltd.
1982   *Chinese Ideas of Life and Death: Faith, Myth and Reason in the Han Period (202 B.C.–A.D. 220)*. London: George Allen & Unwin Ltd.
1994   *Divination, Mythology and Monarch in Han China*. Cambridge: Cambridge University Press.

Lufrano, Richard
1997   *Honorable Merchants: Commerce and Self-Cultivation in Later Imperial China*. Honolulu: University of Hawaii Press.

Lynn, Richard John, trans.
1994   *The Classic of Changes: A New Translation of the I Ching as Interpreted by Wang Bi*. New York: Columbia University Press.

Machle, Edward J.
1993   *Nature and Heaven in the Xunzi: A Study of Tien Lun*. Albany: State University of New York Press.

Major, John
1993   *Heaven and Earth in Early Han Thought*. Albany: State University of New York Press.

Makeham, John
1995   *Name and Actuality in Early Chinese Thought*. Albany: State University of New York Press.

Malebranche, Nicolas
1980   *Dialogue Between a Christian Philosopher and a Chinese Philosopher on the Existence and Nature of God.* Translated by Dominick A. Iorio. Washington, D.C.: University Press of America.

Mann, Susan
1997   *Precious Records: Women in China's Long Eighteenth Century.* Stanford, Calif.: Stanford University Press.

Maspero, Henri
1978   *China in Antiquity.* Translated by Frank A. Kierman, Jr. N.P: University of Massachusetts Press.

Mencius
1984   Translated by D. C. Lau. 2 vols. Hong Kong: Chinese University Press.

Metzger, Thomas A.
1977   *Escape from Predicament: Neo-Confucianism and China's Evolving Political Culture.* New York: Columbia University Press.

Minamiki, George, S.J.
1985   *The Chinese Rites Controversy from Its Beginning to Modern Times.* Chicago: Loyola University Press.

Moran, Patrick Edwin
1993   *Three Smaller Wisdom Books: Lao Zi's Dao De Jing, The Great Learning (Da Xue), and the Doctrine of the Mean (Zhong Yong).* Lanham, Md.: University Press of America.

Mungello, David E.
1977   *Leibniz and Confucianism: The Search for Accord.* Honolulu: University of Hawaii Press.
1985   *Curious Land: Jesuit Accommodation and the Origins of Sinology.* Stuttgart: Franz Steiner Verlag.

Munro, Donald J.
1969   *The Concept of Man in Early China.* Stanford, Calif.: Stanford University Press.
1977   *The Concept of Man in Contemporary China.* Ann Arbor: University of Michigan Press.
1988   *Images of Human Nature: A Sung Portrait.* Princeton, N.J.: Princeton University Press.

Murata, Sachiko
2000   *Chinese Gleams of Sufi Light.* Albany: State University of New York Press.

Needham, Joseph
1954–   *Science and Civilisation in China.* 8 vols. Cambridge: Cambridge University Press.

Neville, Robert C.
2000   *Boston Confucianism.* Albany: State University of New York Press.

Ni, Peimin
   2002   *On Confucius.* Belmont, Calif.: Wadsworth/Thompson Learning, Inc.

Nivison, David S.
   1966   *The Life and Thought of Chang Hsüeh-ch'eng (1738–1801).* Stanford, Calif.: Stanford University Press.
   1996   *The Ways of Confucianism: Investigations in Chinese Philosophy.* Edited by Bryan W. Van Norden. Chicago and La Salle: Open Court.
——, and Arthur F. Wright, eds.
   1959   *Confucianism in Action.* Stanford, Calif.: Stanford University Press.

Obenchain, Diane B., ed.
   1994   "Feng Youlan: Something Happens." *Journal of Chinese Philosophy* 21, nos. 3/4 (September–December 1994).

Paper, Jordan
   1987   *The Fu-Tzu: A Post-Han Confucian Text.* Leiden: E. J. Brill.
   1995   *The Spirits Are Drunk: Comparative Approaches to Chinese Religion.* Albany: State University of New York Press.

Pines, Yuri
   2002   *Foundations of Confucian Thought: Intellectual Life in the Chunqiu Period, 722–453 B.C.E.* Honolulu: University of Hawaii Press.

Prazniak, Roxann
   1996   *Dialogues Across Civilizations: Sketches in World History from the Chinese and European Experiences.* Boulder, Colo.: Westview Press.

Puett, Michael J.
   2000   *The Ambivalence of Creation: Debates Concerning Innovation and Artifice in Early China.* Stanford, Calif.: Stanford University Press.
   2002   *To Become a God: Cosmology, Sacrifice, and Self-Divinization in Early China.* Cambridge: Harvard University Press.

Queen, Sarah A.
   1996   *From Chronicle to Canon: The Hermeneutics of the Spring and Autumn, According to Tung Chung-shu.* Cambridge: Cambridge University Press.

Raphals, Lisa
   1992   *Knowing Words: Wisdom and Cunning in the Classical Traditions of China and Greece.* Ithaca, N.Y., and London: Cornell University Press.
   1998   *Sharing the Light: Representations of Women and Virtue in Early China.* Albany: State University of New York Press.

Ricci, Matteo, S.J.
   1985   *The True Meaning of the Lord of Heaven (T'ien-chu Shih-i).* Translated by Douglas Lancashire and Peter Hu Kuo-chen, S.J. Taipei: Ricci Institute.

Roetz, Heiner
   1993   *Confucian Ethics of the Axial Age: A Reconstruction under the Aspect of*

the Breakthrough Toward Postconventional Thinking. Albany: State University of New York Press.

Rosemont, Henry, Jr., ed.
1991 *Chinese Texts and Philosophical Contexts: Essays Dedicated to Angus C. Graham*. La Salle, Ill.: Open Court.

Rowley, Harold Henry
1956 *Prophecy and Religion in Ancient China and Israel*. London: University of London, The Athlone Press.

Rozman, Gilbert, ed.
1991 *The East Asian Region: Confucian Heritage and Its Modern Adaptation*. Princeton, N.J.: Princeton University Press.

Rubin, Vitaly A.
1976 *Individual and State in Ancient China: Essays on Four Chinese Philosophers*. Translated by Steven I. Levine. New York: Columbia University Press.

Schwartz, Benjamin I.
1985 *The World of Thought in Ancient China*. Cambridge, Mass.: Belknap Press of Harvard University.

Shao Yung
1986 *Dialogue Between a Fisherman and a Wood-Cutter*. Translated by Knud Lundbaek. Hamburg: C. Bell Verlag.

Shaughnessy, Edward L.
1996 *I Ching: The Classic of Changes*. New York: Ballantine Books.
1997 *Before Confucius: Studies in the Creation of the Chinese Classics*. Albany: State University of New York Press.

Shryock, J. K.
1937 *The Study of Human Abilities: The Jen wu chih of Liu Shao*. New Haven, Conn.: American Oriental Society.

Shun, Kwong-loi
1997 *Mencius and Early Chinese Thought*. Stanford, Calif.: Stanford University Press.

Smith, D. Howard
1968 *Chinese Religions*. New York: Holt, Rinehart and Winston.
1973 *Confucius*. New York: Charles Scribner's Sons.

Smith, Kidder, Jr., et al.
1990 *Sung Dynasty Uses of the I Ching*. Princeton, N.J.: Princeton University Press.

Smith, Richard J.
1991 *Fortune-Tellers and Philosophers: Divination in Traditional Chinese Society*. Boulder, Calif.: Westview Press.
1994 *China's Cultural Heritage: The Ch'ing Dynasty, 1644-1912*. 2nd ed. Boulder, Colo.: Westview Press.

——, and D. W. Y. Kwok, eds.
1993 *Cosmology, Ontology, and Human Efficacy*. Honolulu: University of Hawaii Press.

Som, Tjan Tjoe
1973   *The Comprehensive Discussions in the White Tiger Hall*. 2 vols. West-port, Conn.: Hyperion Press. Leiden: E. J. Brill, 1949. Reprint.
Standaert, N.
1988   *Yang Tingyun, Confucian and Christian in Late Ming China*. Leiden: E. J. Brill.
Swann, Nancy Lee
1968   *Pan Chao: Foremost Woman Scholar of China*. New York: Russell and Russell.
T'an, Ssu-t'ung
1984   *An Exposition of Benevolence: The Jen-hsüeh of T'an Ssu-t'ung*. Translated by Chan Sin-wai. Hong Kong: Chinese University of Hong Kong Press.
T'ang, Chün-i
1956   "Chang Tsai's Theory of Mind and Its Metaphysical Basis." *Philosophy East & West* 6 (1956): 113–36.
1974   "The Spirit and Development of Neo-Confucianism." In *Invitation to Chinese Philosophy,* edited by A. Naess and A. Hanny. Oslo: Scandinavian University Press.
Taylor, Rodney L.
1978   *The Cultivation of Sagehood as a Religious Goal in Neo-Confucianism: A Study of Selected Writings of Kao P'an-lung, 1562–1626*. Missoula, Mont.: Scholars Press.
1990   *The Religious Dimensions of Confucianism*. Albany: State University of New York Press.
Thompson, Laurence G.
1958   *The One-World Philosophy of K'ang Yu-wei*. London: George Allen & Unwin Ltd.
Tillman, Hoyt Cleveland
1982   *Utilitarian Confucianism: Ch'en Liang's Challenge to Chu Hsi*. Cambridge, Mass.: Harvard University Press.
1992   *Confucian Discourse and Chu Hsi's Ascendancy*. Honolulu: University of Hawaii Press.
1994   *Ch'en Liang on Public Interest and the Law*. Honolulu: University of Hawaii Press.
Ts'ai, Y. C.
1950   "The Philosophy of Ch'eng I: A Selection from the Complete Works." Ph.D. dissertation. Columbia University.
Tsai, Yen-zen
1994   "*Ching* and *Chuan*: Towards Defining the Confucian Scriptures in Han China (206 BCE–220 CE)." Unpublished Manuscript.
Tu, Weiming
1971   Review of *Hsin-t'i yü hsing-t'i* [Mind and Nature], by Mou Tsung-san. *Journal of Asian Studies* 30 (May 1971): 642–47.

1974 "Reconstituting the Confucian Tradition." *Journal of Asian Studies* 33 (May 1974): 441–54.

1976 *Neo-Confucian Thought in Action: Wang Yang-ming's Youth (1472–1509)*. Berkeley: University of California Press.

1979 *Humanity and Self-Cultivation: Essays in Confucian Thought*. Berkeley, Calif.: Asian Humanities Press.

1985 *Confucian Thought: Self-hood as Creative Transformation*. Albany: State University of New York Press.

1989 *Centrality and Commonality: An Essay on Confucian Religiousness*. Albany: State University of New York Press.

1993 *Way, Learning, and Politics: Essays on the Confucian Intellectual*. Albany: State University of New York Press.

——, ed.

1994a *China in Transformation*. Cambridge, Mass.: Harvard University Press.

1994b *The Living Tree: The Changing Meaning of Being Chinese Today*. Stanford, Calif.: Stanford University Press.

——, Milan Hejtmanek, and Alan Wachman, eds.

1992 *The Confucian World Observed: A Contemporary Discussion of Confucian Humanism in East Asia*. Honolulu: University of Hawaii Press.

Van Zoeren, Steven

1991 *Poetry and Personality: Reading, Exegesis and Hermeneutics in Traditional China*. Stanford, Calif.: Stanford University Press.

Waley, Arthur

1938 *The Analects of Confucius*. London: George, Allen & Unwin, Ltd.

1939 *Three Ways of Thought in Ancient China*. Garden City, N.Y.: Doubleday.

Wang, Aihe

2000 *Cosmology and Political Culture in Early China*. Cambridge: Cambridge University Press.

Wang, Y. C.

1966 *Chinese Intellectuals and the West: 1872-1949*. Chapel Hill: University of North Carolina Press.

Wang Yang-ming

1963 *Instructions for Practical Living and Other Neo-Confucian Writings*. Translated by Wing Tsit-chan. New York: Columbia University Press.

Watson, Burton, trans.

1967 *Basic Writings of Mo Tzu, Hsün Tzu, and Han Fei Tzu*. New York: Columbia University Press.

Weber, Max

1951 *The Religion of China: Confucianism and Taoism*. Translated by Hans H. Gerth. New York: Macmillan.

Williamson, H. R.
   1973   *Wang An Shih: A Chinese Statesman and Educationalist of the Sung Dynasty.* 2 vols. Westport, Conn.: Hyperion Press.

Wilson, Thomas A.
   1995   *Genealogy of the Way: The Construction and Uses of the Confucian Tradition in Late Imperial China.* Stanford, Calif.: Stanford University Press.

———, ed.
   2003   *On Sacred Grounds: Culture, Society, Politics and the Formation of the Cult of Confucius.* Cambridge, Mass.: Harvard University Asia Center.

Wittenborn, Allen, trans.
   1991   *Further Reflections on Things at Hand: A Reader, Chu Hsi.* Lanham, Md.: University Press of America.

Wood, Alan T.
   1995   *Limits to Autocracy: From Sung Neo-Confucianism to a Doctrine of Political Rights.* Honolulu: University of Hawaii Press.

Wright, Arthur F., ed.
   1953   *Studies in Chinese Thought.* Chicago: University of Chicago Press.
   1960   *The Confucian Persuasion.* Stanford, Calif.: Stanford University Press.
———, and Denis Twichett, eds.
   1962   *Confucian Personalities.* Stanford, Calif.: Stanford University Press.

Wu, Pei-yi
   1990   *The Confucian's Progress: Autobiographical Writings in Traditional China.* Princeton, N.J.: Princeton University Press.

Wyatt, Don J.
   1996   *The Recluse of Loyang: Shao Yung and the Moral Evolution of Early Sung Thought.* Honolulu: University of Hawaii Press.

Yang Hsiung
   1993   *The Canon of Supreme Mystery: A Translation with Commentary of the T'ai Hsüan Ching.* Translated and edited by Michael Nylan. Albany: State University of New York Press.
   1994   *The Elemental Changes: The Ancient Chinese Companion to the I Ching, The T'ai Hsüan Ching of Master Yang Hsiung.* Translated and edited by Michael Nylan. Albany: State University of New York Press.

Yang, Lien-sheng
   1957   "The Concept of *Pao* as a Basis for Social Relations in China." In *Chinese Thought and Institutions,* edited by J. K. Fairbank. Chicago: University of Chicago Press.

Yao, Xinzhong, ed.
   2003   *RoutledgeCurzon Encyclopedia of Confucianism.* 2 vols. New York and London: RoutledgeCurzon.

Yearley, Lee H.
   1990   *Mencius and Aquinas: Theories of Virtue and Conceptions of Courage.* Albany: State University of New York Press.

Yeh, Theodore T. Y.
    1969   *Confucianism, Christianity and China*. New York: Philosophical Library.
Yen Yüan
    1972   *Preservation of Learning*. Translated by Maurice Freeman. Los Angeles: Monumenta Serica.
Young, John D.
    1983   *Confucianism and Christianity: The First Encounter*. Hong Kong: Hong Kong University Press.
Yü, Chün-fang
    1981   *The Renewal of Buddhism in China: Chu-hung and the Late Ming Synthesis*. New York: Columbia University Press.
Zaehner, R. C.
    1970   *Concordant Discord: The Interdependence of Faiths*. Oxford: Oxford University Press.

Monographs: Korea

Choi, Ming-hong
    1980   *A Modern History of Korean Philosophy*. Seoul: Seong Moon Sa.
Choung Haechang, and Han Hyong-jo, eds.
    1996   *Confucian Philosophy in Korea*. Kyonggi-do: The Academy of Korean Studies.
Chung Chai-Sik
    1995   *A Korean Confucian Encounter with the Modern World: Yi Hang-no and the West*. Berkeley: Institute for East Asian Studies, University of California, Berkeley.
Chung, Edward Y. J.
    1995   *The Korean Neo-Confucianism of Yi T'oegye and Yi Yulgok: A Reappraisal of the "Four-Seven Thesis" and Its Practical Implications for Self-Cultivation*. Albany: State University of New York Press.
de Bary, Wm. Theodore, and JaHyun Kim Haboush, eds.
    1985   *The Rise of Neo-Confucianism in Korea*. New York: Columbia University Press.
Deuchler, Martina
    1992   *The Confucian Transformation of Korea: A Study of Society and Ideology*. New York: Columbia University Press.
Grayson, James Huntley
    1989   *Korea: A Religious History*. Oxford: Clarendon Press.
Haboush, JaHyun Kim
    1988   *A Heritage of Kings: One Man's Monarchy in the Confucian World*. New York: Columbia University Press.
    1996   *The Memoirs of Lady Hyegyong: The Autobiographical Writings of a Crown Princess of Eighteenth-Century Korea*. Berkeley: University of California Press.

Kalton, Michael C., trans.
1988   *To Become a Sage: The Ten Diagrams on Sage Learning by Yi T'oegye.*
          New York: Columbia University Press.
Kalton, Michael, et al.
1994   *The Four Seven Debate: An Annotated Translation of the Most Famous
          Controversy in Korean Neo-Confucian Thought.* Albany: State Univer-
          sity of New York Press.
Kendall, Laurel, and Griffin Dix, eds.
1987   *Ritual and Religion in Korean Society.* Berkeley: Institute of East
          Asian Studies, University of California, Berkeley Center for Korean
          Studies.
Kim, Sung-Hae
1985   *The Righteous and the Sage: A Comparative Study on the Ideal Images of
          Man in Biblical Israel and Classical China.* Seoul: Sogang University
          Press.
Phillips, Earl H., and Eui-young Yu, eds.
1982   *Religions in Korea: Beliefs and Cultural Values.* Los Angeles: Center
          for Korean-American and Korean Studies, California State Univer-
          sity.
Ro, Young-chan
1989   *The Korean Neo-Confucianism of Yi Yulgok.* Albany: State University
          of New York Press.
Setton, Mark
1997   *Chong Yagyong: Korea's Challenge to Orthodox Neo-Confucianism.*
          Albany: State University of New York Press.

Monographs: Japan

Ackroyd, Joyce, trans.
1979   *Told Round a Brushwood Fire: The Autobiography of Arai Hakuseki.*
          Princeton, N.J.: Princeton University Press and University of Tokyo
          Press.
Bellah, Robert N.
1957   *Tokugawa Religion: The Values of Pre-Industrial Japan.* Boston: Beacon
          Press.
Craig, Albert, and Donald Shively, eds.
1970   *Personality in Japanese History.* Berkeley: University of California
          Press.
Davis, Winston
1992   *Japanese Religion and Society: Paradigms of Structure and Change.*
          Albany: State University of New York Press.
de Bary, Wm. Theodore, and Irene Bloom, eds.
1979   *Principle and Practicality: Essays in Neo-Confucianism and Practical
          Learning.* New York: Columbia University Press.

Elison, George
1973   *Deus Destroyed: The Image of Christianity in Early Modern Japan.* Cambridge, Mass.: Harvard University Press.
Irokawa, Daikichi
1985   *The Culture of the Meiji Period.* Translation edited by Marius B. Jansen. Princeton, N.J.: Princeton University Press.
Kassel, Marleen
1996   *Tokugawa Confucian Education: The Kangien Academy of Hirose Tanso (1782–1856).* Albany: State University of New York Press.
Kitagawa, Joseph M.
1987   *On Understanding Japanese Religion.* Princeton, N.J.: Princeton University Press.
Lidin, Olof, trans.
1970   *Ogyu Sorai's Distinguishing the Way.* Tokyo: Sophia University Press.
1973   *The Life of Ogyu Sorai: A Tokugawa Confucian Philosopher.* Lund: Scandinavian Institute of Asian Studies.
Maruyama, Masao
1974   *Studies in the Intellectual History of Tokugawa Japan.* Translated by Mikiso Hane. Princeton, N.J.: Princeton University Press.
McEwan, J. R., trans.
1969   *The Political Writings of Ogyu Sorai.* Cambridge: Cambridge University Press.
Mercer, Rosemary, trans.
1991   *Deep Words: Miura Baien's System of Natural Philosophy.* Leiden: E. J. Brill.
Najita, Tetsuo
1987   *Visions of Virtue in Tokugawa Japan: The Kaitokudo Merchant Academy of Osaka.* Chicago: University of Chicago Press.
——, and Irwin Scheiner, eds.
1978   *Japanese Thought in the Tokugawa Period 1600–1868: Methods and Metaphors.* Chicago: University of Chicago Press.
Nakai, Kate Wildman
1980   "The Naturalization of Confucianism in Tokugawa Japan: The Problem of Sinocentrism." *Harvard Journal of Asian Studies* 40 (1980): 157–99.
Nakamura, Hajime
1969   *A History of the Development of Japanese Thought from A. D. 592 to 1868.* Tokyo: Japan Cultural Society.
Nosco, Peter, ed.
1984   *Confucianism and Tokugawa Culture.* Princeton, N.J.: Princeton University Press.
Ooms, Herman
1985   *Tokugawa Ideology: Early Constructs, 1570–1680.* Princeton, N.J.: Princeton University Press.

Pollack, David
   1986   *The Fracture of Meaning: Japan's Synthesis of China from the Eighth to the Eighteenth Centuries.* Princeton, N.J.: Princeton University Press.
Sawada, Janine Anderson
   1993   *Confucian Values and Popular Zen: Sekimon Shingaku in Eighteenth-Century Japan.* Honolulu: University of Hawaii Press.
Smith, Warren W.
   1973   *Confucianism in Modern Japan: A Study of Conservatism in Japanese Intellectual History.* 2nd ed. Tokyo: Hokuseido Press.
Spae, Joseph
   1967   *Ito Jinsai: A Philosopher, Educator and Sinologist of the Tokugawa Period.* New York: Paragon.
Taylor, Rodney L.
   1988   *The Confucian Way of Contemplation: Okada Takehiko and the Tradition of Quiet-Sitting.* Columbia: University of South Carolina Press.
Tominaga, Nakamoto
   1990   *Emerging from Meditation.* Translated with introduction by Michael Pye. London: Duckworth.
Totman, Conrad
   1993   *Early Modern Japan.* Berkeley: University of California Press.
Tucker, Mary Evelyn
   1989   *Moral and Spiritual Cultivation in Japanese Neo-Confucianism: The Life and Thought of Kaibara Ekken (1630–1714).* Albany: State University of New York Press.
Yamashita, Samuel H.
   1994   *Master Sorai's Responsals: Annotated Translation of Sorai Sensi Tomonsho.* Honolulu: University of Hawaii Press.
Yasunaga, Toshinobu
   1992   *Ando Shoeki: Social and Ecological Philosopher in Eighteenth Century Japan.* New York: Weatherhill.
Yoshikawa, Kojiro.
   1983   *Jinsai, Sorai, Norinaga: Three Classical Philologists of Mid-Tokugawa.* Tokyo: Toho Gakkai.

Contributors

JOSEPH A. ADLER, Associate Professor of Religion at Kenyon College, received his Ph.D. in Religious Studies from the University of California at Santa Barbara. He is co-author of *Sung Dynasty Uses of the I Ching* (Princeton University Press, 1990) and a contributor to *Confucianism and Ecology: The Interrelation of Heaven, Earth, and Humans* (Harvard Center for the Study of World Religions, 1998) and *Sources of Chinese Traditions*, rev. ed. (Columbia University Press, 1999). He is co-chair of the Confucian Traditions Group of the American Academy of Religion.

JOHN BERTHRONG, educated in Sinology at the University of Chicago, is the Associate Dean for Academic and Administrative Affairs and Director of the Institute for Dialogue Among Religious Traditions at the Boston University School of Theology. Active in interfaith dialogue projects and programs, his teaching and research interests are in the areas of interreligious dialogue, Chinese religions, and comparative theology. His most recent books are *All under Heaven: Transforming Paradigms in Confucian-Christian Dialogue*, *The Transformations of the Confucian Way*, and *Concerning Creativity* (on the thought of Zhu Xi, A. N. Whitehead, and R. C. Neville). He is co-editor with Mary Evelyn Tucker of the volume on *Confucianism and Ecology* published by the Center for the Study of World Religions and Harvard University Press in 1998.

JOANNE D. BIRDWHISTELL is Professor of Philosophy and Asian Civilization at the Richard Stockton College of New Jersey and East Asian Book Review Editor for *Philosophy East and West*. She has published *Transition to Neo-Confucianism: Shao Yung on Knowledge and Symbols of Reality* (Stanford University Press, 1989), *Li Yong (1627–1705) and Epistemological Dimensions of Confucian Philosophy* (Stanford University Press, 1996), and a number of articles. She received her M.A. and Ph.D. from Stanford University and her B.A. from the University of Pennsylvania. Her research interests now focus on comparative philosophy, particularly in respect to environmental and gender issues.

EDWARD Y. J. CHUNG is currently Associate Professor of Religious Studies and Co-ordinator of Asian Studies at the University of Prince Edward Island, Canada. He has also taught at the University of Toronto, where he received his undergraduate and graduate degrees (Ph.D., 1990). His research interests are Neo-Confucianism, modern Korean religion and culture, East Asian thought, and comparative religion (especially Confucian-Christian studies). He is the author of *The Korean Neo-Confucianism of Yi T'oegye and Yi Yulgok: A Reappraisal of the Four-Seven Thesis and Its Practical Implications for Self-Cultivation* (1995) and has published articles and presented conference papers on these subjects. His ongoing research project deals with the Confucian tradition and its modern transformation in South Korea.

WM. THEODORE DE BARY is John Mitchell Mason Professor Emeritus and Provost Emeritus at Columbia University, as well as director of the Heyman Center for the Humanities. He is the author or editor of more than two dozen works on Asian civilizations, including *Waiting for the Dawn* (Columbia University Press, 1993), *The Trouble with Confucianism* (Harvard University Press, 1991), *Confucianism and Human Rights* (Columbia University Press, 1998), and *Asian Values and Human Rights* (Harvard University Press, 1998).

DUNG NGOC DUONG received his B.A. in English at the University of Ho Chi Minh City, his M.A. in East Asian History from Harvard, and his Ph.D. from Boston University in Religious Studies. On returning to Vietnam after graduate studies he was appointed Professor of Religious Studies and Asian Studies in the College of Social Sciences and Humanities at National University of Ho Chi Minh City. His recent publications include *The Training of the Zen Buddhist Monk, An Introduction to China's Cultural History, Oriental Philosophies and Religions,* and *The Classic of Change and the Paradigm of Chinese Thinking.*

DANIEL K. GARDNER is Professor of History at Smith College. He is the author of *Chu Hsi and the Ta-hsueh: Neo-Confucian Reflection on the Confucian Canon* (Harvard University Press, 1986) and *Learning to Be a Sage: Selections from the Conversations of Master Chu, Arranged Topically* (University of California Press, 1990), as well as numerous articles on Chinese intellectual history.

CHRISTIAN JOCHIM is Professor of Comparative Religious Studies and Director of the Center for Asian Studies at San Jose State University. He received his Ph.D. in Religion (and East Asian Studies) at the University of Southern California. He teaches in the area of Asian religions and culture. He is the author of *Chinese Religions: A Cultural Perspective* in the Prentice-Hall Series in World Religions (1986). He has published many articles on Chinese religions and philosophy in *Journal of Chinese Religions, Philosophy East and West, Encyclopedia of Women and World Religions,* and other journals and compilations. Currently, he is studying contemporary Confucianism, especially in Taiwan.

MICHAEL C. KALTON received his Ph.D. from Harvard University in the joint fields of comparative religion and East Asian languages and civilizations. He is professor and director of the Program of Liberal Studies at the University of Washington, Tacoma. He is the author and translator of books and articles dealing with Korean Neo-Confucianism, including *To Become a Sage: The Ten Diagrams on Sage Learning by Yi T'oegye* (Columbia University Press, 1988) and *The Four-Seven Debate: An Annotated Translation of the Most Famous Controversy in Korean Neo-Confucian Thought* (State University of New York Press, 1994).

LIN TONGQI is an associate in the Department of East Asian Languages and Civilizations, Harvard University. His area of research is the intellectual/philosophical discourse in China since 1978. He has published a number of articles on the subject since 1989 and is currently also working on a comparative study of contemporary New Confucianism and Christianity.

LIU SHU-HSIEN was Chair Professor of Philosophy at The Chinese University of Hong Kong from 1981 to 1999. He is now a research fellow (specially invited chair) at The Institute of

Chinese Literature and Philosophy, Academia Sinica, Taipei. He has numerous publications both in Chinese and in English, including *Contemporary Chinese Philosophy: Problems and Characters* (in Chinese), 2 volumes (Global Publishing Co., 1996) and *Understanding Confucian Philosophy: Classical and Sung-Ming* (Greenwood Press, 1998).

ROBERT CUMMINGS NEVILLE is Professor of Philosophy, Religion, and Theology and Dean of the School of Theology at Boston University and has been president of the American Academy of Religion and the International Society for Chinese Philosophy. His works treating Confucianism and/or ecology include *Reconstruction of Thinking* (1981), *The Tao and the Daimon* (1982), *The Puritan Smile* (1987), *Recovery of the Measure* (1989), *Behind the Masks of God* (1991), *Normative Cultures* (1995), *The Truth of Broken Symbols* (1996), and *Boston Confucianism* (2000), all from the State University of New York Press.

WILLIAM YAU-NANG NG is an Associate Professor of Chinese at the National Chang-hua University of Education in Taiwan. He is the author of *T'ang Chun-i's Idea of Transcendence* and editor of several books on Neo-Confucianism and comparative philosophy. He is currently working on the spirituality of contemporary Neo-Confucianism.

VIVIAN-LEE NYITRAY is an Associate Professor in the Departments of Religious Studies and Comparative Literature and Foreign Languages at the University of California, Riverside. She is the author of *Mirrors of Virtue* (1999), co-editor of *The Life of Chinese Religion* (2000), and she is presently completing a manuscript on Confucianism and feminism in Chinese cultural contexts.

YOUNG-CHAN RO is Associate Professor of Religious Studies in the Department of Philosophy and Religious Studies, George Mason University. He is the author of *The Korean Neo-Confucianism of Yi Yulgok* (State University of New York Press, 1989) and co-author of *The Four-Seven Debate: An Annotated Translation of the Most Famous Controversy in Korean Neo-Confucian Thought* (State University of New York, 1994).

JANINE ANDERSON SAWADA teaches Japanese religion and intellectual history at the University of Iowa. She is currently researching religious groups and political coalitions of the late Tokugawa and early Meiji periods. Her past works include *Confucian Values and Popular Zen: Sekimon Shingaku in Eighteenth-Century Japan* (University of Hawaii Press, 1993).

THOMAS W. SELOVER is Assistant Professor of Religious Studies at the University of Saskatchewan. He is currently serving as editor for the semi-annual journal *Religious Studies & Theology*, and as co-chair of the East Asian Religions consultation of the AAR. He is author of *The Kernel of Humanity* (1998). His research interests include Song dynasty intellectual history, interpretations of the *Analects* as sacred text, the Confucian tradition as a mode of indigenous East Asian spirituality, comparative studies in religion, and comparative theology.

DEBORAH SOMMER is currently Assistant Professor in the Department of Religion at Gettysburg College. She received her Ph.D. from Columbia University. Her areas of research include the religious aspects of the literati tradition, especially sacrifice and ritual and the use of images in ritual contexts. She is the editor of *Chinese Religion: An Anthology of Sources* (Oxford, 1995) and is currently working on a book on the religious significance of the iconography of Confucius.

RODNEY L. TAYLOR is Professor of Religious Studies and Associate Dean of the Graduate School at the University of Colorado, Boulder. His books include *The Cultivation of Sagehood as a Religious Goal in Neo-Confucianism: A Study of Selected Writings of Kao P'an-lung, 1562-1626* (Scholars Press, 1978), *The Holy Book in Comparative Perspective,* with F. M. Denny (University of South Carolina Press, 1985), *The Way of Heaven: An Introduction to the Confucian Religious Life* (Brill, 1986), *The Confucian Way of Contemplation: Okada Takehiko and the Tradition of Quiet-Sitting* (University of South Carolina Press, 1988), *They Shall Not Hurt: Human Suffering and Human Caring,* with J. Watson (Colorado Associated University Press, 1989), *The Religious Dimensions of Confucianism* (State University of New York Press, 1990), and *The Illustrated Encyclopedia of Chinese Confucianism.*

MARY EVELYN TUCKER is Professor of Religion at Bucknell University, where she teaches courses in world religions, Asian religions, and religion and ecology. She received her Ph.D. from Columbia University in the history of religions, specializing in Confucianism in Japan. She has published *Moral and Spiritual Cultivation in Japanese Neo-Confucianism* (1989). She co-edited *Worldviews and Ecology* (1994), *Buddhism and Ecology* (1997), and *Confucianism and Ecology* (1998). She and her husband, John Grim, have directed the series of ten conferences on religions of the world and ecology at the Harvard University Center for the Study of World Religions from 1996 to 1998. They are also editors of the book series from these conferences.

TU WEIMING is Professor of Chinese History and Philosophy at Harvard University and the director of the Harvard-Yenching Institute. He is the author of *Neo-Confucian Thought in Action: Wang Yang-ming's Youth* (1976), *Centrality and Commonality: An Essay on Confucian Religiousness* (1989), *Confucian Thought: Selfhood as Creative Transformation* (1985), *Way, Learning, and Politics: Essays on the Confucian Intellectual* (1993), and is the editor of *The Living Tree: The Changing Meaning of Being Chinese Today* (1994), *China in Transformation* (1994), and *Confucian Traditions in East Asian Modernity* (1996).

Photographic Credits

THE EDITORS AND PUBLISHER thank the suppliers of the following photographs:

1. Yin-yang image and characters for "moon" and "sun." Courtesy of Deborah Sommer.
2. Confucian temple in Qufu, Shandong. Courtesy of Deborah Sommer.
3. Main hall of Imperial Academy in Beijing. Courtesy of Deborah Sommer.
4. Main hall of the Confucian temple, Gaoxiong, Taiwan. Courtesy of Chu Ronguey.
5. Main gate to the Imperial Academy in Beijing. Courtesy of Deborah Sommer.
6. Stele commemorating the 900th anniversary of Cheng Yi's commentary on the *Book of Changes*. Courtesy of Cheng Dexiang.
7. Statue and spirit tablets of Zhang Zai, Zhang Zai shrine, Hengqu, Shaanxi. Courtesy of Deborah Sommer.
8. Shao Yong's statue and spirit tablet, Shao Yong shrine, Luoyang. Courtesy of Deborah Sommer.
9. Divinatory diagrams, Shao Yong shrine, Luoyang. Courtesy of Deborah Sommer.
10. Newly renovated shrine to Zhang Zai, Hengqu, Shaanxi. Courtesy of Deborah Sommer.
11. Detail of mural at the Zhang Zai shrine, Hengqu, Shaanxi. Courtesy of Deborah Sommer.
12. Detail of mural at the Zhang Zai shrine, Hengqu, Shaanxi. Courtesy of Deborah Sommer.
13. Detail of mural at the Zhang Zai shrine, Hengqu, Shaanxi. Courtesy of Deborah Sommer.

14. Ritual at the Cheng clan shrine in Taejon, Korea. Courtesy of Cheng Dexiang.
15. Tea ritual at Zhu Xi's grave, Fujian. Courtesy of Cheng Dexiang.
16. Offering of herbs in a rite to Confucius in Jiali, Taiwan. Courtesy of Chu Ronguey.
17. Copies of exam cards placed under incense burners in Zhanghua Confucian temple. Courtesy of Deborah Sommer.
18. Ritual offering by Korean visitors at the grave of Zhu Xi. Courtesy of Cheng Dexiang.
19. New stele at the grave of Zhu Xi, Fujian. Courtesy of Cheng Dexiang.
20. Women dancers and musicians at the Confucian temple in Seoul. Courtesy of Chu Ronguey.
21. Entrance to the Confucian temple, Hue, Vietnam. Courtesy of Chu Ronguey.
22. Commemorative arch in Xinzhu, Taiwan. Courtesy of Deborah Sommer.

Index

Tu Weiming (*cont.*)
on *qi*, 70nn. 22, 23
on religious dimension of
Confucianism, 428–30,
460n. 3
on self-cultivation, 231–32,
294
and self-transformation in
Confucianism, 21
and social Confucianism, 19
and term "anthropocosmic,"
4
on third epoch of Confu-
cianism, 323–24
and third generation of New
Confucians, 324, 400, 426
on vigilant solitariness, 348
on Xunxi, 313n. 16

universe: as purposeful, 163

Van Zoeren, Steven, 69nn. 8, 9
Veith, Ilza, 69n. 13
Vendley, William, 504, 508n. 53
Vietnam
conformist social ethic of,
318n. 64
Confucian spirituality in,
289–319
vigils: of purification, 210–11
virtue, 134–62
and happiness, 325–26
natural, 262
virtues
four central, 30n. 40; 385
five cardinal, 295
vitalism, 166; and Qing
thought, 167
Vu Khieu, 314n. 19

Waley, Arthur, 229
Waltner, Ann, 477n. 9
Wang Chong, 124, 144n. 16
Wang Fu-zhi, 166
Wang Lungxi: doctrine of Fourfold Non-being (*siwu*) of,
340–44, 345–46, 347
Wang Mingsheng, 169
Wang Yangming, 8, 13, 301
Four-Sentence Teaching of,
339–41, 45 (*see also siwu;
siyu*)
on learning of the mind and
heart, 78, 154–59
and Mou Zongsan, 333
and ontological perfection,
344–47
on *ren*, 61
rise of school of, 184, 190

and School of Mind, 382
on self-cultivation, 338–39
on self-sufficiency of human
nature, 389
and spiritual exercises, 157
on unity of heaven, earth,
and humanity, 492–95
wanwei (savoring the text), 57
wanwu (cosmos of all things):
Cheng teaching about,
65–67
Warring States, period of, 49
Watson, Burton, 80nn. 4, 12
Watsuji Tetsuro: on stadiality,
249
Way. *See* Dao
Weber, Max, 22, 32n. 57
Wei Zhengtong (Wei Cheng-
t'ung), 315n. 40
as critic of New Confucianism, 399–404, 407–10
Whitmore, John K., 314nn. 17,
20; 316n. 43; 319n. 67
Wilhelm, Hellmut, 35n. 102
will: philosophy of, 159–61
Wilson, Thomas, 33n. 71
Wolters, O. W., 312n. 1
women
and Confucianism, 463–79
as human manifestation of
yin cosmic principle, 465
identified with hexagram
kun, 465
Woo, Peter Kun-Yu (Wu
Kunru), 412–13, 419nn.
35, 37
words: as symbols, 39
wu (emptiness; void; non-
being), 340
particular things, 42, 51–52
Wyatt, Don J., 35n. 106, 145n.
28

Xia dynasty, 49
xiantian (before Heaven), learning of, 50
xiao (filial piety), 8–9, 126, 187
*Xiaojing. See Classic of Filial
Piety*
Xici (Appendix), 130–31,
135–37, 145n. 28 (*see also
Book of Changes*)
Xie Daoyun, 470–71
Xie Liangzuo, 58, 59, 65–66
on *ren*, 61–63, 68n. 5, 70n.
17
xin (heart-mind), 41
Buddhism and, 73

as category of Confucian
philosophical thought,
149–51
and formation of human
beings, 41, 50–52
as master of self, 207
relation of, to nature and
feeling, 152–54
spiritual exercises of, 150–51
Tang Junyi on, 396n. 32
in Vietnamese Confucian-
ism, 298–300
and Way of Heaven, 497–99
xing (human nature), 41
essence of, 384–86
and formation of human
beings, 41, 50–52
goodness of, 83, 95, 150–51,
206
as perfect, 190
Tang Junyi's notion of,
381–84, 396n. 32
xingzhi (original wisdom):
Xiong Shili on, 362–64
xinrujia. See New Confucianism; New Confucians
xinxue (learning of the mind
and heart), 164
Xiong Shili, 360–64
and Confucian metaphysics,
486–87
as pioneer of New Confu-
cianism, 324, 353,
400–401, 426
xixin (habitual mind): Xiong
Shili on, 363
xu (empty; pure), 145n. 24
Xu Fuguan, 17, 364
liberal criticism of, 408–10
and second generation of
New Confucians, 324,
353, 399, 400, 426
Xunzi (Hsun Tzu)/*Xunzi*, 5, 9,
10, 30n. 42; 124, 424
and distinction between "I"
and "me," 52
on learning, 313n. 16
on *li*, 316n. 46
on orientations, 455–57
and ritual, 454–55

Yamashita, Samuel, 267n. 4
Yamazaki Ansai, 250, 253, 254,
257–60, 266
Yang, C. K., 16, 33n. 71
Yang Shi, 59, 68n. 5
on *ren*, 62, 64, 70n. 17
Yan Hui, 76, 78
Yan Yuan, 166